ULTIMATE HOME SOLUTIONS

ULTIMATE HOME SOLUTIONS

© 2003 Research Machines plc. All rights reserved. Helicon Publishing is a
division of Research Machines.

Helicon Publishing
Research Machines plc
New Mill House
183 Milton Park
Abingdon
Oxon
OX14 4SE

First published by Collins in 2003
An imprint of HarperCollins *Publishers*
77–85 Fulham Palace Road
London W6 8JB

The Collins website address is www.collins.co.uk

Printed and bound in Great Britain by The Bath Press Ltd.

ISBN 0007165986

Editorial team: Barbara Fraser, Carolyn Newton, Darren Ward, Linda Sonntag,
Alyson Lacewing, Sandra Meredith, Lynda Swindells

Illustrators: Andrew Green, Antbits Illustration, Nick Pearson, Lorraine Hodghton

Design: Price Watkins, Lorraine Hodghton

Cover design: Senate Design Ltd

ABOUT THIS BOOK

We're all used to seeing cleverly decorated, pristine homes on TV and in magazines – making your home an expression of personality has become big business. But do you find that the day to day domestic experience doesn't quite match? That the details of life get in the way of the grand plan?

Ultimate Home Solutions is the book to help you sort the practicalities on the way to achieving the home you hope for. Written by experts, topic by topic, it gives straight-forward but detailed guidance on how to make your space work better for you – reorganizing, extending, maintaining, updating. But it also has smart solutions for the domestic issues we all have to deal with, whether we live in a flat or a house, and whether we rent or own – security, cleaning, basic DIY, paying bills, sorting insurance. And if you're planning to buy a property, this book takes you through the process from start to finish, including tracking down the best mortgage.

Wherever it's essential to have professional advice, the writers say so, and explain how to go about finding help. Bear in mind, however, that things change quickly these days. While the publishers believe the material here is accurate at the time of going to press, you should always check for yourself what the implications are of making a major decision relating to your home, especially where it involves committing money. If you're unsure, always seek a professional opinion. To help, there is a list of useful Web sites and addresses at the end of every chapter – if an organization is listed there, it's highlighted in **bold** type when it's mentioned by a writer.

Likewise, before undertaking any of the practical jobs described, think through what skills are required. If you have any doubts, get help from a professional or an experienced friend.

Lastly, there are cross-references throughout the book, but the Contents, listing the topics covered in each chapter, and the Index, are useful tools for checking out where else a subject is covered.

THE WRITERS

Anthony Bailey

A freelance financial journalist and columnist for the *Express*.

Lynn Brittney

A magazine journalist and author whose books include *A Woman Alone*, the *Which? Guide to Working From Home*, and the *Which? Guide to Domestic Help*.

Paul Butt

A solicitor and an Associate Professor at the College of Law, Chester with over 25 years' experience of property law.

Will Garside

Former staff writer on the magazine *Computer Weekly*, who has also written a book on computer troubleshooting, for PC users at all levels.

David Holloway

A long-standing DIY expert and book author who writes for *Practical Householder* and other magazines.

Mike Lawrence

A DIY book author and journalist whose credits include DIY consultant on the BBC's *Changing Rooms* partwork, and contributor to *Practical Householder* magazine.

John McGowan

Editor of *Practical Householder* magazine, who gives advice on insulation and wallpapering.

Joe McShane

Advice Service Manager of the Oxford Citizens Advice Bureau, who has contributed on You and your space.

Elizabeth Martyn

Sole author of *House Beautiful Home Handbook*, and contributor to the *Good Housekeeping Book of the Home*, who has recently written for Tesco, and Channel 4 programme support.

Ann Maurice

Interior designer and presenter of Channel 5's House Doctor series, who contributed on Preparing to sell a property.

Rachel Parma

With experience in local government, she has contributed on You and your council.

Mark Ramuz

Editor of *The Woodworker* magazine, who also writes for *The Mirror*, and *Home*.

Jane Sheard

A former assistant director of the Good Housekeeping Institute, Jane Sheard is a house renovator and specializes in writing about building, renovation, and planning rooms.

Linda Sonntag

An experienced writer and editor whose credits include working on *Superstitch* and *Dish of the Day*. She has contributed to the Everyday Living chapter.

Toby Wallis

Multimedia consultant and Web page designer who has written the section on designing and running a Web site if you run a business from home.

Virginia Wallis

A freelance journalist specializing in personal finance, especially mortgages and tax issues, Virginia writes regularly for the *Observer*.

CONTENTS

CHAPTER ONE

Finding your home

▶ Somewhere to rent

There's been an increasing trend towards renting accommodation. It's the obvious option if you're going to be in an area for only a short period. If you're planning to settle, it gives you time to consider the type of property that would suit you and to save up to buy. Before you rent, make sure you can't get caught out by the small print in the tenancy agreement, so that your time renting goes as smoothly as possible. If you're sharing with friends, there are some special issues about being joint tenants that are worth thinking about at the outset – see p13.

TENANCY AGREEMENTS AND THE LAW

The tenancy agreement you will be asked to sign is a binding legal document. Unlike many legal documents it will not carry a 'health warning' cautioning you against signing it unless you wish to be bound by its terms – but you must not sign it without understanding exactly what you are letting yourself in for.

Under the Unfair Terms in Consumer Contracts Regulations 1999, any term in a tenancy agreement that is deemed unfair by the tenant is void. But the regulations are very vague as to what may or may not be 'fair' and the only way that this can be decided upon is by going to court, which could be expensive and time-consuming. Best not to sign an agreement that strikes you as unreasonable in the first place.

FIVE FLASHPOINTS IN TENANCY AGREEMENTS

1 It's usual for a landlord to require a prospective tenant to pay a **deposit** as well as a month's rent in advance. Normally the deposit will be equivalent to one or two months' rent. You should not agree to pay more than the equivalent of two months' rent as a deposit – this would almost certainly be unfair. The idea behind a deposit is that if you fail to pay the rent, or cause any damage to the house or contents, the landlord can use this money as compensation without the need for expensive court proceedings.

Many tenancy disputes arise out of the repayment of deposits at the end of the tenancy. Landlords sometimes claim that there is damage, which is then disputed by the tenant. Equally, there may be a disagreement as to the amount that should be deducted as compensation for the damage caused. Here the landlord has the advantage – as the tenant you have already handed over your money and it is unlikely to be returned unless you go to court.

The tenancy agreement should make clear the following:

- what the landlord (or the letting agency) can use the deposit for – either just for arrears of rent, or for breakages as well
- whether, if the landlord makes use of the deposit during the tenancy, for the agreed purposes he or she can require you to top it up to the original amount
- whether the tenant is entitled to receive interest on the deposit for the time it is held by the landlord
- that the deposit is held on trust for the tenant. Otherwise there is a risk that the money will not be recoverable by the tenant if the landlord should become insolvent.

The government has introduced a Tenancy Deposit Scheme, which aims to provide security for tenants' deposits and independent resolution of disputes. Ideally, you should ensure that your landlord is willing to participate in this scheme. More details are available on the Department of Transport, Local Government, and the Regions' Web site http://www.housing.dtlr.gov.uk.

2 What **length of tenancy** are you looking for? Be wary of signing up for too long, because if you decide to leave early, you will be liable for rent for the rest of the time you agreed. However, most landlords will take a favourable view if you can find an acceptable replacement tenant for them.

3 If the property is being let furnished, ensure that there is a detailed **inventory** of the contents. This should not

only include everything in the house, but also describe its condition, detailing any damage. Go through it carefully and don't sign it unless you are sure it is accurate. This can save all sorts of arguments at the end of the tenancy when it comes to the repayment of the deposit. The landlord will often make a deduction because of a damaged item, despite a tenant's claim that it was in that condition to start with. A detailed inventory can prevent this.

4 It is usual for a landlord to include in a tenancy agreement various **rules and regulations** that state what you can or cannot do in the property. These will often aim to avoid causing a nuisance to neighbours. Whatever it is you have agreed to, your signature on the tenancy agreement binds you to it. If you do not comply with these provisions, the landlord may well be able to bring the tenancy to a premature end. However, what a landlord cannot do is impose new rules after you have signed the agreement – unless, that is, the agreement allows it.

5 Landlords frequently keep keys to the properties they let, but the law does not allow them **right of entry** unless this is specifically stated in the agreement. A landlord may arrange to come round to see what repairs need doing, but otherwise, he or she has no more right to enter the property than a stranger has. The whole essence of a tenancy is that the tenant has the right to exclude anyone and everyone from the property – including the landlord.

SHORTHOLD OR ASSURED TENANCY?

Most lettings these days are what are called **shorthold** tenancies (sometimes called **assured shortholds**, but they are the same thing). Unless your tenancy agreement states expressly that it is an **assured tenancy** with no mention of the word 'shorthold', then it will be a shorthold. In the case of a shorthold, the landlord will have an absolute right to possession of the property at the end of the tenancy, as long as he or she gives you two months' notice. Although the landlord cannot evict you without obtaining a court order, he or she will have an absolute right to such an order.

If your tenancy is an assured tenancy, then the landlord can only obtain possession if he or she can prove the existence of one or more 'grounds for possession', that is, circumstances which justify him or her requiring possession. These are many and various and outside the scope of this book, but include non-payment of rent and breaches of other terms of the tenancy agreement. Some grounds are 'mandatory', which means that on proof of the ground, the court must make an order for possession against the tenant. Other grounds, however, are discretionary, so that even if the ground is established, the court has discretion whether or not to order possession.

If you have an assured tenancy and you receive a notice claiming possession, you should immediately seek legal advice as to your rights.

THINK BEFORE YOU SIGN

It cannot be stressed enough that you must read the tenancy agreement carefully and thoroughly before signing it. If in doubt, seek advice from a **Citizens Advice Bureau** (CAB) or free housing aid centre if there is one in your area. Be wary of pressure to sign immediately because of a queue of eager applicants behind you. There may well be others waiting to snap up the property, but any reasonable landlord will give you time to make sure you understand what you are signing – after all, this is in the interest of both parties.

FINDING A PROPERTY

Through an agent:

If possible, ask friends in the area who have rented property before to recommend an agent.

- Use an agent who is a member of a professional body, such as the Royal Institution of Chartered Surveyors (RICS) or the Association of Residential Letting Agents (ARLA). These bodies have professional standards to uphold and membership shows a commitment to behaving professionally.

- Remember that the agent is the landlord's agent and although the existence of a buffer between landlord and tenant can help in settling disputes, the agent is in the pay of the landlord.

- When you sign up with an agency they will want to see evidence of your identity, such as a passport, and at least two months' pay slips. They may check with a credit reference agency to see if you have a satisfactory credit rating. They may also ask for an administration fee for signing the tenancy and a further fee at each renewal.

Let direct from the landlord:

- Many landlords advertise privately in the small ads of local papers.

- Beware of landlords who insist on rent payments in cash – their disregard of the tax laws might mean they would disregard your rights too.

- If the property is in poor condition when you look round, think twice before signing up for it. The landlord may promise to carry out the repairs when you have signed the agreement, but a good landlord would have done the repairs before advertising it. Once you have signed up, the landlord will have little incentive to carry out repairs.

RESPONSIBILITY FOR OUTGOINGS

All outgoings on the property – council tax, gas, water, electricity, and telephone bills – will normally be your responsibility as the tenant, whether or not this is stated in the tenancy agreement.

TAKING IN A LODGER OR SUBLETTING

If you are yourself a tenant and want to sublet all or part of your accommodation, then you will probably need your landlord's consent. The law says that you can sublet or take in a lodger unless your tenancy agreement says otherwise, however most tenancy agreements contain a prohibition on subletting. If you don't comply with the terms of the agreement, your landlord will probably have the right to go to court and seek your eviction from the property, even if the tenancy agreement has not yet expired.

Remember also, that if you grant a sublease, you will be taking on the role of landlord to that subtenant. So you will need to check up on references and make sure that you have a proper agreement, just like any other landlord.

As a landlord you will be liable to that subtenant to carry out repairs when they need doing, and you will be liable if a gas fire is defective. Of course, your own landlord may be liable to you to carry out those repairs, but that is between the two of you. Your tenant will look to you and you alone for compensation. See p46–9 for more on letting, and p77 for more on renting out a room to a lodger.

TENANCY RIGHTS AND OBLIGATIONS

Your rights and obligations as a tenant are, to a large extent, governed by the terms of the tenancy agreement, but the general law may also sometimes be relevant.

RESPONSIBILITY FOR DAMAGE AND REPAIRS

The Landlord & Tenant Act 1985 places the obligation for repairing the structure and exterior of residential properties on the landlord. This is so in cases where the tenancy is for a term of less than seven years – which will cover most tenancies – and applies even if there is a provision in the tenancy agreement saying that the tenant must carry out the repairs. The same Act also provides that the landlord must keep in repair and proper working order the installations in the property for the supply of gas, water, electricity, and sanitation. This includes sinks, baths, toilets, and drains, though if drains are blocked because of the tenant's unreasonable behaviour, then the tenant is responsible for unblocking them.

The words 'structure' and 'exterior' are not defined by the Act, but will include the main fabric of the house, such as walls, roof, window frames, gutters, drainpipes, and paths and steps that form the main access to the house. Interior decorations and fittings are not included in the Act.

The landlord will not be liable for damage that was the tenant's fault – say the tenant cracked a washbasin by dropping something into it. The landlord will equally not be liable to repair items other than those within the Act, or to redecorate, unless stated in the tenancy agreement. You as a tenant are liable for matters not covered by the Act if you have agreed to such repairs in the tenancy agreement – another reason for reading it through carefully.

If the agreement does not deal with the repair of an item that does not feature within the Act, then neither landlord nor tenant is under an obligation to repair. However, if the damage was the tenant's fault, the tenant is responsible.

GETTING REPAIRS DONE

Landlords can be expected to do repairs only if you tell them what needs doing – until you have done this, they are not liable. Many landlords are very conscientious about maintaining their property. It is, after all, in their interests to keep it in good condition. But some landlords are not helpful and repairs can remain outstanding for a long time, often at great inconvenience to the tenant.

Going to court to force your landlord to do repairs is an option (see p96 for how to do this), but can be lengthy and expensive. What you cannot do is simply stop paying the rent – the fact that the landlord has failed to do the repairs is not grounds for defence if he or she sues you or tries to evict you for non-payment.

If persuasion, or persistence, does not work, you can warn the landlord that unless he or she carries out the repairs, you will have them done and then deduct the cost from future payments of rent. In such a case it is obviously safest to get at least two estimates first and send these to the landlord in advance, so there can be no argument that the cost is excessive.

Tenants are entitled to compensation in reduced rent for disruption while major repairs are carried out.

THE GARDEN

Neither landlord nor tenant is responsible for the garden – unless the tenancy agreement states otherwise. In the absence of this the tenant need not keep it tidy, and the landlord can't be forced to either.

ALTERATIONS

Often a tenancy agreement will forbid alterations, but if it does not and you as the tenant make improvements, you are allowed to remove them at the end of the tenancy. If they are left in place, the landlord does not have to pay you compensation.

INSURANCE

The landlord may well insure the structure of the building, but he or she will not insure your contents. If these are lost, stolen, or damaged, for instance by fire, you will have no comeback against the landlord. So consider taking out your own contents insurance.

UNLAWFUL EVICTION AND HARASSMENT

The landlord cannot evict you without first obtaining a court order – even if your tenancy has come to an end. If he or she tries to do so, or threatens or harasses you into leaving by unreasonable behaviour, such as excessive noise or cutting off services, he or she is liable to criminal proceedings. You can also bring legal action against a landlord to claim compensation and reinstatement to the property if you are evicted.

SHARING WITH OTHERS

If you plan to share with others, you may be asked to sign the same agreement and become **joint tenants**. This means each tenant can be held responsible in full on all the terms of the agreement. The landlord can claim the full monthly rent from any of you – he or she is not bound by any arrangement you have made to each pay a contribution. And if one tenant leaves, the rest will still have to pay the monthly rent between them.

A joint arrangement also means that if one tenant breaks the terms of the agreement by causing damage, the landlord can again claim against any one tenant for that loss, or retain some of the deposit at the end of the letting. If you end up paying more than your share, or losing your part of the deposit because of another's breakages, you can claim that amount from that person – if you can find them and if they will pay up. If court proceedings are necessary, these may be expensive.

If one joint tenant leaves, the rest will almost certainly need the landlord's consent to bring in another person to share. If you do this without consent, the landlord might well be able to obtain possession of the property.

Alternatively, you may be asked to sign a separate agreement each, promising to pay a specified amount of rent. If one of the tenants leaves your liability doesn't change – but it is up to the landlord to find a replacement tenant. You might want quickly to find a replacement who is acceptable to the landlord.

In the case of breakages or damage, although each occupier has signed a separate agreement, it will be impossible in practice for the landlord to know which of the occupiers actually caused the damage. Usually the agreement will allow the landlord to hold any tenant liable for any damage, no matter who caused it.

GAS, FIRE, AND ELECTRICAL SAFETY

There are various government regulations dealing with safety. The landlord is responsible for the safety of the electrical system, any oil or solid-fuel heating, and any appliances included in the let. There are criminal penalties for supplying unsafe electrical equipment.

If the property is let furnished, upholstery, soft furnishings, and mattresses must comply with various flammability criteria. Older furnishings that have no swing ticket or label showing compliance with the regulations are illegal, unless classified as antiques.

If the property contains a gas appliance, the landlord must ensure that it and any flue or pipe serving it is maintained in a safe condition. The appliance must be inspected at least once every 12 months by a CORGI-registered plumber and a record of these inspections kept.

The landlord must produce this record to the tenant on the grant of the tenancy and within 28 days of each annual inspection. **If you are not shown this record when taking a tenancy, or it cannot be provided when you ask, do not take the tenancy.**

WHEN CAN LANDLORDS INCREASE THE RENT?

The amount of the rent, and your ability to pay it, is a crucial factor to consider before entering into a tenancy. But once you have signed the agreement, can the landlord increase the rent?

- In the case of a letting for a fixed term (usually six months) there can be no rent increase, unless it is built into the tenancy agreement. So again, read the agreement carefully – you will be bound by any provisions contained in it that allow an increase.

- In the case of a periodic tenancy (one that lasts from week to week or from month to month), the law does allow a landlord to increase the rent even if there is nothing in the tenancy agreement permitting this. But in order to increase the rent, the landlord must follow the correct procedure. This involves him/her serving a two-months' notice on you in the form laid down by the Housing Act 1988, stating the proposals for the new rent and detailing your right to refer the increase to the Rent Assessment Committee (a government body) to see if it is fair. You need not agree to any increase where the correct procedure has not been followed.

- Landlords are not entitled to increase rent after carrying out repairs, such as replacing an old gas boiler with a new one, but an improvement, such as installing central heating when it wasn't there before, could be a reason for reviewing the rent. The landlord would then need to follow the procedure of notice, as above, again giving you the right to refer the increase to the Rent Assessment Committee.

Assessing funds to buy

Buying a home of your own could be the biggest financial commitment you ever make. So it's not something you should rush into – especially if you don't envisage staying in the same place for at least three years. Buying will be a realistic option, however, only if you can amass the substantial amount of cash you'll need to meet the costs involved.

SHARED OWNERSHIP – A HALFWAY HOUSE

If property prices in the area you like are out of your reach, it could be worth considering a shared-ownership scheme. These are usually run by housing associations. Instead of buying a property outright, you buy a share, with the help of a mortgage, and pay rent on the remaining share owned by the housing association. You then have the option of increasing your share as you can afford to.

Whether or not a shared-ownership scheme is an option depends on whether you meet a particular housing association's eligibility criteria. Preference is usually given to housing association and council tenants, and first-time buyers. Get more details by phoning the **Shared Ownership Advice Line** or contacting the **Housing Corporation**.

NO STAMP DUTY

You can buy property costing £150,000 or less in some 2,000 'disadvantaged' areas of the UK without having to pay stamp duty. Details from the **Stamp Office**.

FIVE REASONS TO BUY

1 Buying can be cheaper than renting – largely because mortgage interest rates are the lowest they have been for over 25 years. According to research by Abbey National, even taking into account the costs involved in maintaining a property, on average it is 57% cheaper to buy than rent over 25 years.

2 Owning your home gives you security. Providing you keep up your mortgage payments, you will know that you can stay in your home as long as you like.

3 When you have paid off the mortgage, you will have acquired a substantial financial asset and a home that costs very little to live in.

4 Because lenders are so keen to attract new customers, especially first-time buyers, many offer to help out with some of the upfront costs involved in buying a property, such as valuation and legal fees, either by refunding them if the mortgage goes ahead or by providing a cash lump sum. For more on finding a good mortgage deal, see p18–21.

5 Providing your property goes up in value, buying your own home can mean that if, in the future, you want to finance home improvements – or any other large purchase, such as a car – you can extend your mortgage rather than using more costly types of loan.

CAN YOU AFFORD TO BUY?

The biggest single cost you face when buying a property is the cash deposit. The deposit needs to be at least the difference between the purchase price and the size of mortgage a lender is prepared to grant you. Most lenders will not lend more than 95% of the valuation of the property, so the minimum deposit you will need is 5%. If you plan to buy at auction (see p31), you will need a deposit of at least 10% of your maximum bid price.

Your income also affects how big a mortgage you can get. If you are buying on your own, the most you can borrow is typically 3–3½ times your annual income, although some lenders will lend up to 4 times your income. So if you earn £20,000 a year, you could get a mortgage of between £60,000 and £80,000. Assuming you could borrow 95% of the value, this would buy you a property costing between £63,150 and £84,200, for which you would need a deposit of between £3,150 and £4,200. You also need to budget for:

■ stamp duty, which you will have to pay if the property costs more than £60,000. The rates are: 1% on properties worth £60,001 to £250,000; 3% from £250,001 to £500,000; and 4% on £500,001 or more

■ Land Registry fee, which is a flat fee of: £40 if the purchase price is up to £40,000; £60 from £40,001 to £70,000; £100 from £70,001 to £100,000; £200 from £100,001 to £200,000; £300 from £200,001 to £500,000; £500 from £500,001 to £1 million; and £800 on property costing more than £1 million

■ search fees, which cost an average of £126 and pay for general checks – such as whether or not the property is in the path of a planned road development

■ legal fees, of around £400 to £1,000, depending on the value of the property (see table). However, your lender may cover this expense.

■ upfront mortgage costs, which can vary according to the size of the mortgage and the type of deal you choose. For more details, see p16.

MOVING UP THE LADDER

If you already have a foot on the property ladder but are considering a move, the costs you face are the same as those for a first-time buyer (see table), with one major difference. As long as your current home has risen in value since you bought it, the sale proceeds will provide you with the deposit for your next property. How big a deposit depends on how much you have left after:

- negotiations with your own buyer – you may end up reducing the asking price by as much as 10%

- paying off what you owe on your current mortgage – together with any charges for repaying early (if applicable, though these charges may be waived if you take out your next mortgage with the same lender)

- paying the estate agent – unless you choose to sell privately (see p38)

- meeting the legal fees involved in selling – unless you do the conveyancing yourself (see p37)

- covering the costs involved in buying the next property, as well as removal expenses.

If all these costs reduce the potential sale proceeds to zero – and you have no other way of paying the costs – trading up is not an affordable option. You will need enough out of what's left to put down a deposit of at least 5% on the new property, and of course you must also earn enough to get the size of mortgage you need.

IMPROVE YOUR CHANCES

- If you plan to buy a home, saving up a deposit should be your top priority. Although the minimum you are likely to need is 5% of the property value, if you can save a deposit of at least 10% you will be in a much stronger position when it comes to finding a good mortgage deal.

- Before applying for a mortgage, pay off as much of any existing debts as you can. Although most lenders base what they are prepared to lend on your annual salary, they also look at your ability to repay the loan. The more debt you have in the form of overdrafts, outstanding credit card bills, and personal loans, the less income you will have available to make mortgage repayments.

- Work out whether you can afford the regular monthly costs of buying a home. This includes not just the mortgage repayments (see p16) but the cost of insurance (see p17).

- If buying a place of your own doesn't seem affordable, and you don't want to get involved in shared or joint ownership (see opposite), consider taking a lodger to help pay the mortgage. Currently the first £4,250 of rent taken each year is tax-free. Some mortgage lenders will take the rent into account when they calculate your mortgage related to your earnings, but are more likely to do so when assessing your ability to repay, which looks at all income and outgoings. For practicalities, see p77.

AVERAGE COST OF BUYING IN ENGLAND & WALES

Property price (£)	5% deposit (£)	Administration costs (£)				Total administration costs (£)	Total funds you will need (£)
		Solicitor/ Conveyancer	Land Registry fee	Searches	Stamp duty		
25,000	1,250	434	40	144	nil	618	1,868
50,000	2,500	409	60	144	nil	613	3,113
60,000	3,000	417	60	144	nil	621	3,621
80,000	4,000	436	100	144	800	1,480	5,480
100,000	5,000	463	100	144	1,000	1,707	6,707
150,000	7,500	523	200	144	1,500	2,367	9,867
200,000	10,000	571	200	144	2,000	2,915	12,915
300,000	15,000	699	300	144	9,000	10,143	25,143
500,000	25,000	899	300	144	15,000	16,343	41,343

Source: *The Woolwich Cost of Moving Survey 2002*.
Figures compiled by the University of Greenwich, School of Land and Construction Management. This table gives the average costs of buying in England and Wales with a 5% deposit. Actual costs vary by region and tend to be highest in the South East and South West of England.

UPFRONT MORTGAGE COSTS

As well as budgeting for all the costs involved in buying a property (see p15), make allowance for the fees you may be charged for setting up your mortgage. These include:

- **Valuation fee**, which pays for a professional mortgage valuation – the figure on which the lender will base your final mortgage offer. You can avoid this fee by choosing one of the special deals where the lender bears the cost of the valuation or refunds the fee if the mortgage goes ahead.

- **Arrangement fee**, to cover the administrative costs of setting up the mortgage, although not all lenders charge a one-off fee for this.

- **Booking fee**, which you are likely to have to pay if you choose a mortgage deal where the rate of interest is fixed, capped, or discounted. For more details on interest rates, see p20.

- **Legal fees**, for the cost of creating the mortgage document, unless – as it usually is – this work is undertaken by your conveyancer and so already included in the other legal fees.

ADDING UP THE MORTGAGE COSTS

Just as important as working out whether you can afford the one-off costs of buying (and selling, if you have to do that too) is checking that you will be able to meet the ongoing monthly cost of home ownership. To give you an idea of what your mortgage repayments will be, the table below gives the monthly cost, for different sizes of loan, of a repayment mortgage paid back over 25 years.

Sharing the cost of buying a property with another person can make the upfront costs more affordable and also increases the size of mortgage you can apply for. Most lenders will either consider lending the same income multiples as if you were buying on your own, plus one times the second person's income, or they will lend 2½ – 2¾ times your joint income.

If you share the purchase of a home with a friend, make sure that you own the property as 'tenants in common'. This means that you each own a distinct share in the property (the sizes of the shares should reflect how much you each put into buying it). You should also ask a solicitor to draw up a trust deed to set out what happens if one of you wants to sell but the other doesn't. This costs about £75.

Being tenants in common also allows each of you to specify who will get your share if you die. This is not the case if you own the property as 'joint tenants' – ownership of the whole property automatically passes to the other if one partner dies. However, a joint tenancy is worth considering if you are buying with a significant other and you would want him or her to be able to continue living in the property after your death.

WHAT WILL THE MORTGAGE COST EACH MONTH?

(£)	Interest rate (£)					
Size of loan	3%	4%	5%	6%	7%	8%
30,000	144	160	177	196	215	234
40,000	192	213	236	261	286	312
50,000	240	267	296	326	358	391
60,000	287	320	355	391	429	469
70,000	335	373	414	456	501	547
80,000	383	426	473	522	572	625
90,000	431	480	532	587	644	703
100,000	479	533	591	652	715	781
125,000	599	666	739	815	894	976
150,000	719	800	887	978	1,073	1,172
200,000	958	1,066	1,182	1,304	1,430	1,562
250,000	1,198	1,333	1,478	1,630	1,788	1,953

Source: MoneyFacts.

WHAT INSURANCE DO YOU NEED?

Although your lender may offer the types of insurance detailed below, you will not necessarily need all of them.

BUILDINGS INSURANCE

This is a must – without a suitable policy you won't get your mortgage. If you don't take the policy offered by your lender, you may have to pay an administration fee of around £25, although the insurer you decide to use may pay this fee for you.

CONTENTS INSURANCE

Covers the cost of replacing (or repairing) belongings if they are lost, stolen, damaged, or destroyed. If you are moving, you'll need a new policy for your new address.

LIFE INSURANCE

Lenders like you to have life insurance because it pays off the mortgage if you die. Paying for life insurance is unavoidable if you choose an interest-only mortgage backed by an insurance-based savings plan (see p18). But with other sorts of mortgage you usually have a choice. If you are unattached and dependent-free, you don't need life cover. If you have a joint mortgage and/or children, you probably do.

CRITICAL-ILLNESS INSURANCE

Critical-illness policies pay out a lump sum if you are diagnosed as having one of a defined list of life-threatening or seriously debilitating conditions (such as cancer, multiple sclerosis, loss of limbs/eyesight/ hearing/speech). Whether you need critical-illness insurance or not depends on several factors: the likelihood of serious illness striking before your mortgage is paid off, how it would affect your finances, and what other resources you have available.

COMBINED LIFE AND CRITICAL-ILLNESS INSURANCE

An drawback of critical-illness insurance is that, typically, it will not pay out if you die within 28 days of the diagnosis of a serious illness. So, to plug this gap, many lenders sell policies that combine life with critical-illness cover. If you decide you need both, combined cover tends to be cheaper.

MORTGAGE PAYMENT PROTECTION INSURANCE (MPPI)

Also called 'accident, sickness, and unemployment' (ASU) cover. It aims to meet your mortgage repayments for up to 12 months (sometimes 24) if you're not earning as a result of redundancy or illness. So you don't need it if your ability to meet your monthly mortgage repayments would be unaffected by illness or unemployment. If you're self-employed, having a policy that pays out if you are too ill to earn could be useful, but you're unlikely to benefit from unemployment cover. The reverse may be true if you are an employee with a decent sick-pay scheme. You are unlikely to benefit from MPPI if already out of work, work fewer than 16 hours a week, have not been in continuous employment for at least six months, or are a contract worker.

SEVEN WAYS TO SAVE

1 Before you make your mortgage application, check whether you will be charged a 'high lending fee'.

2 Don't assume that taking the insurance that a lender offers will improve your mortgage chances.

3 Get insurance quotes from independent providers to compare with your lender's quote.

4 Don't assume that because a mortgage offer gives quotes for insurance, you have to buy it.

5 Don't borrow from a high-street lender. Lenders operating by phone or over the Internet are more likely to give you a free choice of insurer.

6 Don't be panicked into buying MPPI and/or critical-illness cover.

7 Find out what your employer offers in life insurance, sick pay, and pension in the event of early retire-ment due to ill health. Check how much you would get if made redundant.

THE COST OF 100% MORTGAGES

One very good reason for making sure that you have as big a deposit as possible to put towards your property purchase is the fact that if you don't have a lump sum of at least 5% of the value of the property, you may face a 'high lending fee'. This is almost certain to be the case if you can scrape together only the difference between the purchase price and the mortgage valuation and so have to take out a 100% mortgage.

The high lending fee pays for an insurance policy called a mortgage indemnity guarantee (MIG), which protects the lender from the risk of not being able to recover the full amount of the loan if you fall behind with your mortgage repayments and the property has to be repossessed.

A limited number of lenders do not charge a high lending fee and you are unlikely to face a fee if you borrow less than 75% of the lender's valuation of the property. But if you need to borrow more than 90–95%, you can generally expect to be charged 5–9% of the difference between 75% of the valuation and the amount of your loan. With a mortgage of £95,000 on a property valued at £100,000, paying for your lender's peace of mind could cost anything from £1,450 to £1,790. If you borrow 100% of the valuation, the fee can be as much as 12% of the amount of the loan over 75% of the valuation. If you can't pay this fee up front, it is added to the loan, which means that you end up paying interest on it too.

As an added precaution, as well as charging a high lending fee, some lenders will make buying mortgage payment protection insurance (see opposite) a compulsory part of the mortgage deal.

Choosing a mortgage

The days are long gone when everyone paid pretty much the same mortgage interest rate and you could get a mortgage only if you had dutifully saved with the same financial institution for a number of years. These days, lenders vie with each other to attract business with a constant stream of new deals for both first-time buyers and borrowers looking to switch mortgages, resulting in hundreds of mortgage deals to choose from. See How to get a good deal, p21, for where to look on the Internet for interactive advice on what type of mortgage might be appropriate for you.

FLEXIBLE MORTGAGES AND WHO THEY SUIT

Unlike traditional loans, where you pay a set amount each month over a fixed number of years (typically 25), flexible mortgages allow you to vary your monthly payments and make extra, lump-sum payments. This means that you can pay off your mortgage more quickly and so reduce the total amount of interest you pay.

This sort of mortgage may not suit first-time buyers on a tight budget, for whom choosing a low rate of interest is a top priority, but flexible mortgages can be very attractive for anyone with unpredictable earnings, for example people who are self-employed. This is because, as well as allowing you to make overpayments, most flexible mortgages also allow you to make underpayments or even stop making payments for a while.

REPAYMENT OPTIONS

The most important decision you have to make when choosing a mortgage is how you will repay it. There are two ways of doing this. Which of these you choose depends to a large extent on your attitude to risk. The stability of your income and whether or not it may rise or fall over the foreseeable future is also a consideration when deciding on a mortgage,

REPAYMENT MORTGAGES

A repayment mortgage – sometimes called a capital repayment mortgage – is the only **risk-free** way of making sure that you (rather than your lender) will own your home after the mortgage has come to an end. With this type of repayment method, part of your monthly mortgage payment is used to pay interest and part is used to pay back the capital you have borrowed, although in the first few years most of your monthly payment is interest (however, see Five mortgage myths). This means that you gradually pay off the loan and – providing you keep up your repayments – you are guaranteed to have repaid it in full by the end of the mortgage term. If you

don't want to take any chances with your mortgage, this is the repayment method to go for.

INTEREST-ONLY MORTGAGES

More risky than a repayment mortgage, as there is no guarantee that you will pay off the loan and so own your home when the mortgage comes to an end. This is because, instead of paying back the loan little by little, the whole of your monthly mortgage payment is made up of interest. None of the capital you have borrowed is paid back until the end of the mortgage term, when you will be expected to pay off the entire loan in one go.

To make sure that you have a sufficiently large lump sum to be able to do this, as well as making mortgage payments you should make payments into some kind of savings plan (see below for the options). The risk you take is that the savings plan may not produce the lump sum you need to repay the mortgage, although if your investments do exceptionally well you could end up with more than you need to clear your mortgage debt.

BACKING UP AN INTEREST-ONLY MORTGAGE

If you are attracted by the idea of combining the purchase of a property with the discipline of regular, long-term saving, you will need to decide on the kind of savings plan you are going to use to back the mortgage. Lenders make it very clear that it is your responsibility to make sure that you are saving enough to build up the lump sum you will need to repay the loan. If you fail to keep up the payments into the savings plan, or you don't pay into a savings plan at all, when the mortgage comes to an end the lender can make you sell your property if that is the only way you have of raising the cash needed to repay the full amount of the loan.

WITH AN ENDOWMENT

In the past, the most popular form of savings plan to back an interest-only mortgage was an endowment policy. This is essentially a life-insurance policy linked to stock market investments. The main disadvantages of this kind of savings plan are that it includes life insurance that you may not need and you are tied to paying the monthly premiums for the full term of the mortgage. If you don't, you risk getting back less than you paid in.

Even if you do manage to keep up with the monthly premiums, there is no guarantee that your savings will grow sufficiently to

produce the necessary lump sum. In recent years, thousands of people have been told that their policies are not on track to repay their mortgages because the underlying stock market investments have not performed as well as had been expected. This 'endowment scandal' has prompted most lenders to give up recommending interest-only mortgages backed by an endowment, in favour of ISA-backed mortgages.

WITH AN ISA

The attraction of a mortgage backed by an Individual Savings Account (ISA) is that an ISA is a more flexible and tax-efficient way of building up a lump sum than an endowment, and it doesn't have to include life insurance (see p101 for more on ISAs). The main disadvantage is that your investments are still linked to the stock market, so there is still no guarantee that you will build up the lump sum you need. You also need to be prepared to keep an eye on how well your investments are performing.

In addition, at the time of writing there is no guarantee that ISAs will continue after 2009, which means that you might have to look for another savings plan at some stage.

WITH A PERSONAL PENSION

Using a personal pension to back an interest-only mortgage is tax-efficient but also very risky. The idea is that you pay into a personal pension (which includes stakeholder pensions – see p89) with the aim of building up a fund that will be used both to pay you a pension and pay off your mortgage. However, only 25% of this money can be used to pay off the mortgage, so the fund built up in the pension plan has to be at least four times the size of your mortgage.

You should also be aware that if you have more than 25 years to go before retiring, you will have to pay mortgage interest for longer than you would with a mortgage linked to another sort of investment – you'll be paying until you decide to take your pension.

Also, if you join an employer's pension scheme, you may have to find another way of saving to pay off your mortgage, because you cannot normally pay into an employer's pension and a personal pension at the same time.

FIVE MORTGAGE MYTHS

1 You have to pay back your mortgage over 25 years.

You can arrange a shorter or longer mortgage term than this. The shorter the term of the mortgage, the lower the overall cost of the loan.

2 In the first few years of a repayment mortgage, you pay off hardly any of the money you have borrowed.

Not true. After five years of a repayment loan of £70,000, for example, you would have paid off around £6,000 of the loan. By contrast, with an interest-only loan you would have paid off nothing after the same number of years.

3 Repayment mortgages cost more than interest-only mortgages.

Interest-only loans only seem cheaper. Once you add the amount you have to pay into the savings plan to the monthly mortgage interest, the total mortgage-related payments on an interest-only mortgage are higher.

4 Interest-only loans are better if you plan to move in the future, as they are more flexible than repayment mortgages.

There's no difference in flexibility between the two types of mortgage. And a repayment mortgage can be better because you will have a smaller capital sum to pay back when the property sells, releasing more funds to put towards the purchase of your next property.

5 Endowment-backed mortgages are still suitable for some people.

The only people who benefit from endowment mortgages are the advisers who get paid commission for selling them.

CHECK ON PENALTIES FOR SWITCHING

If you choose a special mortgage package, such as a fixed, capped, discounted, or cashback deal, there are usually strings attached in the form of (sometimes quite hefty) fees if you decide to pull out of the deal early. Most lenders charge a penalty only if you change your mortgage during the period of the special deal, but some will tie you in beyond that period.

This is not a worry if you plan to stay with the same lender, but if it's possible you'll want to change lender, or repay some or all of the mortgage early, look for a deal that has a short penalty period.

WHAT IF YOU'RE NOT A STANDARD BORROWER?

If there's a chance that you will be refused a mortgage because you don't fit the standard borrower profile of a full-time employee with a regular salary, you shouldn't give up on the idea of buying your own home. Using a mortgage broker can increase your chances of getting a mortgage, as can approaching one of the growing number of lenders who offer:

- **self-certification mortgages**, for people who can't supply evidence of two years' worth of earnings, such as the recently self-employed, new contract workers, or divorcees living on maintenance from an ex-spouse
- **impaired-credit mortgages**, for people who have had problems with credit in the past, which may even have led to a county court judgement (CCJ) or bankruptcy.

THE OPTIONS FOR PAYING INTEREST

Once you have decided how you are going to repay the mortgage, you need to choose the type of interest deal that will best suit you. The type of interest deal you choose can affect how long you are tied to the same lender and the kind of penalty fee you may have to pay if you move house or switch lenders in the future (see left).

STANDARD VARIABLE

All lenders offer mortgages where the interest is charged at their standard variable rate (SVR), which goes up and down in line with interest rates in general. In terms of monthly mortgage payments, this is unlikely to be the cheapest deal available, but there is usually no penalty to pay if you decide to switch your mortgage.

DISCOUNTED VARIABLE

As the name suggests, with this type of deal you pay a lower than normal variable rate for a fixed period of time, which can be as little as six months or as much as five years. Some deals keep the same discount for that period, while others gradually reduce the discount each year. A discounted rate is worth considering if you don't mind the fact that your repayments will still rise and fall in line with interest rates in general, and you like the idea of paying less for your loan to begin with.

BASE-RATE TRACKER

This is a variation on the standard variable theme. The difference is that the lender guarantees that the interest rate you pay will never be more than a fixed percentage above bank base-rate (the rate set by the Bank of England on which lenders base the rates they charge) and that changes in base rate will be passed on immediately. This is an advantage when interest rates fall, but not so good when they rise.

FIXED

With fixed-rate deals, the interest rate you are charged is fixed for a certain number of years – you are guaranteed to be able to pay that rate irrespective of changes in interest rates in general. At the end of the fixed-rate period, you revert to paying the lender's SVR. Fixed rates are ideal if you are on a tight budget and want the security of knowing that your mortgage payments won't go up and down for the first few years. However, you need to be aware that you are generally locked into a fixed-rate deal, so you won't benefit if there is a fall in interest rates in general.

CAPPED

With a capped-rate deal, the rate you pay is semi-fixed in that it is guaranteed not to go above a certain level – the 'cap' – during the period that the capped rate applies. With some deals, there is also a lower limit – the 'collar' or 'floor' – which means that the interest rate you are charged cannot go below a certain level either. A capped-rate can be more attractive than a fixed-rate mortgage if you have some flexibility in your budget (allowing you to cope with limited rises and falls in interest rates) and you want the certainty of knowing that there is a limit on how much interest rates can go up and down.

CASHBACK DEALS

As well as offering different ways of paying the interest, several lenders have special deals that give back, as a cash payment shortly after the loan starts, a percentage of the amount you have borrowed. Providing the monthly payments are manageable, the attraction of this kind of deal is that you get a lump of money to spend as you wish. The disadvantage is that the lender may want some of the money back if you decide to move or change lenders within five or so years of taking out the mortgage.

FIVE STEPS TO A SUCCESSFUL APPLICATION

1 Register to vote When assessing your application, as a way of confirming your current address, lenders will check that you are on the electoral register. Not being registered to vote can count against you.

2 Have your papers ready When applying for a mortgage, you will need to produce between three and six months' worth of payslips or bank statements that show how much you were paid. If you are self-employed, lenders usually want to see your accounts or tax statements for the past two or three years. If you currently rent your home, you may also be asked to provide evidence that you pay your rent on time and a reference from your landlord.

3 Clean up your credit record Most lenders consult a credit reference agency to find out what other debts you have, how good you are at keeping up repayments, and whether you have ever been credit blacklisted. So, in the months leading up to applying for a mortgage, be scrupulous about paying all your bills on time, and – if possible – reduce overdrafts and credit-card balances.

4 Apply early You don't have to have found a property to apply for a mortgage – many lenders will make an 'in principle' mortgage offer based on your earnings. This is worth having because it establishes the price of the property you can afford to buy, reassures prospective sellers that any offer you make is genuine, and helps to speed up the buying process.

5 Be realistic If you apply to borrow more than you can afford, it's very likely that your mortgage application will be turned down. This will show up on your credit record and may deter other lenders from giving you a mortgage. See p14 for working out costs.

THE MORTGAGE CODE

Until October 2004, when the sale of mortgages will be regulated by the Financial Services Authority, lenders, and other mortgage advisers, have to abide by the Mortgage Code. This is a voluntary code of practice that aims to improve the quality of mortgage advice and service levels from lenders, brokers, and other mortgage advisers. Under the Code, every potential borrower must be given a copy of the leaflet *You and Your Mortgage* (which explains your rights under the Code) as early on in the buying process as possible.

Lenders and mortgage intermediaries must tell you what kind of service they offer, which can be:

■ information on one type of mortgage deal, which may apply if you have made up your own mind about the mortgage you want

■ information on different mortgages but no specific advice about which one is best – you use the information to make your own choice

■ advice and a recommendation as to the most suitable deal, following in-depth questions about your current circumstances and future plans.

In addition, mortgage intermediaries must tell you whether they:

■ search the whole market looking for the best deal

■ look only at mortgages offered by a limited number of lenders

■ only make recommendations about mortgages offered by one lender.

An intermediary who searches the whole market is more likely to find a competitive deal than one who looks only at the mortgages of one particular lender.

HOW TO GET A GOOD DEAL

■ Check the personal finance pages of the weekend press for up-to-date information on the best mortgage deals available.

■ Look beyond the high street. Some of the best deals available are from small building societies and the banks who operate only over the telephone or Internet.

■ Use the Internet. One of the big advantages of going online to find a mortgage is that most mortgage Web sites provide interactive comparison tables – you enter your preferences and are presented with a list of possible mortgages. Useful sites include: http://www.charcolonline.co.uk, http://www.marketplace.co.uk, http://www.moneynet.co.uk, and http://www.moneysupermarket.com.

■ Look out for CAT-standard mortgages. CAT (charges, access, terms) marks are a government-backed initiative designed to make it easy to spot a mortgage that is low-cost and penalty-free. Although CAT-standard mortgages aren't guaranteed to be the cheapest, you can be confident that there are no nasty surprises lurking in the small print.

■ If you don't have the time or inclination to search for a good deal, consider using a mortgage broker, who can search the market for you. Brokers usually charge you a fee, but may also be paid a fee by the lender. If so, the Mortgage Code says they must tell you that the lender is paying a fee and disclose the exact amount if it's more than £250.

Looking to buy

In the property world location means everything – it's the cornerstone of the asking price. But your decision to buy will be based on what the location means to you and how long you plan to stay there. Is this property going to be a stepping stone to a larger home, or will you stay in it for the foreseeable future? Are you buying to let a property in an area that will appeal to a particular type of tenant, such as students or business people? Think carefully about your needs and how they might change, how an area may change over time, and keep in mind possible resale values.

WHAT YOU NEED FROM WHERE YOU LIVE

Make a list of the facilities you need or would like to have nearby and rate every property you view against it. The list might include good access to:

- public transport
- a motorway
- school
- college
- hospital
- workplace
- family and friends
- the countryside
- swimming pool or gym
- golf course
- shops
- cinemas and restaurants.

CHOOSING THE LOCATION

After finding an area that offers what you want, focus on specific locations within it. You might even compile a list of streets that you particularly like. Consider not just how a property will suit you while you live there, but how local features will affect its value when you come to sell. The Web site http://www.upmystreet.com gives extensive local information by postcode.

- **Near a public house** This may offer a handy extension to your social life, but pubs can generate traffic and noise, particularly at closing time.

- **Near a school** If places at the school are sought after, the property could have a good resale value to a family with school-age children. In the meantime, how will you be affected by noise from the playground and school-run traffic?

- **Rivers and flood plains** Since the bad flooding in 2000, we're all more aware of the dangers of low-lying areas. Check the past history of the area with the Environment Agency at http://www.environment-agency.gov.uk/flood.

- **Local amenities** Unfortunately, many villages are losing their shops and post offices. Could a lack of local amenities be restricting for you? And would it affect resale value?

- **Public transport** Does your area provide good transport links?

- **On the sea front** Still a dream for some, but consider the possibilities of coastal erosion before you buy.

- **Proposed building projects** You or your solicitor needs to do a thorough local search to ensure that there are no major building projects planned. Future road creation or widening schemes would dramatically affect traffic levels. However, not all projects are bad news financially. The creation of giant shopping malls, which employ hundreds of people, and extensions to the London rail system have been known to push up property prices.

- **Electricity pylons or mobile phone masts** There is currently a debate about the health issues of living close to pylons and phone masts. Check out if the property you like has pylons or cables nearby by contacting http://www.home-envirosearch.com.

- **Crime rate** Click on http://www.upmystreet.com to check out crime rates in your area.

- **Seasonal traffic** Be aware of how traffic in the area changes. It may come alive with tourists in the summer, or host an arts festival in the winter.

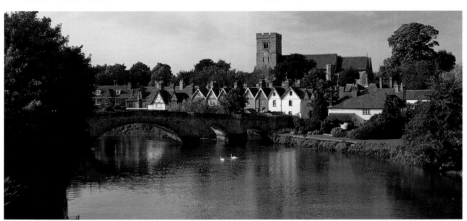

STARTING YOUR PROPERTY HUNT

There are many more options open to the house-hunter now than just the local estate agent. The Internet has opened up a whole new way of discovering and viewing properties. Other possibilities depend on the type of property that interests you.

- **The estate agent** Still most people's first port of call. Be firm about your requirements and price range but be prepared to receive details of properties that don't quite fit all your specifications. Estate agents know that would-be buyers will often compromise, or even change their mind on what they're looking for. It's worth stressing to estate agents that you are genuinely looking to buy, and make it clear what you're hoping to find. Developing a good working relationship with an individual at each agency makes it more likely that they will think of you when a new property comes onto their books.

- **The Internet** Useful if you are planning to move some distance away and can't easily visit local estate agents. You can download details of properties from their sites and register at the same time. They will then e-mail or post you details of other suitable properties that come on the market.

- **Private sales** Some people prefer to sell their property without incurring an agent's fee. Check advertisements in the local paper. More unusual properties, or those in very popular locations, may be advertised in the national press – or on the Internet.

- **Property developers** If you are interested in a newly built property it is worth contacting the **National House Building Council** for a list of members. Check whether any of them has building projects in your chosen area. Most of the larger companies advertise their new projects in local papers. See p30 for more on the implications of buying off-plan.

- **Buildings at risk** You may be hoping to renovate a building that is in need of extensive repair or even reconstruction. Estate agents are usually reluctant to handle such properties. Contact your local authority or try **English Heritage**. **The Society for the Protection of Ancient Buildings** and the **Scottish Civic Trust** publish lists of such properties in Scotland.

- **Auctioneers** Auction houses often have unusual properties on their books that may be in need of renovation or have a sitting tenant, and would not easily sell on the open market. Look in *Yellow Pages* for details of local property auctioneers and register your interest. You will be sent information about future auctions and can purchase the catalogues. See p31 for more on the process of buying property at auction.

- **Self-build** Not quite as DIY as it sounds, though some people do choose to build their own. Basically, you buy a plot of land which already has outline planning permission, then approach one of the many companies that design and make self-build houses. The manufacturer recommends a builder in your area who can construct the house to the required specifications. Self-build companies usually handle planning applications if the house you want doesn't fit your outline planning permission. See p30 for more on buying this way. Useful Web sites include http://www.ebuild.co.uk and http://www.selfbuildit.co.uk.

- **Shared ownership** Some housing associations operate a rental scheme in which a proportion is taken from each monthly payment and put towards eventual ownership of the property. See p14 and contact the **National Housing Federation** for more information.

Viewing a property

Try to visit a property for the first time in daylight. If the place appeals to you, arrange to view it again at another time of day, so you can see it in a different light. Take a good look at the immediate neighbourhood and drive past at commuting times to check the traffic. Give the inside and outside a thorough check – any potential problems you see may affect your decision whether to make an offer, how much you are prepared to pay, and what professional advice you will need.

SEE ALSO Boundaries and Neighbours, p78

WHAT TO ASK THE SELLER

Be friendly and ask questions, whether you're with an agent or not. Many of your queries will relate to the specific property, but general questions may include the following.

- Why is the seller selling?
- Has he or she another property to move to?
- Is the seller's move dependent on another property purchase – in other words, is there a chain?
- Does the seller want a quick sale?
- How long has he or she lived there?
- Has the seller made any improvements or changes to the property?
- What are the neighbours like? Have there been any disagreements about boundaries, access, and so on?

LOOKING AT THE OUTSIDE

This is something you will need to do thoroughly if you're interested in buying. Check the structural soundness and security, and imagine what it would feel like to live there.

STRUCTURE CHECKLIST

- Are the walls in good repair? Does brickwork need repointing? Are there any dark patches on render that may indicate damp?
- Is the chimney stack straight? Ask the seller if it works.
- Does the guttering look sound? Can you see any damp patches that may be caused by leaky gutters?
- Is the roof in good shape? Ask the seller if there is a roof guarantee certificate.
- Do windows and sills look rotten or rusty? In a Conservation Area, there are restrictions on replacement windows – see p255.
- If there is a conservatory, is it generally in good repair? Do the foundations look sound and is the flashing, the metal strip where the conservatory roof abuts the house, intact?
- Are there any large trees nearby that might damage foundations with their roots or block the light? The trees could have a preservation order on them – check with the planning department of your local authority.

LOOKING INSIDE

Go prepared with a tape measure, pen, and paper so that you can note fixtures that the seller wants to either leave or sell. It may be useful to have rough measurements of your current accommodation for comparison, and sizes of any bulky furniture. Then ask yourself some searching questions.

- Can you see any shared elements with neighbours, like a drive, right of way, or flying freehold (where part of one dwelling is built on top of a neighbour's property)?

ACCESS AND SECURITY

- If there is shared entry for a block of flats, is there an entry phone or electronic pass card system? Does the door shut automatically? Ask whether there is a resident or part-time caretaker.
- A public walkway or footpath through the garden or round the boundary of the house might compromise your security.

Is access to the property or garden awkward?

Might anyone need to get through a front or back door with a bike, pushchair, or wheelchair? Is access to the property and up the stairs generally easy for removals? Is it straightforward to get to the garden?

Is there enough storage?

If there are no built-in cupboards or wardrobes, you may need to install some or buy freestanding storage. Either way, it will reduce the size of the rooms.

Is there space for your furniture?

Is there enough space in the kitchen/dining room for the size of table you need? You might need to move radiators to make your furniture fit.

Will the kitchen be suitable?

If you're not planning to replace units, check whether there are enough work surfaces and that the utility area is big enough for your appliances – and any you may want to install in the future.

Which way do the rooms face?

When do they get the sun?

Is there enough water pressure?

Turn on a tap to check, on each storey.

Is there room to expand?

Would it be possible to convert the loft or build an extension? Even if you don't need it yourself, the capacity to expand adds to the value of a property.

USING YOUR SENSES

By using your senses as you walk around the property, you can spot lots of small details that may indicate problems. You can then ask a surveyor to check these out, if you're still interested.

USE YOUR EYES

- If the floorboards are covered up by carpet, ask to see a corner of them in each room, if possible. If you are planning on bare wood floors, rotten wood and boards with big gaps may need to be replaced. Boards in bad condition may also be a sign of dry or wet rot or beetle infestation.

- Look for signs of condensation and mould in the kitchen, bathroom, and toilet. This means that there is a ventilation problem. Windowless bathrooms and toilets should have an adequate extraction system to remove moisture.

- Look around the loft. Check whether it offers good storage space, whether the roof timbers are sound, what sort of insulation it has, and whether the water tank is insulated.

USE YOUR EARS

As you walk from room to room and out into the garden, what can you hear?

Neighbours Visit when the neighbours are likely to be home and check if you can hear them through any party walls. If you are viewing a flat, can you hear people upstairs? Noise carries more easily if a flat has bare wood floors. Although they are currently very popular, some flat leases do not allow bare floors.

Traffic Try to visit when the traffic in the street outside will be at its worst. Can you hear it from the back garden?

Noisy plumbing Run a tap or flush the loo, then listen in the bedrooms. Loud plumbing could mean that the pipes are faulty. Check the location of the boiler. If it's on the other side of the bedroom wall it might wake you up when it comes on in the morning.

USE YOUR SENSE OF SMELL

Try to overlook smells that you will be able to get rid of – cats, dogs, cigarette smoke, or old carpets. It's the smells that may point to problems that you have to watch out for.

Damp A musty odour, rather like potting compost. You would not expect a lived-in property to smell damp unless it had problems such as cracked walls, water penetration, or bad ventilation.

Gas If you think there is a faint whiff around a boiler, then it may need to be replaced.

Toilet If a WC smells dodgy, it could mean there is a leak into the floorboards.

CHECK FOR SAFETY

- A flat above ground level should have a fire escape or some means of exit over a balcony or roof.

- Look at the fuse box. Ideally the fuses should be modern with trip switches – see p60.

- Modern electricity regulations require cables to be housed in plastic trunking.

- Stair banisters should be good and firm. If you may be buying the stair carpet, check that it's not worn and that it's fixed firmly against the stair treads.

POSSIBLE CHANGES

MAJOR EXPENSE:

- new roof
- new kitchen
- new bathroom
- building an extension
- adding a conservatory
- converting the loft
- rewiring the property
- installing central heating
- new boiler
- repointing external brickwork
- replacing a damp course
- replacing windows with double-glazed units.

LESSER EXPENSE:

- redecorating
- adding more units and worktops to the kitchen
- adding a downstairs toilet
- adding fitted wardrobes
- adding shelving or more storage
- insulating the loft
- knocking down walls
- adding a shower.

(See Getting work done, p246–66)

Buying a property

Now you've found the property you want to buy, it's time to get the professionals on board. Your mortgage lender will send a surveyor to do a valuation, and you should commission a more detailed surveyor's report. At the same time, you'll need to appoint a solicitor or licensed conveyancer to deal with the conveyancing – the transfer of the property from the present owner to you. See p29 for more detail. There are a number of documents your conveyancer needs to collect For definitions of some property transaction terms, see p39.

COLLECTING INFORMATION

Your conveyancer will need to assess information about the property. The sources of this information are the seller, the local council, the deeds, and one or more surveyors' reports. The government has plans to make it a legal requirement for the seller to collect this information before putting the property on the market, which would speed up the process. However, the seller will provide relevant paperwork, such as guarantees covering work done on the property, such as timber treatment, chimney repair, electrical work, damp-proofing, repointing of brickwork, roof repair or replacement, tanking (water-proofing) of the cellar, loft or cavity wall insulation, and major plumbing jobs. The seller should also provide any correspondence from the local authority about pending or approved planning permissions or restrictions on parking, removal of trees, change of use, or extending the property.

THE LENDER'S VALUATION REPORT

The purpose of the lender's valuation report is to reassure the bank or building society that the property is worth the money that you want to borrow. It is, in other words, to protect the money lent to you. It is not a detailed survey, but it will establish whether there are any major structural defects that affect the asking price. It assesses the market value of the property, taking into account:

- accommodation and land
- condition of the property
- location
- traffic density
- neighbourhood amenities
- market value of properties in the area
- resale potential.

If, in the surveyor's opinion, the property is overpriced, you have three options. You can find the extra money, taking the risk that you might not get your money back when you come to sell. You can back out and look for another property. Or you can enter into negotiations with a revised offer.

Equally, bear in mind that if you are putting in a sizeable proportion of the asking price yourself, you might want to have the valuation confirmed by a second opinion, as it will be your money that's at risk if the valuation is overgenerous.

COMMISSIONING YOUR OWN SURVEY

If you are buying a new house it should have a National House Building Council certificate. This is a warranty that covers the house for ten years and precludes the need for commissioning your own survey – the lender's valuation report is sufficient. For older properties there are three types of survey:

- Homebuyer's Report and Valuation Survey
- Building Survey
- Specialist Report.

HOMEBUYER'S REPORT AND VALUATION SURVEY

If you are buying a property built since 1900 that has no obvious problems (see Building Survey) it's wise at least to commission your own Homebuyer's Report and Valuation Survey. This will reveal whether there are any hidden defects that might affect your purchase. Most mortgage lenders encourage you to use the surveyor who carries out their valuation report. Most surveyors offer a discount if you book a more detailed survey that can be done at the same time as the valuation report. If, however, you use a different surveyor you will have to pay the full price for the survey, but you will have the benefit of a second opinion on the property.

The report is presented in a standard format of about ten pages in length. The surveyor groups observations under four headings:

1 Defects that are a threat to the fabric or structure of the building, such as subsidence, rotten roof timbers, or other major problems.

2 Defects that could have a significant effect on the purchase price – rotten window frames, central heating not working, for instance.

3 Health and safety aspects, such as wiring requiring replacing or asbestos lagging around a water tank in a loft.

4 Legal matters, for instance whether access is over another person's land, requiring a right of way.

Electricity, gas, plumbing, and central heating are given a visual examination but

not tested. Also, be aware that surveyors cannot usually lift fitted carpets for a floor inspection unless the house is uninhabited or there are obvious signs of dry rot or rising damp. However, they will lift a carpet covering a floor hatch that needs to be accessed. The Homebuyer's Report costs around £300 and takes no more than half a day to complete. For a list of what's checked, see right.

BUILDING SURVEY

For unusual properties and properties built before 1900, a full Building Survey is a good idea. This is not a standard format report, and you can instruct the surveyor to address areas of special concern or, equally, to disregard, say, the condition of the decoration, if you know this needs attention. The survey should cover the condition of:

- the structure of the building (noting any unsoundness, such as subsidence)
- special features, such as beams, thatched roofs, balconies, tanked (waterproofed) cellars
- extensions to the original building
- RSJs – reinforced supporting joists put in to carry a load where a supporting wall has been knocked down
- electrical wiring and plumbing – these will be inspected for health hazards such as lead pipes, but not tested.

The cost of a Building Survey is usually between £400 and £500 and it can take a day or more to complete, depending on the size of the property.

SPECIALIST REPORT

Arising from a Building Survey, the surveyor may recommend that you commission a Specialist Report to examine any serious problem in detail. The specialist concerned could be a structural engineer, or an expert in timber preservation or damp treatment. You may well benefit from a specialist's opinion if the property:

- has been empty for a long time
- is very run down
- has had several extensions added
- is a conversion (say from an oast house or a barn)
- has suffered subsidence in the past or is in a terrace where subsidence has occurred to neighbouring dwellings.

A general surveyor will usually be able to recommend a specialist company that could undertake the survey. Agree the price beforehand, though timber and damp treatment firms should provide a free full report and quote at the same time for any action they recommend.

HOW TO FIND A SURVEYOR

Surveyors can be found through your mortgage lender, in the *Yellow Pages*, on the Internet, or through advertisements in local newspapers, through your estate agent. Ask a friend in the area if you want a truly independent recommendation. Surveyors should be members of RICS (Royal Institute of Chartered Surveyors). The letters MRICS after a surveyor's name mean Member of RICS. After practising for 12 years a surveyor can apply for Fellowship (FRICS). A specialist surveyor could be a member of the Association of Building Engineers (ABE) or the Architects and Surveyors Institute (ASI).

WHAT'S CHECKED IN A HOMEBUYER'S REPORT

THE PROPERTY AND LOCATION

Summary of the type and age of the property, its internal and external construction, and its surroundings.

THE EXTERIOR

Movement Any signs of subsidence, structural movement, or cracking.

Dampness and condensation Whether there is a damp course. Signs of condensation. Moisture readings to check for damp.

Roof, chimneys, and gutters Ground-level inspection.

Walls Whether the walls are true, cracked, or show structural movement.

Windows and doors Condition of frames and panes.

Decoration Paintwork, metal, and timber finishes.

THE INTERIOR

Roof space The internal roof structure, insulation, and ventilation. The surveyor may not go up into the loft if it's not easily accessible.

Ceilings Condition and structure.

Floors Signs of subsidence or settlement are noted.

Walls and partitions What they are made of, and any structural problems.

Fireplaces Not tested.

Woodwork Condition of doors, kitchen fittings, and skirting boards. Signs of infestation, damp, and dry rot.

Decoration Plaster and paintwork.

SERVICES AND SITE

Electricity and gas A visual inspection of meters and outlets.

Water Visible plumbing, storage tanks, cylinders and immersion heaters, and boilers. None of these will be tested.

Heating Central or other heating will be visually inspected but not tested.

Drainage Visual inspection only.

1 Do your research. You need to assess how fair the asking price is, and how fast houses in the area are selling. Scour the property papers and estate agents' windows, and view similar houses in the area. Ask the agent how long the house has been on the market, and whether there have been any other offers.

2 Only offer well below the asking price if you're prepared to irritate the seller and risk losing the property. But if the price is high and you aren't set on getting only that property, it can pay off.

3 Offer slightly less than you think you'll end up paying, hoping to meet the seller in the middle.

4 Sellers normally want a quick sale, so put yourself in as strong a position as possible and emphasize this to the agent or seller: you're at an advantage if you have nowhere to sell, you have a buyer for your current property, you already have a mortgage approved, and if you're flexible on completion dates.

5 Appear serious and committed but not desperate – don't let the agent or seller know that this is your dream house.

6 Make it clear that your offer is subject to contract and survey.

7 Ask the agent (or, if it's a private sale, the vendor) for a commitment in writing to take the property off the market once your offer is accepted. The agent may not be prepared to do this, but it's always worth asking.

8 Use carpets and curtains as a negotiation tool by offering to pay a specified amount over the asking price of the house to include them. Second-hand furnishings aren't much use anywhere else, so don't pay over the odds.

CONVEYANCING – WHAT HAPPENS AND WHY

Conveyancing – the process by which the house or flat changes hands – has developed somewhat haphazardly over the years. A government survey in 1999 found that the system used in England and Wales is the slowest in Europe. However, the good news is that it is also the cheapest. There are two landmarks in a typical conveyancing transaction – exchange of contracts and completion.

PROCEDURE UP TO EXCHANGE OF CONTRACTS

Once you have agreed a price with the seller, the seller's conveyancer draws up a formal contract laying down the terms on which the seller is prepared to sell the house. As well as dealing with the price, it will prove that the seller does actually own the house and state whether there are any restrictions on the use to which the property can be put. The original oral agreement is not legally binding – the law requires that any contract for the sale of property be in writing.

Your conveyancer checks the contract to ensure that the terms are acceptable and that the seller really does own the land. He/she will also make several searches, asking public bodies questions such as:

- Has the local authority any development plans that may affect the house, such as for a new road?

- If the house is in a mining area, has it been affected by subsidence?

- Was planning permission obtained for any building work done on the property? Does this work comply with building regulations?

- Have any restrictions on the use of the house been complied with? Will they affect your use of the property?

You, as the buyer, should also commission a survey at this stage, and your mortgage lender will organize a valuation report (see p26). The object of all these investigations is to discover as much as possible about the house before you legally commit to buy. If you discover something unfavourable (such as plans

for the new M100 at the bottom of the garden), you can withdraw from the transaction without any comeback from the seller. The law does not require the seller to disclose this information to you – it is up to you to find it out. The government has produced plans for a Seller's Pack, in which sellers would be legally required to disclose much more information to a buyer at the start of a transaction, but these plans are at present on hold – see Selling your home, p36.

EXCHANGE OF CONTRACTS

- Once you and your legal representative are satisfied with the house, the contract is drawn up in two identical copies – you sign one and the seller the other.

- The contract becomes legally binding only when the copies are exchanged, so that each party has a copy of the contract signed by the other and both could sue on the contract, should the need arise.

- Contracts are normally 'exchanged' over the telephone – the hard copies are physically sent later.

- If the transaction is one of a chain, each dependent on the next (see right), all the contracts in the chain must be exchanged at the same time.

- You, as the buyer, will be asked to pay a deposit of up to 10% of the purchase price on exchange. This is held by the seller's legal representative until completion and is non-returnable if you decide not to proceed with the purchase.

After exchange, your conveyancer draws up a document known as a Transfer. This is the document that concludes the transfer of ownership from the seller to you, the buyer. Once you have signed it, the Transfer is sent to the seller's conveyancer to be signed by the seller. The seller's conveyancer will keep it until completion (see below). Your conveyancer must ensure that you have the rest of the purchase money ready for the day fixed for completion. Your conveyancer will deal direct with your lender, if you have arranged a mortgage, and will also draw up the mortgage document for you to sign. Some final searches by your conveyancer ensure that there have been no last-minute changes in the legal ownership of the property at this stage.

COMPLETION

On completion, your conveyancer hands over the money and the seller's conveyancer hands over the Transfer deed, transferring the ownership to you. The seller leaves keys to the property with the conveyancer or estate agent for you to collect. But the legal work is still not finished. Your ownership must be registered at the Land Registry (a government body that records the ownership of land) and you must pay stamp duty – your conveyancer will arrange both of these. Stamp duty is a government tax levied as a percentage of the purchase price on all purchases of houses and flats for more than £60,000.

FINDING LEGAL HELP

When you're looking to buy a property, it's worth asking three solicitors or licensed conveyancers to give you a rough estimate of their likely costs, based on the property price and whether there are issues that may require extra time to resolve. These might include leasehold queries on a newly

built flat, for instance, concerning parking, management company responsibilities, and so on, or queries on a repossessed property, where the other party might wish to complete the sale with minimal expenditure of effort. Both of these cases would increase the burden on the buyer's legal representative.

Find a solicitor or licensed conveyancer by:

- personal recommendation
- looking in *Yellow Pages*, or the Internet
- contacting the **Law Society**. You can search on their website, http://www.solicitors-online.com.

THE CHAIN BREAKS

One of the major causes of problems in property sales is the chain. This is where a chain of people are all dependent on selling their existing home before they can proceed with the purchase of their new one – A is buying from B, who is buying from C, and so on. It only needs one sale to fall through for the whole chain to fail. So through no fault of your own, your sale and purchase may fall through, at great expense and inconvenience. This is why exchange of contracts should ideally take place only when everyone in the chain is ready, and why it helps if everyone in the chain can exchange at exactly the same time.

GAZUMPING

As there is no binding contract until exchange, and as exchange often occurs several weeks after you make an offer on a house, there is a time where the seller may back out. If the seller backs out right at the last minute before exchange with the object of forcing up the price, this is called gazumping. The seller may be playing you off against another prospective buyer. You may have incurred expenses in legal, search, and surveyors' fees and feel that you are at the seller's mercy. The government's plans for a Seller's Pac, (see p36) and for electronic conveyancing (see left) are designed to shorten the delay between acceptance of offer and exchange, thus reducing the likelihood of gazumping.

E-CONVEYANCING

Much of the conveyancing process is still paper-based. Although the actual exchange of contracts can be done over the telephone, drafts of contracts and transfers are documents that must be sent through the post, and this can cause delay. The government plans that in the future contracts and transfers will exist only electronically. They will be transmitted and signed via computer, saving time and expense. Some conveyancers already allow you to track your purchase via their Web site, with a password.

A major initiative is the **National Land Information Service** (NLIS), which enables local authority searches to be made online, providing the results in hours rather than weeks. Information held at the Land Registry on the ownership of property can be accessed online. These advances will speed up the conveyancing process dramatically. There may also be cost savings, although the new technology involves expensive investment, which conveyancers may want to pass on to their clients.

BUYING IN SCOTLAND

The legal process for buying property in Scotland is significantly different from that in England and Wales, and is often looked to as a model for a system where chains and gazumping are much less of a problem. See p38.

Buying: special cases

Perhaps you can't afford to buy a standard property on your own, or perhaps you've seen a plot that's being developed and looks just right for you. Here's some help on what to do.

HOW TO GO ABOUT SELF-BUILD

If you want a new property but don't want to buy from a developer, the answer could be to self-build. This doesn't mean that you have to lay the bricks yourself – unless you have the time and the right skills – but that you buy a plot of land, usually with planning permission, and supervise the construction of your own home.

A good place to start is the Web site http://www.ebuild.co.uk, which allows you to search for a suitable building plot on ebuild's UK building plots database, and buy step-by-step guides and home-plan books in their online bookshop. The site also has a directory of building companies manufacturing self-assembly houses, most of whom will help you obtain planning permission, should you need it, and recommend builders in your area who can erect the house for you.

Building your own home takes time and commitment. Over the period of construction you have to either live in a caravan on site or bear the cost of living in one home while building another, as well as devoting your life to being site foreman. You also have to organize a self-build mortgage, which is released in tranches to cover the cost of ongoing work.

Self-build is a route to achieving an impressive property that will cost very much less to build than it will be worth in the end.

BUYING A HOME OFF-PLAN

Developers often sell properties before they have been built, sometimes with exchange of contracts taking place before building even begins – this is called buying off-plan. Sometimes all the purchaser has to go on are the architect's plans, specifications, and drawings, though some developers may have a virtual reality computer programme that allows you to 'walk through' the proposed building, or a show flat or house that you can inspect on site.

When you are ready, you can sign reservation papers to reserve a home in the complex. There will be a reservation fee of a few hundred pounds. Don't put your own house on the market or give notice on a rented home until you have been given an absolute date for completion of building works.

BEFORE YOU COMMIT

1 To help you imagine the space offered in the new property, check the internal and external measurements on the plan against the measurements of your current home.

2 Pay regular visits to the site. Check boundaries and measurements against the plan as soon as possible. If in doubt about the developer's intentions, contact the local planning department to check if specifications have changed.

3 If looking round a show home, note whether artificial light is used during the day. Has the furniture been scaled down to make the rooms look big?

4 Check the small print of the reservation agreement to make sure that the property you are reserving has the same specifications as the show home or the property in the plans.

5 Ask the developer the following questions.

■ Has final planning permission been granted or is it still pending for some aspects of the development?

■ Has the heating system been tested in other developments?

■ What fixtures, fittings, and finishes are included in the total price? Are any of these to be paid for as they are installed? Some developers include decorating, carpets, and even curtains.

6 Make sure that there are penalty clauses if the developer misleads you or is late completing.

HOW TO BUY AT AUCTION

If you want an unusual property or one that needs renovation, the auction route can offer some good bargains. Repossessed homes are often sold by auction, too.

1 Contact property auctioneers in the relevant area and order catalogues for forthcoming auctions. Check when you need to register, should you want to bid.

2 Arrange to visit any properties you are interested in.

3 Make a shortlist and go to the local authority with questions about your chosen properties. Find out if they have rights of way, boundary problems, and so on.

4 Arrange to revisit properties you are still interested in. Organize a survey and ask the surveyor or a builder to advise what, if any, work would need to be done and how much, roughly, it would cost.

5 Visit a mortgage provider to set up a mortgage offer on any property you would be prepared to buy. This has to be done before you go to auction. You can only bid if you have the money available,

or it could be accessed within three weeks of your bid being accepted.

6 The day before the auction, phone the auctioneers to check that the properties have not been withdrawn.

7 Attend the auction having decided the maximum amount of money you can bid, and stick to it.

8 If your bid is successful, your contract to buy the property is binding as soon as the hammer goes down. You will usually be asked to sign a contract, though there is no actual legal need – you are bound anyway. You will be asked to pay a 10% deposit or £1,500, whichever is the greater. You will lose this if you back out later.

9 Insure the property immediately.

10 Pass details of your property to your mortgage lender for fast-track processing.

11 Instruct your solicitor or conveyancer.

12 Completion should take place within three weeks.

SHARED OWNERSHIP – BUY AND RENT

Housing associations and charitable trusts sometimes offer first-time buyers – who may be single people, single parents, or students – the chance to part-buy/part-rent low-cost properties. Most local authority housing departments have lists of shared ownership schemes in their area. If you are eligible for a particular scheme you can fill in and submit an application form. If you are accepted, you will be offered a vacant property or put on a waiting list.

Conditions associated with shared ownership include:

■ payment of a reservation fee, usually a couple of hundred pounds, which is non-returnable but does go towards the price

■ getting a mortgage to buy your 50% or 75% share of the property

■ your mortgage lender will carry out a valuation report (see p26), which will cost you around £150

■ you will need to appoint a conveyancer to carry out the transaction (see p29). This may cost around £400

■ when you move into the property you will be paying a mortgage to the lender and some rent to the association each month

■ after you have lived in the property for a certain time, you can buy more shares in it (until you own it outright), or sell your shares back to the association (at a fair market rate)

■ once you own the property outright, you can sell it on the open market.

BUYING A PROPERTY WITH OTHER PEOPLE

Pooling resources with friends is one way of buying a home that's beyond your means. The problem comes when one party wants to sell their share.

■ Up to four people can be named on a property deed as owners.

■ Get a solicitor to draw up a contract between co-owners so that if anyone wants to leave, the other co-owners get the first option on buying their share. If they can't afford it, there should be a joint effort to find a mutually acceptable replacement.

■ It's simpler if everyone owns and pays equal shares of everything – mortgage payments and other outgoings – even if one of the owners is away a lot. A solicitor can draw up a deed of trust to specify everyone's obligations.

■ All co-owners should have adequate insurance cover that will pay their share of outgoings in the event of redundancy or illness.

WEB SITES AND ADDRESSES

Association of Residential Letting Agents, Maple House, 53-55 Woodside Road, Amersham, Bucks HP6 6AA
phone: 0845 345 5752; fax: 01494 431530;
e-mail: info@arla.co.uk
Web site: www.arla.co.uk

Site has a Buy to Let area with detailed information on the associated charter, what 'buy to let' is, and which lenders will offer the finance. There is detailed information for both tenants and landlords.

Charcol, Lintas House, 15-19 New Fetter Lane, London EC4A 1AP phone: 0800 71 81 91;
e-mail: coe@charcolonline.co.uk
Web site: www.charcolonline.co.uk

Independent financial adviser.

ebuild
email: info@ebuild.co.uk
Web site: www.ebuild.co.uk

For self build, DIY, and house renovation. There is an extensive Web directory of building products and services.

English Heritage, Customer Services Department, PO Box 569, Swindon SN2 2YP
phone: 0870 333 1181; fax: 01793 414926;
e-mail: customers@english-heritage.org.uk
Web site: www.english-heritage.org.uk

Envirosearch Residential
Web site: www.home-envirosearch.com

Government housing information
Web site: www.housing.odpm.gov.uk

General housing information, including government housing policy and the housing choices available to homeowners, tenants, and landlords.

HM Land Registry, 32 Lincoln's Inn Fields, London WC2A 3PH
phone: 020 7917 5996; fax: 020 7917 5934;
e-mail: marion.shelley@landreg.gsi.gov.uk
Web site: www.landreg.gov.uk

Explanation of the role of the land registration agency for England and Wales. There are reports on property prices, links to regional offices, and details of how to obtain online access to registry documents.

Homecheck, Imperial House, 21-25 North Street, Bromley BR1 1SS
phone: 0870 606 1700; fax: 0870 606 1701;
e-mail: info@homecheck.co.uk
Web site: www.homecheck.co.uk

Housing Corporation, Maple House, 149 Tottenham Court Road, London W1T 7BN
phone: 020 7393 2000; fax: 020 7393 2111;
e-mail: enquiries@housingcorp.gsx.gov.uk
Web site: www.housingcorp.gov.uk

Landmark Information Group Ltd, 3rd Floor, Challenger House, 42 Adler Street, London E1 1EE
phone: 0207 958 4999;
fax: 0207 958 4981;
e-mail:
webmaster@landmark-information.co.uk
Web site: www.landmark-information.co.uk

MarketPlace
Web site: www.marketplace.co.uk

Helps you to find the right property, mortgage, loan, pension, investment, or insurance for you.

Law Society, The
Law Society's Hall, 113 Chancery Lane, London WC2A 1PL
phone: 020 7242 1222; fax: 020 7831 0344:
email: info-services@lawsociety.org.uk
Web site: www.lawsoc.org.uk

Enables you to search for a law firm or individual solicitor in England and Wales.

Money Supermarket, 1 Chantry Court, Sovereign Way, Chester, Cheshire CH1 4QA
phone: 0845 345 5708;
e-mail:
moneysupermarket@mortgage2000.co.uk
Web site: www.moneysupermarket.com

Offers comparison tables for personal finance products.

moneynet.co.uk, 4 Cobden Court, Wimpole Close, Stanley Road, Bromley BR2 9JF
phone: 020 8313 9030; fax: 020 8464 1971;
e-mail: info@moneynet.co.uk
Web site: www.moneynet.co.uk

Comprehensive, impartial, and independent advice on the products available in the personal finance sector.

National Association of Citizens Advice Bureaux, Myddelton House, 115-123 Pentonville Road, London N1 9LZ
e-mail: adviceguide@nacab.org.uk
Web site: www.adviceguide.org.uk

Covers advice for England, Scotland, Wales, and Northern Ireland and a wide range of topics from money and employment to housing, education, consumer affairs, and the legal system. Enables you to pinpoint your nearest CAB.

National House Building Council (NHBC), Buildmark House, Chiltern Avenue, Amersham, Buckinghamshire HP6 5AP
phone: 01494 735363
Web site: www.nhbc.co.uk

A warranty and insurance provider for new homes.

National Housing Federation, 175 Gray's Inn Road, London WC1X 8UP
phone: 020 7278 6571; fax: 020 7833 8323;
e-mail: info@housing.org.uk
Web site: www.housing.org.uk

Body representing the independent social housing sector.

National Land Information Service (NLIS), Local Government Information House, Layden House, 76-86 Turnmill Street, London EC1M 5LG
phone: 01279 451625
Web site: www.nlis.org.uk

Royal Institute of Chartered Surveyors, RICS Contact Centre, Surveyor Court, Westwood Way, Coventry CV4 8JE
phone: 0870 333160; fax: 020 7222 9430;
e-mail: contactrics@rics.org.uk
Web site: www.rics.org/public

Information on residential surveys, boundary disputes, and advice on finding a surveyor.

Scottish Civic Trust, The Tobacco Merchants House, 42 Miller Street, Glasgow G1 1DT
phone: 0141 221 1466; fax: 0141 248 6952
Web site: www.scotnet.co.uk/sct

SelfBuildit
Web site: www.selfbuildit.co.uk

Help and advice on building your own house.

Shared Ownership Information and Advice Line
phone: 0345 585757

Society for the Protection of Ancient Buildings, 37 Spital Square, London E1 6DY
phone: 020 7377 1644; fax 020 7247 5296;
e-mail: info@spab.org.uk
Web site: www.spab.org.uk

Stamp Office
phone: 0845 603 0135;
Web site: www.inlandrevenue.gov.uk

Gives details of 2,000 'disadvantaged' UK areas where land and property sales of £150,000 or less are not subject to stamp duty.

UK Property Web, 40 The Woodpeckers, Weymouth, Dorset DT3 5RS
phone: 01305 814721;
e-mail: wendy.hyde@ukpropertyweb.co.uk
Web site: www.ukpropertyweb.co.uk

Dedicated to buying and selling property privately. No commission charge. Also offers a property matching service.

Up My Street
Web site: www.upmystreet.com

Enter your postcode to find information on services in your area.

CHAPTER TWO

Selling, moving, letting

Preparing to sell a property

In today's fast-paced and highly mobile society, it's not unusual to own five or more homes in one lifetime. Home ownership is no longer just equated with shelter – the term has become synonymous with investment. Buying and selling homes has become a national pastime in the UK, with many people amassing a considerable amount of capital by following the adage 'buy low, sell high'. Much of the advice here is relevant if you're preparing to let your home.

THREE KEY INGREDIENTS

Getting the highest and best price for your home usually requires more time and energy than money. However, before getting started, you need three key ingredients:

Commitment Unless you are truly committed to selling your home, and are mentally and emotionally prepared to move on, you will not take all the steps necessary to getting it sold. Be very clear of your motivation before embarking on the marketing process.

Detachment You need to be able to step back and view your home through a buyer's eyes, a vision not clouded by personality, memories, or emotion. You are not selling your home – you are selling a house.

Cooperation Unless you have the cooperation and involvement of any other household members as well as your estate agent, the task at hand will be extremely difficult. It's all energies on board, working toward the same goal – the sale.

BUYERS WANT SPACE, FUNCTION, AND POTENTIAL

Just as you the seller are looking to get your highest and best price for your house, the buyer is also looking to get the best possible deal. Your job is to make the buyer think that your house is just that deal. With the high prices of homes today, buyers have become more and more particular. They want to get the most they can for their money – the most space, function, and potential. Also, today's buyers are usually extremely busy people, and prefer to use what little leisure time they have for recreation. Most of them are looking to pay as much as they can afford for a home that they can move straight into, without having to spend a lot of time or money on alterations. As a seller you need to present your home so that it meets the needs of the greatest buying audience in order to realize your best sale price.

KERB APPEAL – THE FIRST STEP

Begin outdoors. Stand across the road from where you live and assess how your home measures up to the rest of the homes on your street. Does it grab your attention? Prospective buyers are likely to drive past your house first and will only bother to come inside if they like what they see from the street. This is kerb appeal, and it is critical. Your house should be appealing and welcoming, one of the nicest on the street, yet in keeping with the style of the neighbourhood. Fresh paintwork, a well-manicured garden, and the overall first impression of a cared-for home are important factors in getting buyers inside.

CREATE A PLEASING AMBIENCE

Buyers probably make the decision whether or not to buy within the first 60–90 seconds of entering a house. A buyer may not even be aware of this decision because it has been made subconsciously. Although most buyers have a list of requirements for their purchase, the decision whether or not to buy a particular house is usually based on intangibles. The place has to feel right. And if it doesn't, they are out of the door as fast they came in.

What can you do as a seller to make a house feel right? Pay close attention to those subliminal messages, a technique that is used often in advertising. Potential buyers will experience your house with their five senses – sight, hearing, touch, and smell. Ask a good friend to do an inspection before buyers come.

Inside the house, good lighting is essential, both natural and ambient, to create a cheerful atmosphere, and colours should be soft, neutral, and easy on the eye. Cleanliness and order throughout evoke a looked-after feeling in the home. Clean windows, curtains and surfaces, especially in the kitchen, are reassuring.

Soft background music puts the buyer at ease. Subtle fresh scents as well as plants and flowers add life and vitality to a room. A fire in the fireplace on a chilly day creates the feeling of homeliness, as does the old trick of something yummy baking in the oven. If you have a garden, remove weeds and trim plants and lawn. Sweep paths. Pets, children, and sellers themselves should remain unobtrusive in order to let the prospective buyers view the home in a relaxed and comfortable manner.

PROJECT AN IMAGE OF SPACIOUSNESS

Buyers have to be able to imagine living in the house that they are viewing, with their own possessions and furniture. It is your job to make it as easy as possible for them to visualize this. Since space is always at a premium, you need to make the most of what you have.

■ Edit your belongings ruthlessly and arrange furniture to allow freedom of movement. Now, more than ever, 'less is more' (money in your pocket, that is). If a buyer cannot see a room for clutter, there is no chance of them mentally moving in. Clear out all shelves and cupboards, and put everything back in a neat, organized manner. Buyers need to feel that there is adequate room for all their belongings, not get the impression that even you are struggling for space. Take advantage of unused storage areas

in the house, in lofts, basements, garages, under the stairs, and so on, and present it neatly as an asset, not an eyesore. Never, ever, present one of your bedrooms, no matter how small, as a junk room. You will be doing yourself out of money.

■ Pay special attention to the kitchen and bathroom. As these are two rooms that can be the most costly to redo, buyers tend to scrutinize them carefully. Few buyers have the money left over after purchasing their new home for any major renovations, so they need to feel that the kitchen and bathrooms are in good, useable condition. Sometimes it takes as little as a lick of paint on walls or cabinets, new flooring and/or tiling, and some updated lighting to make a kitchen or bathroom look and feel good.

TEN STEPS TO MAKING A SUCCESSFUL SALE

1 Clear away all clutter – see p130. Pack up and store anything inessential. You'll be ahead of the game when moving day comes along.

2 Do a really effective spring clean, whatever the time of year. Pay special attention to kitchens and bathrooms. Take care of any repairs.

3 Fresh paint can do wonders to brighten up a room. Use a light, warm, neutral colour.

4 First impressions are crucial. Be sure your home looks appealing from the front door through the entrance hall. A tidy garden, clean windows, polished door furniture, and a welcome mat will invite buyers to step inside.

5 Indoors and out replace or trim plants that are overgrown or unsightly. Buy fresh flowers for the house.

6 Pay careful attention to subliminal messages: soft music, adequate lighting, and pleasing scents elicit a positive emotional response.

7 Pick a colour scheme, preferably based on something you already own, like a painting or rug, and use these colours as accents to create harmony throughout the house.

8 Now that you have cleared and cleaned, reinstall some of your favourite things. But remember, 'less is more'.

9 If necessary, buy a few accessories to give your house that pulled-together feeling. Things like colourful rugs, fresh towels, decorative cushions, new curtains, and prints can all be taken with you when you move.

10 Finally, the most artful preparation in the world will not sell a house if it is overpriced. Accept that you may need to hire a qualified estate agent, and listen to their advice.

Selling your home

It's easy to feel you lack control when you sell a property, especially if you need a speedy sale and a good price to secure your next purchase. With estate agency fees and legal costs adding up to a significant sum, you could save considerably by selling the property yourself or trying for a house swap. Whichever route you go, do all you can to maximize your property's selling power, be aware of the issues involved in the legal contracts that selling or exchange entails, and if you sell through an agent, choose carefully.

SEE ALSO Buying a property, p26–9

THE SELLER'S PACK

New legislation, likely to take effect from 2004 or 2005, will oblige anyone selling a property to pay to provide prospective buyers with a seller's pack, consisting of:

- a completed local authority search on their property (indicating, for example, whether there are any development plans for the area)
- a full survey of the property – though this will not be a valuation.

While the pack is expected to make the selling and buying process quicker in England and Wales, it may increase property prices a little, to offset the money sellers have to spend on preparing the pack. Banks and building societies will probably still want to conduct their own valuations before lending on the property, and this cost will probably be passed on to the buyer one way or another.

CHOOSING AN ESTATE AGENT

Most property sales are conducted through an agent, whom the seller pays to represent them in the selling transaction. Ideally you should ask three agents to value your property and recommend a selling price. Personal recommendations are a good place to start, especially from someone who has sold a property similar to yours – perhaps a former neighbour.

- Look at the sort of details your chosen agents produce for properties like yours.

- Ask each agency what they see as your home's main selling points, and get detailed information on how they plan to advertise it. How often will it appear in the local paper? Do they have a Web site or do they supply details to a composite Web site, such as www.propertyfinder.co.uk?

- Look for an agent who demonstrates a good knowledge of the area and shows a genuine interest in handling your sale.

- Choose someone you get on with. A good relationship with the agent is important and will make it easier to sort out any problems that may arise.

- Consider using a smaller agency – they may depend more on your sale and make more effort than a large agency, which may have so many properties that they can't give yours their full attention.

COMPARING AGENTS – WHAT TO CHECK

- Look at the charges carefully – most agents charge a percentage of the final sale price, which means you only pay if and when the property is sold, but some may offer a lower percentage and charge fees for advertising, putting up the sale board, and arranging viewings, all of which you may be liable to pay for immediately.

- Check the small print and ask what happens if you sell to a neighbour, friend, or colleague – some agencies claim 'sole selling rights' (not the same thing as 'sole agency' rights, see right), which means you have to pay their fee even if you end up selling the property without their help. This may even apply for a set time after your contract with the agent has expired.

- Don't automatically opt for the agent quoting the highest sale price – they may just be desperate for your business. A difference of 5 per cent is acceptable, but if the estimates are adrift by more than this, ask the agent quoting the highest rate to justify their figure with actual examples of recent sales of similar property in the same area.

YOUR RESPONSIBILITY AS A SELLER

You and your solicitor or conveyancer should together fill in two legally binding documents: the Fixtures and Fittings form, and the Property Information form. These should cover all the basic information about the state of the property and exactly what you're selling.

As the seller, it's best to be honest if a potential buyer asks about something you know is dodgy – for instance, if you know of some dry rot, or have very difficult neighbours. Sellers can be sued for not revealing the truth.

COST OF SELLING A HOME IN ENGLAND & WALES

Property price (£)	Legal fees (£)	Estate agent's fee (£)	Total funds you will need (£)
25,000	381	728	1,109
50,000	396	936	1,332
60,000	399	1,020	1,419
80,000	422	1,253	1,675
100,000	446	1,490	1,936
150,000	502	2,129	2,631
200,000	551	2,851	3,402
300,000	658	4,132	4,790
500,000	867	6,697	7,564

Source: *The Woolwich Cost of Moving Survey 2002*. Figures compiled by the University of Greenwich, School of Land and Construction Management.

Note: This tables gives the *average* cost of selling in England and Wales. Actual costs vary by region and tend to be highest in the Southeast and Southwest of England.

SOLE OR MULTIPLE AGENCY?

- A sole agency agreement, where you let just one agent try to sell your property for a set number of weeks, is the cheapest option. Multiple agency, where you place the property with several agents at the same time, can increase the cost by as much as one per cent of the sale price or even more, and as most buyers will visit or contact all the estate agents in an area, you may not gain much by signing up with more than one.

- If your start with a sole agency agreement and the agent doesn't manage to sell your property within the agreed sole agency time, you can try multiple agency as the next step. Multiple agency may be worth considering from the start, however, if you want to sell very quickly, or if your property falls between two areas of potential buyers (whether districts of a city, or nearby towns) and your first choice of agent doesn't have a branch in both areas.

- An estate agent may well agree to a shorter sole agency period than their terms and conditions state. Try to get this amended when you sign up, rather than challenge it later if they haven't found a buyer.

SELLING PROPERTY WITHOUT AN AGENT

Selling your property privately, without involving an estate agent, may entail more work on your behalf, and you might find it hard to reach as many prospective buyers as an estate agent would. On the other hand, if you're successful, you'll save the commission you would have to pay an estate agent. If you have already signed with an estate agent, however, don't agree a private sale unless you are absolutely certain that you aren't breaching the terms of your contract, or you could still be charged a fee – see Comparing agents, p36.

FIRST STEPS

- Find out how much estate agents are asking for similar properties in your area.

THE LEGAL TRANSACTION

The legal side of selling a house is more straightforward than buying, when you may need extensive legal help you be sure of what you're getting. Ask three solicitors or licensed conveyancers to quote an all-in price to handle the sale. Alternatively, it is possible to undertake conveyancing yourself, though you will need to be able to devote considerable time to the procedure and not be daunted by the paperwork. Consumers' Association publishes a book, *Which? Way to Do Your Own Conveyancing*.

FIND A SOLICITOR BY:

- personal recommendation
- looking in *Yellow Pages*, or the Internet
- writing to the **Law Society** for a list of local registered legal practices. The Law Society also has a web site with the directory of solicitors on it and a search facility for local firms – http://www.solicitors-online.com.

FIND A LICENSED CONVEYANCER BY:

- looking in *Yellow Pages*, or the Internet

See Buying a property, p28 for the sequence of a property sale once an offer's been accepted.

SELLING PROPERTY IN SCOTLAND

The process of selling and buying property in Scotland differs from transactions in England and Wales in several ways.

Property is advertised either at a fixed price or inviting offers over a certain sum. With a fixed price, the first offer of that sum should secure the purchase, though a seller can accept a lower offer.

If more than one buyer is interested in a property, the seller's estate agent may set a date and time for sealed bids to be submitted. The seller can then choose the highest price offered.

The seller's legal representative accepts the chosen offer in writing. There still isn't a legally binding contract, until negotiations on the terms of the contract have been settled – called Conclusion of missives. Once this has been reached, if either the seller or buyer wishes to withdraw, they must pay the other party compensation.

SWAPPING HOMES

Swapping your home is an alternative to selling the traditional way. Several Web sites allow you to advertise the property you have and outline what you're looking for. If you want to stay in the same vicinity, you might even find a neighbour with whom to swap. If the two properties to swap are valued differently, there will be a balance to pay. A significant financial advantage is that in a property swap, stamp duty is payable only on the higher priced property – and you could agree to share that cost with the other owner.

- Pay for an independent valuation from a surveyor.
- Decide the asking price.
- Draw up a short description of the property, using the conventional abbreviations used in the local property paper. Ask a friend to check it, in case you've forgotten anything.

ADVERTISING YOU HOME LOCALLY

- Pay for a small ad in the local paper, giving a telephone number but not your address.
- Drop details into local letterboxes. It's cheeky, but people do it – your home may be just what someone local is looking for, whether it has a special feature, bigger garden, or is simply larger or smaller than their own.
- Ask to display an advertisement on staff noticeboards in large offices, universities, or hospitals.

ADVERTISING FURTHER AFIELD

- Sign up with a company on the Internet. One way Internet companies can afford to advertise your home without charging you or the eventual buyer is by passing your details to other companies who are interested in people who are moving and might want their products/services. You aren't committed to buying any of these. Read the small print carefully.
- Set up your own Web site dedicated to selling the property; see Building your own Web site, p278. This may be worth doing if the value or location of your property makes it of special interest. Don't give the exact address, but emphasise if it's in a tourist area or employment hot-spot, especially if employees come to the area from a long distance or from abroad.
- If you're in a popular area but don't want to go on the Web, an advertisement in a national Sunday newspaper or a magazine may produce a buyer.

SHOWING PEOPLE ROUND

- Create a demand. Estate agents often arrange for several potential buyers to view at more or less the same time, to make the property look popular. Hold an 'open house' viewing on a single afternoon so that prospective buyers find the place buzzing and realize they need to make a good offer quickly.
- **Always** have another person with you when you show round potential buyers.

MAKING A SALE

- Ask for all offers to be put in writing to your solicitor or conveyancer, even if you're being offered the asking price. This gives you time to consider the implications of the offer, for instance, does the prospective buyer have funds already available?
- Insist that any subsequent negotiations on price or contents are done via your legal representative.

ACCEPTING AN OFFER

Work out what you need to make on your sale, so that you know whether an offer is worth accepting. This will depend partly on your circumstances: if you are buying another property you will probably have a specific figure in mind that you need to reach in order to make your new purchase, allowing for all your legal costs of the sale and purchase. If you are downshifting to a smaller home or less expensive area, or moving into rented property, you may be able to be more flexible about what price you accept.

- If the property market in your area is strong, it might be worth making it clear that you won't negotiate: state on the property details that you won't drop the asking price even if a survey reveals minor defects.

- Don't stick to an unrealistically high figure for the sake of it, however – it will probably take longer to find a buyer and you may have to drop the price if the buyer's survey and valuation suggest that you're asking too much.
- Don't jump at the highest offer without thinking it through – more money doesn't necessarily mean a more committed buyer. Opt for a buyer who you feel really wants your home and has the resources to pay for it.

QUESTIONS FOR THE AGENT

If you use an estate agent they will advise whether or not to accept an offer, but you should specifically ask whether your potential buyer:

1 Needs to sell a property before they can buy. The more links there are in the chain, the more delays there are likely to be before completion.

2 Has finance arranged. A genuine buyer will be able to produce proof that a lender has provisionally offered them a mortgage. If they claim to have a large proportion of the purchase price available as cash, ask your agent to check out the details. Buyers desperate to have their offer accepted sometimes promise more than they can deliver.

SOME PROPERTY TRANSACTION TERMS

Completion When title deeds are signed over to the buyer's solicitor/conveyancer and ownership of the property is transferred. Scottish equivalent: Date of entry.

Covenant Usually a restriction in a lease or freehold that prevents the tenant or owner from doing specific things in the property, for example running a business.

Deeds Usually Title deeds. A legal document, signed and witnessed, stating the official owner of a property. Scottish equivalent: Disposition.

Exchange of contracts When seller's and buyer's legal representatives swap contracts; this should be the point of no return. Scottish equivalent: Conclusion of missives.

Fixtures Fixed items usually left in a property, such as baths and toilets.

Freehold Property or land that is wholly owned by the freeholder, who can lease it (rent it) to someone else or sell it outright.

Ground rent An annual sum payable to a landlord who owns the lease on a property.

Land Registry fee Payable to the Land Registry to record ownership of property or land.

Lease A contract setting out the conditions under which the freeholder allows a leaseholder to live in a property or use a piece of land.

Service charge Usually an annual sum paid to a landlord or management company for services provided to tenants, such as cleaning, maintenance, and repairs.

Sitting tenant A person who has a legal right to occupy a property, even though it has been sold by the owner to another person.

Subject to contract Applies to the period between an offer being made on a property and contracts being exchanged.

Subject to tender System whereby property (usually repossessions) are advertised and potential buyers submit sealed bids.

Title deeds The documents that state the name of the legal owner of a property.

Vacant possession Describes a property with no occupants, ready to be occupied by buyers.

IF THE OFFER IS REVISED DOWN

Sometimes, when a seller has accepted an offer, the buyer later reduces his or her offer. This may well be immoral, but gazundering, as this is called, is not illegal. So what can you do about it?

The first thing is to find out precisely why the offer has been reduced. There will usually be some good reason – the survey has revealed problems or repairs that need doing, which justify the reduction. In that case, carrying out the repairs yourself should mean that the offer can be restored to its original amount, but you will still have to find the cost of the repairs.

More often, the house has simply been valued at a lower amount by the buyer's mortgage lender, so reducing the amount of the loan the lender is prepared to make. It is then a case of bluff and counterbluff – how keen are you to sell (at a lower price) and how keen is the buyer to buy (by finding more money from their own funds)?

As a seller you may have little choice but to agree – or risk losing the house that you are buying because your sellers will not wait until you have found another buyer.

ONCE YOU'VE ACCEPTED AN OFFER

- Let your agent deal with the buyer, if you are employing one. If you're selling privately, it's best not to get too friendly with your buyer, however well you appear to get on. This is a business deal and there may be tough negotiations to handle.
- Don't encourage gazumping by accepting a higher offer after you have agreed a price with a committed buyer.

Moving home

Moving home is not only exhausting, it's also an intense experience. It calls for careful planning, plenty of decision-making, and being prepared for hard physical work. If you opt to get help with your move, go for the best service you can afford. The Internet has made it easy to get quick preliminary estimates for how much your move will cost.

SEE ALSO Cutting clutter, p130

SERVICES OFFERED BY REMOVALS FIRMS

Removals firms vary in the services they offer, though all should provide a free quotation – not an estimate, which by definition is not a final figure for the job. Expect to be offered some or all of these services:

- full or part packing service
- full or part loads
- supply of packing boxes, wrapping paper, and travelling wardrobes
- specialist removal of pianos, antiques, clocks, fine art, and Rayburn and Aga stoves
- containerized packing for shipping overseas
- full insurance cover
- seven-day-a-week service
- cleaning of the property you're leaving and/or cleaning your new home before you arrive
- transport of garden equipment, second car, or boat
- organization of temporary accommodation if required.

FIVE STEPS TO EMPLOYING A REMOVALS FIRM

1 Invite several removals firms to provide free quotes. Ideally, get personal recommendations. Firms should be members of the **Road Haulage Association** (RHA) or the **British Association of Removers** (BAR) or both.

2 Company estimators visit your home to take stock of your belongings and requirements, and note any potential problems, for instance large pieces of furniture.

3 Each firm should then send you a clear list of what is to be moved, a step-by-step description of the process, and a detailed price quotation, including clearly explained insurance terms.

4 Compare services and quotes, and get back to the firms with any questions. Consider whether staff are helpful.– an important part of their service is to give you peace of mind.

5 Once you have made your decision, sign the acceptance form.

QUESTIONS TO ASK REMOVALS FIRMS

- How many staff will work on the removal?
- What training have staff had?
- Are coverings used to protect banisters and carpets?
- Are special packing materials, such as acid-free tissue, used to protect valuables?
- Are padded jackets used to pack grand pianos and other awkward items?
- How often are lorries serviced?

QUESTIONS FOR VAN-HIRE FIRMS

- What capacity van do I need, given the size of the property?
- Are vans cleaned between rentals? How regularly are they serviced?
- How much fuel will the van have? Must it be returned with the same amount?
- Does it have a hydraulic loading-lift?
- Are blankets provided?
- Are there side straps to secure upright items?
- What are the insurance terms?

QUESTIONS IF YOU HAVE TO USE STORAGE

- What's the monthly rent and what are the insurance terms?
- Is storage in bays or containers?
- Are large items of furniture packed individually?
- At what temperature is the storage area kept? Is access restricted?

For self-storage:
- Check what size you will need and what size is available.
- Is there a covered loading area?
- Easy parking, free trolleys?

Ideally visit the premises first to check them out and meet the staff.

COUNTDOWN TO REMOVAL DAY

7 If using a removals firm, give them a provisional date for moving as early as is practical and confirm it as soon as you can.

6 Check in advance what time of day the property will be vacant, so that you won't arrive too early, then arrange times for the move and for keys to be handed over to you.

5 Contact suppliers of water, electricity, and gas at both ends. Arrange for telephone and cable/satellite television accounts to be terminated/opened. Several companies offer services via the Internet, where they handle all the contacting of suppliers when someone moves. All you need to do is register online and select, by tick-box, the suppliers you have arrangements with.

4 Send out change of address cards.

3 Make sure there is adequate parking and access for the removals van at both ends of the journey. Is a parking permit required? Do any overhanging branches need to be clipped?

2 Measure your new home and decide where furniture will go, so that furniture and boxes can be labelled in advance. Check that large pieces will be able to pass upstairs, round corners, through doorways. In some cottages and small terraced houses, there will be a 'coffin hatch', allowing larger pieces to be passed up through the ceiling. It may also be possible to remove a window to allow access. Some pieces of furniture may have to be dismantled and reassembled.

1 If possible, plan for any children and pets to stay with friends for at least the day of the move.

TIPS FOR LOADING A VAN

- Load weight evenly.
- Put large, heavy items on first.
- Use the space above the cab – good for large lampshades.
- Stack flat items (like pictures) and tall items (like standard lamps) at the sides, held in with straps.
- Cover furniture with blankets.
- Put lighter things, like bedding and open boxes of house plants, on top.
- Stand garden pots on the floor of the truck.
- Put the freezer in last.
- Make sure everything is securely wedged or belted in place to withstand cornering and braking.

THINGS TO PACK IN THE CAR

- Kettle, mugs, and everything you need for making hot drinks, including milk.
- Picnic food and cold drinks.
- First-aid kit.
- Nightwear and clothes for the next day.
- Toilet rolls.
- Light bulbs.
- If you have room, bedding.
- Mobile and plug-in phones, plus useful telephone numbers, including that of your conveyancer and the office where you are to pick up keys. Let the removals firm know if you are delayed on your journey. Many removal vehicles have in-cab phones – ask for the number before you leave.
- If children are travelling with you, toys and games they can do on their own.
- Champagne and glasses.

MOVING PETS

Caged pets will settle quickly once the move is complete. Make sure that cages are secured during transport, and that animals inside are protected from bangs and bashes. Special boxes can be bought for transporting birds safely.

Dogs will usually settle easily too, but don't leave them alone in the new property until they seem confident.

Move aquariums with extreme care. The **fish** should travel separately in special water-bags stored in a polystyrene box, both available from an aquatic dealer. Empty the aquarium, but keep the filtration system wet and get it going again within eight to ten hours.

Few **cats** take kindly to moving. They travel best in secure wicker baskets with a familiar blanket, a good air supply, and a restricted view. Place the basket on a wad of newspaper on a plastic sheet, and make sure the basket is wedged or belted in place. Cats fight against the effects of tranquillizers, so they aren't worth using. Putting butter on their paws may distract them for a while, as they lick it off.

If there were previously cats in your new home, buy a pheromone spray that will override their scent and stop your pet from spraying to mark its territory. Sprinkle catnip (catmint, available from pet shops) around the house to make your cat feel at home. Give your cat the free run of your new home straight away, but don't let it out for two weeks. Then let it out ten minutes before feeding time and gradually increase the time outside.

Most removals firms supply packing materials free, or at a nominal charge, even if you opt to do the packing yourself. Some self-move van hire firms may also supply packing boxes. If not, look in *Yellow Pages* under 'Packaging Materials' and 'Boxes, Cardboard'. Be prepared with the following:

- Custom-made packing cases. These are preferable to supermarket boxes, which will be of different strengths and sizes, making it more difficult to load the van evenly and safely. Avoid old-fashioned tea chests, which have sharp corners and get very heavy when full.
- Travelling wardrobes or suitcases.
- Bin bags with ties (for duvets and clothes).
- Acid-free tissue paper.
- Bubble wrap.
- Polythene sheeting (for paintings).
- Packing beans, either polystyrene or biodegradable.
- Masking tape. Better than clear or parcel tape because it's easy to tear, see, and remove. It sticks well on cardboard and, providing you don't overfill the box, is strong enough to hold it shut.
- Felt-tip pen.
- Self-adhesive labels.

PACKING TIPS

- Seal boxes with tape. Label with a brief description of contents and which room they're for.
- Mark which way is up.
- Overfilling a box prevents level stacking.
- If a box is getting too heavy, fill the remaining space with light things, like cushions.

PACKING UP YOUR BELONGINGS

BOOKS

Dust books as you take them down from the shelves. Stack books of similar sizes on their sides, no higher than to make a cube. Wrap each stack in bubble wrap, seal with masking tape, and fit the books on their sides into a tough box. Don't force books in. Only part-fill large boxes, otherwise they will be too heavy. Pack light things, such as pillows or duvets, on top. Pack odd spaces with crumpled paper or packing beans.

CHINA AND CERAMICS

- Wrap each piece individually, including lids. Wrap first in tissue, then in bubble wrap, and secure with masking tape.
- Don't use newspaper, as the print will rub on to the china and you will be faced with a mountain of washing-up.
- Pay particular attention to protrusions, such as teapot spouts and handles. Pad them with wads of rolled or folded tissue.
- Fill hollow vessels with scrunched paper.
- Stack plates flat on top of one another.
- Pack bundles carefully into boxes, filling gaps with packing beans.

CLOCKS (LONG-CASE)

Grandfather and grandmother clocks must be dismantled before moving. If you decide to do it yourself:

1 Wait until the clock has wound down.

2 Remove the hood. (There may be a swivelling catch inside the case.)

3 Lift the weights off their pulleys.

4 Stabilize the movement with one hand on the edge of the face.

5 Lift the pendulum up and back off the suspension block, taking care not to damage the suspension spring.

6 Lift the movement out. In some clocks you will need to unscrew the seat-board first.

7 Wrap the pulleys carefully round the seat-board.

8 Pack the movement in acid-free tissue paper in a padded box.

CLOTHES, BEDDING, AND CURTAINS

Clothes on hangers are best transported in travelling wardrobes. Otherwise, use sports bags or suitcases. Other clothes, bedding, linen, and curtains can be rolled or folded and transported in bin bags. If bedding for the first night won't travel with you in a car, keep it separate and easily accessible.

KITCHEN/UTILITY

- Disconnect the cooker (get a professional to do this if necessary), washing machine, and fridge before the removal van arrives. Secure the washing machine drum with brackets from an authorized agent.
- Empty the fridge and discard or pack its contents.
- Tightly seal jars, bottles, and packets, wrap, and pack upright, wedged in boxes.
- Put the contents of a chest freezer into the minimum number of large polythene bags so they can be quickly put back in the freezer once it's on the vehicle. Switch an upright freezer to fast-freeze first thing on moving day. Unplug freezers at the last minute. They should be the last things to be loaded on to the vehicle and the first to be unloaded. Freezer contents will stay frozen for up to 12 hours. If the freezer will be disconnected for longer, empty and defrost beforehand.

PAINTINGS AND MIRRORS

Protect the corners of framed paintings and mirrors with pads of bubble wrap, then seal in a polythene parcel. Load paintings upright, supported on soft padding and strapped to the van's sides with flat webbing. Crated paintings should also travel upright and be secured.

PIANOS

With a grand piano, the instrument is moved separately from its stand. Rods and linkages must be disconnected, and are sometimes difficult to re-engage. The pedals are loose once the rods have been disconnected – care needs to be taken to avoid catching them on the floor when the instrument is moved. Experts will put the piano in a padded jacket and move it on a trolley. It can take up to five people to negotiate stairs.

RUGS

Never crush a rug by folding it right side in. Roll fringe to fringe, right side outside, so that the pile is stretched, not squashed. For valuable rugs, interleave with acid-free tissue paper.

Roll carpets round a core of PVC or a cardboard roller. It can take three people to roll a large carpet. Clear the carpet of furniture. Stand on the carpet, in a row, facing one end. Lift the edge and walk backwards until about 3 m/10 ft of the carpet is lying face down. Put the roller in position and roll up this part of the carpet. Pick up the roller and walk backwards again, repeating the process until the whole carpet is on the roller.

SILVER

Wrap in acid-free tissue paper. Newspaper is acidic and will cause tarnishing. If you use cling wrap or plastic bags, condensation will form inside.

AREAS TO PACK UP AS EARLY AS POSSIBLE

THE ATTIC

Sort and pack the contents and store in a bedroom where they will not be overlooked. The removals team will want to see the entire scale of your move when they arrive, so they can plan how to load up the van.

THE SHED

Sort and pack the contents of sheds and garages, discarding flammable substances (such as old tins of paint, creosote, and gas bottles), which would invalidate your insurance if put on the van. Clean tools before tying them together.

THE GARDEN

Don't forget patio pots, garden seats, bird tables, and the clothes line.

THE PRIORITIES WHEN YOU GET THERE

- Install freezer.
- Stick labels on doors of rooms to correspond with labels on boxes.
- Plug in phone.
- Unload.
- Chill champagne.
- Make up beds.
- Sort kitchen.
- Leave the rest until tomorrow.
- Open the champagne and toast your new home.

Contact details for organizations given in **bold** appear at the end of each chapter.

TIPS FOR MOVING FURNITURE

- The best time for discussions on manoeuvring is before a piece of furniture is lifted, not after the operation has begun.
- A tape is a more efficient tool for measuring the width of a doorway than the piece of furniture that has to go through it.
- Protect banisters with blankets, making sure there are no edges to trip over.
- Protect your back when lifting by squatting down, getting a firm grip on the object, and lifting from the knees, taking the weight on your legs, not with your back. Put things down in the same way.
- Wear gloves to protect your hands against knocks and dirt, but choose a material that grips well, such as leather.

- Move hi-fis, televisions, video equipment, and computers in their original packing if possible. If not, wrap in bubble wrap and fill gaps in boxes with packing beans.
- Removals firms may require the householder to dismantle and reassemble self-assembly furniture. Have it flat-packed, ready for the move.
- Loop lamp flex and secure with masking tape to the lamp to avoid accidents. Use this method for other electrical items.
- Remove drawers to make furniture lighter and use them as packing boxes.
- Secure cupboard doors to prevent them swinging open while being carried.

▶ Deciding to let

Letting out a property has become an attractive option for long-term investment and a useful short-term solution if you have to move but are reluctant to sell. In the last decade or so, the number of people renting in Britain – and the number of properties available to rent – has increased enormously. This was first triggered by the recession of the early 1990s. More recently, the rise in property prices, especially in the southeast of England, increased the pool of people unable to afford a mortgage, and therefore increased demand for rental accommodation.

WHY MIGHT YOU WANT TO LET?

- If you're moving jobs within a company and need to move to another area, perhaps for a short time, there is a good case for keeping your present property and letting it out in case you need to return. Often the rent you receive will more than cover the mortgage payments you will have to continue making on the property.

- It has become easier to get a mortgage on a property with the specific intent of letting it (see Buy-to-let mortgages, right). This is because in 1989 the security of tenure that previously applied to tenants was relaxed, making a let property less risky for mortgage lenders, who always want to know they can realize their investment if they need to.

BUYING TO LET

The logic behind buy-to-let is simple. Over the years, the value of property has gone up by more than the rate of inflation. If you can buy a property and then let it at a rent that is more than the cost of repaying the loan financing the purchase, then you have the perfect investment – an income-producing asset that will also increase in value. But there are pitfalls you need to avoid.

- Don't get carried away by dreams of wealth. In many parts of the country there is already a surplus of accommodation to let, and thus no guarantee that you will get a tenant or have a steady succession of tenants.

- Buy a property that will be easy to let – size, location, and the rent you will need to charge to make a decent return on your investment will be paramount.

BUY-TO-LET MORTGAGES

Unless you can buy a property outright, you will need to raise the cash by taking out a mortgage with one of the increasing number of lenders who offer buy-to-let loans. These work just like a mortgage you take out to buy your own home (see p18–21), except that:

- you may have to pay a slightly higher interest rate than you would if the loan was for a home for you to live in, although at the time of writing increased competition in the buy-to-let loan sector is bringing interest rates down

- you will usually need to put down a deposit of between 20% and 25% of the value of the property

- Ask letting agents which types of property, and in which areas, are easiest to let, and how much rent these properties will command. Don't just ask the agent who is trying to sell you the buy-to-let loan – go for someone who has no self-interest.

- Like any other business, a letting business has to be run. Be prepared for things to go wrong – burst pipes, for instance, and other problems that need fixing quickly. You will have to organize these, and you will be liable to compensate the tenant if you are not able to act quickly enough. Alternatively, you can delegate the responsibility to an agent, as part of a full management service.

- the size of mortgage the lender will allow you is based not on your personal earnings but on the expected rental income for the year

- the mortgage payments, together with other expenses involved in letting the property, can be deducted from the rental income, which reduces the amount of the income on which you have to pay tax.

You can use an interactive calculator such as that on the Web site of **Paragon Mortgages** (http://www.paragon-mortgages.co.uk) to work out how much money you may make both in terms of rental income and in likely profit from the eventual sale of the property.

RISK ASSESSMENT AND INSURANCE

Letting property can be risky. You only need one bad tenant who stays for six months without paying any rent and then disappears, leaving the house in need of hundreds of pounds' worth of redecoration to bring it back into a decent condition, and your profit for that year – and probably the next – could be gone.

You should take out property insurance, which would cover damage, but the rent is not insurable. If you employ an agent and they failed to check references properly,

you could claim negligence. You can also get legal-costs insurance to cover your costs if you have to sue a tenant.

No matter what happens with your tenant, you will still have to go on paying the mortgage and the other outgoings on the property. If you cannot keep up the mortgage payments, then your lender will have the right to take possession of the property and sell it in order to recover their loan and interest.

TAX IMPLICATIONS OF RENTING OUT

- You will have to pay income tax on any profit you make over and above your outgoings on the property, and will therefore have to inform the Inland Revenue and fill in a tax return every year. These outgoings will include decorating costs, maintenance charges for servicing gas and electricity appliances, buildings insurance, and, in addition for a leasehold property, annual ground rent and any annual service charges made by the management company.

- When you come to sell a property you have let out, you will also be liable for capital gains tax (CGT) on any profit you make on the sale. CGT doesn't apply to your own home as long as you have resided there throughout your ownership.

The **Inland Revenue** publishes the following useful leaflets: *IR87: Letting and your home*; *IR150: Taxation of rents – A guide to property income*; *IR250: Capital allowances and balancing charges in a rental business.*

USING A LETTING AGENT

Having decided that you are going to let, how do you go about finding the perfect tenant? You could simply place an advertisement in your local shop or newspaper and take complete responsibility on yourself for finding a tenant. Alternatively, you can use a letting agent. Before deciding which agent to go with, do your homework.

- Most agents offer two options – full management or just collection of rent. Check their fees and what these fees include. In addition to a percentage of the rent, there will typically be one-off fees for finding a tenant, preparing a tenancy agreement (necessary for each new tenant), preparing and agreeing an inventory, and so on.

- Ask friends and colleagues whether they have any experience of *renting* property through the local agencies – they may be able to tell you which are the most prompt and efficient in dealing with queries.

- Agents vary in how carefully they vet prospective tenants. If you feel up to it, go round the agencies as a prospective tenant to see how efficient they seem at 'selling' the properties they have to let, and what they want to know about you.

- There have been several instances of letting agents holding on to rents received and then either going bankrupt or disappearing, leaving landlords out of pocket. It's therefore wise to go for an agent who is a member of one of the recognized professional bodies – the **Royal Institution of Chartered Surveyors**, or the **Association of Residential Letting Agents**. These bodies have codes of conduct and compulsory insurance schemes to protect clients from problems such as money disappearing due to insolvency or fraud.

Key letting issues

Preparing to let a property takes considerable planning and effort and, even once a tenancy is underway through an agency, you need to be ready to devote time at short notice to talk through any problems. Where you will be living in the meantime may affect your choice of agent – if you'll be a long way away, you may want to choose the most reliable agent you can find, which may also be the most expensive. If you'll be nearby, a smaller or newer agency may be quite adequate.

THE TENANCY AGREEMENT

- Don't rely on word-of-mouth agreements, even if letting to friends. You need the protection of a properly drafted tenancy agreement that covers all eventualities.

- Most letting agents have their own form of agreement. Check that the proposed agreement includes: what the deposit can be used for and whether the tenant is entitled to interest on it; obligations on the tenant not to cause a nuisance or damage the property/contents; that the tenancy can be terminated prematurely if terms are breached.

- If the agreement is too onerous on the tenant, you may well find that no one will want to rent the house. Also, under the Unfair Terms in Consumer Contracts Regulations, any term that is deemed unfair to a tenant will be void and so unenforceable.

- The **Consumers' Association** publishes an agreement that tries to maintain a fair balance between the rights of both landlord and tenant.

SIX THINGS TO THINK ABOUT

Before you sign up with an agent, or start looking for a tenant, there are some important factors you will have to bear in mind.

1 Consent of insurer
Whether you are letting the house furnished or unfurnished, you will need to contact your house insurer (and your contents insurer if letting furnished) to discuss with them your plans to let. It is likely that the insurer would see this as an increased risk and would wish to vary the terms of the policy, often by increasing the amount of the excess and/or charging a higher premium. Failure to get the insurer's consent could result in them refusing to meet any claim you make on the policy.

2 Consent of mortgage lender
Consent to let will be required as a term of your mortgage. The lender will be concerned that the existence of a tenant could reduce the value of the house should they need to sell it to recover their loan. It is possible that the lender may charge a higher rate of interest as a condition of giving their consent. In any event, there is likely to be a fee to cover the lender's administrative costs in deciding whether or not to give consent.

3 Planning permission
This is not normally required to let property, but if you are going to let the house to more than one family group, or divide it into flats, then permission may well be required. You should contact the planning department at your district or unitary council to discuss your plans with them.

4 Length of tenancy
You will need to decide for how long you want to let the property. Is the let intended to be a semi-permanent arrangement (a buy-to-let arrangement probably will be), or is there a chance you may want the house back in a few months'

time, either to live in yourself or to sell with vacant possession? If you let the house on a five-year tenancy, you will not be able to get possession back until the end of that time, unless the tenant agrees, and why should they unless you make it worth their while? Many lets are for 6 or 12 months, which gives you as the landlord some degree of flexibility should circumstances change. However, it may well be that you'll attract a better tenant if you opt for a longer let.

5 References
Every landlord wants a tenant who will look after the property well, pay the rent on time every month, and at the end of the letting will voluntarily vacate the premises without the need for a court order. Insist on references being provided – and be sure, if you use an agent, that they obtain references on your behalf. Ideally, you should obtain an employer's reference, to

show that the prospective tenant is in employment and therefore has the means to pay the rent (this will not, of course, guarantee that they will actually pay it). Many people also recommend getting a reference from a previous landlord to say that your prospective tenant was a good tenant. However, landlords are generally not amenable to giving such references, and insisting on one would rule out someone who has never rented property before. A personal reference as to the person's character is a good alternative.

Be vigilant, however, with *all* references – it's not unknown for people to write their own. Check the names and addresses of all those giving the references, whether employers or individuals. You can search the **British Telecom** Web site for phone numbers and addresses (except for individuals who are ex-directory). Bear in mind that even impeccable references are no guarantee that you'll have a trouble-free time as landlord – there is always an element of luck involved.

6 Guarantors

If there's a doubt over the prospective tenant's ability to pay the rent regularly, it is not unusual for a landlord to insist on the tenant providing a guarantor. A guarantor signs an agreement to the effect that if the tenant does not honour the terms of the agreement (for example, by not paying the rent regularly), then the guarantor is liable. Such an arrangement is often used in the case of a student renting property – a parent will be required to guarantee the obligations under the lease. Again, such a guarantee is only as good as the financial standing of the person giving it, so references should be obtained for the guarantor, too.

WHY IT'S IMPORTANT TO TAKE A DEPOSIT

As well as requiring a tenant to pay rent in advance (usually a month's rent), it is also usual for a landlord to insist on the tenant paying a deposit at the start of the letting. This deposit is usually the equivalent of one or two months' rent.

REASONS

The idea behind the deposit is that if the tenant misses a month's rent, the landlord has the money in hand and does not need to resort to court action to recover it. Similarly, if at the end of the letting there is damage to the house or contents, the landlord can take the cost of the damage from the deposit and only return the balance.

DISPUTES

There are probably more disputes between landlords and tenants over the return of deposits than any other matter. The tenancy agreement should make it quite clear what the deposit is to be used for (whether it is just for rent, or for breakages as well). Also, at the start of the letting, a detailed inventory of the property's contents and their condition should be agreed between landlord and tenant. Otherwise, when the landlord holds on to part of the deposit to pay for damage, there is nothing to stop the tenant claiming that the damaged item was in that condition at the start of the tenancy.

TIPS OF THE TRADE FOR LETTING PROPERTY

1 Decide which market you are selling to and choose finishes accordingly. For students, for example, an inexpensive laminate worktop is fine and you won't get any extra rent for anything fancier. Granite would be more suitable for a top-end corporate let – and the potential rent will be decreased if finishes lack the luxury touch or costs have been cut.

2 At every rental market level, everything must be simple to use and strong. Tenants do not take extra care or make allowances for weaknesses. For example, a shower rail must be robust – tenants won't take the extra few seconds to pull the curtain back carefully. Likewise, if no chopping board is supplied in a 'fully-equipped' kitchen, they will use, and therefore damage, the worktop.

3 Cater for basic needs, like laundry and rubbish removal, with adequate and efficient equipment. With no other option for drying clothes, tenants will have damp washing hanging round, to the detriment of the decoration.

4 Minimize wear and tear on expensive items. A large, good-quality doormat will prolong the life of the hall carpet. A chair rail in the eating area will stop the wall from getting scuffed – and save redecorating the whole room.

5 Tackle problems and have them professionally repaired so that tenants do not take matters into their own hands. Their solution to, say, draughty windows, is likely to be newspaper stuffed into the gaps, or sticky tape.

6 Choose light, bright, non-patterned colours for walls, curtains, and so on (pastels are ideal) to give all types of accommodation a cheerful, positive atmosphere.

7 Tenants like character. Never remove original design features such as fireplaces, cornices, or skirting boards.

Bob MacKinnon, landlord

RECORDS OF EXPENSES

Keep records of all your costs when you set up a property for letting, both for insurance purposes and for setting the costs of running the let against tax on rental income. In the first year you may want to consult an accountant about what you to claim.

In the case of a fixed-term letting, even when the fixed term has expired, the tenant does not have to vacate the house – they are allowed to remain in possession, on the same terms as previously, unless and until the landlord follows the correct procedure to obtain possession.

What the correct procedure is will depend on which of the two following types of tenancy has been granted. It will be obvious that landlords prefer shorthold tenancies.

SHORTHOLD

Unless the landlord has served a notice on the tenant stating that the tenancy is to be an 'assured' tenancy, the letting will be a 'shorthold' (sometimes referred to as an 'assured shorthold') tenancy, no matter how long it is.

The landlord will have an absolute right to obtain possession if he or she follows the correct procedure. They must serve a notice on the tenant, under section 21 of the Housing Act 1988, requiring possession in two months' time.

If the tenant does not vacate at the end of the two months, the landlord will still have to go to court to force the tenant to leave, but the court must order possession – there is no discretion.

ASSURED

If the letting is an 'assured' tenancy, then the landlord must follow a different procedure and must establish a 'ground' for possession – a reason recognized by statute as being sufficient to entitle the landlord to possession. Rent arrears or breaches of some other term of the tenancy agreement may be sufficient.

RIGHTS AND DUTIES

REPAIRS

Under the Landlord and Tenant Act 1985, the landlord is liable for repairing the structure and exterior of the house, and the installations for supplying gas, water, electricity, and for sanitation. As the landlord you cannot avoid this responsibility by trying to put the burden on the tenant in the tenancy agreement. If you do not carry out the necessary work speedily, the tenant may have a claim against you for substantial damages to compensate them for living in an unrepaired house.

GAS, FIRE, AND ELECTRICAL SAFETY

There are stringent safety regulations to be complied with in relation to all of these – see p13 for details.

OUTGOINGS

The tenancy agreement should make it clear who is responsible for paying the council tax, phone, water, gas, and electricity bills. Although the law *implies* that the tenant will normally be responsible, it is best for this to be set out clearly in the tenancy agreement to avoid any disputes.

INCREASING THE RENT

Long lets Once a tenancy agreement has been signed, it is a binding contract between the parties. Just as the tenant is bound to pay the rent throughout the length of the tenancy, so the landlord has agreed to accept that amount for the length of the letting.

The landlord cannot increase the rent without the tenant's agreement – and why should they agree? In a short-term tenancy (for example, six or twelve months) this will probably not be a problem, but in a longer let the effects of inflation will soon adversely affect the value of the rent agreed. Therefore, it's essential for the tenancy agreement for a long let to include a provision allowing the landlord to increase the rent.

Periodic tenancies In the case of a periodic tenancy – one that runs from

week to week or from month to month – the 1988 Housing Act does include a provision that will allow a landlord to increase the rent, even if there is nothing in the tenancy agreement allowing this. However, the procedure for this is slow and complicated and gives the tenant the right to refer the matter to the Rent Assessment Committee (a public body run by the Lord Chancellor's Department on a regional basis), who will have the final say as to what the rent is to be. Even in the case of a periodic tenancy, therefore, it is best not to have to rely on this procedure, and to include a provision in the tenancy agreement allowing the landlord to increase the rent.

Fairness Any provision in the agreement allowing for an increase must be fair, within the meaning of the Unfair Terms in Consumer Contracts Regulations. A provision that allows the landlord to increase the rent at any time, for any reason, and to any amount he or she thinks fit, will probably be held to be unfair and thus void.

EVICTING A TENANT

Even if the tenant is not paying the rent regularly, or is in breach of other terms of the tenancy agreement, the only way you can evict them is by going to court and obtaining a court order for possession. This, of course, will take time and will cost money.

You are not allowed to use or threaten force, or in any other way harass or try to persuade a tenant to leave. Harassment and unlawful eviction are criminal offences and the tenant would also be able to obtain substantial damages from you.

RIGHT OF ENTRY

Many landlords do not realize that although they may well still regard the house as 'their property', once they have granted a tenancy they have no more right to enter that property than anyone else who doesn't live there. If you want to keep a key to the property and be able to look round to check that everything is in order, then this must be provided for in the tenancy agreement. Any provision in the agreement allowing for access by the landlord must still be fair, however, within the meaning of the Unfair Terms in Consumer Contracts Regulations. A provision that allows the landlord access at any time, for any reason, and without giving reasonable notice, is likely to be held to be unfair and thus void.

SETTING UP PROPERTY FOR HOLIDAY LETS

Running holiday lets is similar to any other kind of letting. You will:

- need to obtain consent from your insurers (buildings and contents) and mortgage lender
- be liable for all the repairs, for maintaining gas appliances, and other safety issues
- have to meet all the outgoings.

Many holiday lets are granted fairly informally, but there is still a need for a written agreement to make it clear that the letting is for holiday purposes only. This is often included on the booking form, if the let is offered through an agency, and will prevent a tenant claiming the right to live in the property and thus the right to continue in possession after the end of the let.

When you're choosing furnishings, you might choose stylish, practical tableware and bedding, that can be replaced fairly cheaply, but pay extra for a good-quality sofa and beds (see Buying beds and sofas, p242). You need to budget for:

- dining chairs and easy seating to match the number accommodated
- plenty of crockery and glassware, with spares, plus a full set of cutlery, pans, cooking utensils, and serving dishes
- at least two sets of bedding for each bed – polycotton dries quicker than pure cotton, and anything with pleats or frills will add to the ironing time – plus mattress covers, ample pillows and perhaps new duvets.

Most guests will also expect to find:

- a washing machine and tumble dryer or space for drying clothes
- a microwave
- a dishwasher
- a colour television and ideally a video recorder, which will require a TV licence.

TENANTS RECEIVING HOUSING BENEFIT

Housing benefit is a means-tested benefit, administered by the local housing authority, that can meet some or all of an applicant's rent. Many landlords ask for the benefit to be paid directly to themselves rather than to the tenants, which gives them extra security. Direct payment requires the tenant's consent, and this can be included as a term of the tenancy agreement.

The downside of direct payment is that if benefit is overpaid – as a result of a claimant failing to disclose their full financial circumstances, for instance – the local authority can reclaim the over-payment. If the benefit has been paid directly to the landlord, the overpayment can be reclaimed from the landlord, who would in turn have a right to recover this amount from the tenant – that is if the tenant is still around and there is a chance of successfully suing for the money.

WEB SITES AND ADDRESSES

Association of Residential Letting Agents,
Maple House, 53-55 Woodside Road,
Amersham, Buckinghamshire HP6 6AA
phone: 0845 345 5752; fax: 01494 431530;
e-mail: info@arla.co.uk
Web site: www.arla.co.uk

Site has a Buy to let area with detailed
information on what 'buy to let' is, and which
lenders will offer the finance. There is detailed
information for both tenants and landlords.

British Association of Removers
e-mail: info@bar.co.uk
Web site: www.barmovers.com

Enables you to search and locate a removals
company.

Inland Revenue
phone: 020 7667 4001;
Web site: www.inlandrevenue.gov.uk

Contains detailed information about individual
and business tax, including a separate section on
self assessment. Details of the regional offices are
also provided on the Web site. A range of leaflets
covering letting issues are available from the
Inland Revenue Orderline (0845 9000 404) or
through the Web site.

Law Society, The Law Society's Hall,
113 Chancery Lane,
London WC2A 1PL
phone: 020 7242 1222; fax: 020 7831 0344;
email: info-services@lawsociety.org.uk
Web site: www.lawsoc.org.uk

Enables you to search for a law firm or individual
solicitor in England and Wales.

Paragon Mortgages Ltd, St Catherine's Court,
Herbert Road, Solihull, West Midlands B91 3QE
phone: 0800 375777; fax: 0121 712 2547;
e-mail: mortgages@paragon-group.co.uk
Web site: www.paragon-mortgages.co.uk

Site includes an interactive calculator which
allows you to work out how much money you are
likely to make both in terms of rental income and
the profit from the eventual sale of the property.

propertyfinder.co.uk, 182-194 Union Street,
Union House, London SE1 0LH
phone: 0870 075 8888;
e-mail: info@propertyfinder.co.uk
Web site: www.propertyfinder.co.uk

reallymoving.com
Web site: www.reallymoving.com

Provider of online home-moving services. Gives
information for house buyers on mortgages,
surveyors, solicitors, removals, change of address
services, and home improvements.

Road Haulage Association, RHA Weybridge,
Roadway House, 35 Monument Hill,
Weybridge, Surrey KT13 8RN
phone: 01932 841515; fax: 01932 852516;
e-mail: weybridge@rha.net
Web site: www.rha.net

Enables you to search for a haulier by place or
postcode. One of the categories is removals.

Royal Institute of Chartered Surveyors,
RICS Contact Centre, Surveyor Court,
Westwood Way, Coventry CV4 8JE
phone: 0870 333 1600; fax: 020 7222 9430;
e-mail: contactrics@rics.org.uk
Web site: www.rics.org/public

Useful information on residential surveys,
boundary disputes, and advice on finding a
surveyor.

UK Property Web, 40 The Woodpeckers,
Weymouth, Dorset DT3 5RS
phone: 01305 814721;
e-mail: wendy.hyde@ukpropertyweb.co.uk
Web site: www.ukpropertyweb.co.uk

Dedicated to buying and selling property privately.
No commission charge. Also offers a property
matching service.

Which?, 2 Marylebone Road, London NW1 4DF
phone: 020 7770 7000; fax: 020 7770 7600;
e-mail: which@which.net
Web site: www.which.net

Visit the bookstore area of the site where a
number of publications on selling, letting, and
conveyancing are available.

CHAPTER THREE

Being a householder

Home insurance: how it works

There's an array of different types of insurance policies that between them offer a financial safety net to prevent you losing out on most of life's uncertainties. But in practice, there are limits on how many insurance premiums individuals can afford. When it comes to an insurance priority list, household insurance should be near the top for most people.

SEE ALSO Insurance: buying and claiming, p54

WHAT YOU GET WITH NEW-FOR-OLD COVER

Most household policies will pay out on a new-for-old basis, which is especially important with contents cover. New-for-old means that if, say, your ten-year-old television is stolen, you should get the nearest current equivalent model or enough cash to buy one (though increasingly insurers prefer to replace goods from a named supplier).

No deduction is made for wear and tear. Be wary of policies that pay out on an indemnity basis – they do deduct for wear and tear when you claim.

Traditionally, even new-for-old policies have given only indemnity cover for some items, such as clothes. So if your entire wardrobe were ruined following a burst pipe in the attic, you wouldn't get enough cash to replace everything as new.

But some policies now do give new-for-old cover on clothes – something to watch out for if you like buying designer items.

WHAT IS HOUSEHOLD INSURANCE?

Household insurance falls into two distinct types of policy: contents and buildings. You can choose to have just one type or both.

Buildings insurance protects the structure and fabric of a home you own, including the walls, windows, doors, floors, ceilings, roof, pipes, gutters, decorations, outbuildings, and fixtures and fittings such as baths, basins, radiators, boiler, fitted kitchen cupboards, and the garage. In short, it protects things you couldn't take with you if you moved home.

Contents insurance protects things that you normally keep in your home, whether you own or rent the property. These are items that aren't an integral part of the building, such as furniture and furnishings, carpets and curtains, electrical appliances, kitchen and bathroom equipment, sports equipment, clothes, books, CDs, and jewellery. In short, it protects movable possessions. In certain cases, a policy may cover these possessions elsewhere, for instance while you are away from home (called all-risks, see Policy extensions, opposite), or the place where a student member of the family lives in term-time. Cover can only extend to people who have what the insurers call an identifiable interest in your property, so members of the same family and common-law spouses can be covered by the same policy, but a group of friends sharing a flat, for instance, could not.

WHEN DO POLICIES PAY OUT?

Buildings and contents insurance policies typically pay out for damage and loss caused by fire, flood, storms, theft and attempted theft, vandalism, riots, leaks of oil and water, explosions, subsidence, (though there's usually a substantial excess for subsidence), heave, landslip, earthquakes, and impact – for example by vehicles, animals (but not pets), trees, lamp posts, telegraph poles, aerials, and aeroplanes.

Excess is an initial figure that the insurance company will not pay on a claim – you have to meet this and the insurer pays the balance on the sum you are claiming. The insurer will not meet claims below the excess.

Basic cover also usually includes your legal liability as owner or occupier, for example if a visitor or tradesperson sues you after an injury resulting from disrepair in your home.

It also usually pays for the cost of alternative temporary accommodation, for instance if you were flooded and had to leave your home.

HOW MUCH BUILDINGS COVER?

- Insure for the total **rebuilding cost** – what it would cost to rebuild your home from scratch if, for example, it were destroyed in a gas explosion or burnt to rubble.
- It's rare for anyone to have to claim the total amount. But if you don't insure for total rebuilding costs you'll be under-insured and any claim you submit is likely to be scaled down in proportion to the level of under-insurance.
- Rebuilding costs are based on the size of the property and are not the same as the market value of your property. This

is partly because even if your property were to be demolished, you would still own the land. Don't insure for market value.

- If you have a mortgage, the lender's valuer will usually provide a sum to insure. If you need to work out rebuilding costs yourself, you can get a leaflet from the **Association of British Insurers**.

Alternatively, you could pay for a quotation from a qualified surveyor,

such as a member of the **Royal Institution of Chartered Surveyors** (RICS).

- After some years your original sum insured could be out of date. For example, it may not have been correctly updated each year to match rebuilding cost inflation in your part of the country or you may have carried out major building works such as an extension or loft conversion. Reassess the sum insured from time to time.

HOW MUCH CONTENTS COVER?

- Work out the cost of replacing as new all your possessions, with the possible exception of clothes and household linen, for which you should make a deduction for wear and tear. Which items are to be costed as new and which are to be costed with a wear-and-tear deduction will depend on the policy you are buying (see New-for-old, left).

- The cost of replacing everything (either as new or with a wear-and-tear deduction) is the sum you must insure for. If you under-insure, any claims, including small claims, could be scaled down in proportion to the level of your under-insurance.

- Putting a replacement cost on every item in the home could be huge task and it may involve a lot of guessing, making the final figure an approximation only. Inevitably, many

people make an intelligent estimate. If that's your approach, don't underestimate. You might be surprised at how much you would have to pay out if you needed to replace every item.

- You could err on the side of caution by overstating the replacement cost of all your possessions. Bear in mind that your premium would then be higher than it need be. And while there's a serious disadvantage in under-insuring, when it comes to claiming there's no advantage in being over-insured.

- Many policies automatically index-link your cover each year – that is, they increase the sum insured by the rate of inflation as measured by the retail prices index. Do review the level of cover from time to time. Index-linking may not be sufficient if you are steadily getting more prosperous and acquiring more valuable possessions.

ANY LIMITS ON THE COVER?

Some policies – both buildings and contents – set the level of the premium according to the number of bedrooms in the house. If a room-based policy has no limit on what you can claim, you should be covered. But some room-based policies do

have limits on the cover. Check whether there is a maximum amount of cover and whether your policy would cover the full rebuilding cost in the event of the ultimate disaster (buildings) or the full replacement cost of your possessions (contents).

- Most policies will offer limited cover for **accidental damage**. A contents policy will usually pay out if you damage your television, a hand basin, or the glass in doors, for example. But extensive cover for damage caused by accidents is usually an optional extra, for which you have to pay an extra premium. Check what's covered in the basic policy and decide whether you or your household are sufficiently clumsy to make paying an extra premium worthwhile.

- Other things may be covered by the basic premium or may be covered only if you pay an extra premium – for example, your bike, the contents of a freezer (in case there is a power cut), or a computer you use for work. If these aspects of cover are important to you, check the small print or discuss with the insurer.

- Most policies offer an **all-risks** extension, also known as personal possessions cover, for an extra premium. This protects things you take outside your home and will usually pay out if you accidentally damage or lose them. It could be especially useful if you often have expensive items on you, such as jewellery, cameras, or sunglasses. But it could be an unnecessary expense. For example, you may want this protection only when you go on holiday and you could find similar cover is provided by the travel insurance you buy.

- Some policies cover you when you lose stored oil or metered water. Ask insurers about this cover if it sounds useful.

- Some policies include cover for **legal expenses** as a basic or an extra. Find out precisely what you would get in the event of a claim before you buy this cover as an extra or rely on it if it's included.

Insurance: buying and claiming

Household insurance pays out only on items that are covered and only for certain perils – such as fire and theft. Don't imagine your policy is all-singing-and-dancing. Be aware of exclusions and limits on claims. Getting to know how policies work will improve your chances of buying the right one for you and of claiming successfully.

SEE ALSO Home insurance: how it works, p52

THE BENEFITS OF USING A BROKER

The cheapest insurance tends to come from direct insurers – those that sell direct to the public (usually over the phone and on the Internet) and that don't give commission to a broker or other intermediary. But direct insurers usually cater only for fairly standard risks, and you will have to make all the price comparisons yourself – and check the small print.

What if you are in an area blighted by floods? Or have a holiday home to insure? Or have a home stuffed full of valuable antiques and works of art? Or have other special needs or problems – perhaps a member of the household has a criminal conviction. Consider visiting a competent broker, even if it means you end up paying a higher premium.

A good broker should have a thorough knowledge of the market and be able to match the best policy to your needs. Another advantage is that the broker should be able to help if you ever need to make a claim.

TIPS FOR BUYING BUILDING AND CONTENTS COVER

Household insurance premiums are set by various factors beyond your control, including your **postcode**. Your area may suffer high crime, for instance, pushing up your premium even if your home has Fort Knox-style security. Despite this there are a number of ways to keep the costs down.

- Household insurance offered through a mortgage lender can be expensive. Lenders get a big commission. Get alternative quotes.

- Mortgage lenders require borrowers to have buildings insurance but often let you choose your own insurer if you ask. They may charge £25 or so if you don't use their insurance, but it's often worth paying to get a lower premium. Some insurers will pay this fee for you if you switch to them.

- Buying buildings and contents from the same insurer should ensure there are no gaps in your cover and you will have to deal with only one insurer if you claim. But an insurer that's competitive on buildings premiums may not be so competitive on contents premiums – or the other way round.

- An **excess** is the amount of any claim (loss) you must pay yourself. Most policies have compulsory excesses – and it's worth comparing these – but also let you choose voluntary excesses. You get a reduced premium in exchange for a higher voluntary excess.

- Get several quotes before renewing your policies. In the financial services world, loyalty is rarely rewarded and is often penalized. If you do find a cheaper deal than your existing insurer, tell your existing insurer what you've been quoted, if you would rather stay with the company. It may be able to come up with an improved premium.

- Treat discounts cautiously, for example those marketed at people in particular trades and professions, of a certain age, or in a neighbourhood watch scheme. Compare a discounted premium with other, non-discounted premiums.

- A cheaper policy could have unwelcome gaps in cover. Check the proposed cover carefully. And what's an insurer like when disaster strikes? Keep an ear out for the experiences of people who have claimed. Are some companies worth considering, others to be avoided?

- Check restrictions and exclusions carefully for any that would affect you particularly. For instance, many insurers reserve the right to replace lost items from specified suppliers (see Tips for making a successful claim), and in some cases this extends to jewellery. If you own valuable antique jewellery, or prefer an unusual style, you may not want to replace it from a high-street chain.

FLOOD ALERT

If you live in a UK area at high risk from flooding and are worried about insurance, you should check with your local **Environment Agency** office whether there are plans to improve flood defences in your area by 2007.

The **Association of British Insurers** intends that, if there are plans:

- you should be able to renew insurance with your current insurer, but the premium and excess may increase

- anyone buying your house should in principle be able to get cover from your existing insurer, but this may depend on their claims record.

However if there are no plans:

- insurers may not guarantee to maintain cover. Properties could be considered individually.

TIPS FOR MAKING A SUCCESSFUL CLAIM

- Keep receipts of things you buy, especially of expensive items. These could be useful if you ever need to claim. Consider taking photos of the inside of your home and particularly of high-value items, such as antiques, including jewellery.

- Many insurers offer a no-claims discount. If you have one, find out what it would cost you to lose it, and also the amount of any excess you may have to pay, before you decide whether it's worth making a claim on this occasion.

- People often put in claims for things they are not covered for. But the reverse is also true. You may be unaware that your policy covers you for a particular loss or damage. Read the policy carefully.

- You should put in a claim as soon as possible after you become aware that you have suffered insured damage or loss. Delayed claims may be refused.

- Report all crimes, such as break-ins or vandalism, to the police. The same applies to losses, even if you are sure something has been lost rather than stolen. A claim may be refused if you haven't reported it to the police and been given an incident reference number to quote.

- Don't immediately go out and buy a replacement item, for example a television, without checking with your insurer. Some insurers may want you to replace the TV from a named supplier (from whom they will get a discount for the volume of their business) rather than offer cash. Also, you should be aware that most policies give the insurer the right to repair rather than replace items.

- Ask whether your insurer would agree to upgrade a replacement. Even where insurers give replacement goods rather than cash, some allow you to pay the difference to upgrade your replacement. For example, if your video player were stolen, you could bring forward plans to buy a DVD player.

- After certain types of disaster – such as a flood, fire, or break-in – you should contact your insurer as soon as possible to find out what you can do in terms of immediate repairs and expenditure. After a burglary, for example, you may need to secure the property with new locks or replacement glass. Many insurers have 24-hour phone lines.

- If you can't get hold of your insurance company, keep paperwork relating to any unavoidable emergency expenditure. It's important to limit further damage as far as you can in order not to jeopardize a full pay-out.

- Don't embark on longer-term or less urgent repairs until you have agreement for the work from the insurance company.

- Try and get the insurance company's permission before throwing anything out, for example a carpet ruined by flooding. You may be advised to keep a small sample. The insurer may want to send someone to inspect all the damage.

- If you have access to a camera, consider taking pictures of your home showing the results of the damage and loss. Photos could provide useful evidence to support your claim.

- If you can't agree the value of your claim with the insurance company, consider paying a loss assessor to present your case (not to be confused with loss adjusters, whose job is to value your loss on behalf of the insurance company). To check out the cost and procedure, contact the **Institute of Public Loss Assessors**.

Contact details for organizations given in **bold** appear at the end of each chapter.

IMPORTANT POINTS TO WATCH OUT FOR

- You are obliged to disclose relevant facts when you buy any insurance. Failure to disclose could invalidate the whole policy and something may come to light only when you claim. Volunteer information that's not covered by the questions you are asked. For example, tell your insurer if you work from home and establish how (if at all) this affects your cover.

- Keep your insurer informed of important material facts – for example, if you take in a lodger, let the whole property, or move home.

- Watch for extra endorsements, for example a requirement to fit certain types of locks in high-crime areas. Don't invalidate the insurance by failing meet these requirements.

- Certain types of claim may not be met in full or at all if you are in some way to blame for the loss. For example, with a buildings policy you must keep your home in good repair, while your contents insurance might not cover you if burglars gain entrance through an accessible window you left open.

- Understand the exclusions – for example, you may not be covered for wear and tear, routine maintenance, mechanical or electrical breakdown, damage caused by faulty repair, damage made worse by disrepair, or damage owing to dry rot, woodworm or vermin.

- Certain types of damage caused when your property has been unoccupied for a period, for example 30 days, may not be covered.

- Watch out for limits on single items under a contents policy. You may need to inform your insurer of individual items above a certain value and may have to pay an extra premium to cover each of these.

▶ Making your home secure

Burglary is one of the fastest-growing types of crime. To minimize your risk as a target, check out the security of your building, and examine the security habits (or lack of them) of all the occupants. Many householders make life easy for the would-be burglar by such simple oversights as leaving windows open and doors unlocked, or by advertising the fact that the house is empty. Don't let your home look a likely bet for the opportunist thief.

SEE ALSO Fitting locks, p180 Emergencies, p290

BURGLARY FACTS

- Over a million burglaries are reported to the police every year in England and Wales – almost 2,800 every day, or one every 30 seconds – making up around 22% of all reported crime. It is estimated that a further million burglaries go unreported.
- 80% of burglaries occur when the property is empty.
- Almost half of all successful burglaries take place in daylight.
- 40% of burglaries involve entry via a front or back door.
- 33% of burglars get in through a back window.
- 20% of burglars don't need to resort to forceful entry – they get in through an open door or window.
- Almost 50% of reported burglaries are from sheds, garages, and other outbuildings, rather than from houses.
- Only 9% of stolen property is ever recovered.

WHAT TO FIT

These practical measures will ensure that your property is secure whether you are at home or not, and will satisfy household insurance companies. To improve the security of uPVC windows and doors, seek advice from the manufacturer or a locksmith.

FRONT DOORS

These should be fitted with a mortise lock meeting the requirements of British Standard BS 3621. For daytime security when you're in, and extra security at other times, add a cylinder rim lock (also made to BS 3621) with automatic or key-operated deadlocking. Add hinge bolts to the hinged edge to prevent the door being forced. Fit a door viewer (solid doors only), a door chain, or a door limiter (all available from hardware stores), so you can check the identity of callers. Fit toughened or laminated glass in place of ordinary glass in all glazed doors and side panes.

BACK DOORS

Fit a mortise sashlock made to BS 3621. This combines the functions of lock and latch, allowing the door to be opened without the need for a key when you're in. Alternatively, fit a latch and separate BS 3621 mortise lock.

SLIDING PATIO DOORS

Fit key-operated surface-mounted patio door locks to wooden doors at top and bottom, plus an anti-lift device at the top of the frame if the doors were not fitted with one originally.

FRENCH DOORS

Fit a surface-mounted bolt or a concealed mortise rack bolt to the top and bottom of each door so the bolt passes into a hole in the top and bottom of the frame. Fit a mortise sashlock made to BS 3621 to the door that opens first, and add hinge bolts

to the hinged edge of each door to prevent a burglar punching out the exposed hinge pins and lifting out the doors.

WINDOWS

A wide range of locks is available for wooden windows, and a smaller selection for metal ones. Most are surface-mounted, making them quick and easy to install. Unfortunately, many are supplied with screws that are too short to make a secure fixing, leaving the window prone to forcing. Buy the longest possible fixing screws as extras, if necessary.

The best locks for hinged wooden windows lock automatically as the window is closed and need a key to open them. Fit two locks on windows over about 1 m / 3 ft 3 in high. The best locks for sliding sash windows have dual screws, which pass through holes drilled through the top of the lower sash and the bottom of the upper one. Fit two to each window, close to the sides of the sashes.

Keep keys for window locks nearby but invisible from outside the house, so locked windows can be opened quickly, especially in the event of a fire. Make sure everyone sleeping in your home knows where they are kept.

OUTBUILDINGS

Sheds, garages, and other outbuildings are likely to contain tools and ladders, which a burglar could use to gain easier entry to the house. They may also contain valuable power tools and garden equipment worth stealing. Strengthen hinged doors with hinge bolts, a surface-mounted bolt inside the door that closes first, and a five-lever mortise lock to the meeting edge of the doors. Secure up-and-over doors with a floor-mounted ground lock. Fit sheds and greenhouses with a stout hasp, staple, and padlock. Replace vulnerable glass with unbreakable polycarbonate sheeting.

ALARMS

Visible burglar alarms make burglars think twice, and even a dummy alarm box may prove an inexpensive deterrent. Check your insurer's preference before deciding between professional or DIY installation, and ask whether they stipulate regular servicing. A professionally installed wired system linked to a 24-hour monitoring station is the most secure option, but also the most expensive. It should meet the requirements of British Standard BS 4737. There are two standards for DIY systems – BS 6707 (wired systems) and BS 6799 (wireless systems). Don't install a DIY system unless you have the knowledge and practical skill. If fitted badly, it could trigger endless nuisance alarms.

EXTRA MEASURES FOR HIGH-RISK AREAS

Front doors Add door and frame reinforcements to prevent the lock from being forced. These are metal plates that are fixed to both faces of the door over the position of the mortise lock, and metal strips on the frame that prevent the lock keeper from being forced. All these are available from locksmiths.

Back doors Add hinge bolts, security glazing, and door and frame reinforcement. Fit surface-mounted bolts or concealed mortise rack bolts for extra security when you are out and at night.

Sliding patio doors Consider having metal security grilles fitted.

GOOD SECURITY HABITS

Even the best security equipment in the world is no good if you forget to use it. Be security-conscious at all times.

- Close (and lock if you can) all windows including top ventilators when you go out. Shut windows and doors at the front of the house when you are upstairs, in the back garden, or out of earshot.

- Lock and bolt side and back doors and remove the keys from the locks.

- Check that gates are closed and bolted, that outbuildings are secure, and that ladders are under cover or chained up.

- Move tempting portable valuables out of sight, and draw the curtains in any room containing valuable home entertainment equipment – the favourite target of every burglar.

- Set the burglar alarm if you have one.

- Lock the front door and check that the lock is fully engaged. Make sure key-operated rim locks are deadlocked.

- Don't leave spare keys hidden *anywhere* near the front door. Leave spare keys with a neighbour you can trust, but don't put your house name or number on the key tag.

- If you lose your front door key, get the lock changed immediately.

- Identify callers before opening your front door, using a door viewer or door chain, and always ask unknown callers to produce identification before letting them in. Don't let small children open the front door.

- If you are going out in the evening, draw curtains and leave lights on and a radio playing, to give the impression that the house is occupied.

- Use a security marker to identify valuable items in the house with your postcode and house number (or the first two letters of its name), and photograph items you cannot mark.

GOING ON HOLIDAY

- Ask a neighbour or a nearby friend or relative to keep an eye on the property while you're away, clearing the letter box and checking for unexpected deliveries. If they have a key, ask them to draw curtains and put lights on at night. Otherwise, use automatic time switches to operate lights in the hall or on the landing.

- Cancel newspaper and milk deliveries. Do this on the phone, so you're not overheard.

- Leave small valuables with friends or relatives, or on deposit at your bank. Don't leave larger valuables where they are visible from outside the house.

- Set a burglar alarm if you have one and tell the police who your appointed keyholder is. Make sure the keyholder knows how to use the burglar alarm.

- If you'll be away for more than a couple of weeks, arrange for someone to mow the lawn in spring and summer and sweep up leaves in the autumn.

SECURITY IN FLATS

- The front door to an individual flat can be forced if an intruder gains access to the building, so make it as secure as you can.

- In flats with a communal entrance door, make sure the door closes properly, preferably on a spring.

- Windows and back doors in basement and garden flats are vulnerable, especially when out of sight of the road. Make sure all possible entry points are locked, and consider installing external grilles or sliding internal grilles for extra security.

Checking that all's well

It pays to be vigilant for deterioration in the fabric of your home, and its inside components, before problems become serious. Making the regular checks given here won't take up much time. The section on Basic DIY, starting on p159, gives detailed advice on curing many problems yourself.

SPRING AND AUTUMN CHECKS INSIDE

CENTRAL HEATING

A low or empty feed and expansion tank is a common problem. Another is corrosion inside the heating system, which causes gases to collect in radiators. Check that:

- the feed and expansion tank is about one-third full when the heating is on
- the ballvalve moves easily
- radiators feel hot all over.

Top up the feed and expansion tank as necessary. Use silicone grease to lubricate the ballvalve so it moves freely.

See p192–5 for more on central heating.

TRAPS

Piping under baths, basins, shower trays, and sinks has a water seal to keep out drain smells. Check for:

- blockages caused by soap, hair, or other debris
- evidence of water drips beneath fittings.

Unscrew traps and clear any debris. Replace faulty sealing rings to stop drips.

ANNUAL CHECKS INSIDE

CENTRAL HEATING BOILER

Regular servicing prevents boilers from becoming noisy, inefficient, and dangerous. To reduce noise:

- lower the pump speed by switching its control to a lower setting
- add descaling liquid (from plumbers' merchants) to the feed and expansion tank. Call a CORGI-registered gas fitter or your gas supplier if the boiler is constantly switching on and off, or if there is any sign of soot round the flue, which might be a sign of carbon monoxide escaping. See p147.

INSULATION

Loft insulation keeps houses warm and saves on fuel bills. Insulation on tanks and pipes prevents freezing. Check:

- there are no gaps between lengths of loft insulation, and no dampness
- pipe and tank insulation is correctly fitted.

Reposition loft insulation if necessary. Remove any damp insulation first, then lay new insulation. See p199.

SMALL ELECTRICAL APPLIANCES

If these appliances are moved frequently, flexes and plugs may become worn. Check that:

- flex sheaths are undamaged, and that

the sheath continues inside plugs and appliances.
- connections to plug terminals are sound
- plugs have the right fuse for the appliance's wattage rating.

Replace damaged flex, making sure sheath is secured in the flex grip of the plug. Tighten loose plug terminal screws. For appliances under 700 W fit a 3 amp plug fuse. Fit a 13 amp fuse in other appliances.

SMOKE DETECTORS

Test smoke detectors regularly and keep them free of dust and cobwebs. Replace batteries annually.

STOPVALVES

The stopvalves on your incoming water supply pipe and any other gate valves and servicing valves on your system can jam open if left unused for long periods (see p67 for where to find these). This can be dangerous if there is a leak and you need to turn the water off or isolate part of the system. Check that:

- the main stopvalve turns off easily – leave it a quarter turn from fully open
- all servicing valves work – leave them fully open.

Apply light machine oil or lubricant spray to the spindles of stiff stopvalves and servicing valves. Get a plumber to replace any that are difficult to turn.

ANNUAL CHECKS OUTSIDE

GULLIES

Debris blocks these in-ground collection points for waste pipes and rainwater downpipes. Check that gully gratings are intact and clear of debris and the gully trap itself is clear of debris. Replace missing gratings and clear debris. Flush with water.

ROOFS

Tiles on sloping roofs can be damaged by wind, and heat and frost can damage any roof. Inspect sloping roofs with binoculars and flat roofs from a ladder. Repair damage to felted roofs with bituminous mastic or waterproofer. Call in a roofing contractor to fix a sloping roof.

TV AERIAL/SATELLITE DISH

Use binoculars to check that the dish or aerial:

- is securely fixed to the chimney or wall
- is pointing in the right direction (compare with nearby houses).

Check the downlead is securely attached to the wall. If you have suitable equipment for working at heights, you can do repairs and adjustments yourself. Otherwise call in a specialist.

EXTERNAL REVIEW EVERY OTHER YEAR

CHIMNEYS

Check the actual structures, and have chimneys swept regularly if you burn coal or wood. Using binoculars, look for:

- cracked or leaning pots
- damaged pointing (mortar)
- loose or missing flashings
- any sign of the stack leaning from the vertical.

Use professionals to fix chimney problems. Call a builder to fix masonry, and a chimney sweep to clear soot build-up in the flue.

DRAINS

Underground drains seldom cause problems. Above ground you can check for:

- cracked inspection chamber covers
- debris or standing water over inspection covers.

Remove debris from inspection chamber covers. If the drain is blocked, see p190–1.

EAVES

Eaves woodwork – the vertical fascias to which the gutters are fixed, and the horizontal soffits that fill the space between fascia and wall – is exposed and prone to rot. Check that:

- the woodwork and any decorative finish are in good condition
- gutter bracket fixings are secure.

Cut out and replace any rotten woodwork, or get a builder to do this. Remove and re-fix gutter brackets as necessary.

EXTERNAL WALLS

Damaged walls allow damp to penetrate, and subsidence can cause problems with the basic structure. Check that:

- brickwork and mortar (pointing) are in good condition
- rendering is not cracked or loose
- mastic round door and window frames is continuous and intact
- soil in flower beds is kept at least 150 mm/6 in below the level of the damp-proof course in the house walls, to counter the risk of rising damp
- there are no zigzag cracks in walls.

Repair minor defects and call in a builder for bigger problems. Engage a surveyor to inspect and monitor major cracks.

PAINTWORK

Disintegrating paint can allow rot and insect attack to develop, especially in outside walls. Check that:

- paint is intact, and free from cracks and blisters
- there are no signs of wet rot – the wood would feel soft and spongy
- putty round windows is intact.

Strip defective paint back to bare wood, then prime and repaint. Cut out and repair areas of rot, using exterior wood filler or replacement sections of wood. Chip out and replace defective putty.

WINDOWS AND DOORS

Windows and doors should open and close easily without sticking. Check that:

- handles and locks engage properly and operate smoothly
- glass is free of cracks.

Plane down, prime, and repaint any edges that stick. Reinforce sagging window joints with metal repair plates. Tighten loose hinge screws, and lubricate hinges. Replace cracked glass.

SPRING AND AUTUMN CHECKS OUTSIDE

AIRBRICKS

There should be airbricks (bricks with holes for ventilation) about every 2 m/6 ft on external walls.

- are clear of leaves, cobwebs, and other debris
- are clear of soil and not covered by climbing plants.

Replace any damaged airbricks so that mice and other vermin can't get in.

FENCES

Water and wind can weaken fence posts. Check that:

- all posts are secure
- struts are securely fixed to posts
- panel fixings are intact
- there is no rot at ground level.

Bolt a concrete fence support, ideally set in concrete, to rotten or loose posts. Use brackets to fix loose or split struts, and C-shaped clips to secure panels. Treat wood with preservative.

FLASHING

These metal or mortar strips seal joins on roofs, walls, and chimney stacks. Wind and water can affect the seal. Ensure that:

- metal flashings fit closely to roof surfaces and into wall joints
- mortar flashings are intact.

Hammer metal flashings into shape. Replace faulty mortar flashings.

GUTTERS

Leaves and moss may fall into gutters, resulting in leaks that can cause damp. Using a ladder:

- clear gutters and downpipe inlets
- ensure joints between sections of gutter are not leaking. Reseal leaky plastic gutters. Use bitumen mastic to seal joints on metal ones.

Your electricity supply

Electricity flows in and out of homes continuously, with appliances picking up whatever current they need to operate. Most of us take this uninterrupted supply for granted – until there's a problem. You may need to take action if one of the various circuits (shown on the illustration opposite) distributing electricity round the home gets overloaded and the supply cuts off, or if a particular appliance stops working. The faultfinder on p65 will help identify problems, some of which are straightforward to solve. Bear in mind that many electrical tasks may require detailed electrical knowledge. Call in a qualified electrician if you are in any doubt.

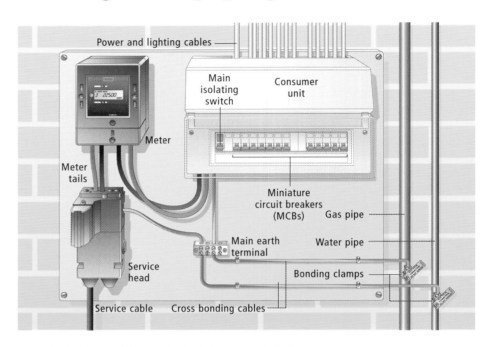

WHEN TO CHECK AND REPLACE WIRING

Have modern wiring systems checked by a professional every five years, and have the wiring checked in any house you buy, unless it is brand new. It may have had amateur work done on it.

Older homes may have several fuse boxes supplying one or two circuits, or circuits that supply power points with round holes. Either system should be replaced without delay.

Other signs of a system in need of modernization are lighting circuits with no earth core in their cables, and cables sheathed and insulated in rubber, or even, with old cables, lead.

HOW ELECTRICITY IS DISTRIBUTED

THE SERVICE HEAD

The electricity supply reaches your home via an underground or overhead cable. After entering the home, the supply cable is connected to a sealed terminal box called the service head or cut-out. You should never tamper with this. The service head contains the **service fuse**, which is there to stop appliances from demanding more electricity than the supply cable can safely deliver without overheating. Most modern homes have a service fuse rated at 100 amps, but a 60 or 80 amp fuse is common in older properties. A lower service fuse rating means you can have fewer high-wattage appliances on at once.

Check for overload To work out how many high-wattage appliances your fuse rating can carry at one time, add up the wattages of appliances that you tend to use at the same time (maybe cooker, dishwasher, washing machine, tumble dryer, as well as lights). Divide the total by 230 (the voltage) to get the maximum

current flow in amps, and check that this does not exceed the service fuse rating.

THE METER

Two cables run from the service head to the electricity meter, which belongs to your electricity supplier and records how much electricity you consume (see How much power are you using?, p63). Modern meters are digital and usage is recorded on a row of figures. Older meters have circular dials. See Reading meters, p62.

If your home uses cheap night-rate electricity to supply electric storage heaters, you will have a dual-rate meter and a timer instead of a single meter wired in from the service head. The timer switches the supply from one meter to the other at pre-set times to record usage at the two different rates.

Some meters nowadays are in a locked unit on an outside wall. You and your supplier should each have a key to get access to the meter. Ask your supplier if you need a replacement key.

THE CONSUMER UNIT

Two cables called meter tails run from the meter to the centre that distributes power around the home, sometimes referred to as the fuse box but more commonly known nowadays as the consumer unit. This contains the system's main on–off switch. Wiring systems older than about 25 years will have circuit fuses that melt if the circuit is overloaded or short-circuited. More modern systems have a row of switches called **miniature circuit breakers** (MCBs) that switch off automatically if a fault is detected. Each fuse carrier or MCB distributes electricity to an individual circuit in the house and controls the rate of current delivered to each circuit: a maximum of 5–6 amps for each lighting circuit, 30 amps for circuits to power points for portable appliances, and 40 or 45 amps for the big fixed appliances such as cookers, water heaters, and electric showers.

THE CIRCUITS

All circuits start at a fuse carrier or MCB in the consumer unit.

Ring main circuit In modern wiring systems the circuits that connect power points run in a loop connecting each power point in turn, finally returning to the consumer unit. Electricity flows in both directions round the loop. Each power point on the ring main can have a branch line spur cable connected into its terminals to supply a single or double power point at the other end of the cable. This makes it easy to add extra power points, if you need them, with the minimum of rewiring.

Radial circuit In older wiring systems the power point circuit is radial, where the cable delivers electricity to each power point in turn and ends at the last one. Lighting, even in modern systems, runs in radial circuits. Most homes have at least two lighting circuits, since the wattage of all the light bulbs together would overload a single circuit.

Dedicated circuit Large, fixed appliances such as cookers and electric showers always have a dedicated circuit, because the amount of power they use is so great that they would overload a shared circuit.

ELECTRICITY SUPPLY TO FLATS

Individual flats within a purpose-built or converted building should each have their own fuse board or consumer unit and independent circuits. In some conversions, however, each flat or bedsit may rely on the building's original systems, which will control supplies from just one point, with usage recorded centrally and billed to one address.

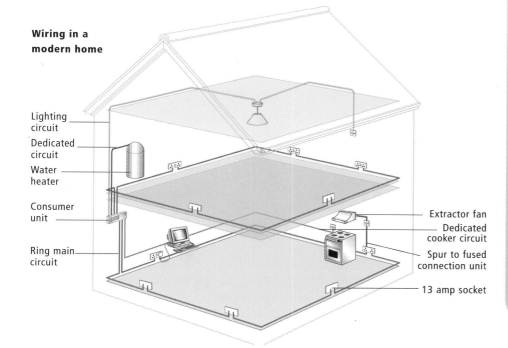

Wiring in a modern home

Lighting circuit
Dedicated circuit
Water heater
Consumer unit
Ring main circuit

Extractor fan
Dedicated cooker circuit
Spur to fused connection unit
13 amp socket

READING METERS

Digital meters show how many units (1 unit = 1 kilowatt hour, kWh) have been consumed since the meter was installed. To check the cost of recent consumption, subtract the reading on your last bill from that on the meter and multiply by the price per unit, given on your bill.

To read a dial meter, start at the left-hand dial recording 10,000 unit/kWh per division, and work across the dials. For each dial, note down the number that the pointer has just passed. If a pointer is directly on a number, you should still record the number below, unless the pointer on the dial to its right is between 0 and 1, in which case note the number the pointer is at. This meter reads 60347.

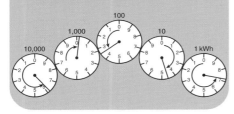

Flex colours

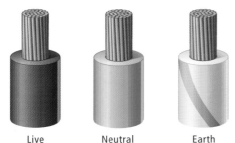

Live   Neutral   Earth

Cable colours

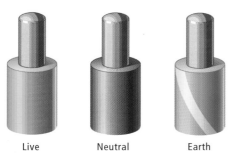

Live   Neutral   Earth

SAFETY FEATURES

MCBs

The MCBs (miniature circuit breakers, see illustration opposite) in modern consumer units allow you to switch off the power to a specific circuit for repairs or alterations, but they also act as automatic protection in the event of overloading – if you plug in more appliances or use more powerful lights than the circuit is designed to supply. When overloading or a short circuit occurs, the MCB automatically switches itself off, and it cannot be reset to restore power until the fault is corrected.

Wiring systems older than about 25 years and not modernized since installation will have cartridge or rewirable circuit fuses instead of MCBs. These contain a length of special fuse wire that will melt if the circuit is overloaded or short-circuited, cutting off the supply to the circuit. See Replacing a circuit fuse, opposite.

RCDs

Modern consumer units also contain a more general safety feature called a residual current device (RCD) that monitors the flow of electric current through the property. If the RCD detects that current has gone to earth – usually because of a leak caused by broken insulation, or because someone has touched a live wire and received a shock – it switches off the

CABLES AND CORES

Every cable in your circuits contains wires (also called cores) that are colour-coded to indicate which way the current is flowing. The red-covered live wire carries the current to where it's needed. The black-covered wire (neutral) carries the current back to where it came from. Both carry electricity at all times. The bare wire in the cable (covered with a green-and-yellow outer sheath when it is exposed at connections) provides a safe path for escaped current, carrying it to earth – see The importance of earthing. Cable outer sheath is usually white or grey.

current in a fraction of a second. This is quick enough to prevent a shock from causing heart failure and death.

Because the area outside a house is not protected by the property's earthing system, RCDs are now fitted in new power points intended for appliances being used out of doors, for instance in garages. If you don't have these, you should buy an RCD adaptor to use when you plug an outdoor appliance into an indoor socket.

THE IMPORTANCE OF EARTHING

Earthing is one of the most important safety features of your wiring system. It can prevent an electric shock, and makes it much less likely that an electrical fault will develop into a fire.

Earthing provides a safe path for any current that accidentally strays from the circuit wiring because of faulty insulation. The escaped electricity is attracted to earth (the ground) because this is an even better conductor than circuit wiring. Given the chance, electricity will flow to earth by the shortest possible route. If there is no earthing system, this could be through your body.

Every circuit is connected to earth via an earth continuity conductor, which is a wire inside the circuit cable, connected to every lighting point, every socket, and every direct appliance connection point (for instance an immersion heater or electric cooker). All the circuit earth conductors are connected to an earth terminal block in the consumer unit or fuse box. This terminal is connected by a cable with green or green-and-yellow insulation, either to a clamp on the sheath of the main supply cable, or to an earth rod driven into the ground beneath or beside the home.

You should also have similar cables connecting metal gas and water pipes, and other exposed metalwork such as sinks and baths, to each other and to the main earth terminal in the consumer unit. These cross-bonding cables ensure that the metalwork is earthed, so that if metalwork comes into contact with a live wire it will not itself become live.

REPLACING A CIRCUIT FUSE

There are two types of circuit fuse – cartridge and rewirable.

Cartridge fuses use enclosed fuses – like those in modern fused plugs, but larger – which clip into the fuseholder or are held in place by its pins. To replace a blown cartridge fuse, turn off the power at the main switch, remove the affected fuseholder, and insert a replacement fuse of the same rating. Cartridge fuses are colour-coded according to their current rating: white is 5 amps; blue is 15 amps; yellow is 20 amps; red is 30 amps; green is 45 amps. All are different sizes (except the 15- and 20-amp fuses, which are effectively interchangeable) making it impossible to fit the wrong fuse in the fuseholder. Replace the fuseholder and restore the power.

Rewirable fuses have a length of wire fitted between two terminals and running across or through a ceramic block inside the fuseholder. In these, the wire itself needs replacing if the fuse is blown. Fuse wire is sold on cards holding wire of three current ratings – 5, 15, and 30 amps – and it's essential to use the correct wire for the circuit concerned. Match the rating stamped on the fuseholder to the size of fuse wire printed on the card it's wrapped around. Loosen the terminals of the fuse so you can release the old fuse wire. Replace it with a new piece of wire, leaving the wire a little slack between the terminals. You will probably need about 50 mm/2 in length – the wire has to be long enough to reach from terminal to terminal and to be wrapped around each.

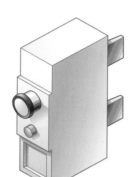

Button-operated miniature circuit breaker (MCB)

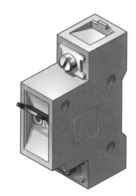

Switch-operated miniature circuit breaker (MCB)

Cartridge fuse carrier

Single-bladed wire fuse carrier

Double-bladed wire fuse carrier

SAVING ELECTRICITY

- Switch lights off when not needed, using time delay switches if necessary.

- Use low-energy light bulbs and low-voltage lighting, especially for lights that stay on for long periods. Dimmer switches don't save money, and you can't use most low-energy light bulbs with them. Compact fluorescent lamps (CFLs) cost more than ordinary bulbs but their cost is recovered very quickly by the energy they save and their longer life. Replacing bulbs in the lights you use most often with CFLs could save you £50 over the lifetime of the bulbs.

- New models of big kitchen appliances are much more energy efficient than older models, especially if you look for one with as high an energy-efficient rating on the label as possible. If your appliances are older than about ten years, replacing them would save you money in the long term.

- Shut the fridge door promptly. For every minute your fridge is open, it takes three minutes to regain its temperature. Keep fridges and freezers as full as practicable.

- Fridge temperature settings should be about 3°C/37°F and freezers around −18°C/−0°F: every degree lower than this adds about 5% to running costs.

- Check fridge and freezer door seals regularly. Empty the fridge and switch it off before going on holiday.

- Defrost freezers regularly – once or twice a year for chest freezers, two or three times a year for uprights – or if buying a new freezer choose one with automatic defrosting. Keep your fridge regularly defrosted.

ALL ABOUT PLUGS

Plugs connect electrical appliances to the mains supply at socket outlets. Plugs used on modern wiring systems have three pins with screw-down terminals inside the plug, to which the cores of the appliance flex are connected. The flex is securely held by a clamp where it leaves the plug casing.

INSIDE A PLUG
Viewed with the plug top unscrewed and the pins facing away from you:

- the **brown (live)** core is connected to the bottom right terminal

- the **blue (neutral)** core is connected to the bottom left terminal

- the earth **(green-and-yellow)** core is connected to the top terminal; some double-insulated appliances, such as irons, marked with ☐ on the flex, do not need earthing, and have no earth core.

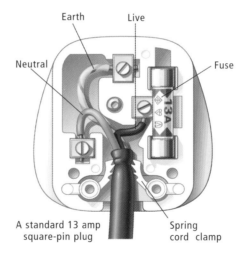

A standard 13 amp square-pin plug — labels: Earth, Live, Neutral, Fuse, Spring cord clamp

The plug contains a small cartridge fuse next to the live pin. Use a fuse rated at 3 amps (colour-coded red) for appliances rated at up to 700 watts, and one rated at 13 amps (colour-coded brown) for more powerful appliances. Use only plugs made to British Standard BS 1363, and fuses made to BS 1362.

All electrical appliances are now sold fitted with a sealed plug. If one gets damaged, cut it off and discard it. Reconnect the flex to a new plug, connecting the cores to the terminals as described above.

ALL ABOUT LIGHT BULBS

General lighting service (GLS) lamps may be clear, translucent (pearl), white, or coloured, and have a tungsten wire filament. The standard lamp has a pear, mushroom, or rounded cylinder shape. Other shapes include pointed candle lamps, compact pygmy lamps, and round golf-ball and globe lamps. Common wattages for GLS lamps are 25, 40, 60, and 100 W.

Large clear and small pearl GLS lamps

Bayonet cap   Edison screw cap

Reflector lamps are used in spotlights. The inside of the glass is silvered to throw light forwards. They come in several sizes, in the same wattages as GLS lamps.

Internal silvered reflector and crown silvered lamps

Compact fluorescent lamps (CFLs) contain small fluorescent tubes instead of a filament, and use much less electricity than a GLS lamp for the same light output. They come in several shapes, with wattages from 3 W to 26 W (equivalent to GLS lamps rated from 25 W to 150 W).

CFL (compact fluorescent lamp) low-energy

Halogen lamps are available in mains voltage (230 V) and low-voltage (12 V) versions. The latter are powered by a transformer wired into the lighting circuit, and come in versions of 20, 35, and 50 W.

Mains voltage halogen lamp

Tubes may be **filament** or **fluorescent**. The former are used for strip lighting, while the latter provide utility lighting to work areas. Filament tube wattages range from 30 W upwards, fluorescent ones from 18 to 58 W.

END CAPS

The brass-coloured end cap, where the light bulbs connect to the fittings, may be the **bayonet cap (BC)** or **Edison screw (ES)** type. Some light fittings take lamps with small versions of these end caps, known as **SBC** and **SES**.

ELECTRICITY FAULTFINDER

This quick checklist will help you trace electrical faults and either fix them – you may need to refer to another page for full instructions – or isolate the cause of the problem if you can't. Don't take on any task if you don't feel fully confident of what you are doing – call a professional if in doubt.

IF A LIGHT WON'T WORK

- Check whether the light bulb works in another lamp; if not, replace.
- Check the circuit fuse or MCB and replace/reset as necessary (see Replacing a circuit fuse, p63).
- If the fuse blows or the MCB trips off again immediately, switch off power, open the lampholder covers with the power still off, and check for loose connections and damaged wires on the flex. Remake or replace as necessary.

IF AN APPLIANCE WON'T WORK

- Unplug it, open its plug, and check for loose connections. Remake as necessary, close the plug, and test the appliance.
- If it still won't work, unplug again, open the plug and fit a new fuse. Close the plug and test the appliance.
- If it still won't work, unplug it again and open the appliance – if you can – to check connections at the terminal block. Remake as necessary.

Replace the flex completely if it is damaged.

IF A WHOLE CIRCUIT IS DEAD

- Check whether the circuit fuse has blown or the MCB has tripped off. If it has, switch off all lights or unplug all appliances as appropriate and replace the fuse or reset the MCB. Restore the power to the circuit.
- Switch on lights or plug in appliances one by one. If one blows the fuse/trips the MCB again, isolate it for checking as outlined above. Check that the circuit is not being overloaded with too many lights/appliances. See Check for overload, p60.
- If you have a split-load unit, supplying electricity at two different costs, check whether the RCD has tripped off. Switch it back on if you can; if you can't, the fault is still present. Locate it if possible by running through the checks above, or call in an electrician.

IF THE WHOLE SYSTEM IS DEAD

- If your system has a whole-house RCD, check whether it has tripped and reset it if possible. If you cannot, the fault is still present (see If a whole circuit is dead, above).
- Check whether there is a local power cut by phoning a neighbour. If there isn't and only your home has no power, call your electricity supplier.

SAVING ELECTRICITY

- Microwave ovens cost up to 70% less to run than conventional ovens and are particularly efficient for reheating food. Fan ovens are 35% cheaper to run and don't need pre-heating. Slow cookers and pressure cookers are also energy-efficient.
- Hang washing up to dry, using a tumble drier only when essential. Tumble dry clothes sorted into heavy and lightweight loads. Dry loads consecutively to use residual heat. Check filters regularly.
- A wash cycle of 40°C uses a third less electricity than a wash of 60°C. Modern wash powders and detergents are so effective that only very dirty washing needs more than 40°C.
- Run washing machines and dish-washers less often with full loads, rather than frequently with part-loads.
- Turn dishwashers off before the start of the drying cycle – dishes will dry in the stored heat – or open the door and let them dry naturally.
- Don't open a heated oven unnecessarily and close it as quickly as you can. It loses about 15°C / 59°F every time you open the door while it's on.
- Switch off appliances such as televisions, hi-fi, and computers instead of leaving them on stand-by.
- Install a timer so that your immersion heater operates only when it's needed.
- If you have cheap night-rate electricity to supply storage heaters, have the immersion heater timed to come on overnight. Avoid using expensive day-time top-ups of storage or immersion heaters.

Plumbing, heating, and gas

Your plumbing system has a number of different parts – the cold and hot water supply, the waste pipes and drains that get rid of the water when you've finished with it, and the heating system, if this relies on hot water to heat the radiators. Knowing how it all works not only helps you to use it sensibly; it also means you can track down the cause of any problems and at the very least minimize the mess that a plumbing disaster can cause.

SEE ALSO Central heating, p192

HOW YOU PAY FOR WATER

If your home does not have a water meter, what you pay for your water supply and the disposal of waste water through the local sewer network depends on the chargeable value of your home. This is a figure based on its former rateable value when everyone paid local rates rather than council tax. Your water company sets a water rate in pence per pound of chargeable value for water supply and waste water disposal, and calculates a supply charge for each service. It then adds a fixed standing charge for each, and computes your total annual bill. You'll be billed for this in two half-yearly instalments, although those who pay by direct debit also have a choice of paying monthly.

If you have a water meter, you pay a quarterly bill consisting of a standing charge plus an amount for each cubic metre (1,000 litres/220 gallons) of water you use.

YOUR COLD AND HOT WATER SUPPLY

Your cold water supply arrives in your home via an underground pipe connected to the water main beneath the road. The pipe is usually buried at a depth of about 750 mm/2 ft 6 in to protect it from frost, and somewhere between the road and your building there is an underground stopvalve belonging to the water company that allows the home to be shut off from the mains supply. In towns this is probably in a small chamber underneath a hinged cover plate set in the pavement, but in the country it may be found anywhere within the property boundaries – it depends on the siting of the nearest water main. Make sure you know where yours is. You are responsible for the pipe as soon as it leaves the water company's underground stopvalve.

After the supply pipe enters the home, it will run to another stopvalve. This allows you to cut off the supply within the home in an emergency or to make alterations to the system. Again, find out where yours is, if you don't already know. From here, the route the supply pipe takes depends on whether your home has an indirect or direct plumbing system.

AN INDIRECT PLUMBING SYSTEM

With this system, found in the majority of homes in the UK, the supply pipe runs up to a cold water storage cistern (tank) in the loft, which fills via a float-operated valve (ballvalve) that shuts off the water flow when the cistern is full. A branch off this so-called rising main supplies mains-pressure, fresh, cold water direct to the kitchen sink for drinking and cooking. Other branches may also be taken off the rising main to supply a washing machine or dishwasher, a garden tap, or an instantaneous gas or electric shower or water heater. An outlet pipe from the storage cistern supplies all the other cold taps in the home. A second outlet pipe

feeds the hot water cylinder, which in turn supplies the hot taps. Each of these two outlet pipes should be fitted with a shut-off valve called a gatevalve.

In an indirect system, the hot water comes from the hot water cylinder. This may be heated by an electric element called an immersion heater, but it is more common for it to be heated by the boiler that operates the central heating system. The cylinder contains a copper coil called a heat exchanger, and this is connected to the boiler by flow-and-return pipes that make up the hot water (primary) circuit for the central heating. This does not mix with the water in the hot water cylinder (secondary circuit).

As hot water from the boiler is pumped through this coil, the coil heats the cold water in the cylinder and the (cooled) water from the coil returns to the boiler to be heated up again. When a hot tap is opened, cold water from the storage cistern in the loft flows into the base of the cylinder, and the pressure drives hot water out of the cylinder via a pipe at the top.

This pipe (from the top of the hot water cylinder) divides into two. One part goes to the hot taps, while the other rises up into the loft and is looped over the main cold water cistern. This pipe – called the open vent pipe – is a safety device and allows air (or steam if the system were to overheat) to escape from the system.

A DIRECT PLUMBING SYSTEM

With a direct system, each cold tap and WC is fed directly from the rising main, so there is no main cold water cistern. Hot water may be supplied either from a hot water cylinder with its own small cold water cistern (sometimes on top of the cylinder), or from an instantaneous gas or electric water heater or a 'combination' gas boiler also connected directly to the

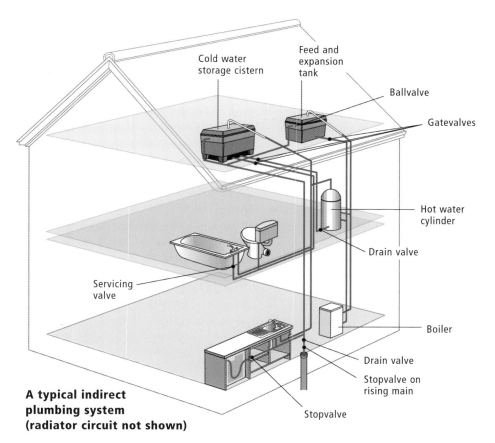

Cold water storage cistern

Feed and expansion tank

Ballvalve

Gatevalves

Hot water cylinder

Drain valve

Servicing valve

Boiler

Drain valve

Stopvalve on rising main

Stopvalve

A typical indirect plumbing system (radiator circuit not shown)

If your system springs a leak, it's vital that you know where to turn the water off so you can minimize the damage caused. On an ideal system you should be able to isolate every appliance and section of pipe, but in practice you will probably have a limited number of controls available to use.

- The most vital is the **stopvalve** on your rising main. Turning this off stops your cold water storage cistern from filling up and allows you to empty it quickly by turning on all your taps. Give the valve handle a half-turn off and on again every six months or so to make sure it hasn't seized up and will work when you need it.

- Find the orange- or red-handled **gatevalves** on the pipes leading from your storage cistern to the cold taps (usually in the loft) and the hot water cylinder (usually in the airing cupboard). Work out which is which and label them. These allow you to isolate key sections of the system pipework.

- On a modern system you should have small **servicing valves** on pipes to individual taps and WC cisterns, and also to washing machines, dishwashers, and water softeners. These valves usually have a small screw, or a red (hot fill) or blue (cold fill) handle that needs only be turned through 90°.

- You may also have a **drain valve** at the rising main. This looks like a tap without a handle and when opened (for which you'll need a small spanner and a hose), drains off water in the pipes that cannot be drained off via a tap.

rising main. Direct systems using combination boilers are more common in flats and conversions than in houses, although they are increasingly used to replace indirect systems in smaller houses. The advantages are that they require less pipework, do not require space-guzzling cylinders and storage cisterns, the amount of available hot water is not dependent on the amount in the cylinder, and they are cheaper to run. Disadvantages are that the boiler itself is more expensive at the outset than the boiler in an indirect system and there is no stored water in reserve if supplies are interrupted for any reason.

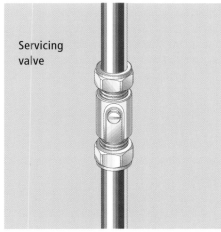

Servicing valve

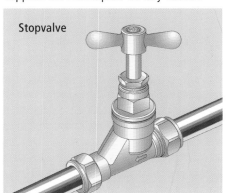

Stopvalve

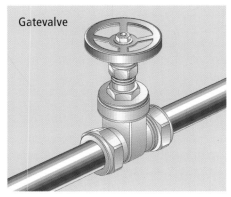

Gatevalve

SAVING WATER

- A five-minute shower uses only a third as much water as a bath.

- Fix dripping taps – see p186. Each could waste the equivalent of a bathful of water a week.

- Run the washing machine or dishwasher only when you have a full load – each full load uses less water than two half-loads.

- Turn off the tap when cleaning your teeth – running water can fill a small bath in five minutes.

- Using the plug every time you run water in a basin or sink could save £15 a year if you have a water meter. Don't leave the tap running when washing vegetables, and wash dirty mugs and plates in a bowl of water at the end of the day rather than one by one under a running tap.

- A third of the average household's water use is flushed down the toilet, and the average household uses the equivalent of two baths a day flushing the toilet. Put a brick in the WC cistern to reduce the volume of water stored. If you have a dual-flush cistern, reduce the flush volume by fitting a conversion cap (supplied with the cistern, or available from plumbers' merchants if you have lost yours) into the hole in the side of the special dual-flush siphon unit.

- Store rainwater in butts for garden usage and throw away your hosepipe.

- A garden sprinkler uses as much water in half an hour as four people use in a day. Use it sparingly, move it often or, better still, get rid of it and use a watering can instead. You must have a water meter installed if you intend to use a garden sprinkler.

STANDARD CENTRAL HEATING SYSTEM

A standard central heating system, which sends heated water from a boiler to radiators and to the hot water cylinder heating coil, has its own small feed and expansion cistern in the loft. This tops up any water losses due to leaks or evaporation and also provides room for the central heating water to expand as it heats up. The cistern is supplied by a branch pipe from the rising main, and fills via a float-operated valve in the same way as the main storage cistern. A second open vent pipe looping over the feed and expansion cistern provides an escape route for air or steam should the heating system overheat for any reason.

YOUR DRAINAGE SYSTEM

When you empty a bath, basin or sink, or flush a WC, the waste water heads for the drains. In a modern home, each water-connected appliance – including the WC – has a waste pipe that runs directly into a single vertical soil stack, normally sited inside the building. In older properties, sinks, basins, and baths empty into ground-level gullies or wall-mounted hoppers, while WC waste is discharged into a separate external soil pipe, and the two parts of the system do not merge until they get underground.

The various waste and soil pipes are connected into underground drainpipes that merge in below-ground inspection chambers with metal covers. The drainpipes then run on, via other connecting chambers if necessary, towards the nearest sewer.

Rainwater from gutters runs via separate downpipes to ground level, and then via underground pipes to the surface water drain under the nearest road, or to drainage pits called soakaways if no drain is nearby.

TYPICAL WATER CONSUMPTION

Below are some average consumption figures for the main water-using appliances. To get your annual water usage in cubic metres, add up how many uses you make of each one per week, multiply the total weekly usage by 52 and divide by 1,000, as there are 1,000 litres in a cubic metre..

As a guide, an average household uses about 160 cu m/35,000 gall of water per year. To find out whether you would save money by having a water meter, contact your water company and ask for details of their standing charges and costs per cubic metre of water used. Work out how much your annual water usage would cost on a meter and compare it with current bills.

Most water companies will install a meter free of charge. Bear in mind that your water consumption may rise if your circumstances change – for instance, if you have children.

Washing, drinking, cooking etc	30 litres/6 gall per person per day
Bathing	80–90 litres/17.5–20 gall per bath
Showering	30 litres/6 gall per shower (80 litres/17.5 gall per power shower)
WC use	9 litres/2 gall per flush (6 litres/1.3 gall for WCs fitted after 01.01.01)
Washing machine	80 litres/17.5 gall per load
Dishwasher	35 litres/7.7 gall per load
Hosepipe (garden)	9 litres/2 gall per minute (540 litres/119 gall per hour)

HOW GAS ENTERS YOUR HOME

If your home has a mains gas supply, it will reach the property through an underground pipe from the gas main in the street. Depending on when it was installed, this pipe will be iron, copper, or yellow plastic. It runs to the gas meter, which is often under the stairs in older homes, or housed in a special cabinet in an outside wall of more recent buildings.

The flow of gas to the property is controlled by the main on-off lever on the supply pipe immediately before the meter. This lever is fully open when its handle is in line with the pipe, and fully closed when it is at 90° to it. It should be left fully open at all times but it is a sensible precaution to check, at least once a year, that it moves freely, so you are sure it can be operated in an emergency. If the supply pipe is metal, it should be fitted with a metal earth clamp which is connected to the main earthing point on your home's wiring system by a cross-bonding cable covered in green-and-yellow PVC insulation (see p62 for why earthing is important).

Iron or copper pipes run from the meter to wherever you need a gas supply within the home. Gas-fired boilers are connected directly to the supply pipework. Cookers are connected to a supply valve with a plug-in bayonet connector or, on older installations, with a screw-on hose fitting. Branch pipes supplying gas fires and room heaters are fitted with a small isolating valve, and a thinner pipe runs on from there to the fire itself.

HOW YOU'RE CHARGED FOR GAS

Gas is charged by unit of consumption, with a standing charge on top. You will normally be billed quarterly, for actual or estimated consumption, but you can opt to pay monthly, by direct debit. See Choosing utility deals, p70.

USING LPG

Around 75,000 homes in the UK use liquefied petroleum gas (LPG) because they have no mains gas supply. LPG is stored in an outside tank (provided and owned by

the gas supplier) that is topped up with regular deliveries by road tanker. A gas pipe fitted with a safety valve and pressure regulator runs from the tank to the home. You may have to buy special appliances to run on LPG, though with minor modifications some mains gas appliances can use it. Your gas supplier will advise you. LPG is 50 per cent more expensive than ordinary mains gas, once the annual tank rental is added to the fuel cost. Switching suppliers to save money is more difficult because the supplier owns the tank. You may need planning permission to have an LPG tank, which must be accessible to the delivery tanker.

GAS SAFETY RULES

It is an offence under the Gas Safety (Installation and Use) Regulations to carry out any work yourself on your gas supply and any appliances connected to it. The work must be done only by a qualified gas fitter or by an installer registered with CORGI (the Council for Registered Gas Installers).

SAVING ON HEATING

- Check your loft insulation and top it up to the level of the joists, if necessary. The recommended minimum thickness is 25 cm/10 in, for new houses and extensions, though existing joints may not be deep enough for this. Loft insulation can save 20%–25% on heating bills. For how to insulate your loft and other parts of the house, see Insulating you home, p198.

- Your central heating thermostat should be no higher than 18–20°C/ 64.5–68°F. Turning it down by 1°C/2°F will make little difference to your comfort and could save £15–£20 on a year's heating bill.

- Cavity wall insulation is expensive but will pay for itself in 3–7 years.

- Draughts can lose up to 15% of the heat from your home. Fit draught strips to all external doors and letterboxes, and consider blocking your chimney flue if you do not use your fireplace. For more detail, see Draughtproofing, p176.

- Fit a reflective panel behind radiators on outside walls to reduce heat loss – you can buy corrugated panels, or use ordinary kitchen foil (much cheaper but not as efficient).

- Radiators do not need to be fitted under double-glazed windows. If you are renovating your central heating system, consider moving radiators so that they are back to back on internal walls, which shortens the pipe.

- Make sure your hot cylinder is well insulated – a jacket costs about £10 and pays for itself in a few months. See Insulating your home, p108.

IF YOU SMELL GAS

If you smell gas at any time, anywhere, call free on 0800 111 999 – there is no charge for the call-out.

Choosing utility deals

We've all seen adverts urging us to switch suppliers of electricity, gas, and telecoms. They promise big savings, especially those trying to get us to switch to a single supplier for electricity and gas. Are there really savings to be made? The answer is yes, for the moment, and it may be less difficult to switch than you think. Even if you don't want to switch, you may still be able to reduce your bills. Phone companies may also provide Internet and cable television access. Before buying or changing, decide what you need and what you're prepared to pay for it.

PRE-PAYMENT METERS

When people fall badly behind with their gas and electricity bills, suppliers will often remove the normal meter from a property and install a pre-payment meter instead. This is to make sure that energy can be used only if it has been paid for in advance – unlike with a normal meter where you pay for it in quarterly or monthly arrears.

If your home has a pre-payment meter you have the right to ask your supplier(s) to change it to a normal 'credit' meter. This is definitely worth doing – pre-paid energy is more expensive and less convenient.

The supplier may ask for a security deposit or that you pay by monthly direct debit. However, if you can prove that you have been a prompt and regular payer in the past, the supplier may be prepared to accept payment by cheque. If your supplier refuses to switch you back to a normal meter, complain to **energywatch** (the Gas and Electricity Consumers' Council).

TELECOMS

Despite the fact that everyone has had a choice of company for their landline telephone for several years now, research by the Department of Trade and Industry showed that, up until June 2000, only 11% of people had taken steps to save on their land phone bills by moving away from **British Telecom** (BT). Choosing a cable company is one option – see p120. If you don't want to have a new line installed, or your street doesn't have cable, you can still save on your bills – up to 20%, for example, by keeping your BT line but changing the company that bills you for your calls.

SAVING ON THE PHONE AND THE INTERNET

There are several ways to save money on your phone bills, none of which involves changing your phone number.

- Stick with BT but switch from its standard line-rental package. Paying a little more each month for the BT Together package gives you a limited number of free calls, halves the cost of national calls, and reduces the cost of your local and international calls. Another alternative is the BT Talk Together package. This has a higher monthly fee, but the first hour of every local call made at the weekend or on a weekday evening is free.

- If you make a lot of national and international calls, you can save a substantial amount by routing them through an 'indirect access' company. You still pay line rental to BT, but you choose another company to bill you for calls. The company will give you a four-digit access code to dial before the number you want to call and/or you will get a special autodialler which you plug into your phone socket to re-route calls.

- You can use different indirect access companies for different types of call, which is worth doing because some are cheaper for daytime national calls, for example, while others specialize in cheap international calls. If you don't want to have to remember several access codes or have a number of autodiallers, consider signing up for 'carrier pre-selection' (CPS), offered by some indirect access companies. This allows calls to be switched through to the relevant company at the telephone exchange, doing away with the need for extra digits or kit.

- If you surf the Internet on a pay-as-you-go basis, it can add a big chunk to your phone bill, especially if you are a heavy user or you access the Internet at peak times. Unmetered access – where you pay a fixed fee per month to an Internet Service Provider (ISP) to cover all your surfing time – can be a much better deal. You can get up-to-date details of ISPs (offering both dial-up and broadband access), together with user comments on the quality of service, by going to http://www.net4nowt.co.uk. Some cable and other phone companies offer similar fixed-fee deals and some offer package deals.

Websites that enable you to compare phone costs – including mobile phone deals – include:
  http://www.buy.co.uk
  http://www.callforless.co.uk
  http://www.saveonyourbills.co.uk
  http://www.uswitch.com.

GAS AND ELECTRICITY SUPPLIERS

HOW TO REDUCE YOUR BILLS

Using less energy will reduce your bills (see energy-saving tips on p000 and p000), but another way of saving money is to change from paying your bills by cash or cheque to paying by direct debit in order to take advantage of a price reduction of between about 5% and 10% (depending on usage and the company supplying the energy).

If your gas supplier is **British Gas**, paying promptly by cash or cheque – which means paying a bill within ten days of the date it was issued – saves about £30 a year. Paying by direct debit is usually still cheaper, but how much cheaper depends on the size of your bill.

You can also save money by changing suppliers. According to figures published by the National Audit Office, people who have switched suppliers have saved, on average, £78 a year on gas and £45 on their annual electricity bills.

And since switching doesn't require any kind of physical upheaval (your gas pipes, electricity cables, and meters stay the same), the only hassle involved – if you want an accurate idea of how much you could save – is working out your annual consumption. See Switching suppliers.

SWITCHING SUPPLIERS

1 Work out your annual gas and electricity consumption by adding up the kilowatt-hours (your electricity bill may call these 'units') on your last four quarterly bills. The energy regulator **Ofgem** estimates that average annual gas consumption is 10,000 kWh in a flat or small house, 19,050 kWh in a medium-sized house, and 28,000 kWh in a large house. The figures for electricity consumption are 1,650 kWh, 3,300 kWh, and 4,950 kWh.

2 Identify which suppliers will save you money. The easiest way to do this is to enter details of your annual consumption into the interactive calculators at http://www.buy.co.uk, http://www.unravelit.com, or http://www.uswitch.com (which usefully gives each company a service rating). Alternatively, use the price information published in the free fact sheets published by **Ofgem**. The fact sheets also give suppliers' contact details.

3 Phone your chosen companies for quotes and to check what kind of contract is offered. With rolling contracts, the supplier is free to change the tariff after giving you 10 days' notice, but you are usually free to change to another supplier without penalty. With fixed contracts, the price can't go up during a set period – usually a year – but you could be charged a fee if you decide to switch again before the end of this period.

4 Sign the contract with your new supplier and tell the old supplier that you want to switch. They may not let you do so until all bills have been paid.

5 Expect the whole process to take about 28 days, during which time either you will be asked to supply a meter reading or your new supplier will take one. Keep a note of this so you can check that the old supplier uses the correct figure when calculating your final bill.

6 You should receive a letter from your new supplier telling you the date that the switch will take place.

GETTING CONNECTED

When you move into a new home, you usually inherit the gas and electricity suppliers chosen by the previous occupant. If you are happy to stick with those suppliers, you should ask the relevant companies for a contract before you move in, as well as arranging to have the meter read when you move in. They will also be able to tell you whether the supply will need to be reconnected and whether there is a charge for this.

Changing suppliers If you want to change suppliers, ask the previous occupants for the gas Meter Point Reference Number and Electricity Supply Number. This helps to speed the change to a new supplier. If you can't get the information from the previous occupants, and you want to find out who supplies your new property, contact the Meter Number Helpline for gas on 0870 608 1524. To find out which company supplies electricity and/or the Electricity Supply Number, contact the local electricity distribution company – listed under 'Electricity' in the phone book – and ask for the Meter Point Administration Service.

If you're renting If you rent a property and pay utilities directly, you may need your landlord's permission to change suppliers. If the landlord charges you for your gas and electricity, you will not be able to change supplier unless you can persuade him or her to do so. Note that there is a 'maximum resale price' for gas and electricity, which is the most your landlord can charge you. This cannot be more than the price he or she has paid per kWh, although the landlord is also entitled to recover any standing charge.

Contact details for organizations given in **bold** appear at the end of each section.

You and your council

Most of us pay our council tax without giving much thought to what our local authority provides in return. Different levels of authority within the local government structure provide a range of services, from the arts to zoo licensing. Knowing which part of a local authority to approach can speed up any contact you have to have. Check your phone directory for direct line numbers for different departments, or look on the Internet for your local authority's Web site, which will also have news of issues in your area.

STRUCTURE OF LOCAL GOVERNMENT

The powers and structure of local government are determined by Parliament.

Scotland, Wales, and parts of England have a single-tier system, in which all-purpose councils have responsibility for all local authority functions. In Scotland, Wales, and parts of England, these bodies are termed **unitary authorities**. In the heavily urbanized areas of England they are known as **metropolitan district councils**. In London there are 32 **borough councils** and the City of London.

In the remainder of non-metropolitan England a two-tier structure exists, in which responsibility for local authority functions is divided between an upper level of **county councils** and a lower tier of **district councils**.

In Northern Ireland, there are single-tier **district councils**.

COUNCIL RESPONSIBILITIES

County councils and unitary authorities are responsible for most local services, which typically include:

- education
- fire and rescue
- cultural services, including the provision of libraries
- highways
- social services
- trading standards
- transport
- waste disposal.

The following services are also managed by unitary authorities and, where local government is shared with another tier of authority, by district and city councils:

- local planning
- planning applications

SOME SPECIFIC SERVICES

WASTE COLLECTION AND RECYCLING

District and unitary authorities are responsible for the collection of household waste and the frequency of the service is up to each individual authority's discretion. The majority of local authorities provide a weekly service, through tendered contracts with waste collection companies.

Many councils now also offer a recycling service. This is normally a weekly collection service of glass, cans, plastic bottles, and newspapers. Schemes are often 'opt-in', requiring customers to contact their authority to register and receive a recycling box. In more remote areas, collection services for recycling may be more basic – for instance of newspapers only.

- housing
- environmental health, including noise nuisance
- minor roads
- leisure and recreation services
- waste collection
- licensing
- electoral registration
- benefits.

At the next level down are town and parish councils, which spend an allocation of council tax on services for their community, such as:

- bus shelters and public benches
- notice boards
- cemetery facilities
- footpaths and car parks
- maintenance of recreational areas.

ELECTORAL REGISTRATION

The electoral register is the list of all local residents who are entitled to vote in the polling district. The register is compiled and maintained by the electoral registration office, which manages the election process. These offices may be based at district, borough, unitary, or metropolitan authorities.

A canvass of every household is conducted in September, October, and November of each year, in order to compile the register. Residents are requested to complete and return a form, giving the names of those individuals in the household on 15 October who are either old enough to vote or will be of voting age before 30 November of the following year. The electoral register is published on 1 December every year.

A rolling register scheme allows people to be added to the register monthly, so you can get your name on the electoral roll as soon as you move to a new area – ask your local council for a form. You can also ask to have your name removed from the register – perhaps you don't want to be approached by any of the political parties. And you can ask for the name of someone who has died recently to be removed, if you provide proof.

Homeless people are entitled to register and vote. The address of a local café, shop, or other business, close to the place where they usually sleep, where they can receive voting papers, can be used.

REGISTERING BIRTHS, DEATHS, AND MARRIAGES

County councils and unitary authorities are responsible for the registering of births, marriages, and deaths.

- **Births** should be registered within six weeks of the birth. In addition to providing the baby's full name, birthweight, and place of birth, you will be required to give the parents' names, and their dates and places of birth, plus the date of the parents' marriage, if applicable. If the parents were not married at the time of the birth, they must both attend to register the birth in order to have the father's details put on the birth certificate.

- **Deaths** should be registered with the registrar within five days. You will be required to provide the registrar with a medical certificate or a coroner's certificate. Other information that will be required is the deceased person's date and place of birth, their occupation, the date of birth of any surviving partner, and, if the deceased is female, the occupation of the spouse.

- Application for a **marriage licence** costs £30 for each partner, paid in advance, plus £37.50 to be paid on the day, though this may be more if a registrar is required to conduct the marriage somewhere other than the registry office. Documents that you will be required to provide include a utility bill or bank statement to prove place of residence. If either of you is divorced, you'll need to show a certificate of decree absolute; if either of you is widowed, a death certificate for your dead spouse.

TRADING STANDARDS

Trading Standards services are designed to ensure that trading in the area is honest, fair, and safe. Services include enforcing and advising on trade and consumer protection laws covering areas such as: credit, prices, weights and measures, labelling of food, product safety, unfair trading, and animal health and welfare. If you have a complaint or comment on local trading in any of these areas you should contact your local office.

EMERGENCY PLANNING

Responsibility for the coordination of an emergency plan lies with your unitary authority or county council, although district councils are also required to have plans in place that feed into the county's overall plan. The plans are generic and are designed as a set of steps that can be put into action in any emergency situation – flood, major accident, or war, for instance.

Emergency plans are drafted in partnership with local voluntary organizations, the emergency services, and any other key organization in the area. Contact your local authority for advice on measures to take if flooding in your area is likely; see also p291.

ENVIRONMENTAL HEALTH

This department of a local authority has responsibility for many health and safety issues we may take for granted, such as checking out businesses dealing with food, ensuring health and safety regulations are adhered to, and disposing of clinical waste. But it also deals with consumer complaints about noise and pollution, repairs needed to private rented property, and any infestations of pests.

COUNCIL POWERS OF ENFORCEMENT

Councils have the power to oblige members of the public to comply with some areas of local government policy. These include:

- payment of council tax – see p75
- application for planning permission.

Before embarking on any building work on your property you should seek advice from the planning department at your unitary authority or district council, as councils have the power to insist that buildings are demolished if prior planning permission has not been sought. Local authorities also have the power to enforce any planning conditions upon which permission was agreed, for instance that premises be used for either commercial or domestic use. See Rules and regulations, p254–7.

PROMOTING WELL-BEING OF YOUR AREA

Under the Local Government Act 2000 councils and local authorities have the power to do anything that promotes the economic, social, or environmental well-being of the area, as long as there is no legislation that prevents it.

WHAT DOES COUNCIL TAX PAY FOR?

The bulk of each pound collected in council tax goes to pay for services such as schools, social services, care in the community, libraries, housing, and highways. A small sum, often just a few pence from the pound, goes to the local police and fire services. A sum also goes to town and parish councils.

CLAIMING COUNCIL TAX BENEFIT

- Council tax benefit is available to people who are unemployed or on low incomes.
- A 'second adult' rebate is available for a council taxpayer whose heterosexual live-in partner is on income support or very low incomes – as long as they do not receive council tax benefit themselves.
- A disability reduction scheme is available where the property is the 'sole or main residence' of a disabled person, as long as the property meets certain criteria. The disability reduction knocks the council tax payable into the band below the one that it would have been in. So someone living in a Band D property who gets a disability reduction would pay the council tax for a Band C property. There is also a reduction if someone lives in a Band A property.

COLLECTING COUNCIL TAX

The 'billing authority' is the local authority that has the power to set and collect council taxes. In England these are district councils (shire and metropolitan), unitary authorities, London boroughs, and the City of London.

COUNCIL TAX BANDS IN ENGLAND, WALES, AND SCOTLAND

| Band | Property value in | | |
	England	Wales	Scotland
A	up to £40,000	up to £30,000	up to £27,000
B	£40–52,000	£30–39,000	£27–35,000
C	£52–68,000	£39–51,000	£35–45,000
D	£68–88,000	£51–66,000	£45–58,000
E	£88–120,000	£66–90,000	£58–80,000
F	£120–160,000	£90–120,000	£80–106,000
G	£160–320,000	£120–240,000	£106–212,000
H	over £320,000	over £240,000	over £212,000

WHAT IS COUNCIL TAX?

Council tax is the tax that pays for a proportion of local council services. The rest are paid for by business rates and central government.

Council tax is a property tax on domestic properties – but the size of the bill also depends on who lives in the home. Taxpayers who live alone get a 25% discount regardless of their income.

COUNCIL TAX BANDS

Each property is banded according to its value, which for these purposes is the amount it would have realized, had it been sold on the open market on 1 April 1991. Properties are assumed to be freehold or, in the case of a flat, to have a 99-year lease. They are assumed to be in a reasonable state of repair.

There are eight council tax bands – see below. The Valuation Office (part of the Inland Revenue) decides which band your home is in by checking details and viewing it from the exterior.

HOW IS COUNCIL TAX CALCULATED?

Each council sets a tax for Band D and the tax for every other band is calculated from it using a standard formula. For example, in every local authority the tax for a property in Band H is always twice the tax for a property in Band D, and the tax for a property in Band A is always two-thirds the tax for a property in Band D.

WHO HAS TO PAY COUNCIL TAX?

Liability for council tax is calculated on a daily basis and there is only one bill for each household. A person who lives in the home can only be asked to pay the bill if:

- they are aged over 18 and
- the home is their 'sole or main residence'.

When there is more than one resident, the resident with the strongest legal interest in the home will be liable for the tax. So, for example, a resident owner would take precedence over any tenants. When a landlord rents property for the sole use of a tenant or tenants, however, the tenant will be liable for council tax.

Where two or more people have the same legal interest in the home, such as joint tenants or co-owners, they are jointly responsible for the bill. Where there are no permanent residents in the home, for example in second homes, the owner is liable for council tax. Reductions in council tax have been possible for second homes, however councils are moving towards charging full council tax for these.

Council tax bills are normally be payable in ten monthly instalments, though councils may offer other arrangements as well. You must keep up to date – see the box, below.

EXEMPTIONS

A property is deemed exempt from council tax if:

- it has been empty and unfurnished for less than six months
- it is empty because the person who would be liable is in hospital or residential care

RISKING A PENALTY

If the local authority sends you a form asking for information to help them determine who is responsible for paying the council tax for your house (the 'liable person'), you must complete and return it.

- it is empty because the person who would be liable is in prison
- it is empty because it is undergoing renovation to make it habitable and has been empty for less than 12 months.

WHAT IF THE BILL'S WRONG?

If you think your council has calculated your bill wrongly – for example has taken account of the wrong number of people in the house – you should contact the council's finance department.

Details of contacts will be given with the demand notice, which is issued in the spring.

If you don't, you may face a penalty of £50. Similarly, failure to give details, when asked, about how many people are in the house may result in an incorrect bill being issued.

COUNCIL TAX DEBT AND RECOVERY

If you do not pay your council tax, your billing authority will take steps to recover the value of your debt, and you may have to bear the cost.

Initially, if you do not pay an instalment of council tax on time, you will be sent a reminder notice. If you pay the arrears when you receive this, your instalments will continue as usual. If however you fail to pay two council tax instalments on time, within a year, you will lose your right to pay by instalments and can be asked to pay the balance for the year. Failing to pay council tax arrears when requested can result in a summons to appear at a magistrates' court. You will have to pay costs for this, even if you settle up before the hearing.

If you appear at the court, you are entitled to explain why you haven't paid, but not having the means to pay will not be considered as a reason. At the magistrates' court, your local authority

may apply for a liability order, which enables it to recover the debt by:

- an attachment of earnings, where your employer deducts a regular amount from your wages or salary and passes it to the authority
- an attachment of income support or jobseeker's allowance, where an amount is deducted from your benefit
- employing a bailiff – see p76.

Volunteering to pay a even a small amount regularly, to discharge the debt, will put you in a stronger position, even if the local authority takes one of the above steps. The liability order may be kept in place as a safety net in case you do not pay the amounts you have agreed. Ultimately, it is possible to be sent to prison for a maximum of 90 days for failing to pay council tax, but the magistrates' court must be satisfied that you have not paid because of wilful refusal or culpable neglect.

THE AVERAGE COUNCIL TAX RATE

In 2003 the average Band D council tax rate – the rate that a local authority sets as a benchmark from which all its other bands of tax are calculated – was forecast to exceed £1,000 for the first time, across Britain. The table below shows how the averages are expected to vary in England, Scotland, and Wales. In England, this represents an increase of £126 in the average council tax bill for a Band D property.

Predicted council tax	
Average Band D bill	2003/04 (£)
England	1,102
Wales	839
Scotland	1,009
Great Britain	1,080

Source: *Chartered Institute of Public Finance and Accountancy (CIPFA), 2003*

COMPLAINING ABOUT YOUR COUNCIL

If you are dissatisfied with a council service or decision, you should first write to, phone, or e-mail the council. Each authority has its own complaints procedure. If the response is unsatisfactory, you should contact your local councillor, who will take the matter further. You might also wish to contact your MP or the **Local Government Ombudsman** (LGO). There are ombudsmen in England, and one each in Scotland and Wales, who are responsible for investigating complaints of local maladministration. The **Northern Ireland Commissioner for Complaints** performs a similar role.

For more information, check on http:// www.open.gov.uk/lgo/index.htm or http:// www.ombudsman-wales.org.

You and your space

Just who does have a right to come on to your property, and under what circumstances? What if someone in your house is being chased for repayment of a debt? And what safeguards do you need if you opt to share your space with a lodger, to raise a bit of spare cash?

ELECTRICITY CABLES AND POLES

An electricity company is able to site telegraph poles on land you own, or put cables across land you own, under what is called a wayleave agreement. Normally this is done with the homeowner's consent, however if the homeowner refuses, the Secretary of State may grant the wayleave.

- Once a wayleave has been granted on a property, there is usually little the householder can do about it. However, it's always worth an enquiry – contact the relevant electricity supplier and ask for 'wayleaves'.

- The wayleave also gives the company the right to come on to the land to inspect and maintain the line or other equipment.

- If a pole carrying an electric cable is sited in your garden, you can get the pole moved to the boundary and the cable relocated underground, though this could cost up to £5,000. You may have to pay all the cost, only part, or nothing, depending on whether the cable supplies you alone, supplies other homes as well, or doesn't supply you at all. Again, contact the relevant electricity supplier.

TRESPASS – NOT WORTH SUING FOR

If there is no right of way or other legal right of access to your land, a person going onto a property you own or rent without either express or implied permission is technically trespassing. Trespass, except in certain very specific circumstances, is not a criminal offence. It is a tort – that is, a civil wrong – and unless you can prove real damage to your property, suing would probably only recover nominal damages.

IF BAILIFFS CALL AT YOUR HOME

Bailiffs are employed by companies, such as lenders, and organizations, such as local authorities, to recover property or to seize property to offset a debt. The vast majority of bailiffs must have a distress warrant (relating to the taking of goods) from the county court or a liability order (sanctioning the intervention of a bailiff, or the deduction of sums owed from wages or benefits) from a magistrate's court.

Bailiffs cannot enter your home by other than peaceful means. This means that they cannot force their way in, although they are allowed to enter if a door is left open, or to climb in through an open window.

Once a bailiff has gained peaceful entry they will 'levy on your goods', which means he or she can write a list of the goods they may take. They may only levy on goods that belong to the person named on the warrant or liability order, so they are not allowed to levy on goods that belong to, say, your children, or other members of your household.

If you agree to make payments to offset the debt, the goods will not be removed. If, however, you default on the payment arrangement, the bailiffs are entitled to come back and seize goods. You may also be charged for their time in doing this.

Although there is no legal definition of harassment by bailiffs, some of the following could constitute harassment:

- threatening arrest or imprisonment
- using bogus court forms
- threatening to call the police – the police play no active role process of implementing a warrant or liability order, although they may be called to prevent a breach of the peace
- asking neighbours to provide information about you.

If you feel that a bailiff is harassing you then this should be reported to company employing the bailiff, the county court, or your local authority's Trading Standards department.

CUSTOMS AND EXCISE CAN SEIZE GOODS

Customs and Excise (C&E) officers are able to seize goods in respect of defaults on payment of VAT, but C&E must first send a written demand for immediate payment. If you fail to respond to the demand, C&E will prepare a distress warrant. This can be done without a court order. The distress warrant must be signed by a higher executive officer and will contain details of the arrears and the name of the person who has been authorized to seize goods.

LIABILITY FOR DEBTS

Generally you are only liable for debts that you personally owe. You are not liable for your spouse's or sibling's debts unless the debt was taken out in joint names, or you acted as a guarantor for the debt.

If you have not heard from a creditor – someone to whom you owe money – contacted the creditor, or made any payments on a debt for over six years, the lender is usually barred from pursuing you. There are, however, some debts that can be pursued beyond six years, such as mortgage shortfalls, secured loans, and joint debts where one partner has been paying, and you should obtain specialist help from an advice agency or solicitor if you cannot deal with these debts.

RENTING OUT A ROOM

Since April 1992, a landlord who rents out one or more rooms in their home can take advantage of the Rent a room scheme. This means that the first £4,250 of income received from renting is usually exempt from income tax. To be eligible the landlord must be an owner–occupier or tenant, and must be letting furnished accommodation in her/his only or main home. The tax relief applies to gross income received in the tax year from the letting, regardless of how many rooms are let. See p44–49 for more about letting property generally.

There are implications of sharing your house with a stranger.

- Always take up references from people who know the person who is renting the room. If possible, get a reference of the person they last lived with – this may be a parent or their last landlord.
- You can check the market rent by looking in local newspapers.

BEFORE A LODGER MOVES IN

Before the lodger moves in, take some photos of the room and draw up a full inventory of its contents. The photos may be useful if the lodger causes damage and you need to claim money for repairs.

You should also decide how often rent will be due – perhaps weekly or monthly – and how this will be recorded. Ask your new lodger for a deposit, typically one month's rent, to be held by you until the lodger leaves. See p47 for more on deposits.

GIVING NOTICE

As long as you have lived in the house, or a member of your family has lived in the house, as your/their only or main home since the beginning of the letting agreement, and as long as you share accommodation with the tenant, then the tenant is likely to be an 'excluded occupier'. For this definition to apply, you must be sharing the use of a room, for example living room, kitchen or bathroom.

An excluded occupier does not have any statutory protection against eviction but you should still give notice at the end of the tenancy. In nearly all cases, four weeks' notice would be considered reasonable. The notice you give does not need to be in any particular form, and could be oral. However, it's best to give notice in writing and keep a copy for yourself.

At the end of a tenancy, you should check the inventory with your lodger, and after you have made any deductions for damage or rent arrears you should return the rest of the deposit to your tenant. You do not have a legal right to deduct money for fair wear and tear – if you tried to do this your tenant could sue you. If possible, get your departing lodger to sign a receipt for the money returned and deductions you have made.

POLICE

Police can enter your home only if they have a search warrant granted by a magistrates' court. They must have significant grounds for entering. These are governed by the Police and Criminal Evidence Act 1984 (PACE).

TELEVISION LICENCE DETECTORS

There are various reasons why **TV Licensing** may believe you have and are watching a television, but have no licence for it:

- the trader from whom you bought the television has informed them of the sale
- your previous licence has not been renewed
- a detector van detects that you are watching but there is no record of your having a licence.

If TV Licensing believes that you don't have a television licence they may send an enquiry officer to visit you. You don't have to let the enquiry officer into your home, but the enquiry officer may apply to the magistrate's court for a search warrant. If the officer does obtain a warrant he or she can return to your property and can if necessary force entry. Any damage caused by the forced entry is your responsibility

You can be prosecuted for installing or using a television set, or a television and a video recorder, and not having a television licence. You can also be prosecuted even if you are not the owner or hirer of the set. In a case in which the set belonged to a husband but was switched on and watched by his wife, for example, the wife was prosecuted.

The exceptions to the licence rule are that: anyone over the age of 75 is entitled to a free licence, even if the present licence-holder for their home is not over 75; people over 74 can obtain a short-term licence; and registered blind persons are entitled to 50% reduction in the licence fee.

Contact details for organizations given in **bold** appear at the end of each chapter.

Boundaries and neighbours

Even neighbours who are the best of friends can fall out over barking dogs or territorial disputes, and there's nothing more likely to spoil your enjoyment of where you are living than acrimony across the garden fence. If you are buying, selling, or improving a property, it is important to know exactly where its boundaries lie. Avoid bad feeling by being clear about your right and responsibilities from the start, and don't rush into action without taking professional advice.

WHAT TO DO ABOUT PARKING TRESPASS

If a vehicle parked on the public highway is blocking your driveway, you should ask the police to deal with it. If, however, a vehicle is parked on your reserved off-street parking space or your driveway, the police class this as a civil offence. They say you can either pay for the car to be towed away or bring a private prosecution against the owner. However, your first step should be to warn the offending motorist of your intention with a note on the windscreen. Giving seven days' notice of your intention to act would be reasonable.

After warning the owner in this way, you are also legally entitled to clamp a vehicle parked on your private property, and to levy a reasonable charge for releasing it – though if you damaged the car the owner would have grounds to claim against you. Wheel clamps can be bought via the Internet and in some motorists' shops.

WHAT TO LOOK FOR WHEN YOU'RE BUYING

THE VIEW

Unless your property deeds state otherwise (which is unlikely), you do not have the right to a view. The local search conducted by your solicitor or licensed conveyancer before purchase will reveal forthcoming developments – you have a right to inspect the plans at your local planning office.

MAINTAINING YOUR PROPERTY FROM NEXT DOOR

If the wall of your property stands directly on the boundary with next door, you may have no legal right to enter next door's property to maintain it. If the neighbour refuses access, you can apply to the local county court (sheriff court in Scotland) for an order. After the works have been done, you will have to make good any damage and perhaps pay compensation for having been allowed access.

RECENT DISPUTES BETWEEN NEIGHBOURS

If you discover that there has been a recent boundary dispute (your solicitor may pick this up, but you should ask the seller for information if you suspect a problem), your solicitor could advise you not to go ahead with the purchase. If you are set on buying, talk to the neighbour concerned to satisfy yourself that the dispute has been settled.

FLYING FREEHOLD

A flying freehold is a property that intrudes into the structure of the property next door. It occurs only in older properties, and it's as well to be aware that the rights and responsibilities of the neighbours it links are notoriously difficult to sort out.

TROUBLE WITH THE NEIGHBOURS

NOISE

If your neighbour annoys you with intrusive noise, they aren't necessarily breaking the law. Try a friendly approach first – they may be unaware that they are disturbing you. Do this in person, then in writing (keep a copy of the letter/s). If this doesn't work, keep a log of the disturbances, noting the date, time, and duration. If possible, ask other neighbours to write statements confirming your report, then send a copy to the Environmental Health (EH) department of your local authority.

If the EH department decides that your neighbour's behaviour is 'unreasonable' and causing a 'nuisance', they can serve a noise abatement order on them. If your neighbour doesn't comply, they may be fined up to £2,000. EH officers may also confiscate equipment such as music systems. In cases of excessive noise between 11 p.m. and 7 a.m., they can issue a warning and follow it up with an on-the-spot fine of up to £1,000. In a block of flats, your neighbours may also be in breach of the terms of their lease or tenancy agreement. Check what your own lease says.

If the EH department fails to act on your behalf, you can take your report to the local magistrates' court (sheriff court in Scotland) and ask for a 'nuisance order' with similar consequences to those above. Alternatively, you can apply for an injunction in the county court (an interdict in the sheriff court in Scotland) to prevent the noise recurring. In the same court, you can claim compensation for the nuisance you have suffered, though this may be a lengthy process and compensation may be small.

PROBLEMS WITH DOGS

If you are regularly disturbed by a neighbour's barking dog, first have a friendly word with its owners. They may be unaware that the dog barks when it is alone, for instance, and may be prepared to help the dog settle by giving it more exercise or leaving it alone less often and in a larger space. Sometimes a dog is less inclined to bark if a radio is left on at low volume, or if the curtains are closed so that it can't see people passing outside. If the nuisance persists, you can apply to the EH department for a noise abatement order, as above.

If you can prove that a dog is dangerous or out of control, a magistrates' court can order that it be kept muzzled or on a leash, neutered, or destroyed. The owner could also be fined up to £2,000 and prevented from owning a dog for some time to come. Contact the police or the **Royal Society for the Prevention of Cruelty to Animals** (RSPCA) for advice.

PESTS

If your neighbour has an infestation of pests, such as mice or rats, and they find their way into your property, call the EH department and suggest to your neighbour that they do the same. A joint visit from the pest control officer would make sense. If your neighbour refuses, EH officers have the power (after giving 24 hours' notice) to inspect premises for pests that are a health hazard. If they are not admitted, they can apply for a warrant and enter by force. If your neighbour is unable to deal with the infestation because of old age or infirmity, contact the social services. See p152 for more on pest control services.

TREES

Trees can damage foundations – their roots take water from the soil, which may cause subsidence. A tree is the responsibility of its owner, so if you have evidence that your neighbour's tree has been the cause of damage to your property, check whether you can make a claim on your buildings insurance policy and allow the insurer to recover the money from next door. The best policy, though, is prevention – talk to your neighbour about pruning the tree before it gets too big, and come to an agreement on cutting back roots and branches to keep it in shape. If you can't agree, you have a right to cut off roots and branches where they cross your boundary, unless the tree has a preservation order on it or you live in a Conservation Area – check with your local authority first.

If your neighbour neglects to prune trees that overhang your property, despite a written agreement that he or she would do so, you can sue through the county court for the cost of pruning the trees, but in order to claim any more, you would have to prove that damage had been caused.

FENCES AND PARTY WALLS

- A fence along a boundary is usually owned by the person who erects it. The deeds or plans to the property may (though in older properties they often don't) show **ownership** – a 'T' mark on a boundary line indicates that a particular partition belongs to the owner of the property inside which the mark has been made.

- Some deeds specify the type of fencing allowed at the property, and its minimum or maximum height. If not, general planning law states that you may not erect a fence more than 1 m/3 ft 3 in high in front of a house or more than 2 m/6 ft 6 in high at the rear. The owner is responsible for maintenance of the fence.

- Dividing walls with supports on both sides belong to both parties, who must share repairs. Under the Party Wall Act, you must give your neighbour two months' notice of an intention to carry out work on the wall, along with details of the proposed work.

EXTENDING YOUR HOME

USING PARTY WALLS

If you plan to use a neighbour's side wall to support the building of an extension on your own property, first check where the boundary is. If the wall belongs entirely to your neighbour, you have no right to use it as a support. If your neighbour is sympathetic and allows you to use their wall, arrange for your solicitor to draw up a legal agreement, or there may be problems when one of you comes to sell. If the property line runs through the wall, it is a party wall – you have the right to use it as a support providing it complies with building regulations. Your neighbour has the right to consult a surveyor, at your expense, to ensure that your building work will not damage their interests.

BUILDING NEAR A BOUNDARY

If you wish to build within 3 m/10 ft of your neighbour's building and lay foundations deeper than those of your neighbour, the law requires you to serve a notice on him/her. Your architect or surveyor will act for you on this. If the neighbour agrees, work can proceed. Otherwise, both parties must appoint a surveyor or surveyors to sort out their differences. See also p255.

FLOOD WATER FROM NEXT DOOR

If flood water from heavy rains drains from a neighbouring property on to yours, your neighbours are not responsible, because they have done nothing to cause it. But if your neighbour builds a patio that drains on to your land, this constitutes a 'nuisance'. If your neighbours refuse to install a drain, you can take action through the courts to force them to do so, and claim for compensation.

WEB SITES AND ADDRESSES

Association of British Insurers (ABI),
51 Gresham Street, London EC2V 7HQ
phone: 020 7600 3333; fax: 020 7696 8999;
e-mail: info@abi.org.uk
Web site: www.abi.org.uk

buy.co.uk, Victoria Station House, 191 Victoria
Street, London SW1E 5NE
phone: 0845 601 2856; fax: 020 7233 5933;
Web site: www.buy.co.uk

Helps you to make savings on your household
bills.

Energywatch, 4th Floor, Artillery House, Artillery
Row, London SW1P 1RT
phone: 08459 06 07 08; fax: 020 7799 8341;
e-mail: enquiries@energywatch.org.uk
Web site: www.energywatch.org.uk

Fax Preference Scheme (FPS), DMA House,
70 Margaret Street, London W1W 8SS
phone: 020 7291 3330; fax: 020 7323 4226;
e-mail: fps@dma.org.uk
Web site: www.fpsonline.org.uk

Register with this company to prevent unsolicited
sales and marketing faxes.

House Contact Centre, PO Box 50, Leeds
LS1 1LE
For general enquiries, phone the number on
the top of your gas or electricity bill;
fax: 0845 604 0304;
e-mail: house@house.co.uk
Web site: www.house.co.uk

British Gas Web site.

Insolvency Service
phone: 020 7291 6895;
Web site: www.insolvency.gov.uk

Help and advice for dealing with personal
insolvency.

Local Government Ombudsman
phone: 0845 602 1982
Web site: www.lgo.org.uk

Local Government Ombudsman for Wales,
Derwen House, Court Road, Bridgend
CF31 1BN
phone: 01656 661 325; fax 01656 673 279;
e-mail: enquiries@ombudsman-wales.org
Web site: www.ombudsman-wales.org

Mailing Preference Service (MPS), DMA
House, 70 Margaret Street, London W1W 8SS
phone: 020 7291 3310; fax: 020 7323 4226;
e-mail: mps@dma.org.uk
Web site: www.mpsonline.org.uk

Register with this company to avoid receiving
unwanted junk mail.

Net4nowt, Home Farm, Cottesbrooke,
Northampton NN6 8PH
phone: 07092 115100; fax: 07092 330090;
e-mail: furtherinfo@net4nowt.com
Web site: www.net4nowt.co.uk

Site that helps you find the Internet Service
Provider (ISP) best suited to your needs.

Northern Ireland Ombudsman, The
Ombudsman, Freepost BEL 1478,Belfast BT1
6BR; visitors: The Ombudsman's Office,
Progressive House, 33 Wellington Place, Belfast
phone: 0800 34 34 24 (free); 028 9023 3821
(switchboard); fax: 028 9023 4912;
e-mail: ombudsman@ni-ombudsman.org.uk
Web site: www.ni-ombudsman.org.uk

Northern Ireland Ombudsman is the popular name
for the Assembly Ombudsman for Northern
Ireland, and the Northern Ireland Commissioner
for Complaints.

**Northumbria Energy Efficiency Advice
Centre (NEEAC)**
phone: 0800 512012;
Web site: www.neeac.co.uk

For advice on cutting your bills by using less
energy.

Ofgem, 9 Millbank, London SW1P 3GE
phone: 020 7901 7000; fax: 020 7901 7066;
Web site: www.ofgem.gov.uk

The regulator for Britain's gas and electricity
industries.

Oftel, 50 Ludgate Hill, London EC4M 7JJ
phone: 0845 714 5000; fax: 020 7634 8845;
email: advice@oftel.gov.uk
Web site: www.oftel.gov.uk

Contact if you have a complaint which you have
not been able to resolve with the phone company
concerned.

Royal Institute of Chartered Surveyors,
RICS Contact Centre, Surveyor Court,
Westwood Way, Coventry CV4 8JE
phone: 0870 333160; fax: 020 7222 9430;
e-mail: contactrics@rics.org.uk
Web site: www.rics.org/public

Information on residential surveys, boundary
disputes, and advice on finding a surveyor.

**Royal Society for the Prevention of Cruelty
to Animals (RSPCA)**, Wilberforce Way,
Southwater, Horsham, West Sussex RH13 9RS
phone: 0870 333 5999; fax: 0870 753 0284
Web site: www.rspca.org.uk

Scottish Public Services Ombudsman, 23
Walker Street, Edinburgh EH3 7HX
phone: 0870 011 5378; fax: 0870 011 5379;
e-mail: enquiries@scottishombudsman.org.uk
Web site: www.scottishombudsman.org.uk

Telephone Preference Service (TPS), DMA
House, 70 Margaret Street, London W1W 8SS
phone: 020 7291 3320; fax: 020 7323 4226;
e-mail: tps@dma.org.uk
Web site: www.tpsonline.org.uk

Register with this company to prevent unsolicited
sales and marketing calls.

TV Licensing Customer Services, TV Licensing,
Bristol BS98 1TL
phone: 0870 241 6468 (to buy or renew a
licence; to notify change of address; for details
of concessions); 0870 241 7167 (for direct
debit applications); 0845 728 9289 (for Cash
Easy Entry payment scheme)
e-mail tvlcsc@capita.co.uk
Web site: www.tv-l.co.uk

Authority in charge of TV licences.

Unravelit, Xelector House, 76 Talbot Street,
Dublin 1, Ireland
phone: 08451 202056;
e-mail: enquiries@unravelit.com
Web site: www.unravelit.com

Helps you to make savings on your household
bills.

uSwitch.com, PO Box 33208, London SW1E 5WL
phone: 0845 601 2856; fax: 020 7233 5933;
e-mail: customerservices@uswitch.com
Web site: www.uswitch.co.uk

Helps you to make savings on your household
bills.

CHAPTER FOUR

Money matters

Time to change banks?

A current account is a must-have nowadays. But because most current accounts offer the same package of cheque book, cash/debit card, direct debits, standing orders, overdraft facility, and the option of accessing your account by phone or over the Internet, it's easy to assume that there's not much to choose between them. That's what the traditional high-street banks would like you to think. However, some accounts – particularly those from stand-alone Internet banks – offer a much better deal than others.

SWITCHING MADE SIMPLE

In the past, switching bank accounts could be a time-consuming and tedious process. However, a recent scheme means that you don't have to endure the hassle of changing your standing orders and contacting all the organizations you pay by direct debit (or who pay you by direct credit) to advise them of the change in your bank details. Your new bank is likely to be able to do all this for you. They will:

- produce a letter for you to send to your old bank authorizing them to pass to your new bank details of all your regular transactions
- set up all your standing orders, direct debits, and direct credits on your behalf
- close your old account (if this is what you want to do) and transfer the balance to your new one.

SIX GOOD REASONS TO SWITCH

1 You have moved or changed jobs and your bank no longer has branches and/or cash machines near to where you need them. Convenience is the most important factor when choosing a current account.

2 You can't remember the last time you set foot in a branch and you would be quite happy running your account by phone or over the Internet. Accounts from branchless banks tend to pay much better rates of interest than those offered on the high street.

3 You have a 'packaged' current account that gives you a range of extras – such as free travel insurance or shopping discounts – in exchange for a monthly fee (that you have to pay even when you're in credit). The extras are rarely worth the £60 to £150 a year that these accounts can cost.

4 You tend to stay in credit and your bank pays no interest or only a paltry

amount. On a balance of £500, for example, switching from the worst rate to the best could mean receiving £25 a year in interest rather than 50p.

5 You run an overdraft and your bank charges a high rate of interest. Many banks charge around 18%, but you could easily halve this. On an overdraft of £500, this would bring the interest charged down from £90 a year to £45.

6 You regularly overdraw and your bank charges a monthly fee as well as interest. Although rare these days, this kind of charge can cost up to £100 a year, assuming you overdraw every month.

COMPARING ACCOUNTS – WHAT TO ASK

- Does the bank provide access to cash machines and have branches where you are likely to need them (if you want branch access)?
- Are there any charges for using the cash machines of other banks and building societies?
- Can you access your account details in a way that suits you – for example, over the phone, via the Internet or WAP phone, or through digital TV?
- Is there a minimum amount that has to be paid into the account each month?
- Can you pay in cheques and cash in a way that you find convenient?
- Does the bank pay interest on credit balances? If so, how much?
- How much interest does the bank charge when you are overdrawn?
- What fees will you have to pay if you overdraw?
- Does the bank charge a monthly fee even when you are in credit?
- Will the bank help you switch your account to them, or will you have to do this yourself?

Extra questions to ask stand-alone Internet banks:

- Does the bank provide prepaid envelopes for paying in cheques through the post, or will you have to pay the postage?
- Is there a charge if you contact the bank by phone rather than by e-mail?

HOW TO GET THE BEST FROM YOUR BANK

- Many people assume that banks don't make **mistakes** – they do. Always keep your own record of all your transactions and check this against your bank statements. Keep cash-machine receipts until your withdrawals appear on your statement.

- Even if you plan never to use it, it is worth arranging an **overdraft** limit on your account in case you overdraw accidentally. Some money may take longer than expected to reach your account, for example. Some banks automatically give you a limit when you open an account, but most expect you to ask for one. If you go over a pre-arranged limit, you will be charged a penalty rate of interest as well as a variety of fees. You will also have cheques bounced and cash withdrawals and debit card payments refused.

- If you lose your cash card and/or debit card, or you suspect that someone knows your personal identification number (PIN), contact your bank as soon as you possibly can. If someone uses your card without your permission, you are liable for the first £50 unless you managed to tell your bank before the fraudulent transaction occurred. Once you have told your bank, your **liability** is zero … unless you wrote your PIN on your card. To avoid writing down your PIN anywhere, choose a number you will remember easily and make use of the option of changing your PIN – an option that the Banking Code (see right) says all banks must offer.

- If you use Internet banking, all the banks say that you will not lose any money if you are an innocent victim of fraud. However, you do need to make sure that you keep secret the security details you use to access your account. Sensible **precautions** include not writing them down without disguising them, not saving your password on your hard disk, and always logging off properly from the bank's Web site after you have finished. This is particularly important if you share your computer, use Internet cafés, or if you access your account from a computer at work.

WHAT DOES INTERNET BANKING PROVIDE?

Most banks offer Internet banking services with a current account. You can't use Internet banking to pay in cheques or withdraw cash, but you can:

- view your balance(s) and recent transactions on screen
- print statements
- transfer money between accounts
- pay bills
- make payments to any other UK bank or building society account
- set up, view, amend, or cancel standing orders
- view direct debits
- order cheque books and other stationery
- send instructions to your bank via a secure e-mail system (which you should use instead of your normal e-mail).

At the time of writing, stand-alone Internet banks – such as cahoot (http://www.cahoot.com), Intelligent Finance (http://www.if.com), smile (http://www. smile.co.uk), or the Internet account from First Direct (http://www.firstdirect.com) – offer all these services but differ from the traditional banks' add-on Internet services in two important respects. They don't have branches, and they pass on – in the form of competitive rates of interest – the cost-savings gained from operating over the Internet. Up-to-date rates are given on the banks' Web sites, which also feature online demonstrations. All stand-alone Internet banks allow you to pay in cheques by post and withdraw cash through cash machines; some also use the Post Office. Check each for the particular services they offer.

THE BANKING CODE

Nearly all banks follow the Banking Code – a voluntary code of practice that, among other things, commits a bank to making sure you have clear information on:

- how you can expect your bank to deal with you
- how your account will be run
- the charges, interest rates, and the terms and conditions governing your account
- the Direct Debit Guarantee (which offers certain assurances regarding your direct debits)
- the steps you must take to protect security information
- how to make a complaint.

If you are not given a copy of the Code automatically, you can ask for one. If you think your bank has failed to follow the Code, contact the **Banking Code Standards Board**, who can also tell you if your chosen bank subscribes to the Code. If you have a complaint about your bank that you are unable to resolve using the bank's own complaints procedure, contact the **Financial Ombudsman Service**.

STANDING ORDER OR DIRECT DEBIT?

With a standing order, you tell your bank to make payments of a fixed amount at regular intervals directly to another UK bank account. With a direct debit, you give your account details to the organization you want to pay and authorize them to collect the money from that account. They can alter the amount, as long as they tell you first.

Contact details for organizations given in **bold** appear at the end of each chapter.

Using plastic

Why bother with a credit card when you can just as easily use the debit card that you got with your current account? One good reason is that a credit card gives you access to free and flexible credit. Another is that because of the Consumer Credit Act, buying with a credit card provides you with a valuable line of defence if something goes wrong with your purchases. The downside of owning a credit card is that it can be a passport to unmanageable and expensive debt.

CHARGE CARDS

They look like credit cards, but charge cards – of which Amex and Diners Club are the most well known – are quite different. Unlike a credit card, a charge card:

- provides unlimited credit, but expects you to pay your bill in full every month – with hefty charges if you don't

- does not provide the protection of the Consumer Credit Act (see Seven benefits of credit cards, right)

- always has an annual fee, which can range from £40 to £150 a year

- can provide access to an automatic overdraft facility of up to £15,000 (for a charge card issued by a high-street bank)

- generally comes with various forms of free insurance – travel or medical insurance, for example

- is unlikely to be offered to you unless you earn at least £25,000 a year.

SEVEN BENEFITS OF CREDIT CARDS

1 One of the main benefits of using a credit card rather than a debit card is the protection provided by the Consumer Credit Act. This says that if you have problems with goods or services – such as a supplier going out of business or failing to deliver – you can get your money back from the card issuer if you can't get it back from the supplier (provided that whatever you bought cost between £100 and £30,000).

2 Some cards provide purchase protection insurance, which pays out if something you have bought with the card is lost, damaged, or stolen within 90 or 100 days of the date of purchase. However, this type of insurance doesn't cover all purchases – secondhand or perishable goods, for example – and there's usually a limit on how much you can claim. This kind of insurance is not worth having if it duplicates cover you already have under your home contents insurance, which it probably will if you have 'all-risks' cover.

3 A credit card can cost nothing – if you pick a card that doesn't charge an annual fee and you always pay the bill in full every month. Most cards charge interest only if you leave part of your balance unpaid.

4 A credit card can save you money if you choose one that earns you cash every time you buy something. How much cash you get back is calculated as a small percentage of the amount you have spent on the card. Some cards offer incentives other than cash – Air Miles or shopping vouchers, for instance.

5 Even if you do not pay your monthly bill in full, a credit card can be cheaper than running an overdraft on your current account, especially if your bank charges a monthly fee as well as interest when you overdraw.

6 Using a credit card can work out cheaper than using traveller's cheques or foreign currency to pay for things abroad. This is because the exchange rate used by card companies to convert foreign spending into sterling is better than normal tourist rates. However, because of credit card charges for cash withdrawals (see Credit card traps to avoid), a debit card is better if you want to use plastic to buy currency, whether over the counter or from a foreign cash-machine.

7 You can give to charity for free if you sign up for a charity credit card. When you first use the card, the card company makes a one-off donation of between £5 and £10. How much the charity gets after that depends on how much you spend, but it's typically 25p per £100 spent.

GET THE BEST FROM YOUR CREDIT CARD

- Always check your statement. Credit card fraud is on the increase, and if you don't spot a rogue transaction you will end up paying for someone else's purchase. This won't happen if you report it to the card company, because the disputed transaction must be removed from your account while it is investigated – and the onus is on the card company to prove it was your transaction, rather than you to prove it wasn't. A rogue transaction is as likely to be an unauthorized payment to an organization you have already paid, as a payment to an unknown destination.

- Hold on to your credit card receipts at least until the transactions have appeared on your monthly statement. This makes it possible to check any payments you don't recognize. Bear in mind that if you query what appears to be a rogue transaction and it turns out that it was yours after all, you may face a charge of up to £10 for the inconvenience to your card issuer. If you use the card to make major purchases, it's a good idea to keep the slips indefinitely.

- Always stay within your credit limit. If you go over it, your card may be refused. You could face a charge of between £10 and £20 each time you exceed your limit. If you are getting dangerously close to your limit, ask the card issuer to increase it. Or cut back on your spending.

- Pay your bill on time to avoid a late-payment charge of up to £25. This type of charge may also be levied if you pay your bill on time but the payment subsequently bounces. To make sure that you pay by the due date, consider paying by direct debit. All card issuers let you pay the required minimum amount each month, and all but a handful let you pay the full amount, by direct debit.

- If you run a debt on your card, keep an eye on the interest rate you are paying. If you have had the card for a year or more, it's likely that you could save on your interest bill by transferring the debt to a different card to take advantage of attractive rates for new customers. Look for these rates in the personal finance pages of the weekend press or on the Internet.

- Keep copies of any letters cancelling standing arrangements made via your credit card (subscriptions, for instance), so that you can prove to the credit card company that you cancelled, should they continue make payment.

CREDIT CARD TRAPS TO AVOID

- Don't use your credit card to get cash. There is usually a minimum charge of £1.50 or £2 for making the withdrawal. Interest may also be charged – at a higher rate than on purchases – from the date of the withdrawal. The best way to avoid temptation is to destroy your credit card personal identification number (PIN) without looking at it.

- Don't use the cheques that several card companies issue alongside their cards. Writing a credit card cheque is like making a cash withdrawal, and attracts the same sort of charges and interest.

Using a credit card cheque rather than the card itself also means that you lose the protection of the Consumer Credit Act (see left).

- Be wary of credit cards offered by shops and large retail groups to be used exclusively in those stores. Store cards are usually an expensive way to borrow.

- Don't be taken in by what looks like a low monthly interest rate. A monthly rate of 2.2% translates into a yearly rate of nearly 30%. On a debt of £500, this would mean paying approximately £150 in interest.

PROTECTING YOUR CARDS

It makes sense to be prudent with your card. Be wary, for instance, of traders who want to keep your credit card (as 'security', maybe) for even a short time. Beyond common-sense measures like this, there are two types of insurance that you are likely to be offered the chance to buy.

Card protection insurance allows you to register all your plastic cards so that if you lose your wallet or purse you only have to phone one number to report all of them missing. You may feel this convenience is worth the typical £10 charge, but the other 'benefits' are of limited value. Most policies, for example, offer up to £1,500 of cover against fraudulent use of the credit card, but the law already protects you against this: your liability is limited to £50 per card until you have notified the card company of the loss or theft. After you have notified them, it's zero. It is also zero if the card never left your possession but someone managed to get hold of and use your card details.

Payment protection insurance promises to pay your credit card bills if you are not earning as a result of illness, injury, or redundancy. However, such policies generally pay only a small proportion – typically 10% – of your outstanding balance, and then only for a year.

Organizing your money

One of the least attractive aspects of being a householder is having to cope with all the bills. The consequences of not paying them can be severe – ignoring utility bills can mean having essential services cut off, while failure to pay your rent or mortgage could lose you the roof over your head. So making sure that you have your regular bills covered should be a top priority. Once you have taken control of your day-to-day finances, you should also consider how you can plan for future financial commitments and meet unexpected demands on your resources.

WARNING SIGNS

A key reason for keeping your finances under control is to avoid the risk of drifting into serious debt. If you answer 'yes' to any of the following questions, you should draw up a budget (see right) and include in your calculations a monthly amount to put towards clearing your debts, starting with the biggest.

- Do you regularly spend more than you earn?
- Are you always overdrawn?
- Do you repay only the minimum amount due on your credit card bill every month?
- Does your overdraft and/or the amount you owe on your credit card go up every month?
- Do you put off paying bills until the final reminder arrives?
- Have you ever missed a loan repayment?

If you answered yes to *all* the above, your debts are already out of control. See Debt action points, opposite.

BUDGETING TO PAY YOUR REGULAR BILLS

Bills have a nasty habit of arriving all at once, which can wreak havoc with your bank balance. One way to avoid sharp dips in your finances is to pay bills monthly by direct debit. But not all bills can be paid in this way and sometimes paying monthly costs more. Insurance companies, for instance, often charge extra if you pay premiums in instalments rather than as a lump sum. So always check before you fill in the mandate.

Another way to deal with bills is to open a second current account into which you pay a monthly amount to cover all your regular bills. To work out how much to pay – or just to get a view of your outgoings – draw up a table as below.

- Put the months of the year across the top and the bills you want to be covered down the side.
- Estimate how much you spend each month (or quarter or year) on each bill or use old bills for approximate figures.
- Enter the figures against each item on the list under the column for the month(s) in which you make payment.
- Total each column to get the total for each month. Add the totals and divide by 12 to give the monthly amount you need to pay into your bills' account.

If you can use spreadsheet software you will find it quicker than using pen, paper, and a calculator. Once it's set up, you can also use your spreadsheet to find out the impact of any additional commitment on your finances.

WORKING OUT HOW MUCH TO SET ASIDE FOR BILLS

	Jan	Feb	Mar	Apr	May	Jun	Jul	Aug	Sep	Oct	Nov	Dec
Mortgage	250	250	250	250	250	250	250	250	250	250	250	250
Council tax		65	65	65	65	65	65	65	65	65	65	65
Buildings insurance	23	23	23	23	23	23	23	23	23	23	23	23
Contents insurance	18	18	18	18	18	18	18	18	18	18	18	18
Electricity	66			60			55			55		
Gas	80			80			65			70		
Water					110						110	
Car insurance	25	25	25	25	25	25	25	25	25	25	25	25
Car tax							155					
Parking permit										35		
Phone	75			75			75			75		
Mobile	20	20	20	20	20	20	20	20	20	20	20	20
TV licence			112									
Pension	100	100	100	100	100	100	100	100	100	100	100	100
TOTALS	**657**	**436**	**613**	**716**	**611**	**501**	**696**	**656**	**501**	**736**	**611**	**501**

Average monthly amount to set aside: **£602.92**

This sample budget shows how to take into account monthly, quarterly, and other bills in order to allocate a monthly sum.

BUDGETING FOR THE UNEXPECTED

It's not just today's bills that you need to budget for – you also need a strategy that will enable you to deal with unexpected bills and continue to meet your living expenses if your income falls because of sickness or unemployment.

1 Aim to clear your **debts** – especially if you are at risk of getting into serious debt (see Warning signs, left). Paying off expensive overdrafts and money you owe on credit cards is a form of saving and makes a lot of sense because the interest you pay on borrowing is invariably higher than interest you earn on savings. (The exception to this is a student loan from the government-owned Student Loans Company.) Being in debt makes you more vulnerable to a sharp drop in income than if you were financially solvent.

2 Take out **buildings and contents insurance**. Insurance policies of this kind will protect you against the cost of dealing with damage or loss caused by things beyond your control, such as storms, floods, theft, or fire. Bear in mind that these policies aren't a maintenance contract – they won't pay out when the boiler breaks down or your washing machine gives up the ghost.

3 Build up your **savings**. A high priority once you have cleared debts is to build up a cash fund that you can fall back on. How big the fund needs to be depends on what you want it to do for you and also on the other measures you have available to protect your income. It could be enough to meet the cost of household repairs, or six months' worth of rent or mortgage payments, or as much as a year's after-tax salary.

4 Check what **financial protection** you have. Many people believe that the state will provide in times of trouble. It may offer some financial help, but state benefits for unemployment and inability to work because of illness or injury are unlikely to cover all your expenses. Building up sufficient savings is one way of making sure that you could cope. Another way is to buy income-protection insurance, which pays a replacement income if you suffer a long-term illness or disabling injury. If you have a mortgage, you could take out mortgage payment protection insurance (see p17). However, if you are an employee, first check the terms of your employer's sick pay and redundancy schemes to see whether buying your own private insurance is strictly necessary.

WHERE TO KEEP FUNDS FOR EMERGENCIES

Although some current accounts pay a reasonable rate of interest, you will be a lot better off if you put cash you are setting aside for the unexpected in an easily accessible savings account. In the past the best savings rates were often paid on notice accounts, which required anything from seven days' to six months' advance warning before withdrawing your money, or you risked losing interest. These days, however, rates paid on instant-access and no-notice accounts, which give penalty-free access, are often as good if not better.

You'll get the best deal by putting your spare cash into a cash Individual Savings Account (ISA). This is a tax-free savings account that allows you to save up to

£3,000 in cash each tax year without paying tax on the interest. The only drawback is that if you take money out once you have paid in the year's maximum allowance, you can't replenish the account with more cash.

If a cash ISA isn't an option – perhaps because you have chosen to invest the maximum in a stocks-and-shares ISA (see p101) – the next best home for your money is likely to be an Internet-based savings account, closely followed by one operated by phone or post. For up-to-date information on the best savings rates, check the personal finance pages of the weekend press or go to http://www.moneyfacts.co.uk.

(see p17)

DEBT ACTION POINTS

If you answered yes to most of, or all, the questions in Warning signs (opposite), your borrowing is already out of control and you need to tackle the problem. Doing nothing in the hope that your debts will disappear could result in your being taken to court, losing the roof over your head, and having essential services – such as gas and electricity – cut off. If you fail to pay your council tax, you could even face prison. Once you have acknowledged the fact that your debts are a problem, try not to accumulate more and start to deal with those you have.

■ Don't be tempted to use the services of a company that promises to reduce your debts by consolidating them all into one big loan – professional debt advisers say that this can lead to worse problems.

■ Cut back on inessential spending – your priority should be to make sure that you can pay your mortgage or rent, utility bills, council tax, and, if you are self-employed, National Insurance and tax.

■ Tell your creditors (the people to whom you owe money) that you are in financial difficulty – the earlier you contact your various lenders, the more sympathetic and helpful they are likely to be.

■ Consider getting free advice from a debt adviser – contact a **Citizens' Advice Bureau**, the **Consumer Credit Counselling Service**, or the **National Debtline** (avoid companies that charge you for help). A debt adviser will help prioritize your debts, draw up a repayment plan, and negotiate with creditors on your behalf.

If you are threatened with court action, don't try to deal with it by yourself. Seek outside help, such as a debt adviser, who can help you to present your case.

THE OPTIONS FOR BUILDING UP SAVINGS

- If you want to save for **up to five years** but may need to get to your savings within that time, the best place to put regular amounts of spare cash is in a savings account (see Short-term investment options, p100).

- If you can tie up your money for **more than five years** and/or you are prepared to see the value of your savings go up and down, you could consider an equity-based savings plan such as a stocks and shares Individual Savings Account (ISA, see p101).

- If you can commit to saving for **at least ten years**, life-insurance-based savings plans – also known as 'endowment' plans – could be an option. You will have to commit to paying regular payments for the duration of the plan, and will have to wait until it comes to an end before being able to touch your lump sum. If you can't, avoid life-insurance-based savings plans.

- For the options available if you have a **one-off sum** to invest, see p100.

PLANNING FOR YOUR FUTURE

If you have any money left over after paying your bills, clearing your debts, setting aside cash against the unexpected, and meeting your day-to-day living expenses, you are in the fortunate position to take steps to plan for the future. Your two main priorities, in order, should be:

- paying into a pension, because the sooner you start, the better (see below)
- building up savings for major expenditure in the future (see left) – such as a holiday, putting down a deposit on a house, buying a car, paying for a wedding, or taking an unpaid career break.

FIVE REASONS TO PAY INTO A PENSION

1 Pension planning is all about saving now to buy an income in retirement. It is vital if you want to live on more than the basic state retirement pension and, for some people, the state second pension (S2P) which replaced the state earnings-related pension scheme (SERPS) in April 2002. How much you get of any type of state pension to which you are entitled depends on your National Insurance record during your working life.

2 The pension you get from the state won't be paid until you are 65 (60 for women born before 6 April 1950). If you don't want to carry on working until you reach that age, you have to save for yourself, otherwise you won't have anything to live on.

3 Paying into a pension is the best way to save for retirement because for every £100 you pay in, the government adds a further £28 in the form of basic-rate tax relief (higher-rate taxpayers get a higher subsidy). And when you retire, you can take part of your pension as a tax-free cash lump sum.

4 The younger you are when you start your pension, the bigger the pension you can expect to get (see table). Even if you can afford to put aside only a small amount, this is better than doing nothing.

5 Joining an employer-run pension scheme (if you can) is like getting a tax-free pay rise. This is because, by law, employers who run their own schemes must contribute to the scheme on your behalf. This is also true of employers who do not run their own scheme but offer staff access to a personal pension rather than a stakeholder pension (see right).

HOW MUCH PENSION WILL YOU GET?

Your age now	The monthly pension you might get at 65 if you pay into a defined contribution scheme and make monthly contributions of:			
	£20	£50	£100	£200
20	£154	£386	£772	£1,544
25	£124	£310	£620	£1,240
30	£98	£245	£491	£983
35	£76	£191	£382	£765
40	£57	£144	£289	£579
45	£42	£105	£211	£422
50	£28	£72	£144	£289
55	£17	£44	£88	£176
60	£8	£20	£40	£81

Source: *The Financial Services Authority*

HOW DO PENSION SCHEMES WORK?

EMPLOYERS' SCHEMES

If you have the opportunity to join an employer's pension scheme, you should take it. The best type of employer-run pension is a **final-salary** scheme – also referred to as a **defined-benefit** scheme. With this type of scheme, your pension contributions buy you a pension that is guaranteed to be a definite proportion – up to a maximum of two-thirds – of your salary at retirement or at the end of the scheme, whichever is earlier. What you pay in is not directly linked to what you get out, because the onus is on your employer to make sure that you are paid the pension you have been promised.

This is not the case with an employer's **money-purchase** scheme (a type of defined contribution scheme), which an increasing number of employers are offering in preference to a salary-related scheme. With a money-purchase scheme, your pension contributions (and the contributions your employer puts in on your behalf) are invested, typically in stocks and shares, to build up a fund. This fund of investments carries on growing until you decide to take your pension. At that point, the fund is converted into cash, the bulk of which is used to buy an annuity – a type of investment which pays a fixed sum to you at regular intervals for the rest of your life.

Some employers offer hybrid schemes – also called **mixed-benefit** schemes – which are a combination of the two types. The pension you get at retirement is guaranteed to be the greater of whichever method of calculating your pension gives the better result.

Whichever kind of scheme your employer offers – and you are unlikely to be given a choice – joining it makes sound financial sense. Because your employer meets the costs of running the scheme and contributes on your behalf, an employer's scheme will provide a bigger pension for the same money than either your own stakeholder or personal pension. It is worth noting that the main cause of the

pensions' mis-selling scandal of the late 1980s was people being wrongly advised to give up the benefits of an employer's scheme to take out a personal pension.

STAKEHOLDER PENSIONS

A stakeholder pension is a type of personal pension and – like other defined contribution schemes – it works on a money purchase basis.

Stakeholders have been available since April 2001. They are aimed at people who do not have an employer's scheme to join. This includes the self-employed and people who do not have a job.

Since October 2001, employers with more than five employees have had to provide access to a workplace stakeholder pension if there isn't already a different sort of pension on offer.

The most important difference between stakeholder pensions and the earlier type of personal pension – which got a justifiably bad name for being expensive and inflexible – is that the government has laid down minimum standards that stakeholders must meet. Old-style personal pensions don't have to meet these minimum standards.

When you invest in a stakeholder pension, you can be sure that the company you buy it from will:

- charge no more than 1% of the value of your fund each year in fund management charges
- let you pay in as little as £20 at a time
- allow you to make both one-off and regular contributions whenever you choose
- not make you pay extra charges if you stop paying in or decide to transfer your fund to a different company.

If you don't currently pay into a pension, you should consider a stakeholder. It is also an option worth considering if you are already paying into either an employer's scheme or a pre-April 2001 personal pension and you want to increase your pension savings.

Borrowing to buy

The best way of financing a major purchase is to save up for it. If you can't wait that long, your only other option is to borrow. But taking out a loan can push up the price of your purchase quite considerably. The interest on a personal loan of £5,000 from a high street bank, for example, could add between £1,400 and £2,600 to what you pay. So if you want to borrow to finance a major piece of furniture or a home improvement, it pays to check the different types of loan available, and the charges involved, before you commit yourself to a lender.

COMPARING THE COST OF CREDIT

All advertisements and marketing material for credit cards, mortgages, and other loans (with the exception of overdrafts on bank accounts) have to show the cost of credit as APR – Annual Percentage Rate. This provides a standardized way of comparing the cost of one loan with another. The APR is not an interest rate – it is an annual rate, and takes into account how much you pay, how often you make payments, and the term or duration of the loan.

As well as the interest you will have to pay on the loan, the APR also covers fees and other charges for arranging the loan and may include the cost of compulsory insurance on repayments. When comparing credit offers, check whether insurance is included or not (see box right).

SIX THINGS TO THINK ABOUT BEFORE BORROWING

1 Don't borrow if you don't have to. Buying on credit can add substantially to the cost of your purchase. You should also think twice before borrowing if you would still be repaying the loan long after your prospective purchase has stopped being of any use to you – if you want to finance a holiday, for example, or buy something that will quickly go out of fashion.

2 Don't overstretch your budget. Although it is best to pay off a loan as quickly as possible to keep interest charges to a minimum, the most important thing is to estimate how much you can realistically afford to repay each month.

3 Check your credit card limit. Provided you have sufficient availability – or you can persuade your card issuer to increase your limit – using a credit card to borrow can be cheaper and more flexible than taking out a personal loan (see below). Of course this is true only if you have a card with a low rate of interest and you are disciplined enough to make regular monthly repayments to clear the debt.

4 Avoid borrowing on impulse. Some retailers use credit promotions to encourage impulse buying. This usually takes the form of some kind of discount if you use their store card (which works like a credit card) or apply for the store's fixed-rate loan (which works like a personal loan). Either way, the interest on the credit is often staggeringly expensive.

5 Beware interest-free credit deals. Although some genuinely are free, others offer interest-free credit for a limited time only – six months, say – and charge a high rate of interest after that. Buy-now-pay-later deals can also end up being expensive. With these, you pay nothing for a few months and then either settle the debt in full or start to make monthly repayments that tend to carry a high rate of interest.

6 Do your homework. It's easy to think that the best place to get a loan is from your bank but this is rarely true, especially of high street banks. You can keep your borrowing costs to a minimum by checking the 'best-buy' tables published in the personal finance pages of the weekend press or by using one of several Web sites that provide information on the various loan deals available.

WHAT SORT OF LOAN WILL SUIT YOU BEST?

A bank overdraft – which is repayable on demand by the bank – is unlikely to be the best way to finance a major purchase, especially if you want to spread the repayments over a number of years. The other main options are described below.

PERSONAL LOANS

If you want to borrow between £500 and £15,000 and you are prepared to pay it back over six months or within up to seven years, a personal loan can be a good choice.

For The monthly repayments are fixed for the duration of the loan, which makes budgeting easier and means that you don't have to worry about facing increased interest rates.

Against If you want to repay the loan early, a lot of lenders charge an early repayment penalty, which is typically the equivalent of two months' interest.

FLEXIBLE PERSONAL LOANS

A handful of lenders offer flexible personal loans, which work a bit like a credit card.

You are given a borrowing limit when you take out the loan, there is no fixed repayment period, and you are not required to make a fixed monthly repayment (although there is usually a minimum regular amount that you have to pay).

For A flexible loan can be useful if you want to be able to vary your monthly payments and you don't have a sufficiently large credit limit with your credit card.

Against Interest rates tend to be higher than with a normal personal loan, so it can be an expensive way of borrowing. If you want this kind of flexibility, and have sufficient credit limit, a credit card can be cheaper.

SECURED LOANS

If you want to borrow to finance home improvements, a relatively cheap option is to extend your mortgage with your current lender. Alternatively, you could take out a loan secured on your home with another lender. However, the interest charged is usually higher than it would be if you simply increased your mortgage.

Against The disadvantage of taking out a secured loan is that you will have to pay a fee to set up the loan. You should also be

aware that with any kind of loan secured on your home, if you do not keep up repayments, you risk having your home repossessed. This is not the case if you take out a personal loan, for which no security is required.

PAYMENT PROTECTION INSURANCE

When looking at the cost of monthly repayments on a personal loan, check whether they include payment protection insurance. This kind of cover aims to meet some or all of your loan repayments if you become ill, lose your job, or, with some policies, if you die before the loan is paid off. However, payment protection insurance doesn't always pay out. Definitions of illness may be very restrictive, often excluding existing medical conditions and stress. Redundancy may be hard to prove if you are self-employed or work part time. So check the details in the small print before committing yourself. Insurance can also add a substantial amount to the overall costs of the loan.

Lenders rarely make buying this kind of insurance compulsory, because if they did it would have to be included in the APR and would make the loan look very expensive, but they do use various ploys to encourage you to take it out. These include:

- making monthly repayments that include insurance look more eye-catching in marketing literature than those without insurance

- using much smaller type for the figures for repayments without insurance so that they are harder to read

- printing payments without insurance over the page where you might not even notice them.

REFUSED CREDIT?

No one has the right to credit. Lenders are likely to refuse you if they think that you are a bad risk and will not be able to repay the loan. This could happen if:

- you scored less than the pass mark in credit scoring – a kind of financial marking system that allocates a score to answers you give when applying for a loan

- the lender consulted a credit reference agency – the main two are **Equifax** and **Experian** – and information on your file suggested that you have had borrowing problems.

If you can't think of a good reason why your application has been rejected, ask the lender. Lenders don't have to reveal exactly why they turned you down but they must tell you whether they checked with a credit reference agency, and if so which one. You can then check with the agency that the information held about you is correct (you can also do this if you simply want to find out what is on your file).

A free leaflet, *No credit?*, from the **Office of the Information Commissioner**, tells you how to go about doing this and explains how to get your file corrected.

LOAN ALERTS

- Don't borrow as a couple – or guarantee someone else's loan – unless you're prepared to pay up if the other person can't (or won't).

- If you buy on hire purchase (HP), you won't legally own the goods until you've paid the last instalment. If you default on payments the goods can be repossessed, and you won't be entitled to any refund.

Parting with your cash

We all want a good deal when we buy goods and services and we need to know that we will be treated fairly if there is a problem. While home shopping and Internet sites have made browsing and buying much more convenient in some respects, it isn't always easy to know who is actually supplying your purchases. The information and advice on the following four pages comes from the Office of Fair Trading (OFT). The OFT runs a comprehensive Web site with consumer rights advice and also runs a telephone service giving information about where to go for help if you have a problem – see Web sites and addresses, p102.

SEE ALSO Making a small claim, p96

YOUR LEGAL RIGHTS

The law says that goods must be:
- of satisfactory quality
- fit for their purposes
- as described.

If you're buying a service, it should be carried out:
- with reasonable care and skill
- within a reasonable time –
  particularly if you have not agreed a completion date.

SALE GOODS

You have the same rights when you buy goods in a sale as at any other time. The seller can't get away with notices saying there are no refunds on sale goods.

YOUR RIGHTS IN SPECIFIC CASES

SAFETY

It is an offence for a supplier to sell you goods – whether new or secondhand – unless they are safe. But this does not apply to antiques or to goods needing repair or reconditioning, provided you were clearly informed of this fact. If you believe you have bought unsafe goods, you should contact the Trading Standards department of your local authority. If new goods turn out to be unsafe you may have a legal claim against the manufacturer.

IF THINGS GO WRONG

If you decide to complain bear in mind how the item was described. A new item must look new and unspoiled as well as work properly, but if the goods are second-hand or seconds then you cannot expect perfect quality. Many shops have goodwill policies that go beyond your statutory rights. For example, some stores allow you to exchange goods that aren't faulty, such as clothes that are the wrong size. If there is something wrong, tell the seller as soon as possible. If you can't return to the shop within a few days, it's a good idea to phone the trader with your complaint.

REJECTING FAULTY GOODS

You have a right to 'reject' faulty goods. If you tell the seller promptly that the goods are faulty and you don't want them, you should be able to get your money back. As long as you have not legally 'accepted' the goods you can still 'reject' them – that is, refuse to accept them.

One of the ways you accept goods is by keeping them without clearly saying that you want to return them after you've had a reasonable time to examine them. What is 'reasonable' however is not fixed: it depends on all the circumstances. Normally you can at least take your purchase home and try it out. But if you delay in examining what you've bought or in telling the seller

that you wish to reject the goods, then you might lose your right to reject.

Even if you signed an acceptance note, this does not mean you have signed away your right to reject the goods. If you agree to let the seller try to put faulty goods right, this also does not affect your rights. Make it clear that if the repair fails, you will be rejecting the goods and seeking a refund. You can insist on a full refund. You do not have to accept a replacement, free repair, or credit note. But if you do accept a credit note you probably won't be able to exchange it for cash later on. Some credit notes are only valid for a limited period.

Once you have, in the legal sense, 'accepted' goods you lose your right to a full refund. You can only claim reasonable compensation. Normally you have to accept an offer to put the goods right or the cost of a repair. But if the faults can't be put right you are entitled to appropriate compensation which, in many cases, may be the cost of buying an alternative.

RECEIPTS

If you lose your receipt your rights still apply. A receipt, however, is important evidence of when and where you bought the goods and, if you don't have a receipt, some alternative proof of purchase is likely to be necessary – a credit card bill or bank statement might do. If you received faulty goods as a present, ask the person who bought them for the receipt or proof or purchase, or to complain for you.

SENDING GOODS BACK

You're not legally obliged to return faulty goods to the seller at your own expense, unless you agreed this in advance. If a bulky item is difficult or expensive to return, ask the seller to collect it. This does not apply when you complain about faults after having 'accepted' the goods – or if the goods were a present.

COMPLAINING ABOUT GOODS AND SERVICES

The law says it's up to the seller to deal with complaints about defective goods or other failures to comply with your statutory rights. Don't accept the excuse that 'it's the manufacturer's fault,' although you might also have additional rights against the manufacturer under a guarantee.

If you have to make a complaint about goods to a trader, most will try hard to deal with it properly. Go back to the shop as soon as possible. It's useful to have a receipt or other proof of purchase to take with you. Explain what the problem is, say what you want done about it, and set a deadline. If you're still not satisfied put your complaint in writing. If the shop is part of a chain, write to the head office. Address your letter to the customer services manager. If none of this works, get further advice from your local **Trading Standards** department, a trade association that may be able to offer arbitration, or consider whether you want to go to court (see Making a small claim, p96).

Equally, if you have a complaint about a service, give the supplier a chance to put the matter right. If you're not satisfied put your complaint in writing, saying what you want done, and set a deadline. If you're dealing with a large business, address your letter to the customer services manager or company chairman/woman. Consider withholding any further money until the problem has been sorted out, but check the small print of any contract you've signed.

Be careful about withholding payments if you have a credit agreement. If you stop paying, it could affect your credit rating and so your chances of getting credit in the future. Continuing to pay will not undermine any claim you have against the lender for any unsatisfactory service by a supplier. You might want to take advice on this.

WAYS TO COMPLAIN

If you complain on the telephone:

- make a note of what you want to say
- have receipts and any other documents handy
- get the name of the person you speak to
- note the date and time and what is said
- follow up your call with a letter, particularly if your complaint is serious.

If you complain in writing:

- describe the item or service you bought
- say where and when you bought the item, or when the service was done, and how much it cost
- explain what is wrong, any action you've already taken, to whom you spoke and what happened
- say what you want done to remedy the situation, for example a refund or repair, or the job done again without charge
- consider using recorded/special delivery so you can check your letter has been received
- keep copies of any letters you send – send photocopies, of original documents.

Further tips:

- Consider getting an expert's opinion in writing to back up your complaint. Motoring organizations offer reports on cars, but any reputable trader with relevant experience can count as an expert. You might have to pay for this.
- If you did not fix a price but you think you've been overcharged, get quotes from other traders for comparison when you complain. Some may charge to do this.
- Take photographs if appropriate.
- If you bought the goods or services on a credit card, you might have additional protection.

HOME SHOPPING OUTSIDE THE UK

Shopping in the EU Always check the details before you shop. Your additional home shopping rights in the UK stem from a European Directive and they therefore should also apply in other European countries. However, it may take longer for some European countries to amend their laws to provide you with equal protection. Also, they may not be exactly the same as in the UK.

Shopping beyond the EU In countries outside the European Union, your rights and responsibilities are likely to vary even more – so check these out too. Always try to check out the small print. If anything does go wrong, it might be more difficult to pursue a complaint against a trader who's based outside the UK – and particularly outside the EU.

MISLEADING CLAIMS

If you think a company is making misleading claims or falsely describing goods, it might be breaking the law and you should tell your local **Trading Standards** department. If you think a company has made misleading claims in an advertisement, contact the **Advertising Standards Authority**.

BUYING PRIVATELY AND AT AUCTION

In a private sale, the goods must be as described, but a seller who is not acting as a business is not covered by the rules on satisfactory quality and fitness for purpose. An auction house is, in principle, covered by the rules on quality of goods, but it may be able to get out of this by putting an exclusion clause in its contract. Always read the terms and conditions before you bid.

YOUR RIGHTS WHEN SHOPPING FROM HOME

Under The Consumer Protection (Distance Selling) Regulations you have special rights as a consumer when you shop from home. You still have your normal statutory rights if something goes wrong (see p92).

With home shopping you have the right to:

- clear information before ordering
- written information about a purchase
- a 'cooling off' period during which an order can be cancelled without any reason and a full refund made
- a full refund if goods or services are not provided by an agreed date or within 30 days of placing an order if no date was agreed
- protection against credit card fraud.

FAULTY GOODS

You are entitled to reject the goods and get your money back if the goods:

- are faulty
- are not of satisfactory quality
- do not match how they were described
- are different to the ones you ordered.

If it takes a while before you notice the goods are faulty, you might only be entitled to claim compensation. This could be the cost of repair or the cost of returning the goods for a free repair. Check whether you are covered by a guarantee. Guarantees add to your legal rights – they don't replace them.

RETURNING GOODS

If your contract says that you should return the goods, you will probably have to pay the cost of returning them. If you choose not to return the goods yourself, the supplier can arrange to collect them – but still charge you for this. Before the seller can collect the goods, you must be given a written notice in a letter, e-mail, or fax, at the time the goods are collected, at the latest. While you have the goods, you must not sell them or give them to anyone else. You should also take reasonable care of them and make sure they are not damaged. Your rights may vary when you have a contract with sellers outside the UK. If you cancel, you might have to pay for the cost of returning the goods – and that could be expensive.

HOME SHOPPING SECURITY AND PRIVACY

When you shop from home, you often have to give more information to the trader than you would if you were in a shop. This might include your postcode, your e-mail address, and your credit card details.

This information can't be given to anyone else without your agreement. If the company you are buying from wants to pass on your details to someone else, it must also give you the right to say no. Be sure to do this if you do not want your name passed on. When paying for goods:

- try not to give your bank account numbers, credit card details, or any other personal information to a company you haven't checked out
- use credit cards, cheques, or postal orders – not cash

- if you have to send cash, use registered post
- keep a dated copy of your order
- if you pay for a product costing more than £100 on your credit card (even if you only pay the deposit) you may have a claim against the credit card issuer as well as against the trader if you have a complaint. This can be useful if the trader goes out of business
- if someone uses your payment card fraudulently to shop from home without your permission, you can cancel the payment and your card company must arrange for you to be re-credited in full
- if you discover that someone has used your card dishonestly, tell the card issuer as soon as possible.

BUYING ONLINE

Once you have decided to buy something over the Internet, be sure you know what is being sold, the total price, the delivery date, the return and cancellation policy, and the terms of any guarantee.

Other points to remember are:

- Save all information possible relating to your order. This might be pages from the supplier's Web site (for example the advertisement), the completed order form, and any e-mails. Suppliers in EU countries should provide you with key pieces of information before your order is finalized. For example, they have to give you the identity of the supplier, the main features of the goods or services, the price, the arrangements for payment and any rights you have to back out. All of this must be given in a clear and understandable way.

- The supplier also has to send you confirmation of the order.

- Be wary of giving out your bank account numbers, credit card numbers or other personal information to a company you don't know or haven't checked out. And don't provide information that isn't necessary to make a purchase.

- Good companies are likely to have privacy statements on their Web sites. In these they will explain what they do with the information they have about you and how secure the information is. Such companies will also allow you to say whether or not you want your

information passed on to other companies. Any company that sells or passes on details about you without your consent could be breaking UK and European law. Outside the EU there may be little action you can take against, say, a US-based company that has information about you.

- You may have some extra protection if you pay by credit card. If you have a claim against the seller for breach of contract or misrepresentation – for example, if goods were not supplied or were faulty – you may also have a claim against your credit card issuer. This could also be useful if the seller goes out of business. This applies to goods or services costing more than £100 for one item (but less than £30,000), even if you have only used your card to pay a deposit. You do not have the same protection if you pay by a debit or charge card.

- Many companies allow you to send your credit card details via a secure (encrypted) page and you should aim to buy from companies that give you this choice. You will be able to see on the screen whether the page you are on is secure. Often it will flash up a warning as you enter a secure page and you might see a closed-padlock symbol in the status bar at the bottom of your screen. If a padlock is not there, and there are no other guarantees, you should think twice about buying.

BUYING ONLINE FROM ABROAD

The general advice on buying online should always be followed when buying from abroad. But there are additional issues.

- Standards vary between countries. Ask the supplier to confirm compatibility of, for example, electrical goods.

- Check that any guarantee is valid in the UK, and whether you will have to return the product to the supplier's country if there is a problem.

- Check for hidden costs such as VAT, customs duties, delivery charges, postage, and packaging. The Customs and Excise Web site gives information on when VAT and duty has to be paid. However, if your supplier is based in the EU, prices should include taxes.

- If problems arise, you might have to take legal action in the country of the seller.

ONLINE BUYING TIPS

Many tips for buying on the Internet are the same as for buying from a shop, such as:

- shop around. That great deal might well be on offer somewhere else

- use retailers and services you know about – or ones that have been personally recommended to you.

But there are also other aspects of shopping online:

- a company might have a great Web site but that doesn't mean it is law-abiding

- make sure you know the trader's full address – especially if the company is based outside the UK

- don't assume an Internet company is based in the UK just because its Web address has 'uk' in it – check out the address and phone number

- look for Web sites that have a secure way of paying (known as an encryption facility) – these show a padlock at the bottom of the screen for payment details

- check whether the company has a privacy statement that tells you what it will do with your personal information.

Look for firms that are part of an independent approval scheme such as **TrustUK**. These have signed up to particular standards, including measures to:

- protect your privacy

- ensure your payments are secure

- let you know what you've agreed to

- tell you how to cancel orders

- deliver goods or services within agreed timescales

- protect children

- sort out complaints – regardless of where you live.

There are many trader approval schemes worldwide, so check out what their particular approval means.

Making a small claim

Faced with a genuine complaint, most firms are prepared to exchange goods or give a refund or appropriate compensation without the threat of court action, but some dig in their heels. If you find yourself in a dispute claiming up to £5,000 from a manufacturer, retailer, or service provider, you can take your claim to the county court. The defendant may settle on delivery of the summons, but if not, your case will be considered for the small claims track. Going to court needn't be daunting or expensive as long as you're well prepared and have worked out your costs.

WHAT IS THE SMALL CLAIMS TRACK?

The small claims track is a relatively informal court procedure designed with the do-it-yourself litigant in mind. You don't need a solicitor or any legal knowledge. You won't normally risk big legal costs if you lose.

Claims must be simple and not involve large numbers of expert witnesses or grey areas of the law. There's usually an upper limit of £5,000 for each claim, though see How to sue, right, for claiming over £5,000. The limit on claims for personal injury or housing disrepair is £1,000.

Typical small claims concern faulty goods, services inadequately delivered, bad workmanship, damage to property, road traffic accidents, personal injury, debts, and disputed ownership. You can also use the procedure to force action – for example to compel a landlord to carry out repairs.

HOW TO SUE

You'll need patience if you sue, as your claim may take six months or so to get to court. But before contemplating going to law, give the person or firm you're in dispute with a chance to settle. Then, if you are getting nowhere, send a letter threatening court action. State that if they have not settled to your satisfaction by a certain date – say within seven or 14 days – you will issue a claim in the county court.

In England and Wales, you can go to any county court to start the action. Ask for the claim form *N1* and its notes for guidance. Fill in the form and return it to the court. The fee for issuing a claim will be between £27 and £115, depending on the amount of money you are claiming, or £120 if you are claiming for something other than money.

It is possible to take a claim of more than £5,000 down the small claims track, but only if the defendant agrees with your suggestion and the judge thinks your claim is sufficiently straightforward. The fee for issuing a claim under these circumstances is up to £500.

The court will send the defendant the necessary papers. The defendant must reply within 14 days, and can apply to have up to 28 days to send in a defence. If there is a hearing, it may be in the court for the area where the defendant is based.

THE DEFENDANT'S RESPONSE

- The papers may be returned to the court undelivered, in which case the court will send you a notice of non-service. You will then have to serve the claim form yourself. Court staff can tell you how to do this. You must serve the claim within four months of the date it was issued, or apply for an extension if four months is not long enough – for instance if you're having problems tracking down the defendant's current address.

- The defendant may admit your claim and offer to settle immediately.

- The defendant may challenge your claim at first, but then admit it and offer to settle as the date for a court hearing approaches.

- The defendant may admit your claim and offer a sum of money where you have not specified an amount. If you accept the offer, ask the court for a judgement to be registered. This will allow you to take further steps to enforce the judgement should the defendant fail to honour the promise. If not, a judge will decide the amount of money, possibly at a court hearing.

- The defendant may agree to pay the amount you want but under terms you don't like, perhaps in instalments. Court officials and possibly a judge can impose a solution.

- The defendant may ignore your claim. You can then ask for judgement in your favour. If you haven't specified an amount of money in your claim, a judge will decide the amount. This may require a court hearing.

- The defendant may dispute your claim, saying that you are asking for too much, or rejecting the claim outright. It's only when this happens that you discover whether your case will be channelled to the small claims track. The defendant may also put in a counterclaim, saying that you still owe money for goods or services.

WHEN A CLAIM IS DISPUTED

As explained above, it's only when a claim is disputed that you discover whether your case will be allocated to the small claims track. A judge will decide whether it fits the criteria – see left. If it doesn't fit the criteria, a judge will allocate the case to a different track (fast track or multi-track) of the county court. You'll have to decide whether to proceed or withdraw, taking account of the more formal procedures and the risk of incurring the defendant's costs should you lose the case.

You will be sent a copy of the defendant's case and asked to fill in allocation questionnaire form *N150* to put your case on the small claims track. On the form you can apply to put forward evidence from an expert witness. There is an allocation fee of £80 for claims of more than £1,000.

Assuming your case is accepted for the small claims track, you'll be told when and where the hearing will take place and what you need to do. Sometimes a judge requires a preliminary hearing. If not, there's only one hearing and typically it will last for no longer than an hour. A judge may not even require a hearing if a decision can be taken on the paperwork alone.

If you win but the defendant ignores the judgement, it will be up to you to enforce the judgement, which might require you taking further legal action. County court staff can advise on the procedure.

EIGHT TIPS FOR MAKING A SMALL CLAIM

1 Gather your evidence – brochures, letters, contracts, and other documents, records of phone conversations or visits to a shop, photos, witness statements – and work out how strong your case is.

2 A **Citizens Advice Bureau** may be able to advise on how your case might fare under the small claims track.

3 Find out when your local county court has small claims hearings and whether you can observe as a member of the public. This will give you a feel for how proceedings work.

4 County court staff can advise on procedures and have a range of leaflets on going to court.

5 If you don't wish to speak in court, you can ask someone to do it on your behalf – a relative, friend, advice worker, or even a solicitor if you're prepared to foot the bill.

6 Keep copies of all documents that arise as your case goes forward.

7 Read all court documents carefully. Watch for deadlines, pay fees on time, and don't get to court late – otherwise your claim could be struck out.

8 You may be able to object to or appeal against decisions taken by officials or the judge as your case proceeds, but watch out for time limits at each stage.

The Internet site http://www.courtservice.gov.uk gives a full account of the small claims track and other aspects of using the courts in England and Wales.

SMALL CLAIMS IN SCOTLAND AND NORTHERN IRELAND

The legal process, the small claims limit, and the court fees in Scotland and Northern Ireland are different from those in England and Wales. For leaflets on small claims in Scotland, write to the **Scottish Court Service** or check out http://www.scotcourts.gov.uk. In Northern Ireland, write to the **Northern Ireland Court Service** or look at http://www.nics.gov.uk/pubsec/courts/courts.htm.

REASONS WHY YOU MIGHT DROP A CLAIM

■ Your aim in making a small claim is to get a judgement in your favour, but this might be only the first of many hurdles if the defendant ignores it – or has ceased trading. Don't go to court if you anticipate serious difficulty enforcing a judgement, because the act of enforcement will be up to you. A high-street retailer with a reputation to worry about is more likely to respect the law than a fly-by-night building firm. Before starting the process, you can check whether the defendant is bankrupt. Contact the **Insolvency Service**. To check whether the defendant has any other unpaid judgements outstanding, which might suggest that enforcing any judgement you obtain could be difficult, contact the **Registry Trust Ltd**.

■ Bear in mind the costs of taking the claim to court, and offset these against the likely outcome. The fee for issuing a claim is between £27 and £115, and allocation to the small claims track can cost a further £80. You won't get the money back if you lose the case, or if you win but fail to enforce the judgement. There'll be more fees to pay if you have to go back to court to enforce judgement.

■ Although you are allowed to use a solicitor, you wouldn't normally get the costs paid, even if you won.

■ You might want to use an expert witness, such as a surveyor in a building case. A defendant can be ordered to pay no more than £200 for an expert witness, however, and only if you win.

■ You or witnesses might lose pay when you attend court. You can each claim up to £50 per day, plus travel and overnight expenses – but, again, only if you win.

Tax and inheritance

According to an investigation carried out in 2002 by Tax Action (a company set up to promote independent financial advice), as a nation we paid out nearly £4 billion in unnecessary tax in the year 2001–2002. Well over £80 million went on fines and penalty interest paid by the 808,000 taxpayers who failed to get their tax returns in on time. But most came from people paying more tax than they legally have to. Deliberately concealing income or gains – or claiming bogus expenses – is tax evasion and it's a crime. But taking legitimate steps to avoid tax by exploiting the tax rules is perfectly acceptable.

YOUR TAX OBLIGATIONS

Your obligations as a taxpayer are to be honest, to give accurate information, to keep records, and – if you receive one – to file your self-assessment tax return and pay your tax on time. Even if you don't receive a tax return, you are still legally obliged to tell the Inland Revenue about income and capital gains that have not been taxed. You should also tell the Revenue about taxable work perks (or 'fringe benefits'), such as a company car. However, if all your perks are listed on the P11D provided by your employer, you can safely assume that the Revenue has been informed. The deadline for notifying the Revenue is six months after the end of the tax year in which you made the income or gain or received the work perk.

FOUR TIPS FOR SAVING TAX

1 Check your PAYE **tax code**, which appears on your payslip. If it is wrong, you could be paying too much – or too little – tax. If you have not received a coding notice and leaflet *P3(T) PAYE: Understanding your tax code*, which explains how your code is worked out and what the letter in your code means, request these from your tax office.

2 Avoid incurring a **penalty**. If you fail to file your tax return (and pay any tax due) by 31 January following the end of the tax year to which the tax return relates, you face an automatic fine of £100. This is also the case if you become self-employed, and you fail to register with the Revenue within three months from the end of the month in which you started working for yourself. Ask your tax office for a copy of leaflet *CWL1: Starting Your Own Business?*

3 Make the most of your **ISA allowances** (see p101). Keeping cash in an ISA rather than in an ordinary bank or building society account increases the interest you get by 20%. If you prefer to invest in equities, you get back the 10% tax that is deducted from the income from equities – and there's no capital gains tax

CAPITAL GAINS TAX

As well as having to pay tax on the income you get from savings and investments, you may also have to pay capital gains tax (CGT). CGT becomes liable when you sell assets that have increased in value, such as antiques and investments like shares, unit trusts, and open-ended investment company shares held outside the tax-free wrapper of an ISA (see p101). There's no CGT to pay when you sell your main home (broadly, one you've been living in), but you may face a CGT bill if you sell a property you inherited, or bought to let.

to pay when you finally cash in your investments.

4 If you are asked to make **tax payments on account** – advance payments against tax to be paid at the end of January and July – check that you are not paying more than you need to. The amount you have to pay is based on last year's tax bill, so if your income has gone down, the amount of tax due will also fall. You can request that the Inland Revenue reduce the amount of payment required.

The tax bill is based on the capital gain, which is the difference between what the asset was worth when you got it and the price at which you sold it (or gave it away), less any costs – such as share-dealing commission – involved in buying and selling.

For example, in the 2002–2003 tax year, you would have to pay CGT at a rate of 10%, 20%, or 40%, depending on your income on any gains over £7,700. Gains lower than this were tax free for that year.

INHERITANCE TAX: RULES AND LIMITS

You won't have to pay inheritance tax on your own estate (broadly, what you leave behind when you die) for the simple reason that you'll be dead. But you may face an inheritance tax bill if you inherit money, property, or other items of value from someone else. At the time of writing, there would be no tax if you inherited from a husband or wife, or if the total value of the estate of the person you inherited from was worth £250,000 or less, and the death occurred in the 2002–2003 tax year.

If the total value were more than £250,000, whether or not you would have to pay tax would depend on two factors. First, it would depend on how the will was worded. If the will said that:

■ your gift was '**free of tax**' (or didn't mention tax at all), you should get the amount specified in the will and any tax due would be paid for out of what was left of the estate after all other gifts had been paid from it

■ your gift was '**subject to tax**' or 'bears its own tax' – there could be a tax bill.

Second, whether or not there would be a tax bill would depend on the taxable value of the estate. This is worked out by taking the total value of the estate, and then subtracting debts, funeral expenses, and tax-free gifts, including those to a spouse, charity, and/or political party.

To this figure would then be added the total amount of gifts that the person whose will it is made in the seven years before death less tax-free lifetime gifts, which would include:

■ wedding gifts worth up to £5,000 from a parent, £2,500 from a grandparent, and £1,000 from anyone else

■ small gifts of up to £250

■ the first £3,000 of any other gifts made in each of the seven years before death.

If the resulting total were less than the nil-rate band of £250,000, there would be no inheritance tax to pay. If it were more than the nil-rate band, tax at 40% would be charged on the taxable value of the estate less £250,000. So if the taxable value of the estate came to £275,000, tax would be due on £25,000 – £275,000 minus £250,000.

These are the rules and limits that apply for the 2002–2003 tax year. Changes to inheritance tax rules, if any, are announced in the budget, and are generally featured in press budget reports.

AVOIDING INHERITANCE TAX

It's worth bearing in mind that a lot of people worry unduly about inheritance tax, which is paid on fewer than 6% of estates. If you stand to inherit under a will, and you think you could face an inheritance tax bill, your options for avoiding the tax are limited to encouraging the person whose will it is to take steps to reduce the possible inheritance tax liability. But since most of the ways of reducing a potential tax bill involve either giving money and possessions away before death and/or paying for professional advice on inheritance tax planning, you may feel that, as a potential recipient, you could come across as a little grasping. Another barrier is that a lot of people don't like talking about money and death – even to their nearest and dearest.

However, even if someone takes no steps to reduce a possible tax bill, it may not matter, because it is possible to alter someone's will after death by getting a solicitor to draw up a 'deed of rearrangement'. Provided you act within two years of a death and all the beneficiaries agree, rearranging a will – which can mean adding beneficiaries who weren't originally included – can reduce the tax bill. You can also use a deed of rearrangement to create a will for someone who died 'intestate' – without making a will.

WHY MAKE A WILL?

A will sets out what you want to happen to what you leave behind after your death. If you don't make one, the law decides who gets what (unless your heirs draw up a deed of arrangement – see Avoiding inheritance tax). What the law decides varies according to whether you are single, married, have children and/or other close relatives. If you are all alone in the world and fail to leave a will, everything goes to the Crown.

Making a will (or revising an existing will) is essential if:

■ you want to stipulate who gets what

■ you start acquiring substantial assets such as a home

■ you are co-habiting and want your partner to inherit your worldly goods

■ you are divorced and your ex-partner is still alive and/or you have children from a former marriage

■ you have young children and you want your wishes about who looks after them taken into account

■ you marry – marriage automatically revokes any will you made as a single person, unless you specified it was 'in consideration of marriage'

■ you run your own business or farm.

You don't *have* to use a solicitor to draw up a will – costs start at around £50, as opposed to £5 for a do-it-yourself pack – but unless your circumstances are absolutely straightforward it is advisable to get legal advice.

ACTING AS AN EXECUTOR

If you are an executor for someone's will, and their estate is not owned jointly with a surviving partner, you will need to apply in person to a probate office, to get probate – an official form allowing the executors to take charge of the dead person's assets.
If the probate office advises you that inheritance tax is likely to be due, take legal advice, paid for out of the estate.

What to do with a lump sum

If you've built up a solid chunk of savings, you've just had a handsome bonus, or perhaps have been lucky enough to inherit some money or win a few thousand on the lottery, you can be left wondering what to do with the extra cash. A lot depends on your personal circumstances, what you want the lump sum to do for you, and how big it is. But on no account should you make a hasty decision or assume you must rush to invest the money. Take time to explore all the options, and consider getting financial advice.

INVESTMENT TERMS

Stocks and shares Buying shares gives you a share in the fortunes of a particular company. Stocks is a generic term for shares and other investments traded on the stock exchange.

Equities Another word for shares.

Bond A loan to a company for a fixed period for a fixed amount of interest. If you hold a bond to maturity you are guaranteed to get back what you put in plus the interest. If you sell before maturity, you get back what the stock market thinks it's worth, which may be more or less than you put in.

Gilts A fixed-interest loan to the government. There is no risk if gilts are held to maturity. If they are sold before then, the risks are the same as for bonds.

Unit trust A fund manager invests your money on your behalf across a range of companies.

Investment trust You buy shares in an investment trust company, whose business it is to invest in the shares of other companies.

SIX PRIORITIES IN ORDER

1 Clear short-term debts such as bank overdrafts, credit-card debts, and personal loans. Having debts is an unnecessary drain on your finances and the interest you save by paying them off will invariably be higher than the interest you can earn from putting money on deposit.

2 Put some cash aside to cope with the unexpected if you haven't already done this (see p87). You should also consider setting aside enough cash to cover major expenditure in the future, so that you avoid the expense of borrowing.

3 Boost your retirement savings either by starting a pension (see p88) or by paying extra contributions into an existing scheme. If you already belong to an employer's scheme (and, in the 2002–2003 tax year, you earned less than £30,000) you can choose between taking out a stakeholder pension and paying into an additional voluntary contribution (AVC) scheme, which employers have to run alongside their main pension scheme.

4 Buy a home if you are confident that you will be staying in the same place for at least three years. Buying your own home is usually cheaper than renting and by the time you finish paying off the mortgage, you will have acquired a substantial financial asset.

5 Pay off some of your mortgage. Doing this can either help to boost your monthly income or can reduce the mortgage term. The downside of paying off your mortgage debt is that you may not be able to get at your cash again without selling your home or re-mortgaging. However, this is not the case with flexible mortgages that link your mortgage to your savings. Instead of paying you interest on your savings, the lender offsets your savings against the amount you owe, which in turn reduces the amount of interest you pay – while still giving you ready access to your cash. So if you have a £50,000 mortgage and £10,000 in savings, you are charged interest only on £40,000. On a mortgage charging 6% interest, this would save you £600. And unlike interest paid on a savings account, the extra income is tax free. Swapping to a flexible mortgage is no different from switching any other kind of mortgage, although you will of course have to take any penalty clauses into account.

6 Put any money left over after you have covered the basics in an easy-access savings account paying the highest rate of interest you can find, while you consider your investment options.

SHORT-TERM INVESTMENT OPTIONS

Unless you can leave your money untouched for more than five years, you will find that your options are pretty much limited to putting your cash into savings accounts and other products where the value of your money does not rise and fall, but grows by having interest added to it. Short-term, low-risk options include:

■ savings accounts that pay a variable rate of interest (the rate varies in line with interest rates generally)

■ cash mini ISAs (see opposite)

■ term accounts, where you lock your money away for anything from six months to five years

■ fixed-rate deposit accounts

■ local authority bonds, where you lend money to a local authority in exchange for a fixed amount of interest

■ products from National Savings and Investments (NS&I).

LONG-TERM INVESTMENT OPTIONS

The first decision to make is whether you want your savings to provide you with income or growth, or a mixture of the two. Although many investments suit both these aims, some are particularly geared to producing an income while others will be better for producing a larger lump sum at a future date. You must also decide how much risk you are prepared to take on your investment – generally, the higher the risk, the greater the return over the long term.

MEDIUM TO HIGH RISK

If you are happy to see the value of your lump sum go up and down, consider investments that provide capital growth – where the lump sum itself changes in value (as with shares) rather than growing by having interest added (as with money in a savings account). It's generally considered unwise to choose fluctuating investments if you can't lock your money away for at least five years. This is because in the short term there is a very real risk that you will get back less than what you put in. Options include:

- corporate bond funds (investment funds that invest in corporate bonds)
- unit trusts or open-ended investment company shares (OEICS, an investment fund that works like a unit trust)
- investment trusts
- unit-linked insurance (like unit trusts with a bit of life insurance thrown in)
- shares.

LOW TO MEDIUM RISK

With some investments you can be sure of what you get back, provided you hold the investment for a minimum period of time, although the value of your lump sum can fluctuate in the meantime. Long-term, medium-risk investments include:

- gilts (British Government Stocks)
- corporate bonds
- guaranteed growth bonds (offered by life insurance companies, these guarantee to return your lump sum plus

a fixed amount of growth at the end of a fixed period)

- guaranteed income bonds (as above except that they guarantee to pay a fixed amount of monthly income for a fixed period of time)
- with-profits bonds (a unit-linked life insurance that offers a degree of certainty but not a guarantee. Your money grows by having bonuses added. Bonuses vary from year to year, which is why the return is not guaranteed).

VARIABLE, FIXED, OR INDEX-LINKED?

The majority of investments pay a return that is **variable**, which means that the amount of money your investment pays you goes up and down in line with market conditions. However, if you want a degree of predictability, you can choose investments such as Savings Certificates from NS&I, where the return is **fixed**. This can work in your favour if, after investing, interest rates generally fall – but the reverse is true if they rise.

If you choose an **index-linked** return, the return is guaranteed to keep pace with inflation – usually with a bit on top. You won't normally get the highest return possible but you can be certain that your money isn't losing its spending power.

PREMIUM BONDS

One way to gamble, without the risk of losing your stake, is to buy Premium Bonds from National Savings and Investments (NS&I). The money you 'invest' buys you numbers that are entered into a monthly draw. This gives you the chance of winning as much as £1 million or as little as £50 – or of not winning at all. Financial experts are divided over whether premium bonds are a serious form of investing as the actual value of your bonds will decrease (they will not keep up with inflation), so redeeming them will give you less spending power than you put in.

DIFFERENT KINDS OF ISA

Taking out an Individual Savings Account (ISA) is a way of sheltering investment returns from tax. Pick one or more of the three types of account to suit your needs: a **cash ISA**; one that invests in the **stock market** (i.e. shares, unit trusts, and investment trusts); or one that's **life-insurance-based**. Bear in mind, however, that unless you are a higher-rate taxpayer, the charges you will pay on stock and shares ISAs and insurance-based ISAs may outweigh the tax savings.

MINI OR MAXI?

Each tax year you can choose between having one maxi ISA or up to three different mini ISAs – but you cannot have both. If you opt for a maxi ISA, you must use a single provider to invest in stocks and shares. With mini ISAs, you can choose a different provider for each type of investment.

ANNUAL ISA LIMITS

Up to 2006, the most you can save in cash is £3,000 per year, and the most you can spend on life-insurance-based investments is £1,000 per year. If you take out a mini stocks and shares ISA, the most you can invest is £3,000. With a maxi ISA, you can invest a maximum of £7,000 in stocks and shares, but if you do this, you cannot invest in cash and insurance.

CAT-MARKED ISAS

CAT-marked ISAs – the acronym stands for Cost, Access, and Terms – meet certain minimum standards laid down by government. For cash ISAs the CAT mark means that, among other things, the interest paid is guaranteed to be no less than 2% below bank base rate. For stocks and shares ISAs, it guarantees that you pay no more than 1% in charges – for insurance ISAs the maximum charge is 3%.

WEB SITES AND ADDRESSES

Association of British Insurers, 51 Gresham Street, London EC2V 7HQ
phone: 020 7600 3333; fax: 020 7696 8999;
e-mail: info@abi.org.uk
Web site: www.abi.org.uk

Trade association for the UK's insurance industry.

Banking Code Standards Board,
33 St James's Square, London SW1Y 4JS
phone: 020 7661 9694; fax: 020 7661 9784;
e-mail: helpline@bcsb.org.uk
Web site: www.bankingcode.org.uk

Chartered Institute of Arbitrators,
International Arbitration Centre, 12
Bloomsbury Square, London WC1A 2LP
phone: 0207 421 7444; fax: 0207 404 4023;
e-mail: info@arbitrators.org
Web site: www.arbitrators.org

Consumer Credit Counselling Service,
Wade House, Merrion Centre, Leeds LS2 8NG
phone: 0800 138 1111;
e-mail: duty.counselling@cccs.co.uk
Web site: www.cccs.co.uk

Equifax Credit File Advice Centre, PO Box 1140, Bradford BD1 5US
phone: 0870 010 0583
Web site: www.equifax.co.uk

Area of the site dedicated to your credit file and how to obtain a copy.

Experian, Consumer Help Service, PO Box 8000, Nottingham NG1 5GX
phone: 0870 241 6212
Web site: www.experian.co.uk

Area of the site dedicated to your credit reference file and how to obtain a copy. Also provides information on why you may be being declined credit.

Financial Ombudsman Service, South Quay Plaza, 183 Marsh Wall, London E14 9SR
phone: 0845 080 1800;
e-mail: enquiries@financial-ombudsman.org.uk
Web site: www.financial-ombudsman.org.uk

Financial Services Authority, Public Enquiries Office, 25 The North Colonnade, Canary Wharf, London E14 5HS
phone: 0845 606 1234;
e-mail: consumerhelp@fsa.gov.uk
Web site: www.fsa.gov.uk/consumerzz

Regulates financial services. For information on stakeholder pensions, go to the Financial Services Authority (FSA) Web site.

HM Customs and Excise
phone: 0845 010 9000
Web site: www.hmce.gov.uk

Useful information source on VAT.

Inland Revenue
phone: 020 7667 4001
Web site: www.inlandrevenue.gov.uk

Insolvency Service
phone: 020 7291 6895
Web site: www.insolvency.gov.uk

Law Centres Federation, Duchess House, 18–19 Warren Street, London W1T 5LR
phone: 020 7387 8570; fax: 020 7387 8368
e-mail: info@lawcentres.org.uk
Web site: www.lawcentres.org.uk

Information about Law Centres, which provide free legal advice and representation to the most disadvantaged members of society.

Moneyfacts Group, Moneyfacts House, 66–70 Thorpe Road, Norwich, Norfolk NR1 1BJ
phone: 01603 476476; fax: 01603 476477;
e-mail: enquiries@moneyfacts.co.uk
Web site: www.moneyfacts.co.uk

Independent provider of financial data.

Money Supermarket, 1 Chantry Court, Sovereign Way, Chester, Cheshire CH1 4QA
phone: 0845 345 5708; e-mail:
moneysupermarket@mortgage2000.co.uk
Web site: www.moneysupermarket.com

Offers comparison tables for personal finance products.

MX Moneyextra, Customer Services, 66 Queen Square, Bristol BS1 4JP
phone: 0845 077 7085; fax: 0117 943 7693
e-mail: customer.services@moneyextra.com
Web site: www.moneyextra.com

Offers news and guidance on the full range of financial products including independent advice on mortgages.

National Association of Citizens Advice Bureaux, Myddelton House, 115–123 Pentonville Road, London N1 9LZ
e-mail: adviceguide@nacab.org.uk
Web site: www.adviceguide.org.uk

Enables you to pinpoint your nearest CAB.

National Debtline, The Arch, 48–52 Floodgate Street, Birmingham B5 5SL
phone: 0808 808 4000; fax: 0121 703 6940
Web site: www.nationaldebtline.co.uk

Northern Ireland Court Service,
phone: 028 9032 8594; fax: 028 9023 6361;
e-mail: informationcentre@courtsni.gov.uk
Web site: www.courtsni.gov.uk

Office of Fair Trading, Fleetbank House, 2–6 Salisbury Square, London EC4Y 8JX
phone: 08457 22 44 99; fax: 020 7211 8800;
e-mail: enquiries@oft.gsi.gov.uk
Web site: www.oft.gov.uk

Office of the Information Commissioner,
Wycliffe House, Water Lane, Wilmslow, Cheshire SK9 5AF
phone: 01625 545745; fax 01625 524510;
e-mail: data@dataprotection.gov.uk
Web site: www.dataprotection.gov.uk

Site has an area dedicated to guidance and publications. The leaflet 'No Credit' can be downloaded.

OPAS, 11 Belgrave Road, London SW1V 1RB
phone: 0845 601 2923; fax: 020 7233 8016;
e-mail: enquiries@opus.org.uk
Web site: www.opas.org.uk

Independent organization providing advice on the full range of pensions.

Pensionguide, Department for Work and Pensions, Correspondence Unit, Room 540, The Adelphi, 1–11 John Adam Street, London WC2N 6HT
phone: 020 7712 2171; fax: 020 7712 2386
Web site: www.pensionguide.gov.uk

For information on your pension options, including forecasting your state pension.

Registry Trust Ltd, 173–175 Cleveland Street, London W1P 5PE, phone: 020 7636 5215;
e-mail: info@registry-trust.org.uk
Web site: www.registry-trust.org.uk

The trust operates the public-access Registry of County Court Judgments for England and Wales.

Solicitors-online
Web site: www.solicitors-online.com

Law Society site enabling you to search for a solicitor by name or by postcode.

Scottish Court Service, Hayweight House, 23 Lauriston Street, Edinburgh, EH3 9DQ
phone: 0131 229 9200; fax: 0131 221 6890;
e-mail: enquiries@scotcourts.gov.uk
Web site: www.scotcourts.gov.uk

Trading Standards Institute, 4–5 Hadleigh Business Centre, 351 London Road, Hadleigh, Essex SS7 2BT
phone: 0870 872 9000; fax: 0870 872 9025;
e-mail: institute@tsi.org.uk
Web site: www.tradingstandards.gov.uk

Official government Web site. Covers UK consumer rights and can help with situations relating to goods and services.

TrustUK, 2nd floor, DMA House, 70, Margaret Street, London W1W 8SS
phone: 020 7219 3345; fax: 020 7323 4165;
e-mail: secretariat@trustuk.org.co.uk
Web site: www.trustuk.org.uk

A non-profit organisation, to protect consumers making online transactions.

CHAPTER FIVE

The technology revolution

Understanding technospeak

Many modern households have sophisticated machinery – computers, modems and broadband, washing machines with fuzzy logic, and so on. Soon we may be tripping over robot vacuum cleaners. All this technology comes with words and abbreviations that are confusing. In this glossary, what an acronym stands for and what the thing is used for may come before a technical definition.

AGP

Stands for accelerated graphics port. Improves the performance of 3D applications in a computer. AGP technology provides a high memory 'fast-lane' for graphics data by providing a dedicated high-speed port for the movement of data between a PC's graphics controller and system memory. Without AGP, data has to be fetched and held in a computer's limited local video memory.

ADSL

Stands for asymmetric digital subscriber line, loop, or link. Used for transmitting data through existing copper telephone wires. An existing telephone line signal is effectively split into two, one for voice and the other for data. ADSL technology can transmit data 10 to 40 times faster than a normal telephone modem (depending on the service available). British Telecom (BT) introduced ADSL in 2000 for business and household customers.

application

Computer program or software designed for a particular purpose. Programs used in businesses and households include word processors, desktop publishing programs, databases, spreadsheet packages, graphics programs, e-mail programs, and Internet browsers.

bandwidth

In computing and communications, the rate of data transmission, measured in bits per second (bps).

bits and bytes

Bit stands for binary digit (0 or 1); the smallest unit of data in a computer. The speed at which information is transmitted is measured in bits per second (bps).
Eight bits make a byte – enough computer memory to store a single character. In the ASCII code system used by PCs, for example, the capital letter A would be stored in a single byte of memory as the bit pattern 01000001.

broadband

Technology that provides fast data transmission for communications – it has a high bandwith, so can transmit lots of bits per second (bps). With broadband connection, you can have a computer, television, and phone all working simultaneously on one line. This means the Internet is always on, response times are short, and audio and video media are received in high quality.
Cable modem broadband is commonly used in homes because installation is easier and cheaper than alternative broadband technologies such as xDSL, fixed wireless, and satellite.

browser

Computer program used to navigate (browse) the Internet and to read HTML files, for example Microsoft Internet Explorer and Netscape Navigator.

bus

A set of parallel tracks – an electrical pathway – that carries digital signals within a computer's central processing unit and to peripherals (components outside the computer such as printers and scanners). The electrical pathway could be copper tracks laid down on the computer's printed circuit boards (PCBs), or an external cable or connection.

cable modem

Box supplied by cable companies as part of a cable connection to television, telephone, and network services, including the Internet. The advantages of cable modems over traditional modems, which operate over standard telephone lines, are greatly increased speed of communications, the ability to transmit video and two-way audio, and lower costs.

cathode-ray tube (CRT)

An essential component of televisions and computer monitors (the bit with the screen); slowly being replaced by LCD. It is a vacuum tube in which a beam of electrons is produced and focused onto a fluorescent screen. The electrons' kinetic energy is converted into light energy as they collide with the screen.

CD-ROM

Stands for compact-disc read-only memory. A medium that can store programs, pictures, sound, movies, and other data. A computer needs a CD-ROM drive to be able to read a CD-ROM. Being superseded by DVDs. The disk is made of plastic-coated metal, on which binary digital information is etched in the form of microscopic pits. The disk is read optically by passing a laser beam over the disk. CD-ROMs typically hold over 600 megabytes (MB) of data.

CD writer

A computer component that allows you to write to, or copy to, CD-ROMs. Some CD-ROMs can only be written to once (CD-R); others can be written to repeatedly (CD-RW).

central processing unit (CPU)

The 'brain' of your computer – it executes individual program instructions and controls the operation of other parts. Sometimes called the central processor or a microprocessor.
The speed of a CPU is measured in megahertz (MHz) – the greater the MHz, the faster the computer will work. A modern home computer might have 800 MHz or more.
The CPU has three main components: the arithmetic and logic unit (ALU), where all calculations and logical operations are carried out; a control unit, which decodes, synchronizes, and executes program instructions; and the immediate access memory, which stores the data and programs on which the computer is currently working.

chip

A complete electronic circuit on a slice of silicon (or other semiconductor) crystal only a few millimetres square.

configuration

The way in which a system, whether it be hardware and/or software, is set up. A minimum configuration is often referred to for a particular application, and this will usually include a specification of processor, disk and memory size, and peripherals required.

digital

Information coded as numbers and transmitted as electronic pulses.

digital camera

Takes pictures that are stored as digital data rather than on film. Pictures can be downloaded onto a computer for retouching, storage, and printing.

DIMM

Stands for dual in-line memory module. A DIMM is a double SIMM (single in-line memory module).

Dolby system

Used in sound systems to improve sound quality of tapes. Electronic circuit that reduces background high-frequency noise during replay of magnetic tape recordings. The higher frequency signals are boosted, and then reduced in a filtered form, helping to eliminate 'hissing'.

download

To transfer data – programs, pictures, movie clips – from the Internet to a computer, or from a component such as a digital camera to a computer.

DVD

Stands for digital versatile disk or digital video disk. Medium for storing digital information. DVDs can hold 14 times more data than CDs, but they work in much the same way. A pre-recorded DVD can hold a full-length feature film.

Ethernet

A networking standard used for connecting several computers to make a local area network.

firewall

A security system built to block access to a particular computer or network while still allowing some types of data to flow in from and out onto the Internet. The firewall is often the first line of defence against hackers.

FireWire

A high-speed connection between as many as 63 electronic devices – computers, camcorders, digital television sets, DVD players, scanners, and colour printers – in one system. An implementation of the IEEE 1394 electronics standard for connecting devices to personal computers.

Flash

A popular browser-independent vector-graphic animation technology, which allows complex multimedia animations to be displayed on Web pages, as long as the browser is equipped with the necessary plug-ins.

games console

A computer for playing games, which are supplied as cartridges or CD-ROMs that slot directly into the console. In 2001, Sony dominated this market with PlayStation and PlayStation2 (PS2), which connects to the Internet, as does Microsoft's Xbox. Nintendo's GameCube is sold as a 'pure games console' and not a personal computer.

gigabyte (GB)

A measure of memory capacity, equal to 1,024 megabytes (MB).

hard disk

The main storage media in a computer – data are read from and written to the hard disk by means of a disk drive.
The hard disk may be permanently fixed into the computer or removable. Hard disks vary in capacity – the hard disk on a new home computer might have anything from 20 to 100 GB depending on your needs.

hardware

The mechanical, electrical, and electronic components of a computer system, as opposed to the various operator programs, which are software.

HTML

Stands for hypertext markup language. The standard for structuring and describing a document on the Internet. It provides labels for parts of a document such as headings and paragraphs, and permits the inclusion of images, sounds, and links to other documents.

IDE

Stands for intelligent drive electronics or integrated drive electronics standard. It is the most popular interface used for mass-storage devices where the controller is integrated into the disk drive (either a hard disk, a high-capacity removable disk drive, or a CD-ROM drive).

interface

The point of contact between two computer programs or pieces of equipment.
A printer interface, for example, is the cabling and circuitry used to transfer data from a computer to a printer, and to compensate for differences in speed and coding.

Internet

Global computer network connecting governments, companies, universities, and many other networks and users. The World Wide Web (WWW) allows seamless browsing across the Internet via hypertext links.

ISDN

Stands for integrated services digital network. Internationally developed telecommunications system for sending signals in digital format. It involves converting the 'local loop' – the link between the user's telephone (or private automatic branch exchange and the digital telephone exchange) – from an analogue system into a digital system, thereby greatly increasing the amount of information that can be carried.

ISP

Stands for Internet service provider. To access the Internet, you connect your computer via your phone line or broadband connection to an ISP, which is connected to the Internet. ISPs provide this access for a regular monthly fee or for free. They also host Web sites, bulletin boards, information services, and so on. Commonly used ISPs include BT Internet, Demon Internet, Freeserve, and AOL.

JPEG

Stands for Joint Photographic Experts Group. A graphics file type used to display images on the Internet. Images can be highly compressed to enable rapid transmission.

kilobyte (KB)

A unit of data equal to 1,024 bytes – enough to store about 1,000 characters of text.

LCD

Stands for liquid-crystal display. Used in calculators, watches, laptop computer screens, digital cameras, miniature TVs, and so on. The display is produced by molecules of a substance in a semiliquid state with some crystalline properties, so that clusters of molecules align in parallel formations.

link

Short for hyperlink. A link allows you to click with the mouse on underlined text or graphics and connect to another site in a Web or computer document.

Mac

Short for Macintosh, a range of computers manufactured by Apple, a US computer company. Often preferred to PCs by those who do lots of graphics work, such as graphic designers and cartographers.

megabyte (MB)

In computing, a unit of memory equal to 1,024 kilobytes (KB). Often called 'meg'.

Microsoft

US corporation that dominates the personal computer market with Microsoft Windows and related applications, including recent innovations for the Internet.

modem

Short for modulator/demodulator. Modems are used for linking one computer to another anywhere in the world using an analogue telephone network. Current maximum data transfer speeds are 56 Kbps.

motherboard

Also called a mainboard. Printed circuit board (PCB) that contains the main components of a microcomputer. The power, memory capacity, and capability of the microcomputer may be enhanced by adding expansion boards to the motherboard.

MP3

Stands for MPEG (Moving Pictures Expert Group)-1 Audio Layer 3. A way of compressing digital sound and audio files while retaining quality, allowing fast transmission via the Internet. MP3 no longer has the best audio quality. Competitors are MP4, and Microsoft's Windows Media Audio (WMA), which is capable of producing a similar sound quality to MP3, with half the file size.

network

Method of connecting computers so that they can share data and peripheral devices, such as printers. The main types are classified by the pattern of the connections – star or ring network, for example – or by the degree of geographical spread allowed; for example,

local area networks (LANs) for communication within a room or building, and wide area networks (WANs) for more remote systems. One of the most common networking systems is Ethernet, developed in 1973 (released in 1980). Subsequent developments have included Fast Ethernet and ATM (asynchronous transmission mode).

NTSC

Stands for National Television Standards Committee, the television and video standard used in the USA and Japan. Programs made for NTSC won't work properly on PAL systems.

operating system (OS)

A program that controls the basic operation of a computer. A typical OS controls the peripheral devices such as printers, organizes the filing system, provides a means of communicating with the operator, and runs other programs. Many operating systems are written to run on specific computers, but some are available from third-party software houses and will run on machines from a variety of manufacturers. Examples include Apple's OS 9, Microsoft's Windows, and Unix.

PAL

Stands for phase alternation by line, the television and video standard used in the UK, other parts of Europe, and China. PAL has a higher definition and different screen format than NTSC. Programs made for PAL won't work properly on an NTSC system.

parallel device

A device that communicates binary data by sending the bits that represent each character simultaneously along a set of separate data lines, unlike a serial device.

PC

Stands for personal computer, another name for microcomputer.
Used to mean IBM personal computer and came to include all computers compatible with it. Most desktop computers are PCs – a Mac is not a PC.

PCI

Stands for peripheral component interconnect. Used to connect a computer processor and its peripherals.

PDA

Stands for personal digital assistant. Handheld computer designed to store names, addresses,

and diary information, and to send and receive faxes and e-mail.

peripheral

A device that connects to the computer and performs a role in its functions, such as modems, printers, and monitors (screens).

pixel

Stands for picture element – a single dot on a computer screen. Screen images are made up of a collection of pixels, with each pixel being either off (dark) or on (illuminated, possibly in colour). The number of pixels available determines the screen's resolution.

Typical resolutions of microcomputer screens vary from 640 x 480 pixels to 800 x 600 pixels to 1,024 x 768 pixels.

plug-in

A small additional file that enhances a computer program's operations. Plug-ins can be downloaded from the Internet.

port

A socket in a computer that enables the processor to communicate with an external device. Computers may have ports for monitors, printers, modems, digital cameras, and less commonly for hard disks and musical instruments (MIDI, the musical-instrument digital interface).

Ports may be serial (capable of transferring only one bit of a data at a time), parallel (capable of transferring multiple streams of data at a time), or USB (capable of faster data transmission than the other two). There are input ports (for joysticks, for example), output ports (for printers, for example), and input/output (i/o) ports.

program

A set of instructions that controls the operation of a computer. There are two main kinds: applications programs, which carry out tasks for the benefit of the user – for example, word processing; and systems programs, which control the internal workings of the computer.

public-domain software

Any computer program that is not under copyright and can therefore be used freely. Should not be confused with shareware, which is under copyright, and may be freely distributed for evaluation purposes but needs to be purchased to use in the longer term.

RAM

Stands for Random Access Memory. Used by the computer to temporarily store information going to and from the processor. RAM chips are written to and read by the computer. Their contents are lost when the computer is switched off. RAM is measured in megabytes (MB). Modern computers come with 128 MB or more.

RealPlayer

Software for broadcasting live or pre-recorded sound and video over the Internet, sold by RealNetworks Inc. Microsoft's equivalent to RealPlayer is Windows Media Player.

ROM

Stands for read only memory. Loaded with permanent data and programs during manufacture. The computer can read ROM chips but not write to them.

Scart socket

Stands for Syndicat des Constructeurs des Appareils Radiorécepteurs et Téléviseurs (syndicate of radio receiver and television equipment manufacturers). A 21-pin audio/video connector used in electronics equipment such as television sets and video recorders. Scart cables are often the preferred method for connecting video games consoles to TV sets.

SCSI

Stands for small computer system interface, pronounced 'scuzzy'.
A method for connecting peripherals to a computer. A group of peripherals linked in series to a single SCSI port is called a daisy chain.

search engine

Computer program used for indexing, and therefore finding, information on the Internet. Commercial search engines such as AltaVista, Google, Lycos, and Yahoo work in different ways but all provide a range of potentially relevant Web sites in response to a key word or phrase.

SECAM

Stands for système electronique couleur avec mémoire (electronic colour system with memory); or séquentiel couleur à mémoire (sequential colour to memory).
Television and video standard used in France, some states in Eastern Europe, and a few other countries. It is broadly similar to the PAL system used in most of Europe.

serial device

A computer device that communicates binary data by sending the bits that represent each character one by one along a single data line.

shareware

Software distributed free via the Internet or on disks given away with magazines.
Users have the opportunity to test it and check its ability to meet their requirements before paying a small registration fee directly to the author. This may bring additional functionality, documentation, and occasional upgrades. Shareware is not copyright-free, unlike public-domain software.

SIMM

Stands for single in-line memory module. Small printed circuit board carrying multiple memory chips. A double SIMM is a DIMM.

software

A collection of programs and procedures for making a computer perform a specific task. Software is built into the computer or distributed on a suitable medium, such as CDs. Computers need two types of software: application software and systems software. Application software, such as a browser or a word processor, is designed for the benefit of the end user. Systems software is the high-level means of talking to and configuring the hardware components of the computer. For example, a systems program might control the operation of the display screen, or control and organize backing storage.

SVGA

Stands for super video graphics array.
A graphic display standard for computer screens providing resolutions of either 800 x 600 pixels or 1,024 x 768 pixels.

USB

Stands for universal serial bus. Transmits data more quickly than serial or parallel devices, and allows devices to be connected and disconnected without switching off the computer.
Allows up to 127 peripherals – including joysticks, scanners, printers, and keyboards – to be daisy-chained from a single socket, offering higher speeds and improved plug-and-play facilities.

URL

Stands for uniform resource locator – a Web site address. A series of letters and/or numbers specifying the location of a document on the Internet. Every URL consists of a domain name, a description of the document's location within the host computer, and the name of the document itself, separated by full stops and backslashes. Thus *The Times* Web site can be found at http://www.the-times.co.uk/news/pages/home.html.

vector-graphic

Graphic stored in computer memory using geometric formulae, allowing the images to be transformed without losing picture quality.

VGA

Stands for video graphics array. A graphic display standard for computer screens providing 16 colours and a resolution of 640 x 480 pixels, or 256 colours and a resolution of 320 x 200 pixels.

virus

Software that can replicate and transfer itself from one computer to another, without the user being aware of it. Some viruses are relatively harmless, but others are very dangerous and can damage or destroy data. Anti-virus software should be installed on all computers, and kept up to date. This is especially important for home computer users connected to the Internet via broadband or those who share files by e-mail or floppy disk. Commonly used programs include VirusScan, Sophos, and Norton Antivirus.

Windows

In computing, originally Microsoft's graphical user interface (GUI) for IBM PCs and computers running MS-DOS. Windows has developed into a family of operating systems that run on a wide variety of computers from pen-operated palmtop organizers to large, multi-processor computers in corporate data centres.

WAP

Stands for wireless application protocol. Used for transmitting data between Web sites and mobile phones.

WWW

Stands for World Wide Web. Hypertext (linking) system for publishing information on the Internet. WWW documents (Web pages) are text files coded using HTML to include text and graphics, and are stored on a Web server connected to the Internet.

Buying or upgrading a PC

Buying and upgrading a personal computer (PC) has become simpler, with high-street chains now offering after-sales support. Some of the larger stores even offer fully guaranteed upgrades.

Although many computer experts still say that having a PC built to your specification, or building your own, offers the best value, high-street chains can often undercut specialist shops through sheer purchasing power. Before buying a PC, it's a good idea to check what the various components do and which PCs are best suited to different types of tasks.

UPGRADABILITY

When buying a PC, upgradability is a key factor in ensuring that your PC doesn't slip into obsolescence too quickly. Check that what you're buying:

- has at least two free PCI (peripheral component interconnect) slots that will allow you to add internal upgrades such as a graphics accelerator card, a secondary sound card, or just the next big thing – whatever that may be

- has at least one free RAM (random access memory) slot. Adding more memory will generally give a flagging PC improved performance

- has not already been upgraded to its maximum level. Often, 'bargain' PCs will have a respectable basic specification but further enquiry may reveal that you will not be able to upgrade the processor, or add more memory.

WHAT DO YOU GET IN A PC?

OPERATING SYSTEM

This is the software that controls the basic operation of a computer. A typical operating system controls the peripheral devices such as printers, organizes the filing system, provides a means of communicating with the operator, and runs other programs.

CENTRAL PROCESSING UNIT

The central processing unit (CPU), often called a processor, is the heart of any PC. Essentially it controls how fast applications run. Processors are classified in three ways:

- By manufacturer, of which Intel is the most common. Intel is the market leader, but rival AMD offers processors that are fully compatible with Intel chips and are often cheaper.

- With a description of the processor's class. The class is generally either a name or a number describing the level of advancement. For example, an Intel Pentium 4 is the fourth version of the Pentium-class chips and will have more features than a Pentium 3. However, some of the features of the Pentium 4 may not be relevant for home users or may work only with very specific applications.

- With a speed rating measured in megahertz (MHz) or gigahertz (GHz). This is similar to the litre rating on a car engine. A 1.1 litre Vauxhall Metro has less horsepower than a 2.4 litre Volvo estate. In the same way, an Intel Pentium 3 650 MHz processor has less power than an Intel Pentium 3 running at 850 MHz. The gigahertz rating means that the unit is measured in thousands, so an Intel Pentium 4 runs at 1.8 GHz (1800 MHz).

The speed of the processor is not the same as the speed of the PC because, like a car, the PC is the sum of all its parts. A fast CPU will be hampered if the rest of the PC is unable to keep up with the speed and performance of the processor.

> **Upgrading tip** Processors are upgradable but you should consult the manual for details of the PC motherboard before upgrading, as this will have crucial information about the types of processor your PC can use and which settings you will need to change. Without this information you may end up destroying your CPU.

HARD DISK

The hard disk drive is used to store all your software and files. There are two main criteria for hard disks.

- Type – normally either SCSI or IDE. SCSI is only used where speed is of the essence and is not normally found in home PCs. IDE is found in over 90% of home PCs.

- Storage capacity – this is measured in gigabytes (GB). Typically even the largest games or applications will not use more than 1GB of hard disk storage. Most hard disks will start at 40 GB but if you're on a tight budget, even an 8 GB hard disk will allow for plenty of applications to be installed on your PC. If you are running out of hard disk space, provided you have the original CD-ROM disk that installed your software, you can always remove software from your hard disk and reinstall it as required.

> **Upgrading tip** Adding a second hard drive, although time-consuming, is a relatively simple upgrade. Nearly every PC will have at least one free connection for another disk. Hard-disk manufacturers such as Seagate or Western Digital provide full installation instructions for their drives.

A TYPICAL PC SPECIFICATION

Operating system	Windows 2000/XP
Processor	Intel Pentium 4 – 2000 MHz (2 GHx)
RAM	256 MB
Hard disk size	40 GB
Graphics card type	ATI 8500 LE
Graphics card memory	32 MB
Devices	Samsung CD-2412 CD-ROM drive
	1.44 MB floppy drive
	Sound Blaster 16 sound card
Interfaces	2 serial; 1 parallel 2 USB

RAM MEMORY

Random access memory (RAM) is used by the PC to execute applications. A simple rule of thumb is the more the merrier. RAM is measured in megabytes (MB) and most applications will need at least 32 MB of memory, but with memory prices dropping constantly, software developers are making their programs more memory-hungry. One word of caution – when buying a secondhand PC, it's wise to make sure that the PC uses the more modern type of DIMM memory, which is easily available, and not older SIMM memory modules, which are increasingly scarce and offer slower performance than DIMM.

Upgrading tip If you use any memory-intensive applications such as action video games or graphics, you may need more memory. Larger memory manufacturers offer a service where you specify the make and model of your PC and they send you the correct memory. Have a look at the Web sites of Hypertech and Kingston Technology.

GRAPHICS CARD

Computer games are the fastest-growing entertainment form. Consequently, the variety of graphics cards for the PC is huge. Graphics card manufacturers are constantly trying to outdo each other and the top of the pack changes weekly. A general rule of thumb is that graphics cards with a lot of memory will often provide good performance. If you're keen to experience fast action games, look at graphics cards costing around £200 from manufacturers such as Nvidia, S3, and ATI. These have the equivalent power of a dedicated games console such as a Sony Playstation 2 or Nintendo Gamecube.

Upgrading tip Whether you are upgrading your PC, building your own, or buying secondhand, you need to make sure that the interface on the graphics card matches the port on the computer's motherboard. The most modern type of interface is called AGP, and provided your PC has an AGP port then any AGP card will work. The older format is called PCI. PCI cards are often found in older PCs and don't accept AGP-based graphics cards.

CD-ROM AND DVD DRIVES

Most new PCs are supplied with a DVD-ROM drive which will allow you to access conventional software and music CDs as well as DVD films. A more common feature now is the ability to write your own CDs or, on more advanced machines, you can create your own DVDs. You can use the CD/DVD-writer to create your own video disks, music collections, or digital pictures, or even to back up your important files.

Both the software and music industries are concerned about piracy and, consequently, using a CD/DVD-writer to make duplicates of copyrighted material is illegal and often difficult to do because of special anticopying features on video, software, and music disks.

Upgrading tip You can add a CD or DVD drive to an older PC using an external interface such as a Firewire or USB port. Although this is slightly more expensive than an internal drive, it doesn't require any special training and can be done in about five minutes.

DISPLAY MONITOR

Monitors comes in two basic designs: a thin LCD, a bit like a laptop screen, or a traditional CRT which is similar to a small TV. LCD displays are great for saving space but can be three times the price of traditional PC displays. All displays come in various sizes, measured diagonally across the screen.

Upgrading tip Unlike a PC, a monitor can't be upgraded or repaired by the keen amateur, so larger displays are often best bought new or at least with a three-year warranty. If you have a 14 in monitor it may be worthwhile to upgrade to a 17 in as the smaller monitor doesn't display higher resolutions very well.

COMMUNICATION ADD-ONS

You can use your PC to connect to the Internet, as an answerphone, or to send and receive faxes. The most common method of adding communication to a PC is through a modem. Most modems come with some basic software for sending and receiving faxes, while other more advanced functions can be added through either free shareware or low-cost software. Most PCs come with a built-in modem (often called a V90) and the standard speed is 56 KB over a normal phone line. This speed can be increased by using a broadband connection, ISDN, or cable modem (see p117 for more details).

Upgrading tip Any new PC will have the latest 56 KB modem as standard. If you're upgrading from an older PC, external modems cost under £40 and can be fitted in a matter of minutes by using the USB or serial ports at the back of the PC.

Choosing the right PC

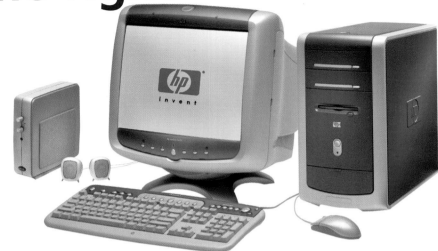

PCs are very adaptable but picking one that fits your current needs is a matter of choosing the right combination of components to suit the type of software you intend to run. Identify what you will use your PC for, then find out what combination will match your requirements. If you want to limit your spend, you may well be able to do without some of the more expensive options on offer, for now, and upgrade later. If the jargon is new to you, check terms in the glossary on p104–7.

BUYING SOFTWARE

Whether you intend to buy a PC, AppleMac, or a personal digital assistant (PDA), software will be required to perform any task. Most computers come with pre-loaded software but this is not always the case.

Before you buy any software, make a note of your computer's hardware specification and type of operating system.

This information should be available on documentation that came with your computer. If it's not, you can either contact the seller or look on the manufacturer's Web site.

If these options fail, you can download free tools such as Sisoft SANDRA 2003 and BCM Diagnostics software from the Internet. These programs will tell you the specification of your computer. Provided the software you intend to buy has an equal or lower specification than your computer, there should be no problem.

WHAT DO YOU WANT TO DO?

I JUST WANT TO PLAY GAMES AND MAYBE SURF THE INTERNET

When looking for a PC for games, a modern processor running at over 1.8 GHz combined with a powerful graphics card such as a Geforce mark 3 is a good start. Memory is key for games, so look for lots of system RAM – 512 MB is recommended. Games are often very memory hungry, so a graphics card with at least 32 MB of video RAM is highly recommended. Generally any PC that can play the latest games will be able to surf the Internet comfortably with the inclusion of a modem. A basic operating system such as Windows 2000 or Windows XP should be sufficient for gaming. Games are generally quite large so a 80 GB hard disk should be a minimum requirement.

Upgrading tip Using an Accelerated Graphics Port (AGP)-based graphics card as a separate component, rather than a built-in one, makes it easier to keep up with new versions.

I JUST WANT TO WRITE LETTERS AND SEND E-MAIL

Word processing and e-mail are very low intensity applications and consequently don't require the fastest PCs. Simple tasks like writing letters and e-mail are the perfect reasons for finding a second-hand bargain. A PC such as an Intel Pentium 2 or an AMD K class processor with only 32 MB RAM and less than 8 GB hard disk space will be able to offer a comfortable level of performance. If you're doing a lot of writing, a larger screen could be a better investment as well as a printer. Look for a PC deal that comes with a pre-loaded application suite such as Microsoft Office or Lotus Smart Suite and a pre-configured modem and Internet connection.

I'M A CREATIVE SORT OF PERSON AND WANT LOTS OF FLEXIBILITY FROM MY PC

The PC is fast becoming the tool of choice for musicians, artists, animators, and video producers. Most creative tasks are quite resource hungry but provided you have a good base to start from, the PC can grow over time to suit the task. Custom-built PCs are most suited to creative tasks. For example, you can specify a PC that can support two CPUs although you needn't have the second processor installed at the time of purchase. Another example of forward planning is to have your hard disk bays fitted in a removable cage, so you can quickly add or switch between hard disk drives for large video files, pictures, or music tracks. If you have a specialist application in mind, it's often worth talking to a local shop about building a machine dedicated to the task, instead of the high street chains that tend to treat PCs as a consumer commodity. For graphics and video, as much memory as possible will help speed things up.

Upgrading tip Upgradability is the key to flexibility. Buying a PC with a highly upgradable motherboard, and a big empty case where all your components will sit, is a good start for a person keen to create their own PC-based music studio or video editing suite.

I WANT TO SET UP A COMPUTER AT HOME SIMILAR TO MY WORK PC

If you want or need to work at home sometimes, it's probably best to pick a PC based on your office specification. This should also include software applications similar to your work PC. Many companies have a person or department responsible for information technology (IT) and, depending on your employer and work role, you may even be able to buy directly through your company (often at a discount). They might also configure your PC to access parts of the company network. The type of PC you need will depend on the type of applications you use at work but most workplace PCs will be devoid of multimedia features such as fast graphics or sound facilities.

I'M ON A TIGHT BUDGET AND JUST WANT A BASIC COMPUTER

The magic number touted by high street chains for a basic new PC is around £1,000, but considering that most of the basic computer applications such as word processing, spreadsheets, databases, e-mail, Internet surfing, and simple games have been around for over a decade, a second-hand PC that is two or three years old is more than capable of performing these tasks.

The main difference is that the applications will need to match the older hardware. The most current version of the popular Microsoft Office application is MS Office XP. However, Office 95 still has 90% of the functions of its more advanced sibling and requires only a Pentium 133 MHz processor, 24 MB of RAM, and less than 1 GB of hard disk space. A PC with this kind of specification can be bought for a couple of hundred pounds. Buy the software first, since it's easier to match the PC to the software than the other way round. Software manufacturers are reluctant to sell older and cheaper software ahead of new expensive packages, but mail-order or second-hand PC suppliers generally also provide older software. Even bigger chains often offer old software at reduced prices. Whatever your source, check the specification sheet for compatibility with the PC you plan to buy.

ANTIVIRUS SOFTWARE

A computer virus is a small program that passes onto your computer without your knowledge or consent, with the intention to cause damage, or to allow an outsider to break into your files. The virus will usually try to pass itself onto another computer by attaching a copy of itself to your e-mails and files. Not all viruses have malicious intent but they can cause the computer to behave oddly and crash.

Antivirus software is available for nearly all types of computers. However, most manufacturers will require you to pay a yearly subscription to provide you with protection against the latest viruses. Without these regular updates, you will be vulnerable to new types of viruses and, in the event of a virus attack, you will not be eligible for technical support from the antivirus company.

Even with antivirus software you are vulnerable to attack, so take these precautions.

- If you receive unsolicited e-mail that has an attached program or document you should, before opening it, check with the sender that it was sent intentionally and not generated by a virus.

- Illegally copied software, often found at car boot sales and markets, is a notable source of viruses and should be avoided.

- If you often use floppy disks, remember to remove them from the disk drive before turning on your PC – floppy disks can carry viruses that can be transmitted as the computer is switched on.

- If you have vital files such as financial accounts, if possible try and copy them to floppy disk as a precaution against a virus attack or hard disk failure.

Alternatives to a PC

Although the desktop PC is the most common type of computing device in the home, it doesn't suit everybody. And if you're especially short of space, or travel a great deal, you might find that a model from the growing choice of laptops and handheld devices is sufficient – or useful to run in tandem with your home computer.

THREE TYPES OF PDA

Personal Digital Assistants (PDAs) come in three basic designs. Some models have a permanently uncovered screen with a stylus pen to access functions, using handwriting recognition for data input. These designs have the advantage of a lighter and more compact chassis but lack a keyboard and inherent protection for the screen. Handwriting recognition is improving all the time and most users have little problem with this system. It's worthwhile testing the different handwriting software before purchase, however.

The second common design is called a clamshell, and looks similar to a condensed notebook with a small keyboard and touch-screen function. This design offers more protection against damage to the sensitive LCD screen than models that have an uncovered screen, but they can be more bulky. Keyboards on clamshell devices vary considerably in ease of use and it's worth testing a few before buying.

The last type of PDA is a combination of a mobile phone and a pocket computer. Although more expensive and bulky than a standard PDA, it allows instant connection to the Internet or down-loading of e-mail at speeds comparable to a desktop PC with a modem.

APPLE COMPUTERS

Apple fans extol the virtues of Apple's easy-to-use operating system, reliability, and sleek design ethic. However, there are far fewer business and leisure applications for Apple computers and accessories tend to be slightly more expensive. To be fair, the more recent Apple computers have tended towards using the more common components found in PCs but the selection is still reduced because, even though an item may have hardware compatibility, not all manufacturers will have the necessary software to make the hardware function.

Apple computers are favoured by many people working in creative fields, and the reliability of the operating system and applications make it a good tool for music, video, and graphic design.

Upgrading tip Apple tend to stock only the latest three or four models, so a lucrative secondhand market has sprung up, although upgrading or repairing older models is often difficult.

iMAC

The iMac has won awards for its design chic and has been popular with first-time buyers who have no preference towards the PC. The design was primarily chosen because of the low build cost and consumer-friendly styling. The iMac comes with built-in Internet connectivity and is one of the easiest computers for the beginner to use.

Upgrading tip The downside to the iMac is the lack of internal upgradability. However, unlike PCs, Apple computers have a second high-speed interface alongside USB, called 1394 Firewire. This allows the iMac to be upgraded with external devices.

APPLE G4/G5 DESKTOP COMPUTERS

Apple has chosen to base its computers on chips developed by Motorola and IBM.

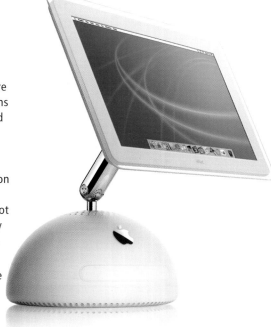

These Power PC class processors use a completely different architecture from Intel and AMD Pentium class chips. Consequently, the associated speed rating for Apple computers, measured in megahertz, is, on paper, often considerably less than Intel or AMD chips. However, in practice, the fastest Apple desktops are normally equivalent to PCs due to the elegance of their design. However, in contrast to very high-specification PCs, which can also double as workgroup servers or powerful workstations, Apple computers tend to be aimed at individual users.

APPLE iBOOK AND POWERBOOK LAPTOPS

Like its desktop counterparts, the Apple notebook range has a striking look, offering light chassis designs and good performance. However, with an effective monopoly on pricing, Apple notebooks tend to be much more expensive than PC laptops that offer equivalent performance. Like its desktop range, Apple has included the high-speed Firewire port in its laptops to provide more external connections, but the range of optional bays is very limited.

CHOOSING A LAPTOP

Laptops have some obvious advantages over desktop PCs. They take up much less space, are highly portable, and tend to hold their value more than desktops. Laptops are more expensive than equivalent desktop PCs, however, and have poorer performance and less storage capacity. Laptops are also more expensive to repair if they break down and the designs are highly integrated, so few of the components can be substituted at a later date without considerable expense. The main elements to consider if you're buying a laptop are:

DISPLAY

The screen on a laptop is permanent, although you can use an external monitor as well which is often better for long-term use. Screens generally come in two types, namely 'Active TFT', found on newer models, or 'Passive TFT', found on older models. Active displays offer a much better picture quality and can be viewed from a more oblique angle. Every display will also have a display size and a resolution. The display size is measured diagonally in inches, with most laptops varying between 12 in and 15 in. The resolution is measured in dots across and dots down and a resolution of 1024 dots across by 768 dots down is pretty standard.

PC CARD SLOTS

PC card slots are used for upgrades such as a modem, network card, or an external hard disk. PC card slots are available as types 1, 2, or 3. Type 1 and 2 slots are very similar, while the type 3 slot is twice the size of a type 2 slot and is used primarily for newer and larger upgrades, such as removable hard disks. If a laptop has only type 1 slots, it's likely to be quite an old model and this will make upgrading or using new hardware add-ons much more difficult.

REMOVABLE BAYS

Most laptop manufacturers will place items like hard disks, CD-ROMs, and floppy disks within removable bays. This allows a laptop user some degree of flexibility with regard to which devices they want to take on the road with them. However, the devices within these removable bays tend to be more expensive than their desktop equivalents. As a general rule of thumb, larger manufacturers such as IBM, Compaq, and Dell tend to have a wider range of items to fill these bays, and tend to keep supplies for older models for a longer period of time.

WEIGHT AND SIZE

If you're lugging a laptop around a lot, weight and size are crucial requirements. The size is generally dictated by the size of the screen, but weight is primarily associated with the price. The price premium on an ultra-light notebook is very high. You can reduce the weight of most notebooks by removing infrequently used bays such as CD-ROM and floppy disk drives, and substituting them for dummy bays when on the road.

WARRANTIES AND INSURANCE

If you're looking at extended warranties, it may be worth the extra cost for laptops considering the high repair charges. However, if you have a very expensive model, talk to your home and contents insurance company about whether the laptop is covered both in the home and on the move. Most companies will require an extra fee for items over £1,000.

> **Upgrading tip** Laptops have similar components to desktop PCs (see Buying or upgrading a PC, p108), such as hard disks, graphics cards, and RAM, but not all of these will be easily upgradable, while those that are, will often only be so at a price.

Personal Digital Assistant (PDA) is an umbrella term that is applied to personal organizers, handheld PCs, or even, to use Microsoft's term, PocketPCs. All these devices:

- typically weigh less than 1 kilo/2 lb
- have a small LCD screen
- have a small internal memory to store a handful of built-in applications and a few optional ones.

Nearly all PDAs can connect to a desktop PC or Mac to allow files such as address books and diaries to be synchronized, and more advanced models have built-in mobile phones, or the ability to connect to a mobile or land-based telephone line. When buying a PDA, you should think through how you may want to use it now and over the next couple of years.

Matching software to systems
Unlike the desktop PC market, which is dominated by Microsoft Windows, there are many operating systems for PDAs, and software will only work on the corresponding operating system. The main rivals are Microsoft PocketPC, Palm OS, and Symbian Epoc – these make up over 90% of the market. Few manufacturers develop software for all three operating systems, so if you have a particular application in mind, it's best to find out about the application's requirements before you decide which hardware to buy.

Each operating system will have basic diary, contact book, word processing, and communication facilities. It's worth noting that PDA versions of popular applications will almost certainly be cut down, and will not offer all the functions of their desktop equivalent.

See opposite for details of the three basic PDA designs.

PC pitfalls to avoid

Whether you're buying a PC, AppleMac, or other kind of personal computer, and whether you're buying new or secondhand, there are a number of potential pitfalls that, with a little vigilance, you can avoid. In particular, it is important to find out what sort of warranty the computer comes with, and what other after-sales care, such as helplines, is available.

SEE ALSO Parting with your cash, p92–5

NOT ALL HELPLINES ARE FREE OR CHEAP

Larger PC manufacturers will offer a telephone helpline. Normally, if you've got a **hardware** problem you can call for advice either on a freephone, local-rate, or national number rate.

With most companies, this service is offered for the life of the PC, although some major manufacturers restrict this to as little as 90 days after purchase.

Software problems, however, are often not covered by these low-cost helplines and some manufacturers' software helplines use a premium-rate number which can result in hefty call charges, especially if you're kept waiting in a queue.

If your PC came with software already installed, then you will have to phone the PC manufacturer for help, not the software developer. This is particularly important for programs like Windows and Microsoft Office. If your copy of Windows came with your PC, Microsoft technical support will refer you back to the PC manufacturer.

UNDERSTANDING THE JARGON OF WARRANTIES

After-sales service is a vital part of your computer purchase but home computer warranties tend to have a language of their own.

ON-SITE WARRANTY

An on-site warranty is the best type to have because, if there's a problem, a computer engineer will visit your home to fix it. On-site warranties vary so always check what's included in the cover. Some may only cover **hardware** problems, and exclude **software** glitches, while some companies may charge an additional call-out fee if the problems are due to improper **configuration** or use of software.

COLLECT-AND-RETURN

Next down the scale is a collect-and-return (C&R) warranty. In this type of warranty the manufacturer will arrange for a courier to collect the machine, fix the problem, and then return it to you. There is no cost except for the inconvenience of having to stay in for couriers and being without your PC for a while.

RETURN-TO-BASE

Bottom of the list is a return-to-base (RTB) warranty. This is similar to C&R in that the machine must go back to the manufacturer for repair, but this time you must arrange and pay for transit. A variation on this type of warranty is return-to-dealer (RTD), used by manufacturers who do not sell direct but through authorized dealers. If you've bought from a local dealer, it may be more convenient to return the machine yourself.

EXTENDED WARRANTIES

Deciding whether to have an extended warranty is difficult. Following complaints in the past, the **Office of Fair Trading** (OFT) has investigated extended warranties and has given guidelines to sellers to avoid high-pressure selling, and to give customers proper information about what

is covered by an extended warranty. The best guideline is to consider how quickly a personal computer's value depreciates over time. A five-year extended on-site warranty may cost £300 on a £1,000 PC, but you should bear in mind that, due to depreciation, your PC will only be worth around £200 by the fourth year. PC monitors tend to hold their value, so if you're buying a 21-inch or larger monitor, an optional five-year warranty that at least covers parts and labour is a good idea.

Upgrading tip If you decide to upgrade your PC substantially over the period of the warranty, you may find that your warranty will be invalidated, or that few of the original components will be covered.

TURNAROUND TIME

With all warranties, you should find out if there is a guaranteed time for repairs. Most on-site warranties pledge to have an engineer to your home within two working days, although you can often get a faster service for an additional payment. If the machine has to go back for repair through a C&R or RTB service, most companies will return it within a week or a fortnight. However, even the most respectable manufacturers may only guarantee a 28-day turnaround time. Any company that refuses to say how long a repair will take or warns of repairs taking 'up to six weeks' doesn't have the resources to offer a decent service and is probably trying to sell you an extended or on-site warranty.

Assuming a reasonably quick turnaround, a return-to-base warranty is adequate for most home users. However, if you're running a home business, on-site maintenance may be essential. On average, an extension from the standard manufacturer's one-year warranty to three years on-site cover will cost around 20% of the purchase price.

BUYING MAIL ORDER

Buying by mail order is becoming more common, and can mean very competitive deals because direct vendors have centralized delivery mechanisms, without the need for expensive high-street locations.

Mail order is generally pretty safe, and horror stories about companies who take a stack of orders before disappearing are very rare. However, protecting yourself is relatively easy. Always buy from a reputable company – you can tell these from most computer magazine reviews, which look not only at the merits of hardware but also at the delivery, support, and service a manufacturer provides.

Another tip is to pay by credit card. If the computer you've ordered does not arrive, the Consumer Credit Act states that the card issuer is jointly liable for any private purchase between £100 and £30,000, ensuring you get your money back. However, this protection does not apply to credit cards first issued before 1971, nor to most debit or charge cards (for example, Switch and Visa Delta).

Many computer magazines will offer a Mail Order Protection Scheme (MOPS) for purchases made from advertisers within the magazine. Although a worthy idea, MOPS does not offer a great deal of protection against an unscrupulous manufacturer. It is hedged with restrictions, and a strict cash limit is imposed for claims against any one vendor.

SIX TIPS FOR BUYING SECONDHAND

Buying a secondhand personal computer is a bit like buying a secondhand car – you can often pick up a bargain but there is a risk. Secondhand PCs, Apples, laptops, and handheld computers can be found in free ads papers like *Loot* and *Micro Mart*, secondhand shops, and auctions. You can also try online auctions such as http://www.ebay.com.

1 If you're buying from a secondhand shop or at an auction, make sure that you get some kind of warranty with the system. If you get to test the machine first, some of these sellers will only give a seven-day warranty but, if the items are not tested, 90-days parts and labour is pretty standard but make sure this also includes the software on the machine.

2 Before paying out any money, get a printed specification of the system you intend to buy. This should include the manufacturer and model number for the base unit and monitor, the size of the hard disk, the amount of RAM, the type and speed of processor, and what software is included in the price. If the machine you receive does not match this specification, you have the right to a refund.

3 Be cautious of PCs that do not come with an operating system such as Microsoft Windows 98 already installed. Getting operating system software to make these older PCs work may be difficult, especially if the original PC manufacturer is out of business.

4 Try to pay by credit card or cheque as this provides a 'proof of purchase' in case the machine was once stolen. In a private sale, get a handwritten receipt that includes a reference number from an official ID, such as a driver's licence or utilities bill.

5 If possible, test a machine before buying. This should include the floppy drive, CD-ROM, and display. If you can, install a piece of software that you intend to use onto the machine before you buy it. A successful software installation is a good indication that it is working correctly.

6 Ask about possible upgrades. If you are told that the system is 'not upgradable' be wary, as it may not use standard parts, making future repairs or upgrades expensive or impossible.

DEVELOP SOME GOOD HOUSEKEEPING HABITS

Modern PCs and AppleMacs are relatively self-sufficient, but developing a few good habits can reduce the risk of computer problems.

Do Keep the rear of the machine well ventilated. The fan that cools the power supply and components needs to vent hot air from these slits.

Do Buy a power regulator that will smooth out electrical power surges, because computers are susceptible to fluctuations in electrical power. Choose one with a built-in battery to give you time to shut down your computer safely in the event of a power failure. They cost around £50.

Do Use a screensaver because it protects the screen from burn-out.

Do Perform a regular disk clean-up and de-fragmentation. These software tools recover wasted space and fix hard-disk problems automatically, and are located under the Start > Programs > Accessories > System Tools menu of Microsoft Windows-based computers.

Don't Move your computer or even a laptop with the power on. The hard disk inside a computer is sensitive to movement and it may develop major and unrecoverable problems if it crashes while being moved.

Don't Switch the power off unless you have safely shut down your Windows-based PC or Apple computer. However, this may be unavoidable if your system has crashed.

Don't Try to upgrade or fix the computer with the power on. Also, never open the monitor as it has no user-serviceable parts and, even with the power off, a monitor can still carry a hefty residual charge.

Don't Expect the keyboard and mouse to last forever. Even good-quality ones get dirty or unresponsive after a time. Both items can be cleaned with an alcohol-based solution.

Accessing the Internet

The Internet originated in the 1970s with a handful of universities and government organizations passing information around in a private network. Having taken off in 1993–4 with the development of the World Wide Web, the Internet now comprises millions of pages of information on almost every conceivable subject, often including pictures, video clips, music files, and software. People without PCs can use digital and cable TV services to surf the Web.

SEARCH ENGINES

To find something on the Web, you need to use a search engine. These free services index Web pages and search them using your query. For example, typing in the words *used car dealers in London* will find Web pages – possibly hundreds of thousands of them – that feature any of these words. However, if you surround the words with quote marks, the search engine will look for the exact phrase. This produces more precise results but requires a Web site to use that exact phrase on its main page. A compromise is to use the plus sign between the words – *+used +car +dealers +London*. The plus sign means the search engine will find Web pages that contain all of the words, but not necessarily in that order.

Search engines often offer different results and features. Have a look at: http://www.google.com, http://www.Yahoo.com, http://www.Excite.com, http://www.Altavista.com, and http://www.Yell.co.uk. Type in the query *search engine* to get a list of others.

CHOOSING A SERVICE PROVIDER

Whichever way you choose to get on to the Internet, you will also need to decide what type of Internet Service Provider (ISP) you wish to use. For some types of connection, you may be forced to use a certain type of ISP, but generally you can mix and match.

FREE ISPS

Following the phenomenal success of Freeserve, launched by Dixons as a free ISP in 1998, other providers started to offer access to the Internet without a monthly charge. These services have relied on users reading the numerous adverts on the ISP's main Web site, and buying things through the services available there.

Few of these sites offer unique content, but collect content found elsewhere on the Internet into one convenient place. Typically, free ISPs will use fixed national rate numbers, and, because of the large number of users, connection speeds are often not as fast as those of ISPs that charge.

Many free ISPs cannot guarantee a high level of service, and some require that you connect only at off-peak times of day.

E-MAIL SERVICES

Basic e-mail software is free and is included as standard with Windows or Apple computers. Like sending a letter, you just need to type in the e-mail address of the person you wish to correspond with, and click on the 'send' button. A typical e-mail address will look something like 'John.Smith@freeserve.co.uk'. The e-mail will not be delivered if you fail to place any of the full stops or the @ sign correctly. E-mails can also contain attached files, although some ISPs place a limit on the size of the attachments you may send. Most ISPs have a Web mail service that allows you to access your e-mail from any Internet browser, which is great if you move around a lot. Have a look at http://www.hotmail.com, which is currently the most popular Web mail service.

Many ISPs also offer un-metered Internet access using a normal modem and telephone line. The connection speed is still slow compared to broadband but for people who want to avoid varying charges, for a fixed fee of between £10 and £20 a month, you can connect to the Internet whenever you want.

FEE-PAYING ISPS

There are still many people who pay for Internet connectivity. The average cost lies between £5 and £15 per month for a no-frills service. One advantage of fee-paying ISPs is that they tend not to bombard customers with advertisements. Also, these services generally have more incoming telephone lines available, so you can connect even during busy times. With established providers, such as Demon and Pipex, you can connect even when travelling to other countries. These services are generally aimed at home workers and small-business Internet users.

CONTENT-PROVIDING ISPS

Content providers, also called portals, require a monthly charge, provide services such as interactive games, blocking junk e-mails, restricting access of inappropriate material to children, and a host of other features available to members. However, some users complain about the 'big brother' mentality of some of these ISPs. Pricing is typically between £10 and £20 per month. AOL and MSN are the largest two content-providing ISPs in the UK.

EQUIPMENT FOR ACCESSING THE INTERNET

Type	Approximate hardware cost	Approximate running cost	Performance	Notes	Availability
PC with modem and standard telephone line	Nearly all PCs come with a built-in modem, but if you need to add a modem, it should cost about £30	Using a modem costs the price of a local-rate telephone call, and phone companies are under increasing pressure to reduce the cost for Internet users	Using a modem is the slowest method of connecting to the Internet, with a maximum speed of about 5 KB per second, or 56 kilobaud per second (Kbps)	Modems have a built-in facsimile ability and are great for people who just want to send the occasional e-mail or fax	Huge number of service providers, with many offering free connection
PC with DSL adapter and DSL-equipped telephone line	Digital Subscriber Line, often called broadband, will have an initial set-up fee of about £100, and may require an additional telephone line	DSL is an 'always-on' Internet connection, and is not charged by the minute, although there will be a monthly charge of between £25 and £40	DSL offers better performance than a modem, but is subject to a drop in performance when many users within the same local geographical area are all using their DSL at the same time – speeds vary between a minimum of 12 KB (128 Kpbs) and 50 KB (512 Kbps)	DSL is not available in all areas because of the slow and expensive process of upgrading telephone exchanges, and inferior copper wiring, to DSL-compatible alternatives – the most DSL-friendly locations are major cities; many companies require you to sign up for a minimum of one year	Only a handful of service providers offer DSL, mostly in larger cities
PC with ISDN adapter and dedicated ISDN telephone line	ISDN is an established technology favoured by small businesses; the set-up cost, including both hardware and installation, can run to several hundred pounds	ISDN is, like DSL, an 'always-on' technology, but telephone companies also charge fees for sending and receiving data – however, this is less than a telephone call and, although the average cost for ISDN is about £3,000 a year, this is dropping rapidly	ISDN performance ranges from 12 KB (128 Kpbs) to 96 KB (768 Kpbs), depending on how many channels you buy, and, unlike DSL, there is no drop in performance with a high density of local users, so that ISDN is suited for dozens of PCs all sharing one connection	ISDN is expensive just for Internet usage, and always has a one-year minimum sign up, but ISDN lines are very reliable	Most large telephone companies can offer ISDN across the whole of the country
Cable modem connected either to a PC or a set-top box with a keyboard	Normally sold as part of a cable television system, set-up costs are generally less than £100	Cable modems are an 'always-on' connection, and have no running cost besides a fixed monthly fee, which is comparable to DSL but often slightly more owing to the faster connection speeds	Cable modems perform at speeds up to 2,048 Kbps (2 MB), which is faster than DSL, and, although performance can suffer from a high number of local users, this loss of performance is negligible	Cable modems are becoming increasingly common with the two largest providers NTL and Telewest providing services in most major cities. However, because of the residential nature of cable modems, they are often not designed for small-business use	Limited to areas that can receive cable
Satellite modem connected to a PC	Although still rare in the UK, satellite transmission of requested Internet pages is catching on in the USA and Europe, but the initial costs of equipment and sign-up fees are high – between £500 and £1,000	Satellite systems have monthly charges similar to DSL, but many companies also charge for the amount of data you download, with current prices of about £1 per 100 MB	Satellite modems have a receiving speed starting at 2,048 Kbps (2 MB), but can theoretically run as high as 41,448 Kbps (40 MB), although services such as Europe-Online only allow you to download shareware, or to look at a selection of Web sites or digital television channels	Satellite modems offer the fastest download speed for people who download shareware, movie trailers, or music, but are not suitable for Internet browsing	No UK suppliers, although it is available through mail order to connect to several European services, such as http://www.europeonline.com or http://www.starspeeder.co.uk
Digital set-top boxes such as Sky digital, with a keyboard	Although the equipment is often free, setting up may require an installation fee and a one-year payment in advance	Cost of a phone call, but often at a fixed rate, irrespective of the time of day	Performance varies between services, ranging from speeds equivalent to a traditional PC modem in a box, to performance similar to DSL	Useful services for those who just want very limited access to e-mail and the Internet, but the set-top box is not upgradable, you can't run the latest games, and picture quality is very poor compared to a computer monitor	Available across the UK

▶ Linking up equipment

Most electronic entertainment devices can be linked together to allow you to create a complete multimedia centre. The huge range of equipment and number of models has forced manufacturers to standardize many of the connections. Newer types of device, however, such as MP3 music players, and hybrid devices, such as hi-fi systems with combined DVD players, may perform well in themselves, but not all can be connected to other devices.

CHECKING OUT THE CONNECTORS

PHONO JACK

Used primarily to link separate audio and video equipment. Usually has colour-coded cable – yellow for video, with red and white reserved for the left and right audio channels respectively.

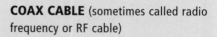

COAX CABLE (sometimes called radio frequency or RF cable)

Often used to carry combined audio and video signals, as in a television aerial. May also be used with digital equipment.

For more on connectors, look at http://www.maplin.co.uk

CONNECTING YOUR TV TO:

VCR Use the coax cable, also called radio frequency (RF) connection normally used for the external aerial, or, with modern TVs, the 21-pin Scart socket.

DVD player/recorder These tend to use only Scart connections.

Computer Many computers have a video 'out' socket that can be altered into a Scart socket using a £5 adaptor.

Camcorder/digital still camera Video and still cameras can both use separate video and audio phono jacks, or a combined S-VHS connector. If your TV only has a Scart socket, ask an electrical store for a kit to convert between S-VHS, Scart, and phono jacks.

Hi-fi Most broadcasts use NICAM- or Dolby-based audio enhancements, so it's worth connecting your TV to your stereo hi-fi. However, owing to the limited number of Scart or audio sockets on each device, you may need a separate 'home theatre' appliance to connect together more than just a TV and hi-fi. If your TV has an audio 'out' socket, you will need a cable that will connect to the audio 'in' (often called 'Line In' or 'AUX') socket on your hi-fi – unfortunately this socket doesn't have common standards. Check the pictures of connectors to work out which cable you require. Often the cable will comprise two phono-to-phono cables for the left and right audio channels.

CONNECTING YOUR VCR TO:

Another VCR Making copies of video cassettes, using two machines, is not illegal provided you don't distribute the copies to anyone else. However, commercial videotapes use a form of copy protection called 'Macro encoding' to prevent accurate duplication. Non-protected video cassettes can be copied by connecting two VCRs using a Scart cable.

DVD player/recorder DVDs are protected with a system similar to the antipiracy Macro encoding on VHS tapes. Some manufacturers argue that DVD recorders should allow people to archive their home VHS tapes onto DVD. A Scart cable is the most common method for connecting DVD players and VCRs.

Computer There are two methods of connecting a PC to a VCR. The first is to place a video capture card into the PC (see Buying or upgrading a PC, p108), and record video on the PC or vice versa. Another, more elegant, solution is to use a high-speed digital connection called an

IEEE 1394 serial bus, such as Apple's FireWire or Sony's iLink. Although at the time of writing few computers or VCRs have these built in, the number of models that do is increasing.

You can also buy a device that will convert your Scart VCR and TV sockets to accept input from a digital video device. If you want to use analogue devices with digital ones, you need a video converter such as the highly rated Dazzle Hollywood DV-Bridge (about £200), or the professional-quality, Datavideo Dac-1 pro (around £1,000).

Camcorder/digital still camera Most digital video and still cameras are equipped with either a video 'out' or an S-VHS socket. The socket will be built into the camera, and a suitable cable will allow playback from the camera to a VCR. Check the pictures of connectors to establish which type of sockets your VCR and camera are equipped with.

Hi-fi The popularity of Dolby and Nicam sound on VHS movies means that most mid-priced VCRs will also support these features. Provided a VCR supports one of the improved audio standards, any hi-fi with audio inputs can be connected, so that films may be played back with better quality sound than you would get from ordinary TV speakers.

CONNECTING YOUR DVD PLAYER/RECORDER TO:

Another DVD player/recorder Connecting two DVD players or recorders together is possible but not advisable, unless you are copying audio disks. You can't make a direct copy of a video DVD because much of the information on the playing disk is not visible to the recording unit. A Scart cable is commonly used for connecting DVDs to copy audio.

Computer Nearly all new PCs have a built-in DVD player. Trying to use a consumer DVD player as a data reader for a computer is impractical because only very expensive models have the interfaces required to carry out both video playback and data transfer. To record a video DVD onto your PC, see the section on connecting your VCR to a computer.

Camcorder/digital still camera DVD recorders can capture any video source. However, unlike VHS tapes, writable DVDs can only be written to once, and they are ten times as expensive. The process for connecting a digital camera to a DVD player or recorder is the same as for VCRs.

Hi-fi All modern DVDs are equipped with the latest audio standards, and most are equipped for connections directly to a hi-fi, or feature separate speaker sockets.

CONNECTING YOUR COMPUTER TO:

DVD player/recorder See above.

Camcorder/digital still camera All digital still cameras have a method for connecting to a PC. The most common medium is the USB port. Using a single, easy-to-fit cable, you can transfer pictures in just a few seconds. Older PCs, without a USB port, will use the serial port, which operates at a slower rate. For connecting a camcorder to your computer, see the section on connecting VCRs.

Hi-fi The growth of 'music via the Internet' services such as Napster and Gnutella spawned the new MP3 portable music players. Consequently, hi-fi manufacturers are beginning to add computer connectivity to their equipment, although generally only in the very expensive, high-specification models.

Even though a PC may have the standard 'speaker out' and 'line in' connectors, the biggest obstacle for this connection may be the positioning of the appliances within the home. The most convenient method for bringing digital music to your hi-fi is to write (burn) your own CDs. However, not all older hi-fis can use these CDs, so it's wise to test a copied CD-ROM disk on your hi-fi before investing in a CD burner for your computer.

CONNECTING YOUR HI-FI TO:

Another hi-fi Hi-fi systems are easily connected using phono connectors. However, when copying between different audio sources, such as CD, MiniDisc, vinyl, or audiotape, clarity of sound can be lost.

For keen audio fans, an optical line is the connection of choice, because this reduces any possible signal degradation. Only high-specification devices tend to support optical connectors.

CHECKING OUT THE CONNECTORS

STEREO JACK

Normally reserved for the headphone jack on stereos, this is also a fairly common connector for computer audio inputs and outputs.

SCART

The most common universal connector for audio and video equipment.

USB

The most common type of high-speed connector for computers and hand-held digital devices.

STEREO VIDEO COPYING KIT

A universal connector kit for audio and video equipment is highly recommended for linking devices, and can be found in high-street electronic goods shops for under £15.

S-VHS (S-VIDEO)

Commonly found on camcorders and high-specification VCRs, this combines video and left and right audio channels into a single, round, three- to five-pin connector.

▶ Moving pictures

For over half a century, broadcast television was the hub of home entertainment. Now cable and satellite TV, DVDs, and VCRs allow a wider choice of viewing, we can be much more in charge of what we watch, but the options when it comes to buying hardware and services can be confusing.

CHOOSING BETWEEN CABLE AND SATELLITE

While there is nothing to stop you having both cable and satellite, the expense and complexity of setting up two services make this a combination for the serious TV junkie only. If you're thinking of subscribing to either cable or satellite services, the table below explains the main differences between them.

DVD PLAYERS

The digital versatile disk (DVD) player is challenging the VHS (video home system) player as the preferred method of watching films at home, and it is also capable of playing music CDs. The latest generation of games consoles, such as Microsoft's Xbox and Sony's Playstation 2 (see p123), not only play video games but also play DVDs and CD-ROMs.

Like VHS tapes, DVDs and most DVD players are able to work only within the territory in which they were bought or rented – the three territories being Europe, America, and Asia. This measure was introduced because film companies were worried that cinema takings would be damaged if films that had not yet been released in the cinema in one country were available on imported DVDs from another.

In practice, many models of DVD player can be bought without region encoding, and some models can be 'upgraded' to ignore region encoding. This does not always mean that a disk will play. Antipiracy and region enforcement software built into the disks can detect if a machine is not running region encoding and may refuse to play.

Feature	Cable	Satellite
Picture quality	Good (slightly better than terrestrial TV) with little interference	Similar to cable TV but with very rare, slight picture degradation due to atmospheric activity
Sound	Supports the common audio standards, but is dependent on the broadcast programme	Similar to cable TV. Many satellite broadcasters offer multiple language support and subtitles, and more plan to offer this facility
Number of channels	At time of writing, cable TV offers 30 to 70 channels – fewer than satellite TV. Cable stations are limited to what is on offer from the service provider (e.g. NTL or Telewest), and it is not possible to receive from multiple providers on the same set-top box	Satellite TV generally offers far more channels than cable. With more advanced satellite dishes, you can subscribe to pan-European networks, providing hundreds of channels
Internet connection	Many providers offer combined Internet services that deliver connection speeds 10 to 40 times faster than a cable modem. The main advantage of these services is that they are 'always-on', and don't incur phone charges. These Internet services cost about £25 per month on average, plus charges for specific television channels	Although it is possible to download shareware software over satellite, surfing is still not possible. Satellite services that offer Internet connectivity use a traditional phone line and have poor connection speeds in comparison with cable modems
Services	Most cable providers offer pay-to-view services such as sports and movies. Newer digital cable services also allow for interactive shopping, banking, and TV guides	Satellite TV has had a headstart in providing services; the Sky digital service offers the widest choice of shopping, financial, information, and interactive services from a broad range of suppliers
Cost per month	£20 to £50, depending on channels taken. Often includes a phone line offering discounted calls to other local cable customers	£20 to £60, depending on channels taken. Often sold with a phone line at standard BT rates
Availability	Only available in major cities, with limited choice of provider across the UK	Services available from Sky and half a dozen European service providers

WHAT TO LOOK FOR IN A NEW TV

Feature	Options	Comments
Screen size	■ Between 10 in and 30 in, measured diagonally	Size of screen is the main determining factor in price. In TVs larger than 30 in, those with back-projected screens (using a system similar to cinema screens) may have fewer problems than curved screens, but may offer inferior picture quality
Broadcast standard	■ PAL (phase alternation line) ■ NTSC (National Television System Committee) ■ SECAM (système electronique couleur avec mémoire)	PAL is the UK standard; other standards apply in Europe, Asia, and the Americas. Choosing a multi-standard TV is not important if your VCR or DVD player converts to PAL from other standards. Multi-standard TVs that support NTSC are useful if you want to connect up to the latest, or more obscure, games consoles, which tend to be available only from Japan or the USA (both NTSC territories). SECAM is the French standard
Picture ratio	■ 4:3 (standard ratio) ■ 16:9 (widescreen)	Width of screen in relation to height. Based on the ratio of the human eye, widescreen is the format of cinema films. In picture quality, widescreen and standard ratio TVs are the same. DVD technology enables films to be seen on TV in their full cinema ratio. Normal TVs can also show films in widescreen by imposing black bars at top and bottom of screen. Widescreen TVs are considerably more expensive than standard 4:3 models
Audio formats	■ NICAM ■ Dolby Digital 5.1 (AC-3) ■ Multichannel television sound (MTS) ■ Digital theatre systems (DTS)	NICAM dominates terrestrial and satellite transmissions; Dolby is more common on DVD and VHS movies. If you have a VCR or DVD player that supports one of these audio enhancements and has separate audio outputs, you will not need a TV with extra audio features. High-specification TVs and those with larger screens often have improved sound support. Although some imported TVs support MTS and DTS, these standards are not widely used in UK terrestrial TV broadcasts, but are more common on satellite and cable services
Inputs and outputs	■ Scart socket set-top box connection	The Scart socket is the best connection method between any video device and a TV (see p118). Some high-specification TVs contain a built-in set-top box, or will allow for a direct connection to one. These are rare in the UK
Digital features	■ Picture-in-picture (PIP) ■ On-screen programming (OSP)	PIP allows you to watch several channels on the screen simultaneously, but you can only get one channel of sound. Most modern TVs allow you to set up channels and alter picture quality using on-screen messages. Beware large-screen TVs that do not offer OSP features; they may be much older than they appear
High-definition or increased horizontal lines	■ 625 lines ■ 700 lines ■ 1000 lines	High-definition TV has more lines of information on the screen, potentially providing a better picture. UK TV broadcasts and DVDs use 625 lines only; there is no guarantee that high-definition TVs available at the time of writing will comply with whichever standard is generally adopted within the next five years
Flat-panel TV	No options available	Flat-panel TVs use computer laptop screen technology. Advantages include less depth and weight and a slightly sharper picture than large-screen TVs. Cost can be five to ten times that of normal TVs of similar size; advances in use of light-emitting polymers may bring costs down within five years

(see p118)

DIGITAL TELEVISION

Terrestrial (as opposed to satellite) digital television broadcasting is planned for most of the UK, with traditional analogue broadcasting expected to cease, probably by 2010. Every UK household will be expected to buy a new box to receive terrestrial digital television channels. Freeview, launched in 2002, offers BBC1, BBC2, ITV, Channel 4, and Channel 5, but the new, wider spectrum contains other free channels as well.

Part of the reason for introducing terrestrial digital television is to increase the choice open to licence payers. Digital television broadcasts should reach all but the most remote areas of the country. If your area had difficulty receiving BBC2 when it started, however, the same may be true of terrestrial digital.

BUYING A VCR

■ VCRs (video cassete recorders) come with either two, four, or six heads. A four- or six-head model offers steady pauses and smoother transitions when editing from a video camera. Audio dub allows you to lay a separate sound track over a video cassette.

■ The playback standard of the VCR is important if you plan to watch videos from abroad – see left.

■ The Videoplus feature allows you to program the VCR to record from terrestrial, satellite, or cable channels, but recording from satellite and cable is not always straight-forward. For more information look at http://www.gemstar.co.uk.

■ If you are planning to connect a lot of devices to your VCR, such as a satellite receiver, games console, and hi-fi, look for a model with dual Scart sockets.

New-generation devices

There are a number of consumer electronic devices that don't fit neatly into the traditional TV, video, or hi-fi categories. Few of these new-generation items are radically different to previous ones – usually they combine the functions of different items into a single device. Examples include music players built into mobile phones and other lightweight items, and the modern video games console, which allows the user to watch films, listen to music, or surf the Internet.

TIVO/SKY PLUS

Tivo or Sky Plus is described as a 'tapeless' VCR that records television programmes digitally onto an internal disk drive. About the same size as an average VCR, Tivo allows you to watch the start of a programme that you are recording, while the recording continues. It is even possible to record one programme while watching another pre-recorded programme. However, the Tivo appliance is limited in functionality without the optional service charge that costs around £10 per month. This enables functions such as an online television guide for easy programming, automatic series recording, and the ability for Tivo to ascertain the types of programmes you like to watch and to record them automatically for you. By linking the separate Tivo box to a VCR, you can transfer recorded programmes to VHS tape, without adverts if you prefer. One word of warning about Tivo: it is quite complex to set up. Some larger retailers offer an installation service for about £50.

MP3 – A NEW FORM OF MUSIC STORAGE

The 'convergence' of music players with computers has led to a new format of music storage called MP3 (MPEG Audio Layer 3). MP3 is a type of audio file that may be stored as digital data on any type of memory or storage device. Advantages of this include the potential for very small playback devices – small enough to fit into a watch for example – and the fact that music can easily be copied to different devices.

MP3 players come in all shapes and sizes. They are both light and durable, they offer very good battery life, and they aren't susceptible to knocks and jolts that might distort playback on a cassette or CD player. These days MP3 players can be found in many different types of device, including mobile phones, watches, car stereos, PDAs (Personal Digital Assistants), and digital cameras. Normally the MP3 audio function must be built in when the device is manufactured. PDAs are an exception because some models can download a software-based MP3 player. Check your PDA manufacturer's Web site to see whether this is possible.

AUDIO FORMATS

MP3 is the emerging leader among several rival audio standards, such as Windows Media Audio (WMA), Universal Disk Format (UDF), Advanced Audio Coding (AAC), and RealAudio. MP3 is used in preference to these other formats by the largest number of players, and there are more tracks available in this format than in any other. MP3 is a free standard, requiring neither licensing cost nor permission to use it. The music industry prefers the rival formats because they offer anticopying technology, so that electronic music can be sold in the same way as physical CDs and tapes. The music industry also fears that the use of

MP3 will lead to more piracy and loss of revenue because music fans will download music for free, instead of paying for it in the traditional way.

Sound quality is the same across all these formats, but if you're buying any MP3 or digital audio device it is wise to look for a device that can be upgraded to support new or emerging formats. Despite the objections of the music industry, MP3 may survive in favour of other formats because its early adoption and easy modes of distribution have led to huge numbers of MP3 software encoders and players being bought, and many MP3-related services on the Internet.

SOUND QUALITY

At the highest quality setting, MP3 music is similar to CD. However, you can record MP3 with lower quality to allow more songs to be squeezed onto a device. At the lower setting, music still sounds quite good, though intricate details within the track may be lost. If you are looking for improved audio quality, look for a device that uses a standard headphone socket. This allows you to buy separate, high-quality headphones or to replace headphones easily if the supplied pair should break.

CAPACITY

The number of songs you can record onto an MP3 player is dictated by how much memory it has. One hour of high-quality music requires 32 MB of RAM. Some devices allow you to add more memory. The most common memory upgrade is a Flash memory card, which slots into many devices like a small credit card. A typical 32 MB Flash module costs about £100. A few manufacturers overcome the high cost of Flash memory by using 8 cm/3 in

COMPARING DIFFERENT VIDEO GAMES CONSOLES

Name	Description	Range of games	Video capacity	Audio capacity	Internet capacity
Nintendo GameCube	GameCube is a dedicated video console from the creators of the video game Mario	There are few games at present but the quality of games is very high. Aimed at the family audience	Uses a proprietary disk, which reduces the cost of manufacture and makes piracy almost impossible, but cannot play videos	Cannot play CD music (see video capacity)	Internet access will be possible using existing consoles but is not yet available
Microsoft Xbox	Essentially a fast PC with a DVD player but without the complexity of a home computer. Microsoft's first attempt at the games console market	Owing to its similarity with the PC, a huge number of games for the Xbox are based on existing PC games	Includes a DVD player and support for hi-definition TVs. The DVD player is not as advanced as a dedicated model, but Microsoft provides an optional upgrade to improve features	The audio CD quality is comparable to the average hi-fi. Connectors allow separate speakers to be added	An Internet connection is available as an optional extra. Built-in Ethernet support makes it well suited to broadband connections
Sony Playstation 2 (PS2)	Successor to the most successful games console ever – the Sony Playstation (PS1)	PS2 has the most games of any current console, with a range for all age groups	DVD player with Dolby and DTS (Digital Theatre Systems). Doesn't have as many features as a dedicated DVD player	The audio CD quality is comparable to the average hi-fi. Connectors allow separate speakers to be added	Internet access is possible but not yet available
Sega Dreamcast	No longer made by Sega, though available in specialist games stores. Design was sold to Pace Electronic; can be bought as part of a satellite/cable television set-top box	Few games at present, with limited new titles, though of a high standard	No DVD playback owing to the antipiracy disk format	No CD audio playback	Has a built-in 56 K modem, but performance is slow
Sony Playstation (PS1)	The most successful games console ever; over 100 million players sold. Still manufactured	PS1 has widest choice of games on the market. Although older games are hard to find new, a big secondhand market exists	Not equipped to play DVDs but does play the rare video CD format popular in the Far East	Has CD audio playback but with few features and poor audio support	Not available
Nintendo N64	Last of the consoles based on cartridges (similar in size to an audio cassette). Still available from specialist shops and by mail order	Has a small range of games, rated by some fans as the most playable and timeless console games	Uses cartridges, to reduce loading time; no video function is available	No audio function available (see video capacity)	Not available

CD-writable disks that provide 200 MB of storage, equivalent to six hours of music. Music can be recorded onto these disks using a normal CD-writer. They cost in the region of £1 each.

COMPUTER CONNECTION

To download music to your MP3 device you will need a computer. The most common type of connection is through USB, and this will transfer each song in a few seconds. Some devices use the computer's serial port for MP3 transfer, but this is a much slower process with each song taking about 30 seconds to transfer.

TELEVISION ON DEMAND WITH A SET-TOP BOX

'Television on demand' is a radical departure from scheduled programming, offered by a privately owned company, Homechoice. Although the service is only in its infancy, it gives the option to select programmes for immediate viewing from categories such as sports, drama, lifestyle, and comedy. Full-length feature films from an extensive back catalogue can also be delivered at any time of the day.

The system uses powerful computers to send your selected programme down a high-speed digital phoneline to a set-top box. Television on demand is also supplied with an 'always-on' Internet connection that is twice the speed of a traditional modem and can be used while watching television programmes. At the time of writing, the service costs between £20 and £40 per month, which is expensive compared to satellite or cable equivalents (see p120).

On the downside, Homechoice is at present available in major cities only, and, although programmes from BBC1 and BBC2 have been plentiful, few programmes from ITV, Channel 4, Channel 5, or the cable and satellite channels have so far been available.

WEB SITES AND ADDRESSES

AltaVista
Web site: www.altavista.co.uk

Popular Web search engine.

Apple
Web site: www.apple.com

Makers of the Macintosh range of computers.

Buying and Using Personal Computers
e-mail: admin@thepcyoubuy.com
Web site: www.thepcyoubuy.com

Digital Television
e-mail: digitaltelevision@culture.gov.uk
Web site: www.digitaltelevision.gov.uk

Government guide to digital television.

download.com
Web site: www.download.com

Access to a whole host of add-ons, new applications, upgrades, and games available as downloads from the Internet.

Ebay
Web site: www.ebay.com

Online auction service.

Excite
Web site: www.excite.co.uk

Web directory and search engine.

Google
Web site: www.google.com

Popular Web search engine.

Hotmail
Web site: www.hotmail.com

Free Web-based e-mail service.

Macintosh Operating Systems
Web site: www.macos.about.com

Collection of articles on using the various Mac operating systems exclusive to the Apple Macintosh range of computers.

Maplin Electronics plc, National Distribution Centre, Valley Road, Wombwell, Barnsley, South Yorkshire S73 0BS
phone: 0870 264 6002;
e-mail: customer.services@maplin.co.uk
Web site: www.maplin.co.uk

Providers of electronic equipment, accessories, and components.

Office of Fair Trading, Fleetbank House, 2-6 Salisbury Square, London EC4Y 8JX
phone: 08457 22 44 99;
e-mail: enquiries@oft.gsi.gov.uk
Web site: www.oft.gov.uk

The Consumer Information section of the site contains advice on buying a PC.

PC World Magazine
Web site: www.pcworld.com/magazine

Contains articles, reviews, and advice on PCs and associated accessories.

Using the Internet
Web site: www.sofweb.vic.edu.au/internet

Guide to using the Internet for beginners.

Yahoo
Web site: www.yahoo.co.uk

Web directory and search engine.

Yell
Web site: www.yell.com

Online classified directory service.

CHAPTER SIX

Everyday living

Information overload

The amount of post coming through UK letter boxes has doubled in the last 20 years, and the number of e-mails sent is still rising. As e-mail and land addresses are increasingly traded between companies, unsolicited offers and catalogues threaten to swamp the items we genuinely want to read or keep – and they eat into our time. You may not want your home to feel like an office, but you can still usefully apply business systems to incoming mail and accumulated paperwork: make a firm decision on every item as soon as you can, store only what you have good reason to keep, and be ruthless in what you throw away.

WHAT TO KEEP?

- Since taxation self-assessment was introduced in 1996, it's been a **legal requirement** that you keep records of income and expenditure relating to work for at least two years after the year to which they apply, and for six years if you are self-employed. If you are in any doubt, check with the Inland Revenue before disposing of financial records.
- Sort carefully any correspondence relating to past events such as house purchases and job searches, and don't throw out any contractual documents.
- If you can't bear to throw out personal letters and old greeting cards, pack them in a box out of sight so you can enjoy rediscovering them another time.

KEEP ON TOP OF ADMIN

SORTING MAIL

- Accept that this takes a little time, and don't put it off.
- Open post near the bin and throw away unwanted items immediately. Sort post into stacking trays labelled 'respond now', 'needs action before responding', 'for reading', and 'for filing'.
- As you read post, annotate it – 'book tickets', 'check with S before accepting' – to avoid rereading.
- Tackle the 'respond now' tray daily, and empty it.
- Before keeping any communication, ask yourself whether you really need it. Is there any real likelihood of you going to the event, or buying the item on offer? Could you get the information elsewhere if you did need it?
- To make retrieving important e-mails easier, and free up memory space, create folders in your e-mail inbox and file there only what you really need to keep. Set your computer to empty your 'delete' file every time you log off.

RESPONDING TO MAIL

- When calling service centres, choose off-peak times to cut costs and time spent in a telephone queuing system.
- Keep a stock of plain postcards headed with your address (print them on a computer or order a set of sticky labels) near where you open the post and use them for instant replies. Buy books of postage stamps so you always have some on hand.
- Stockpile items that can wait a while, and deal with them every weekend.
- After answering invitations, clip them to your calendar or put in your diary so that you can find them on the day.
- Note non-confidential details that you may need when filling in forms – such

as National Insurance number and doctor's address – in your diary or personal information manager.

GETTING INFORMED

- Keep things you intend to read in one place. If items are still unopened after a set time – two days, two weeks, two months – throw them out.
- Always carry reading material with you and use every opportunity to catch up.
- When reading, practise following the printed line with your finger to keep the eye from being distracted and increase speed.
- If you're job hunting, check whether newspapers or magazines covering your field offer an online career manager service, which will e-mail job ads to you automatically.
- If you end up throwing out newspapers unread, get a quick news fix from online news sources or from weekly digests (produced as supplements by some newspapers).

START A FILING SYSTEM

A small filing cabinet is good for organizing household papers, but a portable file box may be all you need. Put papers into plastic or card folders labelled by subject, so that you can take out everything to do with a particular subject in one go.

Named files might include: bank and credit cards (keep bank statements in ring binders of the correct size, available from your bank); clubs/societies; employment; financial planning; garden maintenance and equipment; holidays; household equipment (staple receipts and warranties together and clip to the instruction book); household repairs and maintenance; utilities; insurances (household and personal); investments; loans; medical/dental records; mortgage; pensions; personal documents such as birth and exam certificates; pet records; receipts for smaller purchases (in case you have a credit card query or need to take something back); savings; subscriptions; tax.

- Stick a list on the front of the file box or, in the case of a filing cabinet, each drawer, indicating files inside.
- File papers as soon as they are dealt with. Don't put them back in the in-tray.
- Before filing, write a 'destroy' date on each piece. Purge your files every time you go to them, or every month.
- Start a new file rather than putting an item in a file that only approximates its subject, where you'll have difficulty finding it.
- Tackle a filing backlog for just ten minutes at a time. If you get bored, you'll be more likely to stuff papers in the wrong files, to get rid of them.

ESSENTIAL SECURITY

- Note bank account and credit card numbers, photocopy driving licence and other vital documents, and keep them locked away together with a list of phone numbers to ring in case of loss. Join a credit card protection scheme if you want one organization to notify all your card issuers of card loss, to save time. Some credit card insurance deals offer this service.
- Keep important documents such as house deeds, wills, share certificates, and passports in a secure, fireproof container.

STORING OTHER ITEMS

- Don't buy storage containers unless you are clear about how you plan to use them – otherwise they will merely create more clutter.
- **Magazines, mail-order catalogues**
  Keep in cardboard holders, which sit on a shelf. Throw out a magazine whenever you put a new one in.
- **Items needed occasionally**
  Pin details of sports clubs, medical/dental surgery hours, takeaway menus, and so on to a small noticeboard, or put together in bulldog clips and hang from hooks under a shelf.
- **Coupons, special offers, affinity card discounts**
  Clip together and keep in your wallet, so they don't get left behind.
- **Addresses and phone numbers**
  Even if you store addresses electronically, you might find it useful to have a card index box or small indexed ring binder of contact details near the phone. List emergency numbers – plumber, vehicle rescue, family contacts – on the front, in case someone else has to phone.

JUNK MAIL

- Get your name removed from direct mailing lists by writing, telephoning, or e-mailing the **Mailing Preference Service**. It may take three months for your request to be implemented, and may not prevent all unwanted mail, as the system depends on the cooperation of the companies sending material.
- Check any document that asks for mail details and tick the box requesting that you do not receive further mailings. Read the text next to the box carefully – some wily companies require you to tick if you do want mailings.
- Use prepaid reply envelopes to send back requests to be taken off the mailing list.
- When you receive mail from a source that doesn't interest you, take a minute to send a postcard, headed with your address, asking to be taken off their list.

USING TECHNOLOGY

- Manage your bank accounts online with an Internet banking facility – you can pay bills and make transfers between accounts from your desk. A quick daily check of your balance keeps you in control.
- There are plenty of money management software packages, if you can face inputting the figures. To create your own low-maintenance system, see p86.
- Personal information managers (PIMs) are powerful organizing tools. Everything you enter can be downloaded on to your computer. As well as storing phone numbers, appointments, and things to do, a PIM can keep track of budgets, timesheets, and expenses on spreadsheets.

Making the most of time

The British now work the longest hours in Europe, and pressure to get things done has become one of our biggest stresses, carrying serious implications not just for health, but for relationships, and wellbeing. Many of us spend so much time dealing with work priorities, that we have too little time left to devote to things that are personally meaningful. To get out of this rut, step back and think about what's really important to you, and have the courage to make this a priority in your life. Then, check that you're using time productively, so that you can quickly switch into 'efficient mode' when you need to. Decide which of the techniques here could work for you.

THE INTERNET AND E-MAIL

- Using the Internet instead of another means of communication, for instance to make bookings, can save time, but it helps to know what you are looking for and where to find it. Keep your 'Favourites' up to date.

- The flood of data on the Internet is diverting, but much of it is trivial – recognize it as such.

- Few e-mails are so urgent that they require an instant response. If you're working on the computer trying to get another task done, respond to e-mails in batches once or twice in the day, rather than replying to each one as it arrives.

TIME IS LIFE – VALUE IT

Books on time management proliferate, but most carry the same fundamental message – work out what's truly important to you. Think about where you want to be with each of your aims, big and small, in one year, two years, and five years. Whether you'd like to get fit, redecorate, find a new job, or change direction, the same advice applies. Then work out steps to move you gradually in the right direction, and keep these in your mind as a priority. With very simple time-management techniques, you can win a few minutes here, a few minutes there – and minutes soon add up to hours. Spend these furthering your aims, whatever they are, and you will get a sense of taking charge of your life.

LISTS AND DIARIES

- Use the same diary for home and work commitments to avoid confusion.

- Using weekly and yearly planners can help map progress on long-term goals.

'TO-DO' LISTS

Some time-management specialists advocate using two 'to-do' lists – a master list, plus a daily one that is updated each night. Others say the more complicated your system, the less likely you are to use it, so one list is all you need. Either way, categorize listed items in order of importance, using labels such as 'must do', 'want to do'. Bear in mind that the most

TAKE CONTROL OF THE TV

- Many time-management experts identify flopping in front of the TV as a major cause of lost time, fatigue, and dissatisfaction. How often do you watch programmes you don't enjoy?

- Watching programmes by habit gobbles up time. Study viewing guides and mark what you want to see most.

urgent may not be the most important. If you routinely do trivial but urgent jobs first, you may have less quality time for important things. Try to allot some of your most productive time each day to important tasks that will further your long-term aims.

Decide how to tackle each task by applying the 'four Ds' principle:

Ditch it Put the task on trial: does it really need to be done?

Delegate it Am I the best person to do this task?

Delay it Would it be better to do this when I am less tired, or after I've finished more important tasks?

Do it Prioritize, following these criteria:

- Do the worst job first. Procrastination is a great time-waster.

- Schedule the most demanding job for your best time of day.

- Actually doing something, like ringing the plumber, can be quicker than writing it on a list for the fifth time.

- Make big jobs, such as redecorating a room, less daunting by breaking them down into manageable segments.

- Alternate dull tasks with interesting ones and physical activities with mental ones.

- Performing routine tasks, such as tidying, is effective in short, intense bursts.

- Use a VCR and watch recorded programmes when you really feel like it.

- Don't habitually turn on randomly, in the hope of chancing on something interesting.

- How many channels do you really need? Consider cancelling subscriptions and removing the satellite dish.

FOOD SHOPPING AND PREPARATION

- Examine your food-shopping routine. Most of us shop on the run, making an average of three 30-minute supermarket dashes each week. Consider using local shops to top up rather than driving to a supermarket every time. Reduced toll on your nerves and time makes up for smaller choice and higher prices. Or order via the Internet, and have the goods delivered.
- Bulk-buy staple dry goods – pasta, rice, noodles.
- Divide shopping lists into sections according to the layout of stores, such as fresh produce, refrigerated goods, and the rest. Pack the bags at the till bearing in mind where things will be put at home.
- If you're planning to cook something versatile like bolognese sauce or ratatouille, buy and cook double the amount and freeze the extra portion.
- Put used dishes and utensils straight into the dishwasher.

RUNNING THE HOUSEHOLD

- Don't try to clean the whole house in one go. Tackle one room at a time, or one aspect of one room, such as kitchen drawers. Be systematic, and jobs will get done.
- Know when to stop. Spend a set amount of time on cleaning, then move on to something else.
- Wipe down baths and sinks immediately after use.
- Keep a small squeegee in the shower to wipe down walls and door after each use.
- Put a waste bin in every room.
- Keep cleaning materials together in a box or bucket to carry where they're needed.
- Store laundered bedclothes in sets, with a bottom sheet folded round the duvet cover and pillowcases.
- When visitors come, don't rush to complete all preparations before they arrive – let them join in and help you create the occasion.

TIME FOR YOURSELF

- Add time for yourself into your daily and weekly plans, and value this as much as other tasks.
- Give yourself regular time every day to exercise and relax, and to get in touch with things you really care about.
- Be selective when catching up on chores. Are they all essential?
- Aim to leave work behind when you finish for the day – find absorbing interests that take over from stress.
- Just because a request is reasonable doesn't mean you have to comply with it. Saying yes to others means saying no to yourself.
- You don't need to know everything about everything. Give yourself a break from the news and do something you enjoy more.
- If you're not already doing so, make time for fun: films you want to see, new restaurants to try, interesting books and CDs to buy or borrow, places to go.
- Regularly use quiet time alone to think about your goals.
- Enjoy the moment. Don't waste time hankering after the next house, job, or holiday. Look at the things and people around you and enjoy their presence.
- Don't forget how to be spontaneous.

WHAT THE EXPERTS SAY

Mark Forster, author of *Get Everything Done – And Still Have Time to Play*, says:

'I believe … if we do not find time to play our work suffers, and correspondingly our personal lives are enriched by work well done. I believe that working in a concentrated and purposeful way is less stressful than working in a distracted or unfocused way, and that we can do more and better work when we deliberately limit our working hours.'

Nicky Singer and Kim Pickin, authors of *The Tiny Book of Time*:

'You can regain control over your life not by cramming more in, but by changing the way you think. Work up a sweat putting weed killer on the lawn, or lie in a deckchair and admire the daisies – it's mind over matter.'

Dr David Lewis, psychologist specializing in stress:

'Without specific and well-defined life goals, you will never really know how best to invest your time or whether that investment is worthwhile. Goals help you to focus your efforts, clarify your thoughts, establish priorities, and improve your motivation.'

TECHNOLOGY AND TIME

Technology that is designed to make life easier also increases the pressure to be in touch and react. Hands-free sets mean we can talk on the phone while driving or jogging. Work-related calls come on the mobile at home, at the weekend, on the train. E-mails can be picked up anywhere. The answer is to turn off your mobile and pager when travelling or at home. Don't take them, or your laptop, on holiday. Maintain the distinction between work and leisure, and your health will benefit as you regain a sense of balance.

Cutting clutter

We have more possessions than any previous generation, yet the stuff we devote so much time and energy to accumulating can become a source of underlying annoyance when the home silts up with piles of items that we don't fundamentally need or want. 'Dejunking' has become an almost spiritual movement in the USA, and the same looks set to happen in the UK. The process uses commonsense techniques, but also seems to have a positive effect psychologically, creating a sense of freedom and renewed energy.

SEE ALSO Storage and space-saving, p132, Information overload, p126

WHAT IS JUNK?

Rubbish is junk. Most of the stuff piled on kitchen tables is simply rubbish that hasn't been thrown away yet. Likewise dried-up shoe polish, shampoo dregs, odd earrings.

Broken gadgets are junk. So are things with bits missing or that were never quite right.

Miscellaneous jumble is junk. Odds and ends left on a shelf will only gather dust. Separate unrelated items and put them in the right place or chuck them out.

Ancient history is junk. Not just yesterday's phone messages, curling sticky messages, and last year's calendar, but unwanted gifts, too.

Half-finished stuff is junk. Will you ever really finish making that picture-frame?

Recognizing junk is an important first step to clearing it out.

WHY DEJUNK?

CLUTTER TAKES UP VALUABLE SPACE
Get rid of clutter before you start to think of reorganizing your storage.

CLUTTER NEEDS CLEANING
American dejunking guru Don Aslett reckons 40% of time spent cleaning actually goes into shifting clutter, plus cleaning things that you don't use.

CLUTTER IS DISTRACTING
Too much clutter can distract you from what you really want to do, and indecision and fear of regret can get in the way of tackling the junk.

YOU WANT TO MOVE FORWARD
Work out what you hope to gain from clearing out your junk. What are you making the space for? Identify the things that make you feel relaxed and happy about your home, and use these as a guide to what to get rid of and what to keep.

CLUTTER SOLUTIONS

- Treat shopping for goods as passé. Spend the money on eating out, going to the theatre, holidays. Every time you do succumb to a new purchase, throw out a similar, old item. One pair of shoes in, one pair out.

- Have a ten-minute tidy every night before you go to bed. Throw out newspapers, magazines, unwanted mail. Don't let clutter reaccumulate.

- Gather together old packs of photo-graphs. Pick the best from each batch and make them into framed collages, or put into albums. Throw the rest away.

- It's said that 80% of people wear only 20% of their wardrobe. Examine your clothes with a ruthless eye. Part company with items that haven't been worn for over a year, including jewellery. Bag clothes that no longer fit, and label with a date six months away. Still not fitting after six months? Take the bag to a charity shop. After that, keep a 'chuck bag' permanently in the wardrobe to fill with things for the charity shop.

- Avoid accumulating a pile of clothes on the bedroom chair. Put your clothes on your bed as you undress every night, then put them away or into the laundry basket before you get into bed.

- If you feel totally overwhelmed by the amount of junk you need to clear, consider calling in a decluttering expert, who may charge an hourly or daily rate to help you with the clear-out. Try the **National Association of Professional Organizers**.

SIX STEPS TO GETTING RID OF CLUTTER

1 Start by equipping yourself with four boxes: one for items to throw away, one for stuff to recycle, one for things you want to keep but that are in the wrong place, and a 'maybe' box for those difficult objects whose fate is undecided.

2 Go round each room, systematically looking in every drawer and cupboard, clearing every surface and shelf. Take it slowly – an hour at a time is enough. Maybe put on a CD to time yourself (when the music stops, so do you). Give yourself one day off every week, and allow yourself a treat when you've sorted out a particularly daunting area.

3 Make 'a place for everything, and everything in its place' your mantra. Put items you want to keep straight back where you found them, or in the box for sorting and rehoming. Set up demarcation zones – a place for eating, a place for working, a place for relaxing – and store close at hand the things you use most frequently in each place. Then decide on just one place to keep the most commonly used items – notepads, pens, scissors, sticky tape, writing paper, envelopes, and stamps.

4 You will need to get into the habit of regularly throwing things away, and for a lifelong clutter freak, this is the really hard part. Ease yourself in gently – start off by chucking out a couple of bags of things you've been meaning to get rid of for ages. Take the process seriously. Don't keep pens that leak, a dodgy watch, a ten-year-old guidebook. If it's ugly, or broken, bin it.

5 Deal with the 'maybe' box. It's almost inevitable that the thought of throwing out some things will be quite difficult. Many of us find it hard to let go of the past. But you don't have to throw everything away immediately: have a trial separation. Put items you're unsure about into the 'maybe' box, seal it up, and label it with a date six months away. On that date, reconsider. If you haven't thought about the items in the box since you put

them away, you're ready to get rid of them. Don't even let yourself open the box. If the idea of losing those items still upsets you, put them away for another six months and check out how you feel then.

6 Find a creative way to deal with items you've been keeping for sentimental reasons. First look at each piece individually and think about why you want to keep it. Don't keep anything that doesn't make you smile. One way to move forward is to mount and frame part of whatever it is you're holding on to – a few scraps from a dress, one or two letters – then throw the rest away. Or take and frame a photo of a special item before you part company with it. This can be useful for anything large, such as a piece of inherited furniture, that has important sentimental meaning but doesn't fit into your life as it is today.

- Mess therapist Yvonne Surrey: 'Ask yourself, what is the clutter doing to you personally? Is it affecting your creativity, exhausting you, making you depressed, causing rows?'

- Elizabeth Hilliard, interior design specialist and author of *Perfect Order: 101 Simple Storage Solutions* (Kyle Cathie), says decluttering is 'a good way to cleanse the mind and soul, and very cathartic. It's not just about shelves and files, it's a whole new attitude to life. Rid yourself of the burden of unwanted possessions.'

- Psychologist Oliver James agrees. 'We have many times more possessions than our parents' generation, yet rate ourselves as less satisfied with our lives.'

- Dejunking guru Don Aslett explains why this is. He believes that we can become addicted to our belongings, believing that they represent love or security.

'In childhood we think that objects, like teddies, can make us happy. In adulthood, the message becomes, if one little thing makes us feel secure, surely more things increase our pleasure. We look for ways to make ourselves more impressive to other people, and that includes getting and keeping more stuff.'

Aslett sees getting rid of clutter as crucial to well-being.
'Junk is everywhere. It's on us, in us, and around us and we have to take back our control of it. When you get all the junk out of your life, everything improves – mentally, physically and emotionally.'

Contact details for organizations given in **bold** appear at the end of each chapter.

Storage and space-saving

Despite trends towards minimalism, most of us have more possessions than we have space to store them. New houses often have limited storage areas, while older properties may have awkward spaces that don't lend themselves to straightforward solutions. If you want to impose more order on your belongings, first assess your current and future needs realistically, then search out suitable products, rather than buy items on impulse. Creative use of dead space, such as above a kitchen door or under the stairs, can increase available storage without creating clutter.

SEE ALSO Cutting clutter p130, Shelves and doors p170–172

WHERE TO BUY

Many mail order companies specialize in storage items. Check catalogues and Web sites for trunks, boxes, and baskets; CD, video, and magazine racks; units specially designed for computers, TVs, and video recorders; corner desks, nesting tables, and trolleys. Some mail order brochures are dedicated to kitchen storage. Before ordering, work out where you would put each item, and measure available space to be sure of fit.

Hardware shops are a good source of small storage items. Superstores and department stores sell a wide range of storage solutions from shelving and cupboards down to inexpensive fitments that make the interiors of drawers and cupboards more organized.

ROOM BY ROOM

THE KITCHEN

■ The storage space you need depends partly on your shopping routine. If you rely on daily shopping at local or convenience stores, you'll need less space than if you buy a trolley-load of groceries once a month. How heavily do you depend on frozen foods? Can you manage with a small freezer compartment above the fridge or can you justify a more substantial freezer?

■ Make the most of wall space by fitting a wire storage-grid, peg rail, or row of hooks for frequently used utensils. Position within easy reach, but far enough away from the hob to avoid grease splashes. A wall-mounted wooden or metal plate rack provides permanent storage for crockery. Ceiling racks can hold colanders, jugs, ladles, and even pans, though be sure to leave enough headroom.

■ Make use of kitchen unit add-ons. Possibilities include adjustable shelves for cupboards, clip-on baskets, and trays for pan lids. Many items fit any standard unit. Also look for drawer dividers to sort cutlery and utensils; covered tidies for cleaning materials; tiered racks and carousels for pans, lids, crockery, baking tins, and groceries. Augment existing kitchen units with free-standing cupboards, extra shelves, or a drop-leaf table that could act as a food preparation area.

■ A kitchen trolley on castors can be parked under a table when not in use. For extra flexibility choose one with a butcher's block on top and drawers or shelves below. Folding bar stools provide breakfast seating that can be stashed away.

■ Regularly consign newspapers, bottles, and cans destined for recycling to the garage, shed, or cellar, if you can. Avoid storing in thin plastic carriers, which tend to split. Instead, use stackable plastic crates or baskets, or, if floor space is at a premium, hang plastic laundry bags or canvas holdalls from hooks, and sort your papers and rinsed bottles and cans as you discard them.

THE BEDROOM

Bedrooms are often home not just to clothes and associated accessories, but to sports equipment, extra bedlinen, luggage, and ironing equipment. Ease the pressure by utilizing other spaces. A boxroom, wide landing, or understairs alcove could accommodate, for example, a trunk, cupboard, or chest of drawers.

■ Buy a bed with drawers underneath. Failing that, fill the space under the bed with zipped, breathable duvet and blanket bags, or plastic boxes and crates with lids. Vacuum storage packs fit into small spaces. Fill with clothes or bedding, then shrink down using suction from a vacuum cleaner.

■ If you're short of wardrobe space, sort clothes by season, and store those not

currently in use in breathable bags under the bed. Hang clothes of the same length together. Many items – jackets, shirts, short skirts, folded trousers – only use half the height of a standard hanging-rail, allowing you to fit a second half-height rail below the original one. Add a shelf at the top for luggage and bags. Hang ties and belts on the inside of the wardrobe door.

- Short of drawers? Canvas hanging-holders, divided into generous slots for T-shirts or sweaters, use only 30 cm/12 in of wardrobe width. Pocketed organizers are useful in shallow drawers, to segregate underwear and other small items.

- Get shoes off the floor and on to racks or in to narrow, purpose-built cupboards. Hanging pockets that hook over the top of a door are a cheap solution for shoe storage, and hung inside a wardrobe can be used for scarves, socks, or underwear.

LIVING ROOM

You may have books, newspapers, magazines, TV, videos, remotes, sound system, CDs, and hobby paraphernalia. If your living room doubles as an eating area, you'll also have dining essentials to accommodate. If space permits, invest in built-in or free-standing storage units.

- Don't have too many shelves in the living room. Necessary for books, and good for displaying decorative items, they can also act like a magnet to assorted clutter. Better to add some concealed storage, such as drawers and chests, where unattractive or rarely used items can be kept.

- A small wire-mesh trolley is useful for cutlery, table mats, and so on, and can be moved to wherever it's needed.

- Mini chests of drawers are good for keys, stamps, and other small items.

THE BATHROOM

- Plastic or stainless steel wire baskets that hang from shower attachments or stand in the corner of the bath get bottles off the edge of the bath, which makes cleaning easier.

- Bathroom cabinets are useful for storing medicines and cosmetics but can be very expensive. Buy a plain cupboard, have a mirror cut to fit and screw it into the doors for a cheaper solution.

- Attach a wire grid (often sold in kitchen departments) to the wall and hang wire baskets on it for bottles, face cloths and towels. Or, hang string bags on hooks.

EXTRA STORAGE IDEAS

- Open shelving is relatively cheap to install. Check the weight of the items to be shelved and buy the correct thickness of wood to avoid bowing (see p171). Timber suppliers will advise. Look to fit shelving where you have unused space. A deep shelf above the kitchen door, for instance, is good for bulky but infrequently used equipment. Buy a small set of steps so that you can reach things safely. Put corners to good use with triangular shelves for cookery books. Mount a glass shelf above or across a window for trailing house-plants – especially good if the view is uninspiring.

- Hooks that hang over doors need no permanent fixings and provide a place for umbrellas, towels, tools, or bags. For outdoor clothes, add a second row of coat hooks at waist height to accommodate jackets.

- Cast an eye over existing furniture to see where it could work harder. Swapping a side table for a low cupboard, for instance, retains a useful flat surface while adding storage space.

(see p171)

BUILT-IN OR FREE-STANDING?

Whichever type of storage you go for, be generous and allow space to store items you might acquire in future as well as those you already own.

BUILT-IN STORAGE FURNITURE

- Built to fit it looks neat and makes maximum use of floor space.

- If custom-made by a joiner, it can fit your exact requirements and match your decor.

- Wardrobes need a minimum depth of 60 cm/24 in to allow clothes to hang freely.

- Off-the-peg ranges come in a wide choice of styles and prices.

- Cheaper built-in furniture can be updated by adding new handles and painting over a melamine finish – wet first and rub down lightly (just enough to roughen the surface without penetrating the melamine) with fine, waterproof glasspaper, before applying vinyl silk or matt paint.

- Built-in storage can add to the value of your home, but is probably only worth the outlay if you plan to stay for several years.

FREE-STANDING STORAGE FURNITURE

- Individual pieces or sets give a warmer, more furnished look than built-in units, and are particularly appropriate in period properties.

- Free-standing furniture is usually less expensive than built-in, particularly if you buy second-hand and revamp it.

- Individual items can be made to fit in with existing built-in furniture by filling gaps at sides and above with fascia-boards.

- You can take it with you when you move – though there is a risk that it will not fit the style or available spaces in your next home.

Cleaning up

Cleaning is one of the most resented chores, and can cause friction if you're sharing space. The key to handling household chores is to stay on top. Little and often is the most effective way to clean, making the job easier when you have time for a blitz. Manufacturers know we want an easy life, and they are developing more and more products that, while convenient, are also expensive. Before you spend your money on them, consider some alternatives.

SEE ALSO Laundry kit and tips, p140, Stains and marks, p138

KEEPING SAFE

Always handle cleaning preparations with care.

- Some products, such as oven cleaner, give off noxious fumes, so always use in a well-ventilated room.
- Keep labels on, and never decant cleaners into other containers.
- If you have young children, or have them as visitors, store cleaning products on a high shelf or in a cupboard with childproof catch.

DESPERATE MEASURES

Run out of something vital? Try these quick alternatives.

Air-freshener Burn a match in the bathroom to disperse unpleasant smells.

Descaler Fill kettle with water and add a tablespoonful of vinegar or lemon juice. Bring to the boil, then rinse.

Scouring pads Use scrunched up kitchen foil.

CLEANING AGENTS: WHAT YOU NEED

There's no need to have a huge stock of specialist cleaning agents, as most basic items have a range of uses. With the following selection, you can cope with all the demands of everyday cleaning.

Non-abrasive cleaner Liquid, spray, or cream, for cleaning floors and other surfaces.

Abrasive cleaner Usually comes as a cream, and is good for ceramic sinks and baths. Don't use on acrylic surfaces, which it might scratch.

Lavatory cleaner Leave cleaner for an hour or two, or overnight if bleach-free.

Furniture polish Spray or solid polish. No need to use too often, since regular dusting keeps furniture shiny.

Metal polish Liquid or cream. Check the label for any restrictions on use – don't use silver polish on stainless steel.

Glass cleaner Spray or liquid. Use sparingly to avoid smearing. (Also see Store-cupboard money-savers.)

Scouring/sponge pads Use non-scratch pads on delicate surfaces.

Washing-up liquid Best kept solely for washing dishes.

Limescale remover Essential in hard-water areas. Use regularly around taps and plugholes to keep scale from building up (see Store-cupboard money-savers).

Air-freshener Gels, blocks, or sprays.

Bleach Used sparingly, it is good for disinfecting dishcloths and floorcloths. Bottles with nozzles are less likely to splash bleach on your clothes than the bigger, screw-cap bottles.

STORE-CUPBOARD MONEY-SAVERS

Some of the old-fashioned cleaning methods work just as well as the latest products, and are a fraction of the cost.

Bicarbonate of soda is good for removing unpleasant smells.

- For smooth surfaces, such as inside a fridge or freezer, wet area slightly, sprinkle on bicarb, leave for 30 minutes, then wipe off with a wet cloth. Alternatively, sprinkle bicarb on a damp sponge, wipe round, then rinse off.
- For removing odour from fabrics, dampen area, sprinkle on bicarb, leave for 30 minutes or longer, then launder.

- On carpets that smell, ensure carpet is dry, sprinkle bicarb generously and leave for at least 30 minutes (overnight in bad cases) before vacuuming off.

Salt can prove very handy.

- To get rid of black stains left by eggs on cutlery, rub the area with a damp cloth sprinkled with salt.
- Revive dingy carpets by sprinkling salt generously, leaving for an hour or two, then vacuuming.
- To unblock drains without using a caustic cleaner, pour in 70 g/2½ oz salt and 70 g/2½ oz bicarb, followed by a

litre/2 pints of boiling water. Leave overnight, then flush thoroughly with water. Alternatively, try 70 g/2½ oz bicarb and 100 ml/3½ fl oz white vinegar. Cover drain and leave for a few minutes, then pour boiling water down to flush. Don't use either of these remedies if a proprietary drain-cleaner has already been used.

Vinegar is versatile:

- Paint white vinegar onto stubborn price tags on china and glass. Leave to soak in, then rub the tag off.

- Wash dull kitchen floors with a solution of 200 ml/7 fl oz vinegar in 2 1/4 pt water.

- To slow grease build-up, wipe out your oven with a cloth dampened with water and vinegar.

- Cover limescale deposits round taps and plugholes with kitchen roll soaked in vinegar. Leave for an hour, then scrape off the softened scale using a blunt knife tip. Another method is to use a flour and vinegar paste.

- For streak-free windows, wash with a mixture of equal parts warm water and white vinegar, and dry with a soft cloth. Don't clean windows when the sun is shining on them.

- To unblock a clogged shower head, soak for an hour in a solution of equal parts hot water and white vinegar.

Ice cubes applied to fresh grease spots on a wooden floor will harden the grease, which can then be gently scraped off with a round-edged knife.

Lemon juice and vegetable oil in equal parts is a good mixture for treating furniture scratches. Rub gently into the scratches with a soft cloth. A blend of two parts oil to one part lemon juice makes an effective and fragrant furniture polish.

Methylated spirit removes grease and grime from telephones and piano keys. A little on a damp cloth gives extra shine to mirrors and glass.

Mustard powder and water can deodorize bottles and jars. Just rinse – no need to soak.

Stale bread, rubbed on gently, can clean dirty marks from wallpaper or leather.

Upholstery nozzle

Dust brush

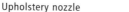
Crevice nozzle

TEN WAYS TO A CLEANER HOME

- Rather than trying to blitz the whole house, do one room at a time and do it thoroughly.

- Share chores – get everyone to do the jobs they prefer.

- When dusting, start at the top of the room and work down.

- When washing walls, start at the bottom of the wall and work up, since water trickling onto dry surfaces can create indelible streaks.

- Tidy daily to make cleaning easier

- Don't let dirt build up or splash marks set. Wipe the stove top clean.

- Put a waste bin in every room and aim to empty daily.

- Place a large doormat inside every external door.

- Keep sets of cleaning equipment in the bathroom and bedrooms to make spontaneous cleaning simple.

- To keep rooms smelling fresh, open windows daily.

The equipment you can't afford to be without:

Vacuum cleaner Buy the most powerful you can afford. Cylinder cleaners are good for tackling stairs and tricky corners, while uprights are good for large rooms. Stick cleaners are another type of vacuum cleaner, designed to polish hard floors and vacuum rugs.

Make use of the cleaner's attachments – an upholstery nozzle is small and wedge-shaped with no bristles, good for getting pet-hairs or crumbs off dining chairs, sofas, and armchairs. The dusting brush has soft bristles and is suitable for curtains and lampshades, as well as window sills, hearths, and other smooth surfaces. The crevice nozzle is long and slender for getting into corners and between sofa cushions.

Long-handled soft and hard brooms Easier to use than a brush and dustpan on large floor areas. Use soft broom on wood, vinyl, or tiled floors, hard broom on concrete surfaces or patios.

Sponge mop Choose one that wrings out the sponge.

Bucket Buy a large one, for less-frequent refills. Rectangular buckets are easier to use with wide mop-heads than round buckets.

Scrubbing brush Handy for removing ingrained dirt on quarry tiles or other tough surfaces.

Chamois leather Especially good for glass and windows.

Dusters and soft cloths Use old cotton T-shirts – they don't shed fibres.

Dusting brush Good for tackling cobwebs, awkward corners, and light-fittings. Choose between a short or long handle, with dusting head made of fleece, feathers, or sponge. Antistatic dusters and brushes are designed to repel dust from TV and computer screens.

Some 40% of the UK population suffers from some form of allergy, the most common of which are asthma, hay fever, and eczema. One reason may be house dust mites, tiny bugs that live in bedding, furniture, and carpets. The **National Asthma Campaign** gives the following advice:

- open windows for a few hours daily – good ventilation helps disperse allergens; ionizers and humidifiers can make allergy symptoms worse
- wash bedding often at 60°C/140°F
- don't keep pets
- in a property that has had pets, steam-clean furniture and carpets
- if you suffer badly, consider replacing carpets with wooden floors, and reducing soft furnishings.

Vacuum cleaners Buy one with powerful suction and an efficient exhaust that doesn't put dust back into the atmosphere. According to the Campaign, there is no proof that special types of vacuum are more effective than other models. Vacuum frequently and thoroughly. Uprights pick up allergens better than cylinder models, but cylinders clean the edges of rooms more thoroughly. If you have a bagless model, ask a non-sufferer to empty and clean it.

Mattress covers It takes dust mites only four months to colonize a new mattress. For a new or existing mattress, fit a special cover that encloses the entire mattress and will not let mites through. Vacuum or wipe covers regularly. Cheaper covers may do the job just as well as expensive types.

Pillows and duvets Mites may actually prefer synthetically filled pillows and duvets, though if you are allergic to feathers you have no choice. Use special covers that enclose pillows and duvets and reduce contact with potential allergens.

CLEANING ROUTINES AROUND THE HOUSE

BATHROOMS
Baths and basins

- Check labels of proprietary cleaners and stain removers – not all of them are suitable for all materials.
- Wipe round baths, basins, bidets, showers, and taps straight after use, while still warm. Wipe off toothpaste splashes immediately – some brands, particularly those containing fluoride, can harm the glaze on vitreous china. Oily bath additives create rings round the tub – rinse off immediately after emptying bath. Dried-on rings can be removed with a damp sponge sprinkled with bicarbonate of soda or vinegar.
- Use an old toothbrush or baby's bottlebrush for cleaning overflows and round plugholes.
- Rinse soap dishes often to prevent a build-up of hardened soap on basin, bath, or shower.
- Treat light scratches on acrylic baths by rubbing gently with metal polish.
- Never leave washing to soak in detergent in an enamelled bath or basin.

Limescale

Take care with limescale removers, and check on the pack that they are suitable for the surface you want to treat. Enamel is easily damaged, even by mild solutions. You can use a paste of flour and lemon juice or vinegar, but even these can eat into the surface below the limescale, so check frequently and remove as soon as possible. Once the limescale is softened, wash off completely. Try rubbing stubborn deposits with the flat end of a wooden clothes peg, but go easy to avoid scratches.

WCs

- Scrub daily, including under the rim, with a lavatory brush.
- Wash lavatory brushes in hot soapy water, then rinse with hot water plus a shot of disinfectant.

- Don't mix different toilet cleaners, and never mix a cleaner with bleach. Don't use bleach if you are also using a cleaner block in the cistern.
- Flush away bleach cleaners after no more than an hour – they can discolour the glaze below the waterline if left for too long.

Taps and showers

- Be gentle when cleaning these, as the finishes are easily damaged. Avoid abrasive cleaners – use warm soapy water instead. Dry taps after cleaning, and polish with a soft cloth.
- Clean glass shower doors with a damp sponge sprinkled with white vinegar.
- Before hanging it, soak a new shower curtain in a salt water solution to help prevent mildew forming.

Tiling

- Dirt comes off tiles far more easily when loosened by steam, so run a hot shower for a few minutes before you start. Open a window when you've finished.
- Wipe tiles with warm soapy water, rinse, and dry with a soft cloth. Don't use abrasive cleaners, which might damage the glaze.
- Clean blackened grout with a proprietary antifungal cleaner, or paint carefully with a mild bleach solution, leave for a few minutes, then rinse off. Do not attempt to clean with wire wool, which can produce rust stains. Avoid mould growth by ventilating the bathroom (see p000).

LIVING ROOMS AND BEDROOMS
Carpets

- Vacuum regularly to remove dirt before it becomes ingrained.
- On smooth, cut-pile carpets, an upright cleaner with a 'beater bar' that raises dust and dirt gives the best results. For loop-pile (such as Berbers) and deep-pile carpets, a cylinder suction-cleaner is better.

- If carpets still look grimy after vacuuming, consider deep cleaning with either a shampooer or spray extraction-cleaner. Both can be hired, or the job can be done professionally – check the *Yellow Pages* for local contractors.

- Carpets treated with stain repellent, either during manufacture or after laying, are easier to clean.

- Use a stain remover on small spots, or try a washing-up liquid solution – cheaper and often just as effective. Either way, test on a hidden spot first.

- Tackle carpet stains immediately. Don't rub wet stains, but blot them with a white cloth. Rinse thoroughly, as deposits of stain remover left behind can attract more dirt.

Wooden floors

Make up a solution of 120 ml/4 fl oz cider vinegar in 4 l/8 pt warm water. Squeeze out a soft cloth in this solution until just damp, then wipe floor. Dry with another cloth to bring up the shine.

Vinyl floors

- Sweep or vacuum with hard-floor attachment to remove loose debris, then mop with a solution of dishwasher detergent in warm water. Tackle ground-in grime with a white nylon scourer. Polish or wax the surface occasionally to help prevent dirt penetrating.

- Remove heel marks from solid floors with a pencil eraser.

Curtains and blinds

- Use the vacuum cleaner dusting brush (see p135) to remove dust from curtains and blinds.

- Clean venetian blinds by wiping slats with a damp cloth or using a special brush designed for blinds.

Furniture

- A soft, clean paintbrush is good for winkling dust out of carved or awkward parts of furniture. An old toothbrush gets into really tight corners.

- Regularly move furniture to vacuum underneath.

Cane and wicker

Vacuum with dusting brush. Wash down occasionally using a solution of 30 ml/1 fl oz ammonia to 4 l/8 pt warm water. Wear rubber gloves and rinse well. Leave to dry outside, avoiding direct sunlight.

Dusting

- Speed up by putting an old sock on each hand and dusting with both simultaneously.

- Don't forget the tops of doors and pictures, light fittings, mouldings on doors, and skirting boards.

- Remove dust from wallpapered walls by vacuuming lightly with the dusting brush attachment.

- To reduce the static which encourages dust to collect on TV and computer screens, wipe them with a dampened fabric-softener sheet.

Lampshades

- Vacuum fabric and pleated lampshades with the dusting brush. Don't let dirt accumulate, as it may create grubby marks that are hard to remove.

- Plain fabric lampshades can be dunked in warm soapy water, rinsed, and dried. Treat with caution any that are trimmed or edged with a different colour, as the colour may run.

Glass table tops

Rub over glass with a little lemon juice on a soft cloth, dry, then polish with scrunched newspaper.

KITCHEN

Sinks

Stainless-steel sinks and drainers sparkle if wiped with a little vinegar on a cloth.

Worktops

- Remove everything, then sweep up or vacuum crumbs, using crevice nozzle in corners.

- Use an all-surface cleaner in warm water to wash down worktops and tiling, tackling any hard deposits with a white nylon scourer. Dry and polish with an old cotton T-shirt.

CLEANING SCHEDULE

EVERY DAY

- Tidy all living areas.
- Chuck old newspapers, or store for recycling.
- Empty rubbish.
- Wipe sinks, baths, basins, and showers.
- Put dirty clothes into laundry basket.
- Hang clothes up.

EVERY WEEK

- Clean worktops and other surfaces with all-purpose cleaner.
- Dust and polish.
- Vacuum floors.
- Wash kitchen floor.

EVERY MONTH

- Clean out fridge.
- Wipe kitchen cabinets, inside and out.
- Move furniture and vacuum underneath.
- Dust walls, furniture, light-fittings.

KITCHEN EQUIPMENT

- Let burnt saucepans stand overnight filled with a strong salt-water solution, then bring to the boil slowly. The burnt material will come away easily.

- Clean the outside of cast iron pans with oven cleaner spray. To prevent rust, rub vegetable oil on the insides after washing. Remove rust spots with scouring powder.

- After cooking scrambled eggs, immediately soak the pan for 15 minutes with water plus a dessertspoonful of dishwasher detergent. Use plain cold water for porridge pans.

- Rub a chopping board with a cut lemon, or a squirt of lemon juice, to kill smells.

Stains and marks

Spills and stains on clothes and carpets are best dealt with as quickly as possible. Luckily, many modern fabrics are easy to care for, and there's a wide range of products that deal kindly and effectively with most everyday stains. For stains that prove more stubborn, there are some specialist techniques to try.

SEE ALSO Cleaning up, p134, Laundry kit and tips, p140

PUT TOGETHER A STAIN-REMOVAL KIT

Special stain-removing products for laundry include:

- branded stain removers in bottles, usually with a foam applicator or rollerball top
- pre-wash sprays in guns
- soaking solutions
- stain-removing powders and liquids to use with ordinary detergents
- everyday detergents with extra stain-removing properties
- biological detergents (it's worth having a small quantity in the cupboard, even if you don't normally use one)
- soap bars (cheap and often effective).

Some of the treatments in the A–Z on the right involve traditional stain removers, available from pharmacies, such as methylated spirits, glycerine, eucalyptus oil, bleach, and borax.

For stains on carpets or upholstery, specialist carpet stain removers are available as sprays or mousses.

FIRST RESPONSE

Using the right technique on a specific stain can make all the difference to your success. If you don't know what caused the stain on a garment, take the item to a dry cleaner's. Be sure to point out the stain, which otherwise might be missed.

For most stains on **washable fabrics** an overnight soak in cold water can be an effective initial treatment. If this doesn't clear the stain, use the branded stain remover of your choice and follow, if necessary, with a wash on the correct cycle for the fabric, using biological detergent. Most common stains will respond to this treatment.

For **stubborn or tricky stains**, try the techniques in the A–Z below. Give a DIY remedy a good chance to work before trying another method. If you use stain-shifters like glycerine or eucalyptus oil, work them well into the stain for maximum effect, but do it gently.

A–Z OF TRICKY STAINS

Ballpoint ink Many of the specialist stain removers deal with ballpoint ink. Alternatively, soak a pad of cotton wool in methylated spirits and hold it under the stain. Use dry cotton wool to dab from above in order to draw the meths up through the fibres and shift the stain. Another option is to apply a couple of squirts of hairspray to the stain, then rub gently with a dry cloth. Either way, launder as usual after treatment.

Beer Leaves a brown mark if left to dry. Sponge gently with vinegar and warm water, then wash as usual. On dried stains, try rubbing gently with methylated spirits.

Bird droppings Clean washing is the usual victim. Scrape off any deposit, and rewash. Berry stains may be stubborn – use a stain remover before washing, or soak in a solution of biological washing powder.

Blood Rinse garments repeatedly, or soak them, in cold salty water. Remove as much of the stain as you can before machine washing. Dried blood is much harder to remove. Try a soak in a cold-water solution of biological washing detergent. Sponge carpets and upholstery with cold water, then use a carpet shampoo.

Candle wax Leave until set, then chip and scrape off as much as possible. Next use a medium-to-hot iron, depending on the fabric, over a doubled sheet of white kitchen paper or a single sheet of brown wrapping paper (an opened-up brown envelope will do) to remove the remaining wax. You can also sandwich the stain between absorbent paper, then apply the hot iron to the top layer of paper. Any residual stains from coloured wax should respond to stain remover.

Chewing gum Don't be tempted to pick, as you will end up pressing the gum deeper into the fabric. Rub the area with an ice cube wrapped in a plastic bag to harden the gum, or place the entire garment in a plastic carrier and put it in the freezer overnight, then chip off the frozen gum. Use dry-cleaning fluid to remove residues, then wash as usual.

Chocolate Scrape off as much as you can. Use a specialist cleaner, or apply glycerine to loosen the stain before washing. If you have neither, work neat

liquid detergent into the stain, then rinse thoroughly with tepid water. Wash in biological detergent, or have non-washables dry-cleaned.

Coffee Rinse or blot as much as possible. You may need to use a stain remover if milk in the coffee leaves a grease stain. Soak washables in biological detergent solution before laundering.

Curry The combination of turmeric and oil that features in most curries creates a stain that can be very hard to remove. Try to keep the area wet. A speedy application of glycerine can keep the stain from setting. Rinse repeatedly with tepid water, or a mixture of 300 ml/½ pt warm water with 10 ml/2 tsp borax.

Dye Red sock syndrome, where one non-fast coloured item sneaks into a load of whites and lightly colours the lot. You might get away with washing everything again immediately, with a generous dose of detergent, before laundry has had a chance to dry. If any colour is still left, you could try a branded run remover – unfortunately these can also affect the original colour of the garment. For whites, wash again with 20 ml/4 tsp bleach in the detergent compartment of the washing machine – check the care label first to make sure the garments can withstand such strong treatment. Never use bleach on acetate, polyester, drip-dry cottons, silk, or wool.

Felt-tipped pen If you're lucky, the ink will be water-soluble and will come out with cold water. If not, try a branded stain remover.

Fruit juice Very hard to shift once dry. Wash through in cold water. Apply glycerine, leave for one hour, then sponge repeatedly with warm soapy water.

Grass If the fabric will take it, soak in a mild bleach solution (follow directions on the bottle). Alternatively, apply glycerine, leave for several hours, then sponge well with warm soapy water and launder.

Grease Dab immediately with dry-cleaning fluid on a pad of cotton wool, or sponge well with warm soapy water before laundering.

For colourless grease stains on leather or upholstery, sprinkle on fuller's earth (an earthy powder available from chemists), cover, and leave overnight. You may need several applications. Or use a specialist leather cleaner.

Lipstick Try dry-cleaning fluid, followed by warm soapy water. Or apply eucalyptus oil, let it soak in and loosen the lipstick, then blot away the stain. Dry clean, or for washable fabrics, sponge with soapy water as hot as the fabric can stand, then launder.

Mud Leave until completely dry, then brush off and then launder.

Pets Wipe up puddles immediately, then wash the area with a tablespoon of vinegar in 500 ml/1 pt water. For solid offerings, remove as much as possible from the surface. Wipe off thoroughly with kitchen paper. Sponge the area well with warm water, or use a carpet spot shampoo, testing first. To remove the unmistakable odour left by cat spray, sponge the area with a mixture of half warm water, half white vinegar.

Tea Apply glycerine immediately, then sponge with warm soapy water and launder. For dried stains, leave glycerine on for longer before sponging.

Vomit Remove deposit, sponge well with warm soapy water, then launder as usual. On carpet, sponge with a teaspoonful of borax mixed with 500 ml/1 pt warm water.

Wine For red wine, quickly pour over some white wine or mineral water, then dab off with a cloth and, with luck, the stain will have disappeared. If not, apply glycerine to loosen the stain before laundering. Be wary of applying salt to red wine stains – although it works on some fabrics, on others it sets the stain permanently.

Act fast – fresh stains are far easier to shift than old, dried ones.

- Never dab at a stain with a coloured cloth or paper – the dye might run and make the problem worse. Use plain white kitchen paper or cloths.

- Carefully scrape off any surface deposit before you start treating the fabric.

- Test any stain-removal product on the least obvious corner of fabrics, to make sure that the colour doesn't run.

- Use mild treatments before moving on to stronger ones.

- Avoid the temptation to rub vigorously at a stain, as you may damage the fibres and leave a permanent mark. Instead, dab carefully, and be prepared to treat the stain several times, until it has completely disappeared.

- Start work at the edge of the stain, moving gradually to the centre.

- For a really bad stain, take the item straight to the cleaner's rather than having a go at it yourself.

- Silk is particularly delicate, and is better treated by a professional, as are velvets and lurex.

TIPS OF THE TRADE

To clean the grimy bottom of a shower curtain, hang in a bucket of cold water mixed with two capfuls of bleach. Check every ten minutes to see when it's ready to remove.

Cover smears of bicycle or engine oil on clothes with a generous amount of neat washing-up liquid and work it in well, before wiping off with a clean cloth. Gently rub with warm water, then launder.

Beryl Gordon, house cleaner

Laundry kit and tips

Ever thought that clothes get a much harder time in the wash than when they're being worn? Some simple routines will limit the damage to garments on their journey from dirty clothes basket to cupboard, not least matching the wash cycle to the fabric. And if you're looking to buy a new washer or dryer, use these checklists to pinpoint the features that will be genuinely useful.

SEE ALSO Stains and marks, p138

THREE DRYING TIPS

1 Sort clothes for tumble-drying into batches and dry similar fabrics together, on the correct setting, to avoid shrinkage.

2 Fresh air is free. Peg clothes so that they hang the same way as you would wear them – skirts and trousers pegged at the waist, shirts at the shoulders – to reduce creasing.

3 Lie heavy jumpers flat on a towel or drying rack so that they don't stretch or lose shape. A short spin first will make the process quicker, but check the care label.

THREE IRONING TIPS

1 Check care labels and sort clothes before ironing, doing those needing the coolest iron first.

2 Ironing clothes inside out means you're less likely to get shiny patches or scorch marks showing.

3 Never iron over plastic or glittery decorations – they'll probably melt and be ruined.

CHOOSING LAUNDRY EQUIPMENT

WASHING MACHINES

Look for the energy label displayed on every machine, giving a rating for energy consumption ranging from 'A' (the best) to 'G' (very poor). Washing machines are also rated A–G for washing and spinning performance. A good spin rating, A–C, means that tumble-drying will be quicker and cheaper.

Some washing-machine features are far more useful than others. Don't be tempted to pay over the odds for an impressive array of programmes, for instance – most people stick to the same three or four.

Automatic timer Some machines can be loaded then left to turn themselves on automatically – useful for taking advantage of off-peak electricity, or for getting the washing done while you're out.

Extra rinse Worth considering for anyone whose skin reacts to detergent traces left in clothes.

Fuzzy logic Many machines come equipped with sensors that monitor the wash and alter different aspects of the performance accordingly. A machine with fuzzy logic might adjust the water intake and temperature, add an extra rinse to clear excess foam, and choose the best spin speed for the load. These machines cost more than standard models, but they do make the most economic use of energy, and will save you money if you do more than three full loads each week.

Life expectancy A few machines, made from top-quality materials and using sophisticated electronic technology, claim to have a life of up to 20 years, rather than the 5–10 year life expectancy that is realistic for other machines. These machines are at the top end of the price range, but over time could prove to be worth the extra initial investment.

Machine size Compact machines can squeeze into a small space, but have a smaller capacity and a limited range of programmes. Top-loaders are not as wide as front-loaders, so are useful if you're short of space. They can be awkward to use, however, if they have to be wheeled out from under a worktop, and they can be noisy. Some standard-sized machines have a large drum that can accommodate 6 kg/13 lb of laundry rather than the usual 5 kg/ 11 lb. Only useful if you regularly do a large amount of washing.

Quick-wash or economy settings Useful for lightly soiled clothes.

Spin speed Higher spin speeds mean drier washing, so look for a machine that offers a top speed of 1,100 revolutions per minute (rpm) or more. Some machines have variable speeds, so you can give fabrics that crease badly a very slow spin.

TUMBLE-DRYERS

The main choice is between air-vented and condenser dryers. Air-vented are cheaper and dry washing faster, but the steam is removed through a broad hose that has to be ducted through an external wall or hung out of a window or open door, restricting where you can put the machine. Condenser dryers are a little more expensive, but you can position them anywhere. They work by condensing the steam back into water, which collects in a built-in container that you empty when necessary. If you can position the dryer near a sink, it can be plumbed in so that the water goes down the drain.

Automatic timer As for washing machines.

Filters All machines have these fluff traps, which need regular cleaning. Choose a machine with a filter that is easy to get at.

Heat settings Most people use just two: a low setting for synthetics, high for cottons. A cool phase at the end of the cycle allows clothes to cool down gradually and helps prevent creasing.

Reservoir warning A light that comes on when the container in a condenser dryer is full. Prevents overflows.

Reverse tumble This fairly standard feature prevents tangling. It may be missing from economy-range compacts.

Size Compact machines are handy if you have limited space, but can handle only 2 kg/4½ lb rather than the standard 5 kg/11lb load.

Start button Designed to prevent an automatic start-up when the door is shut, in case children or pets climb into the dryer.

WASHER-DRYERS

Two machines in one can be the answer if you are short of space or cash. Drawbacks:

- these machines don't dry as fast or as efficiently as a standard tumble-dryer

- the whole process takes longer, because the dryer can only dry half a normal wash-load at a time. And, of course, you have to wait for a wash to finish before you can dry anything.

GETTING THE BEST FROM YOUR WASHER

SORT WASHING CAREFULLY

- Ideally you should separate your laundry into three groups by colour: whites, light colours, and dark colours, so that whites stay white, and dark dyes from black and navy garments don't turn paler colours dingy. If you don't have enough for three loads, at least keep whites separate – it's worth doing a half load.

- It pays to wash items of certain fabric types together. For example, synthetics need a cool rinse and short spin, whereas heavy cotton items like towels, can take a hotter wash and longer spin.

LOADING THE MACHINE

- Don't be tempted to overload the drum. Performance will be reduced and your

machine will suffer greater wear and tear. The motor might even burn out if you overdo it too often.

- Empty pockets and remove badges, brooches, or any loose buttons before you wash. Small loose items can lodge in the machine and cause considerable and expensive damage.

IMPROVING PERFORMANCE

If your washing machine consistently produces poor results, pour a little bleach into the detergent compartment, then let the machine run empty through a complete warm wash cycle.

The bleach will remove any clogged soap scum in the machine and should improve washing and rinsing.

DETERGENTS AND SOFTENERS

The first choice is between detergent in powder, tablet, or liquid form. Tests carried out by the Consumers' Association found that powders and tablets are more effective at removing stains than liquid detergents. Beyond that, the choice is between different types of product, designed for different uses.

Biological Excellent for stain removal, even at low temperatures.

Non-biological Good for sensitive skins (including babies) – especially for anyone

with an allergy to enzyme detergents. May not remove deep staining.

Colour Lower bleach content means colours are less likely to fade.

Wool wash A liquid that's appropriate for delicate fabrics, particularly silk and wool.

Fabric softeners Produce fragrant, soft garments that shed creases more easily and may need less ironing.

Water-softener tablets Stop the limescale build-up that damages the insides of washing machines.

WHAT CARE LABELS MEAN

The International Association for Textile Care Labelling (GINETEX) developed a language-independent care-labelling system in 1975. There are five basic symbols for washing, bleaching, ironing, dry-cleaning, and tumble-drying. Symbols refer to the maximum treatment the textile can bear without irreversible damage.

 40°C Mechanical action normal; rinsing normal; spinning normal

 40°C Mechanical action reduced; rinsing at gradually decreasing temperature; spinning reduced

 40°C Mechanical action much reduced; rinsing normal; spinning normal

 40°C Handwash only

 Do not wash

 Chlorine-based bleaching in a cold and dilute solution is suitable

 Iron at a maximum temperature of 200°C

 Iron at a maximum temperature of 150°C

 Iron at a maximum temperature of 110°C (steam iron may be risky)

 Drycleaning in all solvents normally used for dry-cleaning, with normal procedures

 Drycleaning in all solvents normally used for dry-cleaning, except trichloroethylene, with normal cleaning procedures. Self-service cleaning is possible

 The bar placed under the circle indicates strict limitations on the addition of water and/or mechanical action and/or temperature during cleaning and/or drying. Self-service cleaning is not recommended

 Tumble-drying possible at lower temperature setting (60°C maximum) after a washing process

 No restrictions concerning the temperature of tumble-drying after washing

In the kitchen

Food scares involving salmonella and E. coli have highlighted the need to be careful about the food that we buy and how we store, prepare, and cook it. By making simple hygiene rules a habit, you can reduce the risk of food from your kitchen making you ill.

KEEPING THE KITCHEN CLEAN

Clean worktops frequently by wiping down with an all-surface cleaner that contains bleach, diluted according to directions. Hot, soapy water is also good for cleaning worktops, but may not kill all bacteria. Water on its own removes visible marks, but doesn't affect bacteria.

There is as yet no convincing evidence that anti-bacterial products are more effective than standard disinfectants, such as chlorine bleach.

Keep cloths and sponges clean, and replace them often. Wash out frequently in hot, soapy water and hang up where they can dry. If left wet and crumpled they provide an excellent environment for bacteria to grow.

Bits of food easily become trapped in the plughole and overflow of the kitchen sink, where damp conditions mean they become full of bacteria. Clean the sink daily, and pour a solution of one capful of bleach in 1 litre water down the drain once a week.

After washing up, leave everything to dry in the air rather than using a cloth, which can harbour germs. If you leave dishes to soak, pour away the water and use fresh, hot water and detergent to wash.

PREVENTING FOOD POISONING

There are some 4.5 million cases of food poisoning a year in the UK, partly owing to increased reliance on takeaways and convenience food. The World Health Organisation (WHO) has identified four main causes of food poisoning:

- preparing food several hours before it is needed and leaving it in a warm place
- not cooking or reheating food thoroughly enough
- not having sufficiently high standards of hygiene in handling and preparing food
- cross-contamination between raw and cooked foods.

At home, all of these are easy to avoid.

GOOD FOOD HYGIENE

- Always buy pasteurized dairy products, such as milk and cheese. Vulnerable groups (the very young, the elderly, pregnant women, and anyone who is ill) should also avoid unpasteurized juices.
- Read and follow the storage instructions on products. Avoid food that is past its 'best before' date, especially if it contains meat or fish.
- Wash your hands with hot water and soap before preparing food. Wash them again if you stop cooking to change a baby's nappy, use the toilet, or if you touch a household pet. Always wash hands after handling raw meat.
- All animals, including dogs, cats, birds, and especially reptiles, can harbour germs which could contaminate food. Keep them away from food preparation areas.
- Fruits and vegetables that are to be eaten raw should be washed and/or scrubbed well and rinsed under running water.

- Clean the inside of the refrigerator and freezer regularly. Keep worktops scrupulously clean.
- Always cook food thoroughly, especially poultry, meat, and eggs. Check that meat juices run clear and eggs are set. Defrost meat, poultry, and fish completely before cooking.
- Eat foods while still piping hot. If allowed to cool to room temperature, they provide the perfect environment for bacteria to multiply.
- If you need to cook in advance, or keep leftovers, store the cooked food either above 60°C or below 10°C. This is vital if the food is to be kept for more than four to five hours, because microbes can thrive in warm food over this length of time. Baby food ideally should not be stored at all unless frozen immediately.
- No food, whether perishables, prepared dishes, or leftovers, should stay out of the fridge for more than two hours.
- Cooked foods are easily contaminated by contact with raw meat — keep them separate at all times. Store raw meat at the bottom of the fridge, so that juices can't drip on to cooked foods. Use different chopping boards and knives for raw meat, and wash thoroughly in hot soapy water between uses.
- Store food in closed containers to protect it from contamination by rodents or insects.
- Reheat food thoroughly, until steaming hot right through, and until liquids boil. This is the best protection against food poisoning, since although proper storage slows bacterial growth, only thorough cooking destroys the organisms.

USING THE FREEZER SAFELY

BUYING FROZEN FOOD

- Choose packs that are well below the top line in the shop's freezer.
- Avoid packs that are damaged, icy, or feel at all soft.
- Check the 'best before' date – some foods have a relatively short freezer life.
- Take a cool box to the supermarket and pack all frozen goods into it together to take home, or buy one of the insulated shopping bags many supermarkets now provide.

FREEZING KNOW-HOW

- Food quality deteriorates if kept frozen for too long. Observe the star ratings on your freezer, and always follow recommendations on packs.
- Use frozen foods systematically – first in, first out. Scribble an expiry date on the lid of the container with ink.
- Putting hot food straight into the freezer makes the overall temperature rise, and also affects the flavour and texture of the food. Refrigerate hot food as soon as possible after cooling and freeze after no more than 90 minutes of chilling.
- Never refreeze food, unless it has been cooked in the meantime.
- Don't cram the freezer too full – you'll prevent cold air from circulating.
- Defrost food either in the fridge or microwave, or by placing packages of frozen food in cold water.

IF THE POWER SUPPLY TO THE FREEZER STOPS

- Keep the door closed if the freezer is likely to be on again within 24 hours.
- Consider removing some food to be thawed, cooked, then refrozen later.
- If you have warning of a power loss, turn your freezer on to fast-freeze – if it has this function – for 30 minutes beforehand.

REFRIGERATOR SENSE

- Get into the habit of using a fridge thermometer to ensure that the temperature remains between 0–5°C / 32–41°F. Put a shelf with a built-in thermometer – a useful feature to look for when buying a new fridge – at the top of a larder fridge. Larder fridges tend to be colder at the bottom, while fridges with a built-in ice box have a more even temperature. It's especially important to keep a check if the temperature of your kitchen varies widely through the year, or if the fridge door is opened frequently.
- Don't put large quantities of hot food into the fridge in one container. Foods do not cool right through as quickly as they should to prevent bacteria multiplying. Divide into smaller, shallow dishes, for faster cooling.
- When storing stuffed meats or poultry, remove the stuffing and refrigerate it separately.
- While a well-stocked fridge helps save electricity, don't overfill the fridge – leave enough space for air to circulate freely.

USING EGGS

Eggs sometimes contain the salmonella bacteria, which can cause stomach upsets and can be particularly harmful to pregnant women, babies, elderly people, and anyone whose immune system may be weak. The Food Standards Agency (FSA) advises that eating raw eggs may pose a health risk, and these vulnerable groups should only eat eggs that have been cooked until the whites and yolks are solid. These groups should also avoid foods made with raw eggs, such as home-made mayonnaise and ice-cream.

HOW LONG WILL FOOD KEEP IN THE FREEZER?

Item	Keep for
Pre-packed frozen meals	3–4 months
Home made soups and casseroles	2–3 months
Mince	3–4 months
Bacon	1 month
Sausages	1–2 months
Ham	1–2 months
Beef steaks and joints	6 months–1 year
Lamb chops and joints	6–9 months
Pork chops and joints	4–6 months
Offal	3–4 months
Leftover cooked meats and meat dishes	2–3 months
Gravies and stock	2–3 months
Poultry: whole	1 year
Poultry: joints	9 months

HOW LONG WILL FOOD KEEP IN THE FRIDGE?

Item	Keep for
Ready-made salads	3–5 days
Ready-made convenience meals	1–2 days
Soups, casseroles	3–4 days
Leftover gravy or stock	1–2 days
Raw pre-stuffed meats, such as chicken breasts	1 day
Raw mince	1–2 days
Raw meats such as steaks, chops, joints	3–5 days
Raw poultry, whole or joints	1–2 days
Offal	1–2 days
Cold cooked meats such as ham	3–4 days
Bacon	1 week
Raw sausages	1–2 days
Leftover cooked meat and meat dishes	3–4 days

Safety at home

Every year, more than 4,000 people die and 3 million are injured in the UK through accidents in the house or garden – that's more than are killed or injured in road accidents. Falls, burns, choking, and electric shocks are among the most common accidents, and many involve poorly maintained or badly placed everyday items. Others are caused by the careless use of electrical equipment. Give your home a safety check.

SEE ALSO Children's safety and health, p148, Don't get hurt, p168, Giving First Aid, p284

HAZARDOUS CHEMICALS

- Read labels and follow instructions when dealing with hazardous substances, including wearing any recommended protective clothing.

- Keep hazardous substances in their original containers and make sure the label remains legible. Never put them in old food containers.

- Don't mix chemical products – some react dangerously with one another. A common mistake is to mix bleach with other cleaning products. Rather, choose a cleaning product that already contains bleach.

- Never pour car fuel, engine oil, paint, paint-cleaning products, or similar substances into the ground. They can contaminate the earth and water supply. Likewise, hazardous chemical waste should not be put in the bin or poured down the drain. Check labels for recommended disposal methods, or contact the Environmental Health department of your local health authority.

A ROOM-BY-ROOM GUIDE

KITCHEN

- If you are planning a kitchen from scratch, keep safety in mind – more accidents happen in the kitchen than anywhere else in the home. There should be adequate workspace beside the cooker, so you have plenty of room both to work and to place hot dishes safely. Ideally, the hob should be close to the sink so that pans don't need to be carried far.

- Turn saucepan handles towards the back of the hob when cooking so they are not knocked off.

- Check that all burners are turned off when you finish. Don't test electric hotplates with your hands.

- Don't use wet cloths to pick up hot pots or lids – the water acts as a highly efficient conductor, making the cloth very hot very quickly.

- Don't hang tea towels or oven gloves on oven handles, and keep them away from the hob.

- Be careful when pulling out oven racks with hot dishes on them. Some racks tilt as they slide out, and can tip the dishes towards you or into the back of the oven. Take the dish right out and deal with it on top of the stove or counter.

- Plates and other china can get extremely hot in a microwave – always use oven gloves to take them out.

- Children should always be supervised in the kitchen.

- It's easy to get distracted and leave pans to boil dry. Get into the habit of setting a kitchen timer if you're leaving the kitchen. Be particularly careful when using a chip pan, and never leave frying food unattended.

- Keep kettles, coffee-makers, and toasters towards the back of worktops.

Ensure flexes don't hang off worktops or trail across the hob. Choose coiled flexes when buying new.

- Switch off and unplug the kettle before filling it.

- If a slice of toast is stuck in the toaster, switch off the appliance at the wall before trying to prise the toast out.

- Wipe spills off the floor immediately, making sure the area is completely dry. Spills that contain oil or grease may have to be washed several times with soapy detergent before they lose their slipperiness.

- Keep knives sharp so that they are easy to use without undue force. Store them in a block, or use blade guards if kept in a drawer. Never leave knives or other sharp objects lying disguised in a sink of soapy water. If you use a dishwasher, store knives point down in the machine. Food-processor blades should be treated with the same caution.

- Wash the insides of glasses, jars, and bottles with a brush or bottle-washer – don't put your hands inside in case the glass breaks.

STAIRS

- Wooden stairs can be slippery, especially if polished or waxed. A non-slip matt paint finish would be safer. Fitted carpets are the safest option, though make sure that stair carpets are well fitted and secured, and check edges regularly.

- Don't put rugs near the top of stairs.

- Stairs should be well lit from top to bottom, and there should be a light switch at both ends.

- Don't leave items lying on the stairs.

LIVING ROOM, HALL, AND BEDROOMS

- Ensure that carpet edges at doorways are well secured.
- Either avoid using rugs on polished floors or secure them with carpet tape.
- Arrange furniture so that you have a clear path through the room.
- Keep rooms well ventilated if you use gas, solid fuel, or oil heaters.
- Always use a fireguard on an open fire.
- Don't place burning incense, candles, or cigarettes near beds or curtains, and be careful about using these items late at night, in case you fall asleep with them still burning (see Fire precautions, p146).
- Check electric blankets regularly for wear – some local authorities offer free checks. Turn off an electric blanket before you get into bed.

BATHROOMS

- Plug-in electrical appliances such as radios, hairdryers, and portable heaters should never be used in the bathroom. Low-voltage electric shavers and tooth-brushes that plug into two-pin sockets are fine. Standard battery-operated radios should be put where they won't get wet or fall into water.

FIRST AID KITS

You can either buy a First Aid kit or assemble a kit yourself, but you should store the items in a clean and easily identifiable waterproof container. It is very important to check your kit regularly and to restock items that have been used or replace items that are out of date. It is also advisable to keep a portable kit handy to take to the site of an emergency.

Basic First Aid kit for home:

- Waterproof container for the kit
- 20 assorted adhesive plasters
- 6 medium First Aid dressings
- 2 large First Aid dressings
- 2 finger dressings
- Antiseptic wipes
- 2 triangular bandages

- Baths and showers can become very slippery, particularly if you live in a soft-water area or have a water softener fitted. Use a rubber anti-slip mat to prevent falls.

THE GARDEN

- Put rakes and other tools away after use. Don't leave them where they could be trodden on.
- Uneven paving slabs, broken concrete, and holes in lawns can cause falls.
- Fit plastic caps (available from garden centres) on the tips of bamboo canes to avoid eye injuries.
- Keep garden chemicals safely out of sight and reach of children.
- Use a plug-in residual current device (RCD) when using any electrical appliance (see Your electricity supply, p60, and Don't get hurt, p168). Keep cables well out of the way when cutting grass, and don't use equipment in wet conditions. Always switch off and unplug garden appliances before checking, lifting, or adjusting. Don't clean electrical items by immersing them in water – wipe with a cloth.
- Wear sturdy shoes to protect your feet when mowing or strimming grass.

- 2 eye pads
- 6 safety pins
- Disposable gloves.

Useful additions:

- Blunt-ended scissors
- Cotton wool (never place directly on a wound)
- Tubular bandage
- Tweezers
- Adhesive tape
- Plastic face shield or pocket facemask
- Notepad and pencil
- Blanket, survival bag
- Torch
- Whistle (to attract attention).

TEN ELECTRICITY SAFETY TIPS

1 Broken light switches and sockets are dangerous. Cover with insulating tape as a reminder not to use until mended.

2 Don't leave lamps without bulbs in them – they could cause an electric shock if touched.

3 Water and electricity are a lethal combination. Always switch electricity off at the mains before washing down walls or using water anywhere near light switches or electric sockets.

4 Always dry your hands before plugging in electrical equipment. Don't turn appliances on if you're standing on a wet floor or if your other hand is in water.

5 Keep small appliances where they can't get wet or fall into water. If electrical equipment or plugs get wet accidentally, allow them to dry completely before using.

6 Make sure extension leads are suitable for the intended task – read the manufacturer's instructions. Add up the wattage of the appliances you're plugging in and check that figure against the wattage the extension lead can carry.

7 Don't leave extension leads coiled while in use, as they may overheat. The longer the lead, the greater the danger of overheating – use the shortest lead you can. Don't plug one extension lead into another.

8 Check plugs to ensure that they have the correct fuse.

9 Don't overload sockets with adaptors – have more sockets fitted instead.

10 Have electrical equipment serviced regularly.

All new furniture must by law be manufactured to meet fire-resistance regulations. This means that upholstered pieces must have fire-resistant fillings, the cover fabric must be match-resistant, and the combination of cover and filling cigarette-resistant. Some covers, mostly those made from natural fibres such as cotton or silk, are exempt from the match-resistance requirement. However, items with these covers must have a fire-resistant interliner. Check for details on an item's swing ticket and permanent labels. Secondhand furniture sold privately may not meet the fire-resistance requirements.

If you own upholstered furniture that was made before the regulations came into effect in the UK in 1988, you can improve its fire-resistance.

- Fit secondary covers – all covers sold nowadays must be match-resistant.
- Use a fire-retardant spray. Check that the spray is water-resistant and suitable for the furniture fabric.
- Have the furniture reupholstered with fire-resistant fabric. You could also replace the filling at the same time, or have a fire-resistant interliner fitted between the old filling and the new outer cover.

CHIP-PAN FIRES

- Don't use water or a fire extinguisher to tackle the fire.
- Don't try and move the pan.
- Switch off the heat under the pan only if you can do so without hurting yourself.
- Use a fire blanket or damp tea towel to smother the fire only if it is small.
- If in any doubt – get out and call the fire brigade.

FIRE PRECAUTIONS

Fire is swift, often stealthy, sometimes deadly. In the UK alone, nearly 500 people die in house fires each year and there are around 60,000 accidental blazes. Chip-pan fires are on the increase, as are fires started by candles and aromatherapy oil burners. Even a small fire can be highly destructive, as well as leaving a trail of smoke damage. As precautions against fire, equip your home with smoke alarms and fire extinguishers, make an action plan in case of fire, and get into the habit of making some basic checks before you go to bed.

FITTING AND USING EXTINGUISHERS

There are four main kinds of fire extinguisher, three of which are shown below. Fire extinguishes are colour coded, usually, but not always, as follows.

Red These are water extinguishers, the most commonly used type, but are suitable only for fires of ordinary solid materials such as wood, paper, some plastics, and textiles. Do not use around electrical equipment or on chip-pan fires.

Black These carbon dioxide extinguishers will tackle fires of flammable liquids, such as oil, petrol, and paint, but not chip-pan fires. They need to be used at close range, and work by starving the fire of oxygen.

They can be used for fires involving electrical equipment.

Blue These dry powder extinguishers are effective on fires involving paper, wood, and plastics and for liquids containing grease and paint, but should never be used on pans containing fat, including chip pans.

Cream These foam extinguishers are not recommended for home use.

In addition **fire blankets** are useful for tackling a chip-pan fire in its early stages, providing you can cover the pan entirely and without hurting yourself, and for wrapping round someone whose clothes are on fire.

- Keep at least one 0.45 kg/1 lb dry powder extinguisher on each floor of your home. Place in the hallway, on landings, in the kitchen, and in the garage.
- Mount extinguishers securely near likely sources of fire, though don't put them near radiators or cookers.
- Make sure extinguishers are clearly visible and easily accessible.
- Make sure everyone in the household knows how to operate extinguishers.
- Replace an extinguisher after use or when the five-year guarantee expires.

WATER EXTINGUISHER
Wood, paper, textiles ✔
Some plastics ✔
Electrics ✗
Chip pans ✗

Safety guard
Piercer
Strike knob
Seal
Water

CARBON DIOXIDE EXTINGUISHER
Oil, petrol, paint ✔
Electrics ✔
Chip pans ✗

Operating lever
Control valve
Safety pin
Pressure relief mechanism
Discharge tube
Gaseous carbon dioxide
Discharge horn
Liquid carbon dioxide
Hose
Nozzle

POWDER EXTINGUISHER
Wood, paper, plastics ✔
Grease, paint ✔
Chip pans ✗

Operating lever
Piercer
Discharge tube
Nozzle
Powder

FITTING SMOKE ALARMS

Smoke alarms are essential, since without them there is little chance of escaping a fire that starts when you are asleep.

Ionization alarms are the cheapest type and detect flaming fires before the smoke gets too thick.

Optical alarms cost more and are better at detecting slow-burning fires, such as those caused by smouldering upholstery.

Either type can be powered by battery or mains, and some models can be connected so that fire detected in one spot raises the alarm throughout the house.

Where to fit

- In a single-floor home, fit a minimum of one, preferably optical, alarm in the area between bedrooms and living rooms.

- To protect two or more floors, fit one alarm at the foot of the stairs and another on each landing. For the best protection, use both ionization and optical alarms, and if possible connect them. If you use just one alarm, site it where the noise will be heard throughout the house even when you are asleep, such as at the top of the stairs.

- Don't put smoke alarms in the kitchen, bathroom, or garage.

- Mount as close to the centre of the ceiling as possible, a minimum of 30 cm/10 in from walls and lights.

Maintenance

- Test batteries monthly. Fit new ones annually.

- Keep the casing clean.

- If cooking fumes trigger false alarms, don't remove the battery. Reposition the alarm where cooking fumes won't trigger it, or fit a silencer attachment, which allows you to turn off nuisance alarms without disabling the alarm permanently.

CARBON MONOXIDE POISONING

At least 50 people die in the UK every year from carbon monoxide poisoning, and many more are hospitalized. Even in small amounts, this invisible, odourless gas is harmful. Carbon monoxide is given off by gas-, oil-, coal-, or wood-burning appliances if they are faulty, the room is badly ventilated, or the chimney or flue is blocked.

SYMPTOMS

If you feel drowsy or develop headaches, chest pains, giddiness, nausea, or diarrhoea and stomach pains when there is no obvious cause, carbon monoxide could be affecting you. Turn off all your appliances and see a doctor immediately.

SPOTTING THE DANGER SIGNS

Carbon monoxide causes:

- sooty stains to appear on or just above appliances

- gas flames, which usually burn blue, to burn yellow or orange

- coal or wood fires to burn slowly or go out.

PROTECTING YOURSELF

- Get your boiler and gas appliances serviced annually by an engineer who is a member of the **Council for Registered Gas Installers** (CORGI).

- Keep your home properly ventilated.

- Never let vents or outside flues become blocked, by climbing plants, for example.

- Have chimneys swept regularly.

- Consider fitting a carbon monoxide detector.

CARBON MONOXIDE DETECTORS

- Buy one that complies with the British Standard BS 7860.

- Fit the detector on the ceiling or wall in any room that contains a boiler, fire, or water heater.

- Place it above door and window height and at least 15 cm/5 in from corners.

- Test the alarm to judge whether it is loud enough to wake you. If you don't think it would wake you, fit a second alarm closer to your bedroom.

Children's safety and health

Every week three children die from accidents in the home in the UK, with those aged up to five being at most risk. Annually, domestic accidents bring more than a million children under 15 to a hospital emergency department, while many more have less serious, but often painful, mishaps. Whether you have children living in the house or as occasional visitors, there are effective precautions you can take to ensure that your home is safe for them.

SEE ALSO Safety at home, p144; Giving First Aid, p284; In the kitchen, p142

WHAT SMALL CHILDREN DO WHEN

0–6 months Not fully mobile, but can wriggle or roll into danger. Never leave on a raised surface, even a bed or sofa.

6–12 months Crawling and pulling themselves up. Keep small objects out of reach. Remove or secure free-standing furniture and other items that could topple onto child.

1–2 years Fully mobile, very inquisitive. Never leave unattended. Will probably taste or spill anything they encounter. Take care with hot drinks when near child. Use a fireguard and a stair gate.

2–3 years Can climb, pull, and twist. Will watch and copy. Will run around and knock things over. Keep valuables out of reach. Don't let child see you do anything dangerous.

3 years onwards Child's skills increase steadily. Continued safety training and frequent reminders of safety rules are important.

PREVENTING ACCIDENTS IN THE HOME

The most serious accidents happen in the kitchen and on the stairs. Young children, up to age four, are most at risk, with boys more accident-prone than girls. Younger children are at more risk of burns, scalds, and poisoning accidents, while older children are more likely to suffer fractured bones. Accidents tend to happen in the late afternoon and early evening, and during holidays or weekends, when tiredness, hurrying, distraction, or unfamiliar surroundings may play a part.

BURNS AND SCALDS

Fires cause almost half of all fatal accidents to children, while scalds can cause painful and disfiguring injuries.

- Keep matches and lighters where children can neither see nor reach them.
- Use a full-sized fireguard with fine mesh, secured to the wall.
- A hot drink spill can still scald a small child 15 minutes after being made. Never hold a hot drink while you have a child on your lap, pass a drink over a child's head, or put a drink down on a low table.
- Turn down your boiler's thermostat a couple of degrees. Always run cold water into a bath first, and test the temperature with your elbow before a small child gets in.
- Place pans on the cooker's back rings, and keep handles turned in.

CHOKING AND SUFFOCATION

- Keep tiny items, like marbles, watch batteries, and coins, away from under-threes. Teach older children to keep small toys out of reach of younger ones.
- Children under six should not be given peanuts to eat. If accidentally inhaled, these could lodge in the lung, causing severe illness.

- Flatten and knot plastic bags when using them for storage.
- Pull-cords on blinds and curtains should be short.
- Shut cats out of rooms where babies sleep, and use a pram net or cot net.

CUTS

- Fit safety glass in low-level windows and doors, or make non-toughened glass safer with shatter-resistant film. Buy greenhouses or cold frames that are safety-glazed, or fence them off.
- Put stickers on large expanses of glass, such as patio doors, to draw attention to them.

DROWNING

Small children can drown in less than 3 cm/1 in of water. Always supervise children when in and near water, and be vigilant when visiting gardens and garden centres.

- Fit safety tops on water butts and drain ponds or fence them securely.
- Empty paddling pools between uses.
- Don't leave buckets or bowls of water unattended.
- Never leave babies or children younger than five alone in the bath. Stay in earshot at bathtime at least until they are six.

FALLS

Over one third of all children's accidents are falls, most of which involve tripping. The worst consequences follow falls from a height, including toppling from high-chairs or prams. Always use, and check, safety harnesses.

- Put safety gates, made to BS 4125 specification, at the top and foot of staircases.
- Board up horizontal balustrades and

vertical ones with wide gaps between struts. Discourage climbing.

- Secure carpet and rugs firmly.
- Fit safety locks on all upstairs windows, but make sure you can locate keys swiftly in an emergency. Don't put furniture – or a pram or buggy – under a window if a child could use it to reach the window.
- Never put baby bouncers on tables.

POISONING

- Always keep household or garden chemicals in their original containers. Buy containers with child-resistant caps.
- Keep chemicals and medicines out of children's sight and reach, preferably locked away. Even seemingly innocuous

preparations, such as iron supplements, can be harmful to children.

- Don't leave alcoholic drinks where children could sample them.
- Check, before buying plants, that leaves and fruits are not poisonous.

HOME TREATMENTS FOR COMMON AILMENTS

Colds In babies, the nose may become blocked, leaving them unable to suck properly. Nose drops help to clear the mucus. For babies over three months and young children, liquid paracetamol helps relieve aches and pains.

Coughs Your pharmacist can advise on the right type of cough medicine, depending on whether the cough is dry or not.

Fever Give liquid paracetamol. Make sure you use the correct dosage for the child's age – too small a quantity will not reduce the temperature. You can also give relief by sponging the top of the child's body with tepid water and allowing it to evaporate.

Diarrhoea and vomiting Give plenty of fluids. Babies under six months become dehydrated more easily than older children, so seek medical advice if they refuse liquid.

Tummy ache Children often complain of this when they have colds or other viral illnesses, because glands in their abdominal area swell and become tender. Give liquid paracetamol to ease the discomfort. Tummy ache can also be caused by constipation. Make sure children have sufficient fibre from fruit, vegetables, and wholegrain cereals and bread. They should also have plenty to drink, every day.

GETTING MEDICAL HELP

NHS Direct (see p158) offers healthcare advice over the telephone or Internet. You're asked a set of questions about symptoms, then advised on how to treat the condition at home, or advised to see your doctor. Going online in the first instance may be quicker than using the telephone, and you will still be put through to a qualified nurse.

Many common childhood conditions disappear by themselves over a few days,

without needing medical intervention. Call a doctor if:

- a child has persistent abdominal pain with vomiting, which could indicate appendicitis
- you suspect meningitis – this disease is uncommon, but symptoms include vomiting, headache, sensitivity to light, a rash that does not disappear when pressed, and wanting to lie down undisturbed.

(see p158)

INTERNET SAFETY

The Internet can be a great tool for children, helping with study and research, as well as offering fun. Unfortunately, there are also dangers out on the World Wide Web.

1 Set ground rules and discuss them with children, so that they understand the reasons for them. Display the rules near the computer.

2 Limit the amount of time children spend on the computer. Set a kitchen timer near the computer.

3 Keep the computer in a general living area, not in a child's bedroom, so you can see what they are looking at.

4 Teach children never to give their name, age, address, or phone number to anyone online.

5 Learn enough about computers and the Internet so that you understand what children are doing.

6 Encourage children to tell you which Web sites they are visiting. This promotes trust and respect.

7 Don't let children enter Internet chat rooms unmonitored.

8 Get to know who the children's online friends are.

9 Install software that will block specific Web sites or filter out those that contain suspect keywords.

IMMUNIZATION

The NHS argues strongly in favour of immunization, and offers nine vaccinations against infectious diseases for children between two months and fourteen years. You can get information from your GP and NHS-sponsored Web sites. For arguments against immunization, check out the Web site of **The Informed Parent**.

Dealing with pests

Some pests are health hazards – rats, mice, and cockroaches carry and spread disease. Others inflict painful bites and stings. Many, such as silverfish, are harmless. Any infestation is an unwelcome invasion, but pests get into the cleanest homes. There are three options: DIY treatment, help from the local Environmental Health department, or calling in private specialists. Take precautions to deter pests.

DETERRING PESTS

- Vacuum thoroughly and regularly.
- Clear away food immediately after a meal.
- Store food in the fridge or in sealed containers.
- Empty the kitchen bin daily.
- Put rubbish out in sealed bags.
- Keep the lid on the dustbin.
- Put food for birds where only birds can get it.
- Clear away leftover pet food.
- Get rid of damp in the home.
- Seal cracks in walls and around skirting boards.

IF YOU'RE STUNG

Some people are allergic to the stings of wasps, bees, and hornets. The poison from these stings can accumulate in the body, with the result that future stings will be more dangerous. If you suffer severe swelling, chest pains, or dizziness after a sting, seek urgent medical attention.

A TO Z OF PESTS

ANTS

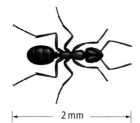

├────── 2mm ──────┤

These will sometimes invade the house in search of food, such as meat or sugar, then establish a trail to the source. Ants are harmless. Store food where they can't get to it. Draw a chalk line across their entrance point to the house to deter them. To exterminate ants, pour boiling water on their nest. If this fails, or the nest is out of sight, use branded chemical treatments, brushing powder into crevices with a small paintbrush. In late summer, newly hatched queen ants swarm from the nest and may enter the house. Vacuum them up.

BEDBUGS

├────── 7mm ──────┤

These insects need warmth, darkness, and a supply of blood from humans or animals to survive. They thrive around the buttons of mattresses and in the crevices of sofas and armchairs, and may also nest behind wallpaper. Their bite does not carry disease but can be extremely irritating, and can cause persistent loss of sleep, resulting in lack of energy, especially in children. Infestations should be treated by a specialist.

BEES

├────── 20mm ──────┤

Never harm a bee – they will not sting unless provoked. Some bees are protected by law – it's illegal to kill them. If a bee is trapped in your house, catch it in a loosely balled tea towel and gently shake free outside. Alternatively catch it in an upended tumbler and slide a piece of paper or card across the bottom. Very rarely, a swarm may settle in a garden away from the hive or even enter a house. Keep children and pets away and phone the police or your local authority. They will contact a registered bee-keeper to come and remove the swarm.

BOOKLICE

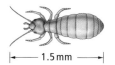

├────── 1.5mm ──────┤

These live on moulds, so attack damp plaster and books, but may also contaminate dry goods such as flour, chocolate, milk powder, and cereals. They are most active between April and November and may come into the house via birds' nests, thatch, or firewood. Treat with a branded insecticide. You will have to throw away all contaminated material. Generally, try to store books in a dry, well-aired room.

CARPET BEETLES

|← 8mm →|

These beetles feed on soiled carpet fibres and may also attack wool, silk, and leather. They thrive indoors in warm, dry conditions. Their larvae may dig long galleries in wood in which to pupate. Vacuum carpets and the floor beneath, paying attention to cracks, crevices, and skirting boards. Check out wardrobes and furniture that has not been moved for a while, too. Spray insecticide into cracks. The eggs are difficult to kill, except by dry-cleaning. If the problem persists, call a professional.

COCKROACHES

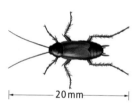

|← 20mm →|

A potential source of serious food poisoning, an infestation of cockroaches can be treated with branded cockroach-killer, but is best treated professionally. Several treatments may be necessary, as the eggs are very resilient and reinfestation is likely. Cockroaches spread bacteria when they walk and excrete. They live in warm, dark places, such as behind a stove or under the floor near central-heating pipes, and also congregate around drains and toilets. They emerge at night to feed on leftovers of human food. If you see cockroaches regularly, in daylight, the infestation will be quite severe. Cockroaches need water, which is why you may find them drowned in a toilet bowl or sink. After eradication, seal cracks, where these insects live. You may be asked to leave treated surfaces for a week, without cleaning, but after that you should clean all surfaces near the infestation, regularly, even those that are out of sight.

FLEAS

|← 3mm →|

Usually brought into the house by cats and dogs, fleas breed fast and their bites can make life a misery for humans. Their eggs, laid in cracks and crevices, are long-lived and difficult to kill. Flea larvae feed on dirt and dust, and the adults feed on blood. Fleas sense their victims' approach by vibrations on the floor, and can jump 30 cm/12 in to land on them. Among the many flea treatments for pets are powders and sprays, dog shampoos, herbal remedies, combing with a flea comb, or using a flea collar. The most effective treatment, available from your vet, is one that is dripped on to the back of the neck. This kills fleas after they bite the animal. Use in conjunction with regular vacuuming. To treat a serious infestation, call a professional.

FLIES

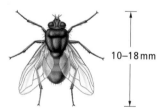

10–18mm

Houseflies feed indiscriminately on excreta and human food, and can transmit diseases and cause diarrhoea. They emerge from their pupae in the warmer weather and breed prolifically, laying eggs in foodstuffs, especially on meat. The eggs hatch into maggots and start to feed. Flies are attracted by the smell of humans and food, and by lower light intensity. Fit fly screens or hang bead or bamboo curtains over open doors. Lace or muslin at open windows will also keep them out. Be scrupulous about food hygiene. Mesh domes used to cover meat are no protection – flies can lay their eggs through the mesh. Uneaten cat- or dog-food is a prime breeding site. Swatting is healthier than fly spray, as is old-fashioned flypaper.

RATS AND MICE

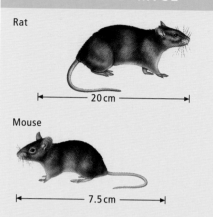

Rat

|← 20cm →|

Mouse

|← 7.5cm →|

THE DANGERS

Rats thrive in sewers. They pose a serious health risk and may be carriers of Weil's disease, which can cause severe muscle pain and even death. Mice can cause serious food poisoning. Both are attracted to easy food sources and to warmth and shelter in which to nest, such as a shed, or a pile of old newspapers under stairs. Rodents can gnaw through cables, pipes, and even concrete. They multiply within weeks of birth, so any infestation needs to be dealt with quickly.

REMEDIES

You can detect the presence of rodents by gnawed material, evidence of droppings, and the smell of their urine. Your best option is to call the experts – local authority extermination services are usually free. DIY remedies are humane traps, baited mousetraps, and dedicated poisons – rodenticides. Keep children away from the infested area. Protect poison bait from pets and wild animals, placing it, for example, in a length of plastic pipe of a diameter small enough to stop a bird or hedgehog from entering (around 2.5 cm/1 in). After rodents have been exterminated, clear out all infected materials, wash the area thoroughly with disinfectant, and block up entry holes. Deter rodents by keeping food in sealed containers.

- **Environmental Health department** (district council or unitary authority). Services and charges vary, but eradication of cockroaches, rats, and mice is usually free. Dealing with other pests costs around £30 (usually half this if you are on benefit).

- **Private firms** Telephone the **British Pest Control Association** on 01332 294288 or visit their Web site – http://www.bpca.org.uk. See also *Yellow Pages* under 'Pest and Vermin Control', but take care to deal with a BPCA-accredited firm – after all, you are inviting someone to use poisons in your home. Get more than one quote. Private firms will be more expensive than the council but will probably offer a quicker response and a wider range of treatments.

DIY TREATMENTS – SAFETY AT HOME

- If you use poisons in the home, don't forget that they can harm or kill other creatures besides your target pest.

- Store poisons in their original containers, away from children and pets.

- Follow the instructions scrupulously.

- Wear a protective mask and rubber gloves. Keep room well ventilated.

- Never use sprays near aquarium fish or near food that is not properly sealed or put away.

- Keep children and animals away from the treated area. Allow the poison to do its work, then wash the area and let it dry. Wash fabrics, and air upholstery thoroughly. Never spray poisons on beds or bedding – call the experts.

FLOUR BEETLES

4 mm

These beetles are occasionally found in flour, cereals, and other dried food stored or bought in unsealed or damaged packaging. Throw out the contaminated food, clean the cupboard thoroughly, and start again, storing food in airtight containers.

HEAD LICE

4 mm

An infestation of head lice can spread quickly through a family, and through a whole class or school. Head lice live on the scalp, biting it and causing inflammation and itching, and laying their tiny pale eggs (nits) near the roots of the hair and behind the ears. Both lice and eggs will die once deprived of the warmth of the scalp. The whole family of a sufferer should use a nit comb and a dedicated non-toxic shampoo, available from chemists and health-food shops. You might want to avoid shampoos containing organophosphates, over which there is some controversy.

MITES

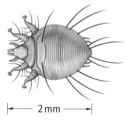

2 mm

Not insects but arachnids (spider family), scabies mites live on blood, burrowing into the skin, usually on the hands. This causes scabies, an extremely itchy rash. The mites are passed on by close contact with a sufferer. Treat with a prescription cream or try tea-tree natural antiseptic oil or ointment. Furniture mites or dust mites, which are harmless in themselves, live in mattresses and elsewhere in the house on flakes of human skin. Their 'dust' or droppings may exacerbate asthma. Vacuum mattresses and upholstery regularly.

MOSQUITOES

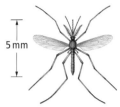

5 mm

Male mosquitoes live on nectar, but the females bite and suck blood from humans and animals. In the tropics, they can transmit malaria and other diseases. In cooler climes, victims may suffer a painful swelling. Mosquitoes are active after sundown, their flight detected by an annoying whine, which stops as they land to feed. Females have lower-pitched whines than males. They lay their eggs on still water – ponds, water butts, even puddles may be breeding-sites. Cover water butts, site ponds away from the house. Be prepared for mosquitoes if you holiday next to a swimming pool. Burn mosquito coils or use plug-in devices with replaceable deterrents. Sleeping with a mosquito net over the bed is more pleasant than using a repellent on the skin. Consider fly screens at the windows.

MOTHS

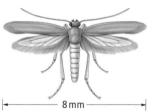

8 mm

Clothes moths lay eggs on wool, then their larvae hatch out and eat it. They will also attack other natural and mixed fibres, especially when soiled with sweat or food. They can damage carpets, bedding, and upholstery, as well as clothes. Brush clothes well to remove eggs and larvae, air them in the sun, and put them away clean in sealed bags or a clean cupboard with sachets of lavender, rosemary, and bay. Camphor mint is a stronger-smelling repellent, but preferable to mothballs – no one wants to smell of naphthalene.

SILVERFISH

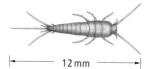

12 mm

These are harmless. They are attracted to damp and can sometimes be found in kitchens and bathrooms, where they feed on cereal crumbs and wallpaper paste. Vacuum them up. Keep food sealed and clean out cupboards. Use an insecticide if necessary. Eliminate damp and they will not return.

TICKS

3 mm

Ticks are arachnid parasites that fasten their mouthparts into the skin of cats, dogs, humans, and other animals. They suck blood and can transmit infections, including Lyme disease, which is rare in the UK, but on the increase. Lyme disease can be serious and even fatal. A red rash of tiny circles is followed by flu-like symptoms. Treatment is with antibiotics. Cover limbs on country walks, and check children's skin and clothing. To remove a tick, grip it with tweezers at the base and twist as you pull. It's important to remove the mouthparts – the old remedy of burning a tick with a lighted cigarette is not recommended. Treat the bite with tea-tree cream or antibiotic cream.

WASPS AND HORNETS

25 mm

Wasps and hornets can give a powerful sting and should be treated with wariness, as their behaviour is unpredictable. Remove as for bees (p150). Alternatively, swat or spray individuals, and remove them carefully once dead. Hornets are rare and their presence probably indicates a nearby nest. Wasp and hornet nests should be destroyed by professionals – don't attempt this yourself. On picnics keep fruit and sweet drinks covered. A glass with a little beer or honeyed water makes an effective wasp trap.

WOODWORM

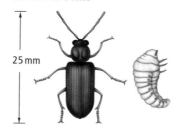

25 mm

Recognize an attack of woodworm by a peppering of tiny holes on the surface of wood – only if there is dust around them are there live woodworm inside. Check secondhand furniture before you buy. Treat a small outbreak with dedicated insecticide. Burn an item you're discarding. Call in professionals if the timbers of the house are infected. See also p196.

See also p196.

NEIGHBOURHOOD ANIMALS

Bats may roost under the eaves of your roof. They feed on insects, they don't damage buildings, and their droppings aren't dangerous. It is illegal to kill or disturb them, or to block their access. For information, contact the **Bat Conservation Trust**.

Birds can be deterred from choosing a nesting site over your conservatory or dormer windows with a wire netting or plastic fringing. Wait until the young have flown before blocking access to nesting places. You could always compensate by siting a bird box on another wall of the house. Bunched wire netting can deter pigeons from perching on ledges. For more details, contact the **Royal Society for the Protection of Birds** (RSPB).

Foxes eat vermin, which may be very welcome, especially in urban areas. Keep outdoor pets safe in cages, and secure runs against burrowing. Secure lids on bins, make bird tables inaccessible. It is illegal to poison or gas foxes.

Moles Deter them with vibrations from a sonic mole-repeller (about £20) or try planting children's windmills in short lengths of metal pipe knocked into the ground. Alternatively, drop mothballs into their holes.

Squirrels Grey squirrels are often regarded as pests. They enjoy nesting in roof spaces, coming and going during daylight. Block up any entrances to the roof space with wire mesh to prevent squirrels from entering. If they have already moved in, call a pest control officer to check there are none actually present, then immediately block up entrances with wire mesh and lop any branches near the roof, which they may be using for access. Use squirrel-proof bird feeders in the garden.

DETERRING OTHER PEOPLE'S PETS

Keep strange cats out of your home by installing a cat flap operated by an electronic tag on your own cat's collar (about £35). People who have no pets of their own can deter dogs and cats with an ultrasonic device called a Dazer. It's harmless but annoying to animal pests, and doesn't affect birds or fish.

The law says that dogs must be kept under proper control by their owners. If a neighbour's dog repeatedly visits your garden and causes a nuisance, and the neighbour does nothing when asked to keep the dog in, call the local police, who will visit the neighbour on your behalf.

Ideas for your garden

There's a lot you can do to produce a garden you want to spend time in, without having to devote too much time looking after it. Start by asking yourself what you want from your garden, how much time and money you have to devote to it, and how much difference you can make in the time you will live there. Ideally, get to know your garden by taking a year to discover what grows there, and which plants thrive best.

COLOUR ALL THE YEAR

Achieve colour throughout the seasons with these plants:

Spring Comfrey (white, pink, or blue flowers and furry grey-green leaves), primula (coloured primroses on tall stems), violet.

Summer Perennial geranium (long-flowering pink and blue varieties), heuchera (pretty green or bronze foliage plant), lavender.

Autumn Gladioli, Japanese anemone (tall stems, pink flowers), scarlet lobelia (scarlet flowers, red foliage).

Winter Dogwood (tall bushes with straight stems in yellow, green, and bright red), bergenia (big leathery green/red leaves, pink or white flowers in early spring), euphorbia (evergreen, lime green flowers).

TIPS OF THE TRADE

Spending even a few minutes every day doing small, routine gardening jobs will stop you feeling a garden is getting out of control.

Peter Turner, retired gardener

LOOKING AFTER A LAWN

If you have just one hour a week to devote to the garden, mow the lawn – a neat swathe of green will throw the wildest flower borders into flattering relief. Edge the lawn by cutting the turf with a spade, or trimming it with long-handled shears or a strimmer.

BUYING A LAWNMOWER

The lawnmower will probably be your most expensive piece of garden equipment. Before you buy one, think about what demands you'll be putting on it (see below). A grass box collects cuttings as you mow – if you don't have one, you'll have to rake them up by hand. Cuttings left on the lawn will die there and get trodden indoors.

Electric hover mowers are lightweight and easy to use. They can manage banks and slopes, and are ideal for very small areas. Not good on long tough grass, or bumpy ground; you may need an extension lead. May not collect grass cuttings.

Petrol mowers will tackle fairly long grass and relatively uneven terrain. With no electric lead, lawn size is no object.

Some have to be pushed along, others move forward as they cut. Many models come with a grass box. They are generally more expensive. They are also much sturdier, but are heavier and more difficult to start. Make sure you can operate the pull-start before you buy.

Strimmers are used for cutting uneven lawn edges and trimming back clumps of weeds. Electric strimmers are lightweight and not up to sustained heavy work, such as cutting nettles. Petrol strimmers are powerful but heavy. Make sure you can operate the pull start before you buy.

ENTERTAINING OUTDOORS

A south- or west-facing patio with durable wooden seating and a barbecue area is good for entertaining. Trellises thick with climbers such as sweet-smelling honeysuckle provide privacy and a certain amount of noise insulation. Shelter a hot spot with a pergola covered with grape vines.

ATTRACTING WILDLIFE TO YOUR GARDEN

- Avoid all chemical pesticides and fungicides and use only organic fertilizer – manure or compost.
- A pond and bog garden will encourage frogs, toads, and newts, as well as snails, tiny crustaceans, dragonflies, and waterboatmen. Provide rocks under which creatures can hide and create shelving 'beaches' to help them get out of the water.
- Nectar-producing flowers attract butterflies, moths, and bees. Try valerian, phlox, buddleia, cornflowers,

evening primrose, snapdragon, hollyhock, and marigolds.
- Birds will come to feed on insects, seeds, and berries. For fruit, try holly, pyracantha, crab apples, rowan, and elder. Hang up feeders of peanuts and wild birdseed – black sunflower seeds are a favourite – where predators can't reach. Encourage squirrels with nuts and seeds, but use at least one squirrel-proof feeder (available from the **RSPB** or pet shops).
- Ground-cover plants, bushes, and climbers give good shelter for wildlife.

PLANNING FOR AN EASY LIFE

HARD SURFACES

Flower beds and lawns require constant attention. Cut down on them by laying hard surfaces that need no more than sweeping, and can provide an extension to the living area and a home for seating, a barbecue, and tubs. Sensitively planned, **terraces, patios, and paths** can offer variety and interest for the eye: consider sweeping and geometric shapes and use a combination of materials to provide features such as borders and radiating patterns. Choose from stone slabs, bricks, paving stones of different shapes and sizes, tiles, cobbles, slate, granite setts (paving blocks), timber rounds, decking, railway sleepers, large and small stones, and many types of gravel. Compare prices at garden centres, quarries, sand and gravel suppliers, and stone merchants (all in *Yellow Pages*), and consider using local stone, particularly any that matches the construction materials of your house.

BOUNDARIES

For permanent, no-maintenance privacy, nothing beats a **brick wall**, if you can afford the outlay. A small, south-facing walled garden provides shelter from the wind and a suntrap in which to relax.

Good fencing is durable and almost maintenance-free. For something more original than standard fencing panels,

consider **reed fencing**, which lasts up to 25 years (like thatch, also made from reeds), as does **woven wicker fencing**, which can be custom-made. Contact garden centres or see *Yellow Pages*.

TUBS AND POTS

Containers soften patio areas and you can take them with you when you move. Build up your collection gradually with spectacular giant pots for specimen plants such as palms and bamboo. The secret for successful multiple planting is fullness. Create an abundant summer display with bedding plants bought in trays or plugs (usually annuals, thrown out when the flowers die), then ornamental foliage plants and trailing flowers. For spring, plant bulbs in tubs at two depths, forcing them to compete with each other for flower space.

EXTRA-LOW MAINTENANCE

Free-seeding flowers (such as evening primrose), self-clinging climbers (such as ivy), and hardy perennials (such as sedum or catnip) need little care.

PICK YOUR OWN

Fruit trees, such as apples and pears, need less attention than soft fruit and most vegetables. It's easy enough, however, to plant a few runner beans with other climbing plants up a trellis, for a fresh summer crop.

PLANTS THAT DO THE WORK FOR YOU

GROUND-COVER

Cotoneaster is a fast-growing evergreen that spreads vigorously.

Creeping juniper is a compact, low-growing evergreen shrub that tolerates shade.

Ornamental dead-nettles spread fast. They have variegated evergreen leaves and spikes of yellow, white, or purple flowers.

Periwinkles have glossy evergreen leaves and spread quickly, producing blue, white, or mauve star-shaped flowers in spring.

Lady's mantle, with light green hairy leaves and lime green flowers, is a hardy perennial (meaning it comes up year after year).

CLIMBERS

On a **south- or west-facing** boundary, try Russian vine – also called 'mile-a-minute'. This deciduous climber may grow 4 m/13 ft a year and reach an eventual 12 m/40 ft. Be prepared to cut it back regularly. Hop is a very fast-growing deciduous climber – up to 6 m/20 ft a year – and the hops make attractive decorations when they are cut and dried.

On **north and east-facing** boundaries, grow a climbing hydrangea – a very tolerant shade-loving plant with delicate white parasols of flowers – or a Virginia creeper, which has magnificent crimson leaves in autumn.

STRUCTURE PLANTS

When planting a bed, first site plants that give a permanent outline of strong shapes. Good choices include barberry (mounds of dark red or green foliage), dwarf conifers, skimmia (evergreen with pink flowers in winter), and choisya (elegant evergreen with scented white flowers in late autumn).

NO MORE WEEDS

Keeping down weeds is the most time-consuming job in any garden.

- Make sure new beds are completely weed-free before planting. Do this without digging, by laying old carpet or stout black polythene over the bed for a whole growing season.

- Lay woven polypropylene before spreading gravel on paths. This allows rainwater to drain away while forming a weed-proof barrier. Create gravel beds the same way, cutting a

cross in the membrane and planting through it.

- Grout paving with cement, or sow cracks with creeping thyme or violets.

- Allow slow-growing shrubs (such as holly and box) to establish by thickly covering the ground around them with straw to stop weeds growing.

- Careful use of ground-cover plants can fill out a bed, leaving no room for weeds (see right). Plant bulbs among them for spring surprises.

TOP EASY-GROW PLANTS

STRUCTURE PLANTS

Yucca Tall palm with spectacular perfumed flower spikes.

Cordyline Long spikes radiate from central growth. Bronze, red, or green. Excellent grown singly in tubs or urns.

Artichoke Tall, grey-green giant. The artichokes develop into spectacular purple thistle flowers. Cut down in autumn to grow again.

SHRUBS FOR HEDGING

Osmanthus Holly-like evergreen. Several varieties, including slow-growing variegated and faster growing green-leaved osmanthus, which has white, delicately perfumed flowers.

Escallonia Evergreen bush with apple-blossom pink flowers.

Box Small-leaved slow-growing evergreen. Ideal for low decorative hedging (parterre).

SELF-SEEDING FLOWERS

Foxglove Tall pink, yellow or white spikes, loved by bees. Grow from seed for flowering in summer.

Verbascum Tall dramatic spikes of yellow or old pink/buff flowers. Grow from seed for flowering in summer.

Borage Tall herb with furry grey-green leaves and vivid blue star-shaped flowers that look wonderful frozen in ice cubes. Attracts bees.

Fennel Tall herb for back of border. Frondy aromatic leaves in green or bronze, yellow flowers, decorative edible seedheads.

PATIO VEGETABLES

Try tomatoes and courgettes in growing bags outdoors – see What to do in summer. Be prepared to buy tomato feed to give every week, and in hot weather water thoroughly at least once a day. Grow baby carrots and radishes in tubs.

THE GARDENING YEAR

WHAT TO DO IN SPRING

- Plant out container-grown shrubs, trees, roses, and hardy perennials (plants that flower year after year). Bare-rooted plants – those grown in open ground and dug up for sale – are best planted in the colder months. Water plants well, then surround with a layer of compost. Do the same for established plants. Deadhead flowering shrubs and remove suckers. Prune shrubs that flower on new shoots to encourage growth. Every few years take out shrubs from patio pots, cut back their roots, and replant in new compost.

- In early to mid-spring, put in snowdrop plants, which take far better than snowdrop bulbs. Plant summer-flowering bulbs in the ground or in pots. In late spring, cut grass as bulbs die down. Never strim bulbs off soon after flowering – they won't reappear.

- In late spring, prune shrubs that flower in winter or early spring.

- Sow seed or lay turf for a new lawn in mid- to late spring.

- Sow vegetable seed, biennials (plants that last for two years), and annuals (plants that last for one season only) in finely raked seedbeds or in containers. Plant seeds of regularly used herbs and salad vegetables in successive sowings.

- Prune back shrubby herbs. Use rooting powder and plant cuttings of woody herbs, such as lavender and rosemary. Plant out container-grown herbs.

WHAT TO DO IN SUMMER

- Water plants – especially those in pots – as necessary. Deadhead flowers unless you want decorative seedheads to develop. Stake and tie tall plants.

- With your thumb and forefinger, remove side shoots of ornamental shrubs to stop them growing into branches. This will produce plants known as standards (a bushy head on a tall stem). Train new shoots of climbers and rambling roses by tying to supports.

- Sow seed of early-flowering perennials (hardy plants that will continue to grow for three years or more), annuals, and biennials.

- Buy tomato plants to grow in bags, with stakes. Remove small shoots between stem and established shoots. Pinch off growing top in August. Train bean plants up a trellis or choose a low-growing variety. Sow purple-sprouting broccoli for spring, and salad vegetables.

- Plant autumn-flowering bulbs by late summer. Stop mowing the grass when they start poking through the lawn. Plant out bulbs grown in pots after the foliage has died down. Lift early-flowering bulbs and divide the clumps to make more plants. Tulips flower better if moved each year.

- Harvest herbs and cut well back after flowering, or earlier if flowers are not to be used. Sow winter and spring crops of herbs in late summer.

WHAT TO DO IN AUTUMN

- Dig open ground to turn over weeds and add organic fertilizer.

- Plant container-grown and bare-rooted trees, shrubs, and hardy perennials. Use a dibber (a tool with graduated depth markings on the side, used for poking a hole in the ground) to plant spring-flowering bulbs, such as daffodils, crocuses, and miniature irises, in pots, beds, or in the lawn. Transplant established shrubs. Lift and divide clumps of perennials that have spread.

- Sow salad rocket and spinach in open ground for picking throughout the winter. Dig over empty beds and dig in well-rotted manure.

- Add organic fertilizer under shrubs and trees. Check stakes and ties to protect plants against wind damage. Protect tender plants against frost – use fleece (a lightweight material available by the metre in garden centres), bracken, or straw, or provide shelter, moving pots of delicate plants indoors.

- Cut and clear all dead and dying growth. Cut hardy perennials right back. Dead-head flowers, unless seed heads are decorative. Prune deciduous shrubs, fruit trees, and bushes. Clip evergreen hedges. Have a bonfire for twigs and diseased wood.

- Lay turf or sow seed for lawns ready for autumn rains.

- Bring winter-flowering plants, such as orchids, indoors.

WHAT TO DO IN WINTER

- As long as the ground is not frozen hard, you can plant deciduous container-grown and bare-rooted trees, shrubs, and hardy perennials. Sow perennial seed in containers.

- Carry out layering – peg down a shoot of a woody plant so it takes root and becomes a new plant in its own right. The new plant can be moved once it is established.

- Protect raised ponds against icing over by laying planks across them or use a plastic cover. Or float a ball on the surface, which you can remove to provide a hole through any ice that does form.

- Service the lawn mower and other equipment.

- Mow grass only if necessary, when the grass is dry, to prevent damage to the lawnmower.

- Prepare seedbeds for spring and summer planting: weed the beds, dig in fertilizer, and rake the surface.

- In an unheated greenhouse or conservatory, keep plants nearly dry to stop roots freezing. If necessary, cover them with fleece or surround them with straw or bracken. Bury small pots in sand.

- Prune ornamental vines and deciduous climbers that flower on new wood.

- Tie up ramblers and climbers loosened by the wind.

WHAT PLANTS LIKE

- Some plants are better suited to some types of soil than others. Buy an inexpensive soil testing kit, or simply choose plants that grow well in neighbourhood gardens.

- Light sandy soils drain freely and benefit from enriching and bulking out with organic fertilizer. Clay soils are heavy, fertile, and retain water. To lighten them, add potash or mushroom compost.

- Vegetables, fruit, herbs, and many flowers need full sun. In general, evergreens and woodland plants are more tolerant of shade.

BUYING PLANTS

- Look for healthy plants with good shape, and plenty of new growth. Don't buy plants with a mass of roots sticking out under the pot, or choked with weeds or moss.

- Swap plants with neighbours or buy from growers at markets and sales for good value.

PLANTING FROM POTS

- Remove plants from pots by holding them securely upside down and banging the pot sharply against a hard surface.

- Dig a hole about twice the size of the root ball or container. Put a layer of compost in the bottom, and sprinkle on fine soil. Put in the plant. If the soil is not wet, fill the hole with water and wait for it to drain away. Pack the hole with soil, keeping the plant upright. Smooth the soil around the plant and tamp down well.

- Soak bare-rooted trees and shrubs in a bucket of water for several hours before planting. Stake young trees while planting.

WEB SITES AND ADDRESSES

Allergy UK, Deepdene House, 30 Bellgrove Road, Welling, Kent DA16 3PY
phone: 020 8303 8525; fax: 020 8303 8792;
e-mail: info@allergyuk.org
Web site: www.allergyuk.org

Allergy UK gives a seal of approval to products found to be beneficial to allergy sufferers, and offers other information, advice, and support.

B&Q
Web site: www.diy.com

Click through to the DIY Advice section for reference information on gardening, decorating, building, carpentry, electrical issues, and plumbing.

Bat Conservation Trust, 15 Cloisters House, 8 Battersea Park Road, London SW8 4BG
phone: 020 7627 2629; fax: 020 7627 2628;
Web site: www.bats.org.uk

Gives information about bats, and includes a section on how they are protected by law.

British Pest Control Association (BPCA), Ground Floor, Gleneagles House, Vernongate, Derby DE1 1UP
phone: 01332 294288; fax: 01332 295904;
e-mail: enquiry@bpca.org.uk
Web site: www.bpca.org.uk

Fire Kills
Web site: www.firekills.gov.uk

Home Office Web site on fire prevention.

FireNet International
Web site: www.fire.org.uk

Contains fire safety advice, including information about the different types of fire extinguisher.

Goldfish, phone: 0800 88 55 55;
e-mail: customer.services@goldfish.com
Web site: www.goldfish.com/guides/guide.html

Buying tips for domestic equipment.

Grandma Knows Best
e-mail: g-k-b@enquire.fsnet.co.uk
Web site: www.g-k-b.fsnet.co.uk

Tips on a wide range of domestic subjects.

HM Land Registry, 32 Lincoln's Inn Fields, London WC2A 3PH
phone: 020 7917 5996; fax: 020 7917 5934;
e-mail: marion.shelley@landreg.gsi.gov.uk
Web site: www.landreg.gov.uk

Explanation of the role of the land registration agency for England and Wales. There are reports on property prices, links to regional offices, and details of how to obtain online access to registry documents.

House Contact Centre, PO Box 50, Leeds LS1 1LE
For general enquiries, phone the number on the top of your gas or electricity bill;
fax: 0845 604 0304;
e-mail: house@house.co.uk
Web site: www.house.co.uk

British Gas Web site.

Immunisation Programme, Department of Health, Room 602A, Skipton House, 80 London Road, London SE1 6LH
phone: 020 7972 3807; fax: 020 7972 5758;
Web site: www.immunisation.org.uk

Information on immunization from the National Health Service (NHS).

Insolvency Service, phone: 020 7291 6895;
Web site: www.insolvency.gov.uk

Help and advice for dealing with personal and corporate insolvency.

Mailing Preference Service (MPS), DMA House, 70 Margaret Street, London W1W 8SS
phone: 020 7291 3310; fax: 020 7323 4226;
e-mail: mps@dma.org.uk
Web site: www.mpsonline.org.uk

Register free with this organization to avoid receiving unwanted junk mail. You can also block unwanted telephone, fax, and email contact via this route.

National Asthma Campaign, Providence House, Providence Place, London N1 0NT
Asthma Helpline: 0845 7 01 02 03;
head office: 020 7226 2260;
fax: 020 7704 0740
Web site: www.asthma.org.uk

Offers news, research, and other information for asthma sufferers.

NHS Direct, phone: 0845 46 47
Web site: www.nhsdirect.nhs.uk

Extensive resource from the National Health Service (NHS). Here you can search the NHS A–Z database for access to medical information.

Office of Fair Trading, Fleetbank House, 2-6 Salisbury Square, London EC4Y 8JX
phone: 08457 22 44 99; fax: 020 7211 8800;
e-mail: enquiries@oft.gsi.gov.uk
Web site: www.oft.gov.uk

Offers information regarding all aspects of being a consumer, help on specific topics, such as general rights, credit, and debt.

Partnership for Food Safety Education
Web site: www.fightbac.org

US-based resource for information on food safety and how to prevent harmful bacteria from spreading. Some of the articles on the site are slanted towards the USA, but most of the material is relevant to any food preparation. Find out about the four steps to safe food preparation: clean, separate, cook, and chill.

Pharmacy Direct, Howarth Lodge, 7 Reading Road, Pangbourne, Berkshire RG8 7LR
phone: 01189 845922; fax: 01189 845846;
e-mail: customerservice@pharmacydirect.co.uk
Web site: www.pharmacydirect.co.uk

Royal Society for the Prevention of Accidents (ROSPA), Edgbaston Park, 353 Bristol Road, Edgbaston, Birmingham B5 7ST

phone: 0121 248 2000; fax: 0121 248 2001;
e-mail: help@rospa.co.uk
Web site: www.rospa.com/CMS

General safety advice.

Royal Society for the Protection of Birds (RSPB), The Lodge, Sandy, Bedfordshire SG19 2DL Tel: 01767 680551
Web site: www.rspb.co.uk

Provides online news and local contact details, as well as information on birds in the UK.

Sort-It-Out, Inc.
e-mail: marshasims@aol.com
Web site: www.marshasims.com

Sort-It-Out, Inc offers quizzes, tips, and products for getting organized and freeing your workspace of clutter.

Surf
phone: 0800 444200
Web site: www.surf.co.uk

Web site of leading detergent manufacturer. There are lots of laundry hints.

Informed Parent, PO Box 870, Harrow, Middlesex HA3 7UW phone: 020 8861 1022
Web site: www.informedparent.co.uk

Publishes a bulletin with information on the arguments against vaccination.

National Association of Citizens Advice Bureaux, Myddelton House, 115-123 Pentonville Road, London N1 9LZ
e-mail: adviceguide@nacab.org.uk
Web site: www.adviceguide.org.uk

Covers advice for England, Scotland, Wales, and Northern Ireland and a wide range of topics from money and employment to housing, education, consumer affairs, and the legal system. Enables you to pinpoint your nearest CAB.

Sleep Council
phone: 01756 791089;
e-mail: info@sleepcouncil.org.uk
Web site: www.sleepcouncil.org.uk

Advice on buying a bed.

Trading Standards Institute, 4-5 Hadleigh Business Centre, 351 London Road, Hadleigh, Essex SS7 2BT
phone: 0870 872 9000; fax: 0870 872 9025;
e-mail: institute@tsi.org.uk
Web site: www.tradingstandards.gov.uk

Official government Web site of Trading Standards. This site gives a broad range of information, from UK consumer rights when buying products to recent safety warnings and product recalls. You can find your nearest Trading Standards Office by typing in your postcode.

CORGI, 1 Elmwood, Chineham Business Park, Crockford Lane, Basingstoke, Hants RG24 8WG
phone: 01256 372200;
e-mail: enquiries@corgi-gas.com
Web site: www.corgi-gas.com

CHAPTER SEVEN

Basic
DIY

The must-have toolkit

You can't tackle any DIY job without the right tools. Start by buying the essential tools needed for the most basic jobs around the home – the must-have toolkit – and add to your collection as your skills and requirements grow. Specialist tools that you rarely need to use can always be rented from a tool hire place – see p162.

ADHESIVES

There are dozens of different adhesives on the market. Many are one-job products, such as wallpaper paste, ceramic tile adhesive, and contact adhesive for plastic laminates. Others are more versatile, and are worth having in your toolkit ready for use.

PVA woodworking adhesive Also known as white glue, this adhesive will cope with almost all woodworking tasks. A waterproof exterior grade is available for use on outside woodwork. It is also sold in large tins for use as a building adhesive and sealer.

Epoxy-resin adhesive This two-part adhesive can be used to stick metal, glass, china, masonry, rubber, and most hard plastics as well as wood and manufactured boards. Too expensive for large-scale projects, it is used mainly for repair work or where a very strong bond is essential.

Cyanoacrylate adhesive Better known as superglue, this adhesive will stick a wide variety of materials including human skin, so must be handled with care. It is a thin adhesive with no gap-filling properties (unlike epoxy-resin adhesive), and used mainly for small-scale repair work, bonding well-fitting parts back together.

THE ESSENTIALS

Power drill Essential for drilling fixing holes in wood and board, and also for making holes in walls when doing jobs such as putting up shelves. Choose between mains-powered or cordless drills, which run on rechargeable batteries and come complete with a battery charger. Mains drills are generally cheaper, but a cordless drill can be used anywhere without needing a mains supply, and can also be used as a power screwdriver. For all-round convenience, choose a cordless drill with variable speed control, reverse gear, and hammer action (for making holes in walls). Battery power starts from 7.2 volts (V). A 12 V or 14.4 model should be powerful enough for most jobs you'll want to tackle. Buy an extra battery so you always have a charged-up spare available when you're using the drill.

Drill bits These fit in the jaws (called the chuck) of your drill and actually cut the hole you're making. You need three types – twist drill bits for small holes in wood, flat wood bits for larger-diameter holes, and masonry drill bits for holes in solid walls. Buy a set of twist drill bits made from high-speed steel (HSS) rather than the cheaper carbon steel, in sizes up to 10 mm/⅜ in diameter. Buy flat wood bits individually or in sets – common sizes are 12 mm/½ in, 16 mm/⅝ in, 19 mm/¾ in, 22 mm/⅞ in, and 25 mm/1 in. Buy masonry drill bits singly as you need them, picking a size (usually 6 mm or 6.5 mm) that matches the plastic wall plug used for making screwed fixings into walls.

Tape measure The best is a retractable steel tape measure. Several sizes are available, from 2 m/6 ft 6 in upwards. The most versatile is the 5 m/16 ft size, which will take most room measurements as well as coping with smaller measuring needs. Tape measures are usually marked in both metric and imperial measurements, so you can use whichever system you prefer. Use

the tape measure as a handy converter between the two systems. Buy one with a lock that holds the tape in the extended position.

Trimming knife You need a sharp knife for a variety of DIY jobs. There's a choice of three types – fixed blade, retractable blade, and snap-off blade. Fixed and retractable blade knives have double-ended blades. When the cutting edge gets blunt, you reverse it to use the other end, before replacing it with a new blade. The retractable blade knife has a blade carrier that can be withdrawn into the knife handle – safer for storage and carrying the knife around. The snap-off blade knife has segmented blades – you snap off the blunt tip to expose a new sharp edge. Retractable-blade knives are the most expensive, but definitely the safest and most versatile.

Screwdrivers Screws come in all shapes and sizes, with three common head types, so you need screwdrivers to cope with all variations. For screws with slotted heads, you need a flat-tipped screwdriver with a blade about 125 mm/5 in long, plus a smaller electrician's screwdriver for coping with small screws like the ones in plugs. Add a No. 2 Phillips cross-tip screwdriver, which will cope with cross-head screws (Phillips and Pozidriv) in the most common sizes. Sets containing a mixture of screwdriver types and sizes are often cheaper than buying tools individually, and you'll get a plastic case to keep them in.

Hammer Essential for driving nails and pins, and for assembling and dismantling things that need a bit of brute force. The best all-rounder is a claw hammer with a metal or glass-fibre handle rather than a wooden one, and a head weight of 16 oz or 20 oz (hammers still come in imperial sizes). Use the claw opposite the head for pulling out old or badly driven nails.

Cordless power drill

Screwdrivers

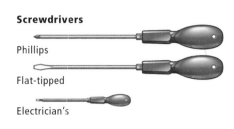

Phillips

Flat-tipped

Electrician's

Crescent pattern adjustable spanner

Countersink drill bit

Masonry drill bit

Tenon saw

Pliers

Tape measure

Hacksaw

Junior hacksaw

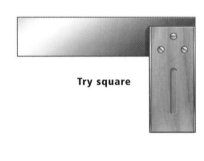

Try square

Claw

Shaft

Claw hammer

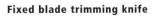

Fixed blade trimming knife

Spirit level

Illustrations not to scale

continued

Local hire shops stock a wide range of hand and power tools and access equipment. If you need a specialist tool for a particular job and can't justify the expense of buying it, or you want to decorate the outside of your house and have nowhere to store a ladder, hiring what you require for the duration of the job is the obvious answer.

Floor sanders You need industrial floor sanders for large areas like floors. They're expensive and bulky. Hire.

Drain rods Useful to have around, but the long rods are unwieldy to store: probably hire.

Power saws Good-quality power saws are fairly pricey, and budget versions are unlikely to last long. If you're planning to do a fair amount of woodwork over the years, invest in a good circular saw and/or jigsaw; otherwise, hire.

Ladders, steps, and access platforms Consider buying a dual- or multi-purpose ladder that converts from a stepladder to a straight or extension ladder. However, you may have nowhere to store ladders, and certainly may not be able to store a ladder long enough for high outside work or platforms for staircase work. It may well be worth hiring these.

Steam wallpaper strippers Recently, compact, lightweight budget versions have come on the market that cost little over £20 and do the job very efficiently. If you're stripping more than one wall, it's probably worth buying rather than hiring.

Concrete mixers Expensive to buy, bulky to store, unlikely to be needed more than once. Hire.

Vibrating plate compactors Petrol-driven plate vibrators ram paving blocks into place. Hire.

Concrete breakers Hire.

Saws You will need a saw for cutting wood to length – to fit a shelf, for example – and the best type to buy is a tenon saw. This has a rectangular blade about 60 cm/ 2 ft long, with a folded strip of brass or steel along its top edge. It's designed for cutting woodworking joints, but will cope with most routine sawing jobs. Add a small or junior hacksaw and some replacement blades to your toolkit, for cutting metal and plastic – things like a rusty screw or a length of curtain track. It will also cut small pieces of wood at a pinch.

Power saws If you plan to work with man-made boards such as medium-density fibreboard (MDF), invest in a power jigsaw. This has a short blade projecting from the base (called the soleplate) of the saw, and cuts on the upstroke. It's a very versatile tool, allowing you to make straight, curved, and angled cuts as well as internal cut-outs away from the edge of the workpiece, such as a hole in a door for a letter box. You can fit different blades for cutting wood, board, metal, plastic, and even ceramic tiles. Buy a jigsaw with variable speed control and a dust bag or vacuum cleaner attachment.

Spirit level Essential for setting things like shelves truly horizontal or vertical. Buy one about 30 cm/1 ft long, with a metal or plastic body, a vial in each edge for setting levels, and another in one end for checking verticals.

Gripping tools A pair of pliers will do all sorts of useful gripping and pulling jobs. They also function as makeshift spanners for small nuts and bolts, and their jaws will cut wire. Buy a pair with insulated handles, as they are more comfortable. An adjustable spanner grips nuts and bolts more securely than pliers and will be invaluable for jobs such as tightening plumbing connections. Pick a crescent-pattern type, with jaws that open to about 30 mm.

Try square A template used for marking cutting lines on wood square to its edges, and for checking that internal and external corners are at right angles. The wood or metal handle (the stock) has a steel blade set at 90° to it.

GETTING SERIOUS

Bolster chisel A wide-bladed steel chisel for cutting bricks and chopping out plaster, this can also be used as a lever for lifting floorboards. It is usually driven with a club hammer, which has a stubby wooden handle and a heavy, squared-off head.

Cartridge gun Forces fillers, mastics, and adhesive out of a tubular cartridge. Bought with the cartridge it's designed to fit.

Filling knife A flexible-bladed tool used to press in and smooth filler when repairing damage to wood and plaster surfaces. Several widths are available – the most useful are 25 mm/1 in and 75 mm/3 in wide.

Nail punch A tapered steel rod about 10 cm/4 in long, which you locate over the head of a nail and strike with a hammer. This punches the nail head below the wood surface so it can be hidden with wood filler.

Power sander Sanding surfaces by hand is hard, time-consuming work, and a power sander will speed things up enormously. Several types are available. One of the most useful all-round performers is the eccentric or random-orbital sander, which moves circular sanding discs in a scrubbing action. They are attached to the sander's baseplate with a Velcro-type fastening. Holes in the discs align with holes in the baseplate so the tool can extract the sanding dust into a dust bag or, via a hose attachment, to a vacuum cleaner.

Surform rasps, files, and planes Shaping tools for wood that have toothed and pierced cutting surfaces, like kitchen graters. They cut wood and clear the shavings very efficiently. The planer file surform is the most versatile, doubling up as a wood plane and a shaping file. Files and rasps are used to shape rough edges, particularly in small areas. A plane smooths broad surfaces of wood.

Nail punch

Bolster chisel

Smoothing plane

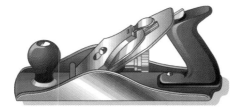

USEFUL EXTRAS

Check out whether these tools might be useful for the jobs you plan.

Firmer chisel

Bevel-edged firmer chisel
Useful for working into angles

Mortise chisel
For cutting mortises (deep slots) into wood for jointing

Cross-cut saw
A general purpose saw designed for cutting timber across the grain

Cross pein hammer
The wedge side is used to start small nails and pins and the smaller head weights (3oz and 6 oz) are called pin hammers

Illustrations not to scale

INVESTING IN A PORTABLE WORKBENCH

If you're planning to do a fair amount of DIY, consider investing in a portable workbench, which can be folded flat when not in use and carried to wherever you are working. It is designed to hold planks of wood steady for sawing, cutting, and gluing. The two planks that form the work surface can be individually adjusted with handles so that they act as a vice, gripping flat or tapered bits of wood between them. Plastic pegs fit into holes on the work surface to hold bits of wood of varying shapes.

If you don't have a portable workbench, you'll need a strong, steady table and a lightweight vice or a bench hook. You can make a bench hook yourself with a short plank of wood and two flat strips of wood glued or nailed on opposite sides and at opposite ends to each other. One of these strips hooks onto a work surface, while the other supports the wood you are working on (see illustration on p165).

Workbench

▶ Useful skills

Mastering some basic techniques will make you competent at DIY. These include working with wood and manufactured boards – the staple ingredients of many DIY projects; assembling things with nails, screws, and adhesives; and making secure fixings to walls, floors, and ceilings. Armed with these skills and your essential tool kit (see p160), you'll be equipped for a surprisingly wide range of jobs and projects.

METRIC OR IMPERIAL?

Many DIY jobs involve taking and working with accurate measurements. Some DIY products (such as wood) are sold only in metric sizes, while others (such as boards) come in metric equivalents of old imperial sizes. Working in metric is more accurate, but if you are more comfortable with imperial measurements, use them. Tape measures are almost all dual-standard, so you can easily convert measurements between the two systems.

If you prefer to use a calculator, 1 in = 25.4 mm and 1mm = 0.03937 in.

TIPS OF THE TRADE

Multi-function power tools seem a good-value option, however it can become irritating to have to adjust the tool for different functions during a job. If you have a lot to do but want to keep down costs, buy one dedicated tool and consider hiring others.

Andrew Jordan, furniture-maker

MEASURING AND MARKING WOOD OR BOARDS

You will need a tape measure, a sharp pencil or trimming knife, a try square (see picture right), and a portable workbench or other firm work surface.

1 Hook the end of your tape measure over one end of the wood you're measuring, pull the tape out beyond the length you want, and make a pencil or knife mark on the wood in the right place. Check the measurement to make sure it's accurate. On wood or boards more than about 150 mm/6 in wide, make several length marks and join them up with a pencil and ruler.

2 Hold the try square with its wooden stock pressed against the edge of the wood and its blade aligned with the length mark. Mark the cutting line on the wood along the blade of the try square, then turn the wood on edge and continue the line down each face.

3 On manufactured boards, measure from adjoining edges of the board to mark the two cutting lines, and use the try square to check that these lines are at right angles.

SANDING

BY HAND

You will need medium- and fine-grade sandpaper, a cork sanding block, some clean cloth and white spirit, and a portable workbench.

1 To sand cut ends, cut a strip of medium-grade sandpaper and wrap it round your sanding block. Keep the block flat on the wood in order to avoid rounding off the corners.

2 Change to fine sandpaper and repeat to finish the job. You can also use fine sandpaper and the sanding block to give planed surfaces a final smoothing.

3 When you have finished sanding, use a vacuum cleaner to remove dust. Wipe the sanded surface with a pad of clean cloth moistened with a little white spirit to remove all the sanding dust.

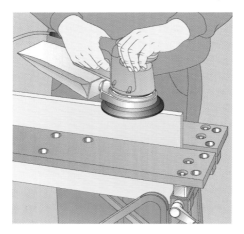

USING A POWER SANDER

You will need a power sander with a supply of sanding discs, a clean cloth and white spirit, and a workbench.

1 Keep the soleplate flat as you sand cut ends.

2 When smoothing planed surfaces, move the sander along the wood in the direction of the grain.

SAWING

HAND SAWS

You will need a tenon saw and a portable workbench. If you don't have a workbench, hand sawing will be easier with a bench hook (see illustration below). See below for how to make one from wood off-cuts. Alternatively, buy a ready-made bench hook.

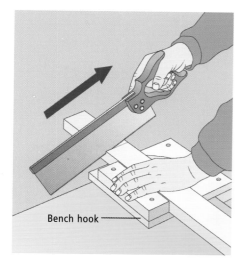

Bench hook

1 Clamp the wood to the workbench or hold it on the bench hook as shown, with the lower block pressed against the edge of your work surface.

2 Any saw cut removes a strip of wood equal to the width of the blade's teeth, so saw on the waste side of the line you have marked. Position the blade of your tenon saw on the waste side of the line, using the thumb of your other hand as a guide, and start the cut with a few light backward strokes (towards you).

3 Once the cut is started, make forward strokes (away from you) with the blade at an angle of about 45° to the wood surface. As the cut deepens, gradually bring the saw to the horizontal and continue cutting. Complete the cut by letting the saw teeth just cut into the bench hook. This stops the underside of the workpiece from splintering. If you are using a workbench, carry on sawing at 45° and support the off-cut with your free hand as you complete the cut.

POWER SAWING

You will need a power jigsaw, a guide batten or fence (see illustration), and a workbench with a clamp.

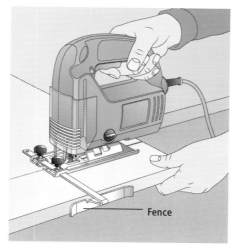

Fence

1 Jigsaw blades cut on the upstroke and can easily splinter veneered or plastic-coated boards, so if using these mark cutting lines on the underside of the board and cut it face down.

2 Clamp the workpiece to your workbench so the saw can't wrench it from your grip. Rest the front end of the saw soleplate on the edge of the wood or board, with the blade to the waste side of the line, and switch the saw on.

3 Move the saw forward until the blade starts to cut. Then push the saw steadily forward with the soleplate flat on the wood, following the cutting line all the way across. Support the off-cut with your free hand as you complete the cut.

MAKING A BENCH HOOK

You can make a bench hook with a short plank of wood and two flat strips of wood glued or nailed on opposite sides and at opposite ends to each other. One of these strips hooks onto a work surface, while the other supports the wood you are working on.

WORKING WITH A POWER JIGSAW

STRAIGHT CUTS

The jigsaw's main drawback is that its slim blade can wander off-line when making long, straight cuts. It also tends to veer off the vertical if forced too hard when sawing wood or boards more than about 12 mm/½ in thick, resulting in cuts with out-of-square edges. There are two solutions:

For cuts close to the edge of the workpiece and parallel to it, fit the adjustable fence guide to the saw soleplate (see illustration near left). Running the fence along the edge ensures a straight cut at precisely the pre-set distance from the edge.

For cuts away from the edge, clamp a timber guide batten across the workpiece parallel to the cutting line and run the edge of the soleplate against the batten to keep the blade on line.

CURVED CUTS

The slim blade allows the jigsaw to cut curves with a radius as little as 25 mm/1 in if driven carefully. Make sure the blade stays on the waste side of the cutting line at all times.

ANGLED CUTS

By adjusting the angle of the soleplate, the saw can make edge cuts at any angle up to 45°. However, using this facility reduces the maximum cutting depth available by up to 30%.

ENCLOSED CUTS

Drill a hole within the waste area big enough to admit the saw blade. Insert it and start cutting, steering the saw out to the cutting line and then along it to complete the cutout. If the cutout has square corners, drill a hole at each corner so the blade can be turned through 90° after cutting each side, and square the corners up with a rasp.

TYPES OF NAIL

Nails come in many different types, shapes, and sizes, but you will need only a few to cope with most DIY jobs. See illustration, right.

Round wire nails have a flat, round head and a round shank, and are used mainly for rough carpentry work, especially out of doors. They come in sizes up to 150 mm/6 in long.

Oval wire nails have an elliptical cross-section and a bulbous head, and are the most commonly used in general woodwork. Driven with the longer axis of the ellipse aligned with the wood grain, they're less likely than round nails to cause splitting. Sizes go up to 150 mm/6 in, but 25 mm/1 in, 38 mm/1½ in, 50 mm/2 in, and 75 mm/3 in sizes are the most widely used.

Ring-shank nails, also known as annular nails, resemble round wire nails but have ringed shanks that grip the wood, making the nail much less likely to pull out under load. Sizes range from 19 mm/¾ in to 100 mm/4 in.

Panel pins are slim, round nails designed for fixing thin panels to supporting frameworks. They can also be used for fixing mouldings and securing small-scale woodworking joints. Sizes range from 15 mm/⅝ in to 50 mm/2 in.

Brads are cut nails that are rectangular in cross-section. They grip better than a round nail. The two most often used are the floor brad, for fixing floorboards to joists, and the much smaller glazing brad, or sprig, for securing glass in frames.

Masonry nails are specially hardened steel nails that can be driven into solid masonry as an alternative to making fixings with screws and wall plugs. Once driven, they are very difficult to remove without damaging the wall. Sizes range from 25 mm/1 in to 90 mm/3½ in.

DRILLING IN WOOD

You will need a cordless drill, a twist drill bit or flat wood bit to match the diameter of hole you require, a try square to use as a drilling guide, and a portable workbench.

1 Clamp the wood you are drilling to the workbench. Fit the bit into the jaws (chuck) of the drill and tighten it.

2 Press the tip of the bit into the wood at the point where you want to drill, and stand the try square upright on its stock next to the drill so that you can use it as a guide to keeping the drill absolutely vertical.

3 Start the drill and push the bit steadily into the wood without forcing it.

4 If you are using a flat wood bit, drill until the point just pierces the underside of the wood. Turn it over, insert the point in the hole, and complete the hole by drilling in the reverse direction. This prevents the cutting edges of the bit from splintering the wood as they emerge.

Drilling a hole from both sides to prevent splintering – see 4 and 5

5 When you have drilled the hole, withdraw the bit with the drill running to clear the waste from the hole.

6 To drill a stopped hole – one that goes only partly through the wood – you need to know when to stop drilling. Either wind a strip of plastic tape round the shank of the bit at the required distance from the tip, or fit a depth stop attachment to it. Drill the hole until the tape or depth stop touches the surface.

DRILLING HOLES IN WALLS

You will need a cordless drill with hammer action, a masonry drill bit to match the size of the wall plug and screw you intend to use, and some plastic tape or a depth stop.

1 Fit the bit into the chuck of the drill and tighten it. Check the depth of hole you need and put a short length of tape or a depth stop on the bit as a marker. Set the drill to hammer action (and slow speed if you have a two-speed drill).

2 Press the tip of the bit into the plaster at the point where you want to drill and start the drill. Push the drill bit into the wall, letting the hammer action do the work.

3 Carry on drilling until the tape or depth stop just touches the wall surface, then withdraw the bit with the drill still running to clear the debris from the hole.

4 Insert the wall plug, ready to receive the fixing screw.

JOINING WOOD

TO NAIL TWO PIECES OF WOOD TOGETHER

You will need oval wire nails, a hammer, a nail punch, and some PVA woodworking adhesive. Make sure you have the correct length nails.

1 Select a nail long enough to pass at least halfway through the piece you're nailing to. If the joint will be under any load, strengthen it by spreading woodworking adhesive on the joining surfaces before assembling.

2   Start hammering the nail into the first piece, with the long axis of the oval head aligned with the wood grain. Position the two pieces carefully and drive the nail in until its head is just proud of the wood surface. Drive the head just below the surface using the nail punch.

3   Plug the hole with wood filler and sand it smooth when it's set.

4   Repeat for the other nails to complete the fixing.

TO SCREW TWO PIECES OF WOOD TOGETHER

You will need countersunk screws, a screwdriver, and a cordless drill, plus twist drill bits and a countersink bit.

1   Select a screw long enough to pass at least halfway through the second piece into which you're driving the screw. For most fixings, a screw of gauge number 8 (a measure of its diameter) will be ideal. Position the two pieces of wood and drill a pilot hole of 2 mm/$\frac{1}{16}$ in diameter through the upper piece and halfway through the lower piece.

2   Separate the two pieces and drill a clearance hole of 4 mm/$\frac{1}{8}$ in diameter through the top piece. Then switch to the countersink bit, and drill out the cone-shaped countersink for the screw head in the mouth of the clearance hole.

3   Reposition the pieces, insert the screw, and drive it in with your screwdriver until its head fits flush with the wood surface.

4   Repeat for the other screws to complete the fixing.

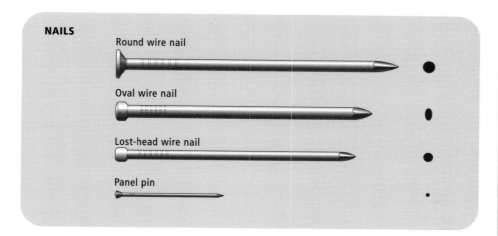

NAILS
Round wire nail
Oval wire nail
Lost-head wire nail
Panel pin

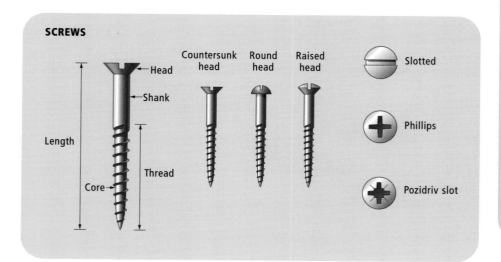

SCREWS
Head
Shank
Length
Thread
Core
Countersunk head
Round head
Raised head
Slotted
Phillips
Pozidriv slot

TYPES OF SCREW

The range of different screws is enormous, but for most jobs you are likely to need just two types – the standard woodscrew and the twin-thread screw. The woodscrew has a plain shank between the head and the thread. The twin-thread is threaded almost up to the head for extra grip, and is quicker to drive. Both types are usually made of steel, which may be coated or plated to resist corrosion. Brass and stainless steel woodscrews are also available.

Head shapes Woodscrews come in three head shapes: countersunk, used where the screw will sit flush with the surface; round head for fixing sheet materials too thin to take a countersink; and raised head (a combination of round and countersunk) for attaching things like door and window fittings, which themselves contain a countersink. Twin-thread screws ('chipboard screws') are made only with countersunk heads.

Slots and crosses Traditional woodscrews have a slotted head and are driven with a flat-tip screwdriver. Many screws are now made with a cross-shaped recess in the head, providing improved grip and driving. Pozidriv, Supadriv, and Prodrive screws can all be driven with a Pozidriv screwdriver. Some screws have a Phillips recess, and require a Phillips screwdriver.

Size and gauge Screws are identified by their length in millimetres or inches, and by their diameter or gauge, either as a number from 1 to 20 or, in the case of twin-thread screws, in millimetres. For most jobs you will be using screws of gauge 6, 8, or 10. Woodscrews are made in lengths from 9 mm/$\frac{3}{8}$ in to 150 mm/6 in, and twin-thread screws in lengths from 12 mm/$\frac{1}{2}$ in to 100 mm/4 in.

▶ Don't get hurt

DIY can be a rewarding activity, but it can also be a dangerous one. Around 100,000 people need hospital treatment for DIY accidents in Britain every year. The two main causes of injuries are failure to read instructions and use tools or materials properly, and carelessness when it comes to commonsense measures such as securing ladders.

EQUIPMENT

Safety goggles (British Standard BS 2092) protect eyes from dust, flying debris, and splashy liquids.

Disposable face masks stop you inhaling coarse dust created by drilling, sawing, and sanding jobs, but won't protect you from fumes. If spraying paint or using chemicals such as timber treatments, use a specialist mask (BS EN149).

Ear defenders or earplugs (BS 6344) protect your hearing when you are breaking concrete or sanding a floor.

Leather gloves protect hands when handling coarse building materials, and **PVC gloves** are for use when using chemicals.

FIRE!

- Take care when using and setting down hot-air guns and blowlamps.
- Don't smoke when using inflammable liquids.
- Don't store inflammable materials in the house, and in particular never under the stairs – a fire there will spread rapidly.

SAFETY WITH TOOLS

Bladed hand tools Use the right tool for the job, and make sure the blade is sharp. You are more likely to have an accident using a blunt tool, because it needs more force to do its job. Keep your hands behind the cutting direction. Fit blade guards when not using the tool.

Power tools Power saws and routers (a tool for gouging) need handling with particular care. With all power tools, read instructions carefully. Never try to remove, bypass, or deactivate a blade guard or other safety feature. Let the motor stop before setting the tool down, and switch off tools whenever you are not using them, even if only for a very short time. Keep clothes and hair away from moving parts. Wear safety equipment when appropriate.

While you work Tie back long hair, wear shoes that protect your feet, and avoid loose-fitting clothes or dangling jewellery. If a job takes longer than you'd anticipated, don't rush or take short cuts. Take frequent breaks – tiredness is the underlying cause of many accidents.

SAFETY WITH DIY MATERIALS

Some DIY materials are dangerous if not used with care. **Paint stripper** and **wood preservatives** may cause skin or eye injury, or give off noxious, inflammable fumes. **Cement** and **glass fibre** insulation can cause skin irritation or eye injuries during prolonged handling. Read the instructions with care, and always wear safety equipment if recommended.

Old materials containing **asbestos** need careful handling and disposal. Grey or grey-blue asbestos may be present in corrugated cement roofing board; cement fascias; soffits (the horizontal boards that cover the gap between the house wall and the guttering under the edge of the roof); gutters; old roof, tank, and pipe insulation; and some old textured ceiling finishes. Wear gloves and a face mask for handling or removing any of these. To minimize dust, soak the surface with water before cutting, drilling, or sanding.

Never dispose of asbestos yourself. Bag up the material, keeping it damp if possible, and contact your local authority – most operate a free disposal service.

SAFETY WITH ELECTRICITY

Power tools Before using, look for damage to the flex sheath, for exposed cores where the flex enters the plug, and cracks in the plug casing. Make sure the tool casing is securely closed and undamaged.

Outdoors Plug power tools into a special socket outlet or a plug-in adaptor with a residual current device (RCD). This cuts off the power supply if you touch any live parts on the tool, flex, or plug.

Wiring work Don't take on wiring projects unless you know what you are doing. Badly executed wiring work can kill. Always turn the power supply off at the main fuse box or consumer unit before you start work. Isolate individual circuits by removing the fuseholder or turning off the miniature circuit breaker (MCB). Double-check all connections have been correctly and securely made.

Cable detector Use this inexpensive battery-powered tool to check the whereabouts of circuit cables (and water pipes) that may be concealed behind walls on which you are working.

USING ACCESS EQUIPMENT

Most falls are from ladders and other access equipment, and almost all are avoidable.

CHOICE OF LADDER

Ladders should be clean and dry, with no damage to the rungs or stiles (the ladder sides), and fitted with safety feet if metal. New or hired ladders should be marked British Standard BS 1129 (wooden) and BS 2037 (metal). BS EN131 applies to both types. The ladder must be long enough for the job, bearing in mind that you should never stand on the top three rungs, and that for climbing on to a roof, at least three rungs should project above the roof edge.

WORKING ON LADDERS

Keep your hands free when going up or coming down a ladder. Carry tools and materials in pockets, a tool belt, or apron. Haul larger things up with a rope and bucket, or have them passed out through a window. Hang paint cans from a ladder hook, and fit a ladder tray to hold tools.

Wear sturdy shoes or boots for comfort and safety. Don't lean out too far – the golden rule is to keep your hips between the stiles, and to hold on with one hand at all times if the job allows. If you can't reach something, move the ladder – never take a chance.

USING STEPLADDERS

Check that the stepladder is fully opened and locked in the correct position, especially if it is a type that can be used in different configurations. Rest its feet on a firm and level base. Set the steps to face the work, not standing alongside it. When you're on the steps, keep both feet on the treads at all times. Overreaching may cause the steps to topple.

USING PLATFORMS

Slot-together platform towers, available from tool hire shops, are generally safer than ladders, especially for long jobs in one location. They must be set up on firm, level ground, and tied to the building if they are more than 4 m/13 ft high. Always fit a handrail and toe boards (to stop you knocking things off) round the platform. Don't climb up the outside of the tower. Either climb up inside it, lifting boards to get to the platform, or use a ladder set against the side of the tower opposite the house wall.

STORING LADDERS

It's better to hang ladders horizontally so that the weight rests evenly on the uprights. If you must hang them vertically, secure the top with a bracket to prevent the ladder from falling. Store wooden ladders off the ground so they are not weakened by damp.

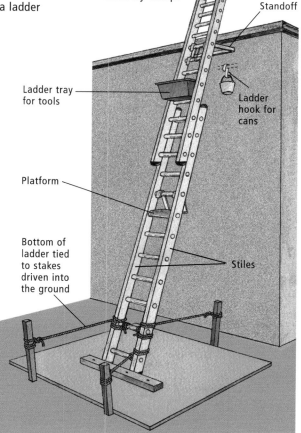

Standoff

Ladder tray for tools

Ladder hook for cans

Platform

Bottom of ladder tied to stakes driven into the ground

Stiles

Ladders are designed for use at one optimum angle, with the foot of the ladder set 1 m/3 ft away from what it's leaning against for every 4 m/13 ft of ladder height. A steeper angle, and you risk overbalancing and falling off. Shallower angles strain the ladder, and its foot may slip away.

1 Set the ladder down flat with its foot against the wall, and extend it to the required height.

2 Lift the top of the ladder and walk towards the wall, moving your hands from rung to rung until the ladder is upright. Rest the top against the wall, then lift or slide the ladder foot out to its final position.

3 Rest the top of the ladder against a firm surface, never against window glass or plastic guttering. If necessary, fit a standoff before erecting the ladder, and rest this against the wall to hold the top of the ladder clear of such surfaces.

4 On uneven or soft ground, place the foot of the ladder on a flat board, securely packed underneath if necessary. Nail a batten along its length for the ladder feet to push against. Never put wedges or packing directly under one stile to get a ladder to stand upright.

5 Secure the ladder at the top and bottom whenever possible. Tie the stiles to stakes driven into the ground beside the foot, and tie them higher up to an open window frame if possible. Don't trust downpipes to be strong enough.

Keep children at a safe distance when you're using tools, and **never** allow children to use or play with them. Always store tools out of harm's way.

Shelves and doors

Putting up shelves is the DIY activity most often attempted after painting and decorating. You can support shelves on individual brackets or, if fitting them in an alcove, on battens fixed to the side walls of the recess. Or you can use an adjustable shelving system. The other job covered here, hanging a new door or rehanging a door that has been removed, is not as difficult as it may seem.

FIXED SHELVING

If your shelves are less than about 750 mm/2 ft 6 in long, first fix the brackets to the shelf. For longer shelves, mark the bracket positions on the shelf and then the wall. Fix the brackets to the wall, then attach shelving.

SHORT SHELVES

1 Using screws that won't penetrate the top of the shelf, screw the brackets to the underside of the shelf at your chosen spacing. Hold the shelf against the wall where you plan to fit it, and rest your spirit level on top. Get the shelf level and use a bradawl to mark the wall through the screw holes in the brackets.

2 Set the shelf aside. Drill the holes and insert wall plugs. Hold the shelf back in place and drive in the top screw in each bracket, then the bottom screw.

LONG SHELVES

1 Mark the bracket positions at your chosen spacings on the edge of the shelf – you are likely to need at least three brackets. Hold the shelf flat against the wall with its rear edge in line with the proposed fixing position. Mark the bracket positions vertically on the wall, using the marks on the shelf as a guide.

2 Hold the first bracket in position so you can mark the wall through its screw holes. Drill and plug the holes, then screw the bracket into place.

3 Rest the shelf on the bracket with a spirit level on top. Get the shelf level – you may need help with this part. Draw a horizontal pencil mark on the wall where the lower back edge of the shelf meets each of the bracket position marks you drew in step 1.

4 Lift the shelf away and fix the remaining brackets to the wall. Finish the job by replacing the shelf on the brackets and screwing them to its underside.

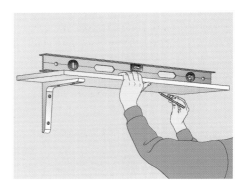

GETTING THE RIGHT SPACE BETWEEN SUPPORTS

Correct spacing between brackets or end supports is crucial to stop shelves sagging.

- With 18 mm/¾ in thick wood or MDF, space the brackets 900 mm/3 ft apart for light loads such as ornaments, and 600 mm/2 ft apart for heavy loads such as books or home entertainment equipment.
- With coated chipboard, reduce the spacings to 750 mm/2 ft 6 in and 450 mm/1ft 6 in respectively.

- If you want wider spacings, use thicker shelves to give extra support, or stiffen the shelves by screwing and gluing a batten to the underside, either flush with the front edge or set back a little way.
- In alcoves, fit a wall-mounted batten to the rear wall of the alcove, mid-way along the back of the shelf.
- Check that brackets are in line vertically before screwing in.

ADJUSTABLE SHELVING

Space the tracks on a solid wall to suit the shelving material and the likely loading. On a timber-framed wall the tracks must be fixed to the studs (see Securing fixings to walls, below)

1 Hold the first track at its chosen fixing position and use a pencil or bradawl to mark the wall through its topmost screw hole. Drill and plug the hole, then drive the screw in part-way so the track can swing freely.

2 Use your spirit level to get the track truly vertical. Then mark the other screw positions on the wall with the pencil or bradawl as before – see illustration. Swing the track aside (or take it down if it's easier), and drill and plug the remaining screw holes. Put the track in position and drive in all the screws.

3 Mark your chosen track spacing on a batten – any thin straight strip of wood will do – then hold it on top of the first track with your spirit level on top. Line up the first mark on the batten with the first track, get the batten level, and mark the wall where the second track should be.

4 Hold the second track up to this mark and repeat steps 1 and 2 to fix the second track in place. Repeat this sequence

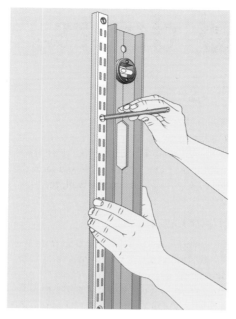

of operations to fix further tracks as necessary to complete the arrangement of shelves.

5 Slot the brackets into place at the intervals you want and put the shelves on them. If you want to screw the brackets to the shelves, hold the shelf down on its brackets and push the bradawl up through each screw hole to make pilot holes in the shelf underside. Lift the shelf and its brackets down, screw on each bracket, and replace.

SHELF MATERIALS

Choose shelves with a thickness of 18 mm/¾ in for both strength and appearance unless your shelves will be very lightly loaded, in which case you can use thinner materials. The most popular materials for shelves are:

■ **Solid wood**, which comes as ordinary softwood – available in widths up to 230 mm/9 in – and more expensive Parana pine or a variety of hardwoods, all available in widths up to 300 mm/12 in.

■ **Coated chipboard**, which is either veneered or plastic coated, with edges and ends finished to match the board surface. It comes in standard widths of 150 mm/6 in, 225 mm/9 in, 300 mm/1 ft, 450 mm/1 ft 6 in, 600 mm/2 ft, and 750 mm/2ft 6 in, and in 1.8 m/6 ft and 2.4 m/8 ft lengths.

■ **MDF** comes in standard 2,440 x 1,220 mm/8 x 4 ft panels, so can be cut to any width you require – a job for your supplier unless you have a circular saw.

SECURING FIXINGS TO WALLS

■ On **solid walls**, use screws and wall plugs to fix shelf battens, brackets, or track. Screws should be long enough to penetrate the wall by a minimum of 50 mm/2 in, and should pass into wall plugs a minimum of 40 mm/1½ in long. Use the thickest screws the holes in brackets or tracks will take. See p166 for advice on drilling holes.

■ On **timber-framed walls**, use screws and cavity fixings – wall plugs that splay out once they pass through the plasterboard, holding the screw in place – to put up single shelves that will carry only the lightest loads.

For all other shelves (and things like kitchen cupboards), locate the vertical timber frame members inside the wall –they're usually at 400 mm/1 ft 4 in intervals – called **studs**. To do this, use a battery-operated tool called a stud detector, or knock on the wall with your knuckles and listen to the sound: hollow knocking turns dull when you reach a stud. Then drive the fixing screws through the plasterboard and directly into the studs. Use screws long enough to penetrate the wall by a minimum of 50 mm/2 in. Starting with the top shelf, fit the screws through the brackets into each shelf.

SHELF SUPPORTS

Fixed shelving is generally supported with L-shaped brackets where one arm is longer than the other – the longer arm is usually fixed to the wall. Continuous aluminium-extrusion shelf supports run the full length of the shelf along the wall and support the shelf almost invisibly (see Invisible alcove supports, p172) and can be used for fixed shelving.

Adjustable shelving has steel, aluminium, or wooden brackets that slot or clip into tracks fixed to the walls. These are good for bearing heavy weights, and the placing of the brackets can be adjusted at any time. Some brackets have a lip at the front to prevent the shelf from sliding forwards.

ALCOVE SHELVING

FIXED SHELVES

The simplest way of supporting shelves in an alcove is to screw wooden battens to the side walls at whatever spacing you need. If your alcoves are wide or your shelves will have to carry heavy loads, you can provide extra support by fixing a third batten across the back wall, between the two side battens.

1 Work out the shelf spacings you need, and mark the shelf positions you want on one side wall. Cut support battens from 38 mm x 25 mm/1½ in x 1 in softwood to a length just less than the shelf width. Drill two clearance holes (to take the body of the screw) in each batten, then use a drill countersink bit to make the recesses at the top of each clearance hole so that countersink screws will fit flush with the batten. Hold one of these battens against the lowest shelf mark on the wall and punch the hole positions in the wall with a bradawl. Drill and plug the holes and screw the batten to the wall.

2 Check whether the alcove side and back walls are square to each other at each point where you want to put a shelf. A try square is the best tool for this. If the walls do form a true right angle, measure and cut the first shelf to length. If they don't, cut out the shape of each internal angle on a piece of card, and measure the width of the back wall. Use the card to mark the first angle on your shelf, and cut that end of the shelf. Next, mark the alcove width along the rear edge of the shelf, then mark the second angle on the shelf and cut it. The shelf should now match the irregular shape of the alcove.

3 Rest one end of the shelf on its support batten, put your spirit level on top, and hold the second support batten beneath the shelf at the other end. Get the shelf level and mark the screw hole positions through the batten as before. Lift out the shelf, drill and plug the holes, and screw the second batten into position. Lay the shelf on it and test its fit.

4 Repeat steps 1 to 3 to fix the other shelves. You may find it easier to work in the alcove if you leave the shelves out until you've finished fixing all the battens. If you want them fixed in place temporarily, nail them to the battens with panel pins.

5 To secure the shelves more permanently, fit brass mirror plates underneath the shelves, see illustration left. First, cut out a recess in the centre of the top of the batten on each side, and screw in a flange. Then, once the shelves are in place, drive a screw through the flange into the bottom of the shelf.

HOW TO HANG A NEW DOOR

1 Check that the door is the correct size (see Getting the fit right, opposite).

2 Screw each hinge to the door frame with a single screw. If the screws don't line up with the old hinge holes in the frame, you will have to drill new holes – use a drill bit slightly smaller than the diameter of the screws. If the new hinge doesn't fit the old recess exactly, rest it on the bottom of the recess and mark where it overlaps around the edges. Cut out the waste wood inside the line with a chisel and mallet.

3 Fold the hinge open. The hinge pivots should protrude from the frame edge. Prop the door in the frame, resting on

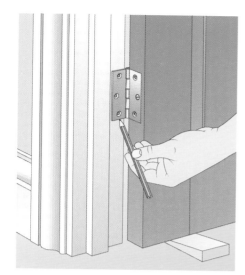

depth as the thickness of the hinge flap. With the bevel (angled edge) of the chisel facing down towards the waste wood, pare away the slivers.

6 Check that the hinges fit flush with the edge. Fix with one screw per hinge so that you can make adjustments easily.

7 Hold the door on wedges, at right angles to the frame, and fix the hinge flaps to the door frame, again with only one screw in each hinge. Check that the door opens and closes easily, then fit the other screws.

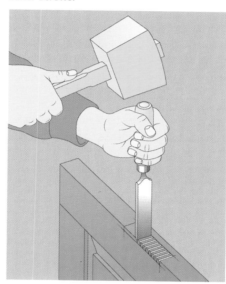

wedges so that there is the correct gap at the bottom. Mark the top and bottom of each hinge on the face of the door.

4 Unscrew the hinges from the frame and lay them on the edge of the door, lined up with the pencil marks. Mark around the hinge flaps and use a straight edge to pencil the thickness of the flap on the edge of the door.

5 Tap around the marked outline of the hinge with a chisel. Cut a series of slivers across the marked section, against the grain of the wood, at 5 mm/³⁄₁₆ in intervals – aim to make the cuts the same

GETTING THE FIT RIGHT

HOW BIG SHOULD THE GAP BE?

Put the door in the frame, supported on two wooden wedges, to check the fit.

- Ideally, there should be a gap of 2–3 mm/¹⁄₁₆–¹⁄₈ in all around the sides and top of the door.

- Usually, the gap at the bottom should be about 6 mm/¼ in, though an internal door with a timber or metal threshold may need a bigger gap – up to 10 mm/³⁄₈ in.

- If there is thick carpet in the room, you will need a gap of 10 mm/³⁄₈ in at the bottom. If you don't want to leave such a large gap under the door, fit rising butt hinges. These are fitted and

look the same as ordinary butt hinges, but the pivot mechanism moves the door upwards by a few millimetres as it is opened.

TRIMMING A DOOR TO FIT

Plane or saw off some of the door if it is too large or the frame isn't exactly square. If you have to reduce the height or width of the new door by more than 6 mm/¼ in, use a panel saw to cut off waste wood, then sand the edge. For smaller amounts, it's easier to use a hand plane or power plane. If the old door was a good fit, use it as a template, but always take off an equal amount of wood from each side of the new door.

REHANGING A DOOR

If a door has been removed for painting, stripping, or planing to fit, rehanging should not take long. Don't rehang a door to open into a corridor or where somebody could walk into it.

1 Check the fit of the door (see left).

2 You should be able to fit the hinge flaps to the door frame in their original recesses. Use one screw per hinge to check that the door opens and closes smoothly. If it does, add the other screws.

3 If the door strains the hinges and doesn't close fully, the hinge recesses are probably too deep. Put pieces of card behind hinge flaps.

USEFUL KNOW-HOW

- Brass screws are soft and can snap easily if they are put under strain as you screw them in. Before fitting the brass screws provided with the hinge, insert a steel screw of the same size into each hinge hole to make the threads in the wood.

- If screw holes in the frame are cracked or too big, fill them with pieces of timber dowel coated with PVA glue and redrill.

Dealing with windows

It pays to give windows with wooden or metal frames a yearly check-up so you can cure any problems before they become expensive. Repaint bare wood or metal areas in the late spring when the frame is completely dry.

EQUIPMENT

- Handsaw
- Screwdrivers
- Drill
- Hammer
- Filler knife and, for leaded panes, a putty knife
- Pliers
- Abrasive paper (for smoothing wood or old paint)
- File/plane
- Old chisel (this work will blunt a new one)
- Tape measure
- Gloves.

LEADED PANES

Rattling glass in leaded windows can be sealed with putty. Knead a small amount of linseed putty, adding black grate polish to make it a dark-grey colour. Force this between the glass and the lead cames (strips) a little at a time with a putty knife. Force the putty further into the gaps with a pointed piece of softwood and flatten bumpy lead by rubbing with the edge of the stick. Use a short-bristled brush to remove loose putty fragments from the glass, working well into the corners and moving in short strokes across the cames.

REPLACING A BROKEN PANE

This describes how to replace a pane of glass in a wooden frame. Follow the same technique with a metal frame but don't add metal glazing sprigs. Get a professional to replace a pane in a uPVC frame.

1 Measure up (height and width) for the replacement glass, using millimetres for accuracy. Take a couple of measurements at different points, as the frame may not be square and the new glass will crack if it is too tight a fit. Use whichever measurement is the smaller in each case, and subtract 3 mm from both height and width to allow for movement.

2 Wearing stout gloves, use an old chisel (the sprigs will blunt a new one) and hammer to chip the putty out of the rebate (the recess for the glass, around the inside of the frame). Lever out headless tacks, called glazing sprigs, with pliers.

3 If bare wood is visible around the rebate, give it a generous coat of wood primer and leave to dry (see tin for advice on how long). Treat rot first with wood hardener and filler.

4 Knead some putty in your hands to make it soft and workable. If the putty is wet and sticky, roll a handful on newspaper to absorb some of the linseed

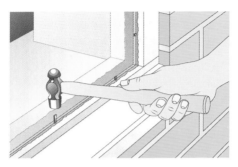

oil. Form it into a sausage shape of about 20 mm/¾ in diameter and press into place all round the rebate, with no gaps.

5 Rest the bottom edge of the pane on the lower edge of the rebate and lift the glass upright, pressing the pane in around all edges to squash the putty and make a weatherproof seal.

6 Tap new glazing sprigs into the edges of the rebate at about 150 mm/6 in intervals. Slide the side of the hammer head up and down against the glass as you gently tap them in to avoid sudden knocks.

7 Press in more putty and use a putty knife to form a neat slope of about 45° between the glass and the frame. Some putty will squeeze out of the rebate, so trim off excess from inside the window. The putty will harden in about 14 days.

ADDING SECONDARY DOUBLE GLAZING

If you want to improve insulation without the expense of replacing windows, you can add secondary double glazing. The most basic form is a **thin plastic film** stuck with tape around the frame and shrunk with the heat from a hairdryer to make it taut. It's cheap and quick to fit, but you can't open the window after.

Clear plastic sheet, available in DIY stores, is better. Some versions allow parts of the glazing to be slid across so you can open the window. The sheet is

screwed to the frame or stuck with double-sided tape. Wash the inside of the window and frame with mild detergent and cut the plastic sheet to size – about 1 cm/½ in smaller than the frame – with a trimming knife or junior hacksaw. Cut the edging strip to fit around the sides and mitre the corners with a mitre box and tenon saw (see Woodstrip flooring, p232). Clip the U-shaped strip over the plastic sheet and fix to the frame. The strip can be drilled to accept screws.

REPLACING A BROKEN SASH CORD

If you have a broken sash cord, the window will be difficult to open and will judder as it is raised. If one of the four cords has broken, replace all. You will need to repaint the window after.

1 Using an old chisel, prise the staff bead (see illustration) away from the interior four sides of the window frame, starting at the middle of the bead. Lean bottom sash into the room from the top.

2 Cut any unbroken sash cord with a trimming knife and lower weight gently to the bottom of its compartment (tie a knot on cut sash cord to prevent it disappearing). Remove inner sash and lever out nails holding the cut-off/broken cords to the sides.

3 Prise away the narrow parting bead and remove the upper sash in the same way.

4 Unscrew the weight pocket – a slip of wood at the bottom of each side of frame – to reveal the weights. There will be two on each side. Lift out the weights.

5 Measure each sash for the new sash cords and cut these to length, allowing a couple of cm for trimming. Where the old (cut off) sash cord is still in place, you can tie this to the new length to draw it through the pulley. Where the cord has broken, tie a small weight (folded lead is ideal, but a bolt will do) on to a piece of string, pass this over the pulley, lower the small weight and then the string can be used to pull the new sash cord through. Tie the new sash cords to their weights using a non-slip figure of eight knot (see picture below) and tie a temporary knot in the other end.

6 Rest the upper sash on the window ledge, pull one of its cords down and use galvanized clout nails (short nails with a large head) to fix the cord into the groove on the side of the sash. Trim the end of the cord. Repeat for second cord.

7 Replace the slip/s of wood at the bottom of the frame, followed by the upper sash, the parting beads, the lower sash (fit cord first), and finally the beading around the edges of the frame (reuse the nails sticking out, though you may need a few more).

TOO MUCH PAINT

If paint has built up over time on sash windows, they can be difficult to open. Plane off thick paint with a power planer or strip with chemical stripper. Where windows have been painted closed, run a trimming knife between the frame and window to break the seal. If this doesn't work, use a paint scraper or old chisel to lever the woodwork apart. For really stubborn areas, brush on a thick coat of paint stripper and leave the paint to loosen for at least 20 minutes.

DAMP WOODWORK

Timber will absorb water over the winter months. This often makes the sashes swell and jam shut. If possible, only try to open them again when the weather is dry. If they are still stuck, lightly tap all around the frame with a mallet and a wooden block placed flat against the frame. Use a small plane or rasp to file away the raised areas on the frame or the opening sash. To find the areas that need filing, run a piece of thin card all around the joint.

RATTLING CASEMENTS

Casement sashes that rattle can be fixed by adjusting the positions of the metal stay (the long arm that holds a casement window open) or the pivoting catch used to lock the window shut. Unscrewing the catch and fixing it closer to the inside of the frame pulls the window more tightly closed. The metal pegs that hold the stay in place can be moved a few millimetres toward the inside of the room to do the same. You may need to fill the old screw holes with short lengths of wooden dowel, glued into place, so that you can make the new screw holes next to the dowel.

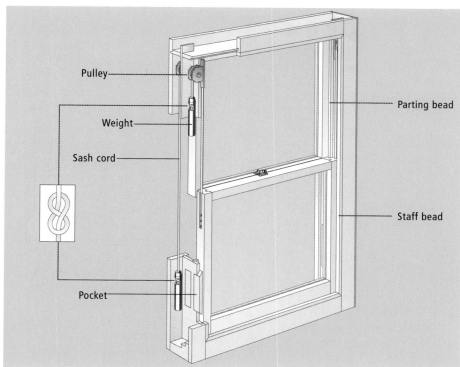

Pulley
Weight
Sash cord
Pocket
Parting bead
Staff bead

Draughtproofing

Draughts account for up to 25% of the heat lost from a home. Add strips of vinyl or foam draught excluder around the outside edge of the frames of doors and windows so that the opening parts close on to it. Foam strips are less hard-wearing than vinyl, so use these for internal doors and windows that aren't opened very often.

SEE ALSO Insulating your home, p198

EQUIPMENT

- Screwdrivers
- Bradawl
- Trimming knife
- Junior hacksaw
- Panel saw
- Bolster chisel (a flat-bladed tool with a sharpened edge)
- Club hammer (a heavy-duty hammer with an oversized head)
- Tape measure.

GAPS ROUND PIPES

Draughts in kitchens and bathrooms are often caused by gaps between pipes and the external wall brickwork, especially around large-diameter soil pipes and extractor fan outlets. Fill these gaps with an aerosol of **expanding foam**. Dampen the brickwork by spraying lightly with water, using a plant sprayer, to make the foam adhere better. Use the long nozzle supplied to force the foam into as much of the gap as possible. When it has set, trim with a sharp kitchen knife and redecorate.

SEALING WINDOWS

Casement windows can be draughtproofed with self-adhesive excluder strips. The available range includes nylon brush, sprung V-strip (a flexible nylon strip with a V-shaped profile that is compressed as the frames meet), and tubular-shaped vinyl. Check the packaging to see which is recommended for a particular gap size. Clean the frames with soapy water, prime and paint bare wood, then press the excluder strip against the parts of the fixed window frame that meet the edges of the opening frame.

Sash windows are harder to seal efficiently because the top and bottom sections must be free to move up and down. Some sash window restoration companies can fit a system of nylon brushes around the frame to keep draughts out. If you want to tackle the work yourself, use a brush seal for the sides and a vinyl tubular strip for the horizontal gaps. Cut the draughtproofing strip with a trimming knife or junior hacksaw to fit the frame part. Some products have a self-adhesive backing; others need to be held with small panel pins. Fix the strip so that the edge is a snug fit against the adjacent frame part.

REPAIRING WOODEN FRAMES

Rotten or badly fitting frames can also cause draughts. Cut out rotten woodwork with a flexible saw and use the old piece as a template to cut the new piece. Soak the new timber in a wood preservative and allow to dry. Glue and screw into place, then prime and paint. You may need to add some exterior wood filler to seal gaps. For cracks between the brickwork and the frame, use an exterior-grade flexible sealant that matches the colour of the frame. It usually comes in a tube that you must fit into an applicator gun, though some come in a flexible tube with a nozzle.

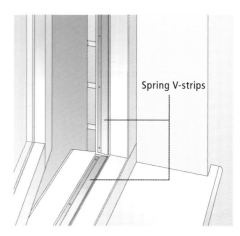

Spring V-strips

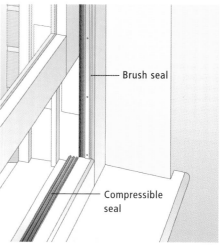

Brush seal

Compressible seal

CHECK THE LOFT HATCH

Stop draughts penetrating the warm parts of the house from the loft by fitting a foam draughtproofing strip around the edge of your loft hatch. Cut the strip to size and press into place around meeting edges. If it doesn't already have one, the hatch will need a simple bolt or catch fitted so that it can be closed firmly against the frame. Draughtproofing the loft hatch is especially important if you have an unfelted roof.

DEALING WITH DOORS

Doors are a major source of draughts. A front door needs a gap around it, but should close firmly against its frame.

If you have a badly fitting door, it may be worth replacing it with a new one (see Hanging a door, p172). If the door does not close properly, try repositioning the door-lock holder on the frame closer to the outside surface of the door.

Even when the door is a good fit, there will be some draught around the edges. Check to find the worst spots by holding the back of your hand close to the gap and moving your hand around the frame closer to the outside surface of the door.

- Fill gaps along the top and sides of the door frame with self-adhesive vinyl or foam strip. Use the tough vinyl strip on external doors. Clean dirt and grease from the frame edges with a nylon scouring sponge and hot soapy water and allow to dry before pushing the draughtproofing strip into place. Some vinyl strips are held with panel pins or nails.

- Fit a draught excluder to the bottom of the inside of a front or back door. These excluders are made of plastic or metal with a flexible rubber strip or nylon brush along the bottom to cut out draughts – smooth rubber strip is better on stone or wood floors, nylon brush is good for carpets. Place the rigid plastic or metal part of the excluder along the bottom of the door and lower until the sealer strip covers the gap below the door. Use a bradawl to mark the two screw holes at the outer edges of the strip. Drive screws through these holes and then drive screws through the remaining fixing holes. If you have thick carpet inside the doorway and don't want to wear the fibres as the door is opened, fit rising butt hinges, which lift the door upwards as it opens. (These are fitted exactly like normal hinges – see Hanging a door, p173.)

- Some door kits consist of a rain deflector, which is fitted on the outside

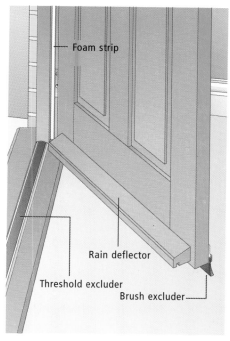

Foam strip

Rain deflector

Threshold excluder

Brush excluder

of the door, and a draughtproofing strip, fitted along the bottom of the doorway (the threshold). The rain deflector is screwed to the door so that the bottom is above the lower edge of the door. The draughtproofing strip is either screwed or nailed directly into the threshold so that a draughtproof seal is formed when the door closes.

DRAUGHTPROOFING THE LETTER BOX

Letter boxes can cause annoying cold spots in a hallway. A draughtproofing plastic flap has nylon bristles around the opening to keep out cold air. The fixed part of the draught excluder is screwed around the edge of the letter box on the inside of the door. Make sure the hinged flap can open and close freely before screwing the excluder to the door. It's also worth fitting a cover plate over a mortise lock keyhole.

BLOCKING GAPS IN FLOORBOARDS

Floorboards in a ground-floor room can often let in cold air.

If your boards are widely spaced, lift and relay to close gaps. Remove skirting boards, then use a bolster chisel and club hammer to lever up floor-boards. Lever up one edge of a sawn board in the middle of the floor and work along the sides to ease away nail fixings. Relay boards so they fit together snugly, replacing any damaged ones.

If most of the boards are close together, use slivers of timber to fill any large gaps. Measure across the ends of the gap to give you an approximate size. To make slivers, use a handsaw to trim edges off a spare board. Brush glue along both sides of a sliver and tap it between boards with a mallet. Plane or sand away protruding edges. Seal small gaps with flexible mastic (waterproof sealant). If you plan to sand and varnish the floor, scrape off excess mastic before it sets. You don't have to do this if you will be laying laminate floor, vinyl, or tiles.

MORE TIPS TO MAKE THE FLOOR WARMER

- If you lift up floorboards to close the gaps, it's also worth fitting rigid insulation. Insulation slabs of 50 or 75 mm/2 or 3 in are cheap and sold in packs to cover around 6 sq m/ 64 sq ft. Tack chicken wire to the sides of joists so that the wire stretches across them, flush with the lower edge. Lay the insulation on the wire before relaying floorboards.

- Mastic can be used between skirting board and floor. Fix quadrant moulding (wood strip that in profile is a quarter-circle) over the joint to hide the mastic, then tap panel pins through the moulding and into the skirting board.

Furniture and flatpacks

Older pieces of furniture can often be repaired to give several more years of service. You can avoid the expense of professional repairs by tackling the simpler jobs yourself. Don't be tempted to use nails for a quick fix of a damaged joint – the nail will soon become loose. Always use glue and screws. Assembling flatpack furniture only requires a few tools but it's worth following some basic assembly tips. Don't rush the assembly, and follow the instructions carefully so you don't miss out any crucial fixings.

EQUIPMENT FOR FLATPACK ASSEMBLY

- Mallet or hammer
- Scrap piece of timber or medium density fibreboard (MDF)
- Screwdrivers
- Adjustable spanner
- Electric drill and selection of bits
- Jigsaw
- PVA glue
- Spirit level
- Router (a high-speed rotating cutting tool that can take various cutters of different shapes) and jig (a hard plastic rectangle with a groove that guides the router's cutter) – both can be hired
- Sash cramp (a metal rod with a fixed jaw at one end and adjustable sliding grip at the other; not as powerful as a vice grip but portable and good for light clamping)
- Try square
- Safety goggles (always wear when hammering or drilling).

REPAIRING FURNITURE

- Before you try to take a piece of furniture apart to repair it, use a small DIY metal detector to find old repairs where nails or screws have been used.

- If a tapered rail or leg is slightly loose in its socket, cut 2–3 mm / 1/16–1/8 in off the end that fits into the socket, then reglue. Because the rail or leg is tapered at this point, the new end-diameter will be slightly larger, so will be a tighter fit.

- If one leg of a chair or table is shorter than the others, you can cure the annoying wobble with a pair of compasses and a handsaw. Stand the piece on a flat surface such as a sheet of plywood. Spread the compasses until the metal point is on the flat surface and the sharpened point of the pencil is level with the bottom of the shortest leg. Transfer this measurement to the other legs and trim them with a saw so that they are all the same length.

- Sticking drawers can often be made to run smoothly by rubbing a candle along the bottom of the drawer sides to lubricate the sliding action. If this doesn't work, you may need to use a plane to shave off some of the sides or top of the drawer. Wobble the drawer up and down to try to find the side that is a tight fit. Keep testing the fit so that you don't take too much off.

- Loose drawer fronts can be reglued with a PVA wood adhesive. Scrape off the old glue with a trimming knife or chisel and spread new adhesive over the joint surfaces. Hold the pieces together with a sash cramp, use a try square to check that they are at right angles, and leave to set.

- You can make your own furniture 'reviver' to clean grimy surfaces. Mix one part linseed oil with four parts white spirit. Wipe on with one cloth and take off the old wax with another. This works on most traditional finishes, including French polish.

- The mortise and tenon joint is a common joint on tables and chairs. A mortise is a square or rectangular recess and the tenon is the part that fits into it. To give repaired mortise and tenon joints more strength, drill a hole through the joint, making sure it passes right through the tenon into the back of the mortise and out the other side. Coat a piece of beech dowel (cylindrical length of wood) with glue and tap it through the drilled hole to peg the parts together. Drill a hole and insert another dowel below the first for extra strength. Use sash cramps – metal bars with one fixed and one movable jaw – to hold the joint firmly together for at least six hours.

Mortise joint

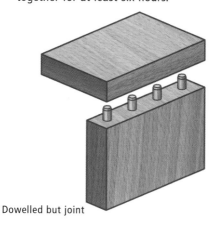

Dowelled but joint

PUTTING IN A FLATPACK KITCHEN

Installing a flatpack kitchen yourself may be an economical option but it requires considerable DIY competence. If you are a DIY novice, there will probably be times when you will need some help, whether from a professional or from experienced friends or family. You will get instructions with the kitchen, but this list explains what has to be done, and in what order. Be prepared for your sink to be out of action for at least two days.

1 Remove all the old units and worktops. You may need to level the floor under the base units so that you have a smooth area for the new ones. If so, buy a powder or ready-mixed pack of floor-levelling compound, spread this over the uneven areas, and leave to dry overnight. If you plan to leave the existing tiling in place, repair any broken tiles around the worktop (see p226). The last job should be to turn off the water supply to the kitchen taps and remove the sink and its surrounding worktop. If these taps don't have isolator valves (valves that shut off the water supply to individual parts of the system), now is a good time to fit them.

2 It's essential that all the base units are at the same level. Measure up the wall from the highest point on the floor and mark the finished height of the units. Hold a spirit level against this point and mark a line around the walls. Base units have screw-in legs so you can adjust the units to be level with this line.

3 Assemble the smaller units outside the kitchen to keep the working area clear. Bring in the units next to the sink area first. You will need to cut the worktop to fit the new sink. Stainless steel sink and drainer combinations come with a template so that you can mark the worktop for cutting with a jigsaw. Mark the underneath of the worktop so that the jigsaw blade doesn't splinter the top surface. If you don't feel confident, call in a professional to tackle this, as making an error will mean having to buy another worktop. Add the base units on either side. Connect up the water and outlet pipes –

again, call in a professional to do this if you are unsure.

4 Check that the units supporting the sink worktop are at the correct level. Use a spirit level to check units are horizontal. Screw the worktop to the units.

5 Work around the other walls, adding all the base units along each wall before fitting the worktop. You will need to use a router (with a straight cutter) and jig to form neat joints between meeting worktop surfaces. This requires DIY expertise, so you may want to call in a carpenter.

6 Assemble the hanging wall units outside. Each wall unit should have a fixing pack consisting of a metal wall-plate and an adjustable connector that is screwed into the rear of the cabinet. Use a spirit level to make a horizontal line around the walls. All the screw holes for fixing the wall-plates should be made along this line.

7 Drill and plug the wall to take the fixing brackets for the wall units (see below if you have hollow walls). Hang the wall units and adjust the fixings so that all the cabinets are aligned and horizontal. Fix adjacent cabinets together with the screws provided.

8 Add the kickboards to the base units and any cornice and open-ended display units.

HOLLOW WALLS

Where walls consist of plasterboard over a timber framework, wallplugs will not be sufficient to hold kitchen wall cupboards.

You will not usually be able to use the studs as for shelving brackets (see page 171) and the best answer is to cut a slot out of the plasterboard to fit a piece of solid timber (say, 75x25 mm or 3x1 in) and then screw the cupboards into that. Use a chisel or router to cut a slot in the timber uprights to accept the timber batten and screw it in place.

FLATPACK ASSEMBLY TIPS

- Most flatpack furniture is made of material that can easily be dented or chipped during assembly. Set your electric screwdriver on a low torque setting and adjust by one click stop until screws are pushed just below the surface. To push together dowel joints – where round pegs in one board fit into pre-drilled holes in the other – place a scrap 10 cm/4 in square piece of softwood over the joint and gently tap with a mallet.

- If you find the framework of a piece of furniture is wobbly or there are gaps around a back or side piece, just add more fixings. Try to match the size of the fixings supplied – longer screws or nails may protrude through the framework.

- If the furniture has doors with adjustable, kitchen-cabinet-style hinges, don't try to correct a misaligned door from one side only – make small adjustments to each side. Hinges can vary, but you will have to make adjustments to the screw fixings on the top and bottom of each hinge, plus a central screw that pushes the door in or out relative to the front of the cabinet.

- Use PVA woodworking glue to fix hardboard backs to the framework and for any other joints between chipboard surfaces that don't have to be taken apart again.

- If all the parts aren't fixed at right angles, the furniture will look shoddy and you may be left with gaps. Most packs use pre-drilled fittings to ensure the pieces join at a right angle, but it's worth double-checking before final tightening – place a try square against the joint and adjust if necessary.

Fitting locks

Fitting the right locks to your doors and windows makes your home far more secure and requires only a few simple tools.

SEE ALSO Useful skills p164–7, Making your home secure p56

SEE ALSO Useful skills p164–7, Making your home secure p56

EQUIPMENT

- Drill and drill bits
- Chisel
- Tape measure
- Pencil
- Ruler
- Mallet
- Screwdriver
- Junior hacksaw
- Masking tape.

LOCKS FOR A FRONT DOOR

For most of us, the front door is what is known as the 'final exit door'. This is the door that can't be bolted or locked from the inside when the last person leaves. The ideal security solution is to fit two locks, one a third of the way from the bottom and the other a third of the way from the top, providing the strongest resistance to attack. The lower lock should be a five-lever mortise deadlock that can be locked from inside or outside. For the upper lock, a cylinder rim lock is usually the best option. It not only locks automatically when pulled closed, but, unlike a simple nightlatch, also deadlocks, making it much harder to force open. See Choosing the best rim lock, right.

INSTALLING A SURFACE-MOUNTED RIM LOCK

Upgrading a non-locking nightlatch to a high-security rim lock is a reasonably simple job, but begin work early so that the door will be secure before nightfall. Fitting a replacement cylinder rim lock should take only about two hours.

A new cylinder rim lock will come in three main sections: the **cylinder** itself, which is the key-operated barrel with measuring bar that fits into the outside face of the door; the lock **casing**, which contains the main body of the workings and the latch; and the **staple**, which provides a casing for the bolt when it is extended into the door frame. The lock kit will also include a **mounting frame**, a metal plate that is screwed onto the inside face of the door to hold the lock casing.

1 Remove your old lock by taking out the screws on the back and edge of the door. Keep all the parts safe in case there's a problem with the new lock and you have to put the old one back.

2 On the outside face of the door, check that the new cylinder fits the existing hole and is the right distance from the edge – the instructions will give the measurements you need. You may need to enlarge the hole slightly with a file or chisel. Too tight a hole may stop the cylinder turning smoothly as the key is turned.

3 Mark the new fixing holes using the paper template provided with the lock. If there are already holes where you need to drill, check that the new screws will grip securely. If not, tap pieces of glued dowel (peg) into the holes to fill them completely. When the glue is dry, drill the new holes.

4 Screw the mounting plate to the inside of the door. Push the cylinder through the door from the outside and check the

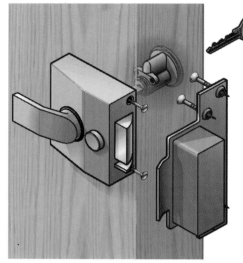

Rim lock

length of the measuring bar against the manufacturer's instructions. You may need to use a junior hacksaw to trim the bar to the correct length.

5 Hold the lock casing in place on the mounting plate and draw around the part of the casing that turns around the edge of the door. Use a sharp chisel and mallet to chop out the waste wood inside the pencil line so that the plate will be flush with the door edge.

6 Assemble the door lock and screw it in place. Check that the key turns smoothly in the lock – enlarge the cylinder hole if it sticks.

7 Close the door and mark the position of the bolt on the door frame. Cut out a recess with the chisel, then screw the staple to the door frame. Temporarily fix the staple with a single screw, and open and close the door to make sure that everything works smoothly. If it does, fit the other screws.

FITTING A RIM LOCK TO A NEW DOOR

If you want to fit a rim lock to a new door, or in a different position to your existing lock, tape the paper template supplied with the lock to the door, and mark the centre of the drill holes for the cylinder and screws.

For most locks, the hole needed for the cylinder will have a diameter of 32 mm/1¼ in, but always check the packaging. Drill through the door with a flat bit and your drill set on a fast speed to reduce splintering. When the point of the drill bit protrudes through the other side of the door, stop and complete the hole from the other side to prevent the wood splintering.

FITTING A MORTISE LOCK INTO A DOOR

Mortise locks are ideal as second locks on a front door (see Locks for a front door, left) and for back or side doors, which are not used as final exit doors. The lock body is fitted into the edge of the door, and the heavy-duty bolt locks into the door frame when the key is turned. You will need to know the width of your door edge when buying a mortise lock.

1 Measure the width of the door edge at a couple of places and join the halfway points to make a vertical line to ensure you fit the lock in the centre. Hold the lock casing (attached to the faceplate) against the edge of the door where you plan to fit the lock, and mark around the casing so that you know where to make the recess.

2 Choose a drill bit that is as close as possible to the width of the casing of the mortise lock, and drill a series of overlapping holes slightly deeper than the depth of the casing along the centre line to remove most of the waste wood. Wrap masking tape around the drill bit to act as a depth stop.

3 Use a chisel to square the edges of the recess until the lock fits. Mark around the faceplate of the lock and chisel a shallow recess so the lock is flush with the door edge.

4 Remove the body of the lock from the recess and hold it against one side of the door. Mark the position of the keyhole. Drill through the recess to the other side of the door (refer to the instructions on the packaging for the size of drill bit to use – usually around 10 mm/⅜ in). To stop the drill bit splintering the wood, clamp a block of scrap wood against the other side of the door. You will need to make two drill holes, one below the other, to allow the key to work smoothly.

5 Put the body of the lock back into the recess and screw in place. Fit the escutcheon (display) plates over the keyhole, using the tiny brass screws provided.

6 Close the door and turn the key to force the bolt onto the door frame. Mark the bolt indent with a pencil and chisel out a recess for the bolt and the striking plate (the metal plate that is fitted to the door frame). Screw the striking plate in place and check that the door locks smoothly.

Mortise lock

Size Rim locks come in backset sizes of 40 mm/1½ in, 50 mm/2 in, and 60 mm/2½ in. The backset is the distance from the centre of the keyhole to the edge of the door. Choose a lock with the longest backset that will fit your door.

Internally lockable For added security, buy a lock that is lockable from the inside with a key. If the door is glazed, or has glazed panels next to it, this is essential to stop the door being opened by an intruder reaching through smashed glass. It's worth buying a lock with this feature for any door – without a key, burglars will not be able to lock the door shut from the inside to prevent disturbance.

Deadlocking Always buy a cylinder rim lock that can be deadlocked. There are several types. Automatic deadlocking is the most convenient – the bolt locks the door shut whenever the door is closed. Double-throw deadlocks shoot the bolt further into the door frame when the key is turned from the outside. External deadlocks lock the door from the outside so that the latch cannot be turned from the inside, preventing an easy escape route through which burglars can carry your possessions.

British Standard mark Check the lock is marked BS 3621. This means it has been tested to simulate 30 years' use and has passed picking and forcing tests.

TIPS FOR LOCKS

- Use the longest screws possible for fixing locks and bolts in place.
- If you have an internally lockable rim lock, always keep a key hidden near the door in case of fire, but make sure it can be reached easily.

- If you have just moved into a house, it's worth changing the locks on all the exterior doors so you know exactly who has keys for your home.

- Save money by replacing just the cylinder of a rim lock. Replacement cylinders cost about half the price of a complete lock.

- A lock is only as strong as the door and frame, so make sure all the woodwork is in good condition. If the frame can be rocked when you push it, add extra wall fixings or have the frame replaced or repaired.

- Oiling a lock attracts dirt and can cause the lock to seize up. Instead, grind the end of a pencil and push some of the powdered graphite into the keyhole.

- Fitting a keypad-operated lock, where you punch in a pin number for access, can be a useful option for a back door. This might be particularly appropriate if people in your household are coming and going a fair amount, or you spend time in the garden out of sight of the door. You should, however, have other locks to ensure security when you are away for any length of time.

- A door lock should be at least 40 cm/16 in away from a letterbox, to be sure no one can reach in. If this isn't possible, the size of the letterbox should be no more than 250 x 38mm/9.8 x 1.5 in.

- The **Master Locksmiths Association**, recognized by the Home Office and the insurance industry, is a useful source of information on recommended types and standards of locks, especially if you have a style of window or door not covered here – for instance tilt and turn windows, and stable doors.

ADDING EXTRA FRONT DOOR SECURITY

DOOR VIEWER

Fit a door viewer and a strong door-chain to improve your front door security. Both are available from DIY stores. To fit a door viewer, drill a hole in the centre of the door at eye level. Most viewers need a 12 mm/ in hole. Use the same technique as for fitting a rim lock to a new door. Push the viewer through the hole, press the parts together from both sides, and tighten by turning the outer ring with a coin.

Viewers have a telescopic body to fit any thickness of door. Screw the chain into the door and frame just below the rim lock.

HINGE BOLTS

These are bolts that fix into the door frame on the hinge side when the door is closed. They offer protection against the use of a jemmy to break a door from its hinges. Fit one near each hinge, using the same method as for rack bolts, below.

ADDING EXTRA BACK DOOR SECURITY

RACK BOLTS

These small bolts, set into the edge of the door, add extra strength on the lock side of a back or side door. They are operated from inside with a key that has a ridged barrel. Fit one rack bolt about a third of the way from the top and another a third of the way from the bottom of the door. Drill a

hole in the door edge big enough to hold the bolt body, then chisel a recess for the metal plate (most come with a paper template – if not, hold the plate against the door). When the bolt is fitted, close the door and turn the key to mark the position of the locking plate on the frame. Drill and chisel out the waste wood to fit.

REINFORCEMENTS

Specially shaped metal strips are available for adding to the strength of any door, and for reinforcing the door frame, so both door and frame can resist tools or kicking. For maximum security, a locksmith can install multipoint locks. These drive bolt-heads into three or all four sides of the doorframe, making it almost impossible to prise open the door.

FITTING LOCKS TO SECURE WINDOWS

Windows need as much protection as doors. Fit at least two locks on an opening window, spaced across the frame so that it is difficult to lever open. Throw away any short screws included with the lock and replace with longer screws with a clutch head. A clutch-head screw has bevelled slots so the screwdriver can drive the screw into the wood but will slip out of the head when trying to undo the screw. They are available from hardware shops. Key-operated locks are the best option, preferably those that lock automatically when shut. To deter burglars, the locks should be large enough to be easily seen. As a final check, push hard on the frame from inside – add a lock wherever it gives.

CASEMENT WINDOWS

Use **snap-shut locks** on wooden casement windows. Fit these on the frame, adjacent to the opening window – usually on the sides. They don't need a key to close so are convenient to use.

Surface-mounted locks are good for securing metal casement windows. They come with self-tapping screws and should be fitted near the centre of the opening edge of the windows. Mark the position of the screws with a bradawl and drill pilot holes with a high-speed steel twist bit. Screw the lock in place.

Metal stays (the long arms that clip over small pegs fitted to the window frame) on casement windows can be reinforced with **stay locks** so the window can be locked partially open for ventilation. These are small metal locks that fit over the pegs. The upright post is threaded. Once the stay is hooked over the post, small locking pieces are threaded over the top and locked.

SASH WINDOWS

Protect sash windows with **screw-through bolts**. Drill holes through the top of the bottom sash and the bottom of the top sash, and insert the brass barrels. The bolt that holds the two sashes together is screwed tight with a key.

As a temporary measure, you could simply screw two long woodscrews through the overlapping horizontal parts of the sash frames so that they are fixed together and the window cannot be opened.

For sashes that you open regularly, it may be worth fitting **sash stops** on the window frame. These allow the window to be left slightly open for ventilation. Hold the faceplate to the bottom of the top sash and mark where the bolt will shoot through. Removing the faceplate, drill a hole for the bolt. Screw the faceplate over the hole, then screw the protective plate in place on the top edge of the bottom sash.

Casement window stay lock

Sash window sash stop

REINFORCING OLD PATIO DOORS

Old metal-framed sliding patio doors generally have too thin a frame to fit a mortise lock. Reinforce them with flush-fitting rack bolts that lock into the top and bottom of the frame to stop burglars prising the sliding parts out of their rails.

CHOOSING LOCKS FOR FRENCH DOORS

French doors are hinged glazed doors that close in a particular order.

- Before buying a central lock for French doors, check that it can be used on outward-opening doors. Special locks are made to suit the rebated edges of French doors.

- On wooden French doors, fit a mortise rack bolt into the top and bottom of each door so that it shoots into the top and bottom of the door frame. Hinge bolts will provide extra reinforcement (see opposite).

- Old metal French doors will need key-operated locks that can be screwed to the surface. Fit them in the same way as surface-mounted locks on metal casement windows (see left).

- Fit key-operated surface-mounted patio door locks to sliding wooden doors at top and bottom, plus an anti-lift device at the top of the frame if the doors were not fitted with one originally.

Contact details for organizations given in **bold** appear at the end of each chapter.

Dealing with appliances

Many small electrical appliances, such as a kettle or an iron, need no installation or wiring. Larger, free-standing appliances – a dishwasher, for example – may need special plumbing, although their wiring is often straightforward. Fixed appliances, such as cookers and extractor fans, are fitted to part of the house and will almost certainly need professional installation. See opposite for what to do when things go wrong with fixed or movable appliances.

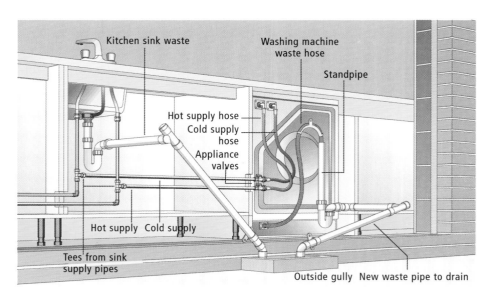

Kitchen sink waste
Washing machine waste hose
Standpipe
Hot supply hose
Cold supply hose
Appliance valves
Hot supply   Cold supply
Tees from sink supply pipes
Outside gully   New waste pipe to drain

INSTALLING A WASHING MACHINE OR DISHWASHER

WIRING UP APPLIANCES

Portable appliances and **free-standing appliances** are usually no problem – you just plug them into the nearest power point, though you may need to extend the flex on a fridge or wire up a washing machine from under a worktop to the nearest power point (see right). **Fixed appliances**, even if they come with a plug, are mostly wired to a fused connection unit on the wall, often with its own switch and a light to tell you that it's on. Fitting a fused connection unit is a job for an electrician, but connecting an appliance to one is no more difficult than wiring up a plug (see p64). You must turn the electricity off at the mains before unscrewing the front cover to expose the live, neutral, and earth terminals. The accessible fuse can be replaced easily if it blows. Most cookers need special wiring, which is a job for an electrician.

WHERE WILL YOU PLUG IT IN?

Washing machines and dishwashers come fitted with a plug, but if the machine is fitted beneath a worktop and the only available power points are above the worktop, you have a problem. Some people solve this by drilling a hole in the worktop to pass the flex through, but this is ugly, lets water and dirt through, and involves cutting off the moulded plug and replacing it with a wired-up plug.

A better answer is to have an electrician install a low-level power point below the worktop, which is connected by cable buried in the wall to a switched fused connection unit, mounted in or on the wall above the worktop. The low-level power point can be a single one and does not need a switch, since you can turn the appliance off at the switched fused connection unit above the worktop.

You will only need to unplug the machine when you pull it out for cleaning behind it or if the fuse in the plug blows. If there is a fault, however, the accessible fuse in the switched fused connection unit should blow first.

WHAT PLUMBING WILL YOU NEED?

Permanent plumbing makes using a washing machine much easier – and is a must for a dishwasher. This means connecting it to the water supply and to the drains.

The first essential for a washing machine or dishwasher is to connect to the hot and cold water supply pipes under the sink (normally only cold for dishwashers – check your appliance instructions). The normal way of doing this is to cut through both water supply pipes and fit compression tee fittings, with new lengths of pipe led to the position of the washing machine, where a pair of special appliance valves (often known as washing machine valves) need to be fitted to take the washing machine supply hoses – see illustration above. If the washing machine is close to the sink, a simpler alternative is to fit a self-cutting tap to each supply pipe in the way described right. The washing machine hoses can then be fitted directly to these taps.

A washing machine or dishwasher needs to have its own waste pipe leading to the drains. The normal method, shown left, is to hook the washing machine drain hose into a new standpipe connected to a trap and then to a new waste pipe taken outside to the drains – usually it can simply be led into the gully outside the kitchen.

If the washing machine or dishwasher is close to the sink, there is a simpler alternative, which is to re-arrange the waste pipes under the sink to accommodate the washing machine waste hose – see the explanation below.

Installing a washing machine or dishwasher shouldn't be too much of a challenge to a reasonably competent DIYer. But if all of this sounds too complicated, get a plumber in to do the job.

WHEN APPLIANCES GO WRONG

■ The first thing to check when an appliance does not work is the fuse in the plug or the fused connection unit. Replace it with a fuse you know is working before going any further. Also check the power point – by plugging in a table lamp that you know works, for example.

■ With many small appliances – such as a toaster, iron, or kettle – if the problem is not in the plug or the power point it may be easier to replace the appliance rather than fiddle about repairing it. For example, a replacement element for a kettle costs around a third of the cost of a new kettle and could take a couple of hours to fit.

■ Problems with the electronics of appliances such as microwave cookers and washing machines are impossible to repair, and you may not have the right test equipment to assess things like a failed thermostat on a refrigerator, and so are likely to need specialist help. Below is a list of some of the things you can check and possibly deal with yourself.

CONNECTING A WASHING MACHINE OR DISHWASHER

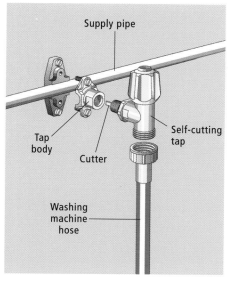

Supply pipe

Self-cutting tap

Tap body

Cutter

Washing machine hose

The following describes only washing machines or dishwashers installed close to the kitchen sink. You will first need to make holes in the side of the kitchen unit under the sink to take the supply and drain hoses.

The washing machine will have to be connected to the water supply pipes using self-cutting taps. These come in three sections: the two sections of the body part are clamped together on each pipe and secured to the wall with screws if required, and then the tap is screwed into the body. As you do this, a sharp cutter on the far end of the tap makes a hole in the side of the pipe to allow water to flow through when the tap is opened. The hoses (red for hot, blue for cold) are then screwed on to the taps and attached to the washing machine. The machine is ready for use once the taps are opened. If the hoses supplied with the washing machine are too short, you will have to replace them with longer ones.

You will then have to connect the washing-machine drain hose. You will normally need to fit a replacement waste trap that can take two connections under the kitchen sink, unless the existing trap has a blanked off section ready to take an extra connection. There are two main ways in which a replacement waste trap will connect to your machine – check the machine's instructions to see which is allowed. The more common method involves adding a short vertical standpipe to the trap into which the washing-machine drain hose can be hooked. The second method is to use a plastic connecting device called a tapered spigot, on to which the machine's drain hose is pushed.

APPLIANCE FAULT CHECKLIST

Problem	Likely cause	Possible solution
Washing machine/dishwasher fails to drain	Blocked pump	Check instructions for details of how to clear
Washing machine fails to spin	Broken drive belt	Remove back cover and replace
Tumble dryer fails to turn	Broken drive belt	Remove back cover and replace
Oven too hot or too cold	Failed thermostat	Call service engineer
Fridge/freezer too warm	Failed thermostat	Call service engineer
Kettle won't work	Element burnt out	Replace or discard kettle
Vacuum cleaner ineffective	Filter clogged Airways clogged Drive belt broken	Replace Clear out Remove cover and replace
Iron won't steam	Scale inside iron	Use descaling fluid or vinegar

Plumbing leaks and drips

Even the best-designed and best-installed plumbing system can leak – usually from a pipe joint, but occasionally from the pipe itself. Taps can drip or stop working altogether and you can get strange noises from the plumbing and heating systems.

FOUR REASONS FOR NOISY PIPES

There are four reasons why plumbing pipes make noise:

- corrosion in your central heating system – see p194 for details
- central heating (or hot water) pipes rubbing on the sides of slots cut in joists under floorboards as they expand and contract. This can be solved by lifting the relevant floorboard and slipping a piece of foam pipe insulation around the pipe where it passes through the slot
- a noisy ballvalve in one or more cisterns. Solve by replacing old piston-type ballvalves with modern diaphragm types. See WCs and cisterns, p188, for more on ballvalves
- water hammer – a thundering noise that normally starts when you turn on a tap, which is actually a shockwave bouncing down the pipe. There is more than one cause of water hammer. The most likely solutions are either to close the main stopvalve slightly (see Cutting off the water supply, right), or to re-washer taps (see Dripping taps, right), or to replace the ballvalve in the main cold water cistern with an equilibrium – or quiet – type.

REPAIRING LEAKS

Leaks need to be dealt with as soon as they are discovered, whether in a pipe, a joint, or from a radiator. Not only do leaks waste water, but they can also cause damage to decorations and to house timbers that may develop rot as a result.

LEAKING JOINTS

Joints between pipes are often the first thing to go when pipework freezes and expanding ice inside the pipe forces the joint apart. If the joint is a compression joint with a nut on each connection, tightening the nuts (clockwise) will normally stop the leak. Always use one spanner to hold the fitting whilst you use another to tighten the nut – but don't overtighten it or it will distort the olive and leak again. If tightening doesn't work, you will need to turn the water off to isolate the pipe affected, dismantle the joint, and replace the compression olives (the shaped brass rings that are compressed to make the seal); the old ones may have to be cut off carefully.

Soldered capillary joints – where the seal is made by a solidified solder between pipe and fitting – are more difficult to repair. They need heat, provided by a blowlamp, first to melt the old solder and then to melt the new solder on a replacement fitting. The easiest thing to do is to turn the water off and cut out the leaking fitting and the pipe on either side, replacing the capillary fitting with a compression or push-fit fitting.

DRIPPING TAPS

When it starts getting difficult to turn a tap off, you can suspect that the washer inside is getting worn – and when the tap starts dripping, you will know it is time to change the washer. Fortunately this is usually relatively simple and inexpensive,

LEAKING PIPES

Copper and plastic pipes do not normally leak unless they have been damaged in some way – either by piercing, typically with a floorboard nail, or by bursting after they have frozen. You can buy pipe repair clamps and repair putties (which set hard) to act as temporary stop-gaps, but the best solution is to turn the water off to isolate the pipe in question (see right), cut out the affected length of pipe, and insert a new length with two straight couplers.

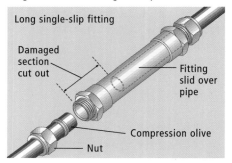

Long single-slip fitting

Damaged section cut out

Fitting slid over pipe

Compression olive

Nut

A proper pipe cutter is better for cutting the pipe, since a hacksaw can leave a jagged edge. You can get special compact cutters to cut pipes next to a wall. If the pipes are rigidly fixed (making insertion of the couplers impossible), make sure at least one of the straight couplers is a slip fitting – this has no internal shoulders, so can be slid up one of the pipes and then slid back into place after the new length has been inserted. You can get long single slip fittings, see illustration, for replacing a short length of pipe.

unless the tap is a modern ceramic disc type that requires only a quarter turn to operate. These are much less likely to go wrong, but when they do, giving more of a stream than a drip, you have little choice but to replace the whole mechanism inside.

REPLACING THE WASHER ON A STANDARD TAP

Old-fashioned pillar taps have a vertical inlet and a rising spindle with a washer at the bottom. They usually have a bell-shaped cover topped by a **capstan head** (four prongs in a cross shape). Conventional modern taps have **shrouded heads** (see right).

1 Turn off the water to isolate the pipe leading to the tap – see right.

2 Remove the cover. With capstan-head taps, unscrew and lift off the head before removing the chromium-plated bell cover (you may need to use a cloth-wrapped spanner if it is tight). Shrouded-head taps and mixer taps usually have a coloured disc in the top of the tap head, which you unscrew by hand or prise out with a small screwdriver to get at the securing screw underneath in order to get the head off.

3 Use a large spanner to undo the largest nut you can see. Use another spanner or a piece of wood to brace the tap as you unscrew this to avoid cracking ceramic basins or baths.

4 Take out the works of the tap. You should see the tap washer on the bottom. Prise this off – you may need to undo a small nut – and replace with a new one of the same size and shape (bath taps have bigger washers than basin taps).

5 Re-assemble everything before turning the water back on.

6 If a tap is leaking from the top when it is opened, tightening the smallest nut

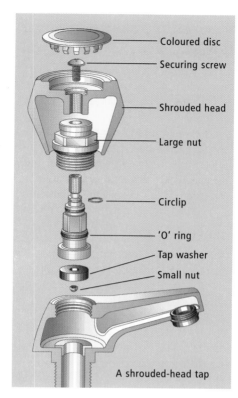

- Coloured disc
- Securing screw
- Shrouded head
- Large nut
- Circlip
- 'O' ring
- Tap washer
- Small nut

A shrouded-head tap

you can see will normally stop the leak, but you may need to dismantle the tap, by undoing this nut, or prising out the circlip, in order to replace the sealing O ring.

MIXER TAPS

Replacing washers on mixer taps is the same as for single taps, though you will need to turn off both hot and cold supplies if you are replacing both washers. Mixer taps can also leak around the spout, caused by a failed O ring. If you can find the tiny grub screw that you undo to remove the spout, replacing this is simple.

CUTTING OFF THE WATER SUPPLY

There are six places you can cut off the water supply in an emergency or when you want to work on part of the plumbing system.

Water company stopvalve Usually at property boundary – see p67. Turns off the supply for the whole house, but leaves the main cistern full of cold water. You may need a special key.

Main stopvalve Usually under the kitchen sink, but may be elsewhere. Also turns off the supply for the whole house, but leaves the cistern full of water.

Cold water gatevalve Usually an orange or red handle, in loft next to cold water tank. Turns off supply to bath and basin cold taps and WC cistern, but allows kitchen cold tap to run. Leaves cistern full of water and all hot taps working.

Hot water supply gatevalve An orange or red handle, normally in airing cupboard close to hot water cylinder. Turns off cold supply to cylinder and so all hot taps. Leaves cistern full of water and all cold taps working.

Servicing valves Found on low-pressure supply pipes to individual taps and ballvalves, they isolate supply to that tap or ballvalve for repair. Small valves without a handle, they have a slotted screw that normally needs only a quarter of a turn to operate.

Stopvalves Found on cold water pipes at mains pressure, leading to garden tap, electric shower (or water heater), washing machine, dishwasher, or water softener. A stopvalve isolates a tap or appliance, when closed.

SEALING ROUND A BATH

Water that gets down the gap between a bath or shower tray and the wall can cause damage to the floor underneath (possibly rot), but can be prevented by applying silicone sealant around the rim of the bath or shower tray.

Silicone sealant comes in white and various colours and requires a bit of skill to apply. You can use either a large cartridge in a caulking gun or a smaller cartridge with its own in-built plunger.

To get a smooth result, do a dry run first: without actually applying sealant, run the cartridge all the way around the edge of the bath or shower tray to check you can do this in one continuous action without having to break to change position.

WCs and cisterns

When a WC doesn't work properly, the problem usually lies in the cistern, not the pan. Fixing WC problems is straightforward, even if you have no plumbing know-how – as long as you understand how the flushing mechanism works. You just need a few basic tools and some inexpensive spare parts. Even getting access to the problem area is easy, just lift off the cistern lid. Cisterns in the loft can have problems, too – usually too much noise or a dripping overflow pipe.

EQUIPMENT

- Wrench
- Pliers
- Screwdriver
- Spare parts as required.

TURNING OFF THE WATER SUPPLY

For some repairs, you will have to turn off the water supply to the WC. See p67 for illustrations of valves.

1 Look for a small servicing valve on the supply pipe to the cistern. If you find one, use a screwdriver to turn its slotted screw through 90 degrees.

2 If there is no valve, and the cistern is fed from the cold water storage tank, turn off the gatevalve on the outlet pipe from the tank, which supplies the cold taps. The gatevalve is usually close to the tank itself.

3 If the cistern is fed direct from the mains, turn off the main stopvalve where the water supply enters your home.

HOW A WC WORKS

When a WC is flushed, two things happen:

- Water in the cistern flows down a connecting pipe into the WC pan. This happens because of a siphon mechanism at the bottom of the cistern, activated by a rod connected to the far end of the flush lever spindle. The siphon action starts when a unit containing a piston and a flexible plastic diaphragm (flapvalve) pushes water through an upside-down U-bend. The piston then drops back, allowing the water to flow past it until the cistern is almost empty and the lack of water stops the siphon action.

- The cistern refills through a ballvalve near the top of the cistern. This valve is operated by a metal or plastic arm connected to a float, which sits on the water. As the water level falls, the float arm falls with it, opening the valve and allowing the cistern to refill. As the water level rises, the float arm rises too, and the valve closes. Similar ballvalves are fitted to water storage cisterns in the loft.

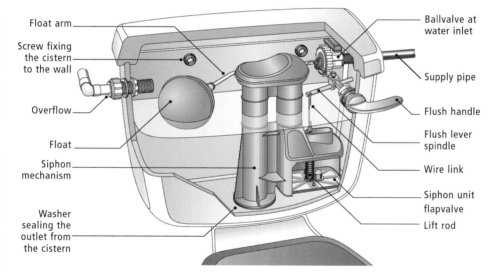

Float arm
Screw fixing the cistern to the wall
Overflow
Float
Siphon mechanism
Washer sealing the outlet from the cistern
Ballvalve at water inlet
Supply pipe
Flush handle
Flush lever spindle
Wire link
Siphon unit flapvalve
Lift rod

IF THE CISTERN DOESN'T FLUSH

Either there's insufficient water, or the siphon mechanism isn't working.

1 **The float arm may be set too low**. Check the water level inside the cistern. It should be about 25 mm/1 in below the bottom of the overflow pipe. The correct level might be marked on the inside wall of the cistern. If the water level is too low, the float arm is also too low, and is closing the ballvalve on the water inlet pipe before the cistern is full. If the float rod is metal and has no adjuster screw, straighten it slightly. If it is plastic, there will be a small adjuster screw on the arm – turn it anticlockwise to raise the arm.

2 **The C-shaped wire link between the flush lever spindle and the lift rod has become disconnected**. Re-hook the wire link on to the flush lever spindle and the top end of the lift rod. If the link is broken, replace it.

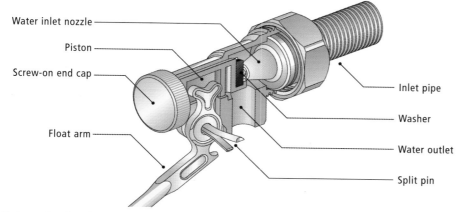

Water inlet nozzle
Piston
Screw-on end cap
Float arm

Inlet pipe
Washer
Water outlet
Split pin

Portsmouth valve, the most common type of metal valve

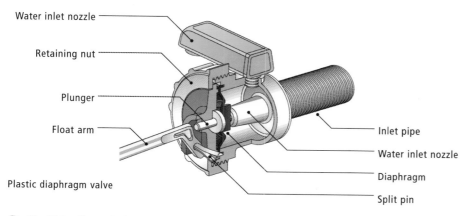

Water inlet nozzle
Retaining nut
Plunger
Float arm

Inlet pipe
Water inlet nozzle
Diaphragm
Split pin

Plastic diaphragm valve

3 If a WC still won't flush effectively, you probably need to **replace the siphon unit flapvalve** (the flexible piece of plastic on top of the perforated plate; see main illustration).

■ On a **close-coupled cistern**, where the cistern and lavatory pan are joined, replacing the valve itself is the same as for a separate cistern, but to get at the nut that holds the siphon unit to the base of the cistern, you first have to remove the cistern from the pan. Turn off the water supply to the cistern (see left). Flush the cistern and mop up the remaining water. Disconnect the supply and overflow pipes from the cistern. Undo the screws holding the cistern to the wall, and also the two wing nuts securing it to the rear part of the pan. Lift the cistern off the pan. Unscrew the siphon securing nut. Unhook the wire link, lift out the siphon unit, lift rod and piston, and replace the flapvalve as for a separate cistern. Reassemble everything and restore the water supply.

■ On a **separate cistern**, where the cistern is joined to the lavatory by a pipe, tie up the float arm to stop the cistern refilling. Flush cistern and mop up the remaining water. Disconnect the flush pipe from the base of the cistern and undo the large nut that holds the siphon unit to the base of the cistern. Unhook the wire link from the top of the siphon lift rod. Lift the siphon unit out and pull out the lift rod and piston from the open base. Remove the old flapvalve and fit a replacement. Cut the new one down to size with scissors if it's too big. Reassemble everything. Untie the float arm so the cistern can refill.

IF AN OVERFLOW DRIPS

If water is dripping or running from an overflow pipe outside, one of your cisterns is overfilling, sending water down the overflow – find out which one before checking the possible causes – see right.

CAUSES OF OVERFLOW

1 **A cistern float arm may be set too high** and is not closing the ballvalve when the water is at the correct level. If the float arm is metal (and has no adjuster screw), bend the end with the float down slightly. If it's plastic, turn the small screw on the arm clockwise so that the float arm is at a slightly steeper angle.

2 If the float is half submerged or more, the **float has let in water** and the arm can't completely shut off the ballvalve. Unscrew the float and empty out the water. As a temporary repair, fit a small plastic bag over the float, squeeze out the air, and tie the mouth of the bag round the arm with a wire tie. Fit a replacement plastic float.

3 The **ballvalve may be faulty**. In a metal valve, the washer in the piston may have perished. In a plastic one, the diaphragm inside may be damaged. See illustrations. First turn off the water supply to the cistern (see left).

■ Replacing a washer on a metal valve: unscrew the valve end cap; you may need a wrench. Use pliers to grip and pull out the split pin that attaches the float arm to the valve. Push the tip of a small screwdriver into the slot where the float arm fitted and use it to push the piston out of the open end of the valve. Push the screwdriver into the slot in the piston and use pliers to undo its end cap. Prise the washer out of the cap. Fit a new washer.

■ Replacing a diaphragm on a plastic valve: undo the large, knurled retaining nut. Lift the float arm and plunger away from the valve body. Note how the diaphragm is fitted before prising it out with a small screwdriver blade. Fit a replacement diaphragm facing the same way as the old one.

Reassemble and restore water supply.

▶ Clearing blockages

The first you are likely to know about a blockage is when a sink, basin, or WC won't empty, or gullies and manhole covers are overflowing outside, usually accompanied by a strong smell. The blockage may be in one of several places – see Where the waste goes, right, for an explanation of the waste system. If there is a strong smell but no evident blockage, ask your local Environmental Health department to check the drains.

PREVENTING BLOCKAGES

It is not a good idea to use chemical drain cleaners to try to clear a blockage – but used regularly they can prevent one. Tip a little chemical cleaner – or some washing soda crystals mixed with hot water – down each waste outlet once a month. Don't do this, however, if you have a septic tank as it may ruin the tank's bacteriological action.

FROZEN PIPES

If a **water pipe** inside the house has frozen and there is no water at the tap, leave the tap open and work back along the length of the pipe, warming it with a hairdryer or hot air gun on a low setting until the water flows again.

Do not, however, use either tool on a frozen **waste pipe**. Instead, soak towels in hot water and drape them over the waste pipes until the water flows away.

WASTE OUTLETS AND PIPES

Sinks, basins, baths, shower trays, or bidets that won't run empty are all indications of a blocked waste system.

PLUGHOLES

The metal grille over the waste outlet – usually called the plughole – is designed to prevent material (such as hair or vegetable peelings) getting into the pipes, so it may get partially blocked quite often. Cleaning it out is simple, but you may need to pull bits of hair out by hand.

WASTE TRAPS

The shaped waste trap underneath a waste outlet remains full of water all the time. It prevents smells from the drains getting into the house and prevents small creatures climbing in. Bottle traps take up less room than conventional tubular P-traps, but are more likely to get blocked – and should never be fitted below a waste disposal unit. If your bottle trap gets blocked regularly, replace it with a P-trap.

Clearing a blocked trap

First try a hand-operated force pump or a simple rubber, cup-shaped sink plunger. This fits over the waste outlet and is pumped up and down vigorously, creating water pressure that may force out the blockage. Hold a damp cloth over the overflow outlet at the top of the basin or sink while using the plunger or force pump to create a vacuum. You may need several goes to clear the blockage.

If a plunger or force pump doesn't work, you can dismantle the trap. Place a large bucket underneath it and undo the nuts holding the ends of the trap on to the waste outlet and the waste pipe leading outside. Be prepared for the contents of the sink or basin to gush out. Clean the trap itself with washing-up liquid and an old bottle cleaning brush (using a different basin in the house) and re-fit it, smearing a bit of liquid soap on to the rubber sealing rings. Empty the bucket outside and check that the trap is clear by running fresh water from the taps.

WASTE PIPES

If plunging and cleaning the trap doesn't work, the blockage is further down the waste pipe. Remove the trap again and use a plumber's snake – a length of flexible wire with a wiggly bit on the end, also known as a sink auger – pushed down the waste pipe to clear the blockage. You can use the wiggly bit to disturb the blockage, pulling and pushing it until you can get the snake all the way along the pipe. Re-fit the trap and test for clear running.

SOIL PIPES

If a soil pipe is on the outside of the house, it may get frozen in the winter, especially if you have a dripping tap inside – see p186 for dealing with this. Otherwise blockages in outside soil pipes are rare. Hopper heads in older systems may sometimes get clogged with soap and hair, but are easy to clean out provided you have a safe way of getting to them. On modern soil pipes, there is usually an access hatch somewhere that you can unscrew in order to get a plumber's snake or a drain rod inside to clean out blockages. Stand well back when you open this – there could be a sudden gush of filthy water.

WCS

A blocked WC is something you will want to deal with as quickly as possible. You can get larger versions of sink plungers and force pumps to use, which have long handles so you do not need to get too close to the blockage. If you have no success with these, there is similarly a larger version of the plumber's snake (see Waste pipes), called a WC auger. Push this down the WC pan until you reach the site of the blockage, which can then be disturbed and cleared.

UNDERGROUND DRAINS

The most obvious sign of a blocked underground drain is an overflowing gully outside, but be suspicious if there is a very strong smell anywhere outside your property, as this could mean there is a blockage in the drain itself or in one of the inspection chambers situated under manhole covers.

THE GULLY

If there is no indication where the blockage is, start by clearing the gully under the kitchen sink waste outlet, where the downpipe from the kitchen empties into the drain. In older houses, this may take the waste from the bath and bathroom basin as well. Be prepared for a horrid job – wear stout rubber gloves to scoop out the gunge from the gully after lifting up the grille. If the blockage is in the gully trap, you may need a plumber's snake (see Waste pipes, left) to winkle it out.

THE DRAINPIPE

If water will still not flow away after clearing out the gully under the kitchen sink waste outlet, lift all the manhole covers and look inside the inspection chambers, some of which may be full. The blockage is in the drain between the last full chamber and the first empty chamber.

Hire a set of drain rods. Join the first couple of lengths to the wormscrew attachment that comes with them and lower this into the last full inspection chamber, feeling for the half drain that runs along the bottom toward the outlet away from the house. Push the wormscrew into the outlet and along the drain in the direction of the empty chamber, adding more rods as you need them, until you reach the blockage. A combination of pulling, pushing, and wiggling the wormscrew should dislodge the blockage, allowing the inspection chamber to empty.

The other attachments that come with a drain rod set – such as a plunger and a scraper – can be used to clean out the drain once the main blockage has been removed. If you encounter an obstruction that will not give way, the drain may be blocked by a tree root or broken drain material and you should call in professional help.

If it is the last inspection chamber before your property boundary that is full – probably by just one third – you have a blockage between this inspection chamber and the main sewer. Rod this inspection chamber as before, pushing the wormscrew along the base of the chamber away from the house, wiggling it until the chamber empties.

If you have a cesspool or septic tank and the last inspection chamber is full, it's time to have the pool or tank emptied.

On some modern drainage systems, you may have one or more 'rodding points' rather than inspection chambers. The small circular covers of these can be removed to allow you to insert drain rods.

USING DRAIN RODS

- Always twist drain rods **clockwise**. Twisting them anticlockwise could make the rods unscrew underground and you could lose one.
- Clean the rods with water and disinfectant after use.

GUTTERS AND DOWNPIPES

Leaves and other debris can be removed from a rainwater gutter with a small trowel (provided you can get safe access to the gutter level). To clear a blocked downpipe, use drain rods from the top – or bottom, if possible – to disturb and dislodge the blockage.

WHERE THE WASTE GOES

1 Water flows out of a sink or basin **waste outlet** – or plughole – which is fitted with a metal grille, and passes through the **waste trap**. Waste traps come in two basic designs: tubular – either an S, U, or P shape – or bottle shaped.

2 Water from the trap under the kitchen sink runs directly outside into a drain with a **grille**, which has a large U-shaped trap, or **gully**, underneath.

3 In older systems, bath and basin water also comes into this drain and gully, having come along two **waste pipes** that join at an open **hopper head**, then through a **downpipe**. In modern systems, the waste pipes from the bath and basin are connected directly to the main external **soil pipe**, which also takes the waste from the WC directly to the **underground drain**.

4 Waste travels through the underground drain past several **inspection chambers** – you get to these by lifting manhole covers, which are metal or plastic lids in the ground.

DEALING WITH AIRLOCKS

If no water comes out of a tap, especially a hot tap, there may be an airlock, usually caused by a misalignment of pipes. Cure an airlock by attaching one end of a hosepipe to the offending tap – you can buy a special attachment for this – and the other to another working tap. Connect hot to hot, or cold to cold, and turn both taps on. If the problem recurs frequently, you will have to get a plumber to look at the pipework.

Central heating

Central heating is wonderful when it works, but can be a nightmare if it goes wrong. A problem may be due to the failure of one or more of the components – boiler, pump, controls, or immersion heater – or something going on inside the system, particularly the onset of corrosion, which is caused by different metals being in contact through water. Many of the problems that arise with central heating can be dealt with relatively simply, but some may call for the services of a professional contractor.

POSITIONING OF RADIATORS

There is a good reason why radiators are put under windows – to counteract the draughts and beat the 'cold zone' that would otherwise result, caused by the rate at which heat passes out through the window. But this applies only to single-glazed windows.

If you have double-glazing (which for most people means replacement windows), radiators can be put wherever it is most convenient in the room given features and furniture (see Saving on heating, p69).

Moving a radiator is quite a major job for which you would probably want to employ a plumber. It will certainly mean draining down the system and possibly re-routing some pipes and you need to know what you are doing to avoid leaks and to avoid leaving air in the system afterwards.

DRAINING AND REFILLING A HEATING SYSTEM

You may need to drain and refill your central heating system if you want to move radiators or replace them with others of a different size, requiring changes to the pipework, or if you want to treat corrosion (see p194).

A central heating system that uses water – the vast majority – will have at least one drainvalve that allows you to empty out the water. The drainvalve will usually be at the lowest point in the system, possibly under the floorboards, but there may be additional drainvalves by the boiler or where pipes are looped down from the first floor to a ground floor radiator – often the case with kitchen radiators.

DRAINING THE SYSTEM

1 Switch off the central heating.

2 Close off the water supply to the feed-and-expansion cistern to stop the system re-filling. To do this you can either turn off the water at the main stopvalve (see p67) or tie up the ballvalve in the feed and expansion cistern – a better option since it allows you to continue using the kitchen cold tap. You can release the ballvalve any time you want to flush the system through with fresh water. You might need to do this after using a cleanser prior to adding corrosion proofer.

3 At each drainvalve – it doesn't matter where you start – attach a hosepipe to the outlet of the valve and lead the hose outside or into a bath.

4 Using a small spanner, unscrew the valve, allowing water to flow out.

5 Unscrew the air bleed valve on every radiator to make sure all the water is removed. You will need to include the air bleed valve on the hot water cylinder. This is usually located on the highest point on the upper of the two pipes that lead from the boiler into the side of the cylinder.

While the system is empty, you might want to remove individual radiators, take them into the garden and flush them through with water from a garden hose.

REFILLING THE SYSTEM

1 Again with the heating system turned off, close all the drainvalves and air bleed valves and release the ballvalve in the feed-and-expansion cistern.

2 As the system fills, bleed each radiator in turn, starting with those on the ground floor and working upwards. You may need to go round the whole system twice, not forgetting the air bleed valve on the hot water circuit next to the hot water cylinder. Corrosion proofer is added on the final fill after cleansing and flushing (check instructions supplied with corrosion proofer for details).

3 When the system is full, turn the boiler on and check that there are no leaks from any of the air bleed valves or drainvalves – tighten any that are leaking.

REMOVING AND REPLACING A RADIATOR

If an individual radiator has sprung a leak – or is too small or large (see Possible problems with temperature, p194) – it is normally a fairly straightforward task to replace it. The easiest job of all is where the replacement radiator has its inlets in the same place and can be hung on the original wall brackets, which is much more likely if it is the same make as the one being replaced. If the existing radiator has an inappropriate heating output, it can be replaced with a different type of the same size (with fewer or more panels or fins) or by one of the same type that is a different height, but not a different length. A new radiator that does not fit the old wall brackets will still not be too complicated to install, but if the new inlets are in a different place from the old, the system will need to be drained so that the pipework close to the radiator can be altered – something that is likely to need the skills of a qualified plumber.

You will need something to catch the water that falls out of the radiator when you remove it – put down towels on the floor and have bowls ready for catching the water from each valve.

1 Close the handwheel or thermostatic valve that turns the radiator on and off – if your radiator has a thermostatic valve, set it to 0 to close it. Remove the cover on the valve at the bottom of the other side, called the lockshield valve – this usually needs a screwdriver – before closing that. If the handwheel from the first valve fits the lockshield valve, you can close it with that, otherwise you will need to use a spanner. With both valves closed, open the air vent at the top of the radiator and unscrew the two nuts that join the valves to the radiator, with the bowls ready

to catch the water. Bend the valves out of the way so that you can lift the radiator off its brackets and tilt it to fully drain.

2 If the new radiator is the same size and make, you should be able to re-use the existing wall brackets, but otherwise you will have to unscrew the old brackets and drill holes in the wall to take wallplugs for the new ones (see Securing fixings to walls, p171). Full instructions should be given with the radiator for getting these in the correct position). Remove the screwed tails (the connections that take the valves) from the bottom tappings of the old radiator and fit them in the two bottom outlets of the new one – you may need a special radiator spanner to do this. Also fit the blanking plug and air bleed valve supplied with the new radiator to the two inlets at the top.

3 Hang the new radiator on the wall brackets and connect up the two valve tails, making sure the nuts are tight. Open up the handwheel and lockshield valves – turn a thermostatic valve to the setting you want – and use a radiator key on the air bleed valve you fitted to the top of the radiator to allow the air inside the radiator to escape once the water starts running into it – see How to bleed a radiator, right.

HOW TO BLEED A RADIATOR

If the tops of the radiators are cold, it's possible that air has collected in the system or that there is corrosion. For prevention and cure of the latter problem, see Corrosion in the heating system, p194.

Air that regularly collects inside any of the radiators indicates a leak – undetected because it is out of sight and the system is kept topped up by the feed-and-expansion cistern. If there is a leak, you can remove air from a single radiator fairly easily by bleeding it. You will need a small radiator bleed key (available in DIY stores) and a cloth.

1 Hold the cloth firmly against the radiator just under the air bleed valve (see illustration) and use the key to unscrew the valve in an anti-clockwise direction.

2 Stop when you hear a hissing sound – the air escaping – and wait until the hissing turns first to a dribble and then to a squirt of water.

3 Close the valve quickly.

If the hissing never turns to water, there is a lack of water in the system, which will almost certainly be because the ballvalve in the feed and expansion cistern up in the loft has become stuck. Because the ballvalve rarely operates in a leak-free system, it may have stuck in the closed position. This leaves the cistern empty because water has evaporated. Ease the ballvalve arm down gently to allow the cistern to re-fill. Don't worry if the level looks low – the cistern should only be around one-third full when cold, to allow space for the water in the system to expand when it is hot. For more on ballvalves, see WCs and cisterns, p188.

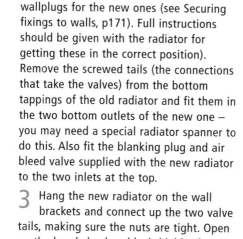

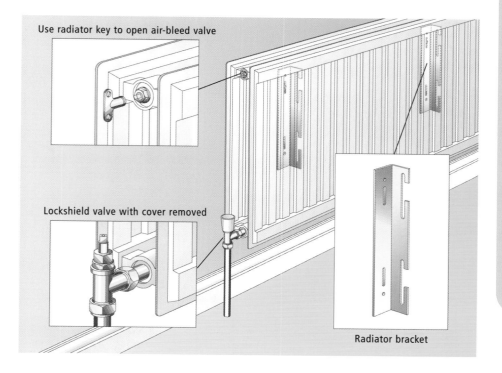

Use radiator key to open air-bleed valve

Lockshield valve with cover removed

Radiator bracket

The boiler appears to be working, but no heat is getting to the radiators or hot water cylinder and you have checked that the system is full of water and not air.

1 **One or more of the motorized valves in your system may have jammed**. This (or these) will normally be positioned somewhere near the pump, probably in the airing cupboard by the hot water cylinder. A motorized valve has a squarish body on top and has either two or three outlets.

- Look for a hand-operated lever – this allows you to override the automatic operation of the valve, so that water can flow along the pipes leading to the radiators and/or the hot water cylinder.

- Move the lever from 'auto' to 'manual'. If this gets the radiators or hot water cylinder warm, you have solved the problem temporarily – except that the valve itself or the operating part on top of it will need to be replaced at some point, which is a job for a central heating contractor.

- Leave the lever on manual in the meantime.

2 **The pump may have failed**. You can tell if the pump is running by feeling it: it will be hot, and will emit a whirring sound and a vibration. If it is not running, it may be stuck, airlocked, or burnt out.

- A stuck pump can be unjammed by applying a screwdriver to the slot provided.

- An airlocked pump can be released by opening the bleed valve on the body (see pump instructions for details).

- A burnt-out pump will have to be replaced by a professional.

POSSIBLE PROBLEMS WITH TEMPERATURE

If you cannot get some rooms to the right temperature, or some rooms are always warmer than others, you may have one of a number of problems.

1 **Some radiators are too large or small for the room**. The heat output of a radiator depends on its surface area, so the larger it is – in other words, the more panels and fins it has – the greater the amount of heat. For the same size (length and height) of standard radiator, there are four choices of design (in increasing order of output):

- single panel
- single panel with fins
- double panel with one set of fins
- double panel with two sets of fins.

You can usually replace the existing radiator with one of the same size but with a higher or lower output.

2 **The radiators are imbalanced**. There may be too great or too little a flow through some of the radiators.

The amount of water flowing through a radiator is controlled by the setting on the lockshield valve. Remove the cover, then turn the spindle of this valve either with a spanner or, if it fits, with the handwheel from the other valve (see Removing and replacing a radiator, p193). Turn the valve clockwise to reduce the water flow and so reduce the heat output, turn it anti-clockwise to increase the flow and output. Getting the balance exactly right requires the use of two inexpensive clip-on thermometers (available from plumbers' merchants), which you apply to the pipes leading to the radiator, but trying different settings may be sufficient.

3 **The room thermostat is in the wrong place.** The heating for the radiators is turned on and off by the action of a room thermostat – an electrical switch which starts the boiler and the pump when the air temperature around the thermostat is too low, and turns them off when the surrounding air reaches the temperature you have set on the thermostat. The thermostat can be fooled if it is in a draught or in direct sunlight, or in a room that has additional heating. If you find that some rooms are too hot and others are too cold, it could be that the thermostat is in the wrong place: the best place is usually in the hall out of direct sunlight and away from draughts. You will need an electrician to move it.

CORROSION IN THE HEATING SYSTEM

A fateful combination of metals in the central heating system can cause corrosion. It will lead to some or all of a number of symptoms:

- leaks, where corrosion has eaten away the steel of the radiators

- cold at the bottom of radiators, from a build-up of sludge

- cold at the tops of radiators, because hydrogen gas has collected there

- malfunctioning pumps and motorized valves, which can jam from corrosion

- various extraneous noises in the pipes and the boiler.

Preventing corrosion is very straightforward in a new system or an old one that is still in good condition by adding corrosion proofer to the feed-and-expansion cistern and allowing it to circulate throughout the water.

Dealing with existing corrosion is a two-stage process: first cleaning out the existing system, and then adding the corrosion proofer. Find out from the manufacturers of corrosion proofers, or a good plumbers' merchants, which cleansing and corrosion-proofing products you need – it depends on the type of boiler you have. Copious instructions are provided with the proofers on how to use them, but you will need to know how to drain down and refill your central heating system – see p192.

PREVENTING FREEZING IN AN EMPTY HOUSE

In a house that is normally occupied during the winter, there should be no danger of frozen or burst pipes. But if a house is left empty for anything more than a day during a cold snap, there is always the possibility that some pipes will freeze and that some may even burst as they thaw. There are specific precautions you need to take to prevent this, depending on how long you are going to be away.

AWAY FOR A WEEKEND

If you are only going to be away from the house for a couple of days, you can either leave the heating on its normal settings and be prepared to pay the fuel bills or, if you want to save money, do the following:

■ set the heating programmer to 24-hour ('continuous') operation

■ set the room thermostat to a low setting – say 5°C/41°F

■ remove or prop loft hatch fully open.

This will allow the boiler to fire to keep the house (and the loft space) above freezing point.

AWAY FOR LONGER

If you leave the house for more than a few days, and want to turn the heating off, you need to drain the hot and cold water systems of all water. If the heating system (which is separate from the hot and cold water systems) has anti-freeze in it, you do not need to drain it.

■ Drain down the cold water system entirely – close the main stopvalve, open all cold taps, and flush all WCs.

■ Drain down the hot water cylinder fully using a length of hosepipe attached to the drain valve at the base of the hot water cylinder (which needs a small spanner to open); put this into a basin or bath, and open all hot taps.

■ When you return, check that all drain valves are closed before opening the mains stopvalve.

■ Close taps as water flows from them – the kitchen cold tap first, then all other cold taps, and then all hot taps.

GENERAL PRECAUTIONS

Whether you are planning to be away or not, it's sensible to take general precautions against freezing in case you are away during a cold snap and haven't been able to prepare for it first. There are two general ways to prevent freezing:

Fit a frost thermostat that brings the boiler on whenever the air temperature drops below a certain level – much lower than the level required to bring the heating on when the house is occupied. This is certainly something you should do if the boiler is situated in the garage or an outhouse that could get seriously cold even if the rest of the house is above freezing.

Add anti-freeze chemical to the feed and expansion cistern so that it circulates around the central heating system. This chemical is made by specialist firms – and is not the same as the antifreeze used in cars.

Adding antifreeze to your central heating system or fitting a frost thermostat are useful general precautions against freezing pipes, but you should still take the specific precautions described above if you go away in the winter to prevent the house water pipes freezing.

MECHANICAL PROBLEMS

The boiler fails to light When boilers stop working, the problem may be that:

1 The fuse in the plug or, more likely, the fused connection unit supplying the boiler, could have failed. The fuse will need replacing.

2 The pilot light could have gone out. See boiler instructions for re-lighting it.

3 If it is an oil-fired boiler, it could have stopped working because of lack of fuel. Having the tank re-filled usually solves the problem.

If none of these simple things provides a solution, it could be that one of the controls – the programmer or thermostat – has failed or something else is wrong with the boiler itself, in which case you'll need to call in a professional heating contractor.

There is no hot water in a system that is heated with an immersion heater. The immersion heater thermostat may have failed.

The immersion heater itself is like a long straight kettle element that fits into the hot water cylinder; the thermostat fits down the middle of it and can be replaced. Turn off the electrical supply to the immersion heater – this is normally a switch close to the hot water cylinder but, if you are uncertain, turn off the electricity at the main switch. Unscrew the cap of the immersion heater (either on the top or the side of the hot water cylinder). Make a note of how the wires are connected to the thermostat, loosen the terminals with a small screwdriver, pull out the wires, and withdraw the thermostat. Take this with you to the shop to make sure the replacement is the same size. Put the new thermostat in place, wire it up in the same way as the old one, set it to 70°C/158°F, replace the cover, and switch the electricity back on again.

Damp, rot, and woodworm

Dampness in houses is a menace – it can ruin decoration and soft furnishings and, if it gets into structural timbers, can create the conditions for rot and woodworm attack. In order to get rid of damp, you need to know where it's coming from. To treat rot and woodworm successfully, you need to identify the problem correctly.

SEE ALSO Insulating your home, p198, Draughtproofing, p176

WHAT TO DO ABOUT WOODWORM

Cause Woodworm is an attack by one of a number of wood-boring insects, normally the common furniture beetle (identifiable by tiny round holes in the wood). See p153 for an illustration of a woodworm.

The beetle lays its eggs in crevices in the wood. It prefers damp wood, but attacks are also possible on dry wood. The larvae then eat their way into the timber before emerging, often years later, as adult beetles. In other words, the tiny holes are made after you have had an attack of woodworm.

Treatment You can treat small areas of woodworm yourself (in plywood furniture, for instance) by brushing on a woodworm killer, but if you have woodworm in the house timbers, or an attack with holes other than small round ones, you should call in a professional firm.

The house will need to be evacuated for a short period while they treat the woodworm attack.

THREE TYPES OF DAMP

Three types of damp can affect houses, and the causes and treatment of each are different.

Rising damp involves moisture rising up through solid floors in contact with the ground, and up walls – apparently defying gravity – as a result of water being drawn up through the tiny holes in bricks in the same way a sponge will fill when laid on water. The normal visible sign of rising damp in walls is a tidemark on the wall decoration.

It can be prevented in floors if an impervious damp-proof membrane (DPM) is laid in the concrete – ruined floor coverings will be the inevitable result if this layer of heavy-duty plastic is damaged or missing.

Similarly, a bituminized felt damp-proof course (DPC) is installed low down in exterior house walls to prevent rising damp – you can usually see this as a thin black layer two or three brick courses up the outside wall. A DPC can become 'bridged' (making a path for water to rise) by earth in flower beds or by careless building work – allowing render to overlap it on the outside of the wall – but if neither of these is the cause of rising damp, the normal remedy is to inject a water-repellent chemical into the brickwork affected, which is definitely a job for the professionals.

Penetrating damp is simply damp that gets into the house from outside – through faulty roof coverings, gaps around doors and windows, solid walls, and through faulty joins between a pitched roof and a chimney, or a flat roof and an adjacent wall. The symptoms of penetrating damp (damp patches on walls and ceilings) are usually worse after rain.

The solution is normally to repair the faulty building component, but if solid walls are letting in water you can damp-proof them yourself (see right). Look to see whether blocked downpipes or leaking gutters outside are making the problem worse.

Condensation is the result of warm moist air meeting a cold surface: when the air is cooled it can hold less moisture, so excess moisture is deposited on the cold surface in the form of water droplets – a familiar sight on single-glazed windows in winter. Condensation has become more of a problem in recent years as we have:

- improved draughtproofing, thus reducing natural ventilation
- improved insulation, making loft spaces colder and so leading to condensation on roof timbers
- fitted double-glazing, making windows warmer and thus transferring the condensation to nearby, colder, walls.

The solutions are to:

- improve ventilation – for example, fitting extractor fans in kitchens and bathrooms, and ventilators around the loft
- improve wall insulation with polystyrene sheeting (see right)
- cut down on the amount of moisture produced in the house, particularly by venting tumble-dryers to the outside and fitting extracting cooker hoods in kitchens.

The airbricks low down on house walls are there to provide ventilation to the timbers supporting ground floors – they should never be blocked. See Insulating your home, p198.

Black mould on walls is usually a symptom of condensation: the mould needs the pure water of condensation to grow. You can remove the mould (see right), but you need to solve the condensation problem to prevent regrowth.

TWO TYPES OF ROT

There are two different types of rot – wet and dry. Both are direct results of dampness. Timber used in new construction is treated with preservative to prevent the development of rot (and woodworm), but many existing timbers will not have been treated.

Wet rot is the more common problem and is identifiable as general decay of the timber, with darkening of the wood and cracking along the grain. It is common in window sills, window frames, and where door frames meet the ground.

If wet rot is extensive, timbers will need to be cut out and replaced (a job for a builder or carpenter), but small areas of damage can be repaired using a wet-rot repair kit. All damaged timber must be cut out, the area coated with a wood hardener, and preservative pellets inserted into holes in the wood, before filling with a flexible (but hard-setting) exterior-grade wood filler.

Once the filler has set and been sanded down, the repaired area can be repainted.

Dry rot is much more serious. It is identifiable by a strong musty smell, thin white strands growing into cotton-wool-like sheets on the cracked grey timber surface, and, in bad attacks, the growth of fungal 'fruiting bodies'.

Dry rot can also spread across and through masonry, and is so serious that all affected timber and masonry must be removed (and the timber burnt) and the area sterilized before new materials are added.

Only professional firms have the expertise and equipment to treat dry rot.

DEALING WITH DAMP AND CONDENSATION

Symptom	Probable cause	Remedy
Damp patches on walls – worse after rain	Penetrating damp	Damp-proof wall inside or outside
Tidemark on wall	Rising damp	Have new chemical DPC (damp-proof course) installed
Black mould on walls	Condensation	Remove mould, improve ventilation, improve insulation of wall
Damp patches on ceilings	Leaking pipe	Check pipes above ceilings
	Roof leaking (penetrating damp)	Repair roof covering
Dampness in timbers of flat roof	Penetrating damp	Repair (or re-cover) roof
Damp patches on pitched roof timbers	Condensation	Seal holes into loft, improve ventilation of loft space
	Penetrating damp	Repair roof covering
Water on inside of windows	Condensation	Improve ventilation, consider double-glazing
Water on inside surface of exterior walls	Condensation	Add wall insulation, improve ventilation
Floor coverings lifting on solid floor	Rising damp	Have new DPM (damp-proof membrane) installed

TREATING DAMP YOURSELF

Although installing a new DPC (damp-proof course) in a wall, a DPM (damp-proof membrane) in a floor, or a new flat-roof covering are jobs for the professional, there are many small jobs you can do yourself to cure damp problems and their symptoms. Simple jobs include:

- applying silicone sealant to the gaps between window/door frames and walls
- using an 'antidamp' paint on a wall that lets in damp, before redecorating – see p205
- adding a clear water repellent to the outside surface of exterior walls and to stone window surrounds that might be letting in damp
- adding polystyrene sheeting 3 mm/⅛ in thick to the interior of outside walls affected by condensation, and covering with new wallpaper
- using a proprietary mould-killer (or home-made bleach solution using one part bleach to five parts water) to get rid of black mould caused by condensation
- using mastic or silicone sealant to seal the holes around pipes passing through the ceiling into the loft, reducing condensation in the loft
- adding draughtproofing around the loft trapdoor to reduce condensation in the loft (see p176)
- fitting small rectangular ventilators in slots cut in timber window frames, reducing condensation
- repairing leaks in gutters and downpipes using gutter repair tape or gutter repair sealant.

Insulating your home

You can't prevent heat escaping from a house but, by insulating efficiently, it's possible to slow down the rate at which it is lost, saving on heating costs. Insulation is more effective in some areas than others. For example, you can cut the rate of heat loss through walls and roofs by around two-thirds, but windows by only half. Overall, effective insulation can cut the heat loss from your house by up to 60 per cent.

SEE ALSO Draughtproofing, p176

VENTILATION

While uncontrolled draughts make living conditions uncomfortable and heating expensive, a house must have a continuous supply of air flowing through it in order to keep it fresh, dry, and safe.

- Airbricks (perforated bricks or grilles) in the outside walls allow air to flow in and prevent dry rot attacking floorboards. The airbricks must be kept clear at all times.

- To protect roof timbers, lofts should be ventilated either with vents fitted in the soffits (the horizontal part of the roof's eaves), through an airbrick in gable end walls, or by tile ventilators that replace roof tiles. Ventilation will automatically be built into new houses, but it's worth checking for in an old house.

- Gas-burning or solid-fuel heaters or boilers must have their own air supply. A ventilator should be fitted as near as possible to the appliance so that a draught is not caused by air flowing across the room to it.

THE HOT WATER CYLINDER

Insulating a hot water cylinder is simple and very cost-effective. A bare copper cylinder should be insulated with a jacket at least 80 mm/3³⁄₁₆ in thick, wrapped around the cylinder and secured with tape. If replacing a cylinder, choose a pre-insulated one – its insulation value will be greater.

THE COLD WATER TANK

Usually in the loft, the cold water tank can be wrapped in a purpose-made jacket. Also, if it doesn't have one, make a lid to cover the tank – use a sheet of expanded polystyrene 25 mm/1 in thick. Where there is a vent pipe from the hot water cylinder below discharging into the top of the tank, make a hole in the polystyrene for a plastic funnel so that any water coming from the pipe will still be directed into the tank. Do not insulate the loft floor below the tank, as warm air rising from the room below will help to prevent the water in the tank from freezing.

PIPES

All pipes – hot and cold – that are exposed to cold air should be insulated. Pay special attention to pipes in the loft that rest on an insulated floor (no heat from the rooms below will reach them) and those that run across outside walls in an unheated room. Because water flows more slowly through bends in pipework, it is more likely to freeze at bends.

Split foam tubing is the most common type of pipe insulation. The split along the side enables the tubing to slip over the pipe. Tubes are available to fit pipework with a diameter of 15 mm, 18 mm, or 22 mm/ ⅝ in, ¾ in, and ⅞ in. If the size you need isn't available, buy a larger rather than smaller size.

- When cutting the tube, use scissors or a knife.
- Push the tubing tightly where pipes enter water tanks and cylinders.
- Butt the lengths up against each other where they need to be joined.
- At bends, cut V-shaped notches in the tube so that it doesn't wrinkle.
- Cut wedge-shaped butt joints at elbow joints in pipework, and where pipes meet at right angles. Secure the tubing with tape.
- Use PVC adhesive tape to secure the tubing at every joint and wherever it is needed to keep the tubing closed.

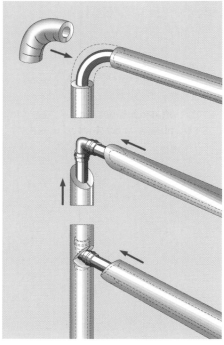

Fitting split-foam tubing

INSULATING A LOFT FLOOR

The current recommended thickness for insulation in new buildings is 250 mm/10 in. If the depth of your joists is less than this, fill to the top of the joists or consider adding wooden battens to the top of joists to extend them. Vacuum the loft before laying insulation – if there is a large amount of dust and dirt, hire an industrial cleaner.

SAFETY

- Never stand between joists. Lay several stout boards across the joists.
- Always wear a dust mask and goggles while cleaning and insulating. A hard hat is also recommended.
- Ensure the area is well lit.

LAYING ROLLS

Glassfibre or mineral-wool insulation is made in two widths – 400 mm/16 in and 600 mm/24 in – so check the distance between your joists before buying. The rolls are usually 100 mm/4 in thick and up to 8 m/24 ft long. Glassfibre can irritate skin so wear suitable gloves and long sleeves when handling it. Run the material under any electric cables on the loft floor, so that the cable will not overheat and is visible. Don't cover downlighter casings or other fittings that illuminate the room below. Don't insulate under the cold water tank; see left. Cold water pipes running between the joists can be covered.

1 Start laying the roll at one end of the loft. If necessary, use a broom to push the end of the roll well into the eaves, but don't block the eaves or any vent.

2 Unroll the material between the joists and press it into the edges, allowing any excess to lap up the sides of the joists. Don't compress the material. When you reach the end of the floor, cut the material with long-bladed shears or a kitchen knife, go back to the other end and start again between the next joists.

3 At the end of a roll, fit the start of the next roll snugly against it.

4 Cut small pieces to fill any odd gaps.

5 Cut a separate piece of insulation to fit the loft hatch and stick it in place with PVA adhesive. Seal the edge of the loft hatch (see Draughtproofing, p176).

LOOSE-FILL INSULATION

Mineral-wool pellets – the only loose-fill DIY product – are useful if the joists are not a conventional distance apart or you are topping up existing insulation but not so good for a draughty loft, as they can get blown about.

1 To prevent the material from blocking the airflow, lay pieces of plywood between the joists near the eaves (enough away from the edge so that the plywood itself does not block the airflow).

2 Pour the pellets between the joists.

3 Level the pellets with the top of the joists by resting a piece of plywood across the joists and dragging it along.

4 The loft hatch is best covered with glassfibre or mineral-wool blanket.

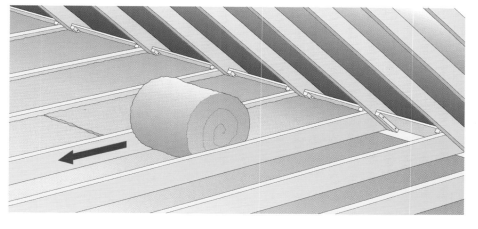

CAVITY WALLS

A suitable insulant, such as mineral wool (glass or rock), polystyrene beads, or polystyrene foam, can be injected mechanically into the cavity in the external walls of a house. It costs around £500 to insulate the walls of a typical semi-detached house. The process can only be undertaken by a professional installer.

GRANTS

The **Warm Front** scheme provides government grants that cover insulation and draughtproofing. Work is usually carried out by qualified local companies but, if you prefer to do it yourself, you may be able to claim £250 to purchase materials.

A grant of up to £1,000 is available to:

- householders who are in receipt of an income-related benefit and have a child under 16
- householders receiving a disability-related allowance.

A Warm Front Plus grant of up to £2,000 is available to:

- people aged 60 or over who are receiving one or more income-related benefits.

INSULATING A RADIATOR

Around a quarter of the heat that disappears through an uninsulated wall can be deflected back into the room by lining the wall behind the radiator with metallic foil. Purpose-made foil is available in rolls or you can use ordinary kitchen foil, which might have to be replaced after a couple of years if it turns black. In either case, stick the foil to hardboard, slightly smaller in area than the radiator, and fix this to the wall with self-adhesive pads.

WEB SITES AND ADDRESSES

B&Q
Web site: www.diy.com

Click through to the DIY Advice section for information on gardening, decorating, building, carpentry, electrical issues, and plumbing.

BBC Homes
e-mail: homes@bbc.co.uk
Web site: www.bbc.co.uk/homes/diy

Step-by-step guides from BBC experts.

DIY Doctor
e-mail: contact@diydoctor.org.uk
Web site: www.diydoctor.org.uk/home.htm

Master Locksmiths Association, 5D Great Central Way, Daventry NN11 3PX
Phone: 01327 262255; fax: 01327 262539;
e-mail: mla@locksmiths.co.uk
Web site: www.locksmiths.co.uk

National Insulation Association, PO Box 12, Haslemere, Surrey GU27 3AH
phone: 01428 654011; fax: 01428 651401;
e-mail: insulationassoc@aol.com
Web site: www.ncia-ltd.org.uk

Royal Society for the Prevention of Accidents (RoSPA), Edgbaston Park, 353 Bristol Road, Edgbaston, Birmingham B5 7ST
phone: 0121 248 2000; fax: 0121 248 2001;
e-mail: help@rospa.co.uk
Web site: www.rospa.com/CMS

General safety advice.

Screwfix, Freepost, Yeovil BA22 8BF
phone: 0500 41 41 41; fax: 0800 056 22 56;
Web site: www.screwfix.com

Mail order supplier of trade tools and hardware products.

Warm Front, Customer Services Manager, Eaga Partnership Ltd, Freepost NEA 12054, Newcastle upon Tyne NE2 1BRl
phone: 0800 316 2808;
e-mail: enquiry@eaga.co.uk
Web site:
www.eaga.co.uk/working_home/working_with_eaga_.html

Details of the Government's Warm Zones initiative.

Readers Digest
Web site: www.readersdigest.co.uk

There is a link through to an online DIY guide. Includes a tip of the day. Site also includes detailed 'gardening year' advice.

CHAPTER EIGHT

Decorating & furnishing

Using colour to best effect

Magazines and TV programmes revel in completely transforming rooms with colour, which can be both inspiring and daunting when it comes to choosing paint schemes for your own home. There are some basic things to take into account, such as the shape and size of the room, features you want to draw attention to or hide, and the effect of natural light. Even subtle variations of shade can have a significant impact on the overall look. There are simple ways to test colours and, even if you get it horribly wrong, it doesn't take long or cost too much to repaint a room.

WHY PAINT AND WHEN?

You may decide to paint because you want to give a room a new look or because the old paint is looking tired, but there are good practical reasons too. Paint is protective, preserving both the inside and outside of a building from the damaging effects of moisture, pollution, sunlight, and everyday wear and tear.

Paintwork also makes your home easier to keep clean, as it seals dusty walls and creates smooth, wipeable surfaces.

The inside of a house usually needs repainting at least every seven to ten years, and the outside every five to seven years, though these times will depend on the property's location, the prevailing weather, and the quality of both the materials and work when the house was last painted.

WHAT TO CONSIDER WHEN CHOOSING PAINT

Colour is a background that complements the furniture, pictures, books, and accessories that make up your home. Colour can add interest to a room without needing to be outrageously bold. Equally, intense, bright shades can be effective without being overpowering. The key to choosing the right colour for a room is taking into account the various factors that will affect its final appearance.

- Choose colours that match the mood of a room and how and when it's used. Vibrant combinations work best in areas where you don't spend much time – the hallway, for example. Rich red walls may be fine in the evening but could look dark and oppressive by daylight.

- Choose calming colours, even if they're dark, for the bedroom, which is the first and last thing you see each day.

- Bold colours can work well in kitchens and bathrooms, but as these rooms tend to have a lot of visual clutter, a simple overall colour scheme will probably work best.

- Natural light affects the appearance of a colour. Whitewashed walls, cool and fresh in Mediterranean light, can look flat and dull in the softer light of northern Europe. Light, ice-blue walls might make a north-facing room look chilly but the same colour in a south-facing room will seem airy and bright.

- Artificial light – especially harsh fluorescent light – can alter colours. Change the lighting or the paint.

- The size of the painted area affects colour. A small patch of lemon yellow looks fresh and clean, but the same colour on an entire wall will start to look green.

- Pale colours maximize the amount of light in a room. The common-sense conclusion is that you should use light colours in small, dark, or poorly lit rooms and darker colours only in bigger, lighter rooms. However, sometimes it's better to do the opposite and emphasize a room's character, enhancing a large, sunny room with light, bright colours, and making a small, dark area warm and cosy with strong, deep shades.

- Colour can give a sense of continuity throughout the house. Even if you use different colours to create an individual mood for each room, you could create a visual link by choosing one colour to appear in every room on, say, the skirting boards or even in the furnishings.

- Don't make switches of mood or style too abrupt. Going from Edwardian to Scandinavian to Mediterranean in the same house would make it feel disjointed and small.

TYPES OF FINISH

As well as the colour, the type of paint finish affects the impression of light in a room.

- **Matt** is the most light-absorbent finish, which makes it a good choice for covering minor imperfections in plasterwork.

- **Satin** gives a degree of reflection and looks livelier than the matt equivalent of the same shades.

- **Gloss** reflects the most light: it's hard on the eyes if used over a large area, but used on relatively small areas it adds sparkle to the overall scheme. It's also the most durable finish, so it's ideal for surfaces that get heavy wear, like skirting boards, window frames, and doors.

LOOKING AT PAINT CHARTS

All colours are derived from three **primary** colours: red, yellow, and blue. Two primaries mixed in equal proportions create a **secondary** colour (red plus yellow makes orange; yellow plus blue makes green; blue plus red makes violet). The shades in between – the **tertiary** colours – are a combination of a primary and a secondary colour.

The colours on the red and yellow side of a colour wheel are often described as 'warm', and those on the blue and green side as 'cool'. With decorating colours, however, the terms 'warm' and 'cool' indicate the amount of red present in various shades of the same colour – so you can have cool and warm versions of all the main colours (see below). It's best not to combine warm and cool shades in a colour scheme, as the warm shades can take on a muddy hue, while the cool ones may look

thin and harsh. Many paint charts are divided into groups of colours that share similar characteristics of, say, warmth, coolness, depth, or intensity, and one of these groups makes a good starting point. The range of colours in each group is wide enough to allow you to experiment with different effects, but because the shades sit comfortably together there's no risk of visual jarring.

TESTING DIFFERENT COLOURS

When choosing a paint colour, the best way to decide what you like and what's suitable for the room you're going to paint is to test a number of different colours.

- Use 1–2 m/3–6 ft lengths of lining paper (plain wallpaper made to be painted over) for each colour. The larger the sample, the better you will be able to judge it.
- Before you apply the paint to the lining paper, write the manufacturer and the name or code number of the colour on the back of the paper.

- Paint the lining paper, taking the colour as close to the edges as possible. Trim off unpainted margins when the paint has dried.
- Stick the samples on the walls and live with them for a while. Look at them in natural light – on both sunny and dull days – and in artificial light, in the darkest corner of the room as well as on the brightest wall. Make sure they work well with the room's carpet, curtains, and furniture.

Cool (left) and warm (right) versions of blue, green, and yellow. Cool shades recede, and generally make rooms look bigger, and sometimes austere, while warm shades appear to come towards you, and will make rooms look smaller and more intimate.

► Choosing paint

Paints fall into two types: oil-based (also referred to as solvent-based) and water-based. Recently there's been a swing towards using water-based paints, for health and environmental reasons, and certainly for the home decorator these are much easier to use, especially when it comes to cleaning up. Water-based paints also offer a great deal of choice: the range of colours is vast and there are a variety of finishes for – literally – floor to ceiling. There are still some situations, however, in which an oil-based paint will give the best results.

WHICH TYPE OF PAINT?

Water-based paints include: matt and silk vinyl emulsions; masonry paints; primers; undercoats; acrylic satin and gloss paints.

- Advantages: quick drying; low odour; clean up with water; less toxic.
- Disadvantages: less durable; more easily marked.

Oil-based paints include: primers; undercoats; satin and gloss paints; masonry paints; metal paints.

- Advantages: hard wearing; gloss retains shine longer; greater resistance to damp.
- Disadvantages: slow drying; strong odour; white spirit or other solvent clean-up.

WHAT'S IN THE CAN?

All paints are made up of pigments suspended in a medium that, once the paint has been applied, forms a solid film that binds the pigments together and sticks to the painted surface. In oil-based paints, the medium is a mixture of oil and natural or synthetic resins. In water-based paints, the medium is made up of water and synthetic resins.

What determines the final appearance of water-based paints is the proportion of pigment to resin. Matt finishes contain the most pigment and therefore have the greatest covering capacity. Gloss finishes have a higher proportion of resin. Generally, the higher the gloss, the more durable the finish is. Various other additives affect the qualities of paint, such as how quickly it dries, whether it's liquid or non-drip, and its shelf-life.

Cheap paints usually contain a lower proportion of pigment, and therefore several coats may be needed to achieve adequate coverage – so they don't necessarily save you money and may cost you far more in terms of time.

PAINTS FOR WALLS AND CEILINGS

PREVIOUSLY PAINTED OR PAPERED SURFACES

These are usually given one of the following finishes:

- **Flat emulsion** (sometimes called flat matt) A non-reflective finish that covers well and hides blemishes. Good for ceilings but marks easily on walls.
- **Matt emulsion** Despite its name, this is sometimes very slightly light-reflective. Good for hiding minor imperfections and suitable for ceilings and for walls in low-traffic areas.
- **Soft-sheen** and **mid-sheen emulsions** Found in ranges for kitchens and bathrooms, they have more reflective finishes.
- **Silk emulsion** Reflects light, is resistant to scuffs, and can be sponged clean. Suitable for most walls, although imperfections will be more conspicuous.
- **Paints for decorative effects** These are for sponging, ragging, and so on. Some have metallic finishes. Most are two-paint systems (which you buy together) – an undercoat followed by a topcoat. Follow the instructions.

- **Textured finishes** These include masonry paint with sand in it. Good for disguising poor plasterwork. The preparation required is similar to that for other painting tasks but you *must* remove wallpaper and mask adjacent surfaces, as splashes are hard to remove once they've dried.

BRAND NEW PLASTERWORK

You can buy paint that's specifically for plaster, which allows the surface to breathe. Don't use standard vinyl emulsion, as it creates a film that prevents the plaster from drying out completely.

DRY, UNPAINTED CEMENT, AND PLASTER FINISHES

These absorbent surfaces can be difficult and expensive to paint – it takes more effort to drag the brush or roller across the surface, and most of the paint will be sucked into the material, rather than form a film on top. Avoid these problems by using a primer sealer, or diluting the first coat of emulsion with up to 10% water (follow the manufacturer's recommendations).

A THREE-STAGE SYSTEM FOR WOOD AND METAL

Bare wood and metal are traditionally treated with a three-paint system – of primer, undercoat, and topcoat – which gives maximum adhesion to these constantly expanding and contracting materials. Buy all three paints from the same manufacturer, as they're designed to work together. Properly applied, the paints are able to withstand climatic extremes.

Primer The first layer of protection. You can buy oil-based and water-based primers. Some primers are for a specific type of surface – wood, metal, non-ferrous metal – but if you have a number of small painting tasks to do, it's most economical to buy a multi-purpose primer.

Undercoat Provides a key – a surface to which the topcoat can adhere – and helps build the depth of colour, so always use the colour recommended for your chosen topcoat. Two coats of undercoat will increase the life of the topcoat, especially on exterior surfaces.

Topcoat Provides a decorative finish and a tough skin that resists moisture, mould, ultra-violet rays, and pollution. Because it also provides a smooth surface, dirt is less likely to stick. The following finishes are available:

- **Satin** A mid-sheen finish. Available in oil-based and water-based paints.
- **Eggshell** A slightly glossy finish – the oil-based equivalent of silk emulsion, but more durable. It can also be used on walls.
- **Gloss** A hard-wearing, shiny finish that resists knocks and can be wiped clean. It highlights surface imperfections. Available in oil-based and water-based paints.
- **Liquid gloss** An oil-based paint that gives the smoothest, shiniest finish. It's the most unforgiving of a less-than-perfect surface and is the most durable finish, so it's suitable for exposed exterior woodwork and metal.

SPECIAL-PURPOSE PAINTS

Kitchen and bathroom paints These are designed to resist moisture and condensation. Some contain fungicide to protect against mould growth.

Floor paints Formulated to be tougher than paints for walls. Water-based versions are good for old wooden, concrete, or stone floors, but for areas of heavy wear – doorsteps, garage floors, passageways – oil-based products are recommended.

Anti-mould emulsions and gloss paints These contain fungicide. They're designed to block out staining caused by minor mould growth and to deter regrowth. They don't solve the underlying cause of mould.

Anti-damp paints These can be applied to damp surfaces before you redecorate with your chosen colour – but they're of lasting benefit only if the source of damp is cured first.

Anti-burglar or security paint Remains permanently slippery. Use it on drainpipes to deter people from trying to climb them.

Slip-resistant paints Recommended for doorsteps and concrete floors, but note that they're not *non*-slip.

PAINTS FOR DIFFICULT SURFACES

Multi-surface primer (as opposed to multi-purpose) Can be used on almost any surface, from MDF (medium-density fibreboard) to melamine, to create a good base for a gloss or satin topcoat.

Ceramic tile primer and paint These give greater adhesion than ordinary paints, so they're good for painting tiles.

Vinyl floor paint Can be used on vinyl and other soft flooring. It's formulated to stick to and flex with the surface.

Wood-grain effect paint Can be applied to most surfaces. It can give a painted door, for instance, a passably natural-looking finish. Saves the hassle of stripping back to bare wood.

HOW MUCH PAINT?

First calculate the size of the surfaces you're going to paint by multiplying the height of the area in metres by the width in metres, to give a figure in square metres (sq m). Most paint labels give a coverage estimate in square metres: divide your total area by this figure. The answer is the number of cans you need. The table below shows the covering capacity in square metres of a range of paints and different sizes of can.

COVERING CAPACITY

Volume of paint	Undercoat (sq m)	Gloss (sq m)	Emulsion (sq m)
500 ml	8	8.5	6
1 litre	16	17	12
2.5 litre	40	42	30
5 litre	80	84	60

PAINTS FOR OUTSIDE

Masonry paints are available as:

- smooth water-based paints, which are like exterior-grade emulsions and provide a dirt-resistant finish
- sand-textured water-based paints, which disguise minor imperfections and give a very durable finish
- moisture-permeable, quick-drying, oil-based paints, which can be applied in damp conditions and give a smooth finish.

Woodwork is usually painted with:

- a three-stage system (see left)
- single-coat exterior-grade gloss
- moisture-permeable paints or woodstains (new wood only, see p220).

Metal can be painted with:

- a three-stage system (see left)
- single-coat exterior-grade gloss
- three-in-one hammered or smooth-finish paint.

Painting equipment

The key to making a painting job easy is to start off with the right equipment. Trying to make do with minimal or unsuitable equipment is false economy – it will be harder to do the job well, and the chances are that three-quarters of the way through the work you'll end up having to get the tools you really need, so you might as well have them at the outset. This doesn't always mean you have to buy the most expensive tools available.

WHAT CAN YOU HIRE?

- **Specialist ladders or trestles** for working in stairwells or high-ceilinged rooms.
- **A steam wallpaper stripper** is much faster than soaking and scraping or chemical strippers. A lightweight budget version will do small areas very efficiently, so may be worth buying. For a whole house, a hired industrial stripper is heavy to handle but will be faster.
- **A wallpaper perforator** punctures the surface of wallpaper, letting steam through to soften paste.
- **A hot-air paint stripper** is the quickest way to remove paint from woodwork. Worth buying if stripping more than one room.
- **A drum floor sander** is the only way to prepare old floorboards for a clear finish.
- **An edge sander** is essential for sanding floors. They're often offered at a discount if you hire a drum sander at the same time.

ESSENTIAL EQUIPMENT FOR PAINTING INDOORS

	Equipment	Materials
For you	Old clothes, including head cover Rubber gloves	
General	Stepladder Dust sheets (see below) Rags – old T-shirts are ideal Dustpan and brush Vacuum cleaner	
For preparation	Bucket Sponges Scrapers Shavehooks Filling knife	Sugar soap Sandpaper (see opposite) Filler Decorators' caulk (flexible filler for gaps) White spirit
For painting	Brushes, paint pads, or roller and paint tray (see opposite) Paint tiles (or old margarine tubs) Screw-top jars for left-over paint	Masking tape Glass scraper Appropriate paints (see p204–5) White spirit (if using oil-based paints)

HOW MUCH TO SPEND?

Good-quality equipment should last a lifetime if you look after it – but sometimes life seems too short to spend time cleaning it. Here are some tips on when to go for the best and when cheap will do.

- With hard-working tools such as scrapers and shavehooks, buy the best you can afford.
- Paintbrushes range in quality and price, from professional animal-hair brushes, through mid-price natural and synthetic brushes, to cheap, disposable brushes. The mid-range brushes are adequate for most DIY tasks: they're durable enough to survive a fairly extensive painting project, but not too expensive to throw away if you forget to clean them, or the bristles become distorted. Disposable brushes are fine for one-off jobs, such as daubing on paint stripper, and for small painting tasks, but they won't

stand up to prolonged use. The cheaper the brush, the more it will shed bristles.

- Paint rollers and trays are often offered as sets at temptingly low prices. If you're only painting one room, they're good value for money. If, however, you're redecorating the whole house, it's worth buying a more expensive roller, which will have a more durable sleeve and a roller mechanism that operates more smoothly.
- Professional dust sheets are heavy and absorbent. Disposable polythene dust sheets are cheap, but because they're not absorbent, paint splashes remain on the surface and inevitably get trodden on and spread further. Newspaper or old sheets and bed covers placed on top of the polythene will absorb most of the splashes, while the polythene protects the flooring.

SPECIALIST EXTRAS

Any of the following might be helpful, depending on what kind of painting job you're doing:

- cutting-in brush for painting window bars (but you can use a 12 mm/½ in brush for this)
- radiator brush or roller for painting behind radiators
- caulk (mastic) gun for filling small gaps where wood and plaster meet, for instance between walls and ceiling
- soft-bristled brush for dusting (but a clean paintbrush will do)
- wallpaper scraper with a long handle and sharp, renewable blades – makes lighter work of shifting the last, stubborn pieces of wallpaper.

Left, a cutting-in brush, for painting window bars, though a 12 mm/½ in brush, centre, is an alternative. A 50 mm/2 in brush, right, is good for painting other woodwork.

WHICH ABRASIVE TO USE?

Sandpaper is used to rub down surfaces and provide a suitable surface (sometimes called key) for paint. It is sold as coarse, medium, and fine, or labelled with a grit number. As a guide: 40G is extra-coarse; 60G is coarse; 80–100G is medium; 120–180G is fine; and 220G+ is extra-fine. Use coarse for rougher surfaces, fine for a smoother finish.

Wet-and-dry paper is made up of silicone carbide particles glued to a waterproof backing. It can be used dry on wood, but is normally dipped in water and used on paintwork. Instead of flying into the atmosphere, the dust forms a slurry that you wipe off. Suitable for rubbing down potentially toxic substances like leaded paint, which you should avoid breathing in as dust.

Garnet paper, distinguishable by its reddish-brown colour, comes in very fine grades. Good for finishing hardwoods.

Flexible sanders have abrasive particles glued to a foam block or sheet. These are not very durable but are good for rubbing down shaped surfaces.

Liquid sandpaper is a brush-on solution that dissolves the surface of sound

paintwork just enough to make it suitable for the new paint. Good for fiddly shapes such as banisters.

Sanding packages are a handy way to buy all the abrasives you need for a particular project – rubbing down metalwork, or preparing to stain and varnish, for example.

Steel wool, like sandpaper, is available in coarse, medium, and fine grades, which are indicated by the number of 0s. Grade 000, for example, is medium; grade 00000 is very fine. Good for stripping old finishes from turned wood (such as table legs rounded using a lathe), and for working wax finishes into the grain. Note, though, that the fine metal dust reacts with and stains some woods. It should never be used in damp conditions, as the metal particles rust.

Paint roller and sleeve

WHAT SIZE OF BRUSH OR ROLLER?

- For painting woodwork, 12 mm/ ½ in, 25 mm/1 in, and 50 mm/2 in paintbrushes will give you optimum control.

- For walls, speed of coverage is important. The bigger the paintbrush or roller, the more paint it can carry – and the less often you have to reload it. In theory, it's quicker and therefore less tiring to paint large surfaces with a 150 mm/6 in brush or 300 mm/12 in roller. But large brushes and rollers are heavy once they're loaded with paint. If you're not used to decorating, you may be better off with a 225 mm/9 in roller and 100 mm/4 in brush.

THE RIGHT ROLLER SLEEVE

Sheepskin-style roller sleeves may be authentic sheepskin or synthetic. Genuine sheepskin holds more paint and is more expensive than synthetic substitutes. Short pile is good for gloss paints on smooth surfaces. Medium pile is used for applying emulsion or satin-finish oil paints to smooth surfaces. Long-pile is suitable for painting rough and textured surfaces. Synthetic versions are perfectly adequate for home decorating and are also available with short, medium, or long pile.

Plastic foam sleeves tend to leave air bubbles in the paint. Avoid them.

Textured or embossed sleeves are designed for use with textured paints.

Preparing to paint

Preparation is the single most important element of decorating anything – from painting a picture frame to tackling a whole room. It's the foundation not just for the immediate project but also for all future redecoration, and poor preparation is the most likely cause of a disappointing result. Taking short cuts is, in the long run, a waste of money and effort. But if you set aside sufficient time, and prepare thoroughly, the actual process of painting will be far quicker and more rewarding.

FILLING HOLES AND CRACKS

There are three kinds of fillers for holes and cracks.

Surface fillers are for plaster and masonry. Interior and exterior grades are available. Powder filler, which you mix with water as you need it, is the most economic. Ready-prepared fillers are more expensive but they're much easier to use and leave a smoother finish requiring little or no sanding.

Wood fillers are available in a range of timber colours; some can be stained. A multi-purpose filler is suitable for most minor repairs, inside and outside. For more serious damage, use a two-part wood filler (you add a hardening agent just before you use the filler).

Flexible fillers, or decorators' caulks, are quick-drying products designed to fill cracks in corners or anywhere subject to shrinkage and movement. Apply direct from the tube and smooth with a spatula, damp cloth, or finger.

GETTING INSIDE SURFACES READY

SOUND PLASTERWORK

- Wash walls and ceilings with warm water and sugar soap. Sugar soap is available in powder, liquid, and concentrated form; follow the recommendations on the packaging. You may need to rub down minor imperfections in brand-new plaster.

- Always wash walls from the bottom up. Water running down on to a damp surface disperses, whereas if it runs on to a dry surface it may leave indelible dribble marks that show through paint.

- Unless the surface is very dirty, you don't need to rinse the walls after washing. If you do rinse, work from the top down.

PLASTERWORK WITH PROBLEMS

- Fill minor blemishes, such as fine cracks or holes left by picture hooks, and allow them to dry.

- Major defects, such as damp, large cracks, or extensive mould, could be symptoms of another more serious problem, which must be put right before you do any decorating (see p196).

WOODWORK

- If the woodwork has been previously painted and the finish is in good condition, wash and lightly sand it.

- If the woodwork has been previously painted and the finish is in poor condition, see p218.

- If the woodwork is unpainted or has been stripped, you can give it a translucent finish (see p222) or paint it (see p205).

METALWORK

- Wash and lightly rub down sound paintwork.

- Remove peeling or blistered paint with a wire brush; treat any rust. Apply a rust inhibitor and an appropriate primer (some preparations combine the two functions) to exposed metal.

- Use a chemical stripper to remove any build-up of paint – especially if, say, it interferes with the action of metal-framed windows.

PAINTING OVER WALLPAPER

Before you decide to remove wallpaper, remember that very often wallpaper is used to hide something and removing it may present you with another problem to solve. If you decide that it would be better not to remove the wallpaper, you may be able to paint over it.

Vinyl paper has a top layer that sometimes peels off quite easily, leaving only the backing. If this is in good condition, you can paint it. With other kinds of wallpapers, it may be possible to paint them, as long as they are still adhering firmly to the wall. Test them by painting a patch about a metre square.

Leave it overnight, and then check whether:

- the wallpaper has lifted away from the wall

- the pattern shows through

- the colour has bled into the paint.

If the answer is 'no' to all three, you can paint over it.

Colours that bleed through can be sealed with an aluminium oil-based paint. If the paper lifts away from the wall, or you don't like the textured appearance, you'll have to strip it off.

GETTING READY TO PAINT OUTSIDE

- Avoid painting exterior surfaces in the winter months as they are likely to be damp. The perfect painting weather is warm, dry, and slightly cloudy.
- Clean and repair gutters and downpipes.
- Wash all surfaces to be painted as for inside walls above. Use a fungicide if there are any signs of mould.

MASONRY

- Use a wire brush to remove powdery or flaking masonry paint.
- Fill cracks and holes with suitable filler.
- Old finishes that feel 'chalky' and new render will both benefit from a coat of stabilizing solution.

WOODWORK

- Rub down sound paintwork with wet-and-dry paper.
- Fill any open joints or cracks with flexible woodfiller.
- Scrape out loose putty from window frames and renew it.
- It's best to remove extensively cracked, blistered, or crazed paint – see p218.
- Cut out any rotten wood and replace it. Treat the new wood with preservative.
- Unpainted woodwork, or woodwork that has been stripped, can be stained (see p220) or painted (see p205).

DEALING WITH OLD PROBLEMS

Lead was used in the manufacture of some primers and woodwork paints until the 1960s. It is potentially dangerous when you disturb it by scraping, sanding, or stripping. To be on the safe side:

- Use wet-and-dry paper with water to rub down paintwork, so that you don't create dust.
- Use a chemical stripper if it's necessary to remove the paint – heat stripping can release toxic fumes.
- Collect all the paint debris, wet-and-dry paper, soiled newspaper, and so on, and seal them in a plastic bag before putting in the dustbin.
- Wash exposed skin and hair.

Lead paint test kits are available from hardware and DIY shops.

Distemper – basically powdered chalk mixed with glue and water – is most likely to be found in old houses. It can't be painted over, and washing it off, though theoretically possible, creates a seemingly endless sludge. Brush off as much loose material as you can and then seal the surface with a stabilizing solution.

Polystyrene ceiling tiles used to be stuck on with five blobs of adhesive. The tiles can usually be prised off with a broad scraper. The adhesive is more difficult to remove. If you can't scrape it off, try, in this order:

- soaking with warm water
- wallpaper stripper
- paint stripper
- soaking with a solution of half a cup of household ammonia and a squirt of washing-up liquid added to a bucket of cold water.

Because you'll be working above your head, protect your face and eyes from splashes. An easier option is to paint the tiles. Use emulsion – never an oil-based paint, as this would increase the risk of fire.

SMART EXTRAS

- Make sure you have a damp cloth for wiping up smears and splashes before they harden. If using oil-based paints, moisten the cloth with white spirit.
- Cut strips of thin card to slide under skirting boards to protect the floor and stop the brush from picking up dust and fluff.

PAINTING TIMETABLE

AS FAR AHEAD AS POSSIBLE

- Choose colours (see p202).
- Work out realistically how much time to allow for painting, including preparation. Take recoat times into account (some gloss paints and varnishes call for 16 hours or more) and allow an hour for clearing up and cleaning equipment.

TWO WEEKS BEFORE

- Measure the room and calculate paint quantities (see p205).
- Make a checklist of all the equipment and materials you need.
- If you have material left over from a previous job, check the quantity and condition.
- Check the availability of hire equipment (see p206) and book it.

THE WEEK BEFORE

- Buy all the materials and equipment.
- Try to deal with any time-consuming tasks that can be done in advance – for instance, filling a deep hole in plasterwork, which will need several thin layers of filler with adequate drying times between each layer.
- Buy quickfix meals and snacks.

THE DAY BEFORE

- Remove as much as you can from the room; including lampshades, curtains, and blinds, so that you can start decorating first thing the next day. If possible, store things where they won't be in the way.
- Move furniture into the centre of the room; cover with a dustsheet.
- Roll up the carpet if possible. If you have a fitted carpet, stick 50 mm/ 2 in masking tape along the edges, placing the tape up to the skirting board. Protect floor with dustsheets or polythene sheets and newspaper.
- Remove all picture hooks and nails from walls.

Putting on paint

When you're painting, working in a logical order speeds up the process and makes you less likely to damage your new paintwork by splashing or scuffing it. It's also worth following a few simple rules, such as always waiting until one stage is dry before moving on to the next, and never touching up an uneven finish before the recommended time for recoating – paint always looks patchy as it dries and a second coat is often needed to give the desired depth of colour.

PAINTING ROUND ELECTRICAL FITTINGS

1 Switch off the electricity at the mains consumer unit (see p000).

2 Unscrew ceiling rose covers, loosen power sockets and switch plates, then paint behind them with a brush.

3 Wait until the paint has dried before replacing the covers.

4 Only when you have replaced the covers should you switch the power back on.

PAINTING RADIATORS

Removing radiators makes painting them and the wall behind much easier – see p192 for how to take them off the wall safely. Alternatively, paint them where they are, using a specially designed radiator brush or roller. Turn off the heating and wait until the surface is cool. You can buy radiator enamel which is baked on when you turn the heat to maximum after painting. Or you can use emulsion or oil-based paint.

TECHNIQUES FOR APPLYING PAINT

Whether you use a brush, pad, or roller is a matter of personal preference. Pads and rollers cover a surface more quickly.

USING A BRUSH

■ To load, dip only the first third of the bristle length into the paint. Wipe the brush on the edge of the can to remove excess paint – unless you're using a non-drip paint, in which case you don't need to remove the excess.

■ Apply the paint with vertical strokes and even it out with horizontal strokes. Finish gloss paints with light upward strokes to prevent sagging and runs.

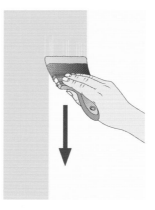

USING A ROLLER

■ To load, fill the dish of the roller tray with paint. Dip the roller into the paint.

Roll it gently on the ribbed section of the tray until the sleeve is evenly coated.

■ Apply the paint in a random criss-cross pattern, working quickly to blend edges. Don't press hard, but keep the roller in good contact with the surface to ensure even coverage.

USING A PAINT PAD

■ To load, dip the pad into its paint tray and pull it across the integral roller.

■ Apply the paint by sweeping the pad in a criss-cross pattern across the surface. Keep the pad flat. Finish gloss paints with light vertical strokes.

THREE GOLDEN RULES

1 **Work in sections**, stopping at logical points – such as a corner or chimney breast – and never in the middle of a wall.

2 **Don't overload the brush, roller, or pad**: the result will be drips, splashes, and uneven coverage.

3 **Stop painting at dusk** if you can. If you work in poor or artificial light a patchy finish is more likely.

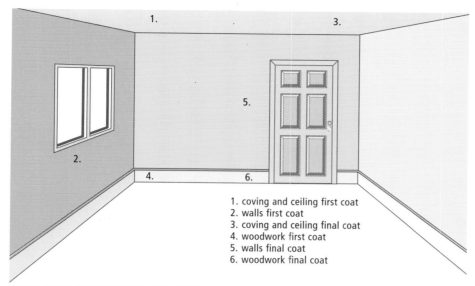

1. coving and ceiling first coat
2. walls first coat
3. coving and ceiling final coat
4. woodwork first coat
5. walls final coat
6. woodwork final coat

SIX STAGES FOR PAINTING A ROOM

This sequence applies for redecorating a room. If you are dealing with new plasterwork and wood, see p204 and p218.

1 Ceiling – first coat

- Start in a corner near the window and work away from the light – this makes it easier to spot any patches you've missed.
- Using a 50 mm/2 in brush, paint the edge of the ceiling.
- With a larger brush, roller, or pad, work from the wet edges in bands about 60 cm/24 in wide across the width of the room, blending the edges together.
- Try not to overlap the walls and ceiling by more than 2–3 mm/⅛ in. If there's coving, paint it at the same time as the ceiling. If it's in a different colour, paint it first.

2 Walls – first coat

- Start at a top right corner (top left, if you are left-handed) and paint the edges with a 50 mm/2 in brush.
- Using a larger brush, roller, or pad, paint areas about 60 sq cm/24 sq in. Work in horizontal bands, blending wet edges.

3 Ceiling – final coat

Repeat stage 1.

4 Woodwork – first coat

If you're using a one-coat gloss, wait until you've given the walls their final coat before painting the woodwork. Opinions vary as to the best order, but there are some common-sense rules:

- Paint any picture rails first. Because they're high, you won't knock them while you're painting the rest of the woodwork.
- Paint opening windows as early in the day as possible to give them time to dry.
- Paint skirting boards last. This is where you're most likely to pick up dirt on the paintbrush and you don't want to risk transferring specks on to more visible woodwork.
- Avoid getting gloss paint on adjacent walls – you'll need a steady hand – as it will show through the next (and any future) coat of emulsion.

5 Walls – final coat

Repeat stage 2.

6 Woodwork – final coat

Remove all dust. Refer to the manufacturer's instructions and, if necessary, lightly sand the first coat. Repeat stage 4.

Clean tools as soon as you finish the job.

- Remove excess paint by blotting onto newspaper.
- Use water, white spirit, or other cleaner, according to the instructions on the paint can.
- If washing tools, do it outside and pour dirty water on the ground.
- Keep solvents in a screw-top jar and wait until paint sinks to the bottom, leaving clean, re-useable solvent at the top.
- Never pour unused paint down the sink. Ask the local council about disposal facilities.

Brushes Flex bristles in the appropriate cleaner (warm water or solvent), loosening paint from the roots. Wash in hot, soapy water. Rinse and shake off excess water. Put an elastic band round the bristles to keep them straight while they dry.

Rollers For water-based paints, remove sleeve and hold under a running tap. Rub a little detergent into the pile and rinse thoroughly. For oil-based paints, pour thinner into tray and roll sleeve back and forth. Wearing rubber gloves, massage pile until paint dissolves. Wash sleeve in hot, soapy water and rinse.

Pads Wash in an appropriate cleaner, massaging pile to loosen paint. Wash in hot, soapy water and rinse.

TAKING A BREAK

You don't have to clean tools between coats or when you stop for a break.

- If using water-based paints, wrap tools in cling film.
- If using oil-based paints, suspend the brush with wire in a jar of water, making sure the bristles are covered. Blot it with absorbent paper before using again.
- If using emulsion paint, put cling film over the paint tray to prevent a skin forming.

Putting up wallpaper

If you haven't put up wallpaper before, choose a paper that is easy to handle and has a pattern that is straightforward to hang. A random pattern is best, because you won't have to do any matching – this will enable you to work comparatively quickly. Read through the problems on p216 before you start, to help you avoid some of the worst wallpapering difficulties. You will need to prepare the wall before putting up wallpaper.

EQUIPMENT

- Paperhanging shears (about 250 mm/10 in long)
- Small pair of scissors
- Paste brush
- Paperhanging brush
- Seam roller
- Plumb line and bob
- Sponge (for wiping unwanted paste from wipeable surfaces)
- Plastic bucket (tie a string across the top, to the handle, to serve as a brush-rest and for wiping off excess paste)
- Water trough (if using ready-pasted paper)
- Sanding block
- Pencil
- Tape measure.

Optional:
- Fold-up pasting table
- Ladder, stepladder, trestle boards
- Chalked stringline
- Steam stripper.

CHOOSING WALLPAPER

- Avoid thin wallpaper as it tends to tear easily when wet with paste and when being positioned on the wall.
- If you have an older property, avoid a very regular pattern such as vertical stripes – few rooms in older houses have true corners or even ceiling lines.
- Wallpaper is normally printed in batches to give colour consistency – buy rolls that all have the same batch number. Examine the rolls in a good light before hanging, none the less.
- Using ready-pasted wallpaper means you won't need to apply paste. The paste is on the back of the paper in dried form and is activated by immersing the paper in water. See Dealing with bubbles, p216, for advice on soaking the wallpaper in a trough and hanging.
- Once you have bought the wallpaper, store the rolls flat. Standing them upright could damage the all-important edges.

ESTIMATING QUANTITY

Use the table, right, to calculate how much paper to buy. The table is based on a standard roll of wallpaper 10.05 m/33 ft long and 530 mm/21 in wide. Since there will be more wastage if you have to match large motifs, add 10% to the table figures for these. If in doubt about the quantity needed, buy an extra roll. If you don't, and later find you need the extra roll, you may not be able to get one from the same batch. Some shops will give you a refund for rolls you don't open.

Purpose-made shears make it easier to cut in a straight line. You will also need a small pair of scissors for making intricate cuts. Keep a jar of warm water and a rag handy to wipe paste from the blades before it hardens and causes irregular cutting.

Seam roller for pressing down seams between adjoining lengths after hanging. Never use on raised-pattern papers.

Paperhanging brush (200–250 mm/8–10 in wide) for smoothing paper onto the wall.

Plumb line and bob. You can improvise with a small weight on a length of string.

PREPARING THE WALLS FOR PAPERING

New plaster Allow to dry for four weeks.

New plasterboard Apply two coats of plasterboard primer/sealer. Depending on the brand, this can take anywhere between 2 and 18 hours to dry.

Wallpaper Remove old wallpaper by soaking and scraping. Allow 10 to 15 minutes for the water to soak through and loosen the paste. The process can be speeded up by adding a proprietary wallpaper-stripping solution to the warm water, though adding a little liquid detergent plus a handful of wallpaper paste is usually sufficient. Many wallpapers are specially made to be easy to strip. Just raise the bottom edge and pull upwards. If a thin backing paper remains on the wall, wet it and scrape off.

Emulsion-painted wallpaper It is possible to break down the surface by scraping or wire-brushing to allow the water to soak through, but it can be tough going. The simple alternative is to use a steam stripper (can be hired), which quickly loosens difficult wallpaper.

After stripping wallpaper, go over the surface with a sanding block to remove small nibs, then wash down with sugar soap and warm water to remove old adhesive and size (sealer).

Dealing with cracks Fill holes and cracks with cellulose filler (use ready-mixed if you prefer, but this is a bit more expensive than one you mix yourself), smoothed level with the surface. Larger holes are more economically repaired with a plaster filler (ready-mixed if you prefer). If the hole is deep, use two layers of plaster, allowing the first to dry before adding a second.

Where there are lots of hairline cracks in an otherwise sound wall, first hang lining paper. This is a thin, white paper hung exactly like wallpaper except that it is used horizontally on the wall. It is important not to overlap edges as these will show as a ridge through the wallpaper. You can hang it vertically if you think you will find handling long lengths of horizontal paper too difficult, but ensure that the joins will not coincide with the wallpaper joins.

Removing fittings Remove fittings such as wall lights, shelves, and roller blinds, because you can't paper around them. Make sure that the electricity is switched off at the mains before removing wall lights and that the power to any bare wires is cut off until wallpapering is complete and the lights are back in place. If you want to replace any fitting in the same position after wallpapering, pop a matchstick into each screw hole, leaving about 12 mm/0.5 in protruding. This will be forced through the paper as it is brushed onto the wall, so you will know where the screw holes are.

HOW MANY ROLLS OF WALLPAPER DO YOU NEED?

Height of room	Total width of walls								
	7 m/ 23 ft	8.5 m/ 28 ft	10 m/ 33 ft	11.5 m/ 38 ft	13 m/ 43 ft	14.5 m/ 48 ft	16 m/ 53 ft	17.5 m/ 58 ft	19 m/ 63 ft
2.5 m/8 ft	4	4	5	6	6	7	8	9	10
2.75 m/9 ft	4	5	5	6	7	8	8	9	9
2.75–3.5 m/ 9–12 ft	5	6	7	8	9	10	11	12	13
3.5 m +/ 12 ft +	7	9	10	12	13	15	16	18	19

PASTE

Wallpaper paste comes in powder form ready for mixing with water according to the manufacturer's instructions. The instructions also state how many rolls the paste will hang. Nowadays, paste is sold as being all-purpose – it will hang any kind of wallcovering.

- The strength of the mix required depends on the type of paper being used – lightweight, heavyweight, vinyl, or whatever.
- If using a vinyl, a special overlap adhesive is needed, as ordinary paste will not stick down overlapping vinyl edges.
- If papering over a wall that was previously damp, or if decorating a kitchen or bathroom, use a paste containing a fungicide. This will inhibit mould growth.

SIZE

'Size' is the term used to describe a sealer that is brushed on a porous wall before wallpapering. The size prevents the paste sinking into the surface, causing some loss of adhesion between it and the paper. The size also leaves the surface slippery so the paper will be easier to push into place when aligning edges.

- Apply the size with a large brush – just 'paint' the wall with it and leave it to dry for an hour before papering.
- Although a specific product can be bought, size is usually made using a weak solution of ordinary wallpaper paste – see instructions on the packet.

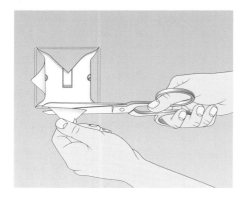

PLANNING WHERE TO START

Normally you should start on the wall adjacent to the window wall and work back into the room. This way, shadows will not be cast if any edges are inadvertently overlapped. The exception is where a large motif is being used and there is a dominant focal point in the room, such as a chimney breast. Here, the motif would need to be centralized on the chimney breast wall.

HANGING THE FIRST LENGTH

1 Use a plumb line and bob to mark a vertical guideline on the starting wall. Presuming you are starting in a corner, make a starting line that will allow 25 mm/1 in of paper to turn back on to the previous wall. Hold the plumb line to the top of the wall – when it stops swinging, mark the line on the wall with a pencil. If a chalked stringline is used, it can be 'snapped' against the wall to leave a vertical chalk line (see Tiling a floor, p228).

2 Cut the first length of paper, allowing 50 mm/2 in at both the top and bottom for final trimming. If applicable, make sure that any pattern will be in the right position on the wall.

3 Place the paper face down on the pasting table with one long edge aligned with a long edge of the table. Brush a generous coat of adhesive lengthways along the centre of the paper, then brush outwards to where the edge of the paper is aligned with the table edge. Then pull the paper to align it with the table's other long edge and complete pasting. Ensure there is complete coverage.

4 Lightweight, washable, and vinyl wallcoverings can be hung immediately. Allow thicker papers to soak for the time recommended – generally until floppy – this can be up to ten minutes with really thick paper. Loosely fold the ends of the paper to meet in the middle, without any creases. Carry the folded paper over your arm as you approach the wall.

5 Unfold the top half of the paper and align its edge with the vertical line. Ensure there is a 50 mm/2 in overlap onto the ceiling. Brush the paper, firmly and quickly but not too vigorously, down the centre and then towards the edges. Then release the lower half of the paper and brush this onto the wall.

6 At the top, gently run the back of the blade of the shears into the ceiling to leave a crease line on the paper. Peel back the edge and cut along this line, then brush the paper back into place. Repeat at the skirting.

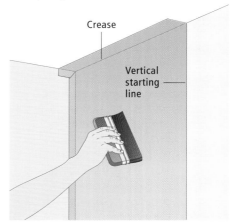

Crease

Vertical starting line

7 Hang further lengths in the same way, matching any pattern and butting the edges of adjoining lengths. Run the seam roller down the join between the lengths of wallpaper.

DEALING WITH FEATURES

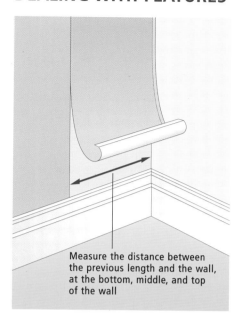

Measure the distance between the previous length and the wall, at the bottom, middle, and top of the wall

CORNERS

Corners are not usually square. Therefore, when less than a full width of paper is needed to reach an internal corner, take three measurements between the edge of the last length of wallpaper and the corner at the top, middle, and bottom. Add 12 mm/½ in to the largest measurement and cut a strip this wide from the next length of paper. Hang this strip, turning 12 mm/½ in of it onto the next wall. Make a vertical guideline on the next wall that will allow the remaining strip to overlap the 12 mm/½ in margin in the corner. You must mark a new vertical guideline every time you take paper onto a new wall.

On an external corner, repeat the process but allow 25 mm/1 in to turn the corner. If the corner is true (check with a plumb line), butt the edges of the two strips of paper. If not, overlap them.

WINDOWS

Cut the various pieces of wallpaper needed to go around a window reveal (recess) before pasting, allowing at least 12 mm/½ in for trimming at the top and bottom of lengths, and ensuring that any pattern matches on both sides of the recess. Paper the sides and top of the reveal first, turning 12 mm/½ in onto the

outside wall. The paper on the outside wall is turned 12 mm/½ in into the reveal to make an overlap. If a reveal is less than about 75 mm/3 in deep, there is no need to hang strips in the reveal, as the paper can be turned into it.

DOORS

Cut an L-shaped piece of wallpaper as required, allowing 50 mm/2 in around the door frame for trimming. Hang the paper above the door first, then make a diagonal cut 50 mm/2 in into the paper at the corner of the frame (the angle of the L). This cut will release the paper so that it can be brushed and creased into place before being trimmed neatly around the frame of the door.

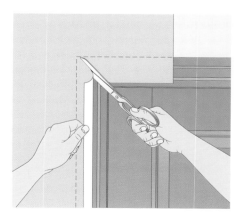

OTHER PAPERING CHALLENGES

FIREPLACE SURROUNDS

Whether you have started in the centre of the chimney breast or have arrived at the breast as you work around the room, you hang the next length as though dealing with a normal wall. The only difference will be that you have to shape the lower half of the paper around the fireplace. Measure and cut a piece of wallpaper, leaving about 50 mm/2 in excess at the edge that will be shaped around the fireplace. Hang the top part of the paper, brushing it into the back edge of the mantelshelf. Make a crease line and cut to fit. Make a short diagonal cut from the top corner of the fireplace surround outwards to release the lower part of the paper (see Doors, left). If the side of the fireplace is straight, simply brush the paper into it, make a crease line, and cut to fit. If the surround has a complicated outline, gradually work downwards, pressing the paper into each shape and using a small pair of scissors to trim along the crease line. If the paste starts to dry out near the bottom, apply more paste with a small brush.

RADIATORS

If you don't want to remove a radiator, cut the paper to shape, allowing about 100 mm/4 in to be smoothed behind the radiator. Cut small pieces for the gap beneath the radiator.

ARCHES

Hang the paper on the facing wall, cutting a series of notches on the edge so you can turn it about 12 mm/½ in into the arch. The paper in the arch is cut in two pieces, which meet at the top. If there is a pattern, you must ensure that the pattern inside the arch matches that on the facing wall.

Wallpapering problems

All problems that occur in wall-papering are avoidable. Correct preparation of the walls is vital, as is careful choice of paper and paste, and following the manufacturer's instructions. Don't underestimate how long a job is likely to take – always work at a comfortable pace.

DEALING WITH BUBBLES

THE OCCASIONAL BUBBLE

If you spot a bubble of air just after hanging a length, pull the wallpaper back past the bubble and brush it on correctly, working from the middle out to the edges. If an odd bubble remains after 24 hours, use a sharp knife to cut an X through it, peel back the four flaps, apply adhesive, then brush the flaps back into place.

LOTS OF BUBBLES

The cause of this is either:

- papering over old wallpaper
- dampness in the wall
- allowing insufficient soaking time.

Remove the paper and prepare the wall properly before repapering, making sure to allow sufficient soaking time.

If a ready-pasted paper is used, bubbling can also be caused by not soaking the paper properly in the water trough. The length of paper should be rolled loosely with the decorative surface outermost and the top edge showing and parallel to the wall. Let the paper soak for the recommended time, then gradually pull the top edge upwards, letting the water reach the entire backing. Leave the tail of the paper in the trough so that excess water runs into it.

PROBLEMS WHILE YOU'RE WORKING

PATTERN FAILS TO MATCH

If the pattern can be matched at the top of the wall but gradually falls out of alignment halfway down, then the paper has stretched irregularly. This can be caused by:

- allowing lengths of paper to soak on the pasting table for different lengths of time
- over-rigorous brushing when hanging
- letting the bottom half of a length drop down when being hung – particularly longer lengths in stairwells.

If this happens, match the pattern at eye level, where it will be most noticeable, or hang a new length.

HANGING PAPER UPSIDE DOWN

With some patterns you can inadvertently hang the whole lot or even a single length upside down. Study any pattern carefully and, before pasting a length, write the word 'TOP' in pencil on the relevant edge on the reverse of the paper.

PAPER DOESN'T SLIDE

It is important that the paper can be easily slid across the wall as the pattern is being matched. If it can't, the cause may be:

- the paste has been mixed too watery – remix the paste correctly and rehang the lengths.
- the paste being absorbed into the wall because it was not sized (a sealer was not applied) in preparation – size the wall then continue to paper.

PAPER LIFTS IN LARGE AMOUNTS

Caused by either:

- not allowing the paper to soak for long enough
- failure to size (apply sealant to) a porous wall
- hanging the paper over gloss paint or distemper (for instance, whitewash)
- the paste being too watery
- dampness or condensation in the wall.

A small area could be remedied by repasting correctly. Otherwise, stripping the paper and rehanging – or in the case of gloss or distemper, removing the old surface – is the only answer.

CREASING

Generally caused by not hanging paper vertically or taking too much around a corner. For a corner crease, cut along the crease, apply more paste, and brush back into place. If the repair is too noticeable, hang a new length. If you are getting creases in straightforward lengths then the paper is not being hung vertically, so you need to start again.

LIFTING SEAMS

Not enough paste was applied along the edges. Raise the seam carefully with a sharp scraper or filling knife, apply paste, and smooth down. Run a seam roller down the edge (though not on a raised pattern). If you've put on too much paste and want to take some off, use a sponge.

PROBLEMS THAT BECOME VISIBLE LATER

STAINED SEAMS

Poor preparation has meant that old size (sealant) remained on the wall. Wiping with a clean, damp rag may help but usually the only answer is to start again, making sure the walls are washed down with warm water to remove old adhesive and size.

GAPS AT SEAMS

The paper has shrunk on drying, caused by the paste being too thin. If the paper is to be painted, you will probably be able to work cellulose filler into the gap with a finger. If the paper is patterned, find a matching coloured pencil and use this in the gap to help conceal it. Alternatively, hang a new length.

SHINY PATCHES

Over-rigorous brushing when hanging is the cause. Rub over with a ball of white bread to lessen the effect.

BROWN SPOTS

Wire wool may have been left on the surface during preparation, or a nail or screw head left just below the wall surface could have rusted. A damp wall on which mould has developed is also a possibility.

Strip off the paper and prepare the wall properly – do not rub down with wire wool. Damp problems must be treated before redecorating. If the wall is prone to condensation, line it first with expanded polystyrene sheeting. Available in DIY superstores, this is thin polystyrene that comes in a roll and is hung like wallpaper. Lining paper is not needed over the polystyrene if you're going to use ordinary wallpaper, but some manufacturers recommend also applying lining before hanging vinyl or woodchip papers. Use the adhesive recommended by the manufacturer – usually their own brand.

FLATTENED EMBOSSING

A paper with a relief pattern may have been flattened by:

- over-rigorous brushing when hanging
- running a seam roller down it.

This can't be rectified – hang new paper.

BE READY FOR REPAIRS

After papering, hang a small amount of the paper in an airing cupboard or wardrobe so that it 'ages', in case you need to do a patch later. If you leave spare paper rolled up it may look too new to use in a repair.

A small torn or stained area can be repaired quite easily. Tear off the damaged area, leaving a solid edge. Find a spare piece of wallpaper to match the pattern. Tear around the edge then carefully remove a 3 mm/ 1/8 in part of the backing paper to leave the patch with a feathered edge. Do not cut out the patch with scissors. Apply paste to the back and smooth into place, brushing outwards from the middle to the edge.

REPAIRING VINYL

Place a patch piece over the damage, matching the pattern if necessary, and tape lightly in place. The patch needs to be 25 mm/1 in or so larger than the damaged area. Using a sharp knife held against a steel rule, cut out a square. Cut through both layers of vinyl. Remove the vinyl from the wall within the square. Paste the vinyl patch and carefully fit it in place.

KEEPING CLEAN

If you are using paste, it's important to remove any excess before it gets onto another surface or dries and hardens.

- Sponge away excess paste from a length of wallpaper as soon you've hung and brushed it.
- Wipe the pasting table after pasting every length. Laying one edge of the paper along the edge of the table helps minimize splashes.
- Wipe and then dry scissors or craft knives as you work.

GETTING ACCESS TO STAIRWELLS

- Erect a safe working platform that will enable you to reach the top of the wall comfortably and without leaning from the ladder or scaffold. Make a sketch of the area and ask the tool hire company for advice on set-up. The arrangement of ladders/stepladders/ trestle boards will vary from situation to situation. You will also probably have to rearrange the set-up as various parts of the stairwell are decorated. When using boards (normally around 300 mm/12 in wide), standard recommendation is that the distance between supports is no more than 1.5 m/5 ft. Above that, a double thickness of board is needed. Planks should be tied to the ladders and stepladders with sturdy rope, and tied together if using a double layer. It's also wise to give long lengths of board some support halfway.

- Alternatively, a narrow DIY scaffold can be erected in a stairwell – they are ideal for anyone who doesn't feel safe on a ladder. Give the dimensions of the stairwell to the tool hire outlet to be sure of getting the best size of scaffold for the job. Before using the tower, check that wheels are fully locked. For safety, always climb up the inside of the tower, moving boards as necessary, and never lean out to the front or side as the tower may topple.

- As you work up or down the stair, measure the length of wallpaper needed from the bottom at the longest side. Trim the diagonal edge after hanging. Long strips of wallpaper can stretch when wet, so keep the time from soaking or pasting each length the same to keep any stretching consistent.

- Paste the paper and fold it concertina-like so that the folds meet paste to paste. If possible, have a helper support the lower part of the long lengths while you hang the top part. If the top of the ladder has to rest against newly papered walls, wrap cloths around it to prevent damage or staining.

Preparing wood to be treated

There could be three reasons why you want to give wood some kind of finishing treatment. You may want to seal new wood, touch up an existing finish, or you may want to strip off an existing finish and start again, perhaps to give the wood a different colour. See p222 for the different types of colour and protective finish and how to use them. But before you apply any wax, varnish, oil, colour, or paint, spend some time on preparation. You'll end up with a smoother, more effective, and more professional finish.

SEE ALSO Sanding p164

WHAT'S THE SURFACE LIKE?

NEW WOOD

All wood that has not been treated – from flat-pack furniture to floorboards – is prepared in the same way:

- sand it lightly with 180 grit/240 grit sandpaper
- remove all dust with a vacuum cleaner
- wipe with a cloth moistened with white spirit to remove any traces of grease.

The wood is now ready for one of these treatments:

- paint
- varnish, oil, or wax, see p222
- colour with wood dye or stain followed by varnish, oil, or wax, see p222
- colour and finish with an all-in-one product, see p222.

If the wood has a lot of knots or is very resinous (oozing sap), the affected areas should first be sealed with knotting solution, which can be brown or colourless. Use a colourless version if you want to apply a translucent finish on top. Applying knotting solution will affect the wood's ability to absorb wood dye and it may be incompatible with some finishes – check the manufacturer's recommendations.

EXISTING FINISHES IN GOOD CONDITION

A finish in good condition is fulfilling its protective role and is best left intact if possible. If you want to change the appearance, consider these options.

- Paint can be overpainted with a different colour.
- Most varnishes can be painted over (check in an inconspicuous place to make sure there is no incompatibility).
- Colourless and light varnishes can be recoated with a coloured varnish. You can apply acrylic varnish over polyurethane varnish and vice versa as long as the old finish has completely cured – two weeks for acrylic varnish, one month for polyurethane varnish. Just sand lightly to provide a good surface for the new finish and remove dust and grease as above.
- With French polish, oil, and wax finishes you can only apply more of the same. If you want to alter the appearance radically, these finishes must be stripped back to the bare wood.

EXISTING FINISHES IN POOR CONDITION

- Cracked, blistered, or flaking finishes are usually found on exterior woodwork and garden furniture. Remove all the loose finish. Use a shavehook and work with the grain, pulling the tool towards you. Rub down with sandpaper. Leave any paint or varnish that is hard to remove unless there is a marked step between the surface of the sound paint and the exposed wood. If there is more paint than wood visible, filling may be a better option than stripping. Use dampened wet-and-dry sandpaper if the paint might contain lead (see p209).
- Oil and wax finishes can be revitalized with several new applications of the same finish.

METHODS OF STRIPPING

Heat stripping is quick and a good first option if you are tackling a large or fixed item, like a staircase, which you can finish stripping with chemical stripper.

Heat the paint with a hot-air gun until it softens enough to be removed with a scraper. The melted paint will still be hot, so collect it in an old metal, rather than plastic, container. Heat stripping is not suitable, however, for paints containing lead (see p209).

Hot-air guns are preferable to blowtorches, which can easily burn the wood. Guns have interchangeable nozzles to direct the heat to where it is needed, including one designed to protect glass.

Chemical stripping is slower but good for small or fiddly projects. It is the best option for paint that might contain lead and can also be used on metal and glass. (Some lacquers are not affected by chemical strippers, and you may need to use cellulose thinners to remove them.) For good results don't skimp on the amount of

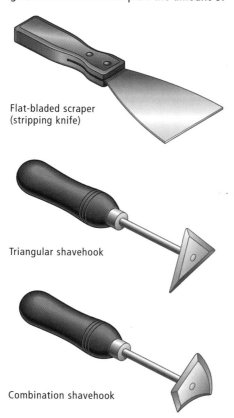

Flat-bladed scraper
(stripping knife)

Triangular shavehook

Combination shavehook

product used, or the time allowed for it to take effect. Remove most of the softened paint with a scraper or shavehook, then use coarse steel wool dipped in the stripper to remove ingrained paint or varnish. Follow the manufacturer's instructions for neutralizing the stripped surface.

When using a chemical stripper, always wear protective clothing and work in a well-ventilated place.

Methylated spirit removes shellac (a hard, glassy varnish) and French polish (the traditional polish found on many older pieces of furniture). To test the finish, rub it with fine steel wool moistened with methylated spirit. If it softens to a treacle-like consistency, the finish can be removed, using steel wool, shavehooks, and copious quantities of methylated spirit. It is even slower and messier than other methods, but kind to the wood underneath. Restoring a French-polished surface is a professional job, although amateurs can achieve passable results on small areas like picture frames or chair legs. Never strip the finish from a potentially valuable item, as you will drastically reduce its worth.

White spirit and linseed oil (mixed in a ratio of 3:1) removes a build-up of dirty wax to prepare for a new wax finish. Apply it with a cloth or steel wool and rub vigorously. Finish by wiping over it with white spirit and leaving to dry. If you want to apply a different type of finish, the surface will need to be thoroughly sanded.

Commercial stripping, in which the item is immersed in a tank of caustic solution, is a tempting option for large or very intricate pieces, but there are serious downsides.

- Caustic solutions dissolve old-fashioned glues, causing joints to loosen and veneers to lift.

- Some woods, such as oak, are badly discoloured by caustic stripping.

Some firms offer a gentler, non-caustic stripping service, but this process is more expensive.

SANDING FLOORS

You'll need to hire a drum floor sander and an edge sander. Prepare the floor *before* collecting the equipment.

- Fill small gaps between boards with wood filler, but if gaps are large, consider relaying the floorboards.

- Nail down loose floorboards (check that you won't hit pipes or wires).

- Punch all nail heads below the surface with a hammer.

Sanders generate a lot of dust.

- Remove furniture, curtains, and lampshades.

- Seal doors with masking tape and stuff newspaper under them to prevent dust from spreading.

- Seal gaps round fitted furniture doors and drawers with masking tape.

- Open windows for ventilation.

ORDER OF WORK

1 Level uneven floors with the drum floor sander. Sand diagonally across boards, using coarse sandpaper.

2 Repeat, working diagonally the opposite way.

3 Fit medium-grade sandpaper and sand along the length of the floorboards.

4 Repeat, using fine sandpaper.

5 Use the edge sander to smooth floor edges.

6 Vacuum up dust and wipe the floor with a cloth dampened with white spirit.

7 Apply finish as required.

SAFETY

- Wear a mask and earplugs or ear protectors.

- Take a ten-minute break every hour to minimize discomfort from vibration.

Colouring wood

Some timbers look fine with just a clear oil, varnish, or waxed finish. Others don't – they may have shade variations that need to be evened out, or the wood may not be the colour you want. If you want to enhance or change the colour of, say, a piece of furniture, a door, or floorboards, without obscuring the pattern of the grain, there's a wide range of products to choose from, but there are important differences between stains, dyes, and varnishes.

SEE ALSO Finishing wood, p222–3

EQUIPMENT

- Sanding block and fine-grade sandpaper
- Steel wool
- Lint-free cloths
- White spirit
- Vacuum cleaner
- Brushes or paint pads to suit the size of the work
- Sponges or foam applicators ('brushes' with foam instead of bristle)
- An old metal or pottery dish to hold the dye (large enough to take your brush or pad)
- Coarse cloth for removing surplus wood dye
- Rubber or disposable gloves
- White spirit, methylated spirit, or cellulose thinners for cleaning up (note that these are not interchangeable; check the manufacturer's recommendations when you buy the product).

CHOOSING THE RIGHT COLOUR

- Check the natural colour: wipe the bare wood with a cloth dampened with water or white spirit to give an idea of what the wood would look like with a colourless oil or varnish.
- Even treated woods will darken with age, so choose a colour one shade lighter than the final colour you want.
- Colour charts and samples are for guidance. The only accurate test for colour is to try it on an *identical* piece of timber – either an offcut or an inconspicuous patch, for example under a table top.
- Take into account the effect of the finish on the colour. Most polyurethane varnishes add a yellow tinge.
- Even the best-quality colourants can vary from batch to batch. Buy sufficient quantities to finish the job. If you need more than one tin, mix them together in a bucket before you start.
- If dyeing, check that the product is compatible with your chosen finish. Play safe by using products from the same manufacturer and from the same range – a quick-drying varnish over a quick-drying dye, for example.

CHOOSING BETWEEN DYES AND STAINS

The key difference between wood dyes and wood stains is that dyes do not protect the wood. Dyes need a finishing coat of varnish, oil, or wax. Overall, a dye gives more control over the depth of colour and, properly finished, will be more permanent.

Wood stains give both colour and protection. And unlike tinted varnishes, which will eventually blister, crack, or flake, wood stains just wear off, making them much easier to recoat or touch up at a future date. They are available for interior and exterior use, vary in density (some are nearly opaque), and come in a fairly limited range of wood colours.

Spirit-soluble wood dyes are available in a variety of timber colours. They penetrate thoroughly, giving a good finish on close-grained hardwoods. You need to wait at least six hours for the dye to absorb before applying the finish.

Quick-drying dyes come in a wide range of shades. While timber tones are 'classics', the availability of other shades tends to be driven by fashion. They may even be marketed under a different name, such as a wash. Shades can be discontinued fairly quickly – another reason for buying enough product to finish the job. Quick-drying dyes are easy to use: they are touch-dry in about 20 minutes and ready for a second coat or the finish after an hour or so.

Concentrated dyes, both water- and spirit-based, give you the flexibility to create your own shades.

ALL-IN-ONE WAXES AND VARNISHES

All-in-one tinted varnishes and waxes colour and seal in one operation. The colour sits on the surface of the wood, rather than being absorbed. This means you have less control over the depth of colour achieved. Any damage on the surface, or imperfections – like runs – will be more conspicuous, and the colour wears off with the finish. These products can be used to alter an existing finish, but check on an inconspicuous place that the old and new finishes are compatible.

APPLYING COLOUR

BEFORE COLOURING

- Remove the existing finish using one of the methods described on p218. If the old finish has deeply penetrated the wood, it might affect the absorption of a dye or stain – seal the surface with clear varnish and then build up colour with tinted varnish.

- Lightly sand stripped or new wood with medium-fine paper (a very fine grade could prevent even absorption). Sand in the direction of the grain of the wood – any scratches across the grain will be conspicuous after colouring.

- Use steel wool rather than sandpaper on shaped surfaces like chair spindles.

- Water-based dyes can raise the wood grain, leaving a rough finish when dry. To prevent this, wipe the wood down with a wet rag. Leave to dry, then sand smooth.

- Remove all dust, using a vacuum cleaner attachment to reach awkward crevices.

APPLICATION

- On flat surfaces use a lint-free cloth – for instance, an old T-shirt folded to make a pad – or, for quick-drying dyes, a paint pad or sponge applicator. Use a brush to carry colourant into corners, mouldings, and carvings.

- Shake the colourant and decant it into an old dish big enough to take your pad or brush.

- Work quickly with the grain of the wood, keeping edges wet and blending them as you go.

- When dyeing or staining floorboards, use a 100 mm/4 in brush and cover two or three planks at a time, stopping at edges and ends.

- Allow the colourant to penetrate for the recommended time, then wipe off the excess, working with the grain.

- Leave until completely dry, then buff with a coarse cloth to remove surplus. If the effect is patchy, or the colour is not deep enough, apply a second coat.

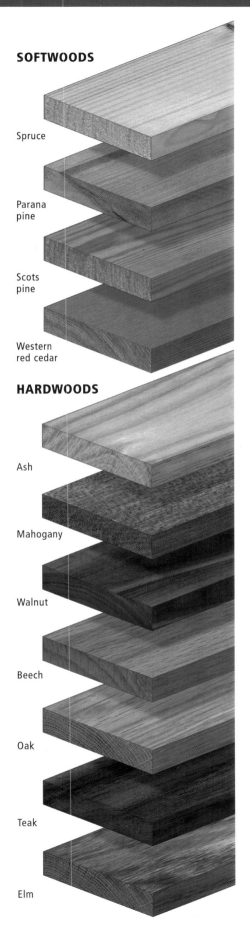

SOFTWOODS

Spruce

Parana pine

Scots pine

Western red cedar

HARDWOODS

Ash

Mahogany

Walnut

Beech

Oak

Teak

Elm

TYPES OF WOOD

SOFTWOODS

Softwoods come from relatively fast-growing coniferous trees that are cultivated and harvested for the building industry. Most floors, skirtings, interior doors, and window frames are made from softwood.

Spruce Also called white wood. Knots can cause problems with dyes and clear finishes, as sealing them with knotting can affect absorption of the colour and the blemishes will show through varnish.

Parana pine The natural pink tinge fades with time and the wood is virtually knot-free.

Scots pine Also called red wood. Knots and resin can spoil the finish (see Spruce).

Western red cedar Used outdoors, untreated, it will weather to a silver-grey colour.

HARDWOODS

Hardwoods, taken from slower-growing broadleaved trees, are generally harder and more durable than softwoods. They offer a greater choice of colour, texture, and grain pattern. Because they take so long to mature, they are expensive and are used for furniture, show wood (such as wall panelling and bench tops), decorative items, and veneers.

Ash Can be stained to resemble oak.

Mahogany Not usually coloured, since it is dark to start with. Grain needs to be filled for a good finish.

Walnut Not usually coloured, best oiled or varnished.

Beech Good with just oil or wax, or can be stained to resemble mahogany.

Oak Can be stained or limed (the grain streaked with white), and is suitable for all finishes.

Teak Naturally oily, so suits an oil finish, though can be coloured, varnished, or polished.

Elm Not usually coloured, this wood suits an oil finish.

Finishing wood

Transparent protective finishes – oil, wax, or varnish – are designed to allow the wood grain to show through. They can be used on bare wood or over compatible dyes but will only be effective if the surface has been properly prepared (see p218). The amount of protection varies from product to product: take into account how much wear the wood will receive, choose a finish that is tough enough to cope, and follow the manufacturer's instructions.

EQUIPMENT

- Brushes to suit the type of finish and the size of the work
- Lint-free cloths
- Fine sandpaper and wet-and-dry paper
- Fine steel wool, 0000 grade
- Old toothbrushes – useful for working wax and oil into carved decoration and mouldings
- Polishing attachments for electric drill or sander – to take some of the hard work out of polishing wax finishes on large areas such as floors, beams, and panelling.

SPONTANEOUS COMBUSTION

When applying an **oil finish**, keep cloths in a closed tin until the job is finished. Then open out the cloths and allow them to dry naturally before throwing them away. There is a genuine risk that folded, oily cloths might burst into flames.

EIGHT TIPS FOR A PERFECT FINISH

1 If you want a smooth, gloss finish on an open-grained wood such as oak, ash, or elm, use **grain filler**. Choose a filler that matches the wood colour, adding a few drops of dye if necessary. Apply one coat of varnish first, and allow to dry. Brush the filler into the wood, working with and across the grain. Remove the excess with a coarse cloth. Lightly sand with the grain when fully dry.

2 Before using **polyurethane varnish**, seal the surface with one coat of varnish diluted by 10% with white spirit. Use a soft cloth pad to work the varnish into the grain, and a brush to get into corners and mouldings.

3 Before applying a **wax finish**, seal the surface with a diluted coat of varnish.

4 All brushes must be clean, as any old paint clinging to the bristles might spoil the finish.

5 Tap excess **varnish** from the brush. Make sure you don't squeeze or scrape the brush against the tin, as this can create air bubbles in the varnish.

6 Whichever finish you are using, allow each coat to dry completely and rub

down with fine sandpaper or wet-and-dry paper before applying the next coat.

7 If, prior to the last coat of any finish, there are imperfections – such as dust, stray bristles, or runs – remove these with wet-and-dry paper when the surface is completely dry, dust, then apply the final coat.

8 If dust settles on the surface you have been working on while the last coat is still wet, let it dry, then use the back of some sandpaper, wrapped the wrong way round a sanding block, to clean off the dust without scratching the surface.

VARNISH – POLYURETHANE OR ACRYLIC?

Polyurethane varnishes are the most commonly used modern varnishes. These varnishes are very hard-wearing and can be used to coat timber inside and outside the home. Acrylic varnishes are nonetheless becoming increasingly popular. Advances in manufacturing methods mean that these, too, are suitable for interior and exterior use, and even for hard-working surfaces like floors.

Although some people maintain that polyurethane still has the edge in terms of durability and glossiness, others are won over by acrylic's user-friendly qualities. Acrylic varnish does not have the unpleasant odour associated with polyurethane, it is non-toxic, it dries more quickly, and brushes used for acrylic varnishing can be cleaned with water.

THE RANGE OF PROTECTIVE FINISHES FOR WOOD

Product	Appearance	Colour range	Properties	Suitable for
Polyurethane varnish	matt satin gloss	clear (slight yellow tinge); mainly timber shades	very hard-wearing; water, heat, and alcohol resistant; slow drying (recoat after 6 hours or longer)	all woodwork; interior, exterior, and flooring grades available
Acrylic varnish	matt satin gloss	colourless (no yellow tinge); timber and non-timber shades	durable; water, heat, and alcohol resistant; non-yellowing; non-toxic; quick drying (recoat after 2 hours)	all woodwork including toys; interior, exterior, and flooring grades available
Wood stain	satin gloss	timber shades	'breathable' finish that does not crack or blister; easy to recoat in the future	all woodwork; interior and exterior grades available
French polish	satin to high gloss	pale (clear); white (light); button (golden brown); garnet (dark brown)	medium durability; difficult to achieve a perfect finish with the traditional method, but 'brush-on' versions are available; requires many coats	furniture and decorative items
Oil	matt to soft satin	clear; slight yellowing effect on light woods	easy to apply; protects against heat, moisture, and alcohol; slow drying and requires several coats; needs to be maintained with further applications	all woodwork, furniture, kitchen and bathroom surfaces, kitchen utensils; food-safe oils available; interior and exterior grades available
Wax	soft, natural sheen	neutral; clear (slight yellow tinge); timber and some non-timber shades	good as a final finish over French polish or oil; needs to be maintained with further applications	furniture and decorative items; also floors but beware of making them dangerously slippery

Preparing to tile

As well as creating a practical surface, tiles are good for covering up imperfect plaster or dated tiles. Before tiling, make sure the surface is dry and reasonably smooth, although minor cracks and bumps will be covered by the adhesive. If there are traces of damp on a wall or floor, the cause must be identified and remedied before you start to tile.

EQUIPMENT

- Spirit level
- Tape measure
- Thin fibre-tip pen
- Tile-cutting jig or manual tile cutter
- Tile nibbler
- Tile saw
- Tile file
- Timber battens (50 x 25 mm/ 2 x 1 in approx)
- Hammer
- Plastic spreader
- Sponge
- Squeegee (to spread grout)
- Dry cloth
- Trowel
- Safety goggles
- Gloves.

You may also need:

- Silicone-carbide paper
- Electric tile cutter
- Ear defenders
- Cold chisel
- Drill
- Chalk line
- Workmate (to hold a tile as you cut it).

BUYING MATERIALS

TILES

Working in either metric or imperial throughout, measure the height and width of the area to be tiled and multiply these figures together. Divide the result by the area of a single tile to give the number of tiles you need (add 10% for cutting and wastage).

For example, working in metric, an area of 4 m by 2 m is 8 sq m, which equals 80,000 sq cm. If your tiles are 10 x 10 cm, they are each 100 sq cm. Dividing 80,000 by 100 gives you 800, which is the number of tiles required before adding the extra 10%. A useful reference is that you need 100 tiles measuring 10 x 10 cm/4 x 4 in each to cover 1 sq m/10 sq ft. The bigger the tile, the fewer you will need.

Buy all the tiles at the same time to avoid any differences between batches, plus a few extra so you can keep spares for replacing broken or damaged tiles in the future. It's almost impossible to match the colour exactly if you buy from a different batch. Shuffle packs of natural or handmade tiles to ensure any colour or pattern differences are spread evenly over the walls or floor.

GROUT

This is the fine filler that is forced between fixed tiles to form a smooth surface. Check the packaging to make sure you use epoxy-based, waterproof grouting in areas likely to get wet. You can also buy coloured grouting, either to contrast with or match the tile colour.

ADHESIVE

Wall-tile adhesive comes ready-mixed in a tub. Again, use an epoxy-based waterproof sealer for bathrooms and kitchens. For floor tiles, choose a dry powder mix – a stronger adhesive that is mixed with water and spread with a trowel. Your tile supplier should be able to recommend the best brand of adhesive for your tiles.

SEALANT

Sealant should be used to form a flexible joint around the edges of a bath or lavatory, for example. Choose a silicone-based clear or white sealant with a fungicide additive to discourage mould. Most are sold in a cartridge but you can also buy rubberized strip that is fixed with a silicone adhesive/ sealant. The rubberized strip is neater but only works well for narrow gaps of a uniform thickness. Sealant in a cartridge is better for uneven walls or awkward areas. See Sealing round a bath, p187.

Tile-cutting jig An inexpensive plastic tool that measures and scores tiles with an adjustable guide. Easier and quicker to use than manual cutters, and better for cutting thin slivers of tile. If you have to cut a lot of tiles, buy or hire an electric tile cutter. These have a small disc that is cooled by a reservoir of water under the cutting table.

Tile cutter Used for making straight cuts. Manual cutters score a line along the tile – the tile snaps along this line when you bend it. Cutters with jaws are useful for breaking thicker tiles.

PREPARING WALLS

Old tiles These are a good base for new tiles. Rub down the glazed surface of the old tiles with coarse silicone-carbide paper to give a key (surface) for the adhesive. Arrange the new joint lines so they don't line up with the joint lines on the old tiles.

Paint Wash with warm water and detergent and allow to dry.

Plaster Repair any large holes with plaster filler and brush on a coat of plaster-stabilizing solution if the surface is powdery. Chip off any lumps with a cold chisel.

Wallpaper Strip back to bare wall before tiling (see p213).

Tile nibbler A pliers-type tool with hardened jaw edges for nibbling away slivers of tile. Use after scoring with a tile cutter.

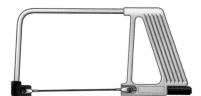

Tile saw A metal-framed saw with carbide blade – use to cut around awkward shapes, curves, and pipework.

Tile file A coarse abrasive tool. Once you have cut a tile, smooth the rough edge with a tile file. It can also be useful for taking off tiny amounts of a tile edge for fitting in tight spots.

Adhesive spreader A flexible plastic tool for applying the adhesive. They are supplied inside tubs of adhesive and have a ridged edge used to make ribbons of adhesive of even thickness on the surface to be tiled.

PREPARING FLOORS

Concrete floors These are ideal for tiling as long as there is no damp. New floors have a damp-proof membrane fitted, but if you suspect damp the floor may need to be coated with a waterproofing compound. Call in a professional for advice. Otherwise, fill any large holes or cracks with self-levelling compound – a powder that is mixed with water and poured over the cracks and hollows – to form a smooth, flat base for the new tiles. Brush a coat of concrete floor sealer over the whole floor. Remove skirting boards and door thresholds before starting work.

Wooden floors Tiles must be laid on a level, firm base because any flexing will crack the grouting. It's essential that there is a flow of air under the floor to stop condensation forming. Check that the airbricks around the external walls aren't blocked with debris or earth. If they are, clear them and check under the floor for signs of damp or mould – such problems will need professional treatment before the tiles can be laid. Replace damaged or rotten boards and cover the floor with sheets of 12 mm/½ in exterior-grade plywood, fixed with rustproof screws at 300 mm/12 in intervals. Pay special attention to the edges and joints. Next, brush on two coats of a PVA-based sealer to stop the plywood absorbing the floor adhesive. Remove skirting boards and door thresholds so you can tile under these. You will probably need to trim some timber off the bottom of the door as well.

Tile gauge For setting out tiles (see right).

Trowel Large adhesive or grout spreader. A trowel is useful for applying a thick layer of floor adhesive.

MAKING A TILE GAUGE

To work out where to place the tiles around obstacles (such as sockets, cabinets, or pipework), make up a tile gauge from a piece of 50 x 25 mm/ 2 x 1 in batten. Lay tiles and spacers along the edge of the batten and mark the tile joints on the wood. You can now hold this batten against the wall to see where the tiles will fall.

MAKING A TEMPLATE

If you haven't got a profile gauge (a metal or plastic tiling jig filled with moveable pins that take up the shape they are pressed against), you can make your own template for cutting tiles to fit round curves or an architrave.

Cut a square of thin card from a cereal packet, then cut a series of notches along one edge, 10 mm/ ⅜ in apart and about 50 mm/2 in deep. Press this edge against the obstacle so that the strips splay and take up the shape. Fold, then cut, the strips to an exact fit and transfer this to the tile. Cut out the shape with a tile saw.

QUICK MAKEOVER

Sometimes new grouting is all you need to transform old tiling. Hire shops can supply an electric grout-remover to rake out old grouting. Regrout with either plain white or one of the new coloured ranges. These are supplied in a tube and are easy to apply. Check the new grout contains a fungicide to reduce the chances of more staining.

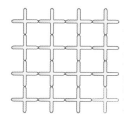

Spacers Plastic crosspieces to hold the tiles at an even distance from each other. You can buy various thicknesses of spacer. Buy the smallest size for 100 mm/4 in sq tiles and larger versions for bigger tiles.

Tiling walls and floors

Tiling a wall or floor requires the same basic skills and it's essential to get the setting out of the tile positions right before starting work. If you plan to lay thick floor tiles, it's worth hiring or buying a diamond-disc cutter. These are very accurate and will cut down the number of wasted tiles. Always wear ear and eye protection when using powered tile cutters.

REPLACING A DAMAGED TILE

Drill three or four holes close together in a line across the damaged tile and use a cold chisel and hammer to break it into pieces that can be levered off the wall or floor. Remove loose grout around the edges. Take a piece of the broken tile with you when buying replacements, as there are many shades of even plain white. Spread some tile adhesive on the back of the new tile, press it into the gap, and then regrout.

CUTTING A SLIVER FROM A TILE

A tile cutter can cut sections bigger than 10 mm/³⁄₈ in from the edge of a tile. If you need to remove a sliver thinner than that, use the tile cutter to score the tile's glazed surface and remove the waste with a tile nibbler. Smooth the cut edge with a tile file or electric sander fitted with silicon-carbide abrasive paper.

TILING A SPLASHBACK

A splashback consists of several rows of uncut tiles fixed to the wall at the back of a bathroom or kitchen fixture or work surface. Even a novice can tackle this job with confidence, as setting out is straightforward and just a few rows of whole tiles should complete the job – you will probably not even need to cut them.

1 Place a tile on the wall, level with the work surface. Rest a spacer on the corner of the tile and pencil a mark along the horizontal edge of the spacer. Repeat at one-metre intervals along the wall.

2 Join up the pencil marks to give a guideline. Using a spirit level, check the line is horizontal. If it isn't, draw a true horizontal line. You will then have to trim slivers off the bottom row of tiles to fit, see left, below.

3 Temporarily nail a batten to the wall right under, and aligned with, the line you have marked. Lightly hammer the nails into the wall so that the batten is held firm but the nail heads are left protruding so that you can lever the batten away later.

4 Spread the adhesive along the area above the batten. It's important that the adhesive doesn't dry out too much, so spread enough to fix only the first row of tiles to start with.

5 Start to tile, pressing the tiles gently onto the wall until you see adhesive squeeze out around the sides. Press spacers into each corner and hold a spirit level across the surface of the tiles to check that it is even.

6 Add more adhesive for a second row above the first, then fix the tiles. Carry on until you have reached the top of the splashback. When all the tiles are fixed, wipe off excess adhesive and leave to dry for at least four hours.

7 Complete the tiling by removing the timber batten and adding the bottom row of tiles, trimming a sliver off the bottom of some tiles if needed. See below left.

8 Use a squeegee to force grout into the gaps between the tiles. Wipe off the excess grout with a damp sponge, rinsed out regularly in clean water. When the grout has dried, polish with a soft cloth.

9 To form a flexible waterproof seal between the new tiles and the worktop or fixture, run a thin strip of waterproof sealant between the lowest tile and the work surface. See Sealing round a basin, p187, for instructions on how to do this.

TILING A WALL

1 Use a tile gauge, held vertically, to plan the positions of the tiles, starting at the top of the skirting board. If you are left with a sliver of tiles at the top, adjust the position of the first row of tiles so that neither the bottom nor the top row is too thin – avoid having less than about a third of a tile's depth. If you want to tile half the wall, for instance up to a dado rail, use the tile gauge to space the tiles so that there is always a whole row of tiles at the top. Make any cuts at the bottom.

2 Temporarily nail a guide batten to the bottom of the wall, level with where the top of the bottom row of tiles will fall. This batten must be horizontal, so check with a spirit level. If you're tiling over tiles, you can drill holes through the tiles to screw on the batten – you will need a masonry drill bit for this.

3 To make sure the tiles are spaced evenly across the wall, find the centre of the wall and mark it with a vertical line. Now use the tile gauge horizontally to

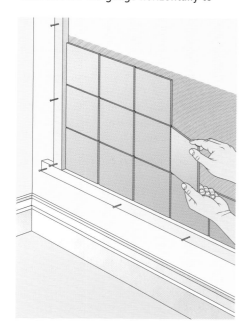

check where the last complete tiles fall at each end of the wall. If there will have to be a thin sliver of tile on one end, shift the tile rows across.

4 Nail a second, upright batten (use a spirit level to make sure it's vertical) along the outer edge of where the last complete tile on the bottom row will be. This will make an exact right angle for you to begin tiling. Work outwards and upwards from the corner formed by the two battens, about 1 sq m/10 sq ft at a time.

5 Use a tile-cutting jig to trim tiles to fit around edges or awkward areas. Measure the gap to be tiled, allowing for any spacers. Using a thin fibre-tip pen, mark the tile to be cut and place the tile on the cutting jig. Hold the tile firmly and use an even pressure to score along the line. Break the tile along the line by pressing down on the arm of the tile cutter.

TILING ROUND A CORNER

INTERNAL CORNERS

The rows of tiles at the adjacent faces of an internal corner will have to overlap so that one is behind the other. Lay the tiles along the face that will fit behind the others first, measuring and cutting each tile to fit the gap. Leave enough space for grout at the edge.

EXTERNAL CORNERS

It is best when setting out tiles to plan for whole tiles at each face of an external corner. If this isn't possible, try to have the whole tile on the face you look at the most. Overlap the tiles at the corner so that the row along one face hides the edges of the row on the other. Again, you should aim to have the full tile on the wall you look at most. You can also buy a

special tile trim that fits around the corner and provides a rounded surface between the two rows of tiles.

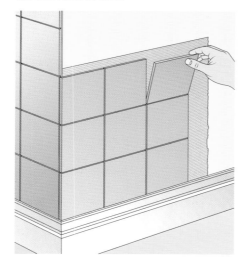

CUTTING AWKWARD SHAPES

HOLES

To make a hole in the middle of a tile, for example to fit around a pipe, mark the centre of where the hole will be on the tile. Using a paper template or something with a diameter slightly larger than the pipe, draw a circle around this point. Then draw a line on the tile through the centre point, and cut the tile in two along this line. Cut out each semicircle with a tile saw, then lay the two halves of the tile together one on either side of the pipe.

CORNERS

Nibble away an area of around 5 sq cm/¾ sq in or less from the corner of a tile with a tile nibbler. This allows you to place the tile on a tiling jig at the correct angle so that you can cut a bigger corner of the correct size.

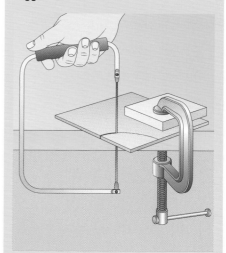

CURVED LINES

Mark the tile with a thin fibre-tip pen and steady the tile in the jaws of a workmate as above. Saw along the line with a tile saw, smoothing the cut edge with a tile file.

MOSAIC TILES

Mosaic tiles are fixed to a mesh or paper backing in sheets at the exact spacing required. These sheets are available in various sizes. Mosaics are fixed to the wall with the same adhesive as other tiles and the setting out method is the same, although you can usually adjust the spacings slightly to avoid cutting the tiles at the edges of a wall. Make sure the tiles are firmly bedded into the adhesive by placing a piece of scrap plywood or medium density fibreboard (MDF) over the tiles and lightly tapping with a mallet. When cutting, use a tile nibbler instead of a tile-cutting jig. You will need to grout over the entire tiled surface once the tiles have been fixed.

MIRROR TILES

If you want to reflect light into a dark area or just want to make a small bathroom look bigger, you could try mirror tiles. Mirrored mosaic tiles can be cut into patterns or used to tile a complete wall. The makers can also supply the special adhesive you will need to fix these. Full-size mirror tiles are fixed with self-adhesive pads in each corner. Make sure the wall is flat to avoid distorted reflections.

METALLIC TILES

You can buy stainless steel tiles – the metal is actually a thin skin over a plain ceramic tile, so they are fixed with ordinary tile adhesive. Before fixing, take care that the grain of the finishes on the tiles runs in the same direction and that electrical sockets don't touch the tiles – call in an electrician to wire up new sockets within the tiled area. Never use a scouring pad or abrasives to clean these tiles.

TILING ROUND A WINDOW

Start tiling a wall with a window from the window recess so that most of the cut tiles can be positioned in less conspicuous areas of the wall.

1 Set out your tiles as for a normal wall, but adjust the height of the horizontal starting batten so that there is a complete row of whole tiles flush with the bottom edge of the window recess.

2 Also adjust the vertical batten position so that the tiles will be evenly spaced on either side of the window recess.

3 Tile the recess so that, if possible, whole tiles are used at the front and any cut tiles are against the window frame. Work along the window ledge and then up the sides.

4 Fit the tiles at the edge of the window ledge in the same way as at an external corner (see p227), with the tiles on the ledge overlapping the edges of the tiles on the wall.

5 Fix the tiles in the normal way. You may need to add a third batten flush with the top of the window recess to support the tiles directly above the window.

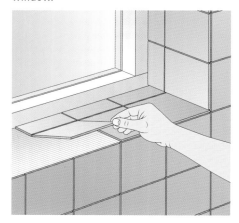

TILING A FLOOR

Floors have to take a lot of wear, and tiles provide a good, hardwearing surface, especially for kitchens and bathrooms. Once you have planned the design and prepared the floor, tiling a kitchen or hallway of around 10 sq m/100 sq ft should take a couple of weekends. It's not a job for the complete novice, but if you have basic DIY skills you should be able to tackle plain floor tiles. There's usually less cutting around awkward shapes than with wall tiles and you're not fighting against gravity. However, if you want to use expensive natural stone, or want a particularly complex pattern, it may be worth calling in an expert.

SETTING OUT

In the setting out stages, it's important to make sure the tiles look straight from the entrance to the room. Often walls are bowed or out of true so check your measurements in several places along each wall.

1 Find the midpoints of the two longest walls. Stretch a chalk line – a length of line covered in chalk – across the room between these points and 'snap' it, tugging it sharply so that it snaps against the floor, to mark a line on the floor halfway along the room. Repeat for the shorter walls but adjust the line so that it passes through the centre of the first line at right angles. Try to work with as many whole tiles as possible, even if it means adjusting the grout line width slightly. To do this, you could either use thicker spacers or simply make the gaps between the last few rows of tiles at the most inconspicuous end of the room slightly further apart or closer together.

2 Lay tiles along the two lines to check they look right from the doorway. If any gaps at the walls are less than half a tile wide, shift the line across to make more of a gap. Also move the guidelines so that tiles around a dominant feature (such as a fireplace or French windows) are symmetrical and there are whole tiles at the doorway. If you can't accommodate all these requirements, opt for symmetry, and whole tiles at the door.

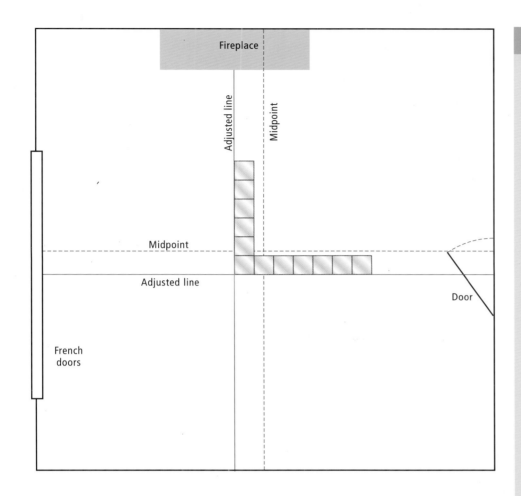

TILING TIPS

- One of the most common mistakes when tiling is to spread on too much adhesive at one time. If the outer edges dry, the bond will be weakened and the tiles may fall off. Only spread on enough adhesive to cover an area you can tackle in about ten minutes.

- To tile the floor of a room that has to be used every day, tile one half of the area at a time so you can walk across the other half while the adhesive sets.

- If your splashback tiles extend beyond the edges of a worktop, support each tile with a nail temporarily tapped into the wall.

- Make screw holes for bathroom accessories with a masonry drill bit. To stop the bit slipping and damaging the glaze, stick some masking tape over the area to be drilled.

- If you want to form a pattern, draw a plan of the room on graph paper to make sure the pattern will look in proportion and symmetrical.

- Diagonal tiling uses the same techniques as normal tiling except that the first tile is placed at 45° in the corner formed by the battens. To achieve this angle, check with a spirit level that the top and bottom points of each tile are in a vertical line.

- Make neat joint lines between the tiles by running a piece of hosepipe over the grouting. This will evenly recess the grout just below the tile surface.

- Don't use wall tiles on the floor – they will not be strong enough to bear the constant wear and weight.

- Most wall tiles come with one or two glazed edges and the remaining edges raw and cut. Use the glazed edges to line borders where they will be exposed, such as the overlapping edges of a window ledge or external corner.

LAYING THE TILES

1 Spread about 1 sq m/10 sq ft of tile adhesive or combined adhesive/grout into one of the right angles made by the two crossing chalk lines. Scrape the notched edge of the spreader across the mix to form ridges of the same thickness.

2 Lay the first few tiles along the edge of the longest centre line. Gently press the tiles into place, making sure they also line up with the other centre line. Add plastic spacers at each corner.

3 Work outwards from the middle of the room until you have laid all the whole tiles on one half of the floor, using a spirit level over every three or four tiles as you lay them to check the tiles are at the same level – not necessarily perfectly horizontal but all surfaces should be flush. Then move across to the other side of the longest centre line and add the rest of the whole tiles. Leave to set for 24 hours – don't

walk on the tiles during this time (see Tiling tips, right).

4 Use the tile cutter to trim the edge tiles to the right shape. Measure the space at both ends of each run of wall in case the walls are uneven, and remember to allow for the grouting gap. Always wear safety goggles and gloves when you are cutting tiles.

5 Leave the adhesive to set for at least 12 hours, then seal the surface if necessary and allow the sealer to dry for at least two hours. Ceramic floor tiles don't need a coating, but unsealed stone, terracotta, slate, and quarry tiles should be protected with a sealer, available from tile stores or DIY centres.

6 Grout between the tiles. Force the grout into the gaps with a squeegee, working from side to side and up and down the tiles. Wipe any grout from the tiles with a damp sponge before it sets hard.

Laying sheet vinyl

Vinyl is easy to wipe clean, waterproof, warmer than tiles, and can deaden noise. Generally, simple, light-coloured designs make a small room feel larger, while bigger patterns are better suited to large rooms. Cushioned vinyl is comfortable underfoot but can be damaged by heavy wear. Thinner sheet vinyl is harder on the feet but longer-lasting. Lino is a 'solid' sheet flooring similar to vinyl but much more difficult to work with, so best laid by a professional.

EQUIPMENT

- Craft knife
- Steel or timber straight-edge
- Tape measure
- Block of wood (75 mm/3 in wide)
- Paint scraper
- Felt-tip pen
- Soft broom.

MEASURING UP

Sheet vinyl comes in 2, 3, or 4 m widths, 1.4–3 mm thick. To find how much you need, measure the room carefully, including any alcoves. If the width of the room is less than 4 m/13 ft 1 in, you will need only a single sheet, and simply need to measure the length. If you will need more than one sheet, it may help to make a scale drawing of the floor, on graph paper, to work out the width and how many lengths you'll need (using as few sheets as possible). Add around 100 mm at each edge for trimming.

PUTTING DOWN VINYL

Vinyl flooring is quite soft – uneven areas underneath will soon show through and spoil the appearance. Before laying the vinyl, vacuum the floor thoroughly and take off your shoes to reduce the chances of grit being trapped under the vinyl and showing through later. Leave the sheeting in the room for at least a day before laying it, either opened flat or loosely rolled. Vinyl is easier to work if warm, so turning on the central heating for a few hours will help.

LAYING A SINGLE SHEET

1 Lay the sheet out in a flat, open area and transfer the markings for the room shape on to the sheet, allowing at least 100 mm/4 in overlap all around. Cut off the larger pieces of waste before taking the vinyl into the room.

2 Unroll the sheet of vinyl and lay the longest edge against the longest straight wall in the room. Allow about 100 mm/4 in of the vinyl to overlap the wall. Adjust so that any pattern is parallel with the wall.

3 Cut slits at right angles to the edges of the vinyl so that it can be pushed into recesses, around chimney breasts, and so on.

4 Press the vinyl firmly into each corner, making a downward cut in the vinyl where it overlaps the wall, directly into the corner. Trim the waste from each side of this line until the vinyl fits into the corner.

5 Where the vinyl overlaps the wall, use a felt-tip pen to mark a line about 25 mm/1 in from the floor. Trim off the waste above this line with a craft knife.

6 Work around the edge of the room, pressing a straight edge against the joint between the floor and the skirting. This will make a crease along which you should cut with a craft knife to give an exact fit. Keep the knife upright.

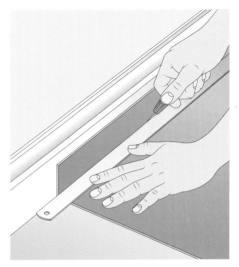

7 Work around door frames or other awkward shapes by pressing the vinyl flat with a paint scraper and cutting around the shape.

8 There are always a few shallow air bubbles at this stage, so use a soft broom to push them out.

9 Use double-sided tape to fix the vinyl to the floor at a doorway, and fit a threshold strip across the doorway to protect the edge of the sheet.

USEFUL KNOW-HOW

To trim the overlap on uneven walls, pull the vinyl away from the wall by about 50 mm/2 in. Hold a pen firmly against a block of wood 75 mm/3 in wide and move the wood along the wall, drawing on to the surface of the vinyl. Cut along the line and push the vinyl back against the wall.

See Soft flooring know-how for more useful vinyl tips.

PREPARING TO LAY NEW FLOORING

Whichever flooring material you choose, it's essential that the floor itself is level, smooth, and dry before work begins. If you can't cure the cause of a damp or rot problem, call in a professional. Most other solid floor or floorboard problems can be easily fixed.

Floorboards The best way of ensuring a wooden floor is smooth and level is to lay hardboard over the top. You can buy 2440 x 1220 mm/8 x 4 ft hardboard sheets from DIY stores. Using the largest paintbrush you have, brush a litre of water over the rough side of each piece of hardboard. Stack the boards back to back, for around 24 hours, in the room to be treated. To cover the floor, cut the boards into 1220 mm/4 ft squares and lay them from the centre of the room outwards. Use as many whole squares as possible to save cutting – you may need to adjust the position of the centre board. Stagger the joints of the squares. Fix with panel pins every 100 mm/4 in around the edge of each board and at 150 mm/6 in intervals in the middle. Make sure the nail heads are flush with the surface. Cut smaller pieces to fit neatly around the edge of the room, cutting around door frames and other obstacles. The best way to cut the board is to hold a straight batten along the marked line and score with a craft knife.

Concrete floors Using a float, spread levelling compound (usually comes in powder form, to be mixed with water) over the floor to fill any holes and provide a smooth surface for the vinyl. Check the instructions for how long you should leave the compound to harden – overnight is best. If in doubt, call in a professional. Use a cold chisel and club hammer to chip off any raised spots. Always wear eye protection when hammering. If there isn't already a damp-proof membrane (a thick polythene sheeting laid on top of the concrete), you should lay one to stop moisture damaging the new floor covering. It's sold in builders' merchants and DIY stores. Use a whole sheet if possible. If this isn't possible, join with a strong, moisture-resistant building tape, overlapping the joints.

Ceramic tiles Spread a 3 mm/⅛ in layer of levelling compound over the joints between the tiles. Remove loose or broken tiles and fill the gaps with levelling compound.

Parquet and cork tiles Remove the tiles or wood blocks with a chisel and mallet. Spread acrylic priming compound (available from builders' merchants and specialist flooring shops) over the exposed surface to a depth of around 3 mm/⅛ in, using the same method as for levelling compound.

EQUIPMENT – PREPARING FLOORS

- Hammer
- Craft knife
- Straight edge
- Tape measure
- Float (a rectangular trowel used to spread floor adhesive and levelling compound)
- Club hammer
- Cold chisel
- Large paintbrush
- Eye protection.

LAYING SHEET VINYL IN STRIPS

If at all possible, avoid making joints in sheet vinyl. If you do have to use more than one width, try to adjust the position so that the joints are in the most inconspicuous place in the room – in alcoves or behind doors, for example.

1 Lay the largest piece of vinyl, trimming the edges to fit around walls and obstacles.

2 Unroll the second piece of vinyl and slide the edge back and forth against the edge of the first section until the patterns are aligned. For larger patterns, such as imitation tiles, you may need to lay the sheet over the top of the first piece until the overlap forms the correct pattern. Lay a straight edge over the double thickness of vinyl and cut through both pieces with a heavy-duty craft knife. Remove the waste strips and press the cut joint firmly together.

3 To join strips of vinyl, peel back the edges and lay a strip of double-sided tape or a vinyl adhesive, sold in DIY stores. Press down the meeting edges with a soft cloth, wiping off any excess adhesive.

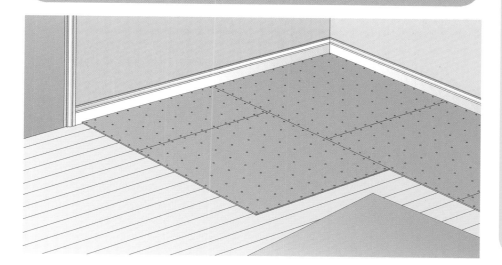

Woodstrip flooring

Woodstrip flooring not only looks good, it's simple to maintain and doesn't harbour dust or other allergy-inducing irritants. Solid wood flooring is the most expensive option and, because it's quite complex to do properly, laying it should only be attempted by very competent DIY enthusiasts. Laminated and wood-imprint planks, though, are easy to lay. Once the planks are in place they form a continuous 'floating' floor, with a gap around the edge that's concealed with lengths of wooden beading. This gap allows the wood to expand slightly if there are changes in temperature or humidity.

EQUIPMENT

- Plank puller (a flat piece of metal with one end bent up and the other end bent down, supplied with the flooring)
- Tamping tool (may be supplied with the flooring)
- Sliding bevel (a tool that marks an angle)
- Heavy-duty craft knife
- Hammer or mallet
- Tenon saw
- Mitre box
- Portable workbench or another support for sawing
- Tape measure
- Drill and flat wood bit.

TYPES OF WOODSTRIP FLOORING

These are the three main types, but individual products can differ – some are preglued, for instance – so check the product details and the manufacturer's instructions.

- **Laminated planks**, where a thin veneer of hardwood sits on top of a cheaper wood, can only be laid over an existing floor. They are already varnished or finished with a vinyl coating, so need no other treatment.

- **Wood-imprint planks** are made by putting a photographed image of

hardwood grain onto thin wood and covering it in hard-wearing resin. They are cheaper than laminated planks, and laid in the same way. They also need no extra treatment.

- **Solid hardwood planks** are the most expensive woodstrip flooring option. Substantially thicker than laminated planks, they can be used in place of floorboards, which is a more complex installation. Most can be sanded and refinished when the finish has worn – check with the manufacturer.

LAYING LAMINATED PLANKS

1 Laminate flooring needs a resilient underlay whether you're laying it over a timber or a concrete subfloor. Your flooring supplier will recommend what to use – usually it's thin foam. Unroll the underlay across the room, trimming it with a craft knife to fit round any obstacles, and tape the lengths together along the seams with heavy-duty adhesive tape.

2 Check whether you'll need to cut any planks lengthwise – see Before you start, right. Lay the first row of planks against the wall, with the tongue side facing out and the spacers provided with the flooring against the skirting board. Use a sliding bevel to transfer the angle of the end wall to the first board so that it can be sawed to fit. When you reach the other end

of the room, measure and saw the last plank to size, allowing room to add a spacer at the end. Slot the plank into place and use the plank puller and a hammer or mallet to make sure that all the joints between the planks are tightly closed.

3 Start the next row with the offcut from the previous row to ensure that the end joints between planks are staggered. Apply PVA wood adhesive along the grooved edge of each plank, fit it under the tongue of the adjacent plank, and use the tamping tool or a board offcut to protect the edge as you tap the plank against its neighbour.

4 When you reach the far side of the room, measure the distance between the last row and the skirting board, then cut planks to the width required, less about 6 mm/¼ in to allow room for the spacers. Use the plank puller to ensure the last row of planks fits tightly against those in the previous row, and insert the spacers against the skirting board.

5 If you need to trim a sliver off the bottom of the door frame to insert the flooring, use a tenon saw held parallel to the floor. Cut the plank that will fit at the

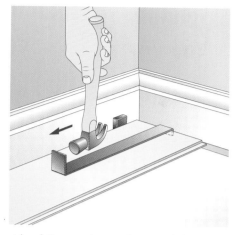

side of the opening to shape and slip it into place.

6 When you have finished laying all the planks, saw lengths of quadrant beading (wooden moulding that in cross section is a quarter of a circle) and fit them to the skirting boards all around the room to conceal the expansion gap. At the corners, saw the beading at 45° (you'll get best results using a mitre box, where the saw is guided at set angles) to create a 90° angle where the two pieces meet. Fix the lengths of beading to the skirting board (not the floor) with panel pins or instant-grip adhesive.

CUTTING TO FIT AROUND A PIPE

1 To fit the end of a plank around a radiator pipe, first cut the plank so that it reaches all the way to the skirting board.

2 To mark where to cut a plank on its short side, lay the plank lengthwise alongside the pipe, with the end of the plank touching the skirting board, and mark where the centre of the pipe is on the side edge of the plank. Then move the plank so that the width end touches the pipe, butt the plank up against its neighbour, and mark the position of the pipe centre on the end of the plank. Draw two straight lines on the plank from the marks so they meet at a right angle. The meeting point marks the centre of the hole you need to cut for the pipe. Use the same method to mark where to cut a plank on its long side.

3 Drill a hole at the meeting point of the two lines, with a flat wood bit fractionally larger than the pipe diameter. With the saw, cut a piece out of the plank at right angles to the edge, as far as the centre of the hole, so you can join both pieces of the plank around the pipe. Glue the joint for a neat fit.

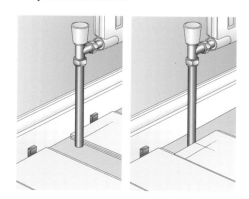

Soft floor-tiles

Soft floor-tiles are the simplest form of floor covering to lay. As they are flexible and relatively thin, it's important to spend time making sure the floor is smooth and flat – covering floorboards with hardboard is essential to avoid ridges wearing through the tiles. When you set out the tiles, loose-lay the first rows to check that the edges are parallel with the walls.

EQUIPMENT

- Heavy-duty trimming knife
- Tape measure and pencil
- Metal straight-edge
- Chalk line
- Timber guide batten (2–3 m/ 6 ft 7 in–9 ft 10 in long)
- Hammer
- Screwdriver.

CUTTING AROUND OBSTACLES

If you need to **cut a curve**, to fit around a basin pedestal for example, make a card template (see Making a template, p225). Transfer the shape to the vinyl (whether tiled or in a sheet) and cut with a craft knife.

If you have to **fit the tiles around piping** that passes into the floor, take a piece of scrap pipe of the same diameter and file one end to sharpen the edge. Use this pipe as a punch to remove neat circles of the floor tile to fit around the pipework. Make a cut into the hole from the tile edge to allow the tile to be slipped over the pipe.

SETTING OUT

1. Prepare the floor in the same way as for sheet material (see p231).

2. Find the middle of the two longest walls and mark across the room between these points with a chalk line (see Tiling a floor, p229).

3. Do the same for the shorter walls, marking a second line on the floor. The centre of the room is where the lines cross. If you have a dominant feature in the room, such as a fireplace, centre the line in the middle of the feature instead of the middle of the wall.

4. Place the corner of one of your tiles in the angle formed by the two lines to check that they are at right angles to each other, adjusting the shorter line if needed.

5. Lay out the tiles, without adhesive, from the point where the lines cross, to check the setting out is correct. If there are thin gaps left at the edges of the room, adjust the lines. If necessary, remove one row of tiles and shift all of them either to the left or the right, leaving a larger gap at the borders – you should aim to leave more than half a tile width at each edge (see Cutting tiles at an edge, right).

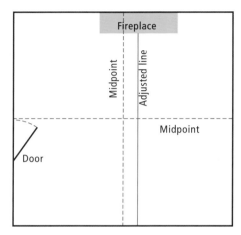

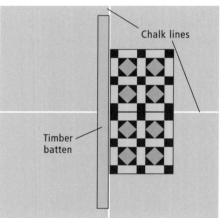

LAYING THE TILES

1. Temporarily nail a straight timber batten along one of the guidelines so that you can butt the tiles against the edge to make a straight line.

2. Use the point where the two lines cross as the starting point for tiling. For self-adhesive tiles, peel away the backing paper of the first tile and press it into place against the batten, flush with the other chalk line. Lay the second tile on the other side of the chalk line, again butted against the batten. If you are using a tile adhesive, spread enough on the floor to fix around 0.5 sq m/5 sq ft of tiles at a time.

3. Work outwards from both tiles, checking that each tile is a tight fit against the fixed tiles. Fit as many whole tiles as possible in one half of the room.

4. Return to the middle of the floor and repeat for the other side of the room. When you have fitted all the whole tiles on this side, work around the wall edges, cutting tiles to fill the remaining spaces (see Cutting tiles at an edge, right).

5. Screw a threshold at each door opening for a neat finish (see Choosing and laying a threshold bar, p237).

CUTTING TILES AT AN EDGE

You are unlikely to be able to fit whole tiles around the edges of the floor area, and will have to cut them to fit (see Setting out, left). When you have fitted all the whole tiles possible, lay a loose tile on top of one of the last whole tiles at an edge. Lay another whole tile on top of this one, and slide it towards the wall until it touches the edge. Mark along the line where the top tile overlaps the loose tile underneath it, then cut this middle tile along the line. The cut-off section will fit into the edge. Cut the tiles along a straight edge with a craft knife held upright.

FITTING CARPET TILES

Carpet tiles are much easier to lay than carpet, and if an area becomes worn or stained the affected pieces are easy to replace. Prepare and lay the carpet tiles using much the same method as for vinyl, with the following differences:

- adjust the tiles so that you have full-size tiles at the door entrance
- lay the tiles in the same weave direction (using the arrow on the back of each tile as a guide) or make a chequered pattern by laying alternate tiles with the arrows in opposite directions
- cut border tiles by making a cut at each edge and scoring across the back with a craft knife (use a metal straight-edge as a guide for scoring) before cutting.

Vinyl tiles provide the same benefits as sheet material but are easier to handle and fit, especially in awkwardly shaped rooms. They are sold in packs to cover about 0.5 sq m/5 sq ft and have a self-adhesive backing. Vinyl tiles are ideal for wet areas, such as bathrooms or kitchens, as they can be easily wiped clean and don't absorb dirt or spills.

Rubber tiles, usually with a dimpled or textured surface for grip, are sold in specialist flooring shops and are laid in the same way as vinyl tiles but with a special adhesive that is spread separately.

Cork tiles have a natural bark texture. They are slightly warmer and softer underfoot than vinyl and can be used in bathrooms, kitchens, or hallways. Cork tiles are fixed with a contact adhesive, sold in DIY stores. You must seal the surface to stop them absorbing dirt – use a clear, flooring-grade varnish.

Carpet tiles are warm underfoot and come in a huge variety of patterns and textures. They can be used in any room, but make sure you buy water-resistant ones if they are to be used in a bathroom or kitchen. These tiles aren't fixed to the floor but it's worth using double-sided carpet-tape across the joints of every third or fourth row to prevent slippage.

SOFT FLOORING KNOW-HOW

- Vinyl and other soft floorings blunt craft knife blades very quickly, so have plenty of spare blades ready. Change the blades regularly as you work.
- Use a straight edge, such as a spirit level about 1 m/3 ft 3 in long, to guide the knife wherever possible.
- If you need to replace a damaged vinyl floor tile, you may find it very difficult to lift the tile. Place some baking-foil over the tile and move a warmed iron over the surface to melt the adhesive. Lift the tile and remove the old adhesive with a scraper.
- Don't wash newly laid vinyl, whether sheets or tiled, for at least a week.
- For a neat finish in a fitted kitchen, take off kitchen unit kickboards and slide the tiles or sheet underneath. You may need to plane a thin strip from the underneath of the boards to be able to refit them.

PAINTING CORK TILES FOR A REVAMP

Painting old cork tiles that are badly scratched or dirty can transform a floor – wash the tiles thoroughly and brush on a couple of coats of floor paint (check the can to make sure it's suitable for cork).

New carpets and offcuts

Carpets add a touch of luxury to any room, as well as reducing noise levels in the rooms below. Choose a grade of carpet according to the amount of wear and tear it will receive. Hallways and stairs need to be very hard-wearing but bedroom carpets can be lightweight. There are moisture-resistant grades available for kitchens and bathrooms. New carpets are expensive so fitting them is generally best left to a professional. However, using a remnant to cover a small floor, or cutting down a larger carpet to fit a new space, is well within the scope of the novice.

EQUIPMENT

- Hammer
- Heavy-duty craft knife
- Tape measure
- Knee kicker (metal tool with square pad that is pushed with the knee to make carpet taut as it is pressed to edges)
- Bolster chisel (100 mm/4 in wide)
- Screwdriver.

NATURAL FIBRE COVERINGS

Manufacturers recommend that floor coverings made from natural materials, such as grasses, should be fitted by professionals, as the material can expand and contract in different conditions.

FITTING A CARPET OFFCUT

1 If you're buying new, prepare the floor in the same way as for sheet vinyl (see p231). If you don't prepare with hardboard, make sure you hammer down any protruding nails and staples in floorboards.

2 There are two ways to secure carpet edges. The best way is to nail gripper strips (lengths of thin plywood batten with angled metal spikes on the upper face) around the edge of the room, about 6 mm/¼ in away from the bottom edge of the skirting board so that the carpet can be pushed into the gap to form a neat edge; see below. Alternatively, when you fit the carpet you can fold the carpet over, as in the illustration on the right.

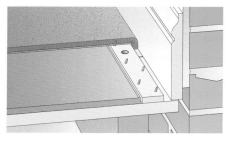

3 If you're fitting a separate underlay, do this now (see below).

4 Align the edge of the carpet with one wall of the room and roll out the carpet. Use a knee kicker (which can be hired) to

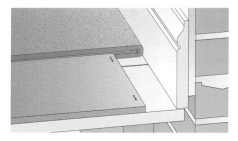

stretch the carpet between this wall and the opposite wall, and push the carpet on to the gripper strip spikes or fold it over.

5 Smooth the carpet from the centre outwards, fixing it along the remaining walls. Use a bolster chisel to push the carpet into the gap between the skirting and the gripper strips. Alternatively, when you fit the carpet you can fold the carpet over, as in the illustration on the right.

6 Join sections of carpet with double-sided carpet-tape. Fix the tape to the floor directly beneath the joint and press the edge of each section of carpet on to it.

7 Trim off excess carpet with a craft knife held at 45° to the wall. If possible, tuck the cut edge under the skirting board with the bolster chisel.

8 Cut the carpet to fit around the door frames, and screw threshold bars across the doorways for a neat finish.

FITTING AN UNDERLAY

It's vital that a good underlay is used under all but foam-backed carpets. It adds to the warmth of the carpet, reduces wear, and helps dampen noise. Never use old newspapers instead. Where there are small gaps between floorboards, put down a layer of building paper – a tough, water-resistant paper sold at builders' merchants – and place the underlay over the top. Buy the best quality underlay available – the foam on cheaper varieties can harden and crumble. Tufted carpets may have their own underlay backing – check before buying.

Try to use a complete piece of underlay for the whole floor. If you have to join sections, butt the edges closely together and fix with a strip of carpet tape, as described in step 6, above. Trim the underlay with a craft knife to fit to the edge of the skirting or the inner edge of the gripper strips. Make sure there are no bubbles or creases in the material, as this will show through the carpet.

CHOOSING AND LAYING A THRESHOLD BAR

To form a neat edge across doorways, fit a threshold bar. DIY stores and flooring specialists stock these bars in a variety of finishes, including chrome and gold. If you are laying carpet, choose threshold bars with upturned spikes on the bottom fixing plate. For laminate or vinyl floors, look for a threshold with a smooth fixing plate. Double-sided bars have a raised T-shaped centre section that overlaps the floor coverings on either side of the doorway.

1 Measure the exact width of the doorway and trim the bar to size with a small hacksaw.

2 Fix to the floor by screwing through the holes in the fixing plate.

3 Tuck the flooring edge into the bar.

FITTING OFFCUT STAIR CARPET

Fitting an offcut of carpet on a stairway isn't difficult, providing you don't rush the work. You will need an extra half a metre (about one and a half foot) of carpeting in length – this allows the carpet to be moved later to even out wear and tear (see step 4).

1 Prise out tacks and nails from old floor-coverings, and repair loose treads (the horizontal 'steps') and risers (the upright sections between each step).

2 Cut a gripper strip to fit at the bottom of each riser and another to fit the back of each tread – fit them so that they abut each other at right angles in the corner of each step, with the spikes facing into the angle made by the strips. Fit on all except the bottom step.

3 Cut a separate piece of underlay to fit on each tread, or buy underlay pads from a carpet supplier (who will cut them to fit your specifications). The front edge folds over the front lip of the step and is tacked to the underside of the tread. Tack the back edge just in front of the gripper strip.

4 Start laying the carpet at the bottom of the stairs. The carpet's pile should face down the stairs so that footsteps don't rub the pile the wrong way. Hide enough extra carpet, by doubling it behind the bottom step, to allow for the carpet to be moved occasionally to spread wear on the nosings (the rounded fronts of the

steps). Tack the carpet to the back of the first tread. Add tacks at the bottom of the first riser and then work up the stairs.

5 Using a wide-bladed cold chisel, push the carpet tightly into the angle formed by the gripper strips at each step.

6 When you reach the top of the stairs, take the carpet to the top of the last riser and trim it with a heavy-duty knife. Tack it in place. You must allow enough upstairs hall carpet to fold down over the lip of the top stair.

CARE OF CARPETS

■ Chairs and other furniture will leave deep indentations in a carpet. Move these items around from time to time to reduce the chances of marking and to even the wear around chairs and tables. For furniture you can't move about, buy small, protective cups sold for the purpose.

■ Cleaning carpets is important to remove ingrained dirt and grit. You can hire steam-cleaning equipment or contact the **National Carpet Cleaners Association**. Heavily used carpets, such as hall carpets, would generally benefit from this kind of cleaning once a year.

TYPES OF CARPET PILE

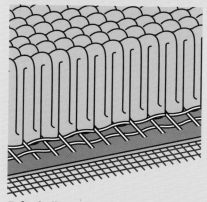

Tufted pile – continuous strands are pushed into a woven foundation secured on an adhesive backing

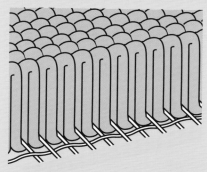

Woven pile – continuous strands are woven into the warp and weft threads of the foundation

Looped pile – ordinary looped pile gives a smooth feel

Twisted pile – looped pile twisted for a coarser texture

Cord pile – loops are pulled tight in against the foundation

Cut pile – loops are cut short for a close-stranded pile

Choosing curtains

When you're doing up a room, curtains represent a considerable part of the expense. Whether you buy curtains ready-made or have them made to fit, you need to measure accurately the window and its surrounds and decide whether to opt for a pole or track. If you are having curtains made, the amount of fabric required will depend on the style of heading you want (see the illustrations below), but also on the length you choose – you have absolute flexibility here. See p240–1 for how to fix curtain poles and tracks.

HOW MUCH FABRIC DO YOU NEED?

1 Measure the width of the curtain pole or track. The width of the finished curtains should together be at least one and a half times this. The fabric width required also depends on the style of heading you choose (see Heading tapes). Allow 4 cm/1½ in for each side seam and any join required.

2 Measure the distance between pole or track and where you want the bottom of the curtain to be. Depending on the weight of the material – heavier fabric needs extra length, to give a longer, flatter hem – allow an extra 15–25 cm/6–10 in for hems and heading. Extra fabric will also be needed if you have to match a pattern. Measure, lengthways, the pattern repeat (from one noticeable feature to the next time that feature appears), and add that amount to each drop (curtain length) of fabric required.

MADE-TO-MEASURE CURTAINS

Whether sewn by you, a friend, or a professional curtain-maker, made-to-measure curtains give you the widest choice of fabric and heading. They may be the only option if your windows don't conform to the standard sizes of ready-made curtains.

CHOOSING FABRIC

Sheers, voiles, and laces are very thin fabrics that give daytime privacy and help screen an ugly outlook.

Medium-weight fabrics, like cotton prints or linen, give privacy after dark but, unless lined, will not keep out the morning light or stop heat loss and draughts.

Heavy fabrics, like velvet, chenille, or tapestry, are good for keeping light out and keeping heat in.

Fabric seconds can be great bargains, but find out what the fault is before you buy. A pattern printed just slightly askew will look conspicuously crooked once it's hanging at a window.

HEADING TAPES

The heading tape hides the edge of the top of the curtain, holds the cords that are used to draw up the curtain fabric to the required width, and provides slots to hold the curtain hooks. These are the most popular heading tapes.

Gathered or standard heading Pulls the fabric into an irregular ruffle. Good for unlined, lightweight fabrics. Allow one and a half to three times the width of the pole or track.

Pencil pleats Suitable for all fabrics. Allow twice the width of the pole or track (three times for lightweight fabric).

Pinch pleats This heading tape makes regular and evenly spaced pleats. This means that you cannot always gather the fabric to exactly the right width, so you must err on the generous side when calculating the fabric required or the curtains won't meet in the middle. Pronged hooks, which are more expensive than standard hooks, hold the pleats in place. Allow twice the width of the pole or track.

Goblet pleats An eye-catching heading, especially if each goblet is finished with a fabric-covered button. Like pinch pleats, they are evenly spaced. Allow two and a half times the width of the pole or track.

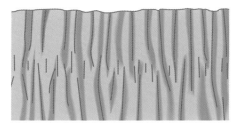
Gathered or standard heading

Pencil pleats

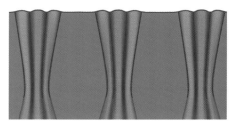
Pinch pleats

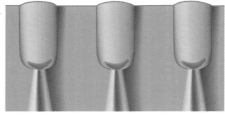
Goblet pleats

BUYING READY-MADE CURTAINS

Ready-made curtains can be much less expensive than professionally made-to-measure ones.

Fabric Obviously, you have to choose from what's on offer. But there are many companies selling ready-made curtains. Shop around.

Heading tape This is usually pencil pleat because it is easily adjusted for different widths and is suitable for both track and pole.

Size Don't give up if the available sizes don't suit your windows. Many suppliers offer, for a fee, an alteration service. It is also possible to shorten curtains yourself without too much hassle (see Tips of the trade). If your window is wider than the maximum width of curtain available, consider buying two pairs of narrower curtains. A few stitches at the top will join them, or you can draw them as four individual curtains.

BENEFITS OF LININGS

Lined curtains:
- hang better
- offer more privacy
- block out more light
- keep in more heat
- give better insulation against noise
- last longer – the lining protects them from fading and dirt

- give a uniform appearance to windows from outside, if the linings match.

In addition to standard lining fabrics, there are flame-retardant linings, and fabrics that totally block out light. A thermal interlining (an additional layer of fabric between the curtain and lining) improves both heat and sound insulation, and makes the fabric look much fuller.

GATHERING THE HEADING TAPE

This involves pulling the cords of the heading tape to draw up the fabric so that it fits the width of the pole or track.

- Heading tapes have two or three gathering cords, and these cords should be knotted together at each end of the tape before you start pulling them.
- Pull the cords from a point 10–15 cm/ 4–6 in from the edge, so the bunched

excess cord will be hidden behind the curtain. If you pull the cords from the ends, they hang at the side of the curtain. With wide curtains, pull the cords from both ends.

- Don't cut off the excess cord – you will have to flatten out the curtains for cleaning in the future. Tie with a knot you can pull out easily.

HANGING CURTAINS

- Don't iron curtains before you hang them – the creases will soon drop out.
- Take the weight of the fabric on your right shoulder (if you're right-handed), draping the curtain so that the heading tape is to the front. This makes hooking the curtains onto the track far less tiring.
- To encourage your curtains to hang evenly, open them and arrange the

hemmed edges into neat folds, 15–20 cm/6–8 in deep. Tie a ribbon or string loosely around each curtain to hold the folds in place, then run your thumb and forefinger up and down each fold to make a sharp crease. Leave the ribbons in position for two or three days before removing them and closing the curtains.

BUYING SECONDHAND

In addition to hand-me-downs, there are other possible sources of second-hand curtains.

Shops dealing exclusively in secondhand curtains:
- On the plus side, the curtains will be clean, are likely to be of good quality, and will probably have been made to measure.
- On the down side, the choice of fabric and size is even more limited than with ready-made curtains. It's worth looking *before* you decorate, as it is easier to buy a paint to match a fabric than the other way round.

Jumble sales and car boot sales can offer bargains, but they are unlikely to have been professionally laundered. Most curtains, especially if they are lined, should be dry-cleaned. Cleaning costs are calculated according to the number of square metres of fabric. Expect to pay in the region of £3.25 per square metre for lined curtains and about £2.50 for unlined, which means it will cost nearly £20 to clean lined curtains for a window 125 cm/4 ft square.

TIPS OF THE TRADE

- If you have to shorten curtains – especially if they're lined and have a professionally finished hem – cut off the excess from the top, rather than the bottom, and attach new heading tape.
- When cutting fabric for curtains, give yourself an accurate line to cut along by pulling out one or two cross threads between the selvedges (the bound edges of a length of fabric).
- Weights stitched into the bottom corners make curtains hang well – leftover foreign coins would do.

Karen Swindon, curtain-maker

▶ Putting up curtains and blinds

Poles and blinds certainly look contemporary, but if you have a bay window, you may have to choose track. Go for a flexible track with a metal core that can be bent to any shape without springing back. If you have to bend a plastic track, warm it first with a hairdryer to make bending easier.

EQUIPMENT

- Hammer drill
- Masonry drill bits
- Bradawl
- Hammer
- Wall plugs or cavity wall fixings
- Screws
- Screwdriver
- Spirit level
- Tape measure
- Pencil
- Curtain track and fittings
- Small hacksaw
- Stepladder
- 25 x 50 mm/1 x 2 in timber batten.

SAFETY

Wear eye protection when drilling overhead (see p168 for British Standard recommendation). If you think there may be a wire or pipe above the window, check the wall with a cable and pipe detector, sold in DIY stores. It's better to buy a combined unit that you can use for other fixing jobs. About £20 will buy a combined metal and stud detector that will also find any timber battens that are hidden behind plasterboard.

CHOOSING POLES AND TRACKS

POLES

Curtain poles are sold in lengths of up to 3 m/10 ft, often with a wide choice of finials – decorative ends that prevent the curtains sliding off. Most poles are supplied as kits with wall fixings. The brackets should be fitted about 10 cm/4 in in from either end of the pole.

- To decide what length to cut the curtain pole, hold it above the window with one curtain attached, and position it with enough pole protruding beyond the frame to allow the curtain to overlap the wall. Allow at least 20 cm/8 in, depending on the thickness of the cloth. Pull the curtain into the open position to make sure it draws right back from the window and lets in the maximum light.

- Telescopic poles save the need for cutting to size, but they are not as strong as solid poles. Check that the pole will take the weight of the curtain fabric you've chosen, including the linings.

- Poles allow you to hang curtains with rings or tabs of material. Tabs are available in kits that include decorative buttons, clips, pins, and iron-on tab templates. Cut leftovers of your curtain material to size and simply iron on the templates to make the tabs.

- Choose slim, lightweight rods for hanging muslin, lace, or voile curtains. Make café blinds by fitting a brass rod across the window, and fixing the fabric in place with pincer clips.

TRACKS

Curtain tracks are sold in lengths of up to 3 m/10 ft and come with fixing brackets, slip-on hooks, end stops, and instructions for hanging the curtains. Some have integral cords to allow you to draw the curtains without handling the fabric. Some are fitted with motorized accessories that allow you to open and close the curtains automatically with a remote-controlled unit. If you want a valance to hide the top of the curtains and the track, opt for a combined track and valance rail kit. Check the track packaging to make sure it will support the weight of your curtains, including linings. As with a pole, track should extend beyond the window frame by at least 20 cm/8 in, depending on the thickness of the curtains, to allow in as much light as possible when the curtains are open.

FIXING THE SUPPORTS

You will need a hammer drill fitted with a masonry bit to make holes in the wall above the window. Masonry bits have hardened metal points that can bore through concrete, blocks, and bricks. Buy a small pack of assorted diameter bits as they are useful for other fixing jobs.

SOLID BRICK OR BLOCK WALLS

Track kits normally include wall plugs for fixing into solid walls. If not, use plugs at least 50 mm/2 in long to give a strong grip for the combined track and curtain weight. Use a drill bit the same diameter as the wall plugs. For a stronger fixing, use the drill bit size that is stamped on the plastic 'tree' that connects the wall plugs.

CONCRETE LINTEL

Concrete is difficult to drill. Instead of drilling lots of holes for the fixing brackets, fix a 25 x 50 mm/1 x 2 in timber batten to the wall with a screw at either end, beyond the lintel ends, and attach the brackets to this.

WOODWORK

You can sometimes attach track (but usually not poles) to the architrave of the window, for instance if the window is in a recess with ceiling straight above. You need to drill holes for the brackets with a wood bit. Screw the brackets into the highest parts of a decorative architrave where it is flat so that the track doesn't buckle. If the window is in a recess, the track can't be extended beyond the sides of the window, and open curtains will bunch up at the edges, excluding light. Where the architrave of the window is flush with the wall, you can fix the track directly to the edges of the window reveal. But the track can be extended only about 50 mm/2 in beyond the window frame, or it will sag, and this is not enough to draw most curtains back fully. To extend the track on to the walls at either side of the window, thus giving more light when the curtains are open, fix a timber batten over the top of the architrave – see Concrete lintel, left.

HOW TO FIX POLES AND TRACKS

1 Decide on the height of the pole or track above the window frame by holding the curtains up to the window. It should be at least 75 mm/3 in. The curtain should be around 12 mm/½ in above the floor to reduce wear on the hem. For shorter curtains, allow at least 50 mm/2 in to drop below the bottom of the window frame, but make sure the fabric does not touch a radiator.

2 Draw a line above the window where the pole or track brackets are to be fixed. Use a spirit level to ensure the line is horizontal. Continue the line beyond each side of the window frame – see Choosing poles and tracks.

3 Fit your drill with a masonry bit the same diameter as wall plugs. Wrap tape around the bit to mark the length of the plug. Drill bracket fixing holes along the pencil line, spaced according to the kit instructions. The end brackets should be around 50 mm/2 in in from the ends of the pole or track to prevent sagging.

PLASTERBOARD WALLS

Buy cavity wall fixings with flanges that open out on the inside face of the plasterboard to give a strong grip in plasterboard ceilings or walls. Avoid heavyweight curtains unless you can fix the track or pole to the timber battens behind the plasterboard.

CEILINGS

Fitting track to a ceiling can be difficult if the joists behind the ceiling run parallel to the window wall, as the nearest joist may be in the wrong position. In this case, you will need to fix cross battens between the joists so that you have something to screw into – which involves gaining access from above, either by going up into the loft or by taking up the flooring above. Once you have access, drill through the ceiling from below at the correct fixing positions, then nail 25 x 50 mm/1 x 2 in battens at right angles to the joists. You will need a special ceiling fixing kit to attach to the brackets.

4 Tap wall plugs or cavity fixings into the drilled holes. If plugs protrude, take them out and make the holes deeper.

5 For poles, screw the pair of end brackets to the wall. You may need a central bracket to support a long pole or very heavy curtains. Attach the curtains to the pole and slot it through the brackets. The end ring or tab should sit between the bracket and the end of the pole to hold the curtains in place as you draw them. Check that the pole ends overhang the window frame equally at either side. Screw the pole securely to the brackets with the screws in the kit. Fit the finials at both ends.

6 For tracks, screw the fixing brackets in place, making sure the track clips are all vertical. Clip on the curtain track. Stand back and check that the track ends overhang the window frame equally at either side. Fit the curtains to the track and add any cord fittings or valance rails. If the curtains are hard to pull, apply a light spray of silicone wax polish to the track.

Blinds can be fitted to the inside of the window frame, to the recess above the frame, or outside the alcove.

1 Mark the positions of the support brackets in the top corners of the window frame. If the blind is to be outside the window frame, make sure the roller is at least 10 cm/4 in wider than the width of the frame.

2 Fix the first bracket. Use wood screws at least 30 mm/1¼ in long for fixing directly to the frame. Use cavity fixings or wall plugs for fixing to the wall.

3 Hold a spirit level on the top of the blind to check that it is level before screwing in the second bracket. Leave enough room for the pull cords to work and make sure they are fitted to the end you can reach most comfortably.

4 For roller blinds, measure the distance between the brackets and cut the pole to fit with a small hacksaw. Stick the fabric to the pole and push in the end caps. Hook the roller into the brackets and check that the blind works smoothly.

A couple of tips for fitting:

- Always cut your blind fabric 3–4 mm/1/16–2/16 in shorter than the cut roller pole length so that it doesn't snag on the brackets.
- Wind a piece of masking tape around the roller pole to give you a precise cutting line when trimming to length.

TIPS FOR DRILLING

- If a wall plug is slightly loose in the hole you have drilled, poke a length of matchstick fully into the hole to give the screw more grip.
- Tape an open envelope under the area you are drilling to catch the dust.

Buying sofas and beds

We spend over a third of our lives in bed, and one that's past its best can seriously affect quality of sleep. When it comes to buying a sofa, it's easy to be swayed by looks, but style and quality are also important if you want to sit in comfort for any length of time and get the wear you hope for. Whether buying beds or sofas, the choice often comes down to something cheap and cheerful for occasional and short-term use, or paying out for quality and durability.

CARING FOR BEDS AND SOFAS

- Turning over mattresses evens out wear and prolongs their life. Every six to eight weeks would be ideal, but even twice a year would help.
- Likewise, regularly turn and reposition the cushions on sofas and armchairs – it's a good idea to do this every time you vacuum the room.
- Vacuum sofas and armchairs using the upholstery attachment every week.
- If you wash loose cushion covers, machine wash on a cool setting and stretch them back into shape while still damp. Try washing a single cover first.
- Read the manufacturer's literature about caring for new furniture, and follow any cleaning information given on labels.
- Trim off any loose threads.
- Jumping on sofas or beds damages springs and other support systems.

SOFAS

Making the wrong choice when buying upholstered furniture can be an expensive mistake, so think carefully about what you want from your sofa before you buy.

QUALITY

Cheaper sofas are upholstered with foam or padding. The frames are made of chipboard and the cushions are supported on straps or springs.

More expensive sofas have sturdy, hardwood frames; thickly padded, sprung interiors; and cushions filled with good-quality wadding or feathers. If you treat a good sofa with care you should get ten years of wear, maybe more, though you might need to renew the covers.

COVERS

Fitted covers are fastened permanently and can't be removed for cleaning. It may be worth having the item treated with stain repellent, although this does add considerably to the cost.

Loose covers are fastened with zips or Velcro for easy removal and cleaning. Buy a second set for a change of colour scheme. More expensive than fitted covers.

Fabrics are usually classified for either light, general, or severe use. Choose leather or synthetic fabrics if your sofa will get a lot of wear.

BUYING A SOFA

- Think about how you and any other members of the household like to sit. Do you want head support from a high back? Or do you like to put your feet up and sit sideways? If the latter, you'll need arms that are high enough to rest your back on comfortably.
- When working out how many seats you need, bear in mind that a two-seater may actually feel small for two people.
- Sit on the sofa for several minutes. Does it support the small of your back properly? Get someone to sit beside you so you can check whether the cushions tip you into the middle.
- Do you struggle to stand up from the sofa? If so, it may be too low or too soft.
- To ensure that the sofa will fit where you want it, check the dimensions of your hall, doorways, and (if relevant) stairs before buying.
- Sofas are often advertised for mail order, but the obvious drawback is that you can't try before you buy. Check that your chosen company offers a trial period – most do – and that, if you reject the sofa for any reason within this time, the company will collect free of charge and give a full refund.

DO YOU NEED A NEW BED?

Beds get a lot of wear, and even the best need replacing after ten years. If you can answer 'Yes' to any of the following questions, it's probably time to buy.

- Has the bed become uncomfortable? Don't wait until a saggy mattress starts interfering with your sleep before you make a change.
- Are the castors bent?
- Is the base sagging?
- Does the bed creak when you turn over? Can you feel bulges or ridges in the mattress?
- Are the divan edges frayed?
- Is the mattress covering torn?
- Does your neck or back ache when you wake up in the morning?
- In a double bed, do you roll towards the middle unintentionally?

CHOOSING A NEW BED

It's tempting to buy a cheap bed base with an expensive mattress, but this can be a false economy. Always consider the two parts together, as a cheap base that wears quickly won't give the support the mattress needs to provide maximum comfort.

MATTRESSES

Interior-sprung mattresses Open springs are found in many mattresses. The price of open-sprung mattresses varies widely according to the filling and covering of the mattress. The wire gauge and number of springs determines how firm the centre of an open-sprung mattress is. Continuous springs are softer and springier than open springs, and mould themselves better to your body shape. Pocket springs are housed individually in fabric pockets. This means they can move independently of each other, which enables them to mould themselves to the body. They give even support, no matter how many times you alter position during the night. Pocket-sprung mattresses are usually more expensive than open-sprung mattresses.

Unsprung mattresses Cheaper than sprung mattresses, and they don't need turning. Made of latex, foam, or fibre. Foam mattresses are hypo-allergenic. When choosing an unsprung mattress, go for a thick, high-quality one.

MATTRESS COVERINGS

Durability comes from the closeness of the weave and the quality of the fabric. A 'micro-quilted' finish is the most usual, where the mattress covering is stitched on to a backing material. Pocket-sprung mattresses are often 'tufted' (a series of tapes having been passed through the mattress and fastened with tags) to hold the mattress filling in place.

BED BASES

A base may be either a divan, usually on castors, which comes down almost to the floor and may have built-in storage drawers; or a bedstead, which may be of traditional design, with a gap between the framework and the floor.

Boarded bases are the cheapest, made of hardboard or even cardboard. They give a firm feel to the bed, but because the mattress is taking all the wear the mattress springs will start to wear out sooner than they would on a sprung base.

Firm-edge bases are made of wood with a heavy-duty spring unit inside. They give good support, both when sleeping and when sitting on the edge of the bed.

Sprung-edge bases are best for comfort and wear, and have a complete spring unit on top of a wooden frame. This helps the mattress to last longer.

Slatted bases provide firm support, but are not recommended for use with a pocket-sprung mattress, as the springs and pockets may get damaged where they are not supported at the gaps between the slats. The slats should be evenly spaced, no more than 8 cm/3 in apart, to provide adequate mattress support.

GUEST BEDS

There are several possibilities for accommodating occasional overnight guests. Ask yourself who will be using the spare bed most often. Older people may find it difficult to get down on to a low sofa bed or futon, for instance.

FUTONS

Buy the thickest, best quality you can afford. Futons need to be rolled up at least every other day, otherwise the filling may become compacted, making the futon flatter and harder. Make sure a futon does not get damp, as the fibres will become matted and lumpy. Buy a slatted base for the futon – more comfortable than using it on the floor.

INFLATABLE / FOLDAWAY BEDS

Inflatable beds to put directly on the floor are inexpensive and can be extremely comfortable. Foldaway beds can be a cheap option, but pricier ones will be bigger and have a better mattress, so are worth considering if wanted for frequent use.

SOFA BEDS

Cheap ones have foam mattresses that unroll onto the floor, and may not be very comfortable. For frequent use, one with a sprung mattress would be better.

BUYING A BED

- Go to the shop prepared to lie on each bed for several minutes.
- Lie as you normally would to sleep, and try turning over.
- When considering a double bed, lie on the bed with your partner, both back to back and facing. Turn over, singly and together. Bigger doubles are significantly more comfortable than the standard width.
- The firmest mattress may not be the best for your particular weight and build. Compare several for comfort.
- Buy the best you can afford.

243

WEB SITES AND ADDRESSES

B&Q
Web site: www.diy.com

Click through to the DIY Advice section for reference information on gardening, decorating, building, carpentry, electrical issues, and plumbing.

Casa Paint Company
phone: 01296 770139;
e-mail: sales@thebluepenguin.com
Web site: www.casa.co.uk/casa.htm

Makers of organic paints.

Crown Paints, PO Box 37, Crown House, Hollins Road, Darwen, Lancashire BB3 0BG
phone: 01254 704951
Web site: www.crownpaint.co.uk

Cuprinol, Wexham Road, Slough, Berkshire SL2 5DS
phone: 01753 550555
Web site: www.cuprinol.co.uk

The How To section has useful practical advice.

Dulux, ICI Paints, Wexham Road, Slough SL2 5DS
phone: 01753 550555
Web site: www.dulux.co.uk

Farrow & Ball Ltd, Uddens Estate, Wimborne, Dorset BH21 7NL
phone: 01202 876141; fax: 01202 873793;
e-mail: info@farrow-ball.com
Web site: www.farrow-ball.com

Manufacturers of traditional papers and paints.

Fired Earth Ltd
phone: 01295 814315;
e-mail: enquiries@firedearth.com
Web site: www.firedearth.com

Suppliers of interior finishes – the Inspirations section has a number of design ideas.

Forest Stewardship Council (FSC),
UK Working Group, Unit D, Station Buildings, Llanidloes, Powys SY18 6EB
phone: 01686 413916; fax: 01686 412176;
e-mail: info@fsc-uk.org
Web site: www.fsc-uk.info

Contains a database of wood products and suppliers certified by the FSC, which is dedicated to promoting responsible management of the world's forests.

Hammerite Products Ltd, Prudhoe, Northumberland NE42 6LP
phone: 01661 830000; fax: 01661 838200
Web site: www.hammerite.com

Makers of specialist metal paints.

International Paints, Plascon International Ltd, Brewery House, High Street, Twyford, Winchester SO21 1RG
phone: 01962 717001; fax: 01962 711503;
e-mail: international@sis.akzonobel.com
Web site: www.international-paints.co.uk

Makers of specialist paints.

National Carpet Cleaners Association (NCCA), 62c London Road, Oadby, Leicester LE2 5DH
phone: 0116 271 9550; fax: 0116 271 9588;
e-mail: info@ncca.co.uk
Web site: www.ncca.co.uk

Ronseal
phone: 0114 246 7171;
fax: 0114 245 5629;
e-mail: enquiry@ronseal.co.uk
Web site: www.ronseal.co.uk

Makers of woodcare products.

Sadolin, Akzo Nobel Woodcare, Meadow Lane, St Ives, Cambridgeshire PE27 4UY
phone: 01480 496868
Web site: www.sadolin.co.uk

Makers of exterior timber treatments.

Sandtex, Akzo Nobel Decorative Coatings Ltd, PO Box 37, Crown House, Hollins Road, Darwen, Lancashire BB3 0BG
phone: 01254 704951
Web site: www.sandtex.co.uk

Makers of exterior masonry paints.

CHAPTER NINE

Getting work done

How much work?

When you own a property, there will be times when you have to pay someone else to work on it. You might need anything from emergency repairs or improvements – perhaps a new kitchen, double glazing, or rewiring – to work of a more structural nature that will increase your living space. This section deals with the basic procedures for finding and dealing with contractors, whatever the level of work.

SETTING A BUDGET

Many renovations end up costing twice as much (and taking twice as long) as originally estimated. The reasons may include appalling weather, problems that become apparent only after work has started, or a misunderstanding with the builder. You may even increase the price yourself by deciding on further improvements as you go along. Follow the guidelines on drawing up agreements (see p253) and don't begin a project unless you have some contingency money available, preferably one-third of the total estimate. If your budget is very tight, check repeatedly that your project is on track financially, and will be completed on time.

What you spend on renovations and improvements should be determined by:

- how much you can afford
- how much the value of your home will increase. This may enable you to extend your mortgage or get a loan to cover the work, but take the repayments into account
- any grants for which you may be eligible (see p256).

WHAT NEEDS TO BE DONE?

There will always be overlaps, but most work is either essential remedial work or home improvement. These deserve more serious consideration than, say, decoration, because they have a lasting impact on the value and saleability of your home.

ESSENTIAL REMEDIAL WORK

There is nothing glamorous about repairing a roof, or curing dampness and rot, but your first priority must always be to make and keep the basic structure of your home sound. Failure to do so jeopardizes the tens of thousands of pounds that you've committed to pay for your home. See p258 for more on how the main remedial treatments are executed and the upheaval they entail. You may choose to have other work done at the same time, to save disruption later.

HOME IMPROVEMENT

The aims of any home improvement should be:

- to improve the quality of your life, giving extra space, light, warmth, or convenience
- to add value to your property.

It's important to keep a balance between these two criteria. Don't put in too much capital – it doesn't make sense to install a kitchen that's worth a third of the value of your flat. And beware of devaluing – replacing traditional period windows with aluminium or uPVC frames is a classic mistake.

To avoid these pitfalls:

- look at neighbouring houses to see what changes have been made, and whether or not they are successful
- talk to local estate agents about the effect your proposed improvements will have on the value of your property. Most agents are happy to give free advice. If not, you need not use them when you come to sell your home.

PRIORITIZING WORK WHEN YOU BUY PROPERTY

If you've bought a renovator's delight that you are not planning to extend, these should be your priorities.

1 Potentially dangerous problems: faulty electrical wiring, old or damaged gas appliances, unsafe structures (from staircases to garden walls), loose chimney pots or roof tiles, unstable masonry that could fall and cause injury.

2 The exterior – if this isn't sound, any work you do inside is likely to be spoiled. Carry out repairs to: the roof, cracked or damaged masonry, damaged gutters and downpipes. Repoint brickwork if necessary. Repair damaged drainage systems. Replace or repair rotted window frames – now is the time to decide whether you would benefit from putting in double glazing.

3 Problems that will get worse if left: rising or penetrating damp, dry rot, and woodworm.

4 Installing new wiring and new plumbing while floorboards are up and before the walls and ceiling are replastered.

5 Putting in a wired security system if you have decided to do this; it will be more expensive to do later.

6 Roof insulation, one of the most cost-effective home improvements. Decide whether you need any sound insulation, perhaps against a party wall.

7 Making good plaster and floors, which will be durable and provide a firm basis for any fixtures.

EMERGENCY CALL-OUTS

Always call the emergency gas line given in the local directory if you suspect a **gas leak** or have problems with your gas supply. Electricity and water problems may not be so clear cut. The supplier owns piping and fixtures up to a certain point, after which they belong to the householder.

If you need to find professional help quickly, look through your local directory or ask neighbours for their recommendations. Choose contractors who are registered with a professional body.

When you phone:

- describe the problem as best you can
- ask what you can do to stabilize the situation until it can be dealt with as a non-emergency
- if the work can't wait, ask what their call-out rate is, what it covers, and what additional charges may be incurred – a punishingly high hourly rate could kick in after, say, the first 20 minutes

- don't accept the first quote. Say you'll get back to them, and make calls to at least two other contractors.

Once contractors arrive:

- ask them to explain what work they propose doing and why. If there's a major problem, ask if they can carry out a holding operation until normal working hours. Good contractors will not leave you without mains services unless there is a very convincing reason, which they should explain
- if new parts are fitted, ask to see and keep the old parts. Get them to point out in what way they are worn or faulty
- obtain a fully itemized receipt, which should offer a guarantee of workmanship and materials, and make sure that it includes the contractor's name and contact number. Ask the person who has done the work for you for their name, too, and write it on the receipt.

FOUR COMMON BUDGET BUSTERS

1 **Upping the specification**
A builder's quote may seem reasonable because it includes such items as ceramic tiles, a bathroom suite, and taps selected off the shelf at the local builders' merchant. If you want something more individual, be prepared to pay extra for quality and design. Visit showrooms and suppliers, get catalogues and price lists, and give your builder the make, size, colour, model number, and price of the items you require. If you don't want to make up your mind just yet, ask the builder to include a realistic but mid-price cost for these items at the outset. Then you will either pay a bit more, or be charged less, depending on the items you choose.

2 **The designer's dream**
Recreating the latest fashion can run away with the pounds, especially when it comes to kitchen and bathroom fittings. What looks right now may appear dated a few years on, and may even have a negative effect when you want to sell. Go for simplicity rather than gimmicks.

3 **The cost of making good**
Discuss clearing up with your builders before work starts, or they may leave you with a heap of rubble and fittings that have been ripped out. You may need to spend some money restoring flowerbeds and lawns that have been walked on or used as a store for building materials.

4 **Follow-on expenses**
You may have a separate budget for major furnishings – curtains, carpets, and furniture – but you should also allow for the smaller, but essential, finishing touches. Light fittings, bathroom cabinets, towel rails, loo roll holders, and door hardware are surprisingly pricey and can amount to several hundred pounds.

Specifying what you want

A good specification is the foundation of any successful renovation or extension project, and a comparison of contractors' quotations is meaningless unless they have all been prepared against an identical specification. The first draft should come from you, the homeowner, though you aren't expected to define thickness of timber or diameter of pipe. It is in your own interests to be clear about what you want – if you don't tell the contractor what you want, you leave the decision to them. You may not like what they choose to use. The final specification should avoid misunderstandings about the work to be done, the materials to be used, and who is responsible for what.

ESTIMATE OR QUOTATION?

According to the Office of Fair Trading, an estimate is generally a rough price, while a quotation is normally a fixed price. The price given on a quotation should not be changed at all without your agreement. With an estimate, unless the specification for work has changed, or new work has been included, this is approximately what you should expect to pay. Legally there is no difference between a written or verbal quotation, but you will have more difficulty settling a disagreement over a verbal one. See Finding a contractor, p253, for advice on getting a signed contract.

THE BASIC STATEMENT

Before you contact any contractors, draw up a basic statement describing the work you want done. This process will clarify matters in your mind and enable you to prepare a useful brief for potential contractors. It also makes a good starting point if you want to hire an architect.

It can be as brief as:
'I have a two-bedroom first-floor apartment, built in the 1950s, which needs rewiring, new plumbing, and central heating installed. Floors and walls will have to be made good afterwards. Do you handle this type of work?'

YOUR SPECIFICATION DOCUMENT

A specification for quotation purposes needs to be more detailed. It requires you to think about how you will be using each room, and how you would like it to look.

Start by taking a separate piece of paper for every room or area that needs work, label it and list the same headings on every sheet. Writing 'not applicable' is better than forgetting something that needs to be done. Make a plan of each room and mark positions of radiators, power points, and so on – see right.

Make several copies of the specification to give to various contractors. Some may be prepared to handle the whole job, others may want you to organize, say, the central heating as a separate job. Ask contractors to indicate which work they are quoting for. Add a clause to the effect that it is the contractor's responsibility to point out errors or omissions in the specification at the time of quoting.

The key headings and issues are:

FOR INTERIOR WORK

Wiring The number and position of power sockets and light fittings, including wall lights and under-cupboard lights. Do you want sockets to be mounted on the skirting (cheaper) or set into the wall (neater)? List any permanent electrical appliances, such as cooker and electric fire. Now is the time to consider installing a security system. By planning ahead, you can make sure all wiring is hidden.

Plumbing Water supply and waste for sink, bath, power shower, bidet, toilet, washing machine, and dishwasher (specify whether cold-fill only or hot and cold for the last two). Do you need an outside tap?

Central heating Specify type and make, if known, as well as number and position of radiators or hot-air grilles. Do you want individual thermostats on each radiator?

Gas Supply for cooker, gas fire, hot water, or central heating.

Floors Repair and replace as necessary. The quality of the work you ask for should reflect the finish you want – greater care has to be taken if you want floorboards polished rather than covered with carpet.

Walls and ceilings Make good as necessary. Even if they are in good condition now, new wiring may have to be channelled in. Do you want coving or a ceiling rose? If you plan to do the decorating yourself, make a note: 'decorating to be done by owner'.

Woodwork Do the window frames need attention? If you live in a period property, specify that architraves, skirting, and doors must match the original.

FOR EXTERIOR WORK

Draw up lists for each elevation – rear, front, north side, south side – and structures such as conservatory or garage. The headings on each list should cover the roof, woodwork, masonry, and gutters.

A TECHNICAL SPECIFICATION

A technical specification, which includes drawings and precise details of materials to be used, is necessary only for new building work or major structural alterations. This will be drawn up by your contractor, based on your initial specification – see left. The more detailed your document, the better.

A SAMPLE SPECIFICATION FOR QUOTATION

Living room	Work required	Responsibility
Wiring	Supply and install 5 x double power sockets as marked on plan	Electrical contractor
	Install new wall lamps	Owner supplies lamps
Plumbing	n/a	n/a
Central heating	Supply and install radiators as marked on plan Contractor to advise on correct sizes	Heating contractor
Gas	Bring supply to fireplace and install fire (owner to specify make and model)	Heating contractor
Floors	Repair and replace floorboards in readiness for sanding	Contractor
	Sand and finish floor	Owner
Walls and ceiling	Make good damaged plaster in readiness for painting	Contractor
	Fit new plaster ceiling rose	Owner to specify style
	Paint walls and woodwork	Owner
Woodwork	Replace damaged skirting to match existing	Contractor
Other	Take speaker wires through to kitchen before floorboards are replaced	Owner

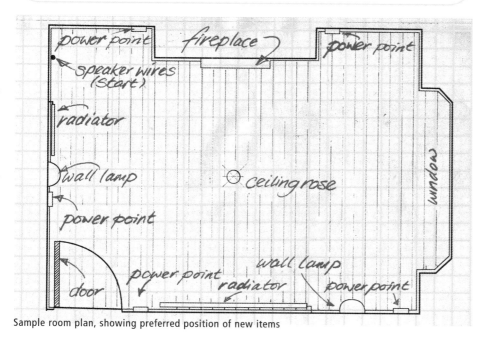

Sample room plan, showing preferred position of new items

SPECIFYING MATERIALS

Misunderstandings about what materials are to be used are a common cause of controversy between contractors and their clients.

■ Basic 'trade' materials, such as electric cable, copper pipe, nails, screws, plaster, and timber, don't have to be specified unless you particularly want, say, thicker than normal plasterboard for soundproofing qualities, or timber from a sustainable resource. Unless you have knowledge of building materials, you have to trust your contractor to supply goods that comply with regulations and will give you the result you want.

■ Generally, visible materials – all the things you tend to take for granted, such as electric switch plates, door hardware, skirting boards, and architraves – are supplied by the contractor. It is your responsibility to make sure they are what you want. Don't assume that the contractor shares your tastes, or automatically uses fittings that are architecturally or environmentally sympathetic.

■ For any item where styling is important to you, specify make, model, colour, and size, or undertake to supply the item yourself. Allow plenty of time for your stockist to order goods so that everything is ready for the contractors the moment they require it. Make sure there is provision for this before accepting a quotation.

■ Bear in mind that good-quality fittings like taps and power showers will function well for years, and the installation costs are the same, whatever the price of these items.

Hiring professional help

Depending on the scale of your project, you may well want to pay for some specialist input, whether it's a one-off consultation with a structural engineer about a load-bearing wall, or the services of an architect to see through a whole extension from start to finish. You need to know what different professionals do, and what to expect if you manage the project yourself.

SEVEN WAYS TO FIND PROFESSIONAL HELP

- Personal recommendation.
- Professional organizations will supply a list of members practising in your area.
- *Yellow Pages*. Look under Architects, Architectural services, Architectural technicians, Building consultants, Computer-aided design services, Draughtsmen, and Surveyors. Make sure the company deals with your type of work.
- Check the Internet for professionals in your area. Some have Web sites with descriptions of recent work.
- Local newspapers often carry small advertisements for architectural consultants, draughtsmen, and specialist companies.
- Magazines and supplements usually have advertisements for specialist companies dealing in kitchens, bathrooms, loft conversions, and conservatories.
- Leaflets through the letterbox may be of use, but only in conjunction with thorough research on your part. Always get at least two other quotes and read the small print very carefully before signing.

DRAUGHTING TECHNICIAN

A technician who puts plans on to paper, often using computer-aided design. Before you enlist any other professional help, consider commissioning a scale plan of your home in its current format, showing its orientation and its position on the site. Then, with tracing paper, a scale rule, and a pencil and rubber, you can experiment with alterations, such as removing a wall to enlarge a kitchen. Ideas generated at this stage make a good basis for an initial consultation with an architect or building surveyor.

WHAT DOES IT COST? To employ a drafting technician to measure up and prepare plans may cost up to £300.

ARCHITECT

To trade as an architect, a person must have a degree in architecture and be registered with the Architects' Registration Council. He or she may also be a member of a professional organization such as the Royal Institute of British Architects.

Architects specialize in different areas (industrial, new building work, and so on), so choose one who has experience and an interest in domestic renovations.

An architect can offer different levels of service tailored to your needs and budget. The first stage is a consultation about the feasibility of and options for improving your home. The second involves drawing up plans and obtaining planning permission or building regulations approval. The third is to take complete control, finding builders and overseeing all work and payments.

WHAT DOES IT COST? The initial consultation is often free, but take it seriously and be prepared to discuss your own ideas, sketches, or plans. For drawing up and submitting plans to the council, a flat fee will be based on the amount of time involved. If you would like the architect to handle the entire project, payment is usually calculated as a percentage of the total cost.

AVOIDING POSSIBLE PITFALLS

- The last thing you want to feel is that the architect's ideas have been foisted on you. Don't employ anyone who fails to lend a sympathetic ear to your thoughts. At the initial meeting, explain clearly what you want to achieve – such as extra living space, or another bedroom – how you envisage the scheme, and how much you want to spend. Find out whether your architect usually teams up with a particular builder, so you can ask around about the builder's reputation.
- Architects' fees rank alongside plumbers' charges in horror stories about costs running out of control.

If you don't want, or can't afford, to employ an architect to handle the whole job, it's important that you both agree their level of involvement from the outset. Ask for a clear explanation of their fees and what service you will receive. If you change your mind as work progresses, check how much extra this will cost.

BUILDING SURVEYOR

Surveyors offer the same sort of services as architects, undertaking anything from consultation to total management. Make sure the surveyor you choose has recognized qualifications and relevant experience. Look for one who is a member of the Royal Institution of Chartered Surveyors or another professional body.

WHAT DOES IT COST? Charges are comparable to architects' fees.

STRUCTURAL ENGINEER

Members of the Institute of Structural Engineers are the people to call when work has to comply with building regulations, but doesn't justify the services of an architect. Structural engineers will also undertake consultation work. For example, when you knock two rooms into one, a structural engineer will specify the type and size of beam that has to go over the new opening. If you are using an architect, he or she will consult a structural engineer as necessary.

WHAT DOES IT COST? There is no fixed scale of fees – charges are negotiated according to the work involved and vary from one part of the country to another.

ARCHITECTURAL CONSULTANT

Architectural consultants may also trade as design consultants or architectural advisers, but never as architects. They don't have to register with any professional body, and therefore don't have to abide by a particular code of conduct. They may not be insured in the event of faulty work. However, many firms work to an excellent standard, and if you find a well-established local firm with good references, they're worth talking to.

WHAT DOES IT COST? An architectural consultant will almost certainly be less expensive than a registered architect.

SPECIALIST FIRM

These firms deal exclusively with one aspect of home improvement – such as loft conversions, conservatories, kitchens, bathrooms, and replacement windows. They offer to handle everything from the design to the installation or construction, usually in a temptingly short period – for example, 'a new kitchen in four days'.

AVOIDING POSSIBLE PITFALLS

- Get at least three specialist firms to submit plans and quotations. Make sure you clarify precisely what they will and won't do. Jobs such as levelling a floor or painting and decorating, for example, may be excluded – in which case their schedule must give you time to have the work done.

- A common ploy of specialist firms is to visit your home, spend several hours coming up with a design and a price, and then offer a substantial discount if you sign up there and then. Don't, unless you have already done enough research to know that the deal represents good value and quality. Explain that you are still considering all options, and that you will get back to them. If they can give you 25% off one week, they should be able to offer the same discount a fortnight later.

- It's true that practice makes perfect, and specialist firms are likely to have encountered, and solved, most problems related to their particular field. But be aware that they might work to a fixed formula rather than giving individual consideration to your requirements.

Managing a building project involving a number of different contractors is almost a full-time job in its own right. It is true that you can save money by being your own manager, rather than hiring an architect or builder to oversee the work, but you must have:

TIME
- To research the materials and quantities you need.
- To source the right materials at the best price.
- To find contractors to do the work.
- To be available to answer queries and make decisions.
- To inspect the quality of the work.

ORGANIZATIONAL SKILLS
- To prepare a schedule of the work.
- To ensure that labour and materials are on site at the same time and at the right stage of the work. Materials delivered too early are likely to be lost or damaged – late delivery wastes expensive labour time.
- To have contingency plans in the event of unexpected problems.
- To manage permissions, approvals, contracts, and payments.

EXPERIENCE
- To be realistic about timeframes and costs.
- To anticipate problems.
- To know if work isn't up to standard.
- To understand problems and discuss possible solutions – otherwise you are at the mercy of the contractor, who may want to do whatever is easiest.
- To stand firm in order to achieve the result you want.

Finding a contractor

Everyone has heard sensational stories about people who have been ripped off by bad contractors, but the majority of tradespeople are honest, reliable, and capable. Some background research will help you find them, and some commonsense guidelines will ensure that you enjoy a good relationship with them. But give yourself plenty of time: good builders, for instance, are often booked up for months in advance, and you don't want to be pressured into choosing someone just because they are available.

TEN QUESTIONS TO ASK

1 Do you do the type of work I require?

2 Have you done a similar job recently and if so, is it possible to see it, or talk to your clients?

3 Can you supply references for similar work?

4 How long have you been in business for?

5 Do you belong to the Federation of Master Builders or any other trade organization?

6 Do you have a full-time team of people – if so, how many?

7 Are there any areas you don't cover, such as central heating or decorating?

8 If you sub-contract, do you regularly use the same people?

9 When would you be available to start?

10 Would you work exclusively on my job, or do you work on two or more sites simultaneously?

WHERE TO LOOK FOR A RELIABLE CONTRACTOR

Nothing beats personal recommendation when it comes to finding professional help, but even that is not foolproof. One person's idea of a job well done is not necessarily the same as another's. So, before you make any decisions about which contractor to hire, check out the options outlined below.

1 **Observation** Walk round your local streets and note any work being done on houses in the area. Try to speak to the owner. At worst, you can knock on the door, though you might be met with initial scepticism. Explain your interest and ask about what they're having done and whether or not they're happy with the builders. Most people love to talk about their renovations and, once they've realized you are genuine, they may be delighted to help.

2 **Small ads** Tradespeople often place advertisements in the local newspaper as one job is coming to an end, so you may have an opportunity to visit their current workplace and assess the quality of the work. Before you phone, prepare a brief outline of the work you

want done (see p248), and a list of questions (see left). Ignore any ads that only give a mobile phone number – they could be cowboys.

3 **Yellow Pages** You may have to make quite a few calls, most of which will be a matter of elimination. But if, after going through your preliminary questions, it is obvious that a company is not suitable for you, ask if they know of anyone who does handle your sort of work. Information of any sort helps narrow the field.

4 **Professional bodies**, such as the Institute of Plumbing, will supply a list of members in your area. Members of the Federation of Master Builders also have to have a good reputation and be able to supply bank references and proof of insurance. Bear in mind that not all bodies may be so stringent in their vetting procedures as these two.

5 Check out **Web sites**, such as http://www.improveline.com – but be sure you're happy with the terms of business indicated on the site.

6 Never, ever employ someone who touts for work on the doorstep.

ASKING FOR QUOTATIONS

- Draw up an initial shortlist of between three and five contractors and make an appointment with each one in turn to meet you on site.

- Give them a copy of your initial specification and go through it with them. Take notes, especially if they suggest any changes. Inform all the other potential contractors of any changes you make at this stage.

- Never tell them what your budget is. Never say you want the job done as cheaply as possible. Never suggest that money is no object.

- Ask each contractor to submit a written quotation. Allow up to 28 days for a complicated job, but phone after a couple of weeks and ask how the quote is coming along. This sends a message that you're seriously interested in employing them and shows that you are not someone who lets things drift.

- Ask each contractor to itemize their costs. This will make it easier for you to see where your money is going, and it will help you agree on payment stages, once you have decided which contractor to employ.

COMPARING QUOTATIONS

There are three main aspects to consider when comparing quotations from different contractors: how much the work is going to cost, what exactly gets done for the money, and how long the job will take.

PRICE

- A high price can be an indication of top-quality work, or it can mean that the contractor doesn't really want the job unless you pay a premium.

- A low price may come from someone who genuinely charges reasonable rates, or it may come from a builder who will demand further funds half way through the job, or use cheap materials.

- VAT, if applicable, makes a huge difference to the final price. Check it has been included.

- A contingency sum of between 5% and 10% should have been included as a matter of course to cover the cost of unforeseeable problems. Check whether this is listed separately or included in the total.

- If a contractor with whom you otherwise felt comfortable offers either a very high or very low price, ask them to go through the specification again to justify the quote. They may have made a mistake, or have misunderstood the scope of the work required.

WHO DOES WHAT

- Will the contractor obtain planning permissions?

- Will the contractor supply materials? If you undertake any part of this, make sure you know exactly what is needed, and when.

- Is the contractor insured for loss of or damage to materials and property, and for injuries to workers and to members of the public?

- Does the quotation cover clearance and removal of rubbish?

TIMING

The quotation should indicate how long the work is likely to take, and approximately when it could be done. If you have any specific timing requirements, you must tell the contractor at the outset.

MAKING AN AGREEMENT

As soon as you've made up your mind, phone the contractor. Confirm the following:

- price and what it includes and excludes

- start date and estimated completion date

- any disruption that would require you to vacate the property, even for a night

- working hours

- number of workers on site

- procedures for changing the brief, the final price, or the completion date. Unless changes are very minor, they should be put in writing

- how payment will be staged, with an agreement to hold back between 5% and 10% until three months after the completion of the job in case of unfinished work, or faulty workmanship that is not immediately apparent.

Put everything you agree into writing and send two copies of the letter to the contractor. Ask him or her to sign and return one copy. This is effectively a contract between the two of you. It will prove a valuable document should serious problems arise (see p265 on getting redress).

Once the agreement has been signed, it's courteous to notify the other contractors who supplied quotes, especially if it was a difficult decision, or was taken because of timing rather than price. It's worth staying on good terms, just in case your chosen contractor lets you down.

A SET CONTRACT

If you would like to work with a professionally drawn-up agreement, you can use the **Joint Contracts Tribunal** (JCT) building contract for homeowners/occupiers. The JCT is an independent body and has produced an inexpensive, four-page, plain English contract to make life easier for you and your builder. It covers all the aspects dealt with on these pages. Some builders may be able to provide the contract, or you can order one direct from the JCT. Not for use in Scotland.

BEFORE WORK STARTS

- Clear the area – your contractor isn't paid to move furniture and take down curtains.

- Remove all fragile and valuable items from the premises, or store them in a lockable room.

- Protect your flooring, removing carpets if possible, especially if they lie between the work site and, say, the bathroom. Builders don't stop to take their boots off.

- Isolate the work area as best you can, using masking tape to seal any doors that can be left closed. Building dust gets everywhere.

- Dig up any precious plants and store them away from the work. Any open space, however small, may be buried under building materials.

BEWARE FALSE CLAIMS

- If VAT is included in the estimate, ask for a registration number and check that it is genuine. If it's not, the contractor gains that extra 17.5%.

- Check that membership of professional organizations is valid and current.

Rules and regulations

Whenever you make a structural improvement to your home, whether it's large or small, check first with your local authority. You may need to apply for planning permission and/or comply with building regulations. An architect or consultant working on your behalf should do this automatically. The rules and regulations can be complicated, but they have the force of law – they exist to provide a pleasant and safe environment for everyone. It's worth being on good terms with the staff of planning and building control offices, who are there to help.

WATCH OUT

- Work that is exempt from **building regulations** may still need **planning permission**.
- Work that does not need **planning permission** may still be subject to **building regulations**.

POINTS ABOUT PLANS

- Site plans should be drawn to a scale of not less than 1:1,250.
- Detailed drawings should be to a scale of not less than 1:100.
- If you cannot give scaled drawings, you should mark all relevant dimensions on your plan. New work or alterations should be crosshatched or coloured on the plan to make the proposed changes instantly obvious.

PLANNING PERMISSION

The purpose of the Town and Country Planning Acts is to protect the character and amenity of an area. In England and Wales, this responsibility lies mainly with local authorities. Scotland and Northern Ireland have similar regulations. In Scotland, these are enforced by the councils. In Northern Ireland, applications should be made to the Planning Service Office of the Department of the Environment. The aim of the regulations is to look after the public interest, not the interest of one individual over another. You do have the right to make some alterations to your property, but the onus is always on you to check whether planning permission is needed.

Operate on the principle that you should take nothing for granted, as interpretations of regulations may vary from area to area. You may discover, for instance, that alterations made by a previous owner mean your home has reached its maximum allowable size (see Volume and area, p257). In a Conservation Area, even repainting the exterior of your house may be controlled. If you don't find out where you stand, you can be forced to undo any unauthorized work and restore the building to the way it was before you started.

SIX STEPS IN APPLYING FOR PLANNING PERMISSION

1 Write to your local planning department to explain what you are hoping to do. Ask if they foresee any difficulties and, if so, what modifications might help get your plans through.

2 If planning permission is necessary, ask for the appropriate application form (some local authorities have them on their Web site, for downloading) and check the following:

- how many copies of the form do you need to return?
- what plans do you need to submit?
- how long will it be before you are given a decision?

3 Check what fee is payable, and what it covers. If the application is turned down, you can usually modify your plans and reapply free of charge within a set time. Equally, if you want to make minor adjustments once work is underway, you may not have to pay a further fee, but you will need to seek permission.

4 Send your completed application forms, necessary plans, and fee to the planning department. Keep copies.

5 The council should acknowledge your application within a few days. It will also notify your neighbours, put up a notice near the site, or advertise the application in the local paper. Members of the public can study your application at the council offices.

6 If permission is refused, you are entitled to know why. Planning staff may be prepared to advise you about changes that might make your scheme acceptable. If permission is granted, work must usually begin within a certain time.

BUILDING REGULATIONS AND CONTROL

The Building Control Service of each local authority has a wide range of responsibility for building regulations, from ensuring safety in public buildings, through naming streets and numbering houses, to making sure that dwellings are structurally sound. Generally, you need to comply with building regulations and get approval from your local Building Control Officer when you:

- erect or extend a building – here size is important, see Volume and area, p257

- carry out structural alterations

- extend or alter a controlled service – for example, water and waste, by putting in a downstairs cloakroom

- change the use of a building – for example, by sectioning off some rooms to create a self-contained flat, or converting a warehouse or barn into a dwelling.

Additionally, building regulations cover some less obvious work, such as having cavity walls insulated. Seek advice as early as possible – unless the work is exempt, you have a legal requirement to tell the council about your intended work. You are entitled to start work two days after giving notice, but for major work it is better to wait until approval has been granted.

HOW TO APPLY FOR BUILDING CONTROL APPROVAL

There are two types of application. The Building Control Service will advise you on the best one for your circumstances.

Building Notice This is suitable for relatively simple work, such as putting in a new cloakroom or removing an internal wall. You need to submit:

- a completed Building Notice application

- a site plan showing the site boundaries and the position of the public sewers if the application is for a new building or a simple single-storey extension. This is available from the council

- the relevant fee. This is calculated according to the type and cost of the work involved.

Full Plans submission Required for more complicated work such as a double-storey extension or where the site presents problems with foundations or drainage. You will probably have to enlist professional help to draw up the plans (see p250). If successful, you will receive a formal notification that the plans have been passed. You need to submit:

- two completed Full Plans applications

- two copies of the detailed drawings of the proposed work. The degree of specification required (such as foundations, roof construction and covering, and thermal insulation) depends on the extent of the work you are proposing

- two copies of a site plan showing site boundaries and the position of public sewers, available from the council

- the relevant fee. This is calculated according to the type and cost of the work involved.

OTHER PEOPLE'S BUILDING PLANS

You have a right to examine any planning application at the council's planning department. Contact the planning department if you think the proposed work would affect your privacy, block your light or overshadow your garden, increase the amount of traffic to an unacceptable level, cause problems with parking, create noise or other pollution (in the case of an industrial development), alter the character of your street, or have any other environmental impact.

Put your objections in writing. There is no guarantee that the development will be stopped, but you may at least win some modifications that minimize its impact.

If your proposed work will affect your neighbours in any way, it is only fair to warn them. This may prevent problems arising.

PLANNING PERMISSION

- Tell your neighbours what you want to do, show them the plans, and listen to any concerns they may have.
- They have the right to object to your application and, whether or not their objections are upheld, it may help your case in the long term to think through any possible modifications in advance.

BUILDING REGULATIONS

Neighbours do not have the right to object unless the 1996 Party Wall Act applies. This covers:

- work on an existing wall or structure, such as the floor in a block of apartments, that is shared with another property, and which could affect its structural strength and support functions. This excludes minor work such as installing shelves or power points
- building on the boundary with a neighbour's property
- excavating near a neighbouring building.

The regulations require that you notify them in writing at least two months before starting work, and obtain their written consent.

WHILE WORK IS IN PROGRESS

- Be considerate (or apologetic) about taking up kerb space with vehicles, building materials, and skips.
- Keep the pavement and road clear of rubbish.
- Let the neighbours know when noisy work is due to start.
- Ask their permission on the day if your contractors need to enter their property in order to access, say, your side wall or roof.

PROOF OF LEGITIMACY

Planning permission Keep all correspondence regarding planning permission in case you ever need to prove that it was granted and whether or not there were conditions attached. A phone call will often establish that planning permission is not required. If you want a record of this, you can obtain, for a fee, a lawful development certificate.

Building regulations If you write to your local Building Control Service it will give written confirmation if work is exempt, and you should keep this. No fee will be charged. If building regulations do apply, you will receive written confirmation of compliance when the work has been finished and inspected. Again, keep this documentation safe.

FINANCIAL ASSISTANCE WITH BUILDING WORK

Grants are few and far between.

- For home maintenance and improvement, they tend to be awarded only to those most in need: the elderly, the disabled, and those receiving state benefits.
- If you live in a listed building or Conservation Area, you may be eligible for a percentage of the cost of repairs directly associated with the historic fabric of the building. But, as with all planning issues, the concern is with public rather than individual benefit. You are more likely to receive help with restoring a significant building that you don't use, than you are for your own home, which it is clearly in your interests to maintain.

Reduced or zero-rated VAT Usually, VAT makes up a hefty proportion of the cost of any building work. The standard rate of VAT is applied to most construction work, but there are some instances, right, when a reduced or zero rate applies to material and labour costs, provided the work is carried out by a builder. If you are doing the work, you will have to pay the standard rate on all materials.

- New building work is zero-rated for VAT. Renovations, improvements, and even new extensions don't count as new building work, but if you are demolishing and rebuilding on old foundations, you may have a case.
- Alterations to make a property suitable for a disabled person are zero-rated.
- Some alterations to listed buildings are zero-rated.

At the time of writing, a reduced rate of 5% applies to the installation of energy-saving materials. This covers:

- insulation for walls, floors, ceilings, roofs, and lofts
- insulation for water tanks, pipes, and other plumbing fittings
- draught proofing for windows and doors
- central-heating controls, including thermostatic radiator valves
- hot-water system controls
- solar panels.

The reduced rate does not cover electric dual immersion water heaters or substantial improvements, such as completely replacing draughty windows.

DO YOU NEED APPROVAL?

The chart on the right is a guide to the permissions required and standards expected for common home improvements. Interpretations of regulations may vary, however, so **always consult your local authority** before starting anything beyond routine decorating and maintenance. If possible, obtain written confirmation that you may proceed. If you live in an area with a two-tier council structure, planning will be dealt with by your district council.

WHICH WORK REQUIRES PERMISSION OR APPROVAL?

Type of work	Building regulations	Planning permission*	Other approval as appropriate
Repairs and decoration	✗	✗	✔ Listed building consent
Replacing an existing kitchen or bathroom	✗	✗	
Creating a new kitchen or bathroom, or altering existing drainage	✔	✗	Must comply with water regulations; contact your supplier
Installing central heating	✔	✗	
Installing unvented hot-water system	✔	✗	
Adding insulation	✔ For cavity-wall insulation	✗	? Listed building consent, for external wall insulation
Adding damp-proofing	✗	✗	
Internal structural alterations	✔	✗	✔ Listed building consent
Replacing windows	✔	✗ Unless they face a highway and project beyond the foremost wall of the house	✔ Listed building consent
Converting loft	✔	✔ For dormer windows and windows over a certain size; check with your local authority ✗ As long as the volume of the house is unchanged and the highest part of the roof is not raised	
Adding extension	✔	✗ Unless it exceeds the permitted increase in volume (see right) ✔ If you live in a flat or maisonette	✔ Listed building consent ✔ Consent of freeholder/ management company
Adding conservatory	✗ Unless floor area is more than 30 sq m/ 323 sq ft in area	? As for extension	✔ Listed building consent
Adding porch	✗	? As for extension	✔ Listed building consent
Adding garden shed or garage	✗ Unless floor area is more than 30 sq m/323 sq ft, or it is within 1 m/ 3 ft 3 in of boundary	? Depends on size and position on the site – consult local authority	✔ Listed building consent
Adding carport	✗	? Consult local authority	✔ Listed building consent
Hardstanding for private vehicle	✗	✗ Unless you live in a flat or maisonette	✔ Consent of freeholder/ management company
Erecting greenhouse	✗	? As for extension	? Possibly listed building consent
Demolition	✗ For total demolition of a freestanding building ✔ For partial demolition	✔	✔ Listed building consent
Change of use (self-contained flat, or office space)	✔	✔	
Removing trees	✗	✗ Unless they are protected, or you live in a Conservation Area	

Key: ✔ = requires permission/approval; ✗ = does not require permission/approval;

   ? = may require permission/approval.

* This column does **not** reflect planning requirements in protected areas, such as Conservation Areas, National Parks, and Areas of Outstanding Natural Beauty, where regulations may be stringent.

THE IMPORTANCE OF VOLUME AND AREA

Volume is a significant factor as far as planning permission is concerned. It is calculated from the external measurements.

- As a general rule, a building can be extended by whichever is the smaller: up to 70 cu m/2,472 cu ft, or up to 15% of its volume on 1 July 1948 (when the legislation came in), or of its original volume if it was built after that date. The allowances are different in Scotland and Northern Ireland.

- Terraced houses and houses in Conservation Areas, Areas of Outstanding Natural Beauty, and National Parks can be extended by up to 50 cu m/1,766 cu ft or 10%, whichever is the smaller.

- If you are thinking of buying a property that you would consider extending, check with the local authority that it has not already been extended to its maximum size.

Area affects whether or not building regulations apply. This is calculated using internal measurements. Small building works, such as the construction of a porch, carport, garage, greenhouse, or garden shed, will be exempt if:

- the building is more than 1 m/ 3 ft 3 in from the boundary and the new floor area does not exceed 30 sq m/323 sq ft.

As an approximate guide, a flat-roofed extension with a floor area of 4 m/13 ft x 4 m/13 ft and a height of 3 m/10 ft would give a volume of 48 cu m/1,695 cu ft.

The floor area of a double garage is usually roughly 30 sq m/323 sq ft.

Disruptive work

Taking up the floor coverings, lifting floorboards, cutting away plaster, and knocking holes through walls are things to do as infrequently as possible. They are unavoidable when you are dealing with urgent problems such as woodworm, damp, or rot, or carrying out improvements that involve plumbing or electrical work. Check out the table to find out what your proposed work will entail, and decide whether there's anything else you can afford to do at the same time. If some jobs will have to be done later, leave access to underfloor spaces – screw, rather than nail, floorboards in place, and don't put down fitted floorcoverings until all the work is behind you.

SEE ALSO Damp, rot, and woodworm p196, Insulating your home p198, Rules and regulations p254

SAVE YOURSELF SOME MONEY

Installing new, or improving existing, systems are expensive projects, but the outlay is justified in terms of comfort, efficiency, and the value added to your home. Much of the cost of using professional plumbers and electricians is accounted for by the hours they have to spend preparing underfloor areas and chipping away at the walls. By having the work done in one go you can at least save the cost of repeatedly lifting the floorboards – and any preparation work that you can do yourself, will save you money.

HOW MUCH DISRUPTION DOES THE WORK INVOLVE?

Type of work	Likely disruption – see key below										Other
	1	2	3	4	5	6	7	8	9	10	
Woodworm Can affect timber in any part of the property	●						●		●		Wait six weeks before laying impervious floor covering such as vinyl
Wet rot Affects floors at ground level and exterior woodwork	●						●				Apply paint or other protective finish to exposed wood
Dry rot Most likely to start at ground level but spreads rapidly	●				●	●	●	●*	●	●	* May need to install airbricks or vents
Penetrating damp Damp patches often indicate source of problem					●	●				●	Gutters may need attention Brickwork may need repointing Check roof for missing slates or tiles
Rising damp	●				●	●	●		●*	●	* For chemical damp-proof course (DPC). Installing/repairing DPC involves drilling into or cutting exterior brick walls
Electrical work	●	●	●	●		●			●		
Plumbing	●	●	●	●		●					Water system may need to be drained
Repairing/ upgrading central heating	●	●	●	●		●				●	Water system may need to be drained

Key:
1. Fitted floor coverings must be removed; floorboards must be lifted
2. Joists and rafters may be notched or drilled to accommodate pipes or cables
3. Solid walls and floors may need to have channels cut into them to house pipes or cables
4. Plasterboard may need to be cut away so that pipes or cables can run behind
5. Damaged plaster needs to be cut out
6. Plaster must be made good/replastering necessary
7. Rotten and weakened timber must be replaced
8. Holes need to be knocked through walls
9. Chemical solutions used
10. Redecoration required

IMPROVEMENTS TO CONSIDER

REPLACING WINDOWS

Ill-chosen replacement windows can seriously devalue a property. Since 2002, new windows must comply with building regulations – and if you live in a Conservation Area, you will need to get planning permission to replace them. Generally, however, a house with double glazing is attractive when it comes to selling, as double glazing reduces draughts and cuts out some noise.

- If your windows are of architectural interest, consider secondary glazing instead of double glazing.

- If your windows are beyond repair and must be replaced, try to replace like with like. A local joiner will be able to make exact replicas – or even sympathetically designed double-glazed windows.

- Even if the new windows are the same size as the old, internal plaster will need to be made good round the frames.

FITTING INSULATION

Insulation is one of the most cost-effective home improvements and, with planning, can be installed as you carry out other work. See also p198.

- Draughtproof gaps round doors and windows with foam or rubber strip, but don't seal the room completely – ventilation is essential. See p176 for how to draughtproof windows, doors and letterboxes yourself.

- Lag hot water pipes and tank to prevent heat loss.

- Lag cold water pipes and insulate cold water tank to prevent condensation and freezing.

- Loft insulation can be bought as rigid sheets, fibre rolls, or loose granules (which are useful for awkward spaces). Install it after all other work requiring access to the attic – plumbing, wiring, roof repairs – has been completed. Make sure the insulation material does not impede ventilation round the eaves.

See p198 for details of materials and techniques for doing this yourself.

- Underfloor insulation is now a requirement for new buildings. In an existing property it is easiest to install it while the floorboards are up. Tack plastic netting between the joists to support the insulation material.

- Double glazing is most effective at preventing heat loss if the gap between the panes is between 8 mm/⅓ in and 20 mm/¾ in.

- Cavity wall insulation should be carried out by a professional. Consult your local Building Controls office before having the work done.

INCREASING THE POWER POINTS

If you're having electrical work done it's worth thinking about how you may be using different rooms in the years ahead, and have extra power points installed now. Bear in mind that adding extra ones later will be far more expensive and disruptive.

Having eight or ten power points in a room is not excessive. Even a modest home office area is likely to need a computer, printer, scanner, and fax machine. Then allow for a desk lamp, perhaps a music system – and you still need somewhere to plug in the vacuum cleaner.

ROOF REPAIRS

A well-built roof will last for decades – if not centuries. Unless the roof structure has been seriously weakened by rot or woodworm, or the tiles and slates have started to disintegrate, most roofs can be repaired. If problems warrant a complete re-roofing job:

- re-use as much of the existing material as possible

- even if you are not in a Conservation Area, try to choose materials that are sympathetic to the original style of your house and the neighbouring properties

- try to do the work during dry weather

- don't undertake any interior work until the roof is sound.

REGULATIONS THAT AFFECT IMPROVEMENTS

Water bye-laws are principally concerned with preventing any risk of contaminated household waste water being siphoned back into the mains supply. Tell the local water supply company about the new installation of a bidet, flushing WC, tap with hose connection or any other fitting which might allow back siphonage. If in doubt, ask.

Building controls apply mainly to the disposal of waste water and sewage. They control the size and type of pipes used, and the angles at which they must fall towards the stack pipe. They specify ventilation requirements for any room with a WC, and also apply to the installation of unvented water heaters.

Building controls also apply to the installation of boilers and unvented heating systems.

Gas connections must be carried out by an employee of British Gas or a member of the Council for Registered Gas Installers (CORGI).

Electrical wiring must comply with the wiring regulations of the Institution of Electrical Engineers (IEE).

Planning permission may be required if you want to install a fuel storage tank on your property, or if you need a chimney or flue that extends above roof level.

FLOOD PROBLEMS?

If you believe your property may be likely to flood, and you are planning major improvement work, you should contact the **Environment Agency** for advice on measures you can take to reduce damage in the future. Examples are: siting all power points and meters above 90 cm from the floor; using waterproof plastering; and tiling and sealing the ground floor.

Combining and dividing rooms

Changing the shapes and sizes of your rooms by taking down or putting up walls often gives scope for dramatic improvements to your home. To explore the possibilities, start with a scale drawing of your existing floor plan, a sheet of tracing paper, and a pencil and rubber. It's also helpful to have scale cut-outs of furniture so you can check it fits comfortably into your new scheme.

DECORATING THE NEW SPACE

If you're combining rooms, think about how the two areas will work together. You might consider:

- laying the same flooring throughout
- making doors and architraves match
- using a screen to partially separate the two spaces.

If you're creating a new room, think about:

- whether you need to add a new focal point
- how to stamp the room with its own clear identity
- using a partition made of glass blocks to provide both light and privacy
- making the space look larger by hanging mirrors or using mirror tiles.

ADVANTAGES/DISADVANTAGES OF REMOVING WALLS

REASONS FOR

- Taking down a wall between two small rooms to make one room of a decent size can make the whole house seem more spacious.
- You may let in more light: knock down the wall that divides a north- and a south-facing room and you have a large south-facing room.
- A separate dining room may be rarely used, which makes it an obvious contender for combining to create a large living/dining room or spacious eat-in kitchen.
- Hall space can be incorporated into the living room.
- Combining two bedrooms may provide room to create a generous main bedroom suite with walk-in wardrobe and en-suite bathroom.

REASONS AGAINST

- Can you afford to lose a room that may be used infrequently, but which offers space for working or reading?
- You may be knocking down just one wall, but in terms of accommodating furniture, shelves, and pictures you are removing two – one from each room. Can you relocate (or do without) the things that used the wall space?
- Will losing a room affect the value of your property? A house that boasts one luxury bedroom suite plus a second bedroom may not be as saleable as a three-bedroom home. Check with an estate agent in your area.

PRACTICALITIES

- The first step is to consult a building surveyor to find out if the wall is load-bearing. If it supports the weight of the floors or roof above, it may not be possible to remove it. If it can be removed, the surveyor will recommend

the correct size and type of beam to span the opening, and the correct way to install and support it.

- The floor in one room is not always level with the floor in the next. If the difference is minimal, you may not discover it until you have created the new opening. A shallow step is likely to cause accidents – the solution may be to raise the level of the lower floor by laying a new layer of flooring.
- Extra work will be involved if there are radiators or wall lights to remove.
- Closing off one door will give extra wall space. The neatest method is to remove the door, frame, and architrave, and infill the opening with stud partitioning.
- Light switches may have to be relocated so that they can be operated from the new, principal doorway.
- There may be times when you would like, temporarily, to re-divide the room. Consider installing French doors in the new opening. If they are glazed, you still benefit from the increased light. Sliding or bi-fold doors use up less floor space but are more expensive.

ADVANTAGES/DISADVANTAGES OF DIVIDING A ROOM

REASONS FOR

- Stud partition walls are quick and relatively easy to build. It is also easy to hide pipes and cables behind the plasterboard. The basic work can be carried out in as little as a day, with extra time for electrical and plumbing work, and for finishing off.

- Dividing a large bedroom to create an en suite bathroom or an additional bedroom can add value to your home.

- A kitchen can be improved if space permits you to section off part of it for a separate utility room.

- It may be possible to create a downstairs cloakroom by, for example, partitioning off part of the hall and using the space under the stairs.

REASONS AGAINST

- If you are dividing one bedroom into two, each new room must have its own window for light and ventilation. You may, therefore, have to install a new window.

- A high-ceilinged room may look terrible when divided in two if the floor space is not adequate. Don't divide a room if the proportions will look wrong.

- Extra walls can make a home darker. Wherever practical, incorporate fanlights over new doorways and fit glazed doors.

- Make sure each room has its own access from a passage or lobby – you may have to sacrifice some floor space to create one.

PRACTICALITIES

- Solid walls offer greater soundproofing qualities than stud partition walls, but are less quick and easy to construct. They also need foundations for support.

- A new stud partition wall will need to be secured at floor and ceiling level. You may have to install extra supports between the joists of the floor below and the joists or rafters of the space above. This would mean lifting floor

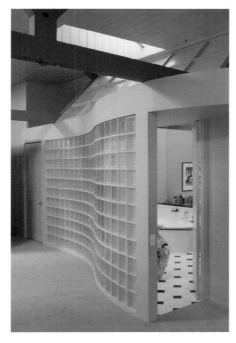

coverings and floorboards, and taking out a section of the ceiling.

- Make sure the new wall does not block future access to the space underneath the floors.

- Plan where to hang radiators, shelves, and mirrors and make sure there are horizontal or vertical timber supports at those places.

- Gas fires and other fuel-burning appliances need a minimum amount of air circulation to function safely and efficiently. Consult your supplier to ensure that, after dividing a room, you will still have adequate ventilation to meet regulations.

- Run wiring and pipework through the wall before you put the plasterboard into place.

- The new wall should look as though it has always been there. Install skirting boards and cornice to match on both sides.

- Take soundproofing into account. Acoustic insulation can be installed between the timber supports. A double layer of plasterboard with staggered joints also reduces noise.

WHEN THE CHANGES INVOLVE PLUMBING

An extra shower room or downstairs WC can make a huge difference when everyone is trying to get ready at the same time – even if 'everyone' is just two people. Separate washing facilities for guests are also a definite bonus.

You must follow building regulations when installing new plumbing (see p000), but there are decisions you can take that will make the work easier, quicker, and less expensive.

- Wherever possible, try to locate the new room close to existing services – directly above, below, or behind the existing bathroom or kitchen, for example. This minimizes the length of new pipework, and makes it easier to connect to your current waste system.

- Reduce plumbing costs when creating a separate utility room by choosing a 'cold-fill only' washing machine.

- If you're installing a new shower, consider an electric one. It requires only a cold water supply, and it won't place an extra strain on your existing hot water tank. However, it's important to check that it will have enough pressure.

- Utility rooms, bathrooms, and cloakrooms do not have to have a window for light and ventilation – although an electric extractor fan connected to the light is a must. Foregoing a window means you can make use of internal spaces that would otherwise be wasted.

OTHER OPTIONS

To alter your living space, consider:

- lowering a ceiling
- raising a floor
- creating a raised area at one end of a room.

Extensions and conservatories

Having an extension built is a far greater undertaking than adding on a conservatory, but they involve similar planning. When you're designing the layout of the new space, consider how you will use the space when it's finished and how that might change in the future. Also, will having the extra room affect the way you use the rest of the house?

CHECK THE IMPACT

Mark the outline of the proposed extension or conservatory with long bamboo canes stuck vertically into the ground. This will give a good indication of the impact it will have on your garden, on neighbours (see p79) and on the view from the rest of the house. It will also show you where shadows will be cast.

CHECK THE FLOW

Unless you are adding a separate 'wing' as a self-contained flat or office, it's important that human traffic flows smoothly between the old and new parts of your home.

- Avoid conflicting interests, such as having to cross the main work area of the kitchen to move from the new room to the back door or downstairs cloakroom.

- If a conservatory is to lead directly off a living room, you may have to rearrange the seating so that you can get to it easily.

- New staircases and passages (even those that are not partitioned off) can eat up floor space.

MAKING AN EXTENSION SUIT THE HOUSE

The reason you need the extra space will dictate whether you choose a single- or double-storey extension and its position on the site. If you can afford only one storey now but would like to build up later, make allowances at this stage with foundations and walls that can support the extra storey.

If the extension will include a kitchen, laundry, or bathroom, how easy will it be to connect into existing waste services, plumbing, and electrical supplies? In a large extension it may be more practical to install independent heating and hot water systems, rather than place an extra strain on the existing system. Design the layout of your extension so that costs of providing new services are kept to a minimum.

LOOKING GOOD

An extension must function well, and it should look as if it has always been there.

Windows and doors If the existing style is not available ready-made, have matching window frames and doors (both external and internal) made by a local joinery.

Bricks Although you should be able to match the colour of bricks fairly closely, modern bricks may not be the same size as old bricks. You may be able to find suitable secondhand bricks, but cost could rule this out. If you are working with different sized bricks, avoid butting directly up to the existing brickwork – even a slight recess will minimize the difference.

Roofing material Slates and tiles can look conspicuously new for years. To achieve an instant weathered look, buy secondhand. If this is not feasible, take old tiles from the least visible part of your roof and use those on the new extension. Put the new tiles in the less noticeable position.

Roof pitch The pitch should match or be sympathetic to the existing slopes and angles of the roofline. A flat-roofed extension on a pitched roof house always looks like an afterthought. If the location or your finances don't allow for a proper pitched roof, raising the roof at an angle for four or five rows of tiles will soften the effect. Alternatively, consider creating a roof terrace (take that decision early as it will affect construction).

MAKE THE BEST OF NATURAL LIGHT

Planning considerations and the layout of your home will narrow down the possible positions for an extension or conservatory. Before you finally decide where to put it, consider how you can best utilize natural light.

- A sunny aspect and good light are vital for a conservatory and desirable for the rooms in which you spend most of your time – probably the living rooms and kitchen. If these rooms currently face north or northeast, it may be possible to switch your floorplan so utility areas and less used rooms are on the darker side of the house.

- If the new extension is to house a garage, laundry, or spare bedroom, locate it so it has minimal impact on the light entering your home. South-facing living rooms sell, but no one is impressed by a south-facing garage.

ADDING A CONSERVATORY

A conservatory can be an effective way to bring more warmth and light into your home without having to change the basic structure of the house. It also provides a way for you to enjoy your garden without having to brave bad weather.

A conservatory requires different materials to most extensions.

- If you want to use the conservatory all year round as an extension of your living space, central heating, lighting, and the type of glass you use are important for its comfort.

- Conservatories can get extremely hot, so allow for ventilation and heat-reflective blinds – which will also give privacy after dark. Automatic venting and blinds systems are effective but expensive.

- Before deciding on a glass roof for a conservatory, think about cleaning. A solid roof with skylights might be more practical, especially if you are building under a tree. It would also make the conservatory cheaper to heat in winter.

THE COMPONENTS

Framework is usually made of timber, uPVC, or metal.

- Timber requires the most maintenance and uPVC the least.

- Timber is sympathetic to older architectural styles.

- Most conservatories are made up of prefabricated panels, and their dimensions determine the final size of the room.

Windows should be double-glazed or the room will be too cold in the depths of winter, when you most want the sun.

- Full height glazing gives the maximum light and sense of space.

- Sill-height glazing gives some privacy and accommodation for radiators. You can also put plants on the sills. The pleasure of a conservatory comes from being able to sit in it and look out to the garden – the internal height of the

sill should be less than 60 cm/24 in or it will obstruct your view.

- All glass that you can fall on to or walk through must be toughened – check with building regulations.

Glass roofing is vulnerable to impact and a major escape route for rising heat.

- Glass must be toughened or laminated – which certainly puts the price up.

- Polycarbonate sheeting is a less expensive option. Choose twin- or triple-wall sheets to reduce heat loss. Be prepared for clicks and creaks as the plastic expands and contracts with changing temperatures.

- Fit guards along the gutters to protect the roof from falling tiles and, in harsh winters, compacted snow falling off the roof or trees.

Flooring depends on how you wish to use the room.

- In Victorian times (when conservatories first became fashionable), tiles were used. If you like the look but not the cold underfoot, consider installing underfloor heating before the tiles are laid.

- Warmer alternatives are timber flooring or concrete, covered with cork, vinyl, or even a fitted carpet.

TEN THINGS TO THINK ABOUT

1 How will you access the new room/s from inside? Can you use an existing doorway, modify a window, or will you need a new opening? Will you have to create a passage or can you conveniently walk through another room with an outside door?

2 Are there obstacles on the exterior wall – such as down pipes, soil pipes, boiler flues – that will have to be repositioned?

3 Can you link the new gutters to your current system, or will you have to make alternative arrangements for dispersing rainwater, such as digging a new soakaway?

4 Are there services or inspection chambers that will have to be repositioned?

5 Is the ground outside at the same level as the existing floors? Will you step down (or up) into the extension, or will you build up (or excavate) the land outside?

6 Do you want access to the new room/s from the outside? Will you need to construct new paths? What are the implications for security?

7 How easy will it be to bring services (electricity, plumbing, drainage, heating) to the site?

8 Will the conservatory affect how you use the garden? Consider adding exterior lighting over new garden doors.

9 Will you still be able to reach the windows, walls, and gutters above the extension or conservatory to maintain them? If the exterior above a new conservatory needs work, do this first, as scaffolding is expensive.

10 Will the new building make upstairs windows accessible to intruders? You may have to fit window locks, or modify your security system to monitor the new roof.

Loft conversions

There is a big difference between boarding over the floor of your loft to make full use of the space for storage, and converting it into a proper room. A loft conversion is a good way to increase your living space without altering the volume or footprint of your property. Although it involves meeting building regulations and possibly acquiring planning permission (see Rules and regulations, p254), loft conversion is quicker and less disruptive than adding an extension.

MAINTENANCE

- Fit windows that flip around to be cleaned from inside.
- Large sheets of flooring are easier to lift than floorboards when you need access to wiring and pipes underneath. Attach flooring with screws, not nails.

FIRE SAFETY

Building regulations require:
- smoke detectors to be fitted in loft conversions
- recommended fire-rated materials and fitting self-closing fireproof doors to prevent the spread of fire
- in a building with two or more storeys, a certain maximum height of windows above floor level and maximum distance from the eaves, to allow escape by ladder.

For details, check with your local authority's Building Office.

IS CONVERSION FEASIBLE?

There are three key factors to consider when contemplating a loft conversion: roof construction, access, and headroom.

Roof construction Traditionally, pitched (sloping) roofs were built on site, using rafters supported by high-level horizontal beams called purlins. The resulting framework leaves the central space unobstructed and makes it fairly easy to incorporate window openings in the roof. Many modern roofs are built with prefabricated trusses, which have lower, horizontal timber braces to give them strength. Unfortunately, these braces make it difficult to move around the loft space. Conversion may be possible, but it will be more complicated and the extra expense may not be justified.

Access Decide where to locate the stairs leading up to the new room. In a single-storey house, space for the new staircase will have to be taken from the hall or one of the rooms. In a two-storey property, the usual location is directly above the existing stairs.

Headroom There must be adequate headroom above the stairs as you enter the new room. To achieve this you may either have to position the stairs to enter the room under the highest point of the roof – which would use up valuable floor space – or build up the wall and raise the roof over the stairs.

In order to move about the loft easily, you need a minimum height of about 2 m/7 ft. Measure the floor area that offers this headroom to check whether it will be adequate. Consider whether you need one or more dormer windows. Lower-ceilinged areas around the edge of the room can be used for storage and for some furniture. A desk, for example, can be tucked against a wall that is less than 1 m/3 ft high, as long as the pitch of the roof allows you to sit and stand up comfortably.

CONVERSION STEP BY STEP

1 The first thing to do is to create safe access to the loft space. Do this where the stairs will eventually be positioned.

2 Will you be able to carry all the materials through the house and through this access? If not, make an opening in the roof – in a place where you will be installing a window. This will also give natural light to work by. Builders should be ready to cover the gaps with plastic sheeting if the window is not fitted immediately.

3 Install services (electricity, central heating, other plumbing) before you put down the new floor.

4 Insulate the roof and the gap between the roof and the sloping walls. Don't block ventilation around roof timbers – building regulations may apply.

5 If you remove insulation from under the new floor, heat rising from the rest of the house will keep the chill from the loft room.

6 If installing skylights, black frames look less obviously new than light timber ones, especially on older roofs. If you build a dormer window, make sure that the pitch, scale, and style are sympathetic to the existing roofline.

Avoiding problems

The more thorough you are when preparing your specification for any contractor, the less likely you are to end up in dispute. You should ideally agree in advance what procedures you'll follow if a dispute does arise. Play your part in maintaining a good working relationship by giving the contractor as much notice as possible, in writing, if you change the specification, or if there is good reason why payments will be late or withheld, and by paying promptly if there are no problems. Here are the six most common complaints about getting work done – and how to avoid them.

1 Undue pressure to have unnecessary work done. You should never agree to have work done that you don't want – but that is sometimes easier said than done. If you're up against someone particularly pushy, buy yourself time by saying that you have a friend or relative with whom you'd like to discuss the proposals, or say you need to obtain a loan to pay for the work and you'll have to submit three detailed quotations. Unscrupulous builders and cold-call salespeople will not risk being put under such scrutiny. See also p247 for dealing with emergency call-out contractors.

2 Over-charging. Confirm every verbal quotation in writing, even if you are only having minor work done and are paying on an hourly basis. Your letter should confirm the hourly rate; whether it includes VAT; how materials will be costed; roughly how long the job should take.

3 Lost deposits. Some firms won't undertake work unless they receive a deposit. If they insist on this, ask for bank and insurance references – and follow them up before work starts.

4 Unnecessary delays. In the absence of unforeseeable problems, you have a legal right to have the work completed within a 'reasonable' time frame. Before you accept any quotation, ask how long

the work should take, when it will start and when it will finish. Include a penalty clause in your agreement, to reduce the bill by a stated amount if the job overruns beyond a set number of days.

5 Unfinished work. Before accepting a quotation, especially for a major contract, check the company's insurance: it should protect you from financial loss although it can't compensate you for the inconvenience of having to find another contractor. For smaller jobs, make sure that, at all times, the money you owe the contractor more than covers the cost of finishing the job – otherwise unscrupulous traders may feel they have nothing to lose by abandoning you.

6 Poor workmanship. Following up references and checking on membership of trade associations is your best safeguard. While the job is on, inspect the work at the end of every day. If you suspect the work is not up to standard, talk to the contractor immediately as it could jeopardize the quality of subsequent work. Hold back the final payment for three months in case problems arise once the contractor has left the scene.

KEEP A DIARY

If there is any dispute a full record will help you present your case.

- Every week, compare actual progress with anticipated progress.
- Keep a record of materials as they are delivered.
- Make a note of all payments.
- Keep a record of all conversations with the builder, especially those in which either of you expresses concern about possible problems.
- Take photographs regularly, ideally with a camera that dates each shot.

SEVEN STEPS TO PROBLEM SOLVING

1 **Talk to the contractor** and give him or her a chance to put things right.

2 **Put your complaint in writing**, if there is no response; see p92 for what to include.

3 **Consider getting an independent expert opinion** to confirm your complaint. Be prepared to pay for this service.

4 **Write to the head office, if there is one, or a trade organization, if the contractor belongs to one.** It may be prepared to intervene on your behalf.

5 **Consider withholding payment** – but check the terms of your contract carefully, particularly if you have a credit agreement with the company. You must inform the lender of any problems.

6 **An arbitrator can be consulted** – but only if both parties agree.

7 **The last resort is to go to court** – though normally you can't do this if you have already gone to arbitration. If you are claiming less than £5,000 (£2,000 in Northern Ireland, £750 in Scotland) the matter can be dealt with under the small claims procedure; see p96.
For larger amounts you may be able to use the small claims track, but the court will decide. If you can't use this route, you will need to employ a solicitor.
Cost can quickly spiral upwards, so be sure of your ground and consider the possible outcomes before embarking on this.

Contact details for organizations given in **bold** appear at the end of each chapter.

WEB SITES AND ADDRESSES

British Wood Preserving & Damp Proofing Association, 1 Gleneagles House, Vernon Gate, Derby DE1 1UP
phone: 01332 225100; fax: 01332 225101;
e-mail: info@bwpda.co.uk
Web site: www.bwpda.co.uk

Chartered Institute of Arbitrators,
International Arbitration Centre, 12 Bloomsbury Square, London WC1A 2LP
phone: 0207 421 7444; fax: 0207 404 4023;
e-mail: info@arbitrators.org
Web site: www.arbitrators.org

CORGI, 1 Elmwood, Chineham Business Park, Crockford Lane, Basingstoke, Hants RG24 8WG
phone: 01256 372200;
e-mail: enquiries@corgi-gas.com
Web site: www.corgi-gas.com

ebuild
e-mail: info@ebuild.co.uk
Web site: www.ebuild.co.uk

A Web directory of building products and services for self build, DIY, and house renovation.

Electrical Contractors' Association
Web site: www.eca.co.uk

Federation of Master Builders, Gordon Fisher House, 14-15 Great James Street, London WC1N 3DP
phone: 020 7242 7583; fax: 020 7404 0296;
e-mail: central@fmb.org.uk
Web site: www.fmb.org.uk

HM Customs and Excise
phone: 0845 010 9000;
Web site: www.hmce.gov.uk

Useful information source on VAT.

HomePro.com, Quadrant House, The Quadrant, Hoylake, Wirral CH47 2EE
phone: 08707 344344;
Web site: www.homepro.com

Has an online directory enabling you to find reputable tradespeople or businesses.

Improveline, Bond House, 347-353 Chiswick High Road, London W4 4HS
phone: 0845 359 3000; fax: 0845 359 3001;
e-mail: info@improveline.com
Web site: www.improveline.com

Includes a directory of tradespeople and enables you to search by postcode.

Institute of Electrical Engineers, Savoy Place, London WC2R 0BL
phone: 0207 240 1871; fax: 0207 240 7735;
e-mail: postmaster@iee.org
Web site: www.iee.org.uk

Institution of Structural Engineers, 11 Upper Belgrave Street, London SW1X 8BH
phone: 020 7235 4535; fax: 020 7235 4294;
e-mail: mail@istructe.org.uk
Web site: www.istructe.org.uk

Joint Contracts Tribunal, 9 Cavendish Place, London W1G 0QD
Web site: www.jctltd.co.uk

If you require a contract with your builder, the JCT have a standard contract that you can use.

National Inspection Council for Electrical Installation Contracting, Vintage House, 37 Albert Embankment, London SE1 7UJ
phone: 020 7564 2323; fax: 020 7564 2370;
e-mail: enquiries@niceic.org.uk
Web site: www.niceic.org.uk

National Insulation Association, PO Box 12, Haslemere, Surrey GU27 3AH
phone: 01428 654011; fax: 01428 651401;
e-mail: insulationassoc@aol.com
Web site: www.ncia-ltd.org.uk

Office of the Deputy Prime Minister (ODPM), Enquiry Service, 26 Whitehall, London SW1A 2WH
phone: 020 7944 4400; fax: 0207 944 6589;
Web site: www.planning.odpm.gov.uk

For information on planning procedures in England and Wales.

Painting and Decorating Association, 32 Coton Road, Nuneaton, Warwickshire CV11 5TW
phone: 024 7635 3776; fax: 024 7635 4513;
e-mail: info@paintingdecoratingassociation.co.uk
Web site: www.paintingdecoratingassociation.co.uk

Planning Service, Clarence Court, 10-18 Adelaide Street, Belfast BT2 8GB
phone: 028 9054 0540; fax: 028 9054 0665;
e-mail: planning.service.hq@nics.gov.uk
Web site: www.doeni.gov.uk/planning

For information on planning procedures in Northern Ireland.

Royal Incorporation of Architects in Scotland, 15 Rutland Square, Edinburgh EH1 2BE
phone: 0131 229 7545; fax: 0131 228 2188;
e-mail: info@rias.org.uk
Web site: www.rias.org.uk

Royal Institute of British Architects (RIBA), 66 Portland Place, London W1B 1AD
phone: 0207 580 5533; fax 0207 255 1541;
e-mail: info@inst.riba.org
Web site: www.architecture.com

Royal Institute of Chartered Surveyors, RICS Contact Centre, Surveyor Court, Westwood Way, Coventry CV4 8JE
phone: 0870 333 1600; fax: 0207 222 9430;
e-mail: contactrics@rics.org.uk
Web site: www.rics.org/public

Scottish Building Employers' Federation, Carron Grange, Carrongrange Avenue, Stenhousemuir, Falkirk FK5 3BQ
phone: 01324 555550; fax: 01324 555551;
e-mail: info@scottish-building.co.uk
Web site: www.scottish-building.co.uk

Scottish Executive, 2H Victoria Quay, Edinburgh EH6 6QQ
phone: 0131 556 8400;
Scottish Executive Helpline: 08457 741741;
fax: 0131 244 8240;
e-mail: ceu@scotland.gov.uk
Web site: www.scotland.gov.uk/planning

For information on planning procedures in Scotland.

Select, The Walled Garden, Bush Estate, Midlothian EH26 0SB
phone: 0131 445 5577; fax: 0131 445 5548;
e-mail: admin@select.org.uk
Web site: www.select.org.uk

Scotland's trade association for the electrical, electronics, and communications systems industry.

CHAPTER TEN

Working from home

Setting up at home

It's estimated that by 2005 over 6 million people will be working at home in the UK. Some will be employed by large companies, but the majority are expected to be self-employed sole traders. If you decide to use your home for work, whether it's the kind of work you already do for someone else, or a new business idea that may involve others, you need to prepare thoroughly.

WEIGHING IT UP

For:

- It's comfortable and pleasant. Your surroundings are your own.
- It's cheap. No more travel costs and no need to rent an office.
- Instead of travelling to work, you can be earning money or doing something else.
- You can tailor the hours you work to your needs and those of your customers. You can generally work at your own pace.
- As your own manager, you are in control.
- No one ever got rich working for someone else!

Against:

- The lease or deeds of your home may prevent you from using it for business.
- You might need extra insurance and home security.
- If you work alone, you could feel isolated.
- You might find it hard to resist distractions.
- Your income may be irregular and you may have to chase late payments.

MAKING THE DECISION

BE HONEST WITH YOURSELF

Working at home can be lonely. It can also become addictive. Have you got what it takes to survive? Try to answer the following questions honestly.

- Could you cope with not having anyone to talk to, to bounce ideas off, or to put things into perspective if something goes wrong?
- Would you miss the social life of colleagues?
- Could you motivate yourself without a manager to give you targets and deadlines?
- Do you have the self-discipline to make yourself work, even if the sun is shining? Equally, would you be able to cut off mentally at the end of the day?
- Can you be organized and keep your work separate from your living space?
- How well would you cope with financial insecurity?
- Could you say 'no' to a client or customer, because the work would overstretch you?
- Will you be able to earn enough?

You should feel confident in all these areas before you start on the practical preparations for working at home.

WILL YOU BE A NUISANCE OR BREAK ANY RULES?

If you plan to work at home, you have to be careful that you won't fall foul of the law or upset your neighbours. In general, if you're engaged in a quiet, desk-based activity, no one is going to mind. But you may find that the terms of your mortgage or lease specifically exclude you conducting any business that creates noise, makes a mess, or involves clients' cars or large delivery vehicles parking in your street. And if you do cause disruption, your neighbours may complain to the local authority, which can take steps to limit what you do. See Make sure it's legal, opposite.

DECIDING WHERE TO WORK

If you are going to function well, you need a proper space in which to operate. It may seem at first that all you need is a desktop for your computer, or whatever major equipment you require for your business, but in reality you need much, much more – so if you're starting from scratch, overestimate your needs.

Whatever your business, try to establish a reasonable-sized area to work in, with enough storage space so that the things you need are close to hand. It also helps, psychologically, to keep everything associated with work separate from the rest of your home: this can make it quicker to settle into a work frame of mind and,

equally, allows you to get away from it all at the end of the day. If you can't shut a door on your workspace, consider putting up a curtain to hide desk and shelves, so you don't feel work is hanging over you (see also Your workspace, p270).

In deciding where to work, and depending on what you do, you may need to consider some of the following.

- Changing or combining the function of rooms to create a dedicated workplace. If you can clear away your things completely when your work is done, a room that isn't used much – a dining room or spare room – could double as a workspace.

- Ensuring there is enough natural light and ventilation – especially if you're thinking of putting a desk on a landing or in an area under the stairs.

- Installing extra shelving and other storage, preferably some that is fireproof.

- Fitting up a basement, attic, or outbuilding. Get estimates for how much this will cost (see Finding a contractor, p252) and make sure there would be sufficient heating. If your business is noisy – for instance if you are a composer or a machinist – you might consider soundproofing. See p272 for more on finding grants and p275 for more on setting capital expenditure against tax.

- Providing safe storage facilities if your work involves hazardous materials.

- Providing parking facilities if customers will be visiting.

- Extra plumbing – for instance sinks or a toilet – if you are offering treatments or physical therapy. You may need a special power supply for machines, or you may have to make structural alterations to install and accommodate heavy equipment.

- Access for deliveries, if you are likely to need regular supplies for your work.

- Extra insurance – see p273. If you are investing in expensive equipment, for example, your insurer could insist on extra locks, security lights, or an alarm.

BASIC FORWARD PLANNING

It would be rash to contemplate starting a business at home without the **finances** to tide you over the early stages as you get yourself established. These could be savings, or a loan, or an overdraft facility (see Money and insurance, p272). When working out your financial needs for the first year, take into account not just your usual bills but also items that you may not have had to purchase before, such as special insurance, licences, maintenance and repair of equipment, and so on. You also need to take into account the fact that your heating, lighting, and phone bills are likely to be higher if you will be at home all day.

Once you've worked out your various commitments, you'll be able to work out **how much you need to earn**. Pricing your product or service may be a difficult task and you'll need to take into account what the competition, if any, are charging or what the target market for your goods or services is prepared to pay. You also need to take account of the fact that there may be periods when you have no work, can't work, or want to go on holiday (although you may have to go without holidays until you're safely established).

Market research is a key part of your preparation. You need to be confident that there will be enough demand for whatever product, service, or skills you hope to sell. It's also advisable to have some customers or potential customers in your sights when starting out, and to be prepared to find the next wave.

Last but not least, inform your local **tax office** (see Dealing with tax, p274). Both tax and National Insurance are now dealt with by the Inland Revenue, so you only need to register your self-employment once.

MAKE SURE IT'S LEGAL

When setting up a business, unless it's small-scale and entirely desk-based, it's best to make thorough enquiries with your local council's Trading Standards department to make sure that you are complying with current laws and regulations.

- Check your mortgage or lease and your house insurance to make sure that there are no clauses prohibiting the business use of your home. Change your insurer if necessary. Many house contents policies now include cover for basic office equipment but there's usually a fairly low limit. If you will be using other types of business equipment such as specialist tools, your normal contents insurance is unlikely to cover it. Also, you should inform all your insurers as a matter of course that you have become self-employed because it may affect premium and/or payment of future claims. This is particularly important if you use your car for business.

- You may need planning permission for change of use if using more than half your home as an office, or an outbuilding as a workplace.

- You may need a local authority or government licence to run your business, particularly if you want to run an agency, look after children or animals, or offer physical therapies or treatments.

- You will have to be inspected by the Environmental Health department or other relevant authority if you work with food, look after children or animals, or offer physical therapies or treatments.

- If clients or customers visit you, you should have public liability insurance and, if you handle money on behalf of clients, you should have professional indemnity and/or fidelity bonding. See p273 for more insurance details.

Your workspace

It's worth investing in quality furniture and equipment so that working at home will be comfortable and convenient. If your work area will be on view to anyone visiting your home, you might want to choose furniture that will blend in with your surroundings and, perhaps, conceal the fact that it's a work area. Good organization is essential – otherwise you may waste valuable time trying to find things.

SEE ALSO The technology revolution p103–124

MAKE YOURSELF COMFORTABLE

Working from home is a great idea, as long as it doesn't eventually damage your physical or mental health because you are working in unsuitable conditions. You should have good lighting and ventilation at your workstation, adequate heating, freedom of movement, room to lay out your work, and suitable storage of papers, files, and work tools close at hand. You should also be able to conduct your work in safety and to guarantee the safety of the public who may visit your workplace.

If you have a room or area dedicated to your work, you need to think about the following:

GENERAL CONDITIONS

Light Working under constant electric light without any natural light has been found to promote headaches and depression. If you don't have natural light, invest in some natural light spectrum bulbs that simulate daylight.

Ventilation If you're working in a room without a window that opens, you should consider a small air conditioner, or – if it is, say, an attic – investigate the possibility of installing a new window.

Heating If a room is cold and damp, it will not only affect you but it will also certainly affect computers, photocopiers, and fax machines, as well as any papers you store. Your computer printer will not feed paper through unless it is completely dry. If you are working in an outbuilding, you will need to insulate it and install some form of heating.

WORK AREA

- Make sure you have a large enough work surface. Computers and computer equipment, for example, take up a lot of room. Do you have desk space to lay papers down and to read or write?

- Do you have enough shelving, filing cabinets, or storage – preferably actually in your work area, so that you can access everything easily? If you work with tools, make sure you have hooks or racks so that you can put the tools away when you have finished with them.

- Make sure your work area is big enough. Can you move around it easily? Can you work without tripping over boxes of files on the floor, and can you open the door properly without it banging into your desk?

- If your work surfaces are too high or too low, you may develop neck, shoulder, or back problems.

- Similarly, you will need a well-designed, adjustable chair to work from.

EQUIPMENT

- Do you have adequate power points for all your equipment? Plugging everything into extension leads is a potential fire risk and trailing cables can cause accidents. Can cables be hidden away?

- You'll probably need a telephone point and extension in your work area. You might want a dedicated land phone number and perhaps a dedicated modem line.

- It's vital to have fire safety equipment handy. You'll need to know what type of small fire extinguisher or fire blanket you need for any special pieces of equipment you have.

- If your work involves preparing food or providing therapeutic treatment, do you know what you need to do in order to meet hygiene standards?

It is a good idea to separate your work from your home life as much as possible. Make it a rule not to take work out of your work area. If your work is going through a difficult patch, you'll be able to lift your spirits simply by closing the door on your workspace.

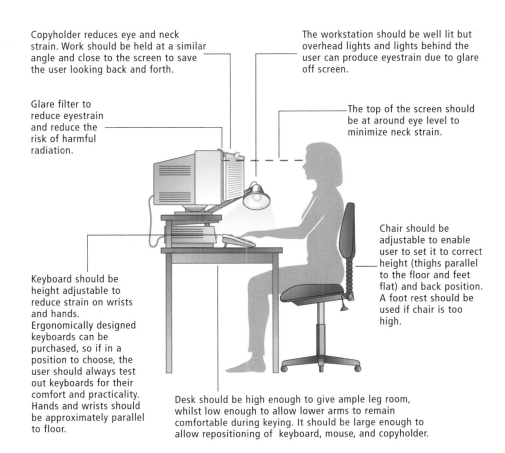

Copyholder reduces eye and neck strain. Work should be held at a similar angle and close to the screen to save the user looking back and forth.

The workstation should be well lit but overhead lights and lights behind the user can produce eyestrain due to glare off screen.

Glare filter to reduce eyestrain and reduce the risk of harmful radiation.

The top of the screen should be at around eye level to minimize neck strain.

Keyboard should be height adjustable to reduce strain on wrists and hands. Ergonomically designed keyboards can be purchased, so if in a position to choose, the user should always test out keyboards for their comfort and practicality. Hands and wrists should be approximately parallel to floor.

Chair should be adjustable to enable user to set it to correct height (thighs parallel to the floor and feet flat) and back position. A foot rest should be used if chair is too high.

Desk should be high enough to give ample leg room, whilst low enough to allow lower arms to remain comfortable during keying. It should be large enough to allow repositioning of keyboard, mouse, and copyholder.

HEALTH AND COMPUTERS

If you're working from home, you'll probably have a computer. The following points will help you use your computer safely.

- Fit a glare filter to protect your eyes from glare and flickering.

- Take a break from working at the computer every hour – otherwise you risk getting headaches, eye strain, and posture problems.

- Look up from your computer every 10–15 minutes and focus on the middle distance, to relieve eye strain.

- Have regular eye tests.

- Guard against repetitive strain injury (RSI), a condition in which prolonged performance or repetitive actions cause pain in tendons and muscles. Stop work if your hands and wrists start aching.

- Ensure that your desk is at the right height so that you can work at your keyboard with relaxed shoulders, with your forearms straight at the wrist, parallel to the floor, and not resting on the keyboard or desk.

- Sit at an adjustable chair when you're working – see above. Your feet should be flat on the floor, your thighs parallel to the floor or with your knees slightly below your hips.

- Make sure that the screen is at the right height so that you're not bending your neck backwards to look up at it, or bending to look down at it.

- Try not to use the computer late at night or have it in your bedroom. Computers throw out powerful electromagnetic fields and can disrupt sleep patterns.

USEFUL EQUIPMENT

Technology has made working from home very much easier, but think carefully about what you need each piece of equipment to do – equipment you already have for leisure use may not be sufficiently fast or reliable for your new work requirements.

If you're buying new, check the small print for technical and maintenance support (and what happens to these if the company goes bust), and what any warranties cover (see PC pitfalls to avoid, p114). Look for good deals but don't skimp on quality.

If specialist equipment is expensive and likely to need frequent upgrading, consider leasing some or all of it.

Computers Be sure your computer system has enough memory for the specific needs of your business and that you can upgrade easily. See Buying or upgrading a PC, p108. For e-mail, which is used extensively in business, you'll need a computer that can connect to the Internet, and an account with a service provider.

Fax machine or a scanner linked to the computer Both enable you to send illustrations as well as text.

Answerphone/voicemail To take messages while you're out.

Mobile phone or WAP phone So that when you're on the move people can contact you and you can contact them, either verbally or with text messages or e-mail.

Laptop computer If you travel a lot, a laptop computer may be a better choice than a desktop, so that you can call up and amend files while you're in meetings or work on a train journey. See Choosing a laptop, p113.

Photocopier A fax machine or scanner can double as a photocopier, but if you need to do lots of copying it's worth getting a photocopier. Small copiers can be leased quite cheaply and are easily upgraded.

Money and insurance

When you're running your own business, it's vital to spend time keeping track of your finances – the money side of things is where many new businesses come unstuck. The key task is to monitor cash flow, but you also need to plan for contingencies, so that you aren't totally floored if you hit a bad patch. The Internet has opened up new possibilities not just for handling money, but for making money too.

SEE ALSO Using the Internet for business, p276

THE BUSINESS PLAN

A business plan is not just a document to present to a bank when you want to borrow money. It's also to show you how your business is going to succeed financially. It should contain some or all of the following:

- what your business produces/provides
- details of the market for the business, with facts, figures, projected market growth, and so on
- whether there's any competition and why you'll succeed against it
- how you'll market your products/services and how much that will cost; allow enough to be able to try different media – national newspapers, magazines, radio, a Web site, for example
- what equipment and supplies you need to start up with
- how you'll price your product/service
- overheads, including rent, mortgage, council tax, insurance, and other regular payments
- projected income and whether you expect to have difficult periods.

FINDING A GOOD BANK ACCOUNT

If you are operating as a self-employed sole trader, you may not need a business account, but you will almost certainly need one if you are going to borrow money. Shop around for the business account that will give you the most flexibility and the lowest charges. Internet banking may be attractive for the various added-value services it offers, such as allowing you to conduct credit enquiries online, receive regular updates of statements, and find new suppliers on the bank's database, as well as make all the usual banking transactions. Online banking can save time, but if you will be banking cash regularly you need to choose a bank that has a branch nearby.

As with all banking, it's vital to keep good records. On bank statements, check that bank charges haven't been changed without warning; that all transactions are included and correct; that all payments into your account have been cleared; and that the balance is correct.

SOURCES OF MONEY

While you may be able to get an overdraft facility from a bank, which is useful for tiding you over when cashflow is tight, you may find you're unable to get a straight-forward loan if you don't have enough security – in other words, you don't have anything that can be redeemed against the loan if you default on your payments. It's inadvisable to offer your home as security against a loan because, if you fail, you risk losing the roof over your head. And if you have a mortgage, you may not own enough of your home to borrow against it anyway – until you've paid off your mortgage you only own a percentage of the property. Start by contacting **Business Link** (see p282) if you're looking for funding.

GOVERNMENT LOAN SCHEME

Your bank may be able to offer you a loan under the government's Small Firms Loan Guarantee Scheme, if it feels that your business is eligible and relatively risk-free. The government guarantee covers 75% of new loans. Loans start at £5,000 and can go up to £250,000. See p282.

GRANTS FROM PUBLIC BODIES

There are nearly 4,000 grants on offer in the UK each year. These are provided by all kinds of public bodies, ranging from local authorities and local and regional arts councils to central government and the European Union. Several publications give details of grants. These can be found in any good business reference library or bought from the **Stationery Office**, which has an online sales service, or try looking on the Internet for information – http//:www.j4b.co.uk is a good place to start.

The amount of a grant is dependent upon a variety of factors and you will certainly have to find a sum of money yourself, as a grant never pays the whole cost of a project. Although there appear to be many grants on offer, getting a grant may take considerable work. Companies called grant consultancies have sprung up to help applicants. There are various types of grant.

- **A direct grant** is a sum of money that is given to a business – usually no more than 50% of a proposed project – and doesn't have to be paid back.

- **A soft loan** is made available to businesses not eligible for commercial loans. It may be interest-free, long term, or offer other benefits. It has to be paid back eventually.
- **A repayable grant** is usually offered, interest-free, for special projects on the understanding that it will be repaid when the project succeeds, but not if the project fails.
- **Support in kind** may take the form of free training, advice, professional services such as research and development, trips abroad for export planning, or something else useful for your business.

VENTURE CAPITAL

The government encourages individuals and businesses to invest in small-to medium-sized companies needing an injection of cash in order to grow. The Inland Revenue gives tax relief to investors who provide venture capital. Nearly £23 billion has been invested in UK companies over the last 15 years. The **British Venture Capital Association** provides information, as does http://venturesearch.co.uk.

BUSINESS ANGELS

Business angels are individuals who invest small amounts in companies in the early stages of development. The National Business Angels Network comes under the aegis of the British Venture Capital Association, which publishes a directory listing all current sources of business angel capital.

WHAT INSURANCE DO YOU NEED?

It's best to consult an independent business insurance broker or go direct to one or more insurance companies – some offer small-business packages that can be tailored to your requirements. These are the main types of insurance.

Home contents insurance All your working equipment must be covered and you must inform the insurer if you add any new equipment, otherwise a claim could be invalid.

Professional indemnity Desirable if you advise or perform a service for clients and the quality of your work could substantially affect their business.

Product liability Important if you manufacture a product, no matter how modest, in case any member of the public is injured because your product is faulty.

Public liability and **third party public liability** The first policy covers you against any injury to the public through your work or in your home. The second type of cover may be relevant if you sub-contract any of your work to others who are deemed to be acting on your behalf.

Employer's liability Required by law if you employ even just one person, to cover you if an employee should be injured in the course of employment.

Business category car insurance Check whether your car insurance covers self-employed business use. You will certainly have to pay higher premiums if the business use of your car involves using the car as a taxi, transporting high-priced goods – for instance samples or stock – or you carry valuable or hazardous equipment.

Private medical insurance Usually offers the option of private medical treatment or, if you opt for NHS treatment, a cash sum to compensate for lost income.

Accident cover This policy will pay you money if you are out of work owing to an accident. Premiums can be quite high if you are in a high-risk occupation, such as the building trade.

Critical illness cover Protection if you are ill and not able to earn money.

Keyman cover A popular policy for very small companies where the loss of one person through illness or injury can greatly damage the effectiveness of the company. The policy covers the cost of a temporary replacement employee.

Dealing with tax

People tend to dislike the notion of tax and tax inspectors: the very words Inland Revenue or Customs and Excise can make even honest people freeze. But this is unnecessary, because tax inspectors can be extremely helpful to the self-employed. So never shrink from asking the Inland Revenue (IR) for advice when you're dealing with income tax, which is an essential part of working for yourself.

COMPLETING A TAX RETURN

You can complete a self-assessment form and return it by post. Alternatively, the IR has an online tax filing service. You can register your intent to file electronically and then download the necessary self-assessment forms and the software program needed to complete and return the information.

If you miss the deadline for submission of tax returns of 31 January each year, you'll automatically incur a fine – currently £100. Further fines and surcharges can be levied if your tax return is delayed any further than that. If it is still outstanding by the following 31 July, you'll be fined a further £100 fine. A 5% surcharge is imposed on any tax bill that remains unpaid 28 days after the due date, and an additional 5% if it remains unpaid after six months.

Contact details for organizations given in **bold** appear at the end of each chapter.

STARTING OUT AS SELF-EMPLOYED

The **Inland Revenue** (IR) classes you as self-employed, and charges tax on your business profits, if you're a sole trader – that is, in business on your own – or in a partnership. The alternative to being self-employed is to set up your business as a limited company that pays corporation tax. This requires the services of an accountant and is beyond the scope of this book.

If you are self-employed and don't register as such with the IR within the first full three months of self-employment, you can be fined £100. There are some exceptions and special rules for certain occupations and industries, like the construction industry, so, to be certain of where you stand, get the leaflet IR56 *Employed or Self-Employed?* from your local IR office, by phoning the Inland Revenue Orderline on 0845 9000 404, or by checking the IR Web site.

After you have registered, the IR will send you a *Starting Up in Business* guide and arrange for you to start paying self-employed flat rate (Class 2) National Insurance (NI) contributions. You'll be sent a quarterly invoice for your NI contributions or you can arrange to pay them monthly by direct debit.

Shortly after the end of the tax year (currently 5 April) in which you started working for yourself, the IR will send you a self-assessment tax return to fill in. This is made up of an eight-page 'core' tax return and supplementary pages that are relevant to your personal situation. So if you have registered as self-employed, the self-employment supplementary pages – where you should give details of your earnings from your business – will be attached to the back of the core tax return. The information you provide enables the IR to work out how much tax and Class 4 profit-related NI you owe, if any. This figure will also set the amount of the advance payments of tax, called 'payments on account', that you have to make for the following tax year.

SELF-ASSESSMENT: THE PRINCIPLES

Different incomes and profits require different supplementary pages to be filled in, but the main points of the self-assessment system apply to everyone:

■ one set of payment dates for tax – 31 January each year. Self-employed people, however, pay tax in two instalments – the first on 31 January made up of tax owed plus first payment on account and the second – the second payment on account – on 31 July

■ fixed, automatic penalties for late returns, and interest and surcharges for late payments (see opposite)

■ clear obligations for keeping records. You must keep records of all financial dealings in support of information given on each tax return for five years and ten months from the tax year to which they relate.

Under self-assessment, you can still ask the IR to work out how much tax you need to pay, in which case you have to send them your completed tax form by 30 September each year.

If you want to calculate for yourself how much tax to pay – or choose to pay an accountant to calculate this for you – the forms are due back by 31 January each year, together with the first payment.

TAX RELIEF ON WHAT YOU SPEND

Employees and the self-employed get the same personal allowances. But the self-employed can usually claim tax relief on more of their work-related expenditure. Buy something for £100 and the real cost after tax relief will be £78 if you're a basic-rate (22%) taxpayer, £60 if you're a higher-rate (40%) taxpayer.

You can claim relief for expenditure that's wholly and exclusively to do with your work. And if you spend money on something that's partly to do with work and partly to do with your private life, you can claim tax relief on the proportion related to your work. For example, you would be able to get tax relief on part of your gas and electricity bills if you work from your home.

As self-employed, you will be dealt with by a local tax office, which can advise on allowances. You might also consider using an accountant, at least when you first start in business, and he or she can give advice on expenses you can claim and, where relevant, on the proportion you can claim.

Tax relief comes in two forms:

- you can deduct from your income in one tax year the full cost of allowable expenses for most work-related expenditure – including gas, electricity, phone, cleaning, insurance, mortgage interest, or rent – or the appropriate proportion of such expenses

- you can deduct from your income capital allowances for capital expenditure – including machines, computers, vehicles, and buildings. But tax relief on most capital expenditure must be claimed over several tax years. If you're a small business you can claim 40% of capital expenditure as a first-year allowance and 25% of the outstanding balance in subsequent years on some expenditure, such as machinery. On other capital expenditure, for example vehicles, the maximum first-year allowance is 25%. However, for computers and related expenditure, small businesses can currently claim a 100% first-year allowance.

SHOULD YOU REGISTER FOR VAT?

You have to register for Value Added Tax (VAT) with Customs and Excise if you supply goods and/or services that are not exempt from VAT and your total sales exceed £55,000 (this is the figure at the time of writing; it may change). You don't have to register if your total sales are less than this threshold, but you can choose to do so. The advantage of being VAT registered is that you can claim back any VAT charged on things you buy for your business, which brings down your costs. This can seem quite attractive if you plan to buy a lot of expensive equipment. For example, if you buy a computer costing £1,175 (including VAT at 17.5%), being registered for VAT means that you can claim back the £175 in tax, so the

computer ends up costing you only £1,000. However, you have to balance this advantage against the fact that you will have to:

- add VAT at 17.5% to all your invoices, which – unless your customers are VAT registered and so able to claim back the VAT they pay – pushes up the price of whatever you are selling

- keep accurate and detailed records and fill in a VAT return, which is usually every three months

- make sure that you have sufficient cash available to pay the VAT you have collected – less the VAT you can claim back – to Customs and Excise.

FINDING A GOOD ACCOUNTANT

An accountant can advise you on tax matters and take on the responsibility of dealing with the IR on your behalf, as well as help you with other financial matters. Conventional wisdom is that hiring an accountant is worthwhile if they can save you the cost of their fee – and preferably more. You can find a good accountant through:

- recommendation from other business people
- your bank
- a professional body of which you're a member
- a business advice source, such as Business Link
- your trade association, if you have one
- a business club, such as the local Chamber of Commerce.

EMPLOYING OTHERS

At some point you may need to have someone to help you with your work. If so, until you have a reasonably large turnover, you should avoid taking on employees. Employment law is complex, and the real cost of hiring an employee may be almost double the salary you offer. Also, it may be difficult for you to offer an employee continued employment, especially if you are in the start-up period. It's better to subcontract – in other words, get another self-employed person to do some of your work – or to contract someone from an agency. An agency will take care of PAYE, National Insurance, and all the other employer's responsibilities. There are plenty of agencies that can provide temporary staff in all employment sectors.

Using the Internet for business

If you will be using the Internet for business, bear in mind that your requirements are more demanding than those of the casual user. It is doubly important that all your e-mails arrive and that your dial-up service always runs efficiently. Avoid the temptation of free Internet Service Providers (ISPs) – they are fine for leisure use but tend to have a very large number of accounts, which can cause problems of service supply. In fact many free services specifically exclude business use.

YOUR TELEPHONE BILL

If you are working from home you'll depend on the telephone quite heavily for business, so it's essential to have a separate phone line for your computer. Many people who have a separate fax line plug their computer into this.

To keep your phone bills as low as possible, investigate cheap-rate or un-metered access dial-up ISPs. Some of these offer a free telephone number for connecting your computer to the Internet for a monthly fee. Even having free access at night and weekends can produce a significant cut in costs if you are building your own Web site.

Broadband connectivity, supplied across normal telephone lines or by cable companies, provides an always on, high-speed Internet connection, plus telephone connection, for a monthly subscription fee. You can use the telephone and remain online at the same time. Find out whether BT supplies broadband where you live by visiting http://www.bt.com. For cable broadband information contact your local cable company.

YOUR OWN DOMAIN NAME

Consider having your own domain name. This is a memorable name for your Internet presence. In business, it's much better to have an e-mail address based on your business name – me@mybusiness.com – than a complicated rigmarole that incorporates your name and your ISP. As with customized telephone numbers, the aim of the domain name is to make it simple for your customers to memorize.

Once you have registered your business domain name, it remains yours wherever you take your Internet account. So if you aren't happy with the service you're receiving from your ISP, you can move to another one but still keep your own e-mail and Web site addresses.

A few years ago registering your domain name was an expensive and complex process, but nowadays it is a lot easier and need cost only a few pounds. You can start by discovering if your chosen name is available – surf to http://www.nic.uk for UK domain names and for global ones (such as .com and .net) to http://www.internic.net. You'll find useful information on these sites about choosing and registering your domain name.

There are plenty of companies with whom you can register. Some even offer 'free' domain name registrations, but look carefully into what's on offer as there may be restrictions on transferring your name to another server. Once again, the advice is to be cautious of free services. Companies that specialize in Internet services for business, on the other hand, often offer good-value package deals.

KEEP YOUR BROWSER UP TO DATE

A Web site is viewed using a special piece of software called a browser. This software accesses the files on the Web site and translates them into a visually coherent page on your computer screen. A browser also enables hyperlink navigation (see How a Web site works, right) and functions such as downloading files, filling in forms, and watching live video.

The two main Web browsers are Microsoft Internet Explorer and Netscape. Some ISPs – AOL for example – provide a specially customized browser that enables you to access additional services available only to subscribers. But the two major browsers are available free on the Web or on CD-ROMs given away with computer magazines. Your computer may have come with a browser already installed. If you plan to take browser software from the Internet, bear in mind that the programs can be very large and take a long time to download. Rather than running up a large phone bill downloading a file, it may be cheaper to buy a magazine offering browser software on a free CD-ROM.

To get the best from the Web it's important to keep your browser up to date. Increasing numbers of Web sites today use advanced features to bring you rich multimedia content and if your browser is an old version you may not be able to access this material. Updates are available on the Web or on CD-ROM and it's a good idea to check for the latest version every few months.

If you're planning to design your own Web site you should bear in mind that different browsers (and different versions of browser from the same manufacturer) are likely to display your Web pages differently. This 'cross-platform compatibility' is the biggest bugbear for the Web designer and if it isn't dealt with correctly it can result in your carefully designed pages looking messy or at worst being unreadable on some computers (see p279).

IS WEB DESIGN FOR YOU?

Some people take to Web design like a duck to water but if you're not a natural technophile, you may prefer to find a good designer and brief him or her thoroughly. It's certainly worth thinking through some of the following considerations first.

- Building a Web site can be time-consuming, and can divert you from more important aspects of your business.

- You may need to acquire and learn how to use several pieces of software, and install additional hardware as well.

- Like any other marketing activity, a Web site works best if it is carefully planned and executed to maximize its effective-ness – it may be difficult to gather enough expertise to do a professional job.

- A poorly designed Web site can reflect badly on your business and discourage potential customers.

A recent technological development has made it possible to create Web pages as easily as creating a Word document. As yet this technology is not widespread, and there are various requirements, but using the system means you can create and update your Web site using any suitable computer with an Internet connection, anywhere in the world. You still need picture-editing software. See Web sites and addresses.

TYPES OF WEB SITE

Web sites range from simple two- or three-page sites with little interactivity to huge multimedia affairs costing tens if not hundreds of thousands of pounds. But most fall into one of the following categories:

- e-commerce sites – where the visitor can purchase goods or services directly over the Internet

- brochureware – informing the visitor about a company's products or services

- news sites – widespread distribution of useful or interesting information

- download sites – sites that supply software such as games or music either free or at a charge

- special-interest sites – such as clubs, trade bodies, or hobby sites.

Each type needs different and specific components that affect the price and complexity of the site. For the do-it-yourself Web designer using standard Web-space suppliers – see p278 for more on these – brochureware is likely to be the most viable option.

HOW A WEB SITE WORKS

A Web site is made up of a number of separate items of data called files. These can be text files (the copy on the page), formatting information files (markings indicating font size, colour, and so on), picture files, sound files, video files, animation files, and document files that the visitor can download to his or her computer and view separately.

Any number of files can make up a Web page, and any number of pages can make up a Web site. Visitors to the site use a browser (see left) that combines all the files into a recognizable form.

The thing that makes a Web page special is the hyperlink. This is a section of text or a picture that replaces one page on your computer screen with another when you click on it. The hyperlink enables you to surf (navigate easily) sites on the World Wide Web.

Once you have designed a Web page on your own computer (see p278 for more on what you need to do this), you publish it by uploading the files to a Web server. This is a computer provided by your ISP and permanently connected to the Internet.

see p278

DOES YOUR BUSINESS NEED A WEB SITE?

Many people assume that a Web site is essential for any 21st-century business. But some activities just don't lend themselves to this type of marketing – or it may be that creating the right Web site would not prove cost-effective.

For example, if you were running a local employment agency for casual labour, your Web site could enable employers to advertise and potential workers to register online. However, updating an interactive site is expensive, and it's unlikely in a small business that it would generate enough additional revenue to be worth the investment. A more realistic option would be a simple Web site advertising the business and the range of jobs catered for, and giving contact details. This type of site is often referred to as brochureware because it is essentially a company brochure published on the Web.

Before investing in a Web site – whether designed yourself or by a professional – ask yourself a few critical questions.

- What extra value will a Web site add to your business for you and your customers?

- How many visitors would your site need to attract to earn an acceptable return on investment? If a Web site is designed to generate cash this is easy to establish. If it is brochureware the returns may be harder to identify.

- Do your clients or potential customers have access to the Internet?

- Can your products or services easily be delivered nationally or even worldwide?

- Can you accept payment by credit card?

- Could a Web site open up a market that you currently can't reach?

Building your own Web site

Building a simple Web site, whether for business or for leisure, can be straightforward, but there are certain hardware and software requirements, as well as hosting considerations, which you should allow for in your budget. You need to decide what to put on your site and how it should look. When it's live on the Web, you need to make sure it works for your business.

WHERE DO YOU GET THE SOFTWARE?

You can get software from a variety of sources. Your local computer shop or superstore may be able to help you and may offer useful advice. Look out for the following, too.

Shareware Software you can try out for a limited period and only pay for if you decide it suits you. The most common way to get hold of shareware is on the Internet or from covermount CDs (see below).

Freeware Smaller pieces of software that cost nothing to obtain and use, often designed to perform a highly specific function, such as creating animations from existing graphics files. These can also be found on the Internet or on covermount CDs.

Covermount CDs CD-ROMs given away with computer magazines are a valuable source of freeware and shareware, as well as demonstration versions of full commercial products. Often you will find articles describing and reviewing the products in the accompanying magazine.

HARDWARE AND HOSTING?

You will need a computer and an Internet connection to enable you to build and upload your site. You should also have enough hard disk space to store your site off-line and to install software you need (see below). To include pictures, you will need either a scanner to digitize printed and photographic material or a digital camera.

When choosing a web space provider, the main options are:

- your existing ISP
- a free hosting service; see http://www.freewebspace.net for what is available (but see comments about free services, p276)
- an independent commercial hosting service; http://www.webhostmagazine. com provides a useful guide.

Check that commercial use of the service is acceptable and take into account:

- any set-up fee, and the monthly cost. This may vary depending on which services you opt for
- how much space will you be given on the server. A basic Web site shouldn't need more than 5 megabytes (MB), but a large product catalogue may need more
- any limit on bandwidth, affecting how many people will be able to look at your site at a time. Limits are unlikely, but it's worth checking, as there could be additional costs if your site is very successful
- whether the host offers all the features you'll need.

WHAT SOFTWARE WILL YOU NEED?

WEB DESIGN SOFTWARE

A Web page is designed using a coding language called HTML (Hypertext Mark-up Language, see Understanding technospeak p104), but you don't need to learn HTML to design a Web page. Your chosen host may offer a template service to help you create your site. Otherwise there is plenty of Web design software available, ranging in price from free to hundreds of pounds.

Macromedia Dreamweaver This professional-level package is one of the leaders in the field, and is the preferred package of many professional Web designers. For the amateur, it can take some time to learn.

Adobe GoLive Another professional-level package from a well-known design software company. Also may be oversophisticated for the amateur.

Microsoft FrontPage Easy to learn and has a WYSIWYG (What You See Is What You Get) editor. It is included in some versions of Microsoft Office. **FrontPage Express** – a cut-down version with fewer features – is available free when you install Microsoft Internet Explorer. They are user-friendly, good value for money, and come with ready-made templates and design styles. But there are some drawbacks: to use some of the features you can only host your Web site on a server with FrontPage Extensions installed. Also, FrontPage uses some features that are only supported by the Microsoft browser – Internet Explorer.

IMAGE-MANIPULATION SOFTWARE

You need to have some software to get the pictures and graphics the way you want them and suitable for your Web site. As well as drawing and painting, your image software should allow you to scan in images; import pictures from your digital camera (if you have one); resize and crop; adjust brightness, colour, and so on; and save your work in a variety of formats (including GIF and JPG – the ones used in Web design). It will take time to learn how to use this software successfully, but it is an essential investment if you are serious about having a good-looking Web site.

At the time of writing the most popular packages are Adobe Photoshop, which is very comprehensive but quite expensive, and JASC Paint Shop Pro, which is comparable but costs considerably less.

SOFTWARE FOR LOADING THE SITE

Having created your Web site, you have to load it on to your Web space so the world can see the result of your efforts. To do this you use a type of software called an FTP (File Transfer Protocol) program, unless you are using a Web design package that uploads your files for you. There are several shareware versions available, and some free of charge, on the Internet. Names to look out for include WS_FTP, CuteFTP, and CoffeeCup.

DESIGN PITFALLS

The main challenge you have in designing your site is ensuring that it looks right on the many variations of hardware and software that will be used to view it. Key differences are browsers and screen resolution.

Browsers When designing your site, it is best to view it using at least Microsoft Internet Explorer and Netscape Navigator. Together, these two products account for over 90% of Web browsers. Use an up-to-date version, as old versions will not necessarily show the site in the same way. Some Web designers keep older versions of Web browser programs so they can check how their sites will look under different conditions. PCs and Apple Macs can show sites completely differently.

Screen resolution Use a common screen resolution – for PCs, it's best to use 800 x 600 pixels, but also view it at the lower resolution of 640 x 480 pixels and the higher one of 1024 x 768 pixels, from time to time. To do this on a PC with Windows, open the control panel on your computer, select 'Display' and then the 'Settings' option. Some software includes a resolution selection feature to help you do this more simply.

TIPS FOR DESIGNING A WEB SITE

- If you are designing a business site, your job is to promote your company's core products, services, and values. Try to adopt a style that reflects your **market image** and ties in with any other material you use to market your business, such as brochures, advertising, and letterheads.

- In general, keep each page as **uncluttered** as possible. Split the information into bite-sized chunks and link several pages together to produce a 'chapter'. Use lots of white space – it is easy on the eye, improves legibility, and looks classy. Smaller pages will also give the user **faster loading** – try to restrict the number and size of images on your pages for the same reason. Some of the more sophisticated Web design packages give an indication of the loading time of a page. If a page takes more than 30 seconds to load using a 56K modem – the most common and fastest modem in general use – the visitor may go to another site.

- Use a **commonly available typeface**. There are really only two choices – serif, which has decorative bits at the end of stems of letters (the most common serif typeface being Times Roman) and non-serif (like this text), where a letter upright is just a single vertical stroke (as in the typeface Arial). Of other fonts, Tahoma and Verdana are particularly popular, but the less common the font you use, the greater likelihood that the visitor will not have it on their computer and therefore that your site will not appear as you intended.

- Make sure your site is **visually consistent**. A jumble of different typefaces and layouts, inconsistent navigation, lots of meaningless flashing and flying images won't impress the visitor, who can go to a more restful and better-designed site at the click of a mouse button.

- Good design is almost always **simple**. That doesn't mean it's easy to achieve, but visual simplicity on a Web page is a really attractive feature that will set your site apart. If you need to put in more information, consider creating a new page rather than expanding an existing one.

INCLUDING METATAGS AND KEYWORDS

Make your pages visible to search engines by adding comprehensive **metatags** and **keywords** – these are words that are not seen by the visitor but noted by search engines and used to index your site. For information about promoting your site in search engines, and specifically to find out more about metatags and keywords, visit http://www.searchenginewatch.com. Some programs will generate metatags and insert them into your Web pages for you.

WHAT TO INCLUDE ON YOUR SITE

If you're designing this Web site for your own business, remember that its purpose is to inform and persuade. Don't get side-tracked into making pictures blink, buttons flash, and everything jump about.

PUT YOURSELF IN THE MIND OF YOUR CUSTOMER

As with all business communications, try to put yourself in the mind of your customer or would-be customer and talk to them in language they understand about issues that concern them. Concentrate on benefits rather than features, what makes you special, and so on.

PLAN YOUR CONTENT FIRST

Planning the content helps you focus on the overall purpose of the site and will help keep that focus as you go through the design process. As well as promoting your products and services, there are some pages that are found on most company Web sites and that you should think about including.

Introduction Welcome, who you are, what you do.

Links page Useful for encouraging visitors to go through your site to other useful sites. Include affiliate links if you have them (see left).

Contact us Make it easy for the visitor to contact you. Include your company address, phone numbers, and e-mail address. More sophisticated features you can include on your Web site enable the visitor to contact you direct by e-mail or have you phone them back. These interactive features require some programming and sometimes extra charges from your ISP as well, so you may want to leave them out until later. Remember also that it is good etiquette, and useful for you as designer, to let people send you feedback about the site.

Our people These days, when it's quite possible to carry out business with people you never see, a bit of personal background and a photograph can do wonders in personalizing your image.

How to find us If you're running a business where people may want to come to your premises, a map and travel directions are useful. If you're concerned about security, consider including these on a page that is not linked to the rest of the site, and give a direction to the page only to people you trust.

HOW MANY PEOPLE ARE VISITING YOUR SITE?

It is important that you know how many people visit your site. Most ISPs will provide some form of statistics – **Web stats** – to help you assess this. But reading Web stats is a skill and without some basic knowledge you can easily be misled.

Most Web stats formats show a count of **hits** on your site. Do not confuse this with the number of visitors to your site – it is actually a count of the number of file requests received by the Web server over the period. Every time a page is viewed all the component files have to be transmitted from the Web site host computer to the viewer's one. Each file request is a 'hit'. A more representative figure, and one gaining popularity, is **page views**. As the name suggests, this shows the number of whole pages delivered by the Web server over the period. Of course, a visitor could view one page or many, so this figure doesn't give you an accurate measure of the number of visitors. Some service providers will provide a figure of the **number of unique visitors**, which is probably the best guide to visitor numbers to your site.

Your ISP will probably be able to supply a variety of additional statistics, which may clarify the situation or cause confusion. In general, the best approach is to select a small number of figures – say, hits and page views – and watch how they develop, rather than rely on absolute numbers. You can then tell if visitor numbers grow steadily, tail off, respond to an offline promotion, and so on.

MAKING YOUR WEB SITE WORK FOR YOU

KEEP YOUR SITE UP TO DATE

Your Web site should be updated and modified continually. It is a simple enough job once you have created the pages, but an aspect that is often overlooked. At all costs avoid **cobwebs** – items that are identifiably out of date. The Web is a live medium, and people notice old content very quickly. For example, if you are running a promotion on your site of 10% discount for new customers, and this promotion ends on Christmas Day, then your site will look out of date if it still has a big splash about the promotion greeting visitors on 26 December.

RESPOND QUICKLY

Similarly, if you get any enquiries from the Web site it is vital that you respond to them quickly. The speed of e-mail means that a delay of more than 24 hours in replying to an enquiry can seem very slow. If you have response mechanisms on the site – for example, a form that sends an e-mail enquiry – make sure they are dealt with just as promptly. Remember that time differences across the world can appear to stretch delays, and even closing for the weekend can have a similar effect to closing your company for an additional day at either end.

Make sure, if you can, that you aren't the only person in the company who can deal with enquiries. You may be out of the office, sick, or on holiday, but the Internet carries on regardless.

MAINTAIN YOUR SITE

You should expect to have to spend some time every week on maintaining your site. Unless you have the time, don't include features that require a lot of maintenance. For example, if you want to include currency exchange rates on the site, it's better to provide a link to a site that specializes in that service rather than have to update a page every day yourself.

MAKE YOUR WEB SITE VISIBLE

You will no doubt want to increase the number of visitors to your site, and the secret to this is visibility. Make sure your Web site is listed on as many search engines as you can find (there are programs that will do this for you automatically, such as the Submission Wizard by Exploit), actively pursue links with other sites by contacting the owner or Webmaster of suitable or complementary Web sites, and make sure your site has plenty of appropriate keywords and metatags (see Including metatags and keywords).

Don't forget the importance of publicity using conventional media. Does your *Yellow Pages* entry include your Web address? What about your stationery, incentive gifts, advertising, Christmas cards? Can you find a 'hook' that will encourage the local or national press to write about your site? A half-page article in a Sunday newspaper can multiply your hit rate by a factor of ten over the weekend. You may feel it's worthwhile to run an advertisement specifically about your Web site. Persevere and be creative. It takes time to build traffic to a site, so keep at it and you will be rewarded.

INTERNET SECURITY

If you are going to spend a lot of time on the Internet, and especially if you're using an always-on connection, your computer is at risk from computer viruses and other forms of attack.

To reduce the risk of these affecting the operation of your computer you should consider installing anti-virus software and/or a firewall, which is a piece of software that blocks attacks on your computer while you are online. The two leading companies in this field are Norton (http://www.symantec.com) and McAfee (http://www.mcafee.com).

If you have ever experienced the effects of a virus or other attack on your computer you will know how important it is to keep your computer secure.

PUBLISHING YOUR WEB SITE

When you are happy with your Web site, you publish it by uploading it to the Web server. You may find it safer to test your site online before going live. To do this create a subdirectory in your Web space to keep your site private. When you have completed the testing phase, transfer all the files to the main directory. Here's an example of how to do this:

1 Say your Web site address is http://www.mybusiness.co.uk, and your live site's picture directory is http://www.mybusiness.co.uk/pictures.

2 Using your FTP software, set up a pre-publication directory called prepub and upload your files to the following addresses: http://www.mybusiness.co.uk/prepub, and http://www.mybusiness.co.uk/prepub/pictures. Test this site.

3 To publish, move the entire contents of the prepub directory, and its pictures subdirectory, to the directories shown in step 1. Your Web site is now live.

LEARNING MORE

- The best way to improve your Web design knowledge is to surf around the Web noting sites or design elements that you particularly like, then use your Web design software to try to introduce a similar effect to your own site.

- Computer magazines are an excellent source of information and have the advantage of being more up to date than textbooks.

- Make use of search engines to explore information sites. You'll find a huge resource of advice, hints and tips and product reviews. And if your ISP provides access to newsgroups (if in doubt, check with them), these can be a good source of advice.

WEB SITES AND ADDRESSES

Better Business, Active Information Ltd,
Cribau Mill, Chepstow NP16 6LN
phone: 0845 458 9485; fax: 01291 641777;
e-mail: info@better-business.co.uk
Web site: www.better-business.co.uk

Free information and guidance for small
businesses.

British Venture Capital Association,
3 Clements Inn, London WC2A 2AZ
phone: 020 7025 2950; fax: 020 7025 2951;
e-mail: bvca@bvca.co.uk
Web site: www.bvca.co.uk

Business Connect Wales
phone: 08457 96 97 98;
e-mail: executive@businessconnect.org.uk
Web site: www.businessconnect.org.uk

Managed by the Welsh Development Agency, the
site provides information for small to medium
businesses in Wales. Provides information on
schemes and grants.

Business Link phone: 0845 600 9006
Web site: www.businesslink.org

A national business advice service. Use this site to
get information for your business needs and to
access business support organizations.

DTI Enquiry Unit, 1 Victoria Street, London
SW1H 0ET
phone: 020 7215 5000;
e-mail: enquiries@dti.gsi.gov.uk
Web site: www.dti.gov.uk

The site contains an area dedicated to business
and small businesses.

Federation of Small Businesses,
Sir Frank Whittle Way, Blackpool Business Park,
Blackpool, Lancashire FY4 2FE
phone: 01253 336000; fax: 01253 348046;
e-mail: ho@fsb.org.uk
Web site: www.fsb.org.uk

Statistics, details of events, and help for small
businesses.

Inland Revenue phone: 020 7667 4001;
helpline for the newly self-employed: 08459
154 515; orderline for leaflets: 0845 900 0404
Web site: www.inlandrevenue.gov.uk

The site contains detailed information about
individual and business tax, including a separate
section on self assessment.

InterNIC
Web site: www.internic.net

Internet domain name registration services.

Invest Northern Ireland, 64 Chichester Street,
Belfast BT1 4JX
phone: 028 9023 9090; fax: 028 9049 0490;
e-mail: info@investni.com
Web site: www.investni.com

Small business scheme in Northern Ireland.

j4b, 51 Water Lane, Wilmslow, Cheshire SK9 5BQ
e-mail: enquiries@j4b.co.uk
Web site: www.j4b.co.uk

Enables you to create your own business profile
and explore the range of funding that might be
available to you.

McAfee Security, Network Associates,
227 Bath Road, Slough, Berkshire SL1 5PP
phone: 01753 217500; fax: 01753 217520:
e-mail: customer_service@nai.com
Web site: www.mcafee.com

Internet security company.

Nominet UK, Sandford Gate, Sandy Lane West,
Oxford OX4 6LB
phone: 01865 332211; fax: 01865 332299;
e-mail: nominet@nominet.org.uk
Web site: www.nic.uk

For the registry of domain names. There is a
database of .uk domain registrations.

SBS Loan Guarantee Unit, St Mary's House,
c/o Moorfoot, Sheffield S1 4PQ
phone: 0114 2597308; fax: 0114 2597316;
e-mail: sflgs@sbs.gsi.gov.uk
Web site: www.sbs.gov.uk

Gives details of the government's Small Firms
Loan Guarantee Scheme.

**Scottish Executive Enterprise and Lifelong
Learning Department**, The Scottish
Executive, 6th Floor, Meridian Court,
Cadogan Street, Glasgow G2 6AT
phone: 0141 248 4774; fax: 0141 242 5665;
e-mail: ceu@scotland.gov.uk
Web site: www.scotland.gov.uk/who/elld

Small business scheme in Scotland.

SearchEngineWatch.com
Web site: www.searchenginewatch.com

Information on how to promote your site in search
engines.

The Stationery Office, TSO, PO Box 29, St
Crispins, Duke Street, Norwich NR3 1GN
phone: 0870 600 5522; fax: 0870 600 5533;
e-mail: customer.services@tso.co.uk
Web site: www.tso.co.uk

Includes an online bookshop with a section
dedicated to business publications.

Symantec (UK), Hines Meadow, St Cloud Way,
Maidenhead, Berkshire SL6 8XB
phone: 020 7616 5600
Web site: www.symantec.com

Internet security company, Norton products.

CHAPTER ELEVEN

Emergencies

Giving First Aid

The First Aid information and illustrations on the next six pages are from St. John Ambulance. These hints are no substitute for a thorough knowledge of First Aid. St. John Ambulance holds First Aid courses throughout the country. To contact your local St. John Ambulance County Headquarters, call 08700 10 49 50 or visit htpp://www.sja.org.uk.

SEE ALSO Safety at home, p144–7, Children's safety and health, p148

RECOVERY POSITION

An unconscious casualty who is breathing but has no other life-threatening conditions should be placed in the Recovery Position, see right.

- Turn casualty onto their side.
- Lift chin forward in open airway position and adjust hand under the cheek as necessary.
- Check casualty cannot roll forwards or backwards.
- Monitor breathing and pulse continuously.
- If injuries allow, turn the casualty to the other side after 30 minutes.

NOTE: if you suspect spinal injury, use the jaw thrust technique to maintain an open airway:

- Kneel behind the casualty and support their head in a neutral position.
- Place your hands either side of the casualty's head, fingertips at the jaw.
- Gently lift and support the jaw, taking care not to move the head.

THE RESUSCITATION SEQUENCE: ADULT

DANGER

Are you or the casualty in any danger? If you have not already done so, make the situation safe and then assess the casualty.

RESPONSE

If the casualty appears unconscious check this by shouting, 'Can you hear me?, Open your eyes' and gently shaking their shoulders. If there is no response, shout for help then follow the ABC Procedure below:

AIRWAY

Open the airway by placing one hand on the casualty's forehead and gently tilting the head back.

Check the mouth for obstructions and then lift the chin using two fingers only.

BREATHING

Spend 10 seconds checking to see if the casualty is breathing:

- Look to see if the chest is rising and falling. Listen for breathing.
- Feel for breath against your cheek.
- If the casualty is breathing, place them in the Recovery Position.
- If the casualty is not breathing, and the condition is due to injury, drowning, or choking, continue with sequence. For any other casualty who is not breathing, call an ambulance, then return to casualty and begin sequence again.
- Give two Rescue Breaths

CIRCULATION

Spend 10 seconds checking for signs of circulation: look, listen, and feel for breathing, coughing, movement, or any other signs of life.

IF THE CASUALTY IS:

CONSCIOUS AND BREATHING:

- Check circulation (including a check for severe bleeding).
- Treat any injuries.
- Get help if necessary.

UNCONSCIOUS BUT BREATHING:

- Place the casualty in Recovery Position.
- Check circulation (including a check for severe bleeding).
- Treat any life-threatening conditions.
- Call for an ambulance.

UNCONSCIOUS – NOT BREATHING:

1 **If circulation is present**, and the condition is due to **injury, drowning, or choking:**

- Give ten Rescue Breaths.
- Call an ambulance, return to casualty, and follow resuscitation sequence again, acting on your findings.

2 If **circulation is present**, and the condition is **not** due to injury, drowning, or choking:

- Call for an ambulance, then continue to give Rescue Breaths until help arrives.
- Check for circulation after every ten breaths.

3 If **circulation is absent**, and the condition is due to **injury, drowning, or choking**:

- Give Chest Compressions together with Rescue Breaths (CPR) for 1 minute.
- Call an ambulance, then return to casualty and follow resuscitation sequence again, acting on your findings.

4 If **circulation is absent**, and the condition is **not** due to injury, drowning, or choking:

- Call for an ambulance, then continue to give Chest Compressions together with Rescue Breaths (CPR) until help arrives.

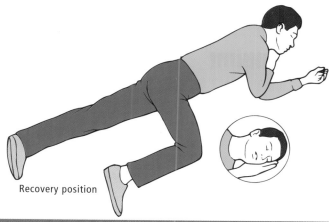
Recovery position

RESCUE BREATHS

1 Ensure the airway is open.

2 Pinch nose firmly closed.

3 Take a deep breath and seal your lips around the casualty's mouth.

4 Blow into the mouth until the chest rises.

5 Remove your mouth and allow the chest to fall.

Do this at a rate of ten breaths a minute. Check for circulation after every ten breaths:

- **If circulation is absent commence CPR.**
- **If breathing starts, place in Recovery Position.**

CPR – CHEST COMPRESSIONS WITH RESCUE BREATHS

Note: Chest Compressions must always be combined with Rescue Breaths.

1 Place heel of your hand two fingers' width above the junction of the casualty's rib margin and breastbone (see right).

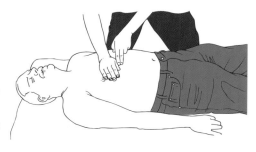

2 Place other hand on top and interlock fingers. Keeping your arms straight and your fingers off the chest, press down by 4–5 cm; then release the pressure, keeping your hands in place (see right).

- Repeat the compressions 15 times, aiming at a rate of 100 per minute.
- Give two Rescue Breaths.
- Continue resuscitation, 15 compressions to two Rescue Breaths.

Only check for circulation if the casualty's colour improves.

If circulation is present, stop the Chest Compressions but continue Rescue Breaths if necessary.

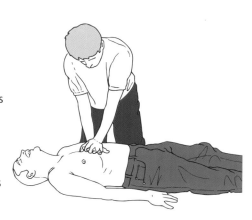

ACTION IN AN EMERGENCY

If you are faced with an emergency, you should:

- **Keep calm and reassure the casualty.**
- **Assess the situation** Is danger still present? Ask the casualty or any bystander what has happened.
- **Make the situation safe** Make sure there is no further danger to the casualty, you, or any bystanders.
- **Quickly assess the casualty or casualties** Act on your findings.
- **Give emergency aid** If there is more than one casualty, treat in the following order:
  - unconscious – carry out the **Resuscitation Sequence (DRABC)**
  - serious bleeding
  - fractures
  - other injuries

Do not move a casualty unless he/she is in immediate danger. Do not give a casualty anything to eat or drink, or allow them to smoke.

- **Get help** Use bystanders to call for help – get them to dial 999 and give the following information:
  - full address or location of the accident, as clearly and precisely as possible
  - describe what has happened
  - describe the injuries found

ST. JOHN AMBULANCE

National Headquarters,
27 St. John's Lane, London EC1M 4BU.

Phone: 020 7324 4000
Fax: 020 7324 4001
www.sja.org.uk

THE RESUSCITATION SEQUENCE: BABY/CHILD

For the purposes of these instructions a baby is considered to be less than 1 year old and a child 1–7 years (inclusive)

 ANGER

- Are you or the baby/child in any danger?
- If you have not already done so make the situation safe and then assess the baby/child.

 ESPONSE

- If the baby/child appears unconscious check this by calling their name and gently tapping their shoulders (children) or tapping the soles of their feet (babies) – never shake a baby or child.
- If there is no response follow the sequence below:

AIRWAY

To open the airway:

- Place one hand on the baby/child's forehead and gently tilt the head back.
- Check the mouth for obvious obstructions and then lift the chin using one or two fingers.

BREATHING

Spend 10 seconds checking to see if the baby or child is breathing:

- **Look** to see if the chest is rising and falling.
- **Listen** for breathing.
- **Feel** for their breath against your cheek.
  - If the baby or child is breathing, place them in the Recovery Position.
  - If the baby or child is not breathing, give two effective Rescue Breaths (see right) and then check circulation.

 IRCULATION

Spend 10 seconds checking for signs of circulation:

- Look, listen, and feel for breathing, coughing, movement, or any other signs of life.

IF THE BABY OR CHILD IS:

CONSCIOUS AND BREATHING:

- Check circulation (including a check for severe bleeding).
- Treat any injuries.
- Get help if necessary.

UNCONSCIOUS, BUT BREATHING:

- Place baby/child in the recovery position.
- Check circulation (including a check for severe bleeding).
- Treat any life-threatening conditions.
- Call an ambulance.

UNCONSCIOUS, NOT BREATHING BUT HAS CIRCULATION:

- Give 20 Rescue Breaths.
- If the baby or child is small enough carry them to the telephone and call for an ambulance.
- If you have left the child to call an ambulance, follow the resuscitation sequence again on your return.

If the baby or child is still unconscious, not breathing, continue to give Rescue Breaths until help arrives.

Check for circulation after every 20 breaths.

UNCONSCIOUS, NOT BREATHING AND HAS NO CIRCULATION:

- Give Chest Compressions together with Rescue Breaths (CPR) for 1 minute.
- If the baby or child is small enough, carry them to the telephone and call for an ambulance.

If you have left the baby or child to call an ambulance, follow the resuscitation sequence again on your return.

If the baby or child is still unconscious, not breathing and has no circulation, continue to give Chest Compressions together with Rescue Breaths (CPR) until help arrives.

RESCUE BREATHS – BABY

1 Ensure the airway is open.

2 Seal your lips around the baby's mouth and nose.

3 Blow gently into the lungs, looking along the chest as you breathe. Fill your cheeks with air and use this amount each time.

4 As the chest rises, stop blowing and allow it to fall.

Do this at a rate of 20 breaths per minute.

Continue to give Rescue Breaths until help arrives.

Check for circulation after every 20 breaths:

- If the circulation is still present continue Rescue Breaths.
- If circulation is absent commence CPR.

If breathing starts, place the baby in the **Recovery Position**.

RECOVERY POSITION – BABY

For a baby less than a year old, a modified Recovery Position must be adopted. The baby should be placed on their side, either in your arms or supported by a small pillow or rolled up blanket. Ensure the position allows for free drainage of fluid and avoids any pressure on the chest which could impair breathing.

For children over 1 year old, the adult Recovery Position should be used.

RESCUE BREATHS – CHILD

1 Ensure the airway is open.

2 Seal your lips around the child's mouth while pinching the nose.

3 Blow gently into the lungs, looking along the chest as you breathe. Take shallow breaths and do not empty your lungs completely.

4 As the chest rises, stop blowing and allow it to fall.

Do this at a rate of 20 breaths per minute.

Continue to give Rescue Breaths until help arrives.

Check for circulation after every 20 breaths:

- If circulation is still present, continue Rescue Breaths.
- If circulation is absent, commence CPR.

If breathing starts, place the child in the Recovery Position.

CHEST COMPRESSIONS WITH RESCUE BREATHS (CPR) – BABY

Note: Chest Compressions must always be combined with Rescue Breaths.

1 Place the baby on a firm surface.

2 Locate a position, one finger's width below the nipple line, in the middle of the chest.

3 Using two fingers, press down sharply to a third of the depth of the chest.

4 Press five times, at a rate of 100 compressions per minute.

5 After five compressions, blow gently into the lungs once.

Continue resuscitation (five compressions to one breath) without stopping until help arrives.

Only check for circulation if the baby's colour improves.

If circulation is present stop the Chest Compressions but continue Rescue Breaths if necessary.

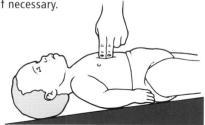

CHEST COMPRESSIONS WITH RESCUE BREATHS (CPR) – CHILD

Note: Chest Compressions must always be combined with Rescue Breaths.

1 Place one hand two fingers' width above the junction of the rib margin and breastbone.

2 Use the heel of that hand and press down to a third of the depth of the chest.

3 Press five times, at a rate of 100 compressions per minute.

4 After five compressions, blow gently into the lungs once.

Continue resuscitation (five compressions to one breath) without stopping until help arrives.

Only check for circulation if the child's colour improves.

If the circulation is present, stop the chest compressions but continue Rescue Breaths if necessary.

RECOGNIZING AND DEALING WITH SHOCK

RECOGNITION

In the case of a serious accident (and once you have treated any obvious injuries and called an ambulance), watch for signs of shock:

- pale face
- cold, clammy skin
- fast, shallow breathing
- rapid, weak pulse
- yawning
- sighing
- in extreme cases, unconsciousness

TREATMENT

- Lay the casualty down and support their legs.
- Use a coat or blanket to keep them warm – but not smothered.
- Do not give them anything to eat or drink.
- Check breathing and pulse frequently. If breathing stops, follow the **Resuscitation Sequence – DRABC.**
- Give lots of comfort and reassurance.

ST. JOHN AMBULANCE

National Headquarters,
27 St. John's Lane, London EC1M 4BU.

Phone: 020 7324 4000
Fax: 020 7324 4001
www.sja.org.uk

DEALING WITH CHOKING

RECOGNITION – ADULT OR CHILD

Difficulty in speaking and breathing. There may also be:

- congested face initially.
- grey-blue skin (cyanosis) later.
- distressed signs from the casualty, who may point to the throat, or grasp the neck.

TREATMENT – CONSCIOUS ADULT

1 Ask the casualty to cough, but if the casualty becomes weak or stops coughing go to step 2.

2 Bend the casualty well forwards and give up to five sharp slaps between the shoulder blades with the flat of your hand.

3 If back slaps fail, try up to five abdominal thrusts. Put your arms around the casualty's trunk. Link your hands below their ribcage (see inset) and pull sharply inwards and upwards.

4 If the obstruction does not clear after three cycles of back slaps and abdominal thrusts dial 999 for an ambulance.

5 Continue alternating five back slaps and five abdominal thrusts until the obstruction clears.

If the casualty becomes unconscious, check breathing and give Rescue Breaths. If you cannot achieve effective Rescue Breaths, give Chest Compressions immediately to try to relieve the obstruction.

TREATMENT – UNCONSCIOUS ADULT

Loss of consciousness may relieve any muscle spasm in the throat. Use the Resuscitation sequence to check the casualty's condition:

- If the casualty is breathing, place them in the Recovery Position.
- If the casualty is not breathing attempt two Rescue Breaths. If these ventilations are effective, check for circulation and carry out Rescue Breaths/CPR as appropriate.
- If these first two Rescue Breaths do NOT make the chest rise, check that the airway is open and the mouth is clear and then try again.

■ If you cannot achieve effective Rescue Breaths after five attempts, commence **CPR** immediately, as this may clear the obstruction.

■ If at any stage the casualty begins to breathe normally, place them in the recovery position and dial 999 for an ambulance.

Monitor and record the breathing, pulse, and level of response every 10 minutes.

TREATMENT – CONSCIOUS BABY

1 Lay the baby face down on your forearm, supporting his back and chin. Give up to five sharp slaps on the baby's back.

2 Check the baby's mouth; remove any obvious obstruction with one finger.

3 Do not feel blindly down the throat.

4 If this fails, turn the baby face up on your arm or lap. Give up to five sharp thrusts into the baby's chest.

5 Check the baby's mouth again and remove any obvious obstruction.

6 Do not use abdominal thrusts on a baby.

7 If the obstruction still has not cleared, repeat steps 1–4 two times, then take the baby with you to dial 999 for an ambulance. Repeat steps 1–4 until help arrives.

If the baby becomes unconscious follow the **Resuscitation Sequence**.

TREATMENT – CONSCIOUS CHILD

1 Encourage the child to cough. Only if they become weak or unable to cough, go to step 2.

2 Bend the child forwards with their head lower than their chest. Give up to five back slaps firmly between the shoulders.

3 Check the child's mouth; remove any obvious obstruction with one finger.

4 If this fails, stand or kneel behind the child. Make a fist and place it against their lower breastbone. Grasp it with your other hand. Press into the chest with a sharp inward thrust. Give up to five of these chest thrusts at a rate of about one every 3 seconds.

5 Check the child's mouth and proceed to step 6 if choking persists.

6 Make a fist and place it against the child's central upper abdomen. Grasp it with your hand. Press into their abdomen with a sharp upward thrust up to five times. Check the mouth and proceed to step 7, if necessary.

7 Dial 999 for an ambulance. Repeat steps 2–6 until help arrives.

If the child becomes unconscious, follow the **Resuscitation Sequence – DRABC**.

DEALING WITH BLEEDING

MINOR CUTS, SCRATCHES & GRAZES

Treatment

- Wash and dry your own hands.
- Cover any cuts on your own hands and put on disposable gloves.
- Clean the cut, if dirty, under running water.
- Pat dry with a sterile dressing or clean lint-free material.
- Cover the cut temporarily while you clean the surrounding skin with soap and water and pat the surrounding skin dry.
- Cover the cut completely with a sterile dressing or plaster.

SEVERE BLEEDING

Treatment

- Put on disposable gloves.
- Apply direct pressure to the wound with a pad (e.g. a clean cloth) or fingers until a sterile dressing is available.

- Raise and support the injured limb. Take particular care if you suspect a bone has been broken.
- Lay the casualty down to treat for shock.
- Bandage the pad or dressing firmly to control bleeding, but not so tightly that it stops the circulation to fingers or toes.
- Treat for shock (see p287).
- Dial 999 for an ambulance.

REMEMBER

- Protect yourself from infection by wearing disposable gloves and covering any wounds on your hands.
- If blood comes through the dressing DO NOT remove it – bandage another over the original.
- If blood seeps through BOTH dressings, remove them both and replace with a fresh dressing, applying pressure over the site of bleeding.

DEALING WITH BURNS AND SCALDS

SEVERE BURNS

Treatment

- Start cooling the burn immediately under running water.
- Dial 999 for an ambulance.
- Make the casualty as comfortable as possible; lie them down.
- Continue to pour copious amounts of cold water over the burn for at least 10 minutes or until the pain is relieved.
- Remove jewellery, watch, or clothing from the affected area – unless it is sticking to the skin.
- Cover the burn with clean, non-fluffy material to protect from infection. Cloth, a clean plastic bag, or kitchen film all make good dressings.
- Treat for shock.

MINOR BURNS

Treatment

- Hold the affected area under cold water for at least 10 minutes or until the pain

subsides. Remove jewellery etc. and cover the burn as detailed above.
- If a minor burn is larger than a postage stamp it requires medical attention.
- All deep burns of any size require urgent hospital treatment.

CLOTHING ON FIRE

Treatment

Stop the casualty panicking or running – any movement or breeze will fan flames.

Drop the casualty to the ground.

If possible, **wrap** the casualty tightly in a coat, curtain or blanket (not the nylon or cellular type), rug, or other heavy duty fabric. The best fabric is wool.

Roll the casualty along the ground until the flames have been smothered.

ON ALL BURNS DO NOT

- use lotions, ointments, and creams
- use adhesive dressings
- break blisters.

FRACTURES

Falls are the most common cause of injury to children in the home. These often result in fractures. The younger the child, the more likely the injury is to be serious.

Treatment

- Give lots of comfort and reassurance and persuade them to stay still.
- Do not move the casualty unless you have to.
- Steady and support the injured limb with your hands to stop any movement.
- If there is bleeding, press a clean pad over the wound to control the flow of blood. Then bandage on and around the wound.
- If you suspect a broken leg, put padding between the knees and ankles. Form a splint (to immobilise the leg further) by gently, but firmly, bandaging the good leg to the bad one at the knees and ankles, then above and below the injury. If it is an arm that is broken, improvise a sling to support the arm close to the body.
- Dial 999 for an ambulance.
- If it does not distress the casualty too much, raise and support the injured limb.
- Do not give the casualty anything to eat or drink in case an operation is necessary.
- Watch out for signs of shock.
- If the casualty becomes unconscious, follow the **Resuscitation Sequence – DRABC**.

ST. JOHN AMBULANCE

National Headquarters,
27 St. John's Lane, London EC1M 4BU.

Phone: 020 7324 4000
Fax: 020 7324 4001
www.sja.org.uk

Fire

Burglary

The advice here comes from the Web site run by the Office of the Deputy Prime Minister, http://www.firekills.gov.uk, which gives useful advice about preventing and dealing with fires, and provides links to other sites.

ALERT EVERYONE

If you become aware of a fire in your home you need to act instantly, swiftly, and calmly. Make sure everyone in your home knows about the fire. Shout. Get everyone together.

DON'T DELAY

You can't afford to waste any time. Don't:

- investigate the fire
- go looking for valuables — whether that's jewellery, photographs, documents, or whatever
- go looking for pets.

SHUT DOORS

As you go out, open only the doors you need to. Before you open a door check it with the back of your hand. If it's warm, don't open it — the fire is the other side. Close any open doors.

GET EVERYONE OUT

Use a set escape route (see p147 for planning this). Stay together if you can.

CRAWL ON THE FLOOR

Smoke is poisonous and can kill you. If there's smoke put your nose as low as possible; the air is cleaner near the floor.

DIAL 999

Once you've escaped, use a mobile, a neighbour's phone, or a phone box. 999 calls are free. Don't call the local fire station's number — it will probably take longer to be answered. You should:

- speak slowly and clearly
- give the whole address of your home, including the town
- say what is on fire (e.g. a two-storey house)
- explain if anyone is trapped and what room they are in.

The more information the fire brigade has, the quicker it can get to you and act when it gets there.

DON'T GO BACK IN

Don't go back in for anything. If there's someone still inside, wait for the fire brigade to arrive. You can tell them about the person and they will be able to find them quicker than you. If you disappear inside the building, that will slow down the firefighters' efforts to rescue anyone else missing, apart from putting your life in great danger.

WAIT NEARBY

Find somewhere safe to wait. When the fire brigade arrives, give them as much information as possible about the fire and the building.

CAN'T GET OUT OF A DOOR?

- Go out of a window if you're on the ground or first floor.
- Throw bedding, etc. down to cushion your fall, and hang at arm's length before dropping.

CAN'T GET OUT AT ALL?

- Get everyone into one room.
- Shut the door and put clothes, bedding, etc. round the bottom of it.
- Open the window and call for help.

CONTACT THE POLICE

If your property has been burgled, contact your local police station, either in person or by phone, and give:

- your name, address, and a contact telephone number
- details of where the burglary has taken place
- the name, age, and address of the owner of the property and where they can be contacted
- if known, the time the crime happened and what type of property is involved
- details of any witnesses, or any people you think may have been responsible for the burglary.

You should make a note of:

- anything you think has been stolen — especially any serial numbers
- any damage to your property caused by the burglars.

Let the police know if you later find:

- an item of property that you thought had been stolen
- that additional items have been stolen.

OTHER CALLS TO MAKE

You may need to contact:

- a locksmith or glazier if locks or windows are broken — see Emergency call-outs, p247, and Fitting locks, p180
- your bank if you notice any credit cards or chequebooks are missing
- your network provider if your mobile phone is missing; the network provider will be able to block the use of the phone
- your insurance company if you plan to make a claim
- the authority that issued personal or official identification papers, such as a passport, if any of these are missing.

Flooding

The information on this page comes from the Environment Agency. You can obtain a local Flood Directory, with a flood map and local contact numbers, from the Floodline, on 0845 988 1188. Tips on how to lay sandbags, and information on repairing and restoring property damaged by flood, are on the Environment Agency's Web site at http://environment-agency.co.uk and are available from the Floodline.

BE PREPARED

In a flood you may find you're without lighting, heating, or a telephone line. The following simple actions will help you to be prepared.

- Make sure you have adequate insurance if you believe your home may be at risk. Check your existing policy.
- Make up a flood kit – including key personal documents, torch, battery or wind-up radio, rubber gloves, wellingtons, waterproof clothing, First Aid kit (see p145), and blankets.
- Keep details of your insurance policy and your insurer's emergency contact number somewhere safe, preferably as part of your flood kit.
- Get into the habit of storing valuable or sentimental items upstairs or in a high place.
- Buy some sandbags or floorboards to block doorways and airbricks. See http://www.environment-agency.gov.uk or call the Floodline.

FLOOD WARNINGS

- Listen out for warnings on radio and TV, and phone the Floodline for more information.
- Move pets, vehicles, valuables, and other items to safety.
- Alert your neighbours, particularly the elderly.
- Put sandbags or floorboards in place – but make sure your property is ventilated.
- Be ready to turn off gas and electricity (get help if needed).
- Co-operate with emergency services and local authorities – you may be evacuated to rest centres.
- Do as much as you can in daylight. Doing anything in the dark will be a lot harder, especially if the electricity fails.

STAY SAFE IN A FLOOD

- Floods can kill. Don't try to walk or drive through floodwater – six inches of fast-flowing water can knock you off your feet and two feet of water will float your car.
- Manhole covers may have come off and there may be other hazards you can't see.
- Never try to swim through fast-flowing water – you may get swept away or be struck by an object in the water.
- Don't walk on sea defences or riverbanks, or cross river-bridges – they may collapse in extreme situations or you may be swept off by large waves. Beware of stones and pebbles being thrown up by waves.
- Move your family and pets upstairs or to higher ground. If the flooding is severe the authorities may move you to temporary accommodation.

Switch off water, gas, and electricity at the first sign of flooding to your property.

IF YOU'VE BEEN FLOODED

- Call your insurance company's 24-hour emergency helpline as soon as possible. They will be able to provide information on dealing with your claim and assistance in getting things back to normal.
- Find out where you can get help to clear up. Check with your local authority or health authority in the first instance, or look under Flood damage in the *Yellow Pages* for suppliers of cleaning materials or equipment to dry out your property.
- Open doors and windows to ventilate your home but take care to ensure that house and valuables are secure. It takes a house brick about a month per inch to dry out.
- Contact your gas, electricity, and water supply companies. Have power supplies checked before you turn them back on. Wash taps and run them for a few minutes before use.
- Throw away food that may have been in contact with floodwater – it could be contaminated. Contact your local authority's Environmental Health department for advice.
- Beware of bogus traders. Always check references and if possible get recommendations. See Avoiding problems on p265, and Emergency call-outs, p247. Contact your local Trading Standards department for advice (see phone book or http://www.tradingstandards.gov.uk).

ILLUSTRATIONS

Key
t = top; b = bottom; c = centre; r = right; l = left

ARTWORKS

Andrew Green: 60; 67b; 164; 165; 170; 171; 172; 173; 174; 175; 176; 177; 184; 185; 186; 187; 188; 189; 193; 198; 199; 210; 211; 214; 215; 227; 228; 230; 231; 233; 235; 236; 237tc

Antbits Illustration: 62; 63; 64; 65; 150; 151; 152; 153; 161 (except for hacksaw; junior hacksaw, claw hammer and tenon saw); 163ct; 163br; 166; 178; 180; 181; 182; 183; 207; 212; 219; 224; 225

Lorraine Hodghton: 61; 67t; 135; 141; 229; 234; 237r; 238

Nick Pearson: 169; 249

St. John Ambulance: 285; 286; 287; 288

PHOTOGRAPHS

Apple Computer, Inc.: 112

Barbara Fraser: 254

Corbis: 10; 15tl (Neil Beer); 19tc (PictureNet); 19tl; 20 (PictureNet); 22; 29; 30; 31 (Image 100); 45 (PictureNet); 48 (Image 100); 49 (David Papazian); 76; 82; 88; 131 (Jeffrey Coolidge); 149 (Chris Carroll); 157tl; 222tr; 250 (Tom Grill); 255; 261 (Neil Lorimer, Elizabeth Whiting & Associates); 278

Ecoscene: 69 (Anthony Cooper); 71bl (Peter Currell)

Freefoto.com: 16r; 24; 27; 37; 156tl;

Getty Images: 15r; 16tl; 43; 56; 71tl; 72; 84; 85; 111; 113; 126; 128–129; 130; 156tr; 232; 263

Hewlett Packard: 110

IPC Syndication: 35 (Trevor Richards); 91 (Richard Powers); 132 (Lizzie Orme); 133 (Ed Davis); 134 (Simon Whitmore); 222b (Paul Massey); 242 (Lucy Pope); 260 (Simon Whitmore); 268 (Ed Reeve)

Lorraine Hodghton: 157tr; 195; 258

Maplin Electronics: 118; 119

MW Scaffolding Ltd: 246

Panasonic: 70

Philips: 120

Red Cover: 46 (Robert O'Dea)